ALICE IN BORDERLAND

STORY AND ART BY

HARO ASO

S0-BCS-891

3

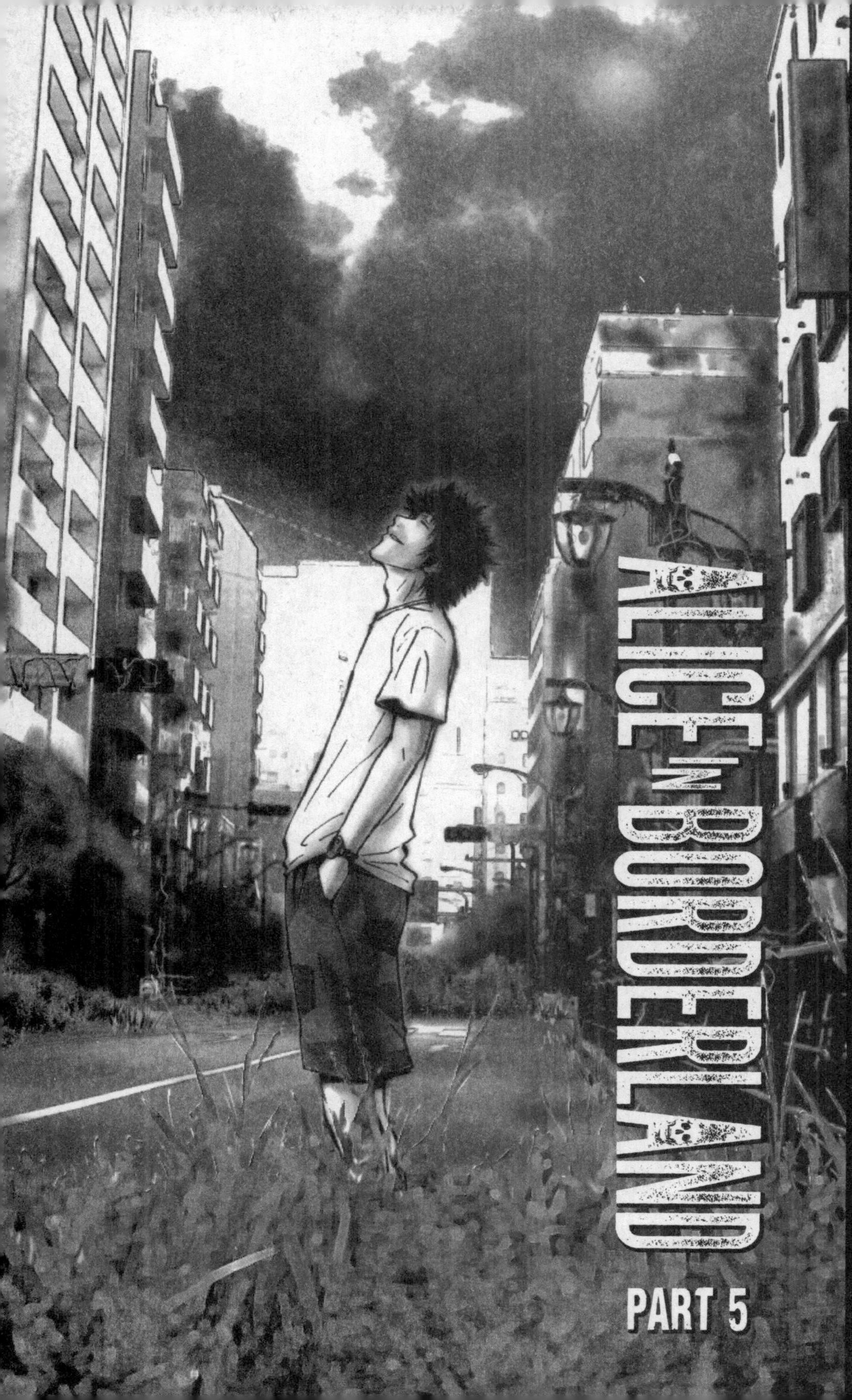
ALICE IN BORDERLAND
PART 5

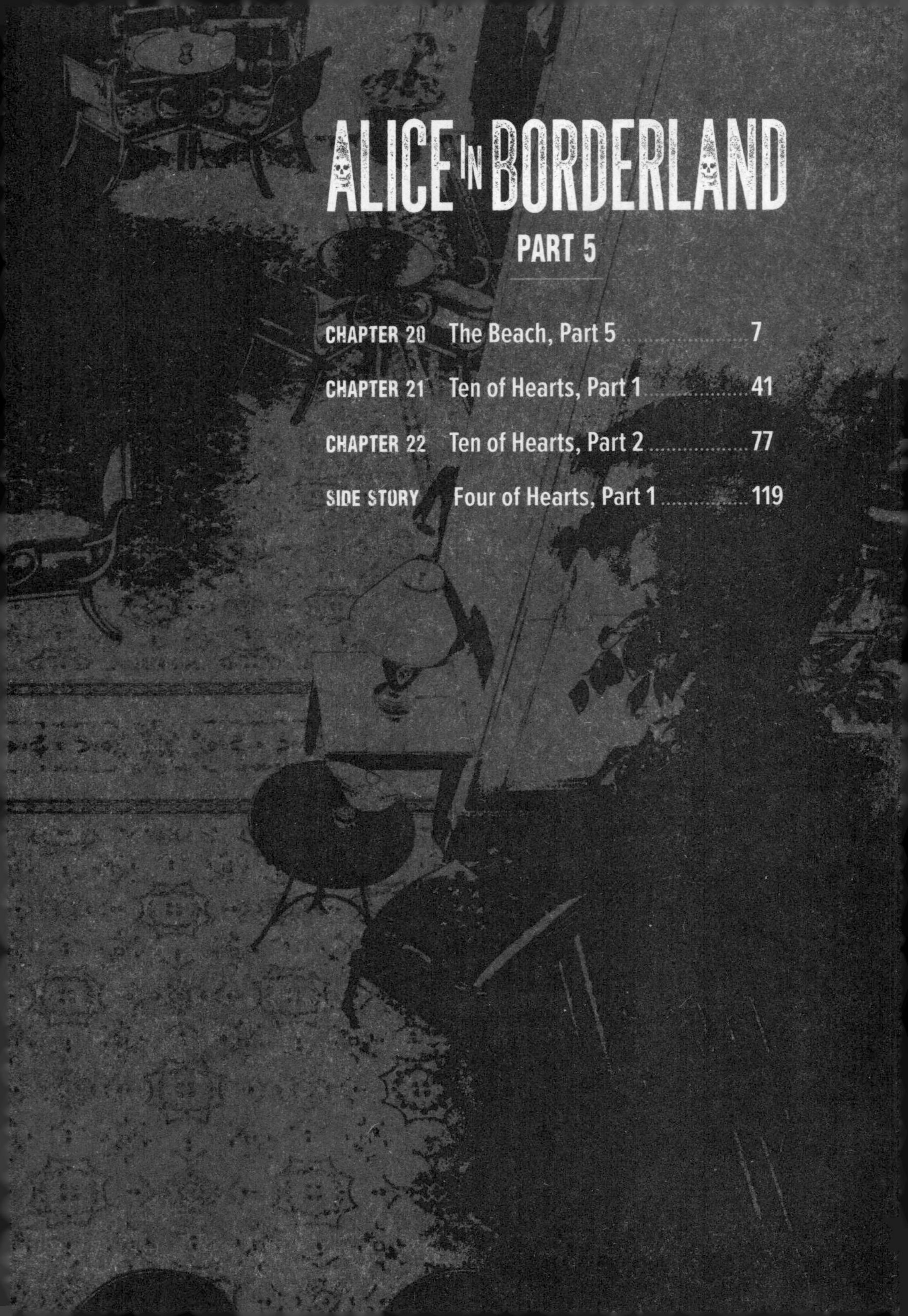

ALICE IN BORDERLAND

PART 5

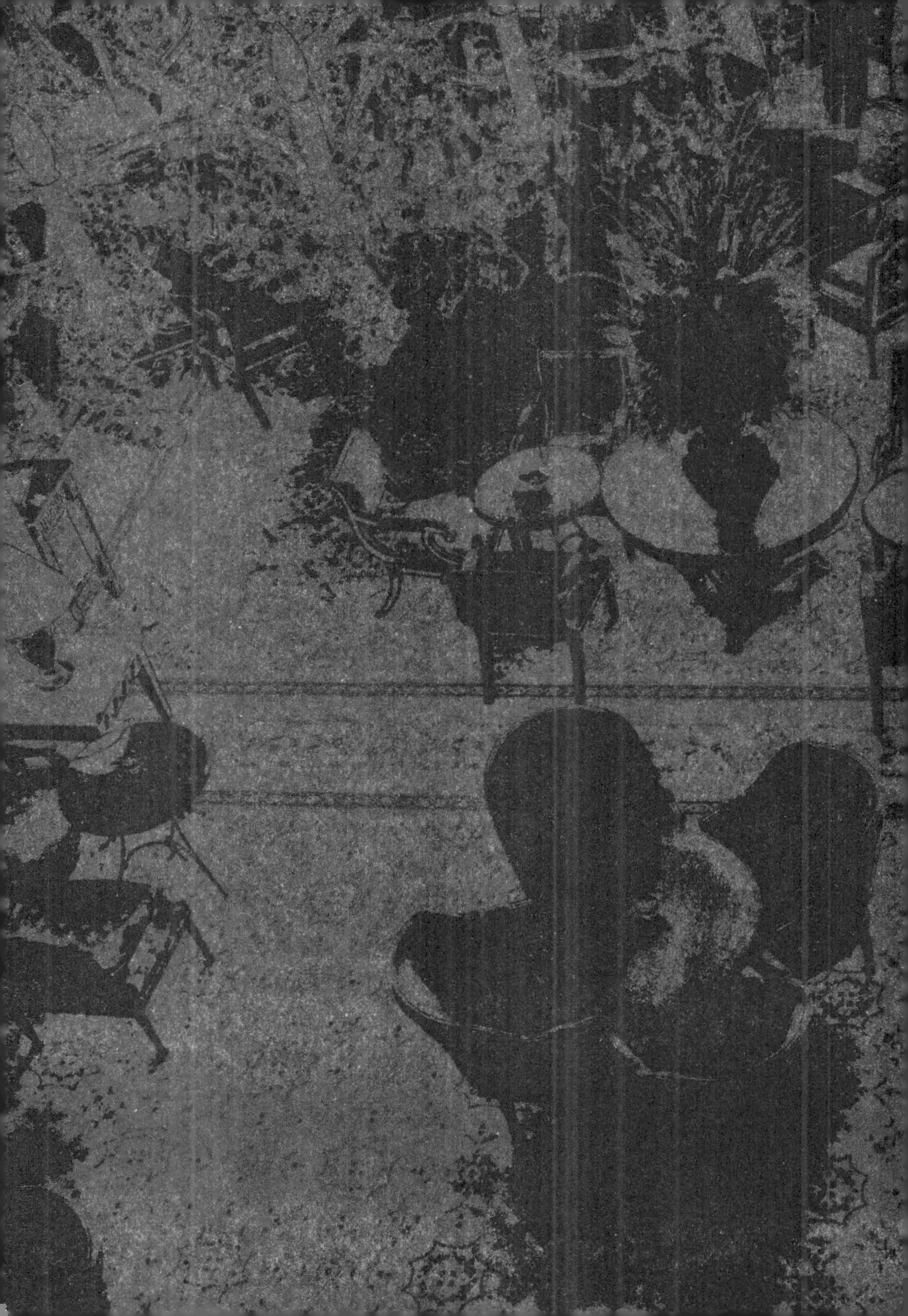

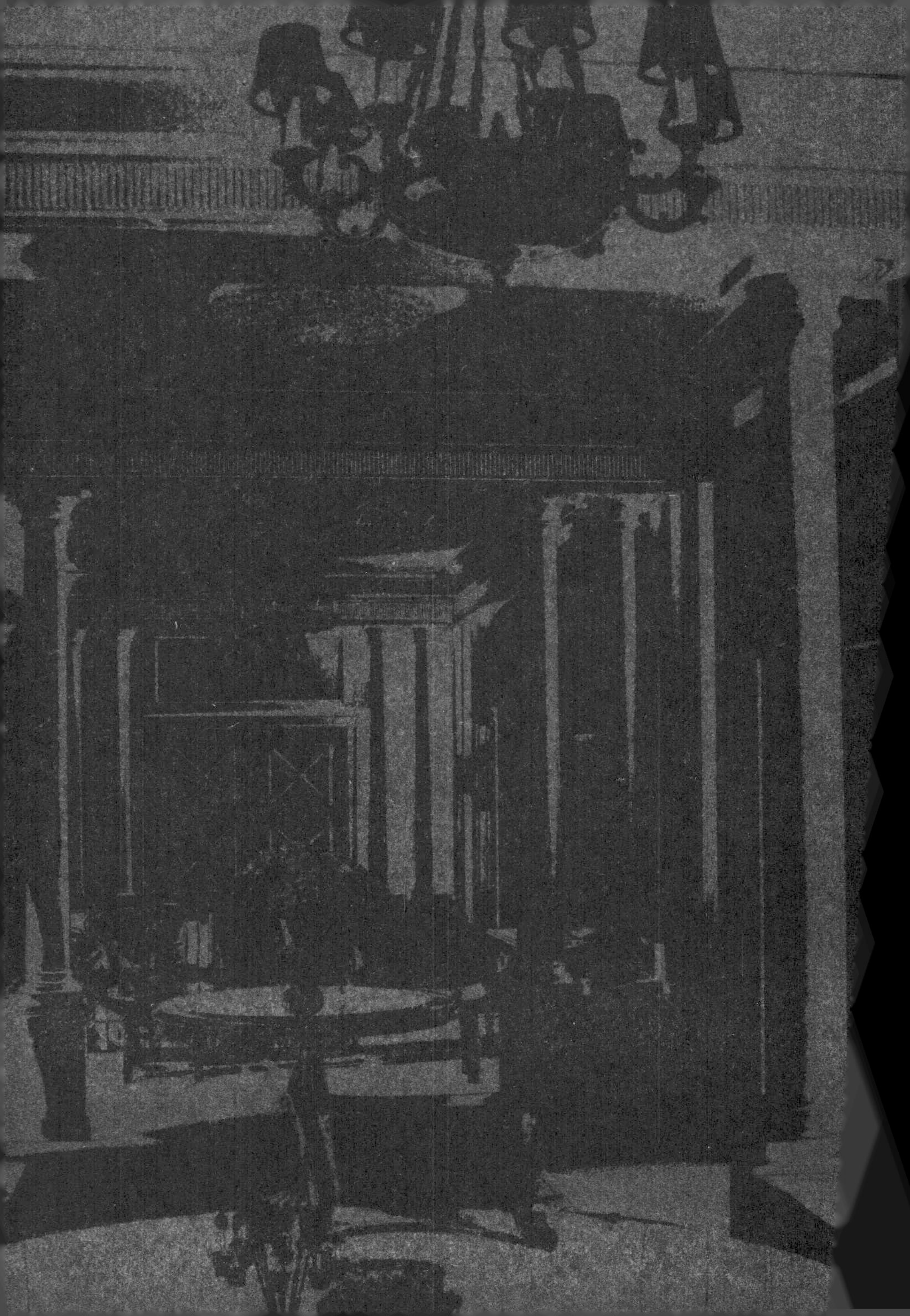

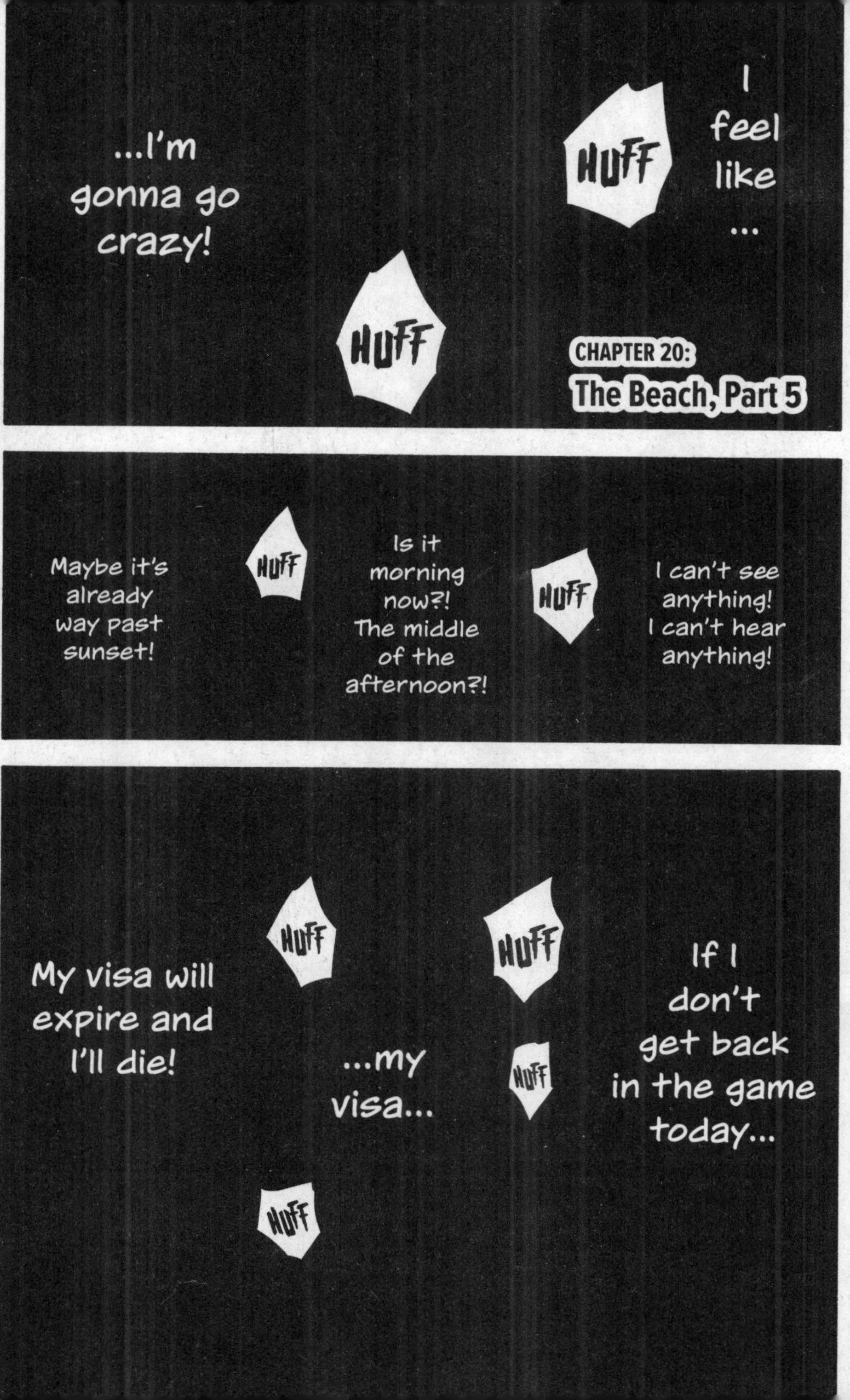
I feel like ...
HUFF
CHAPTER 20:
The Beach, Part 5
...I'm gonna go crazy!
HUFF
I can't see anything! I can't hear anything!
HUFF
Is it morning now?! The middle of the afternoon?!
HUFF
Maybe it's already way past sunset!
If I don't get back in the game today...
HUFF
HUFF
...my visa...
HUFF
My visa will expire and I'll die!
HUFF

CHAPTER 20: The Beach, Part 5

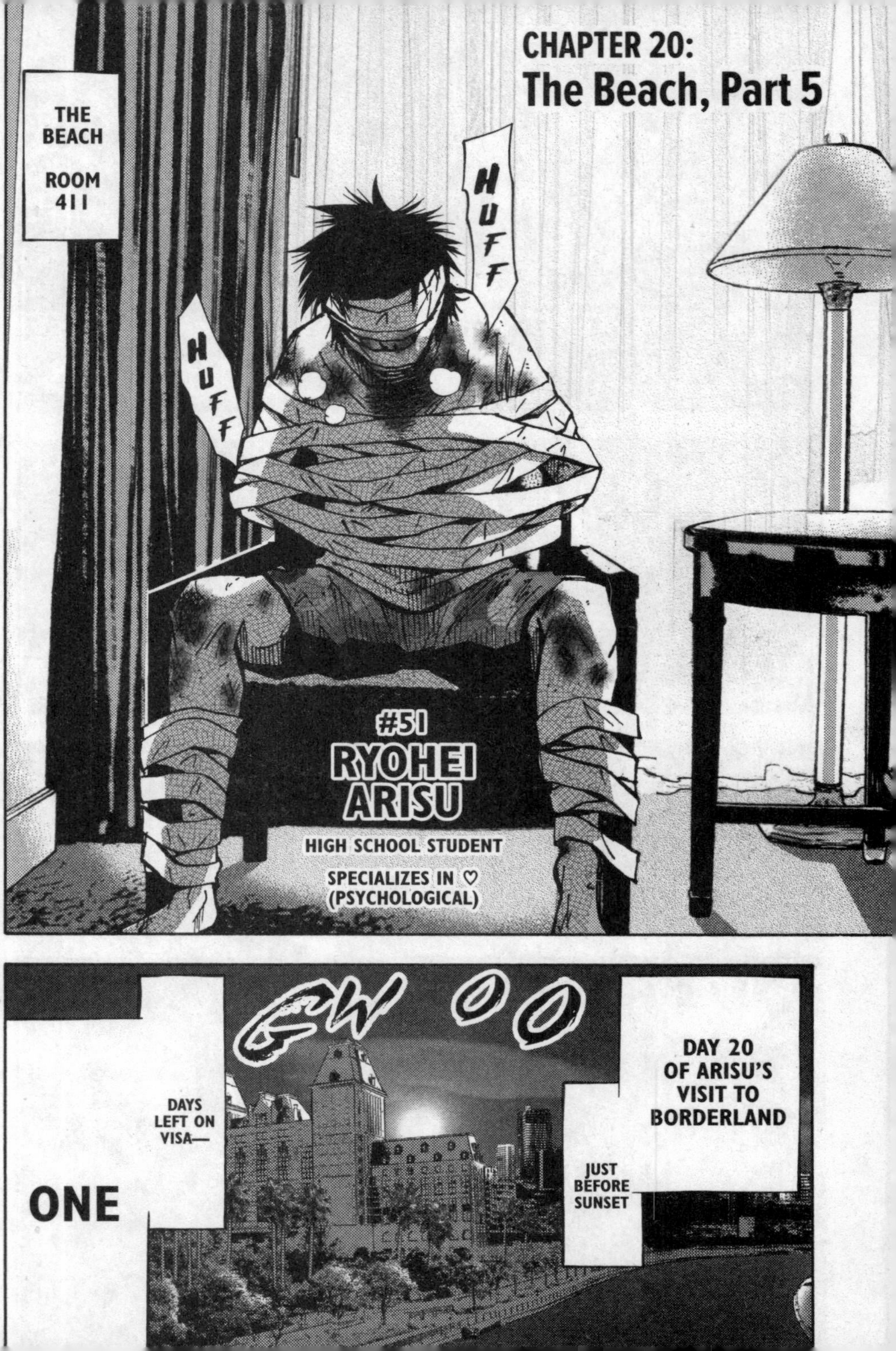
HUFF HUFF
HUFF HUFF
THE BEACH ROOM 411
#51
RYOHEI ARISU
HIGH SCHOOL STUDENT
SPECIALIZES IN ♡ (PSYCHOLOGICAL)
GW OO
DAY 20 OF ARISU'S VISIT TO BORDERLAND
JUST BEFORE SUNSET
DAYS LEFT ON VISA—
ONE

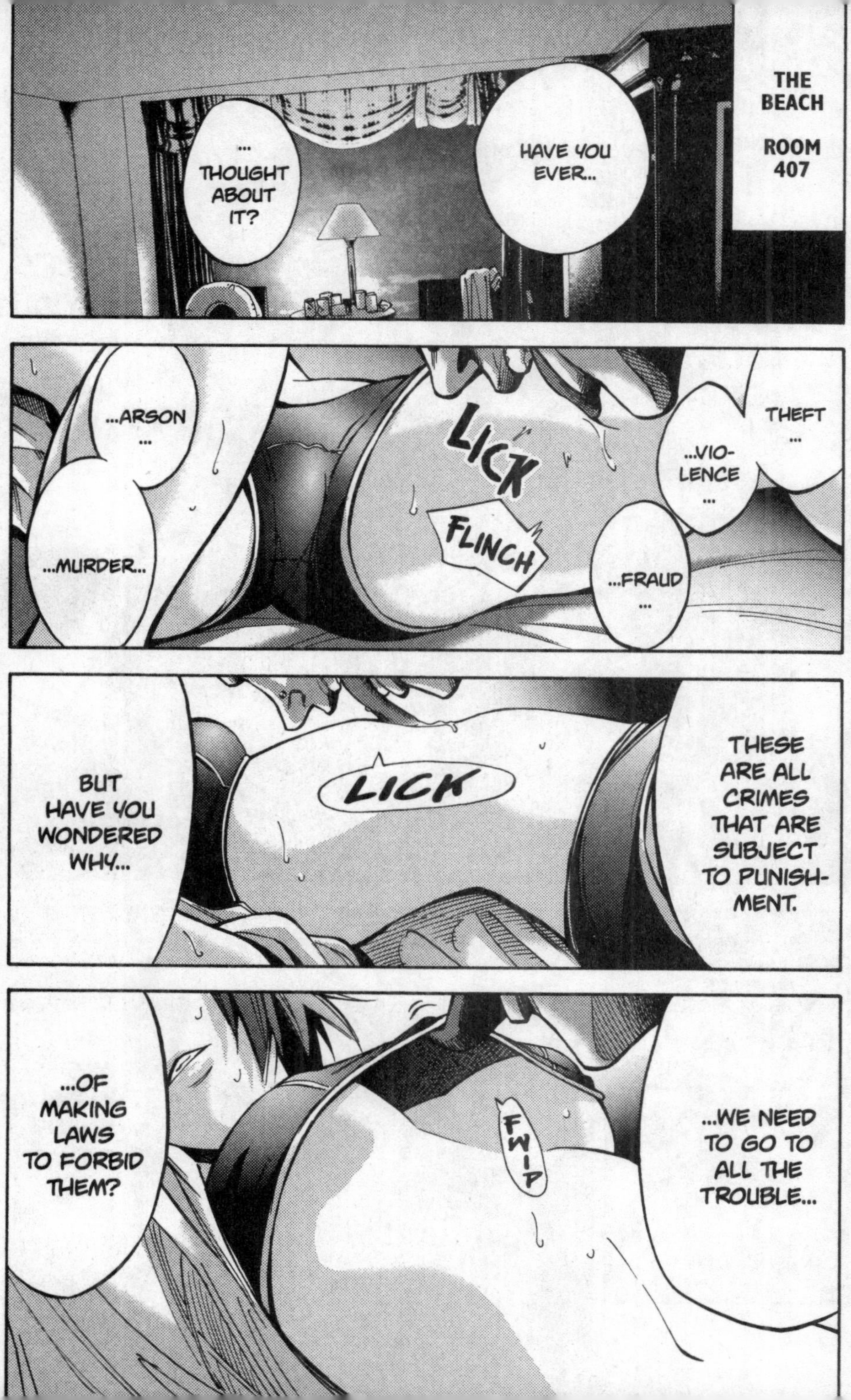
THE BEACH ROOM 407
HAVE YOU EVER...
...THOUGHT ABOUT IT?
THEFT...
...VIO-LENCE...
...FRAUD...
LICK
FLINCH
...ARSON...
...MURDER...
THESE ARE ALL CRIMES THAT ARE SUBJECT TO PUNISH-MENT.
LICK
BUT HAVE YOU WONDERED WHY...
...WE NEED TO GO TO ALL THE TROUBLE...
FWIP
...OF MAKING LAWS TO FORBID THEM?

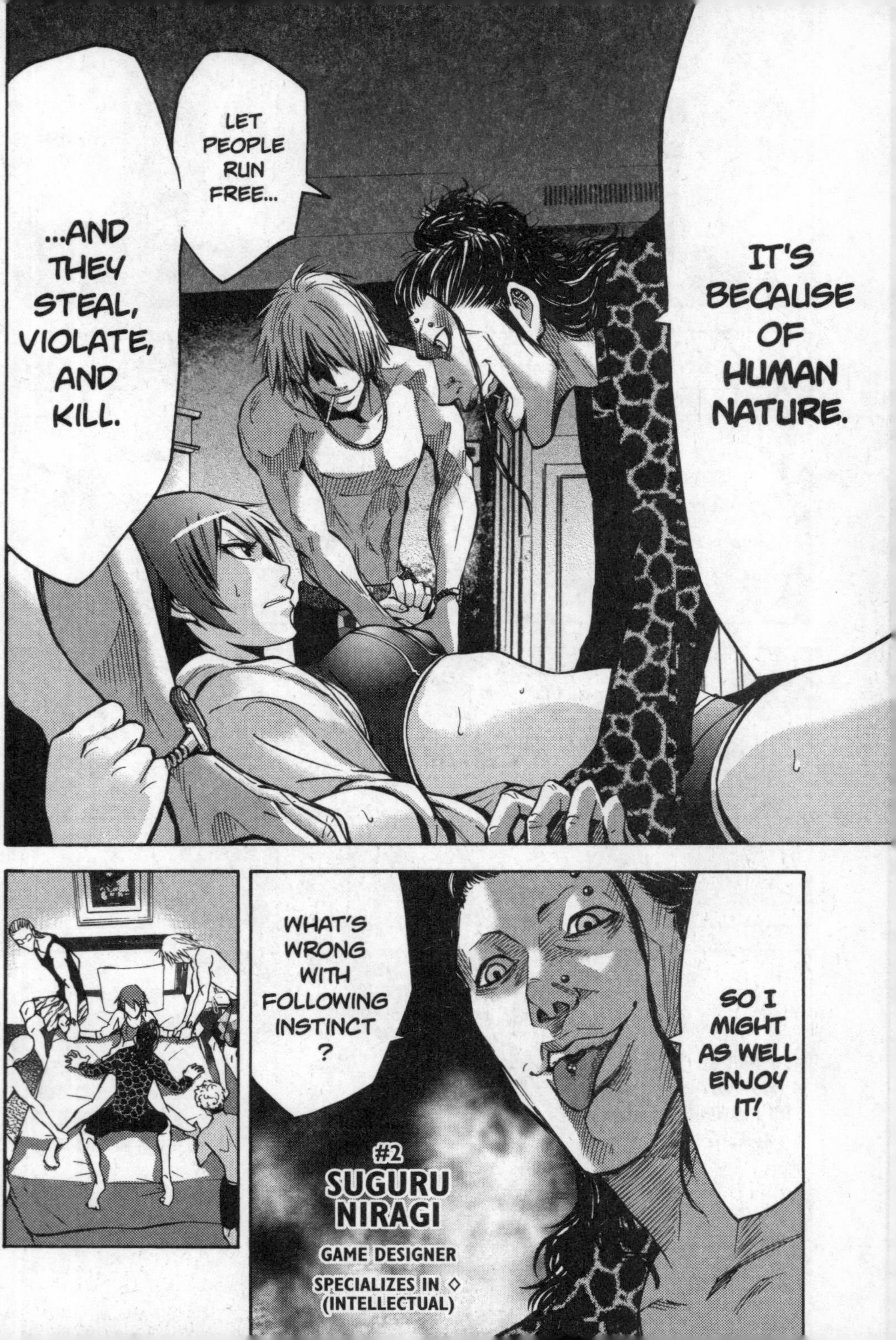
IT'S BECAUSE OF HUMAN NATURE.
LET PEOPLE RUN FREE...
...AND THEY STEAL, VIOLATE, AND KILL.
SO I MIGHT AS WELL ENJOY IT!
WHAT'S WRONG WITH FOLLOWING INSTINCT?
#2
SUGURU NIRAGI
GAME DESIGNER
SPECIALIZES IN ◇ (INTELLECTUAL)

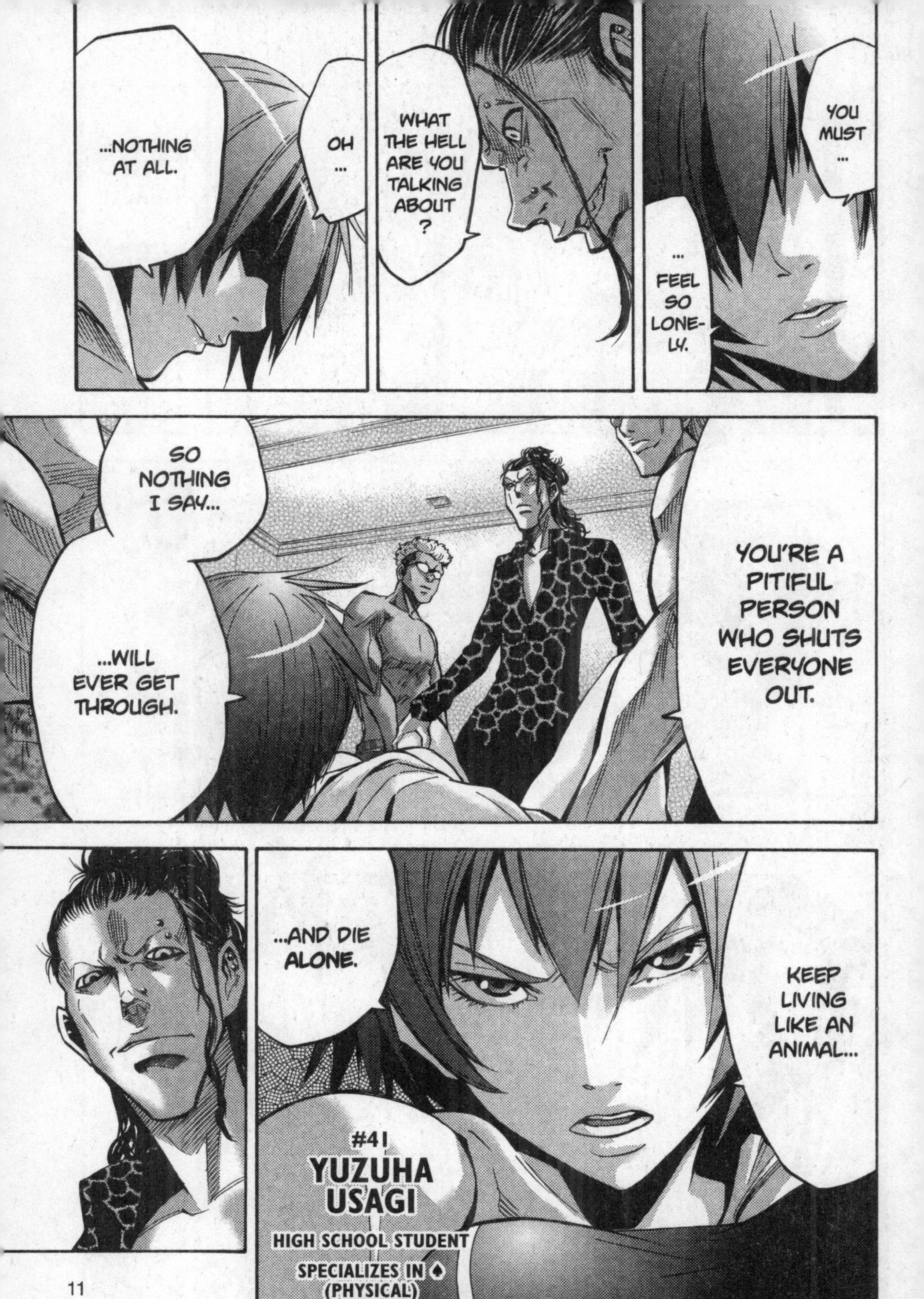
YOU MUST ...
... FEEL SO LONE-LY.
WHAT THE HELL ARE YOU TALKING ABOUT ?
OH ...
...NOTHING AT ALL.
YOU'RE A PITIFUL PERSON WHO SHUTS EVERYONE OUT.
SO NOTHING I SAY...
...WILL EVER GET THROUGH.
KEEP LIVING LIKE AN ANIMAL...
...AND DIE ALONE.
#41
YUZUHA USAGI
HIGH SCHOOL STUDENT
SPECIALIZES IN ♠ (PHYSICAL)

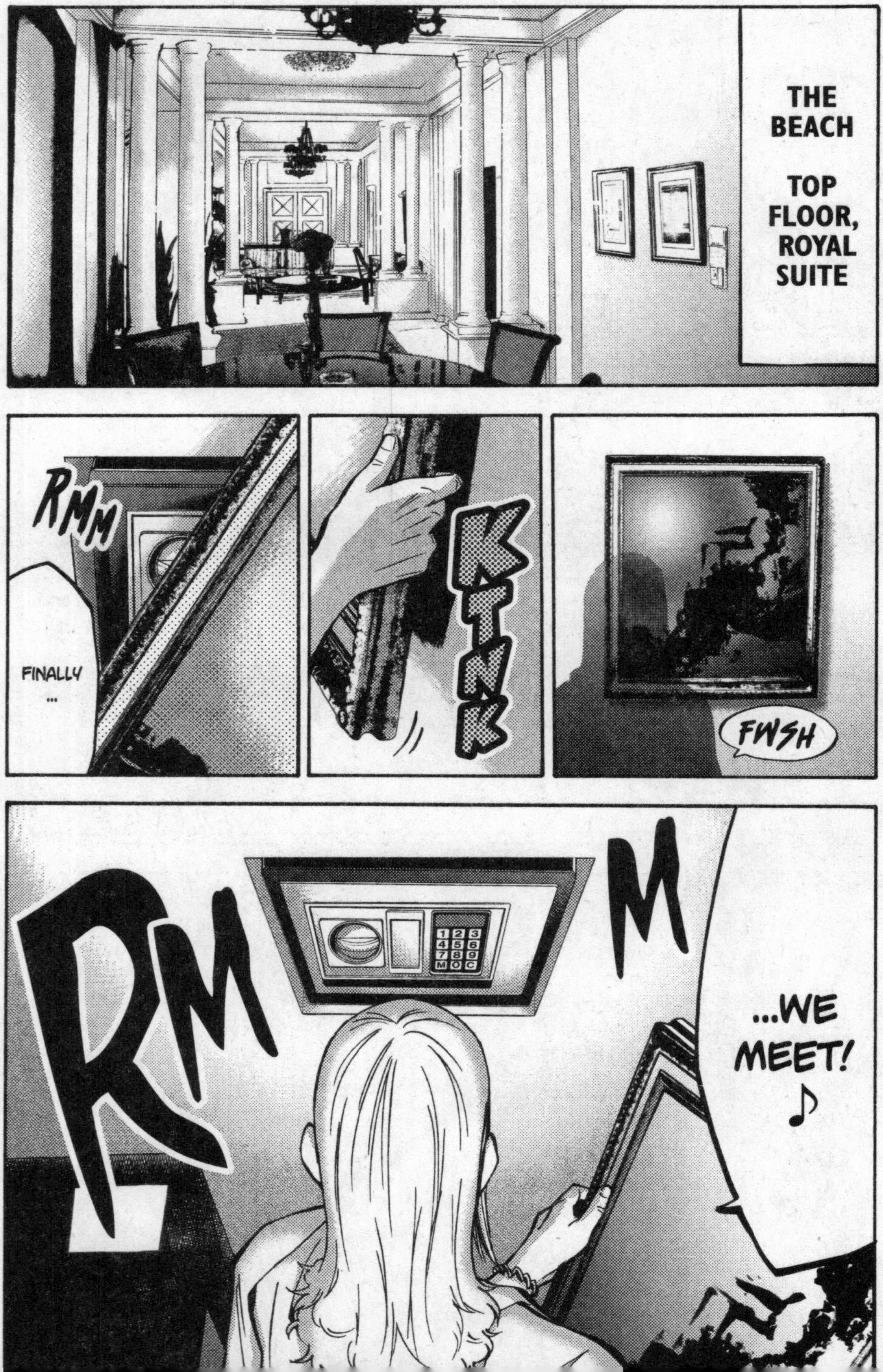
THE BEACH
TOP FLOOR, ROYAL SUITE
FWSH
KTINK
RMM
FINALLY ...
RMM
...WE MEET! ♪

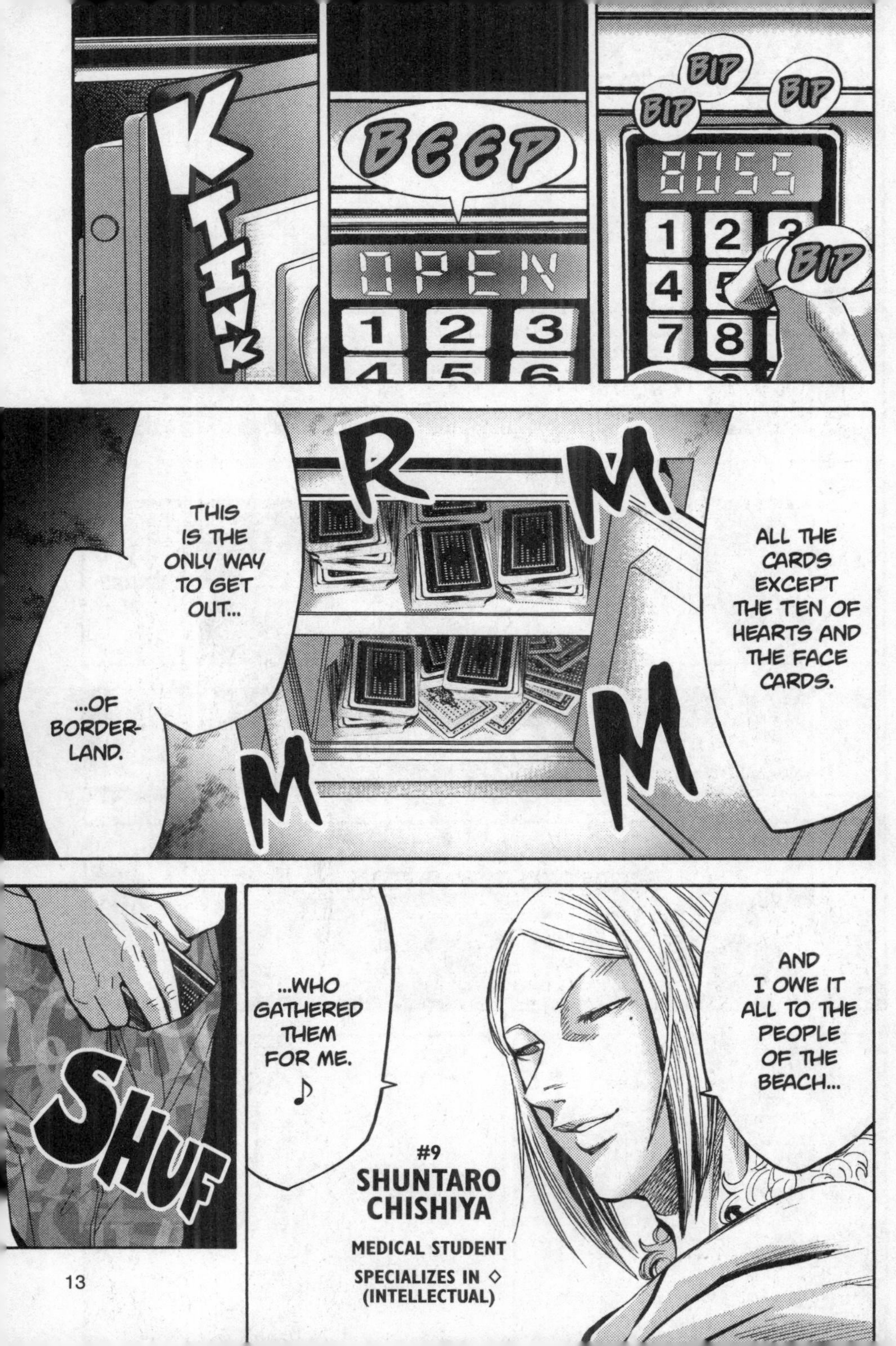
BIP
BIP
BIP
BIP
8055
BEEP
OPEN
KTINK
ALL THE CARDS EXCEPT THE TEN OF HEARTS AND THE FACE CARDS.
RMMM
THIS IS THE ONLY WAY TO GET OUT...
...OF BORDERLAND.
AND I OWE IT ALL TO THE PEOPLE OF THE BEACH...
...WHO GATHERED THEM FOR ME. ♪
#9
SHUNTARO CHISHIYA
MEDICAL STUDENT
SPECIALIZES IN ◇ (INTELLECTUAL)
SHUF

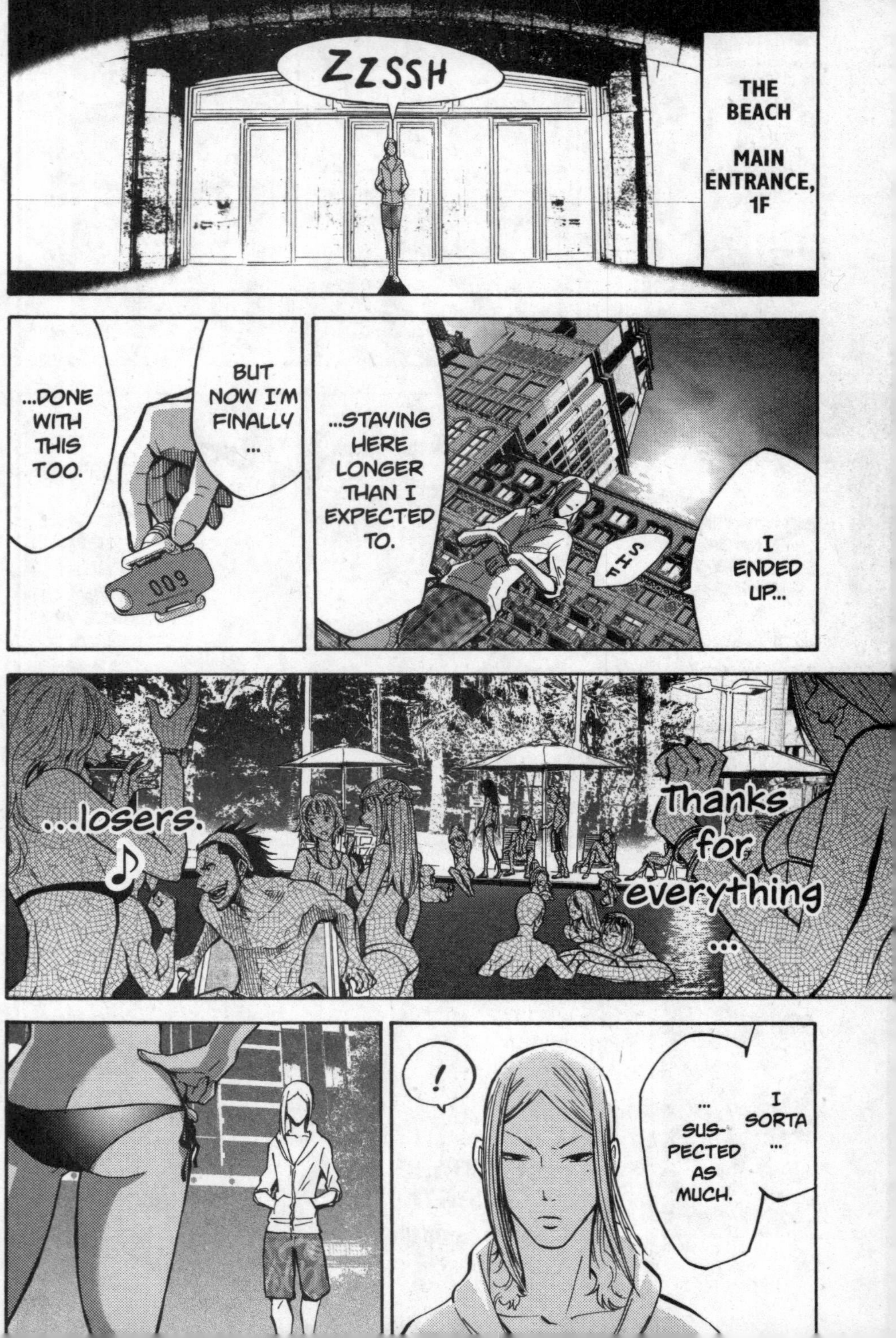
THE BEACH MAIN ENTRANCE, 1F
ZZSSH
I ENDED UP...
...STAYING HERE LONGER THAN I EXPECTED TO.
SHF
BUT NOW I'M FINALLY ...
...DONE WITH THIS TOO.
009
Thanks for everything ...
...losers. ♪
I SORTA ...
... SUS-PECTED AS MUCH.
!

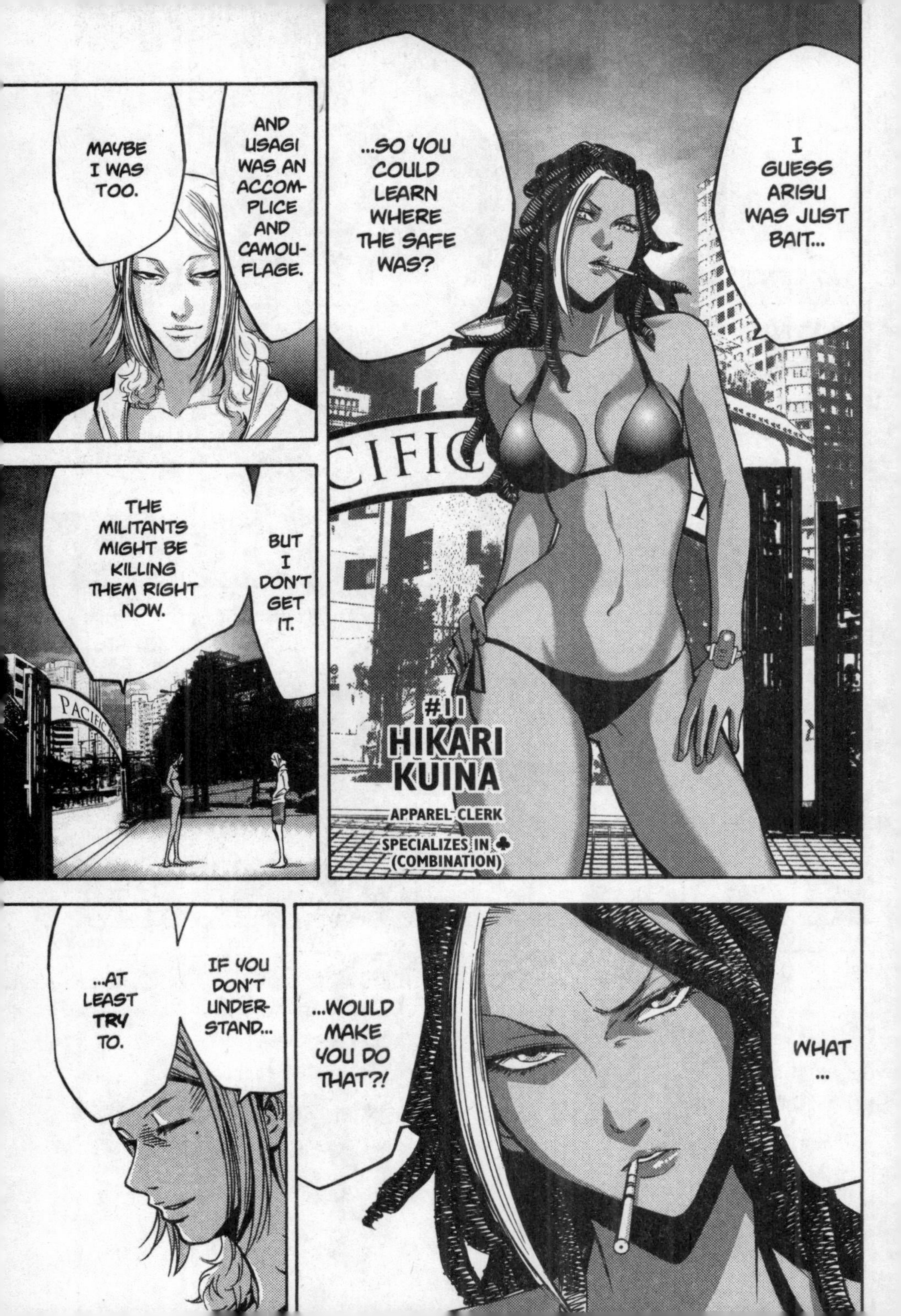
I GUESS ARISU WAS JUST BAIT...
...SO YOU COULD LEARN WHERE THE SAFE WAS?
#11 HIKARI KUINA
APPAREL CLERK
SPECIALIZES IN ♣ (COMBINATION)
AND USAGI WAS AN ACCOMPLICE AND CAMOUFLAGE.
MAYBE I WAS TOO.
BUT I DON'T GET IT.
THE MILITANTS MIGHT BE KILLING THEM RIGHT NOW.
PACIFIC
WHAT...
...WOULD MAKE YOU DO THAT?!
IF YOU DON'T UNDERSTAND...
...AT LEAST TRY TO.

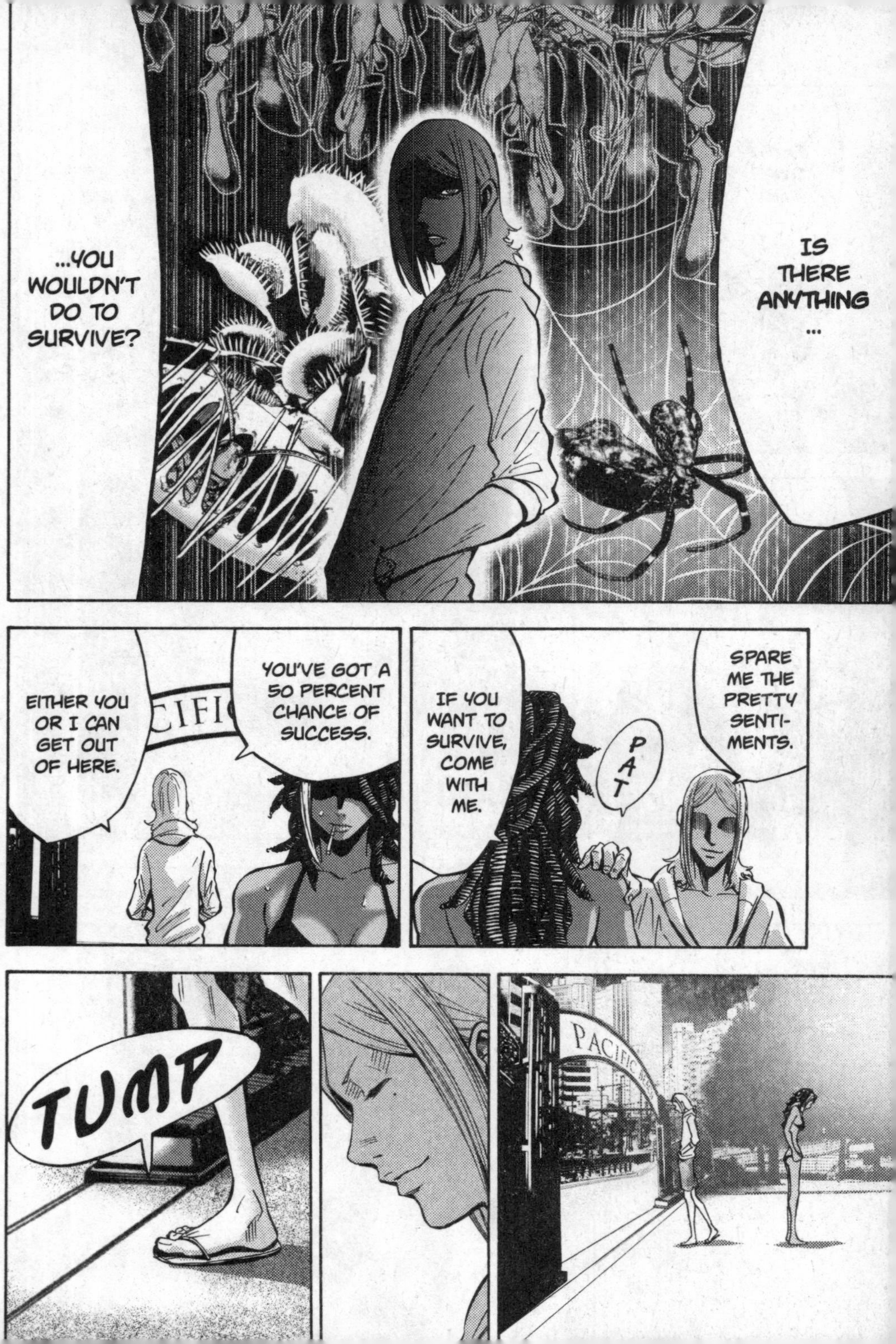
IS THERE ANYTHING ...
...YOU WOULDN'T DO TO SURVIVE?
SPARE ME THE PRETTY SENTI-MENTS.
PAT
IF YOU WANT TO SURVIVE, COME WITH ME.
YOU'VE GOT A 50 PERCENT CHANCE OF SUCCESS.
EITHER YOU OR I CAN GET OUT OF HERE.
PACIFIC
TUMP

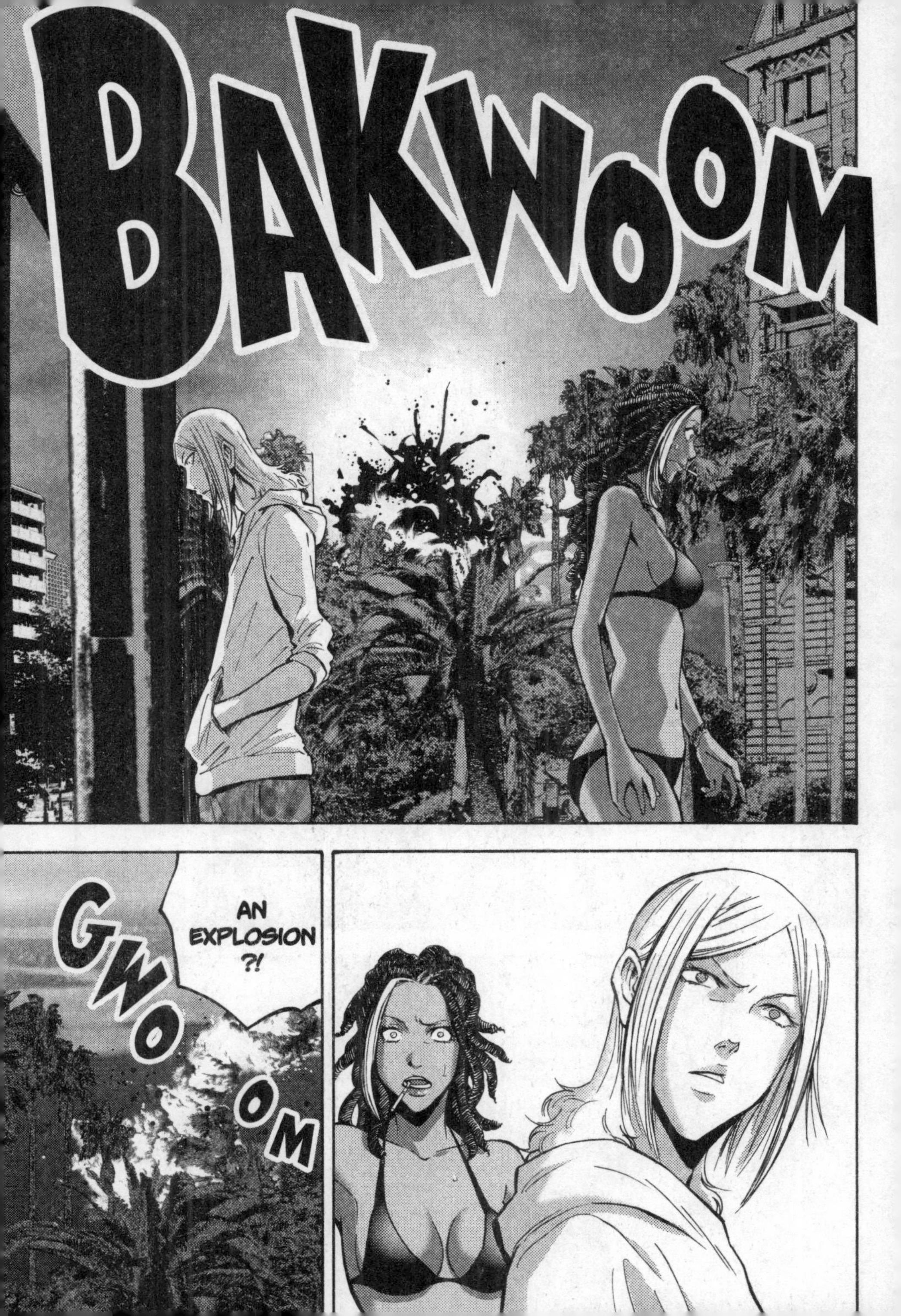
BAKWOOM
GWOOOM
AN EXPLOSION ?!

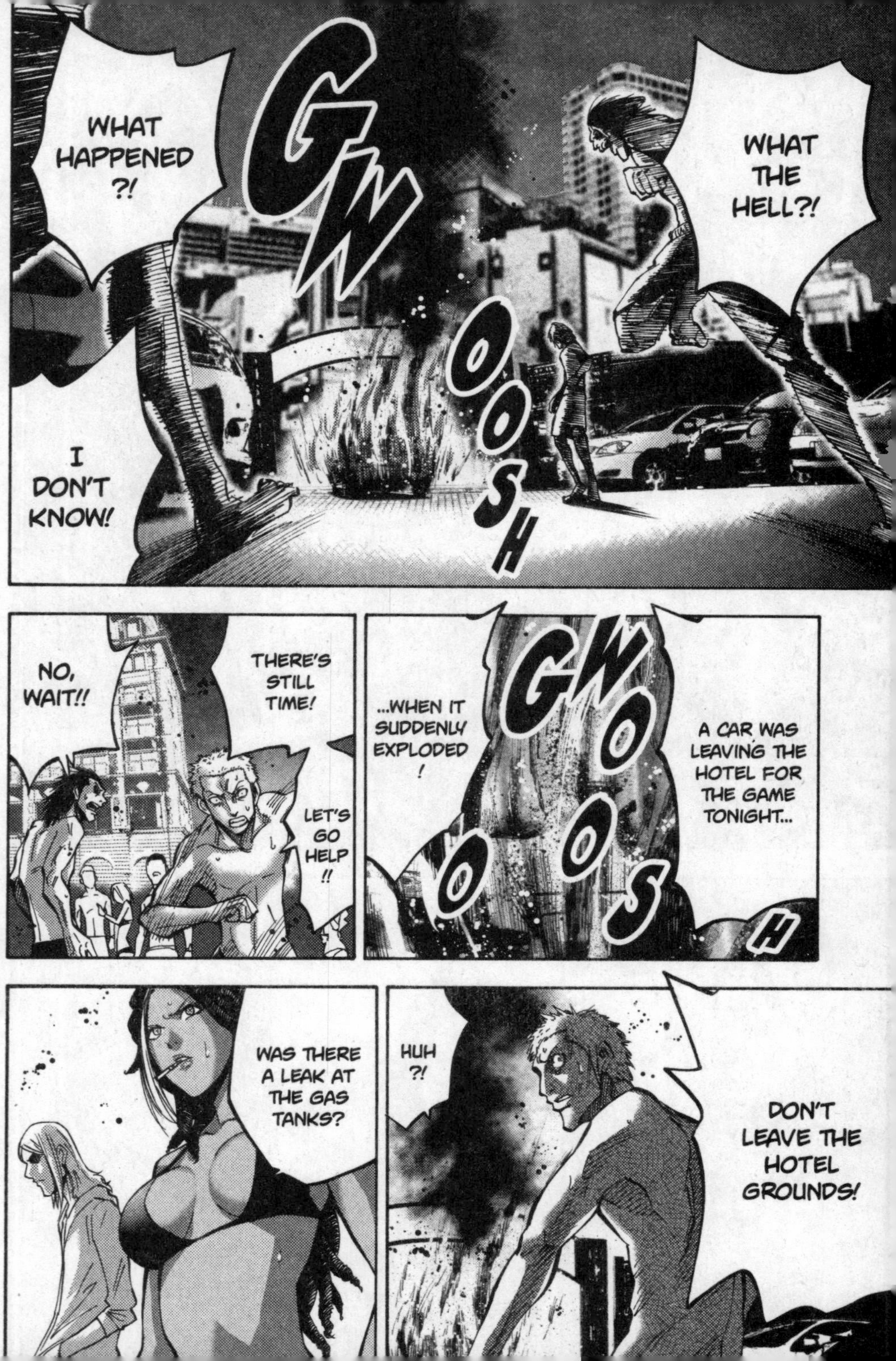
WHAT THE HELL?!
WHAT HAPPENED ?!
GWOOOSH
I DON'T KNOW!
A CAR WAS LEAVING THE HOTEL FOR THE GAME TONIGHT...
GWOOOOSH
...WHEN IT SUDDENLY EXPLODED!
THERE'S STILL TIME!
LET'S GO HELP!!
NO, WAIT!!
DON'T LEAVE THE HOTEL GROUNDS!
HUH?!
WAS THERE A LEAK AT THE GAS TANKS?

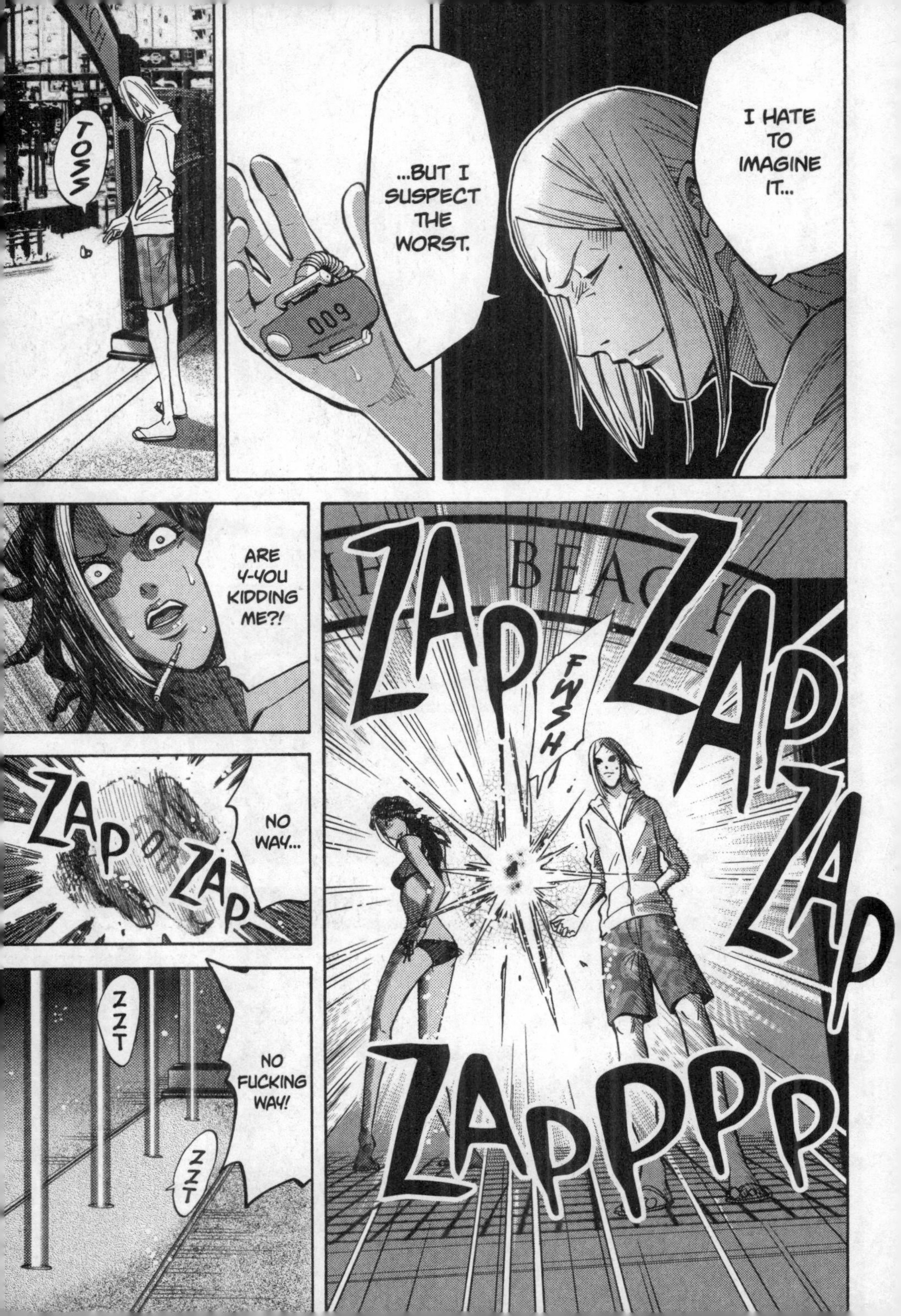
I HATE TO IMAGINE IT...
...BUT I SUSPECT THE WORST.
009
TOSS
ZAP
ZAP
FWSH
ZAP
ZAP
ZAPPPP
ARE Y-YOU KIDDING ME?!
NO WAY...
ZAP
ZAP
NO FUCKING WAY!
ZZT
ZZT

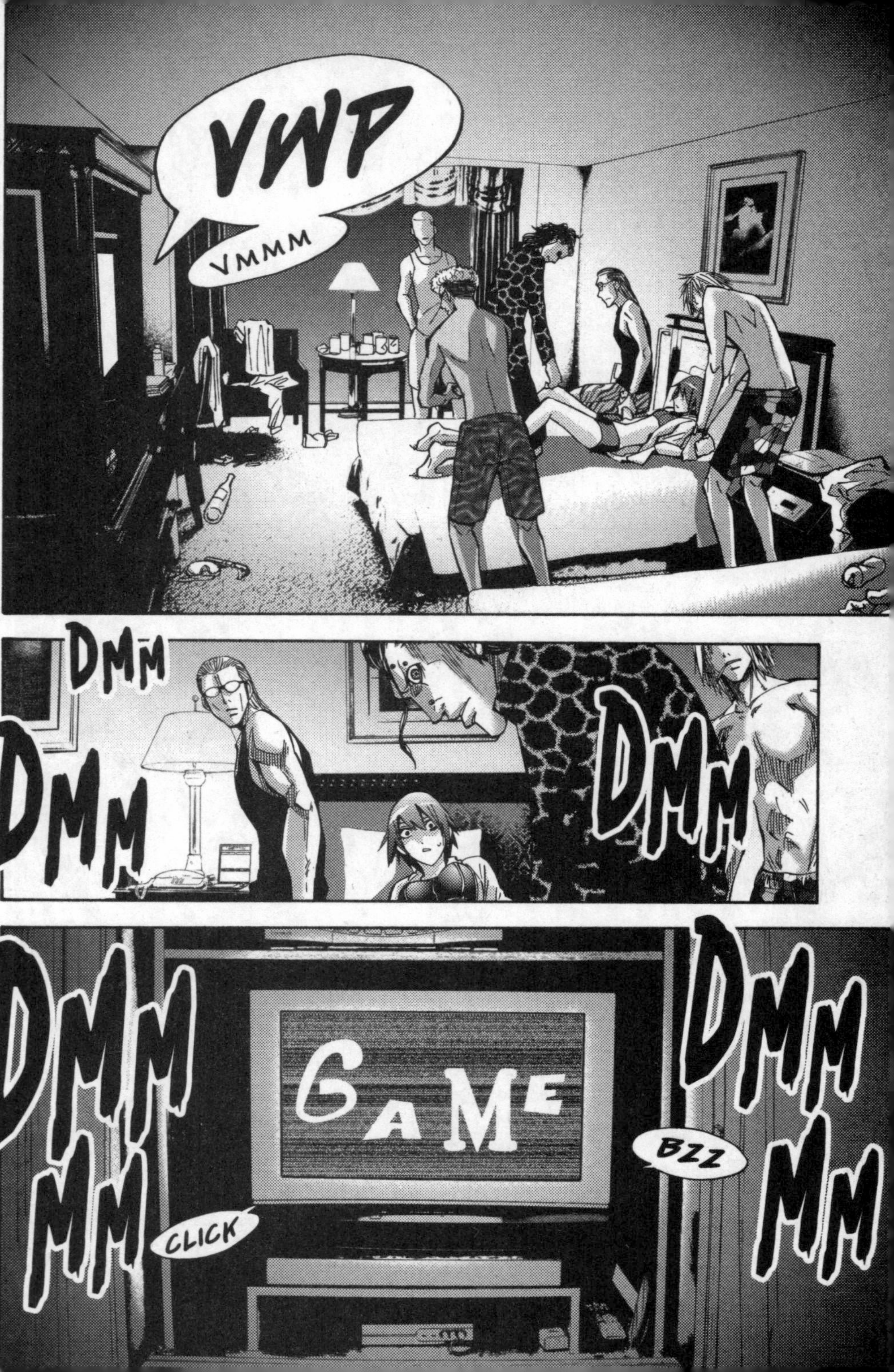
VWP
VMMM
DMM
DMM
DMM
DMM
MM
GAME
CLICK
BZZ
DMM
MM

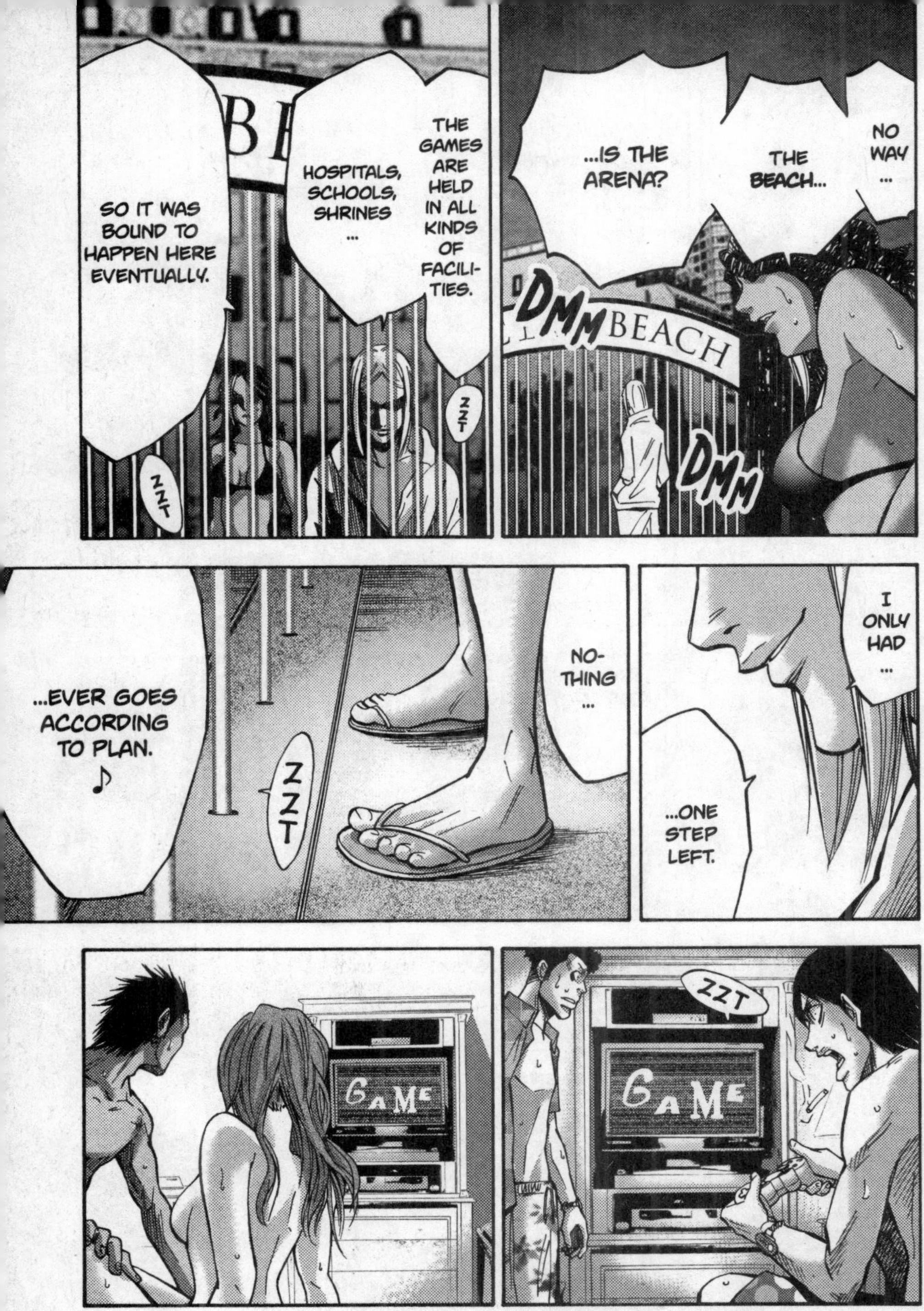
NO WAY ...
THE BEACH...
...IS THE ARENA?
DMM
BEACH
DMM
THE GAMES ARE HELD IN ALL KINDS OF FACILITIES.
HOSPITALS, SCHOOLS, SHRINES ...
SO IT WAS BOUND TO HAPPEN HERE EVENTUALLY.
ZZT
ZZT
I ONLY HAD ...
...ONE STEP LEFT.
NOTHING ...
...EVER GOES ACCORDING TO PLAN. ♪
ZZT
ZZT
GAME
GAME

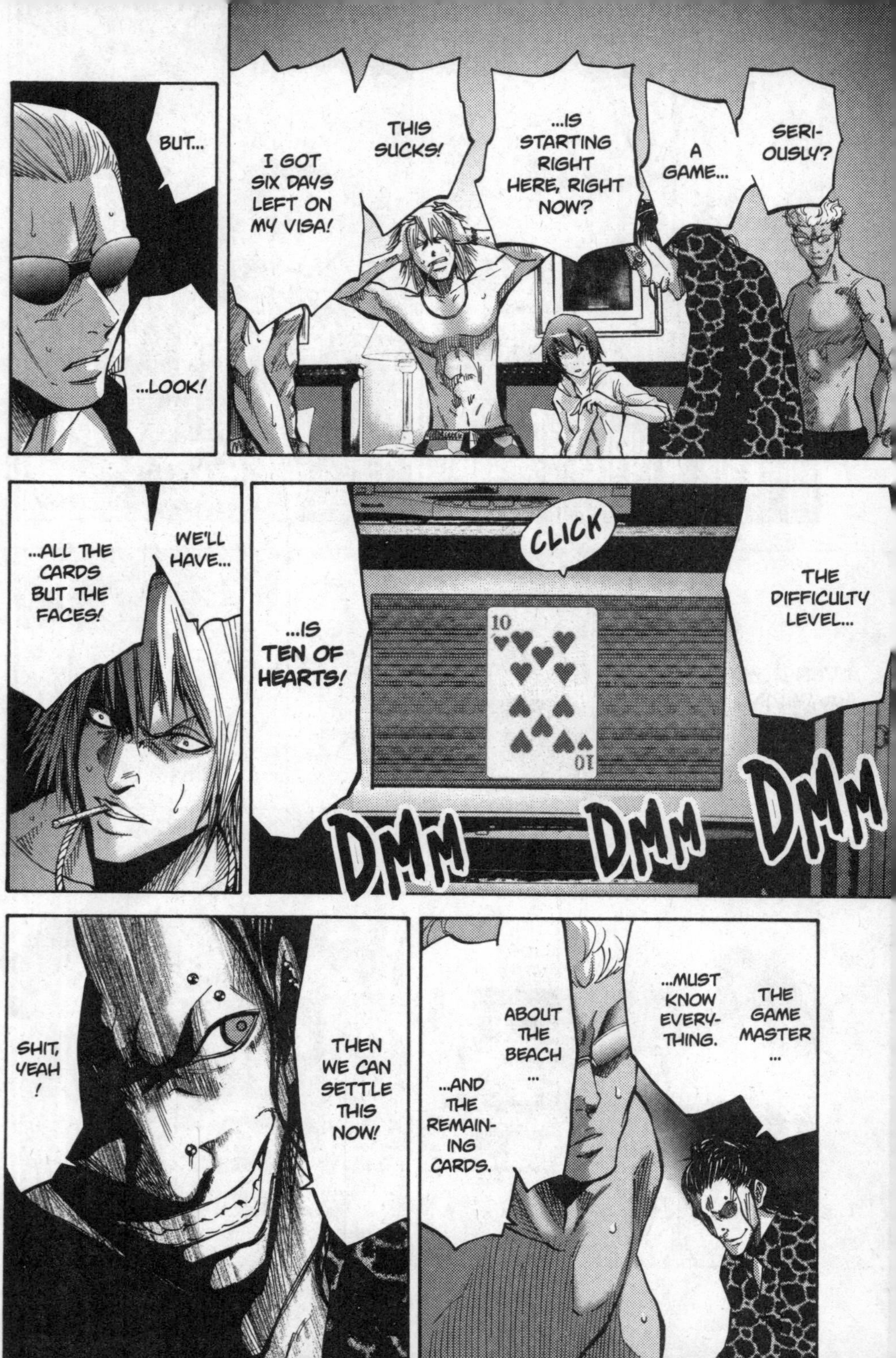
SERI-OUSLY?
A GAME...
...IS STARTING RIGHT HERE, RIGHT NOW?
THIS SUCKS!
I GOT SIX DAYS LEFT ON MY VISA!
BUT...
...LOOK!
THE DIFFICULTY LEVEL...
CLICK
...IS TEN OF HEARTS!
10
10
DMM
DMM
DMM
WE'LL HAVE...
...ALL THE CARDS BUT THE FACES!
THE GAME MASTER...
...MUST KNOW EVERY-THING.
ABOUT THE BEACH...
...AND THE REMAIN-ING CARDS.
THEN WE CAN SETTLE THIS NOW!
SHIT, YEAH!

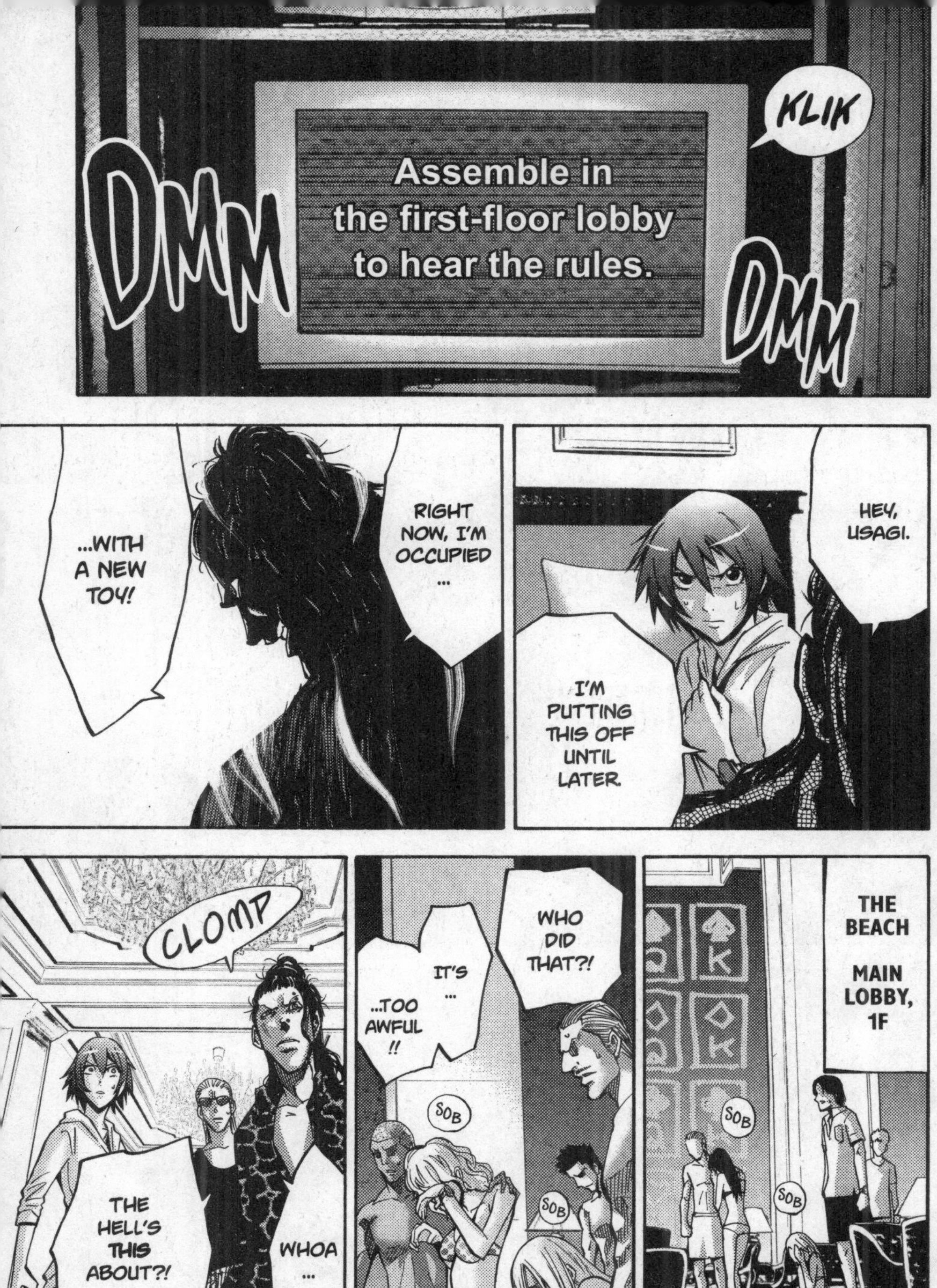
KLIK
Assemble in the first-floor lobby to hear the rules.
DMM
DMM
HEY, USAGI.
I'M PUTTING THIS OFF UNTIL LATER.
RIGHT NOW, I'M OCCUPIED ...
...WITH A NEW TOY!
THE BEACH
MAIN LOBBY, 1F
SOB
SOB
WHO DID THAT?!
IT'S ...
...TOO AWFUL!!
SOB
SOB
CLOMP
WHOA ...
THE HELL'S THIS ABOUT?!

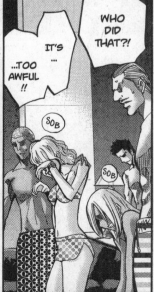

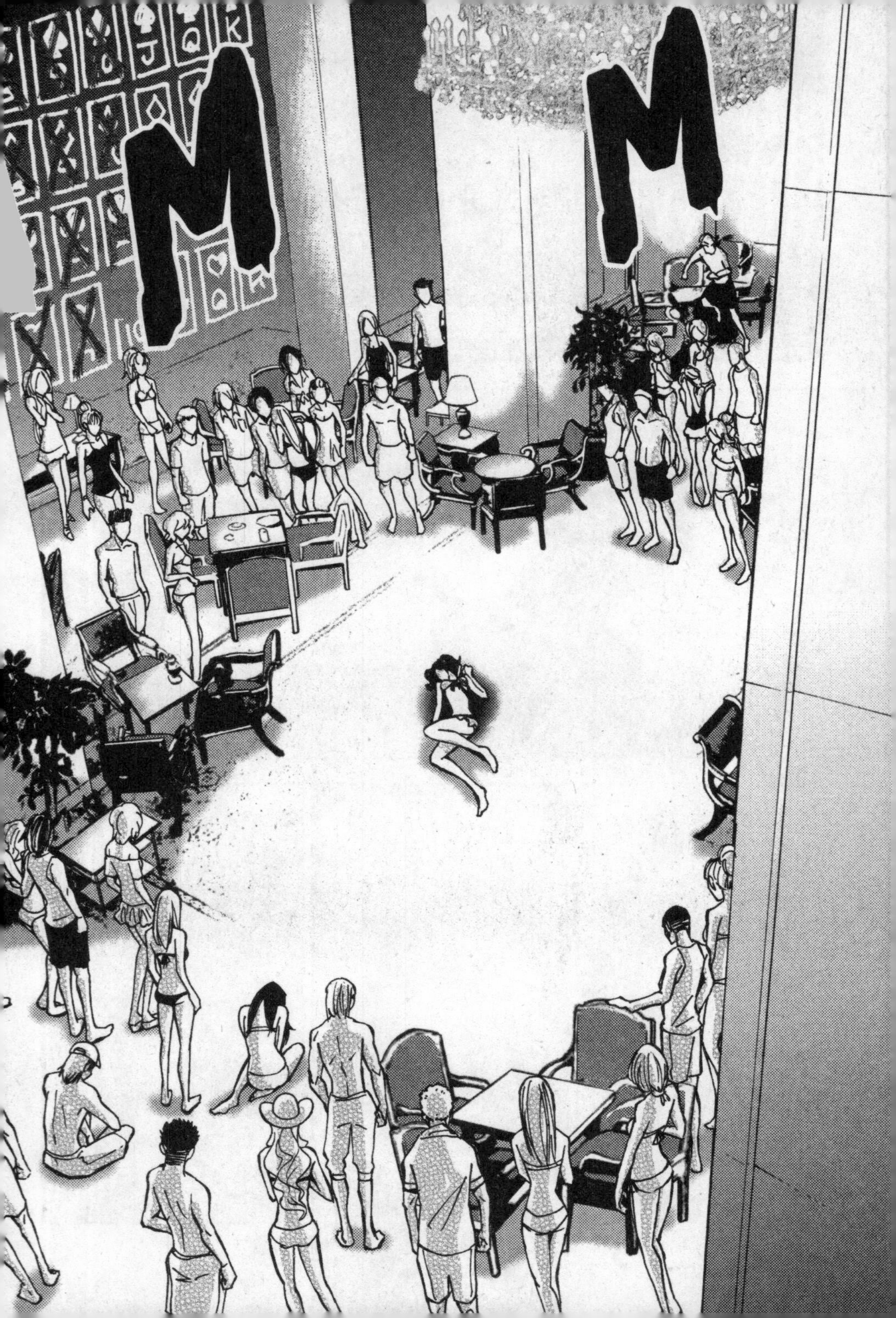
M
M

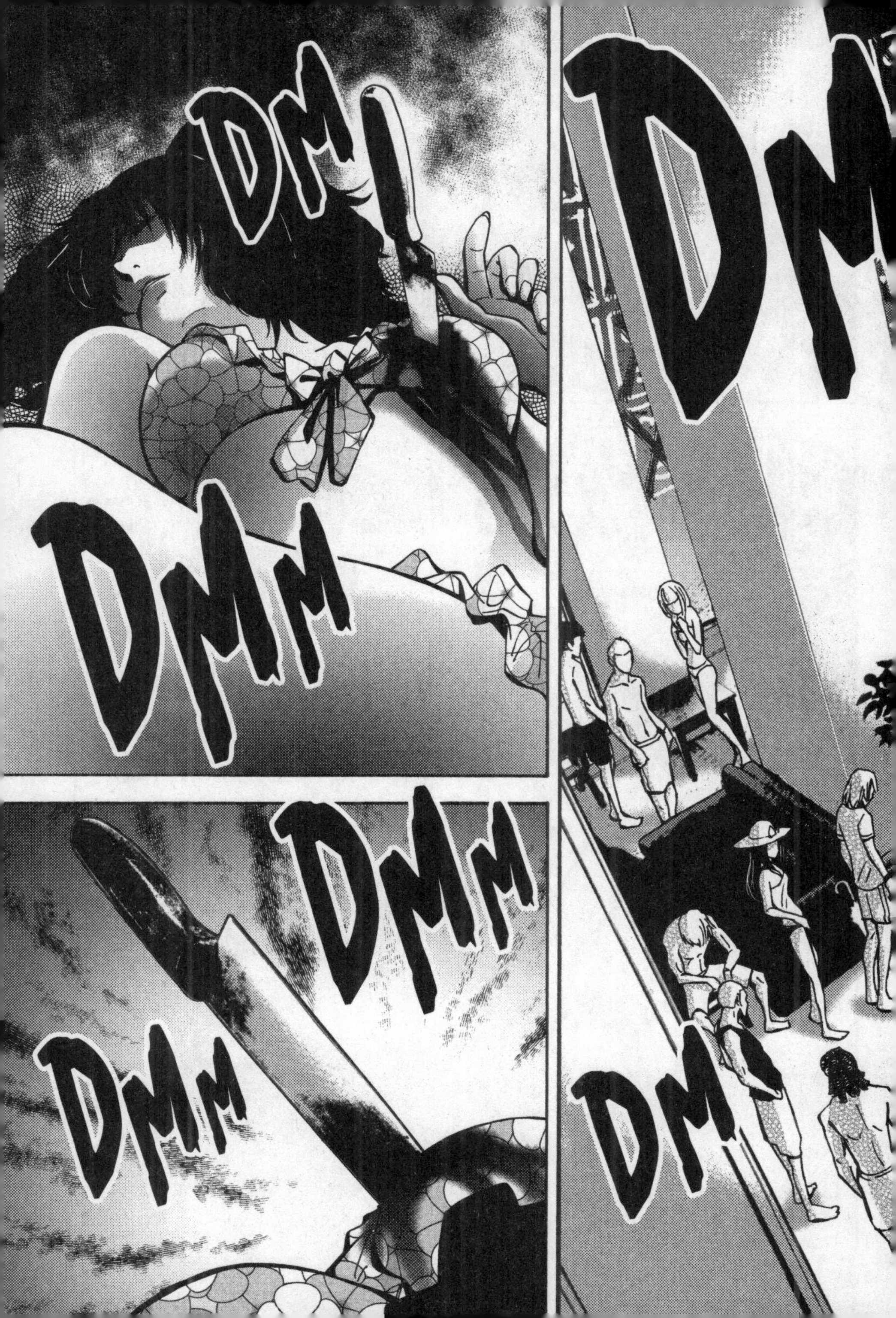
DM
DM
DM
DMM
DMM
DMM

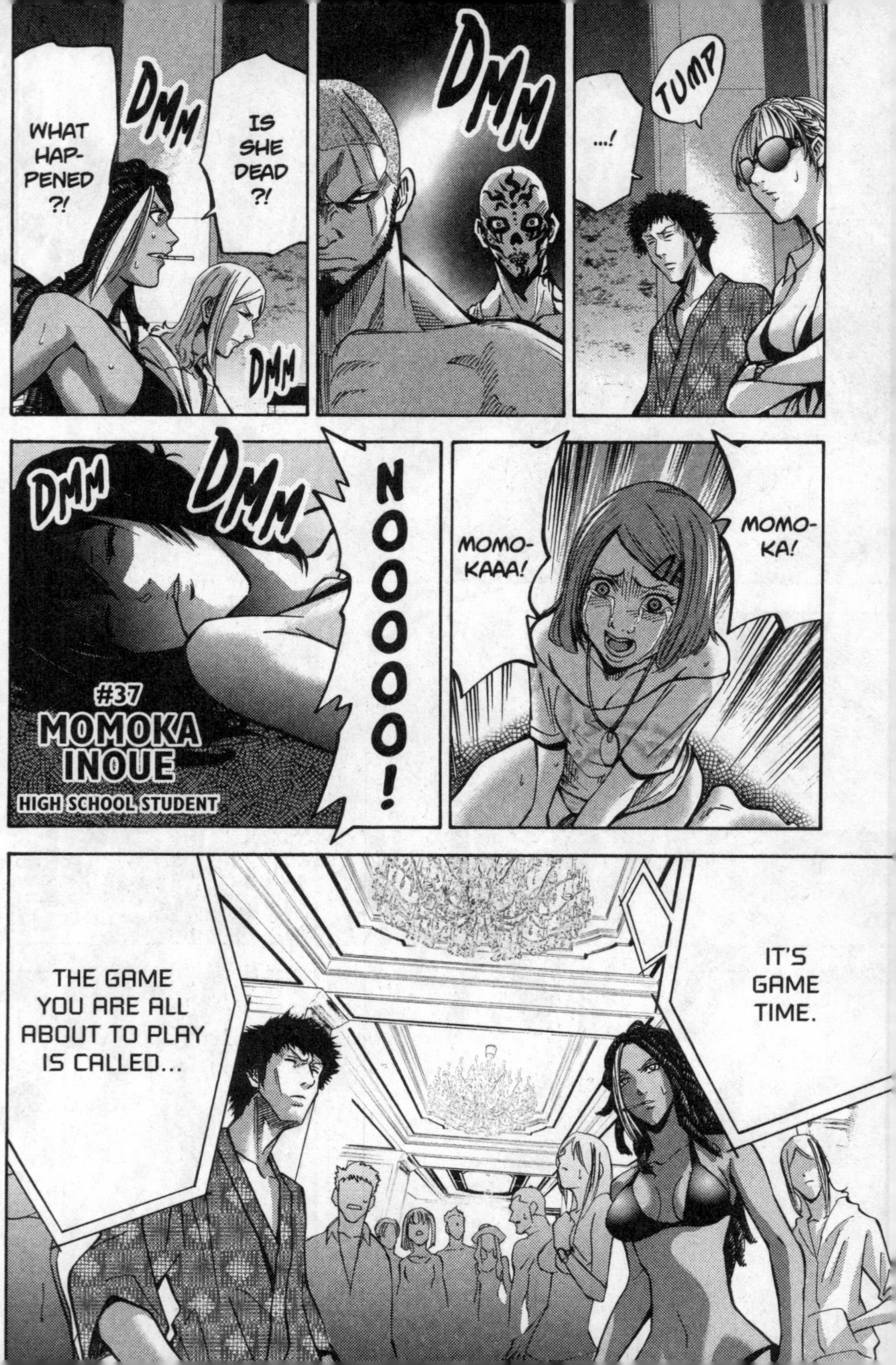
TUMP
...!
DMM
IS SHE DEAD ?!
DMM
WHAT HAP-PENED ?!
DMM
MOMO-KA!
MOMO-KAAA!
NOOOOOO!
DMM
DMM
#37 MOMOKA INOUE
HIGH SCHOOL STUDENT
IT'S GAME TIME.
THE GAME YOU ARE ALL ABOUT TO PLAY IS CALLED...

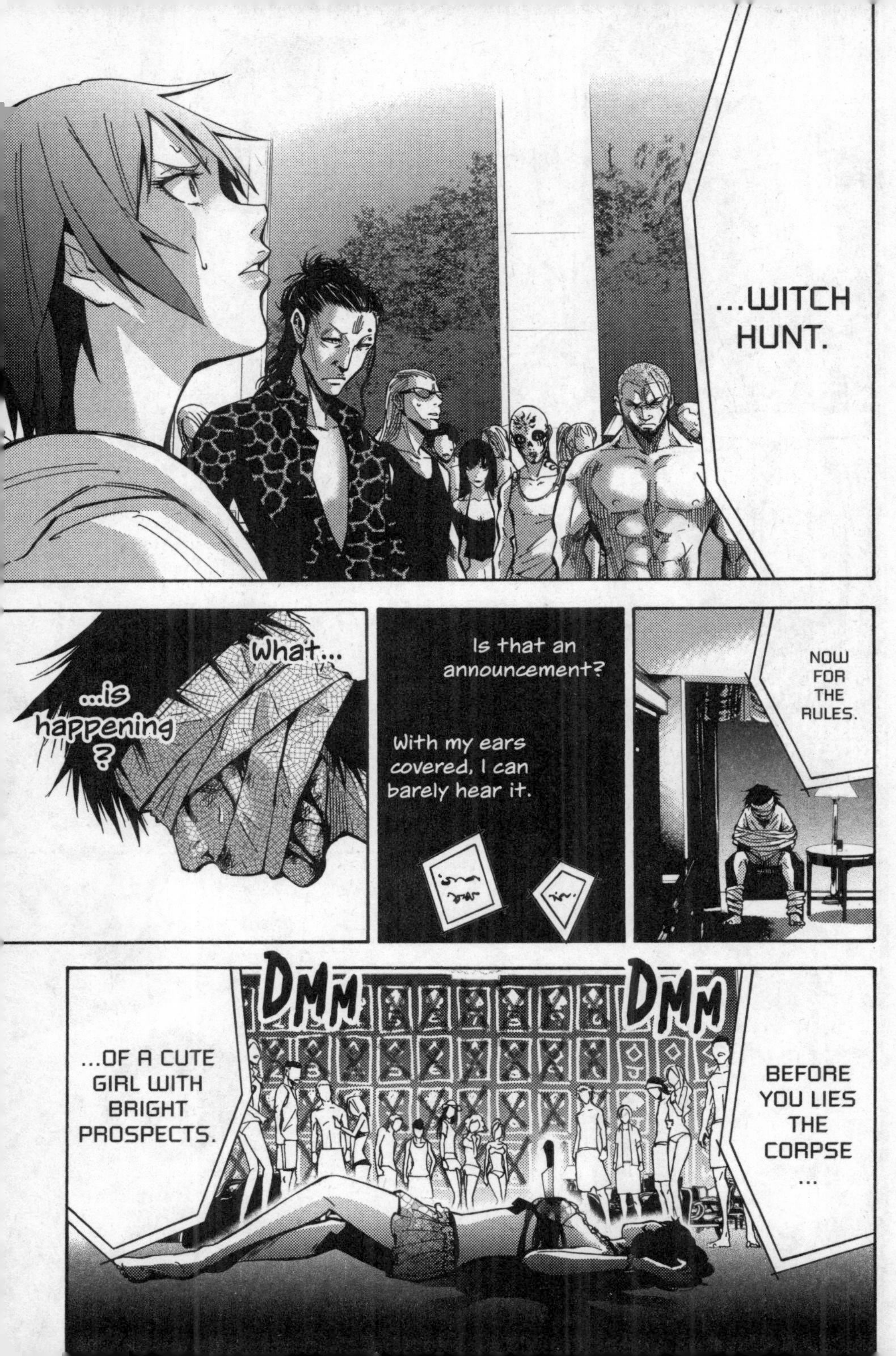
...WITCH HUNT.
NOW FOR THE RULES.
Is that an announcement?
With my ears covered, I can barely hear it.
What...
...is happening?
DMM
DMM
BEFORE YOU LIES THE CORPSE...
...OF A CUTE GIRL WITH BRIGHT PROSPECTS.

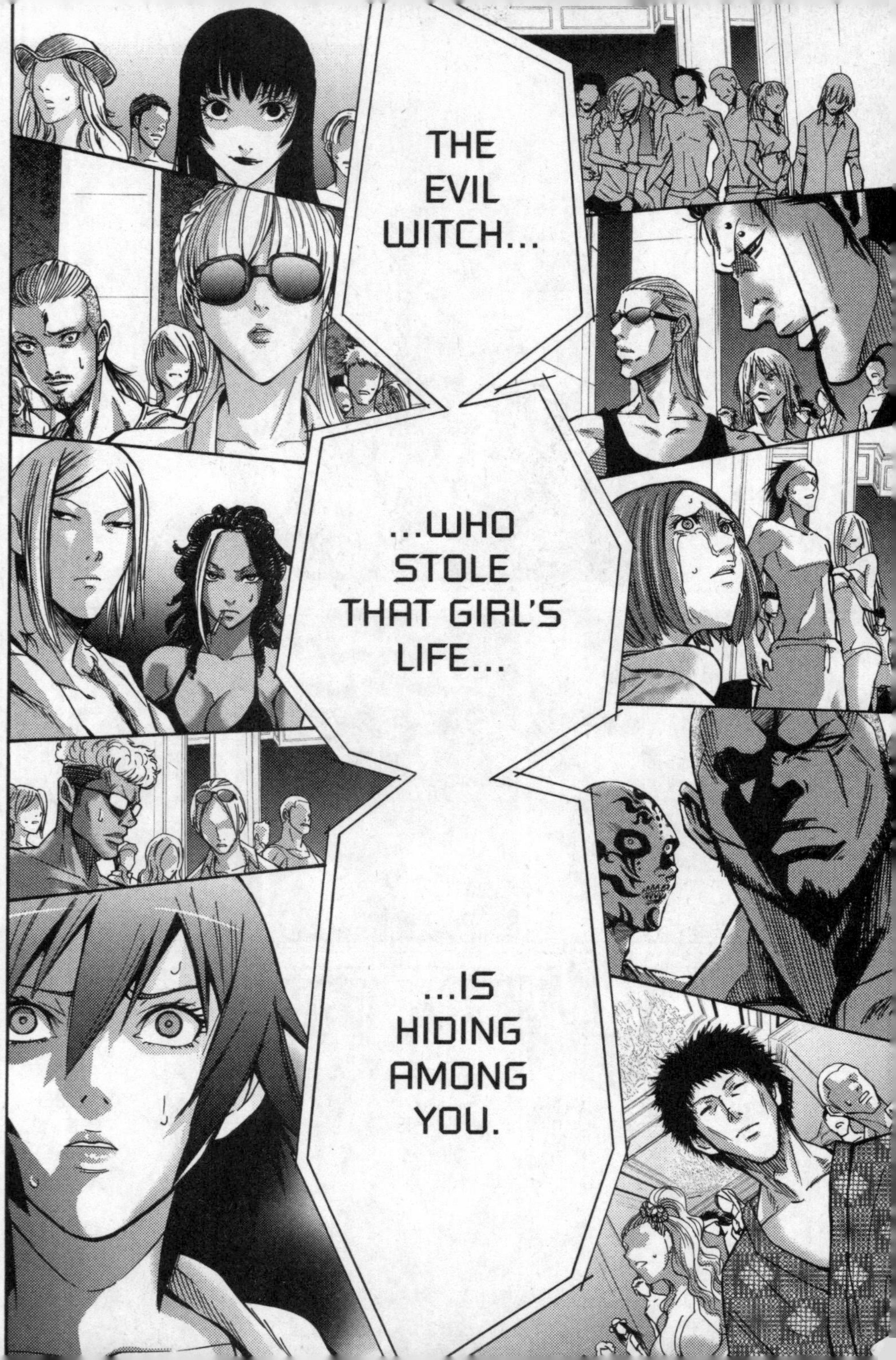
THE EVIL WITCH...
...WHO STOLE THAT GIRL'S LIFE...
...IS HIDING AMONG YOU.

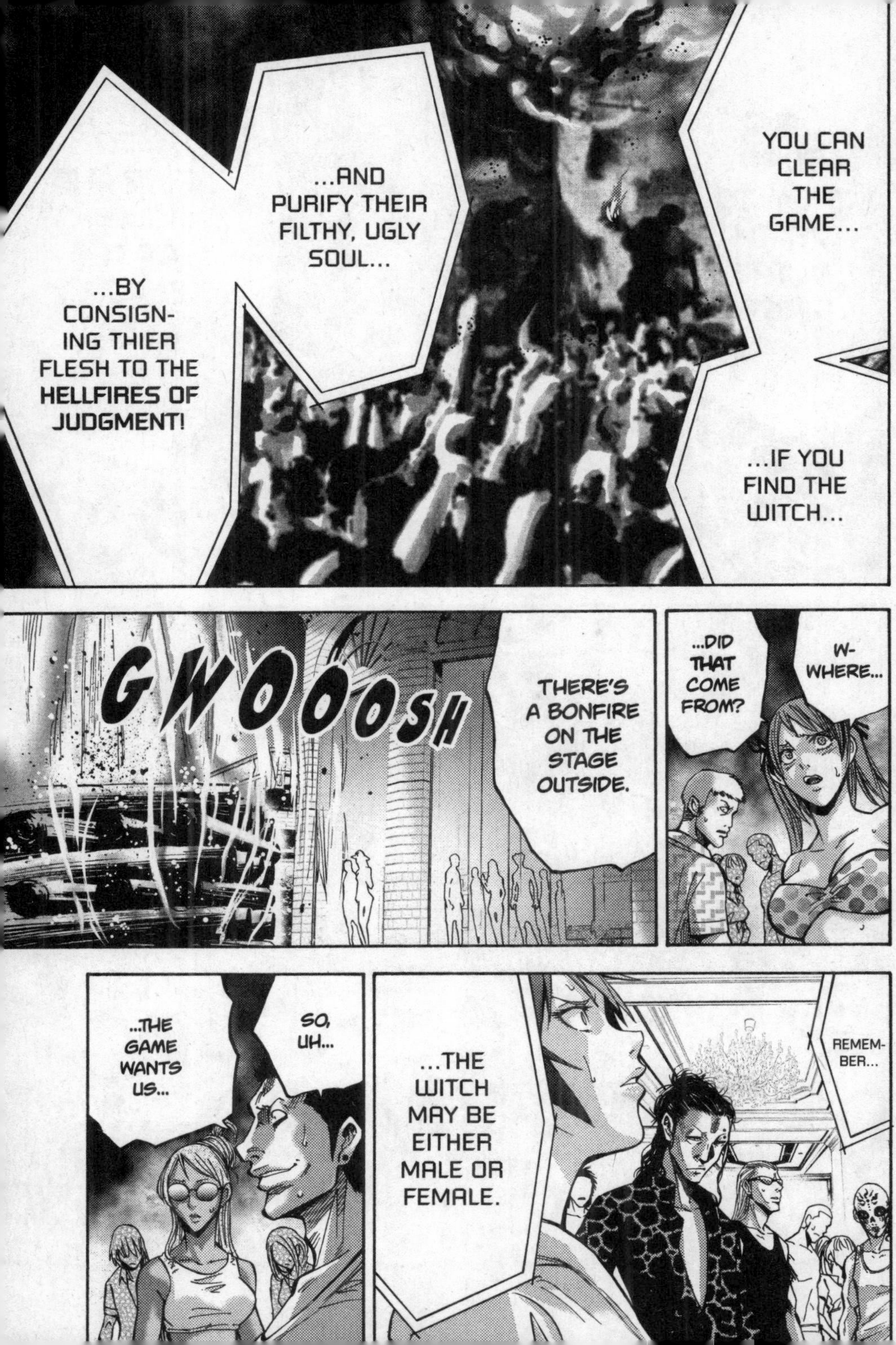
YOU CAN CLEAR THE GAME...
...IF YOU FIND THE WITCH...
...AND PURIFY THEIR FILTHY, UGLY SOUL...
...BY CONSIGN-ING THIER FLESH TO THE HELLFIRES OF JUDGMENT!
W-WHERE...
...DID THAT COME FROM?
THERE'S A BONFIRE ON THE STAGE OUTSIDE.
GWOOOSH
REMEM-BER...
...THE WITCH MAY BE EITHER MALE OR FEMALE.
SO, UH...
...THE GAME WANTS US...

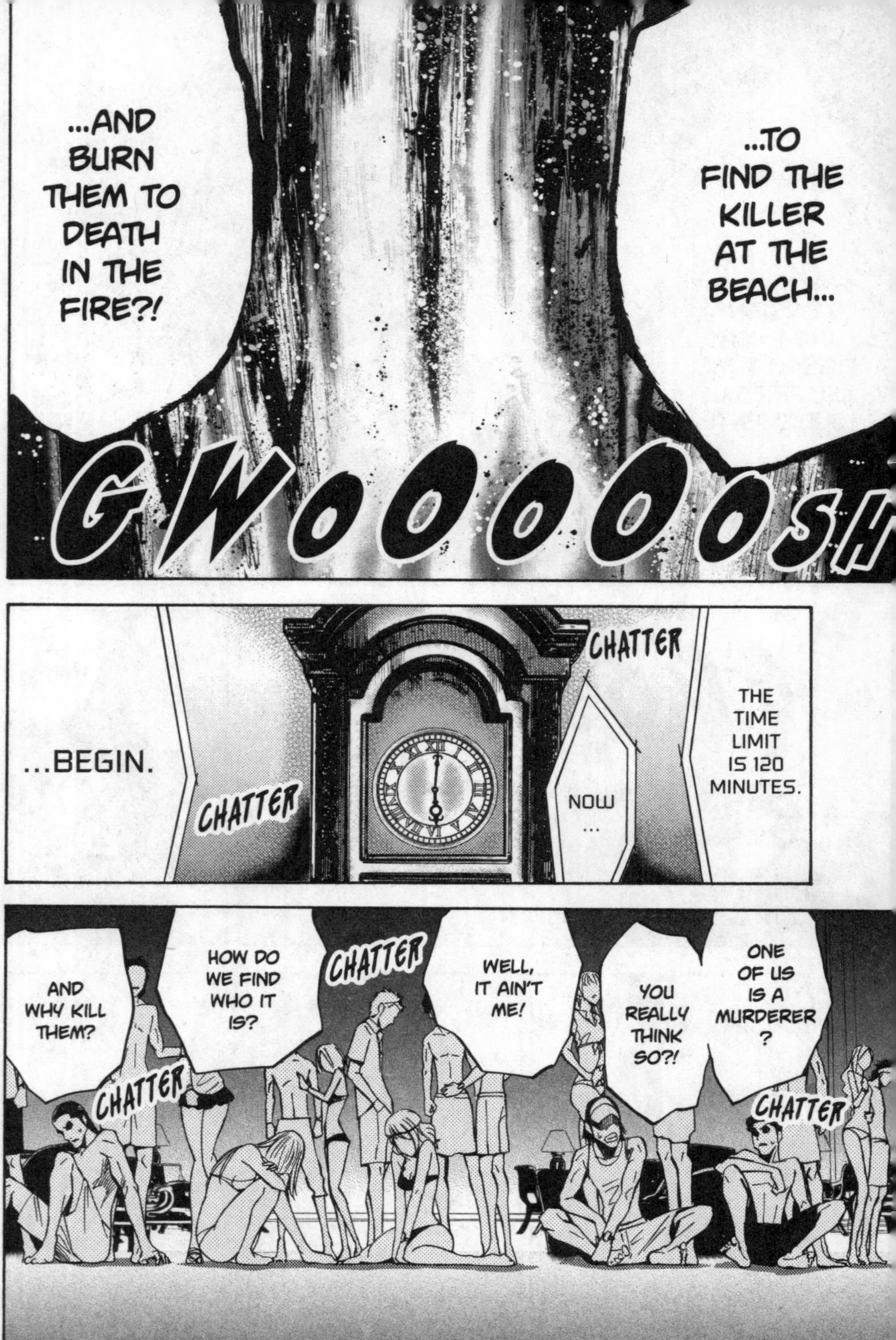
...TO FIND THE KILLER AT THE BEACH...
...AND BURN THEM TO DEATH IN THE FIRE?!
GWOOOOOSH
THE TIME LIMIT IS 120 MINUTES.
CHATTER
NOW ...
CHATTER
...BEGIN.
ONE OF US IS A MURDERER ?
YOU REALLY THINK SO?!
CHATTER
WELL, IT AIN'T ME!
CHATTER
HOW DO WE FIND WHO IT IS?
AND WHY KILL THEM?
CHATTER

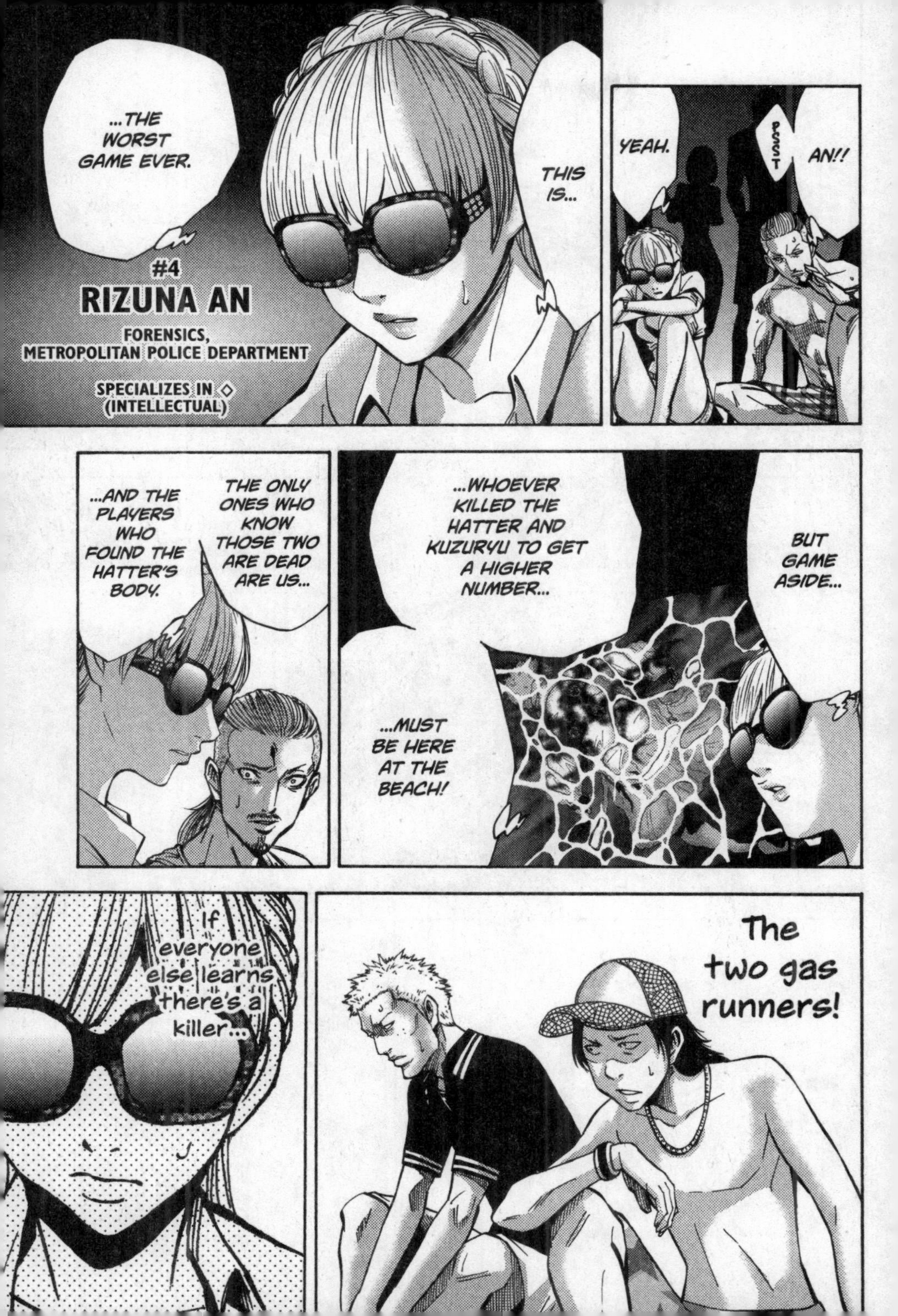
AN!!
PSSST
YEAH.
THIS IS...
...THE WORST GAME EVER.
#4
RIZUNA AN
FORENSICS, METROPOLITAN POLICE DEPARTMENT
SPECIALIZES IN ◇ (INTELLECTUAL)
BUT GAME ASIDE...
...WHOEVER KILLED THE HATTER AND KUZURYU TO GET A HIGHER NUMBER...
...MUST BE HERE AT THE BEACH!
THE ONLY ONES WHO KNOW THOSE TWO ARE DEAD ARE US...
...AND THE PLAYERS WHO FOUND THE HATTER'S BODY.
The two gas runners!
If everyone else learns there's a killer...

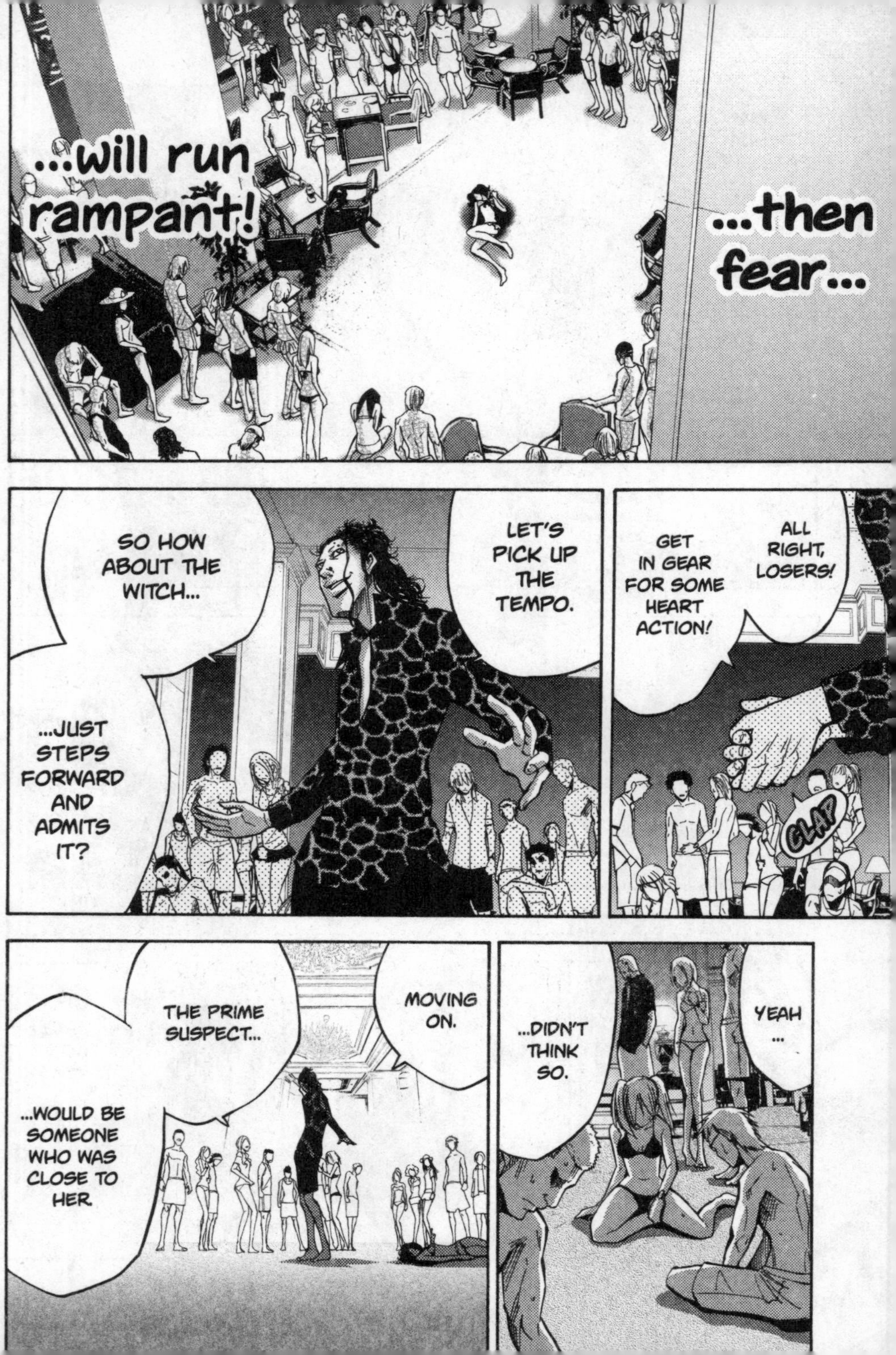
...then fear...
...will run rampant!
ALL RIGHT, LOSERS!
GET IN GEAR FOR SOME HEART ACTION!
CLAP
LET'S PICK UP THE TEMPO.
SO HOW ABOUT THE WITCH...
...JUST STEPS FORWARD AND ADMITS IT?
YEAH ...
...DIDN'T THINK SO.
MOVING ON.
THE PRIME SUSPECT...
...WOULD BE SOMEONE WHO WAS CLOSE TO HER.

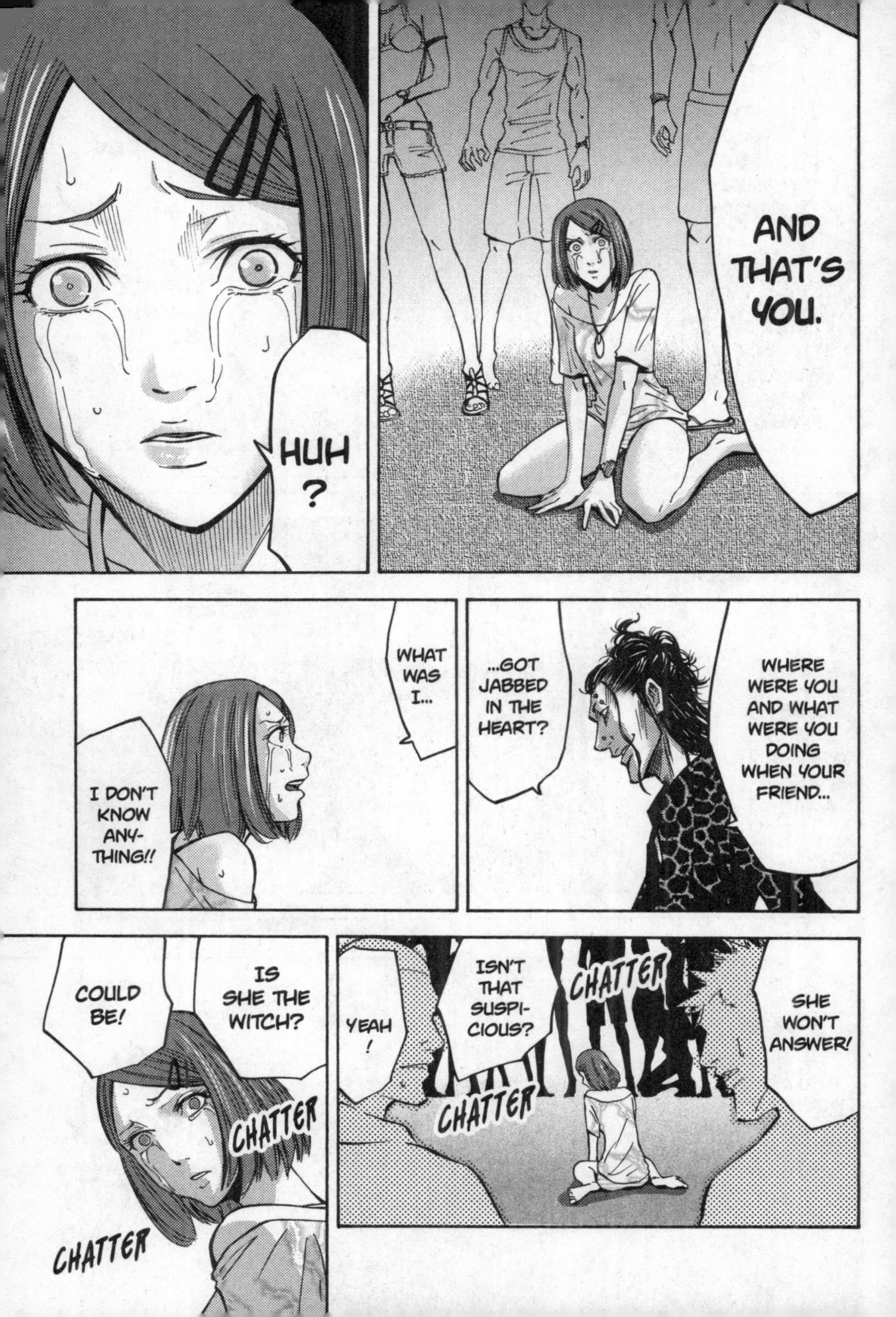
AND THAT'S YOU.
HUH?
WHERE WERE YOU AND WHAT WERE YOU DOING WHEN YOUR FRIEND...
...GOT JABBED IN THE HEART?
WHAT WAS I...
I DON'T KNOW ANY-THING!!
SHE WON'T ANSWER!
CHATTER
ISN'T THAT SUSPICIOUS?
YEAH!
CHATTER
IS SHE THE WITCH?
COULD BE!
CHATTER
CHATTER

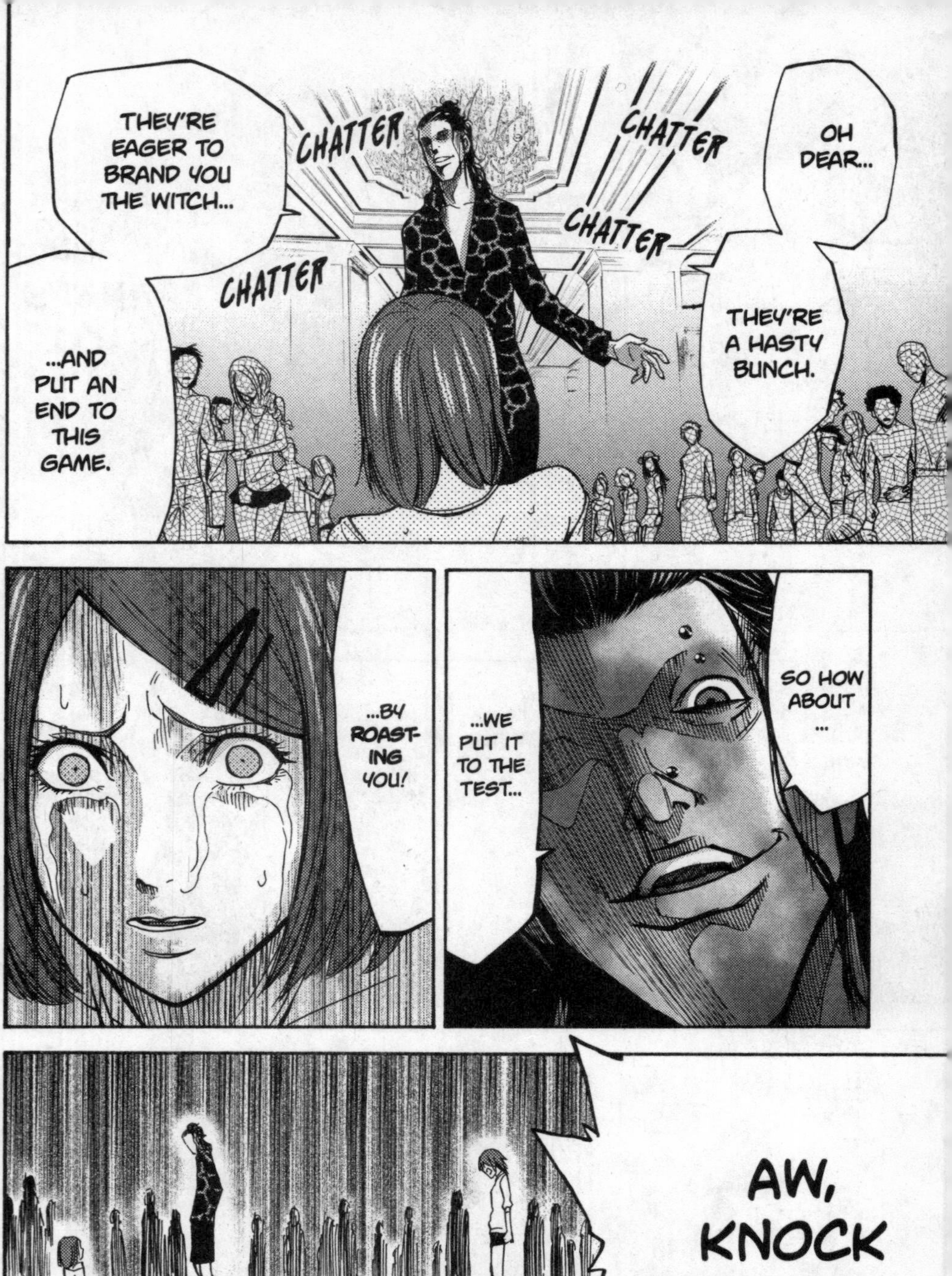
OH DEAR...
THEY'RE A HASTY BUNCH.
CHATTER
CHATTER
CHATTER
CHATTER
THEY'RE EAGER TO BRAND YOU THE WITCH...
...AND PUT AN END TO THIS GAME.
SO HOW ABOUT ...
...WE PUT IT TO THE TEST...
...BY ROASTING YOU!
AW, KNOCK IT OFF!

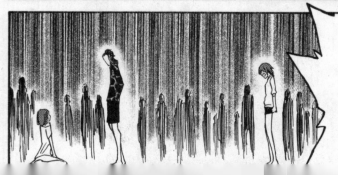

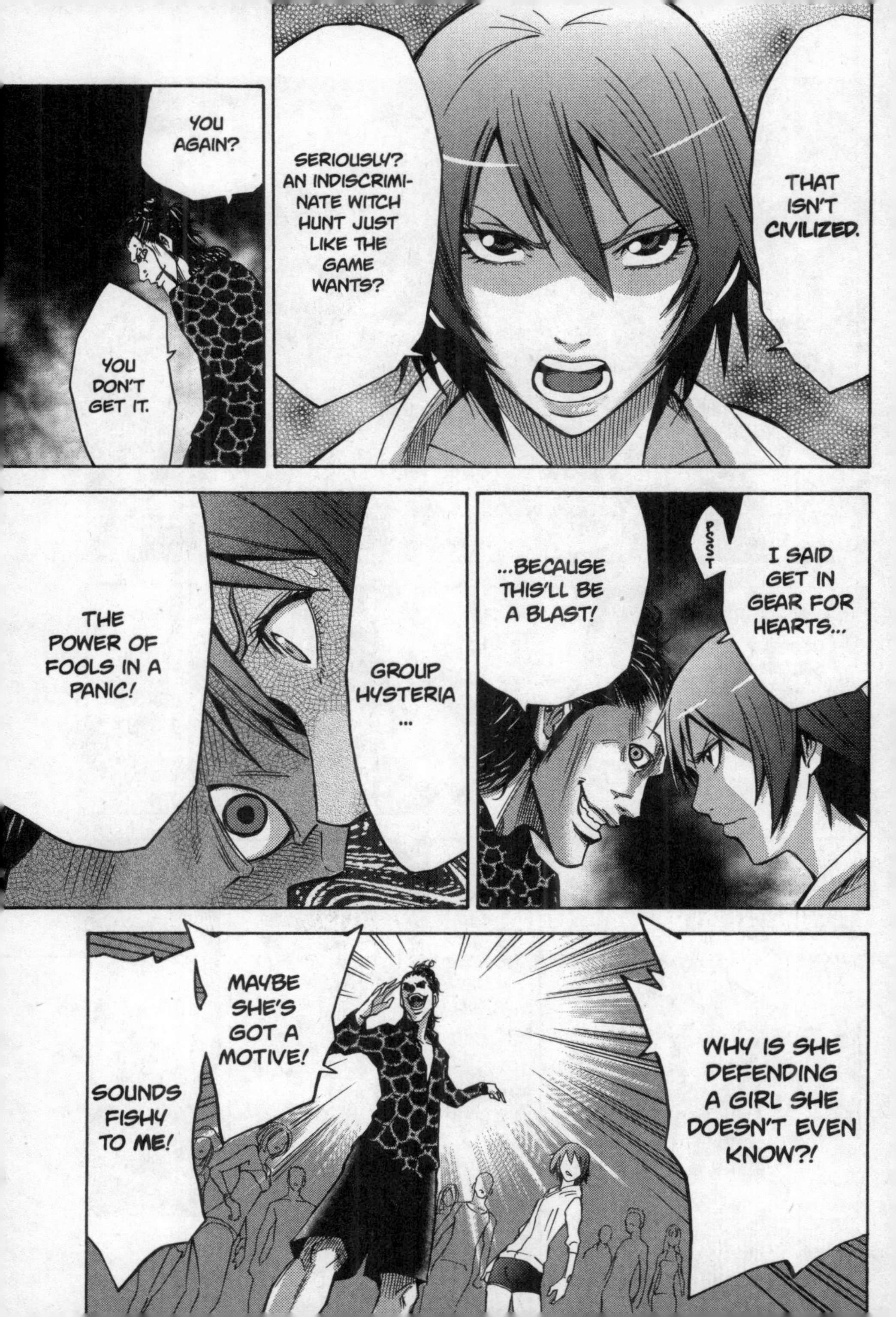
SERIOUSLY? AN INDISCRIMI-NATE WITCH HUNT JUST LIKE THE GAME WANTS?
THAT ISN'T CIVILIZED.
YOU AGAIN?
YOU DON'T GET IT.
PSST
I SAID GET IN GEAR FOR HEARTS...
...BECAUSE THIS'LL BE A BLAST!
GROUP HYSTERIA ...
THE POWER OF FOOLS IN A PANIC!
WHY IS SHE DEFENDING A GIRL SHE DOESN'T EVEN KNOW?!
MAYBE SHE'S GOT A MOTIVE!
SOUNDS FISHY TO ME!

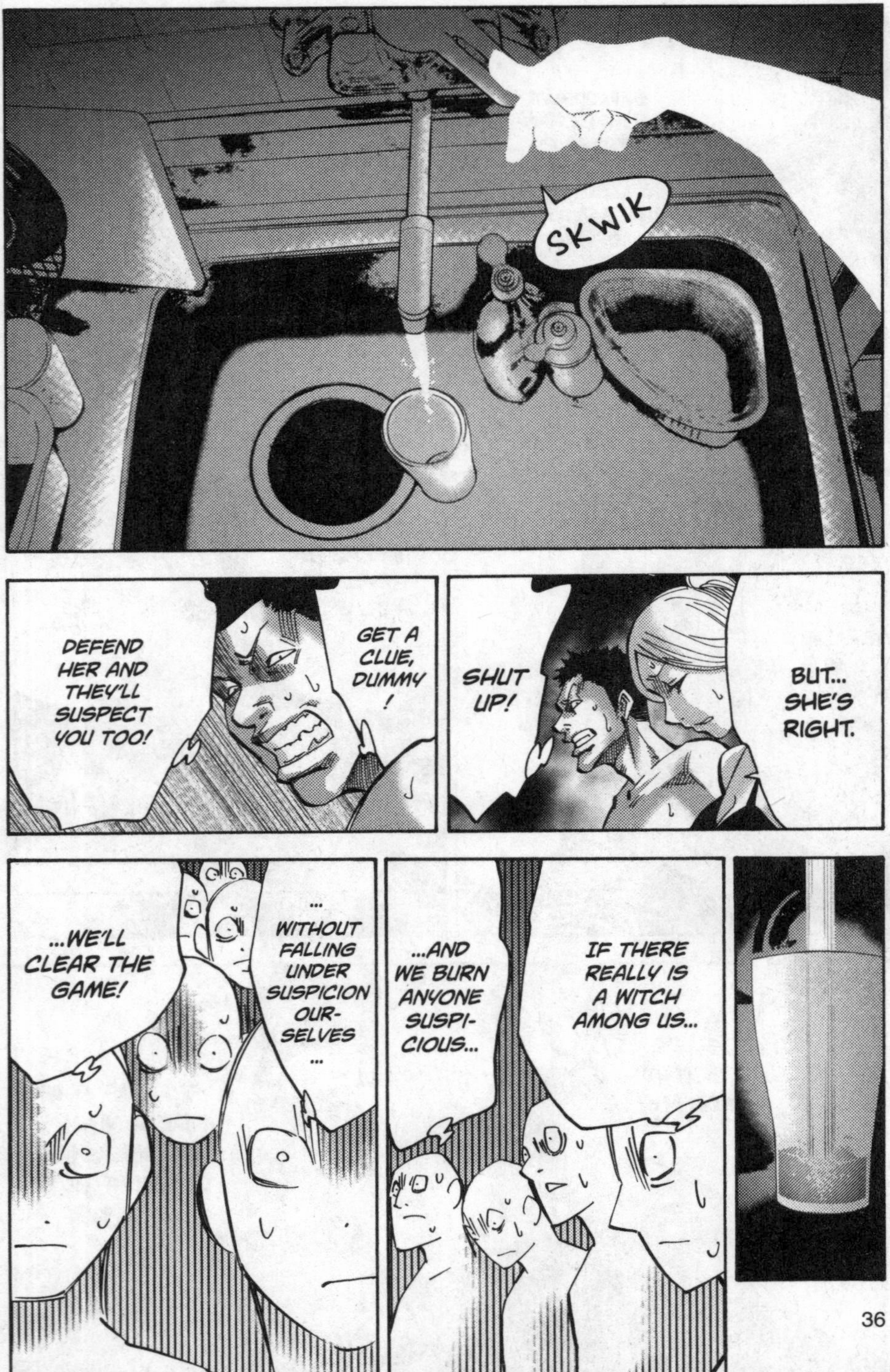
SKWIK
BUT... SHE'S RIGHT.
SHUT UP!
GET A CLUE, DUMMY!
DEFEND HER AND THEY'LL SUSPECT YOU TOO!
IF THERE REALLY IS A WITCH AMONG US...
...AND WE BURN ANYONE SUSPICIOUS...
...WITHOUT FALLING UNDER SUSPICION OURSELVES...
...WE'LL CLEAR THE GAME!

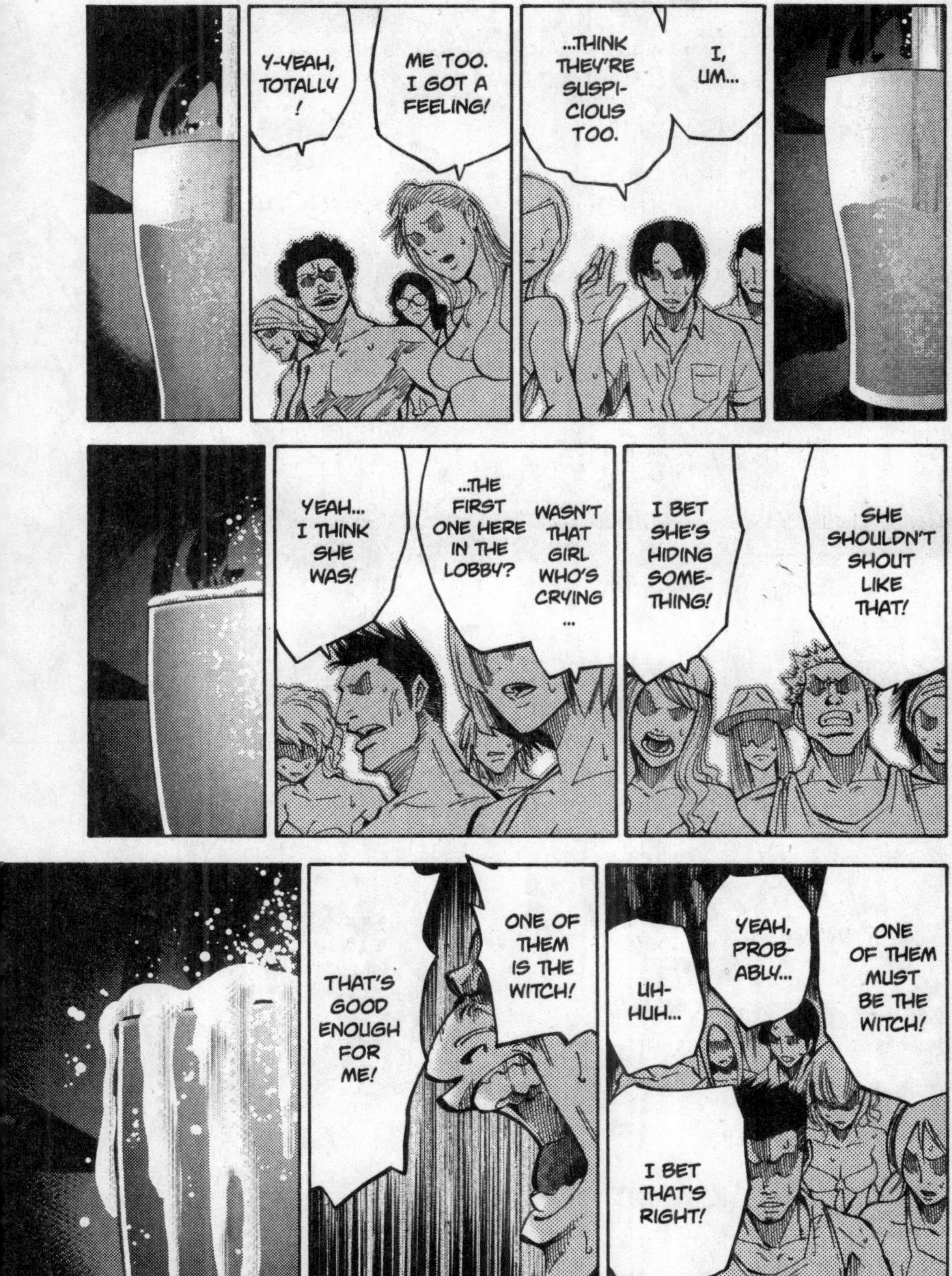
I, UM...
...THINK THEY'RE SUSPICIOUS TOO.
ME TOO. I GOT A FEELING!
Y-YEAH, TOTALLY!
SHE SHOULDN'T SHOUT LIKE THAT!
I BET SHE'S HIDING SOMETHING!
WASN'T THAT GIRL WHO'S CRYING...
...THE FIRST ONE HERE IN THE LOBBY?
YEAH... I THINK SHE WAS!
ONE OF THEM MUST BE THE WITCH!
YEAH, PROBABLY...
UH-HUH...
I BET THAT'S RIGHT!
ONE OF THEM IS THE WITCH!
THAT'S GOOD ENOUGH FOR ME!

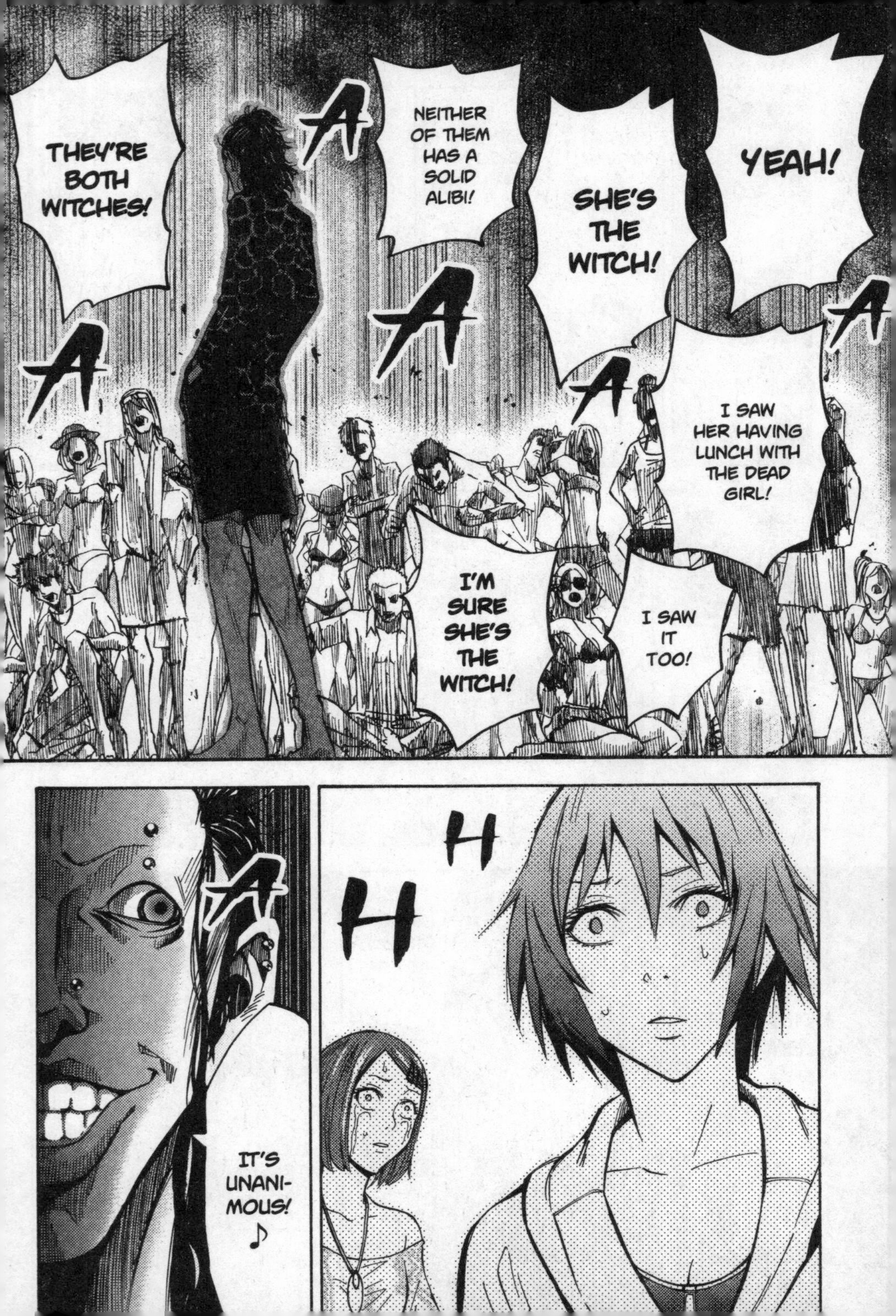
YEAH!
A
SHE'S THE WITCH!
A
NEITHER OF THEM HAS A SOLID ALIBI!
A
THEY'RE BOTH WITCHES!
A
A
I SAW HER HAVING LUNCH WITH THE DEAD GIRL!
I SAW IT TOO!
I'M SURE SHE'S THE WITCH!
H
H
A
IT'S UNANI-MOUS! ♪

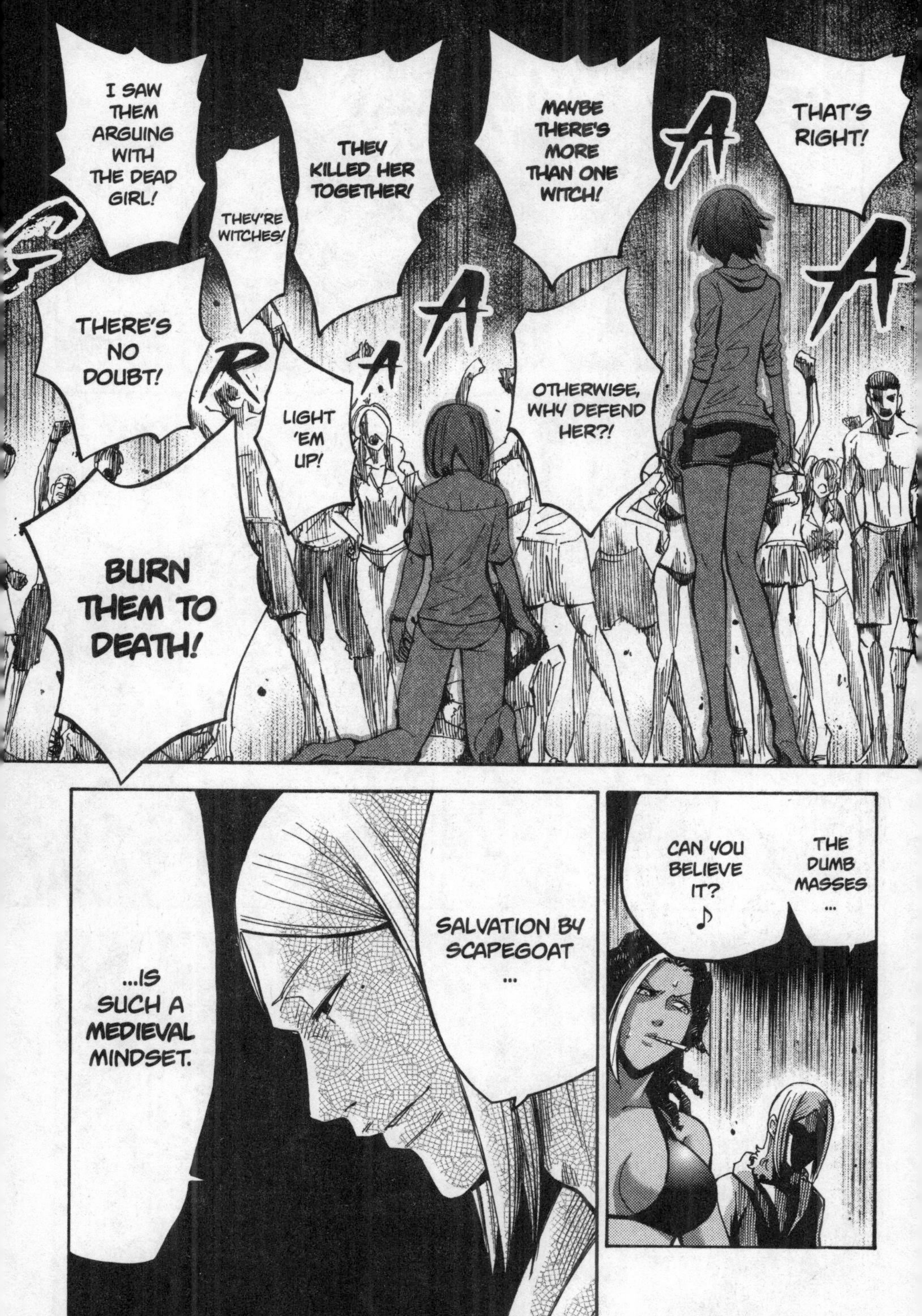
THAT'S RIGHT!
MAYBE THERE'S MORE THAN ONE WITCH!
THEY KILLED HER TOGETHER!
THEY'RE WITCHES!
I SAW THEM ARGUING WITH THE DEAD GIRL!
OTHERWISE, WHY DEFEND HER?!
LIGHT 'EM UP!
THERE'S NO DOUBT!
BURN THEM TO DEATH!
THE DUMB MASSES ...
CAN YOU BELIEVE IT? ♪
SALVATION BY SCAPEGOAT ...
...IS SUCH A MEDIEVAL MINDSET.

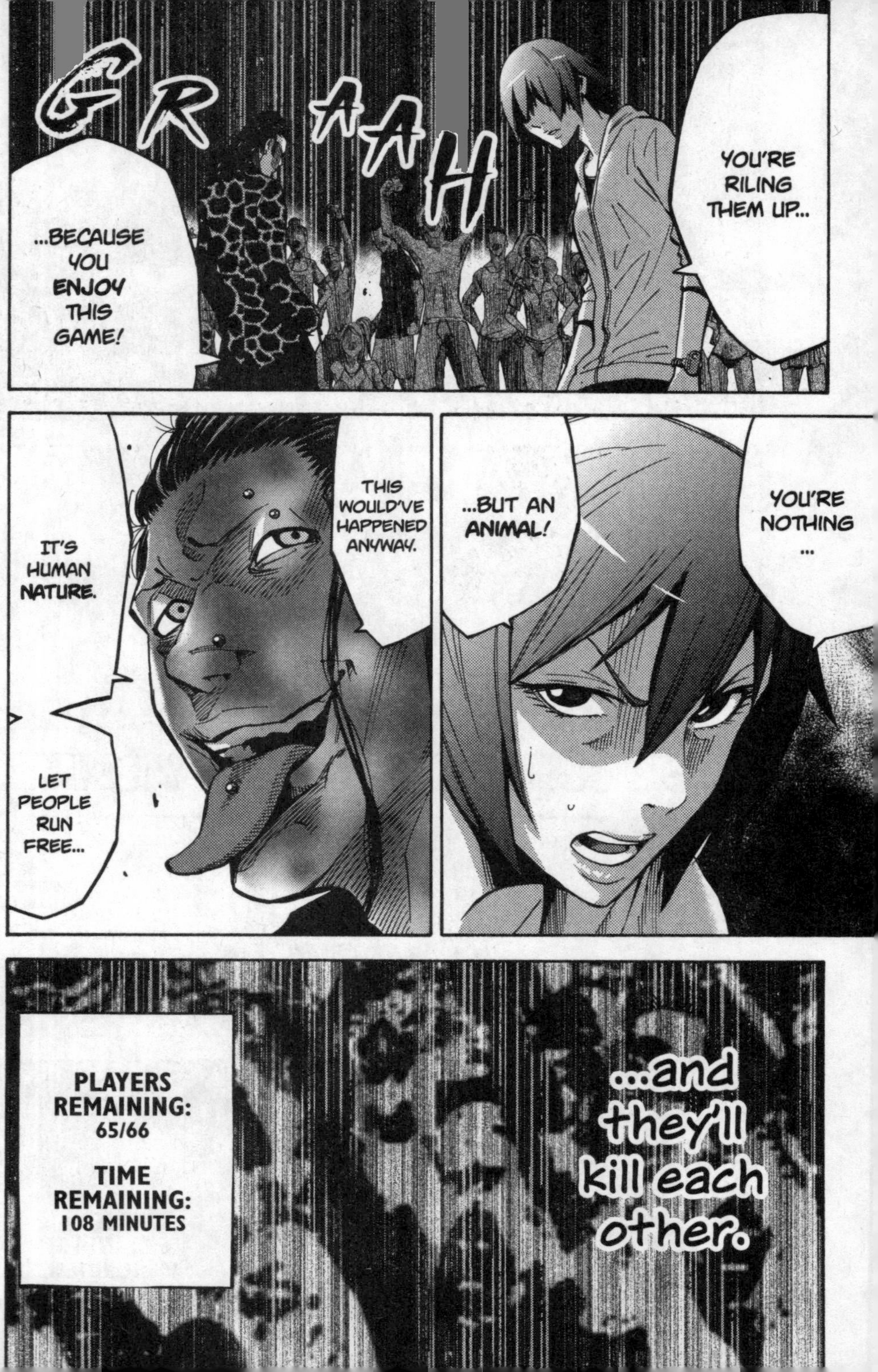
YOU'RE RILING THEM UP...
GRAAH
...BECAUSE YOU ENJOY THIS GAME!
YOU'RE NOTHING ...
...BUT AN ANIMAL!
THIS WOULD'VE HAPPENED ANYWAY.
IT'S HUMAN NATURE.
LET PEOPLE RUN FREE...
...and they'll kill each other.
PLAYERS REMAINING: 65/66
TIME REMAINING: 108 MINUTES

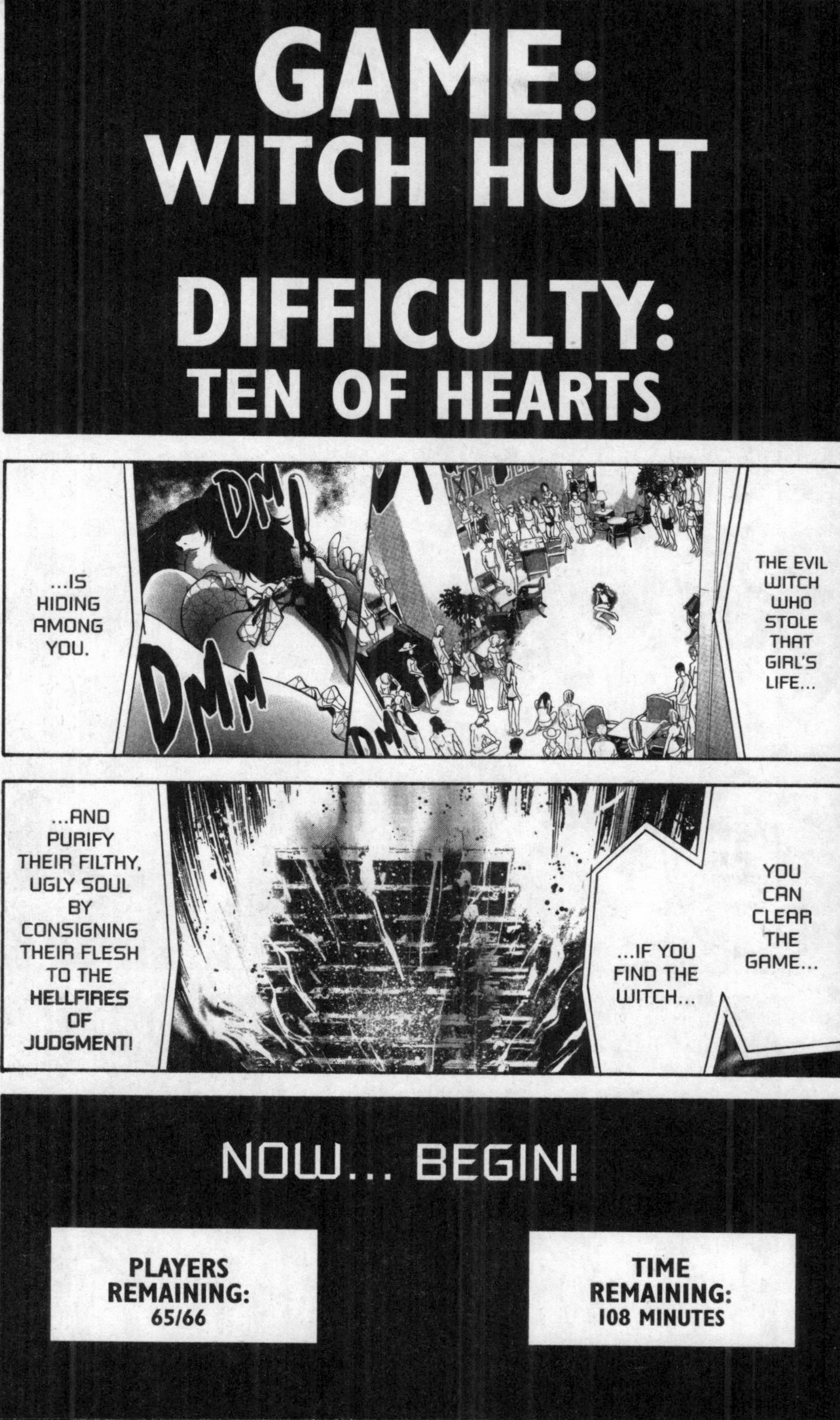
GAME:
WITCH HUNT
DIFFICULTY:
TEN OF HEARTS
THE EVIL WITCH WHO STOLE THAT GIRL'S LIFE...
DMM
...IS HIDING AMONG YOU.
YOU CAN CLEAR THE GAME...
...IF YOU FIND THE WITCH...
...AND PURIFY THEIR FILTHY, UGLY SOUL BY CONSIGNING THEIR FLESH TO THE HELLFIRES OF JUDGMENT!
NOW... BEGIN!
PLAYERS REMAINING: 65/66
TIME REMAINING: 108 MINUTES

CHAPTER 21: Ten of Hearts, Part 1

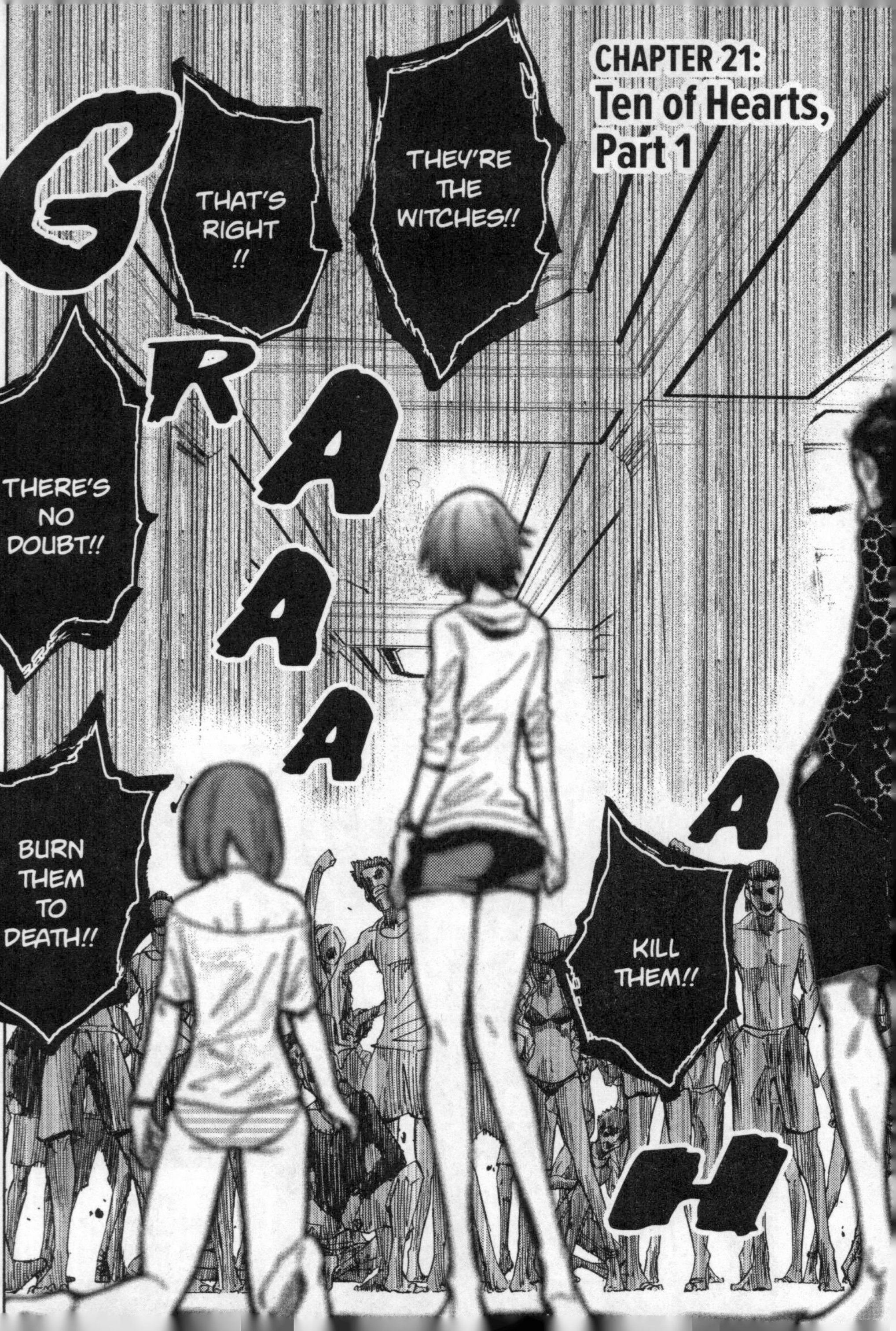

THEY'RE THE WITCHES!!
THAT'S RIGHT!!
GRAAAAAAH
THERE'S NO DOUBT!!
KILL THEM!!
BURN THEM TO DEATH!!

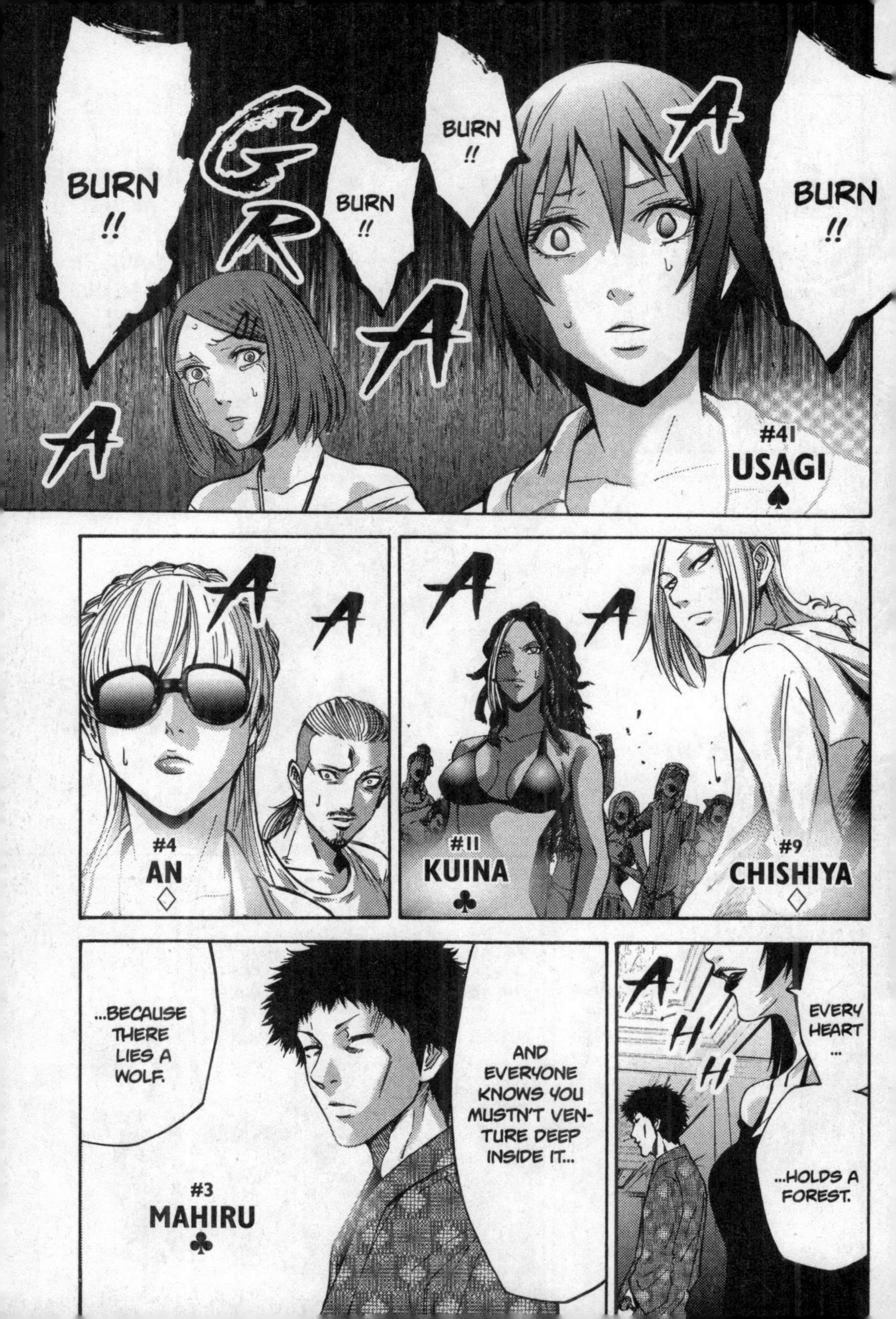
BURN !!
A
BURN !!
BURN !!
GRAAA
BURN !!
A
#41
USAGI
♠
A A
#9
CHISHIYA
♢
#11
KUINA
♣
A A
#4
AN
♢
AHH
EVERY HEART ...
...HOLDS A FOREST.
AND EVERYONE KNOWS YOU MUSTN'T VEN-TURE DEEP INSIDE IT...
...BECAUSE THERE LIES A WOLF.
#3
MAHIRU
♣

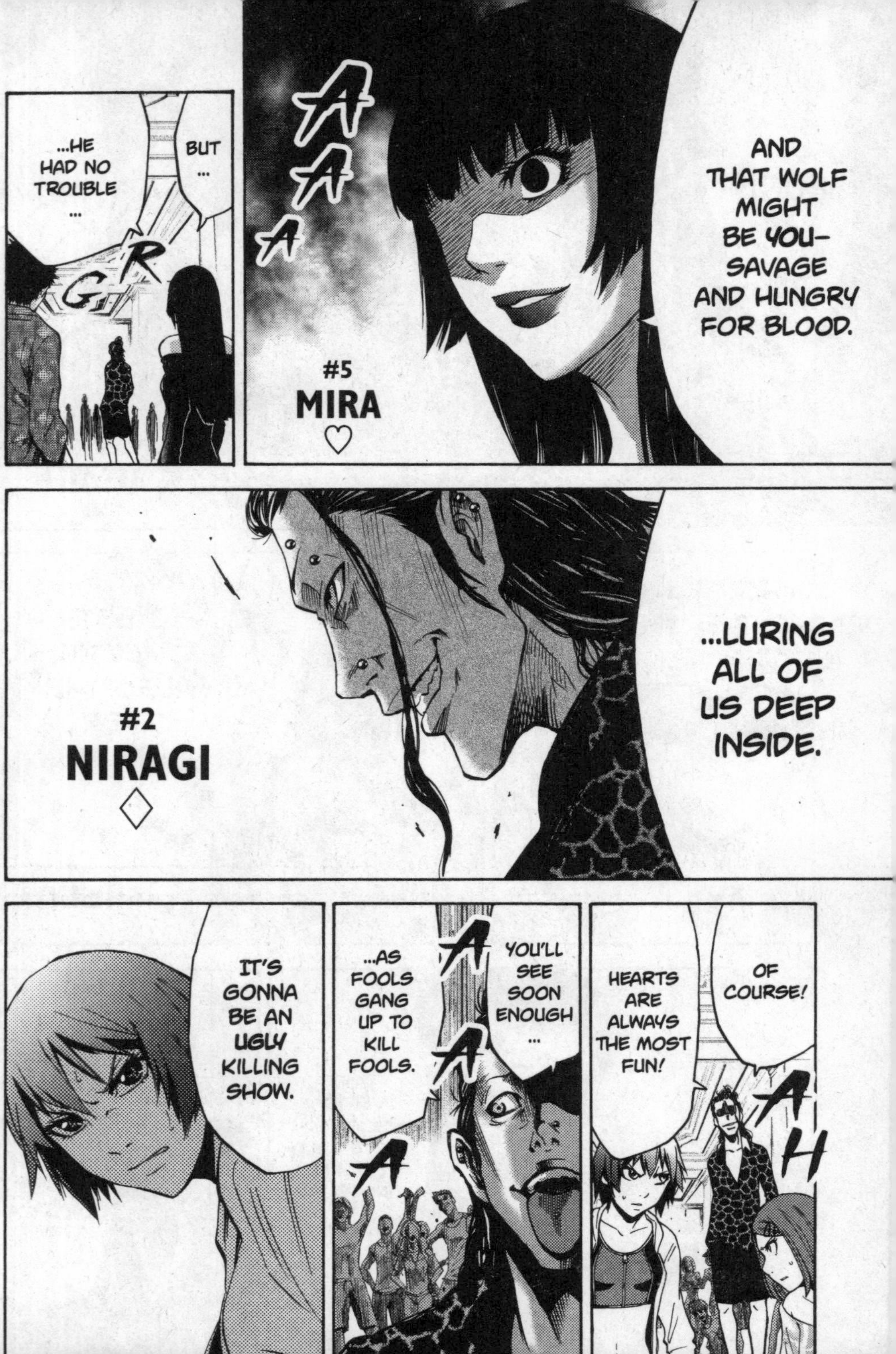
AAAA
AND THAT WOLF MIGHT BE YOU— SAVAGE AND HUNGRY FOR BLOOD.
#5 MIRA ♡
BUT ...
...HE HAD NO TROUBLE ...
GR
...LURING ALL OF US DEEP INSIDE.
#2 NIRAGI ◇
OF COURSE!
HEARTS ARE ALWAYS THE MOST FUN!
AH
YOU'LL SEE SOON ENOUGH ...
...AS FOOLS GANG UP TO KILL FOOLS.
AAA
IT'S GONNA BE AN UGLY KILLING SHOW.

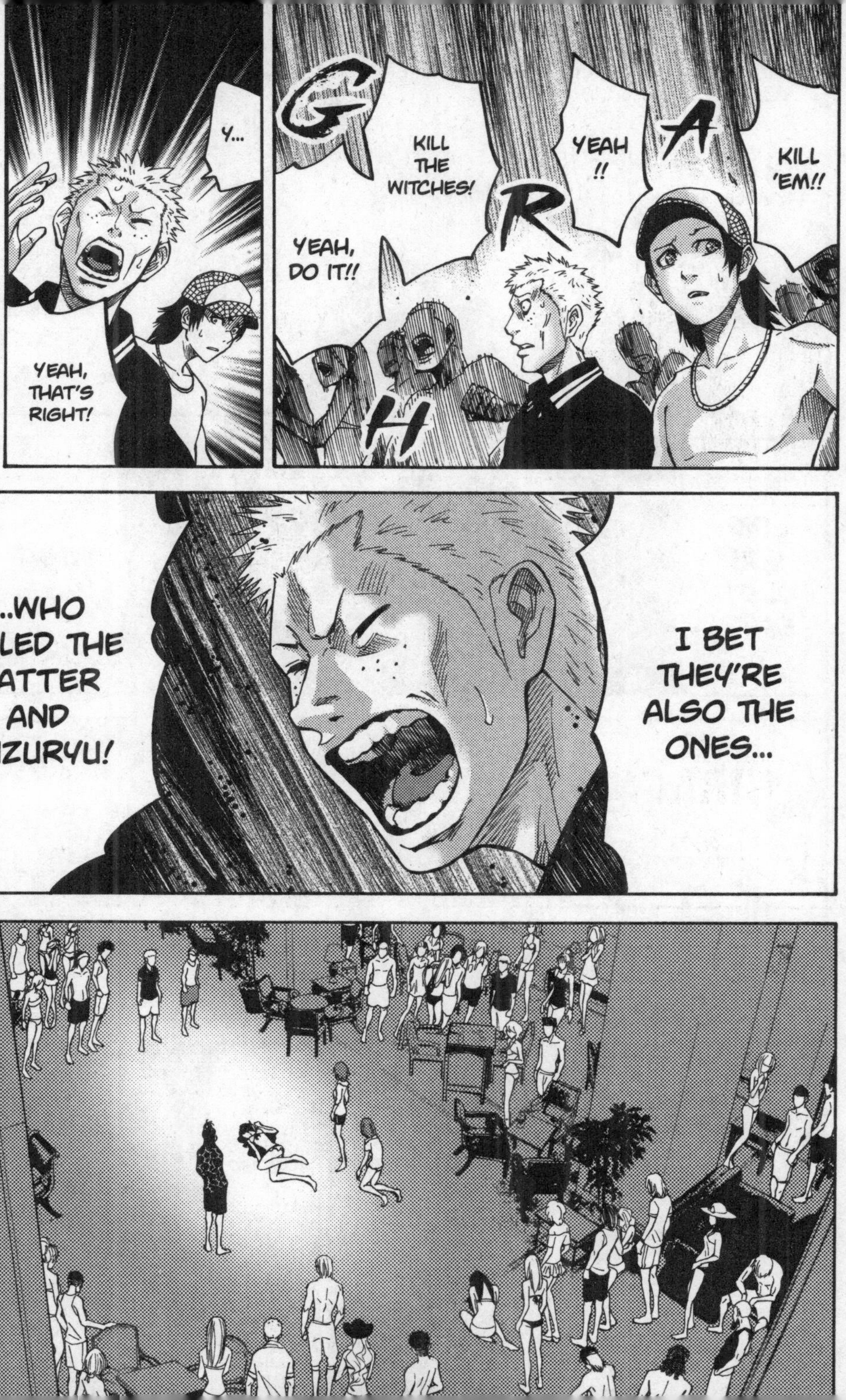
KILL 'EM!!
YEAH !!
KILL THE WITCHES!
GRAH
YEAH, DO IT!!
Y...
YEAH, THAT'S RIGHT!
I BET THEY'RE ALSO THE ONES...
...WHO KILLED THE HATTER AND KUZURYU!

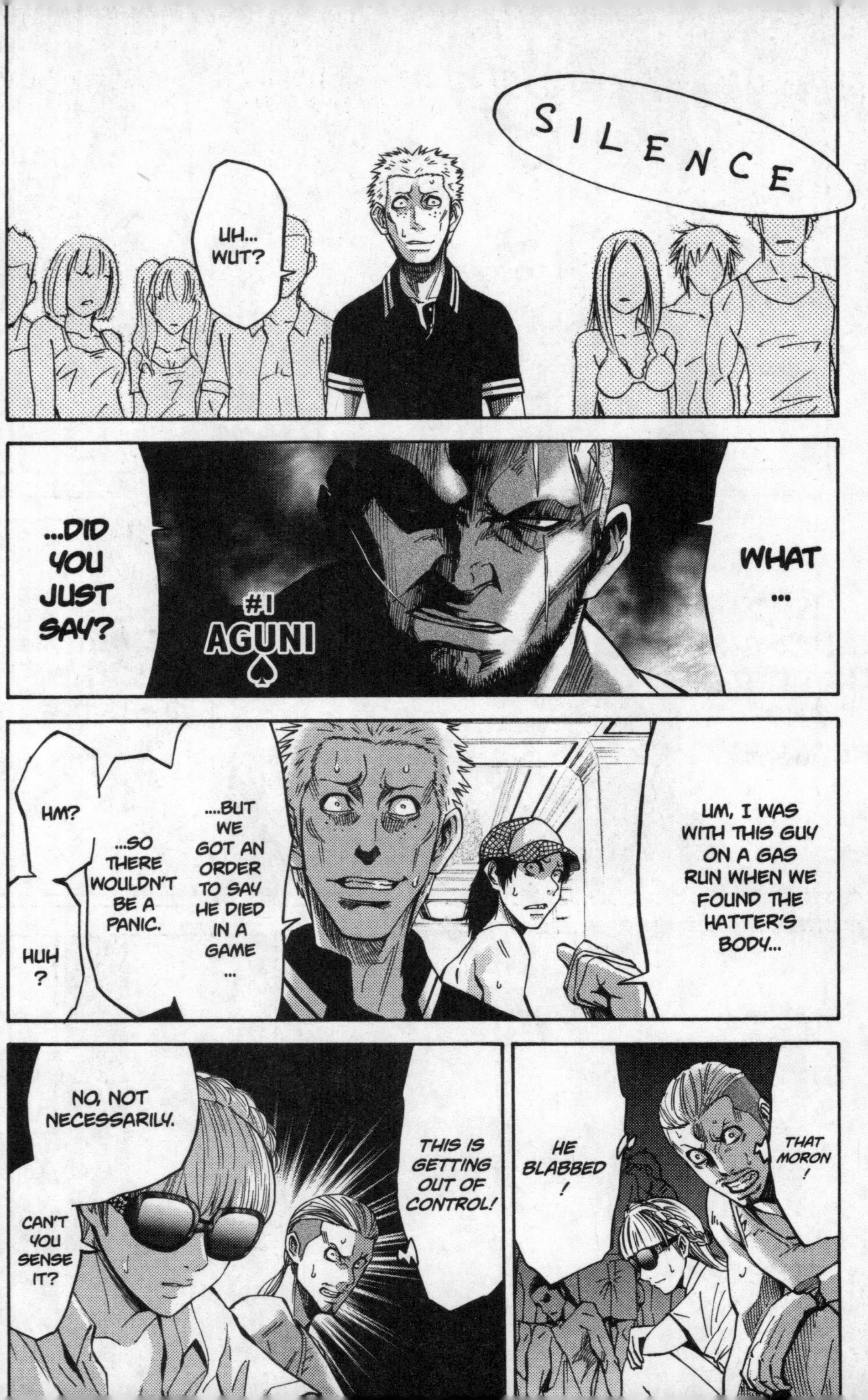
SILENCE
UH... WUT?
WHAT ...
#1 AGUNI
...DID YOU JUST SAY?
UM, I WAS WITH THIS GUY ON A GAS RUN WHEN WE FOUND THE HATTER'S BODY...
...BUT WE GOT AN ORDER TO SAY HE DIED IN A GAME ...
...SO THERE WOULDN'T BE A PANIC.
HM?
HUH ?
THAT MORON !
HE BLABBED !
THIS IS GETTING OUT OF CONTROL!
NO, NOT NECESSARILY.
CAN'T YOU SENSE IT?

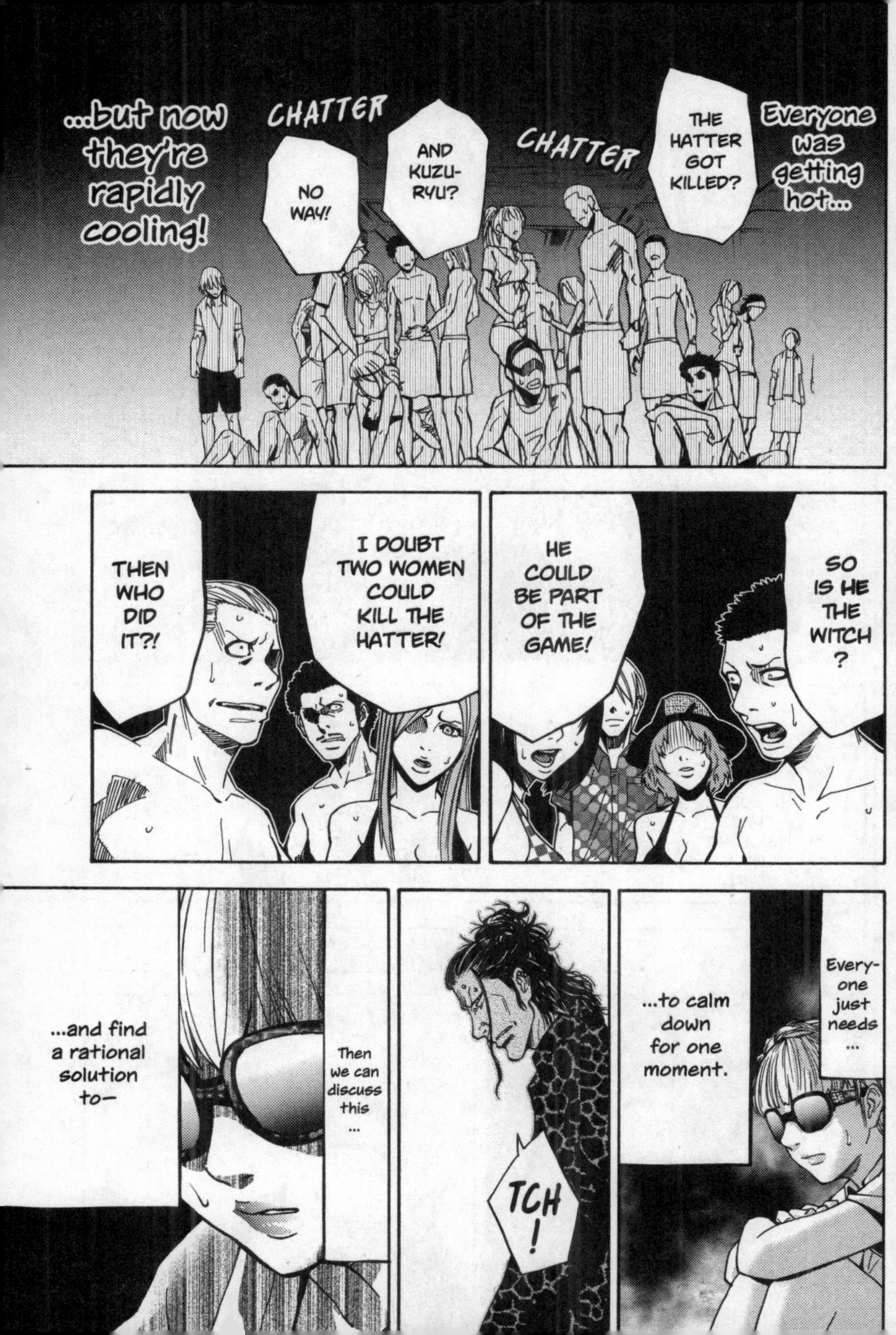
Everyone was getting hot...
THE HATTER GOT KILLED?
CHATTER
AND KUZU-RYU?
CHATTER
NO WAY!
...but now they're rapidly cooling!
SO IS HE THE WITCH?
HE COULD BE PART OF THE GAME!
I DOUBT TWO WOMEN COULD KILL THE HATTER!
THEN WHO DID IT?!
Every-one just needs...
...to calm down for one moment.
TCH!
Then we can discuss this...
...and find a rational solution to—

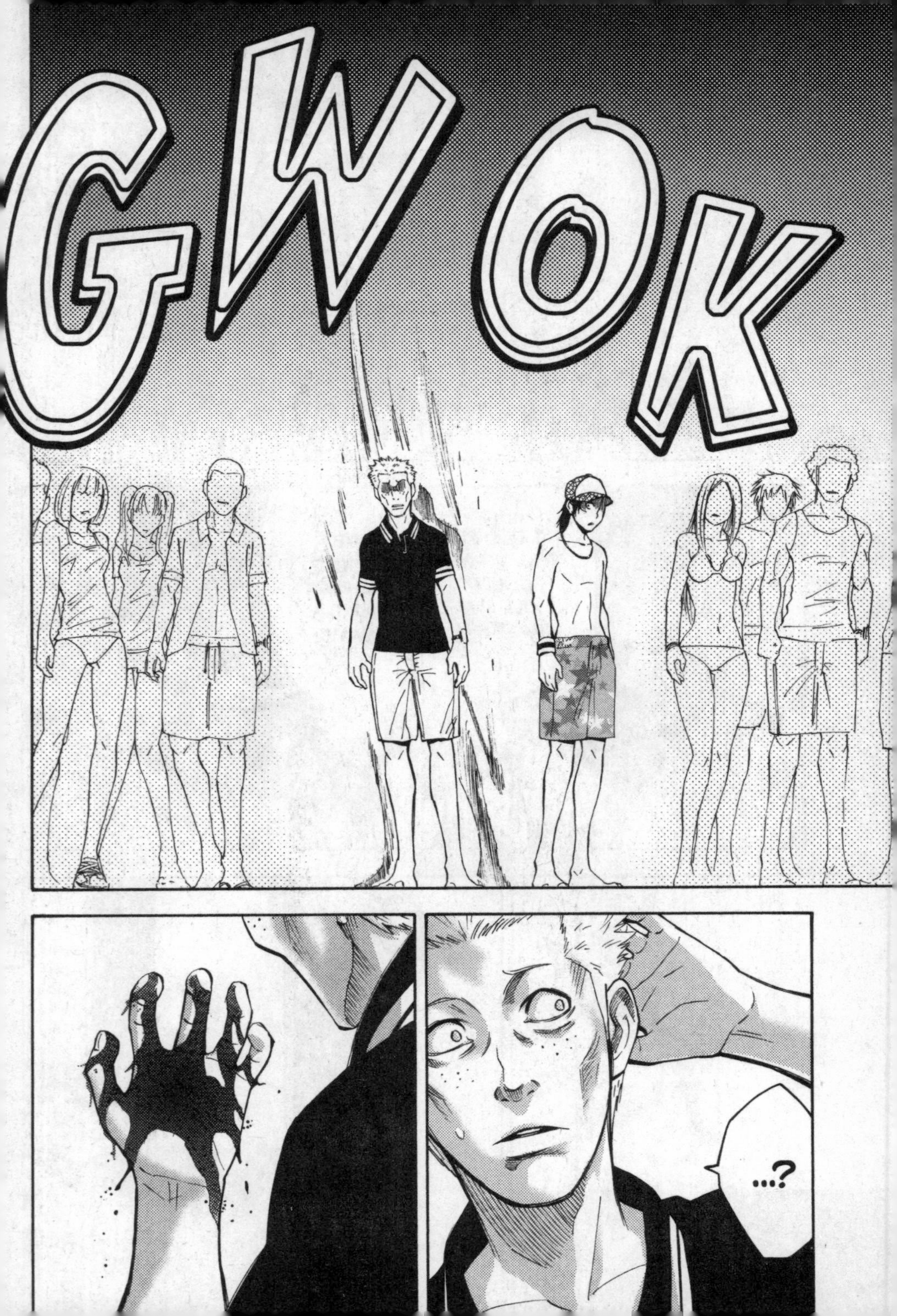
GWOK
...?

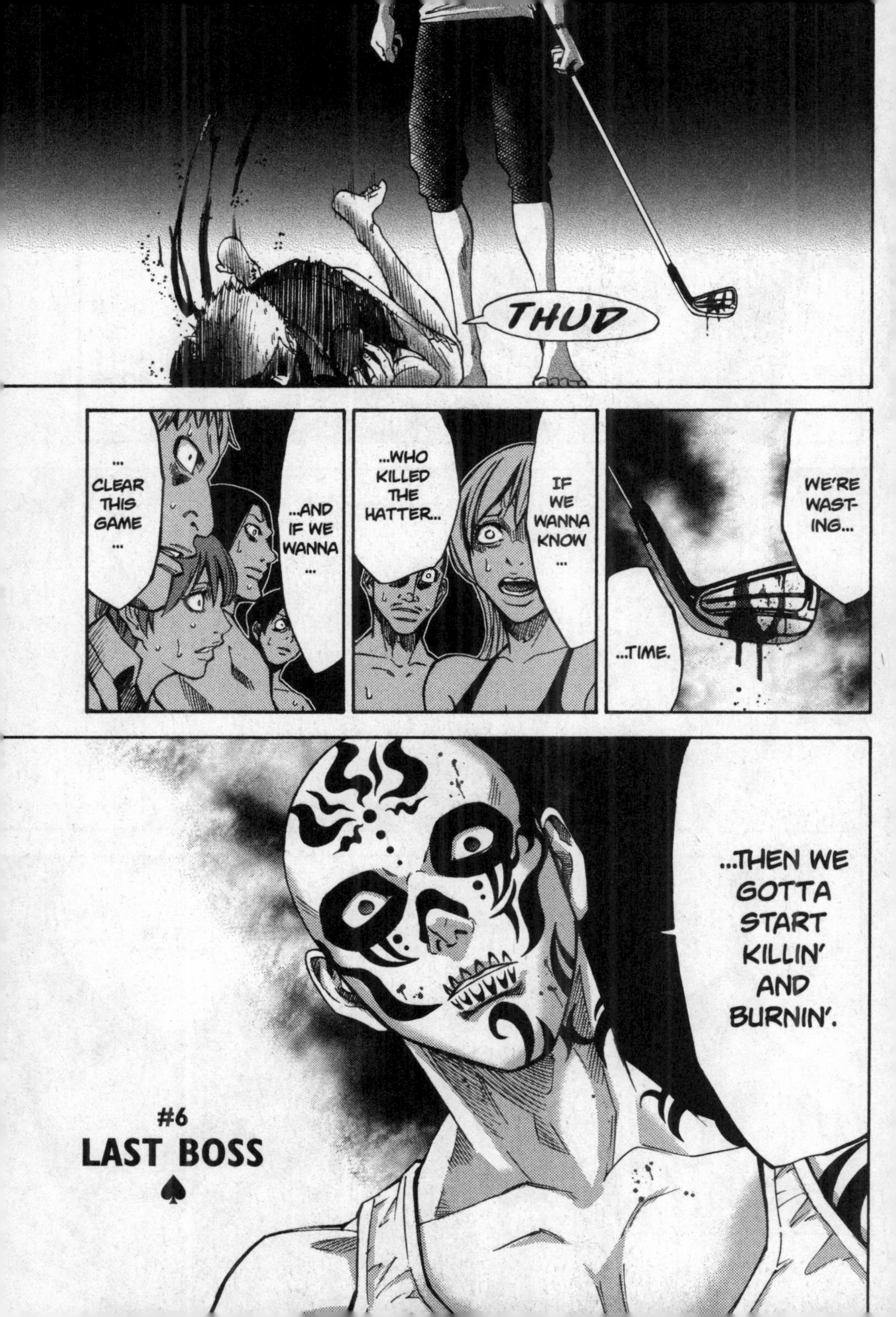
THUD
WE'RE WASTING...
...TIME.
IF WE WANNA KNOW...
...WHO KILLED THE HATTER...
...AND IF WE WANNA...
...CLEAR THIS GAME...
...THEN WE GOTTA START KILLIN' AND BURNIN'.
#6
LAST BOSS

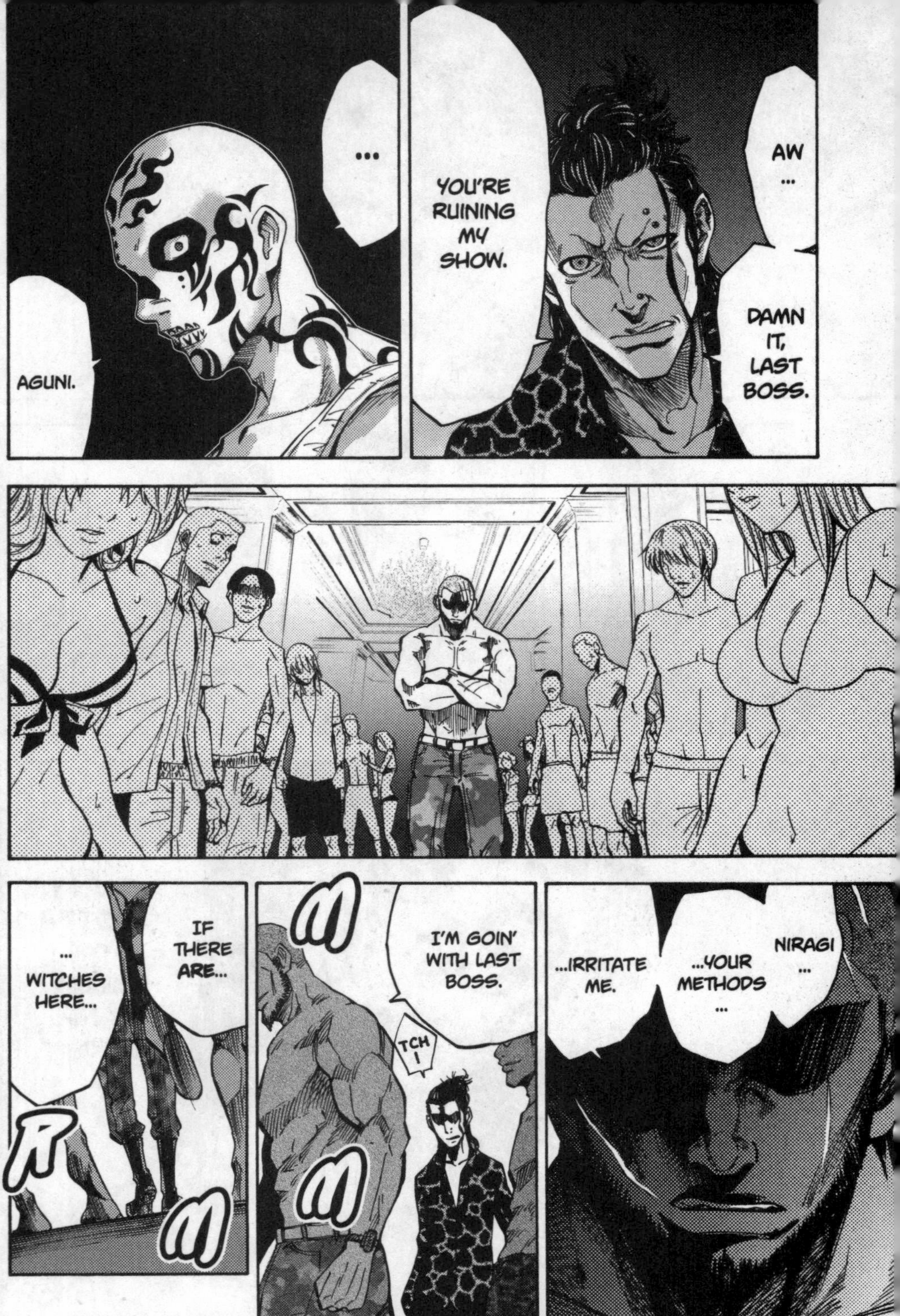

AW ...
DAMN IT, LAST BOSS.
YOU'RE RUINING MY SHOW.
...
AGUNI.
NIRAGI ...
...YOUR METHODS ...
...IRRITATE ME.
I'M GOIN' WITH LAST BOSS.
TCH !
M
M
M
IF THERE ARE...
... WITCHES HERE...
R

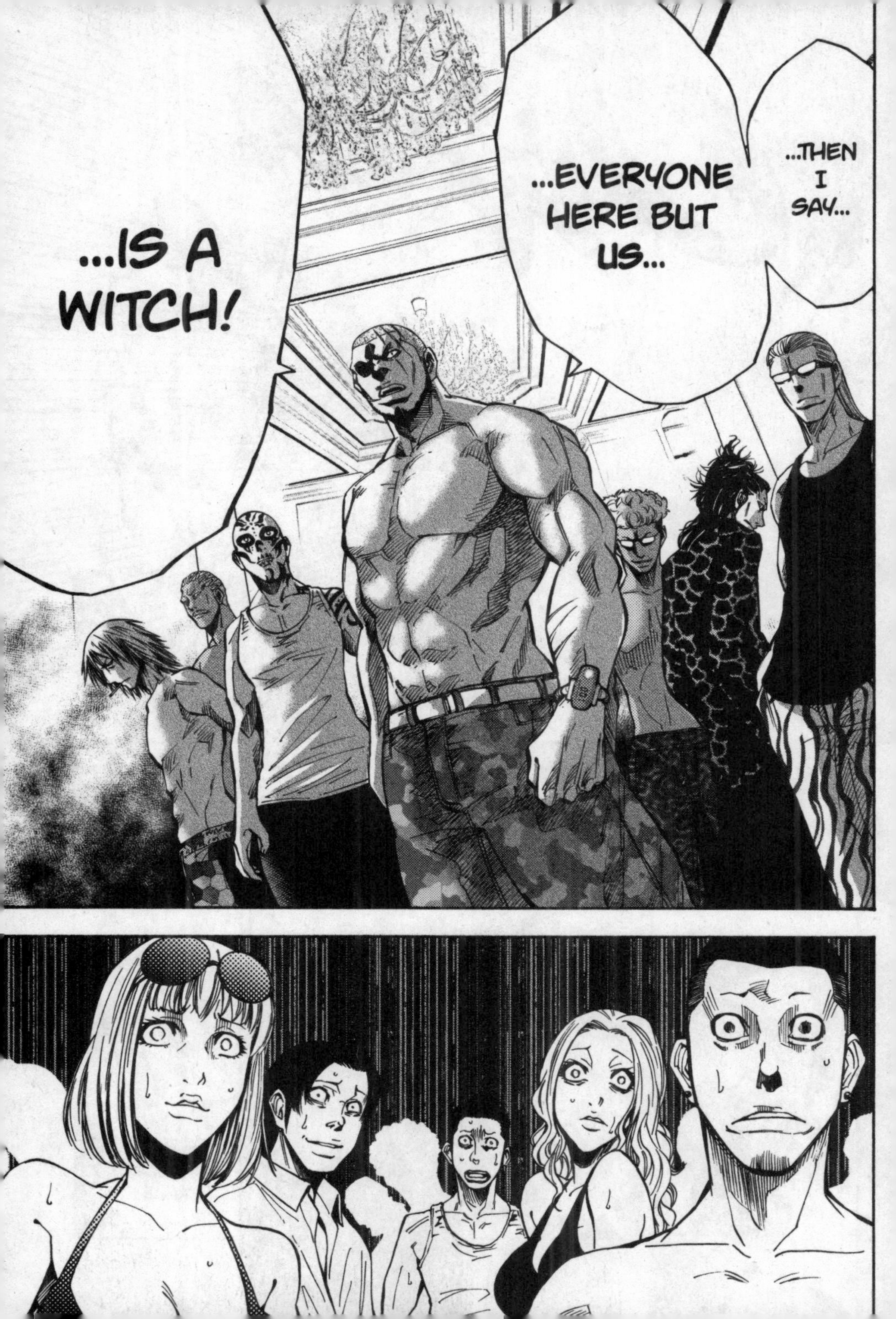
...THEN I SAY...
...EVERYONE HERE BUT US...
...IS A WITCH!

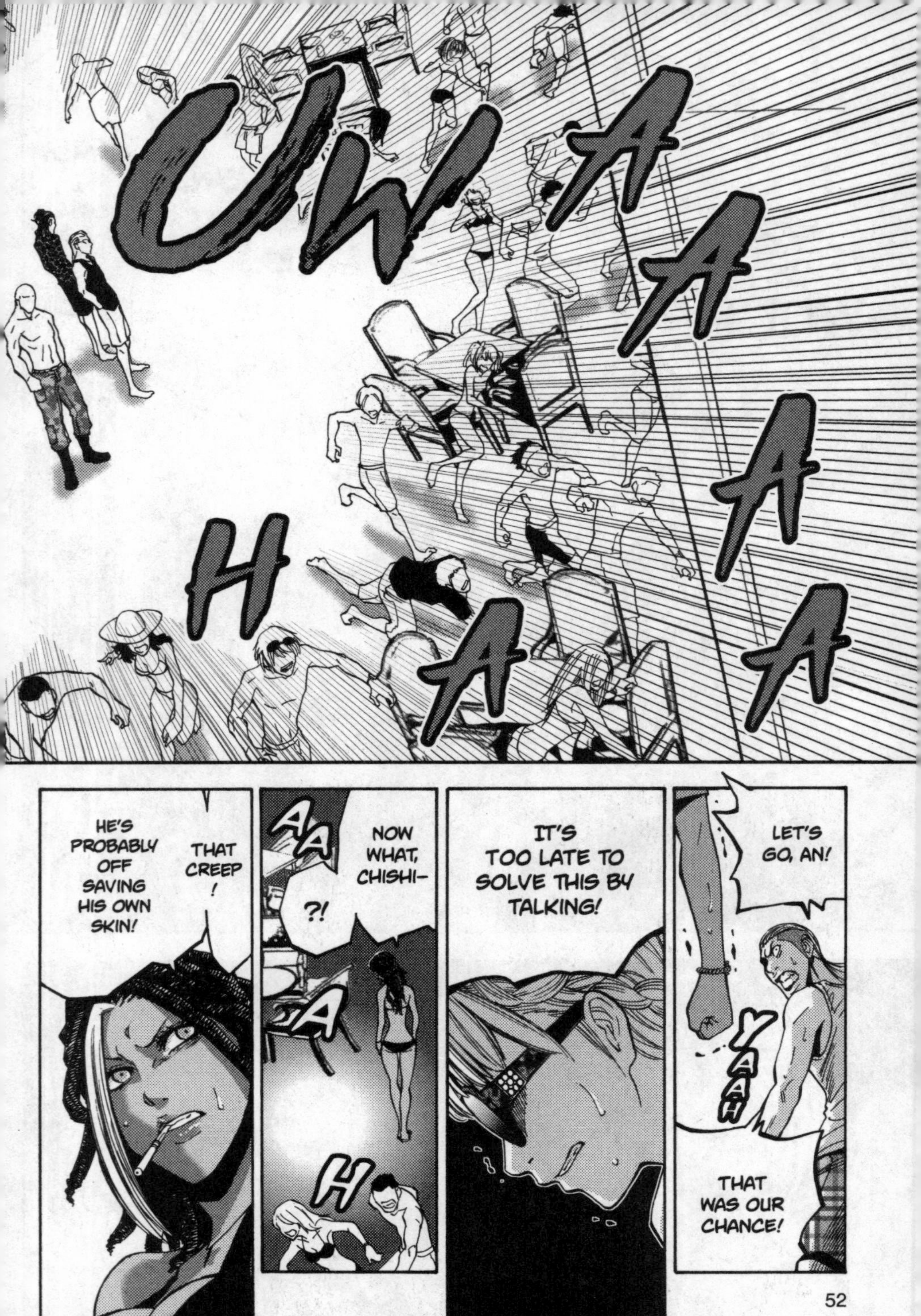
UWAAAAAAAH
LET'S GO, AN!
YAAAH
THAT WAS OUR CHANCE!
IT'S TOO LATE TO SOLVE THIS BY TALKING!
NOW WHAT, CHISHI-
?!
AAAH
THAT CREEP!
HE'S PROBABLY OFF SAVING HIS OWN SKIN!

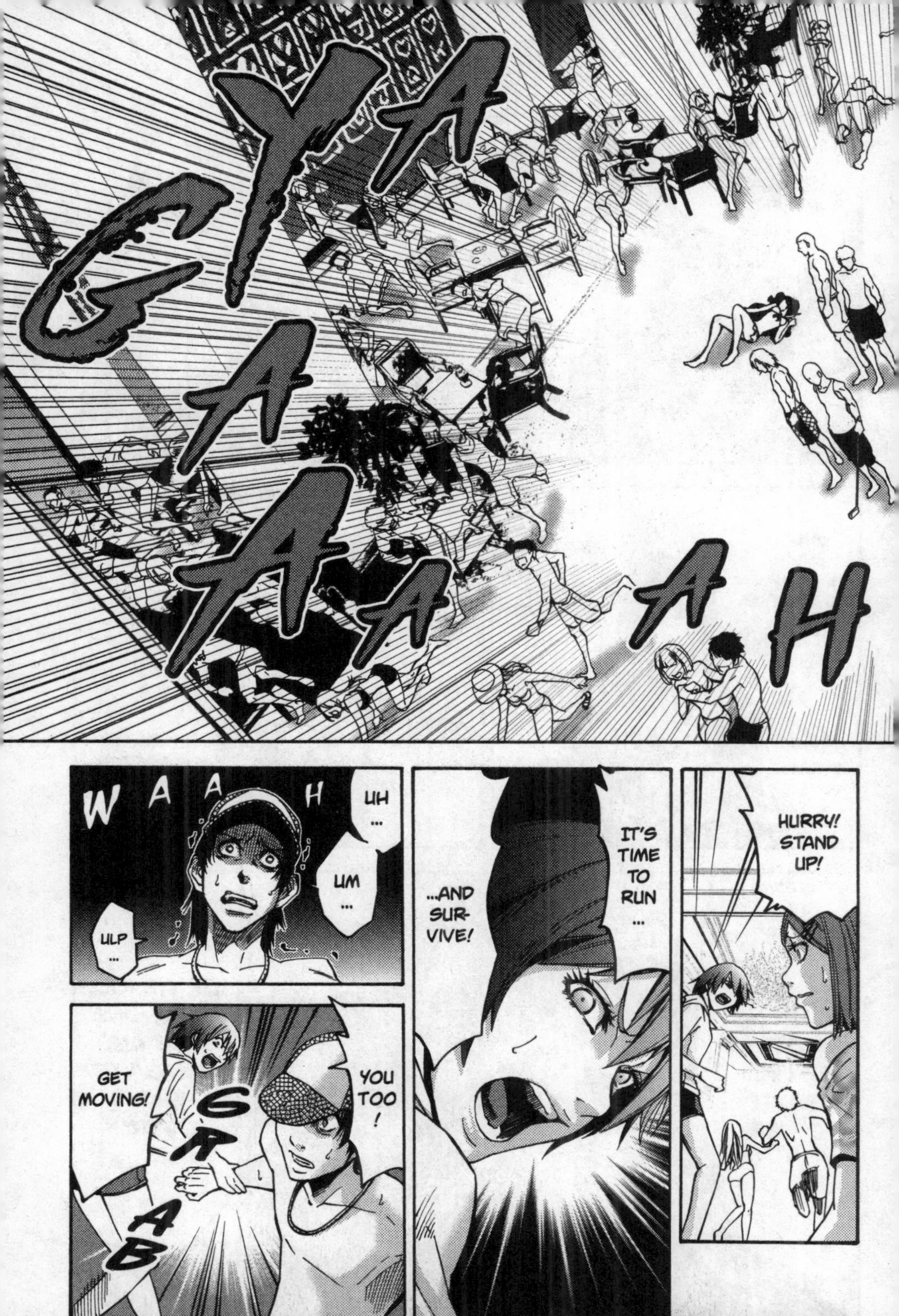
GYAAAAAAH
HURRY! STAND UP!
IT'S TIME TO RUN ...
...AND SUR-VIVE!
WAAH
UH ...
UM ...
ULP ...
YOU TOO!
GET MOVING!
GRAB

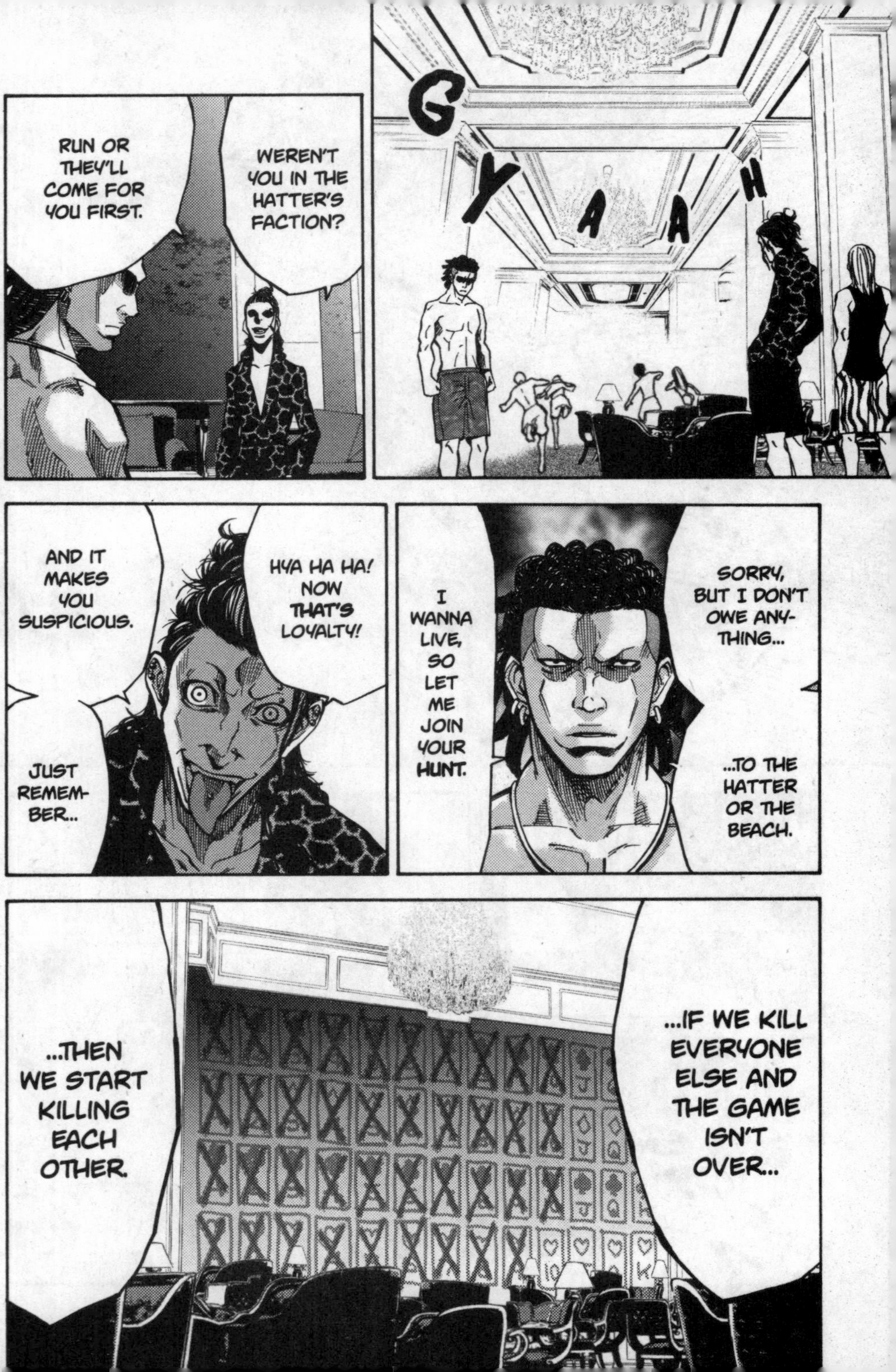
GYAAH
WEREN'T YOU IN THE HATTER'S FACTION?
RUN OR THEY'LL COME FOR YOU FIRST.
SORRY, BUT I DON'T OWE ANY-THING...
...TO THE HATTER OR THE BEACH.
I WANNA LIVE, SO LET ME JOIN YOUR HUNT.
HYA HA HA! NOW THAT'S LOYALTY!
AND IT MAKES YOU SUSPICIOUS.
JUST REMEM-BER...
...IF WE KILL EVERYONE ELSE AND THE GAME ISN'T OVER...
...THEN WE START KILLING EACH OTHER.

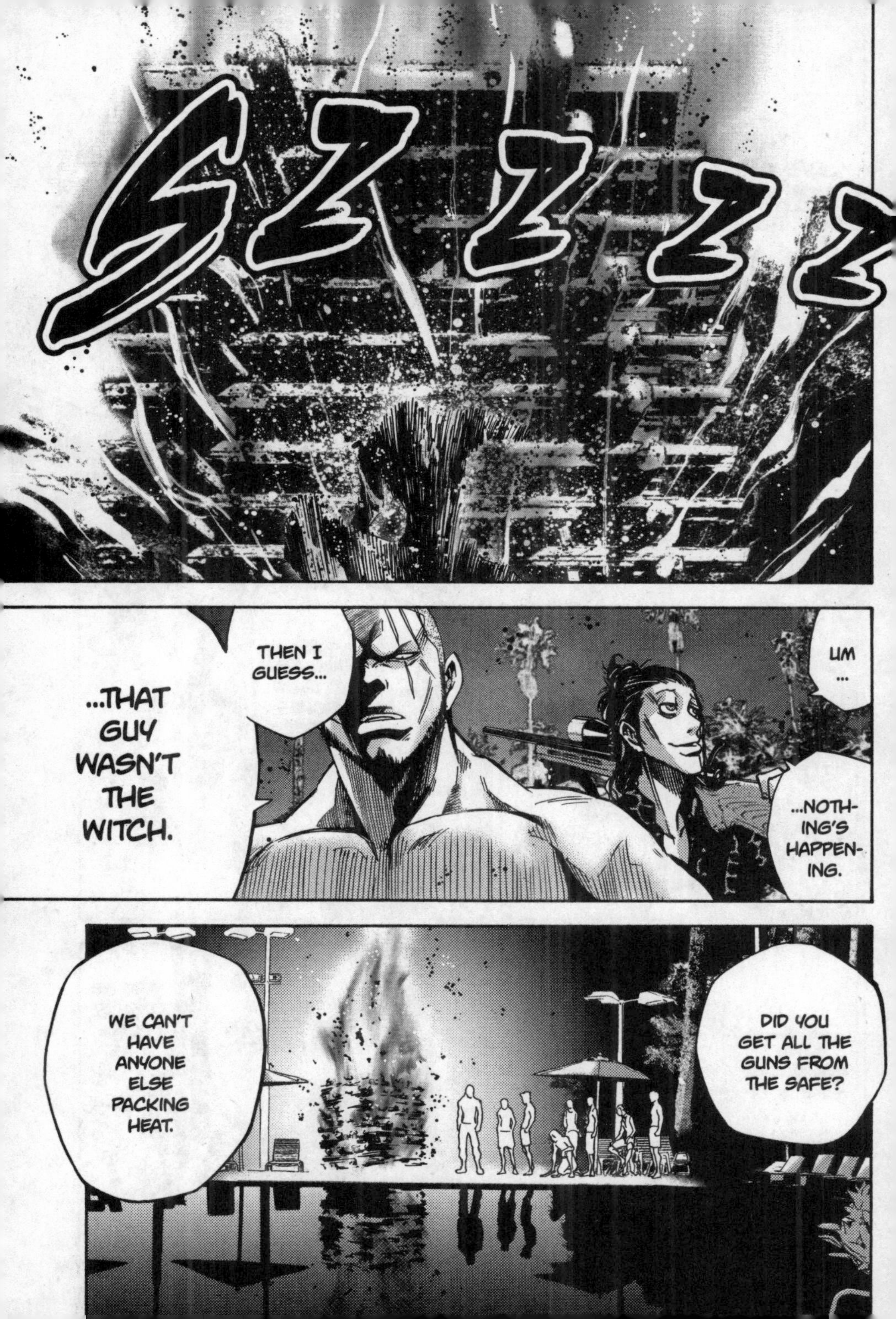
SZZZZ
UM ...
...NOTHING'S HAPPENING.
THEN I GUESS...
...THAT GUY WASN'T THE WITCH.
DID YOU GET ALL THE GUNS FROM THE SAFE?
WE CAN'T HAVE ANYONE ELSE PACKING HEAT.

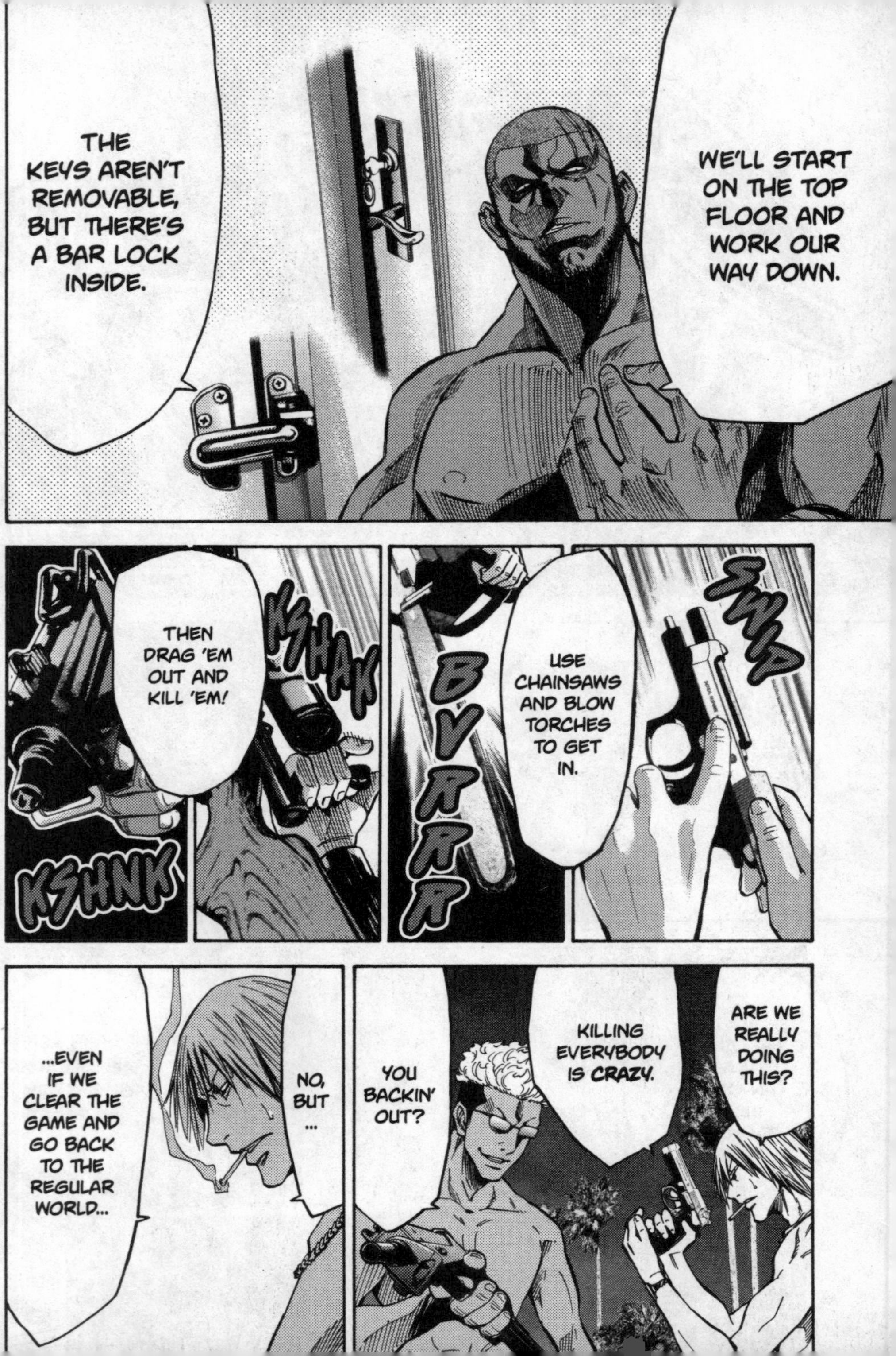
WE'LL START ON THE TOP FLOOR AND WORK OUR WAY DOWN.
THE KEYS AREN'T REMOVABLE, BUT THERE'S A BAR LOCK INSIDE.
SWAP
USE CHAINSAWS AND BLOW TORCHES TO GET IN.
BVRRRR
KSHAK
THEN DRAG 'EM OUT AND KILL 'EM!
KSHNK
ARE WE REALLY DOING THIS?
KILLING EVERYBODY IS CRAZY.
YOU BACKIN' OUT?
NO, BUT ...
...EVEN IF WE CLEAR THE GAME AND GO BACK TO THE REGULAR WORLD...

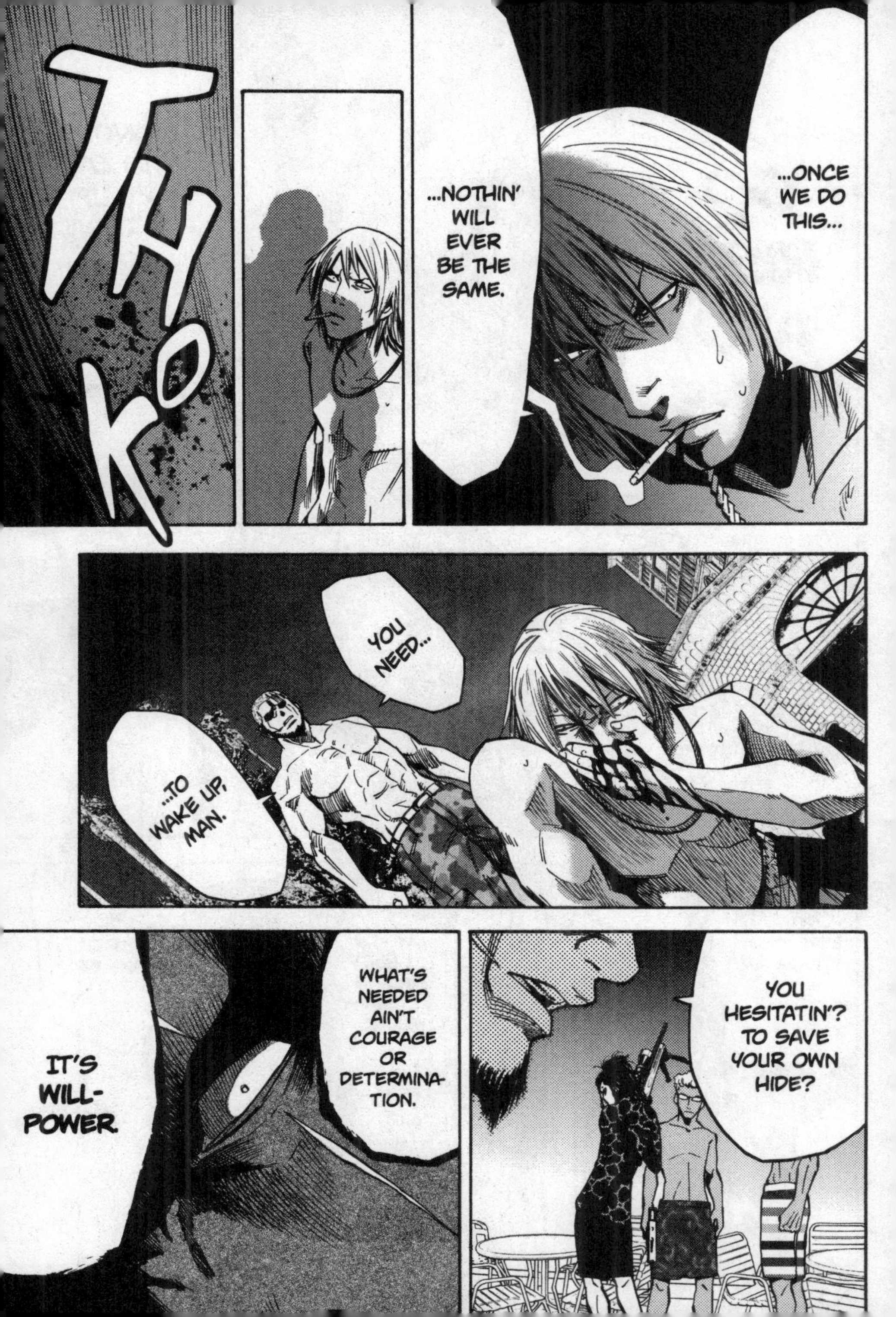

...ONCE WE DO THIS...
...NOTHIN' WILL EVER BE THE SAME.
THOK
YOU NEED...
...TO WAKE UP, MAN.
YOU HESITATIN'? TO SAVE YOUR OWN HIDE?
WHAT'S NEEDED AIN'T COURAGE OR DETERMINA-TION.
IT'S WILL-POWER.

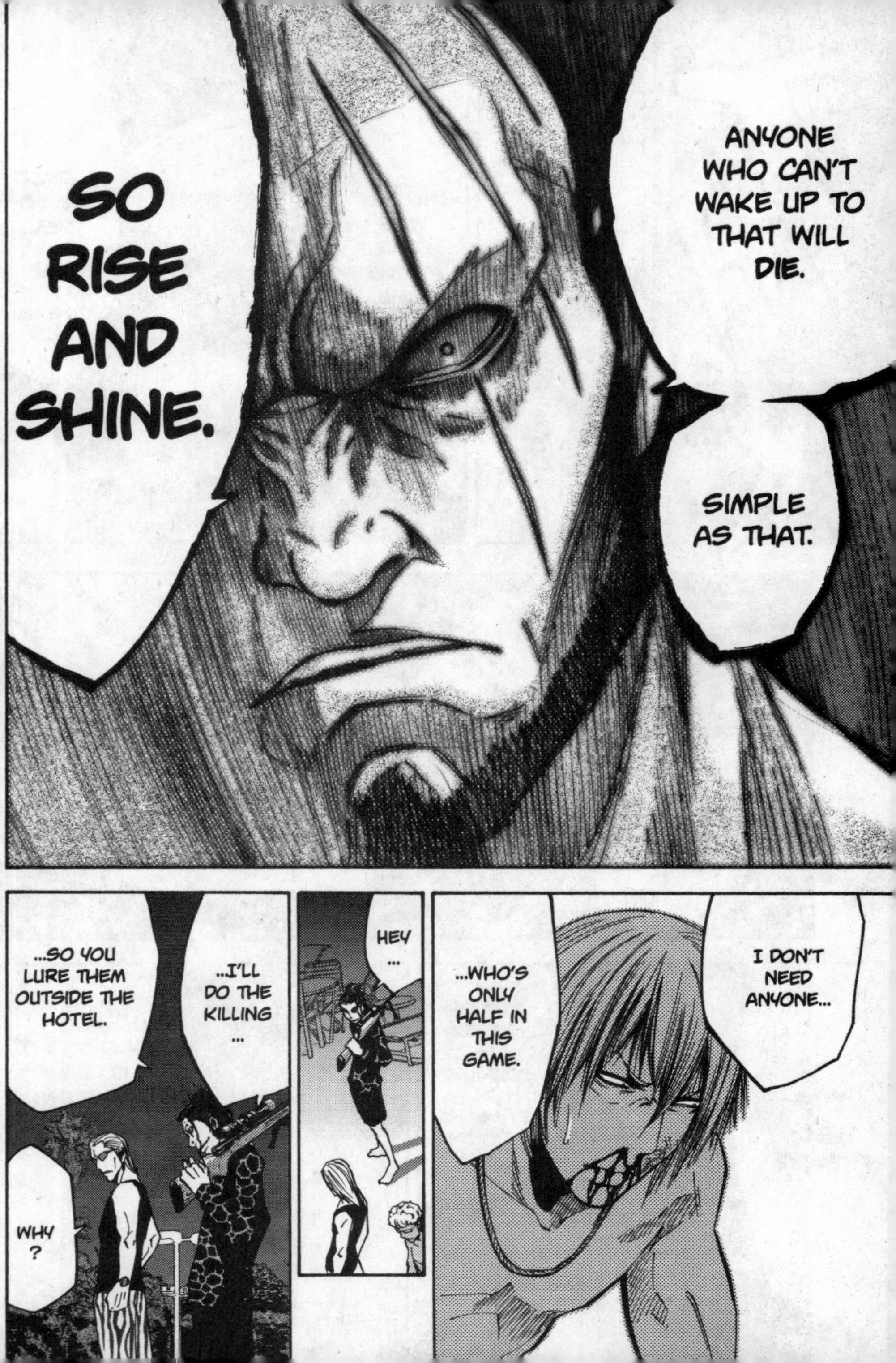
ANYONE WHO CAN'T WAKE UP TO THAT WILL DIE.
SIMPLE AS THAT.
SO RISE AND SHINE.
I DON'T NEED ANYONE...
...WHO'S ONLY HALF IN THIS GAME.
HEY ...
...I'LL DO THE KILLING ...
...SO YOU LURE THEM OUTSIDE THE HOTEL.
WHY ?

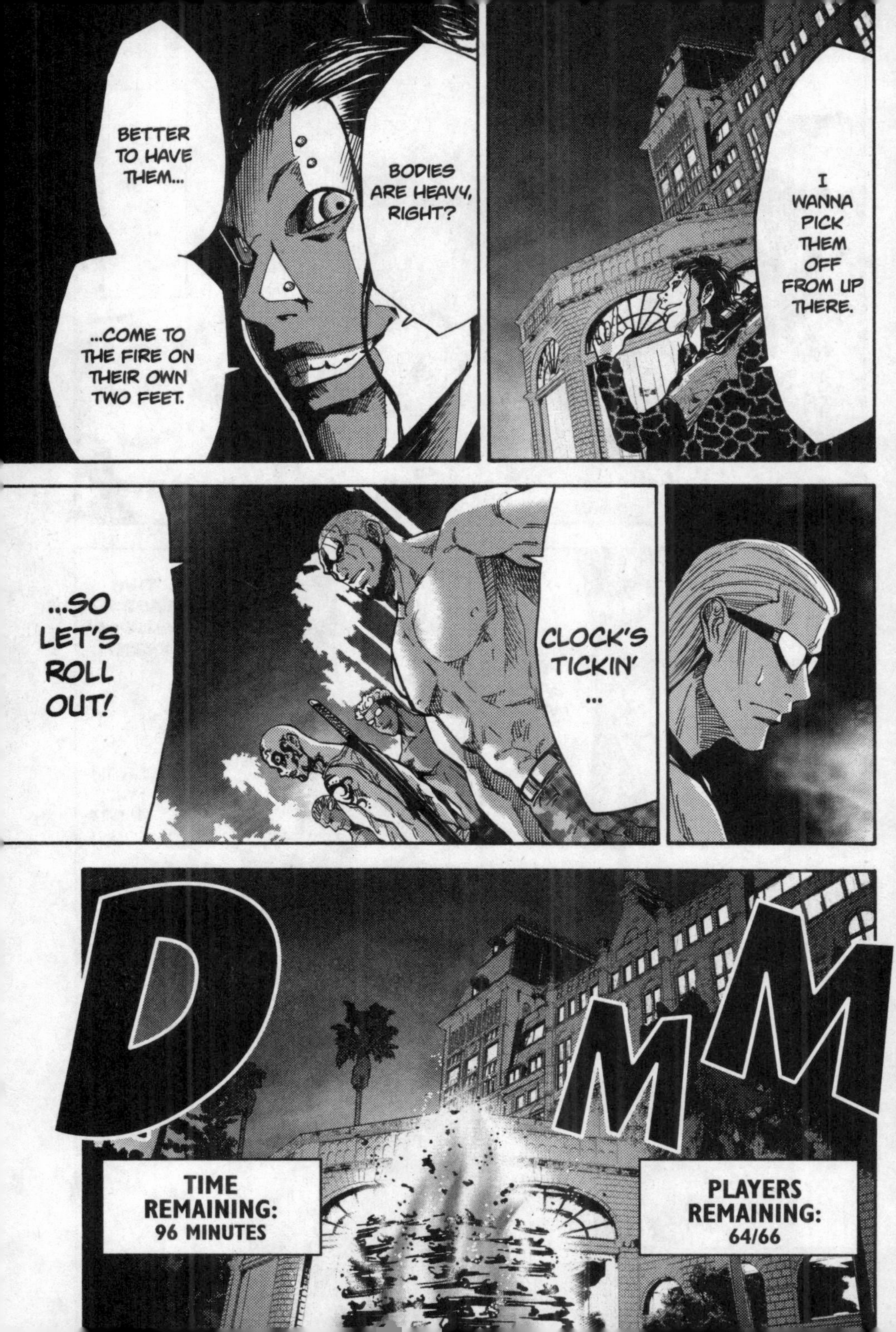
I WANNA PICK THEM OFF FROM UP THERE.
BODIES ARE HEAVY, RIGHT?
BETTER TO HAVE THEM...
...COME TO THE FIRE ON THEIR OWN TWO FEET.
CLOCK'S TICKIN' ...
...SO LET'S ROLL OUT!
DMMM
PLAYERS REMAINING: 64/66
TIME REMAINING: 96 MINUTES

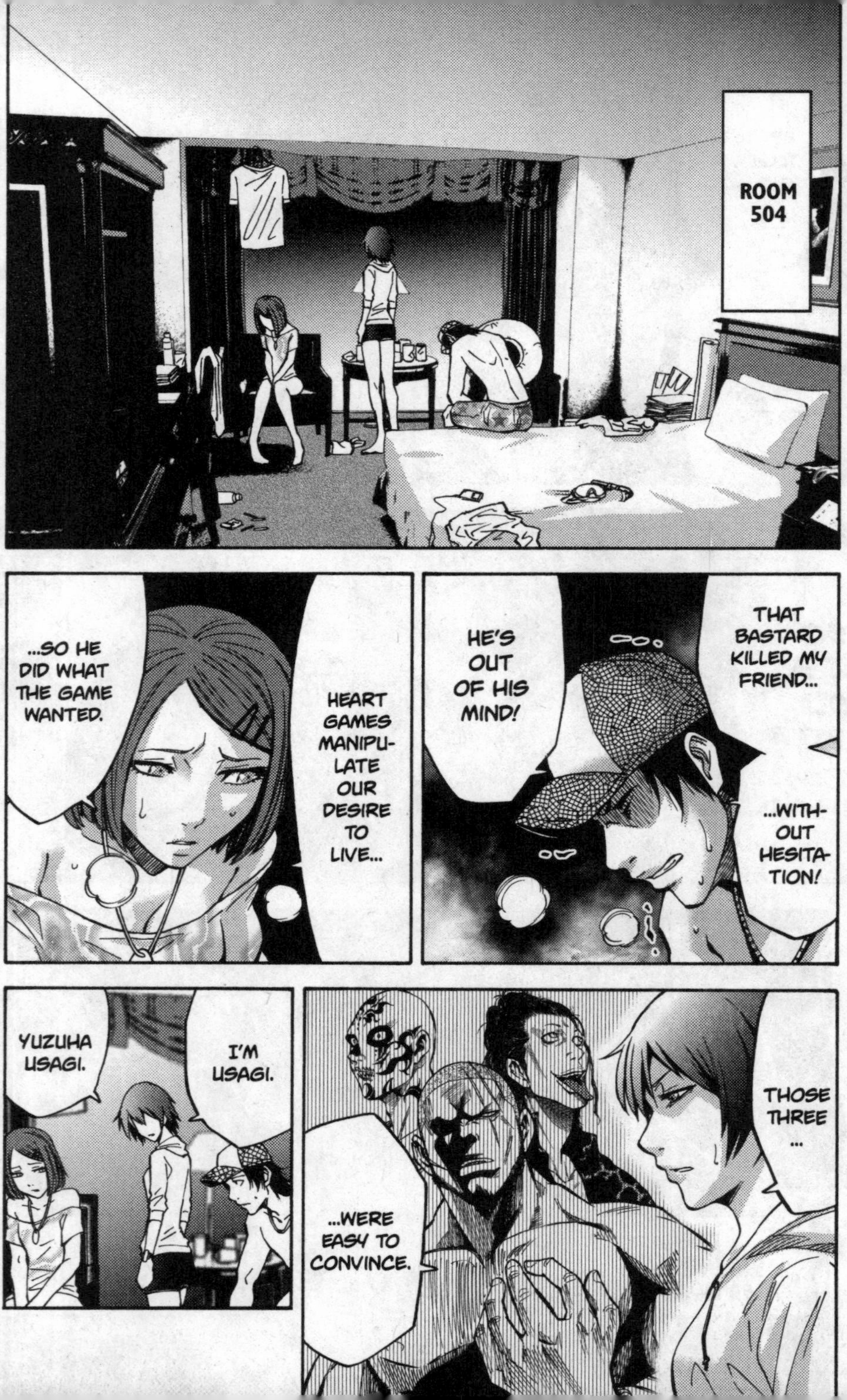
ROOM 504
THAT BASTARD KILLED MY FRIEND...
...WITH-OUT HESITA-TION!
HE'S OUT OF HIS MIND!
HEART GAMES MANIPU-LATE OUR DESIRE TO LIVE...
...SO HE DID WHAT THE GAME WANTED.
THOSE THREE ...
...WERE EASY TO CONVINCE.
I'M USAGI.
YUZUHA USAGI.

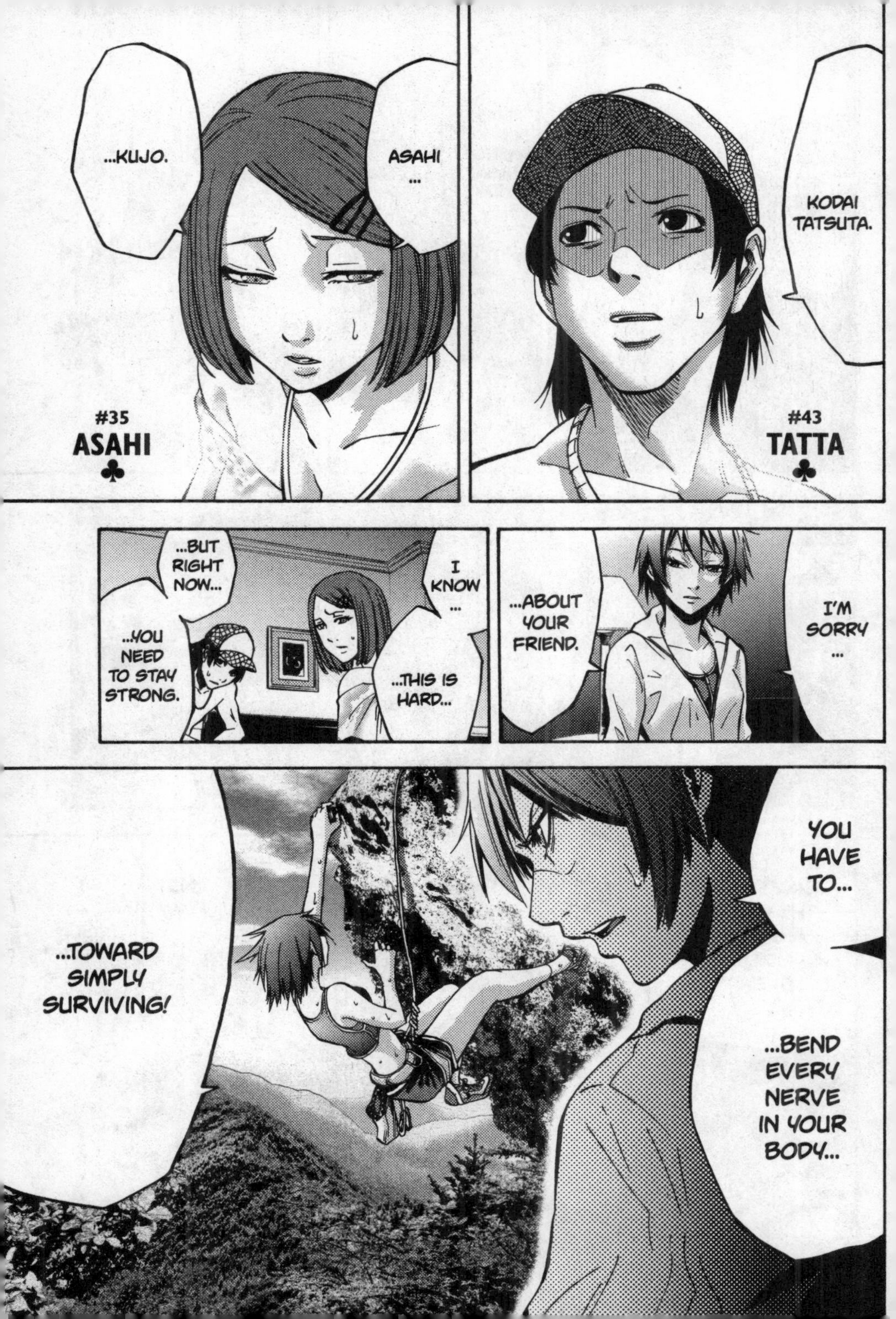
KODAI TATSUTA.
#43
TATTA ♣
ASAHI ...
...KUJO.
#35
ASAHI ♣
I'M SORRY ...
...ABOUT YOUR FRIEND.
I KNOW ...
...THIS IS HARD...
...BUT RIGHT NOW...
...YOU NEED TO STAY STRONG.
YOU HAVE TO...
...BEND EVERY NERVE IN YOUR BODY...
...TOWARD SIMPLY SURVIVING!

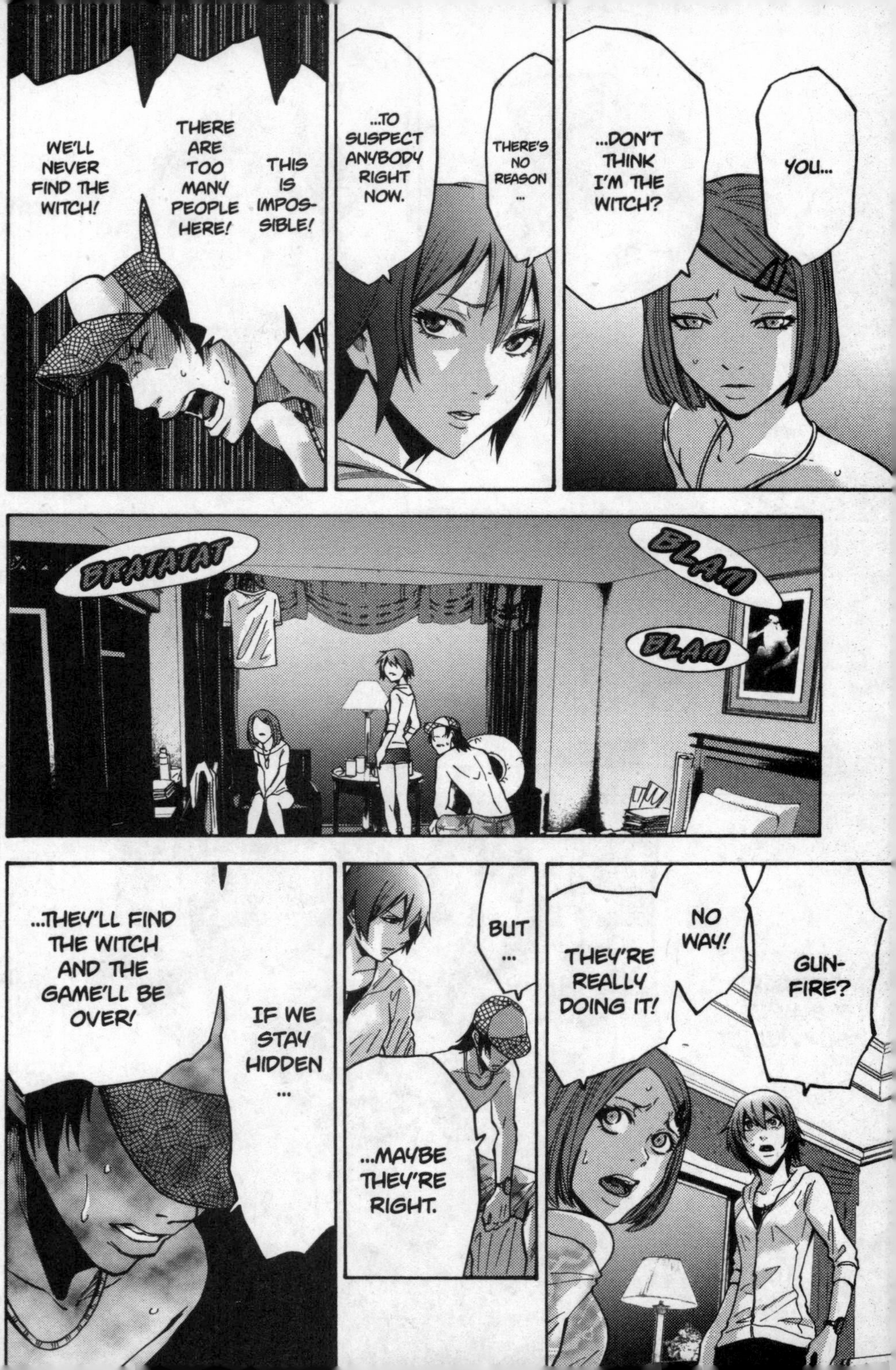
YOU...
...DON'T THINK I'M THE WITCH?
THERE'S NO REASON ...
...TO SUSPECT ANYBODY RIGHT NOW.
THIS IS IMPOSSIBLE!
THERE ARE TOO MANY PEOPLE HERE!
WE'LL NEVER FIND THE WITCH!
BLAM
BLAM
BRATATAT
GUN-FIRE?
NO WAY!
THEY'RE REALLY DOING IT!
BUT ...
...MAYBE THEY'RE RIGHT.
IF WE STAY HIDDEN ...
...THEY'LL FIND THE WITCH AND THE GAME'LL BE OVER!

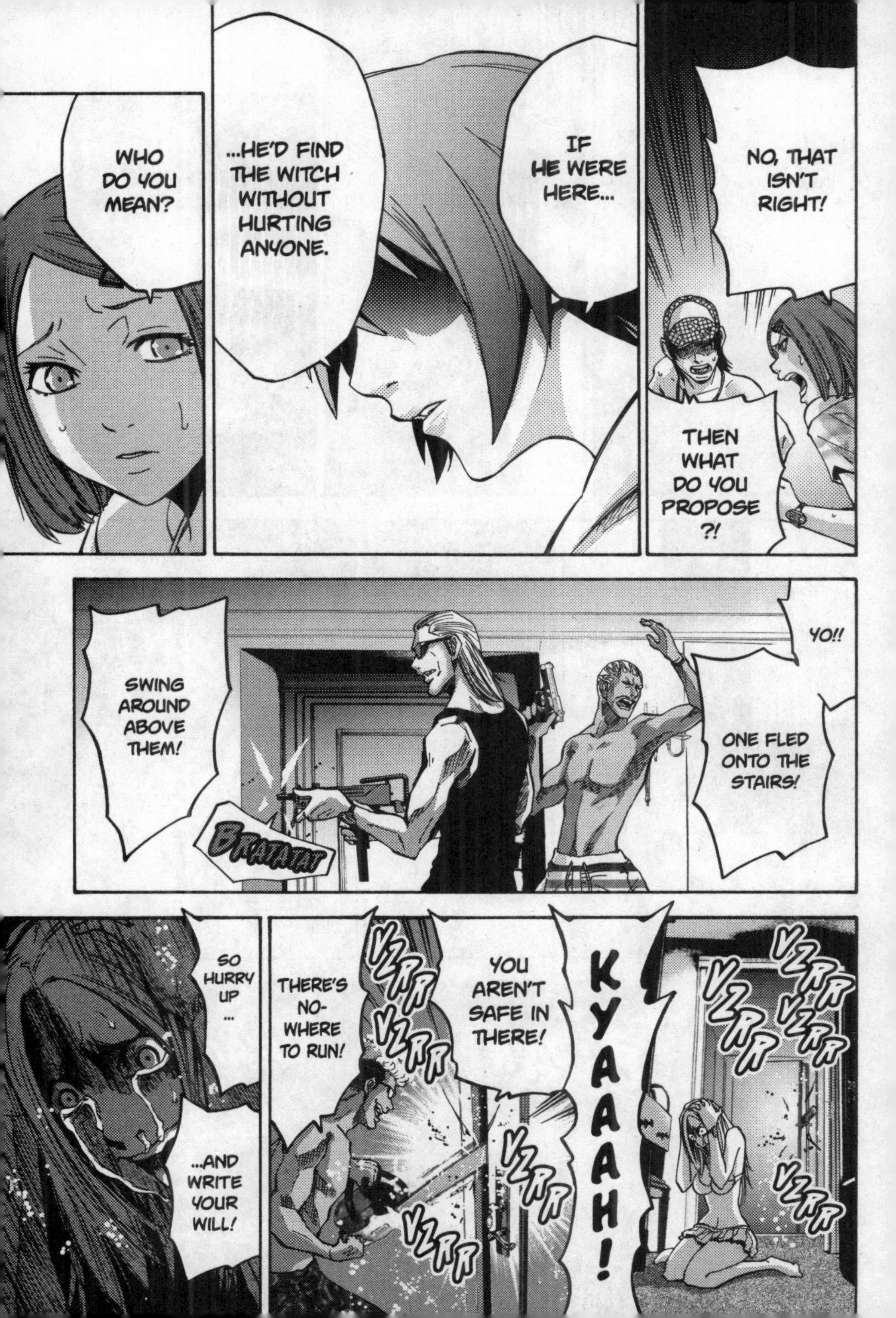
NO, THAT ISN'T RIGHT!
THEN WHAT DO YOU PROPOSE ?!
IF HE WERE HERE...
...HE'D FIND THE WITCH WITHOUT HURTING ANYONE.
WHO DO YOU MEAN?
YO!!
ONE FLED ONTO THE STAIRS!
SWING AROUND ABOVE THEM!
BRATATAT
VZRR VZRR VZRR VZRR VZRR
KYAAAH!
YOU AREN'T SAFE IN THERE!
VZRR VZRR VZRR VZRR
THERE'S NO-WHERE TO RUN!
SO HURRY UP ...
...AND WRITE YOUR WILL!

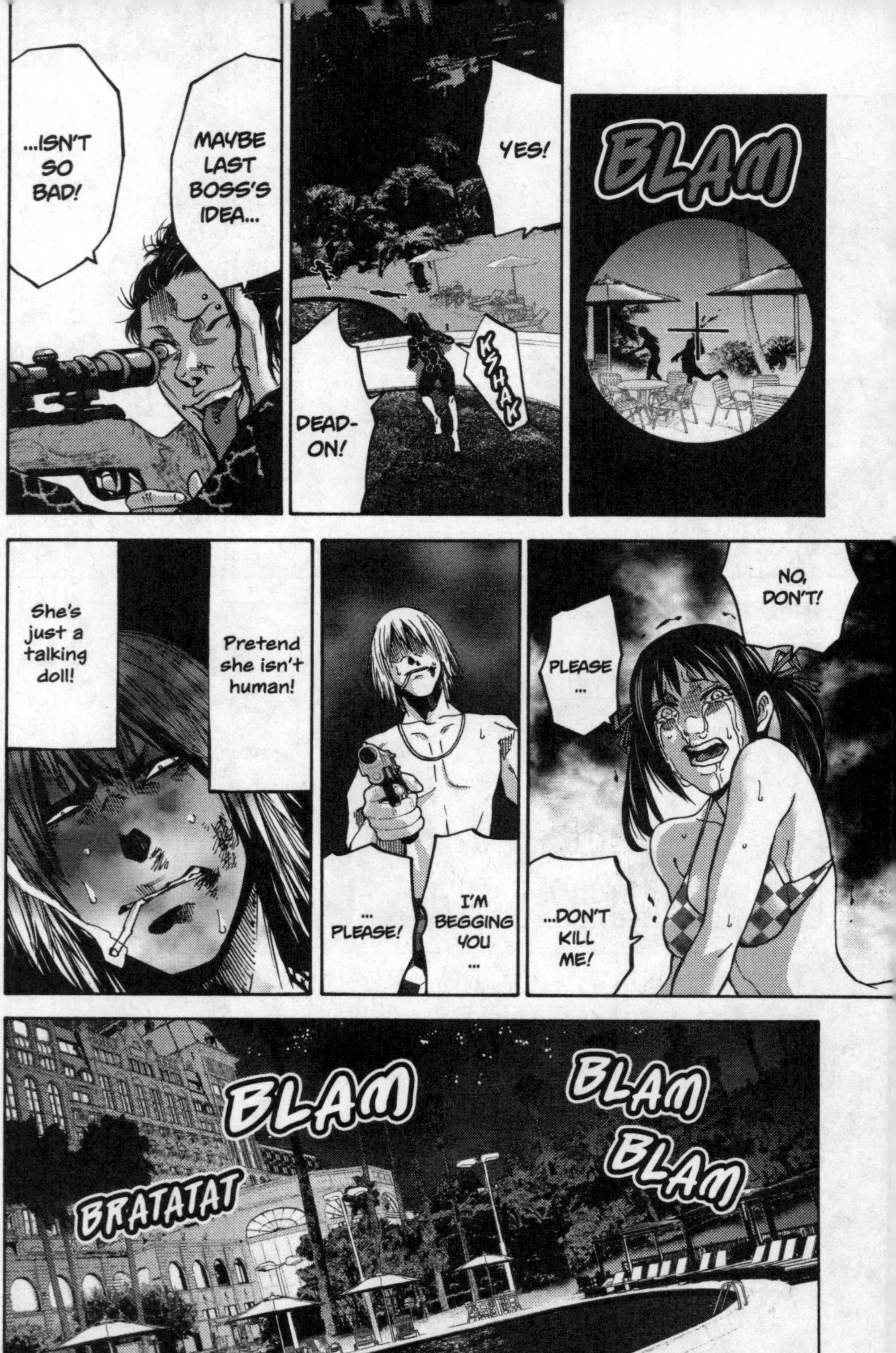
BLAM
YES!
KSHAK
DEAD-ON!
MAYBE LAST BOSS'S IDEA...
...ISN'T SO BAD!
NO, DON'T!
PLEASE ...
...DON'T KILL ME!
I'M BEGGING YOU ...
... PLEASE!
Pretend she isn't human!
She's just a talking doll!
BLAM
BLAM
BLAM
BLAM
BRATATAT

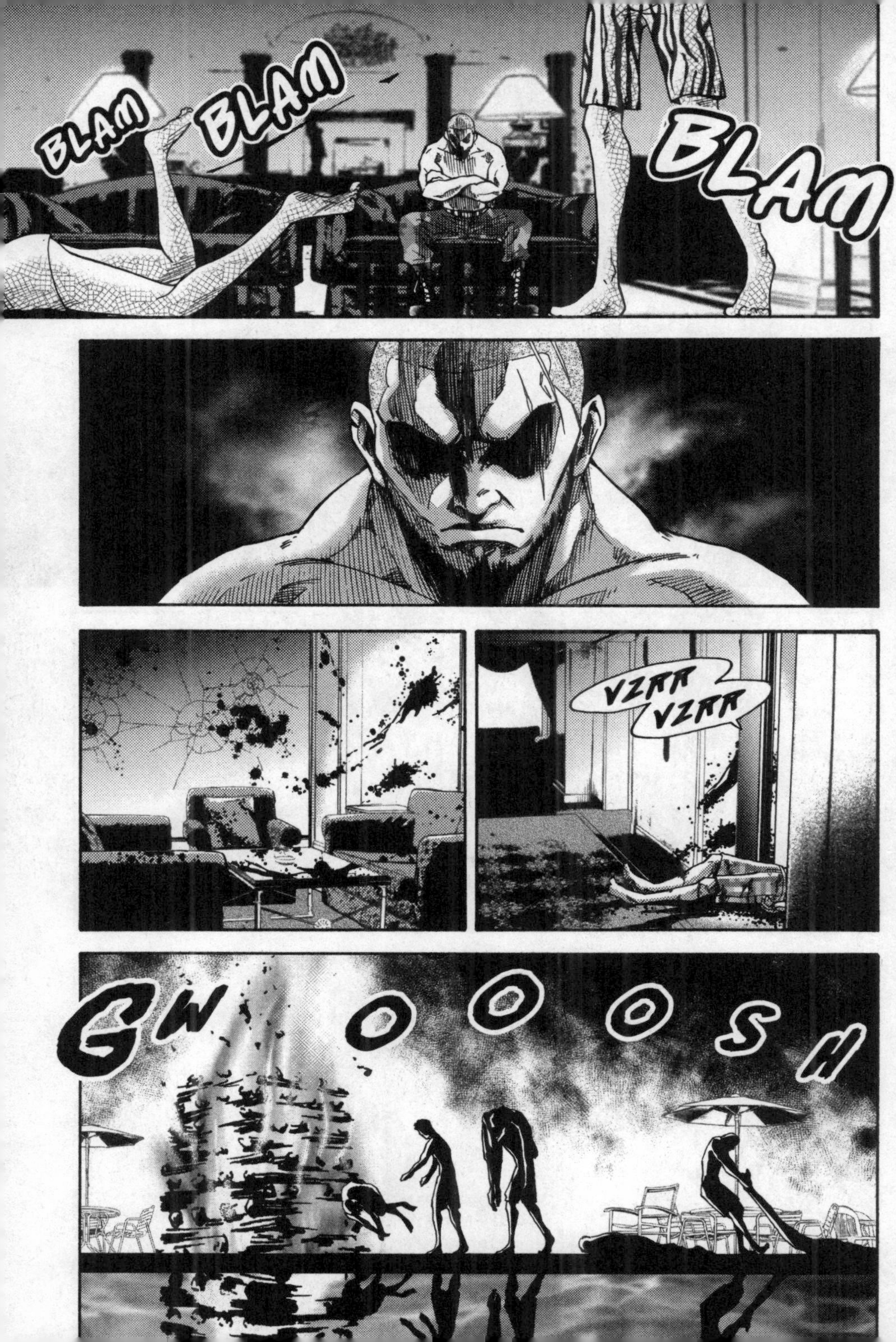
BLAM
BLAM
BLAM
VZRR VZRR
GWOOOSH

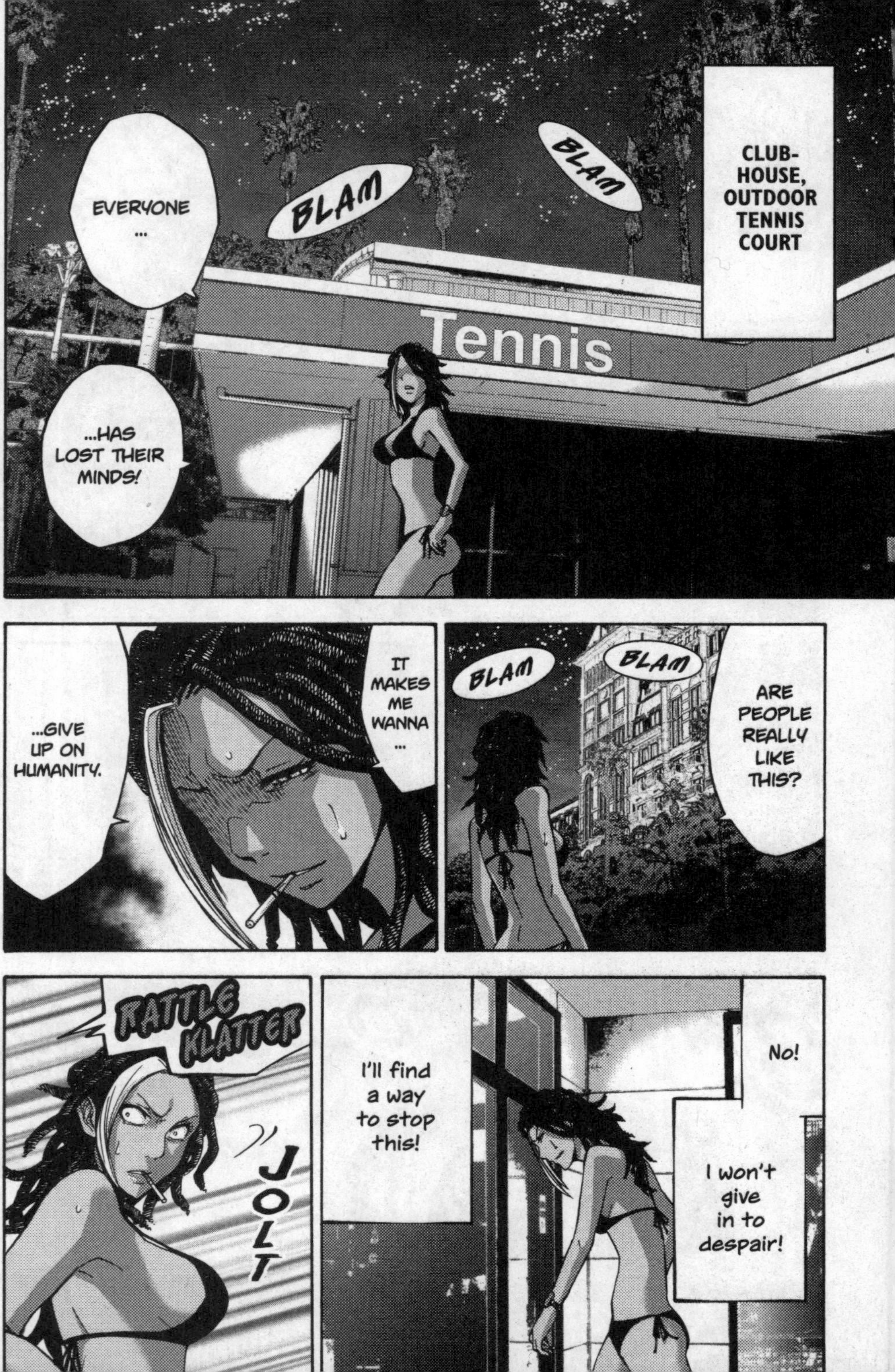
CLUB-HOUSE, OUTDOOR TENNIS COURT
BLAM
BLAM
Tennis
EVERYONE ...
...HAS LOST THEIR MINDS!
BLAM
BLAM
ARE PEOPLE REALLY LIKE THIS?
IT MAKES ME WANNA ...
...GIVE UP ON HUMANITY.
No!
I won't give in to despair!
I'll find a way to stop this!
RATTLE KLATTER
JOLT

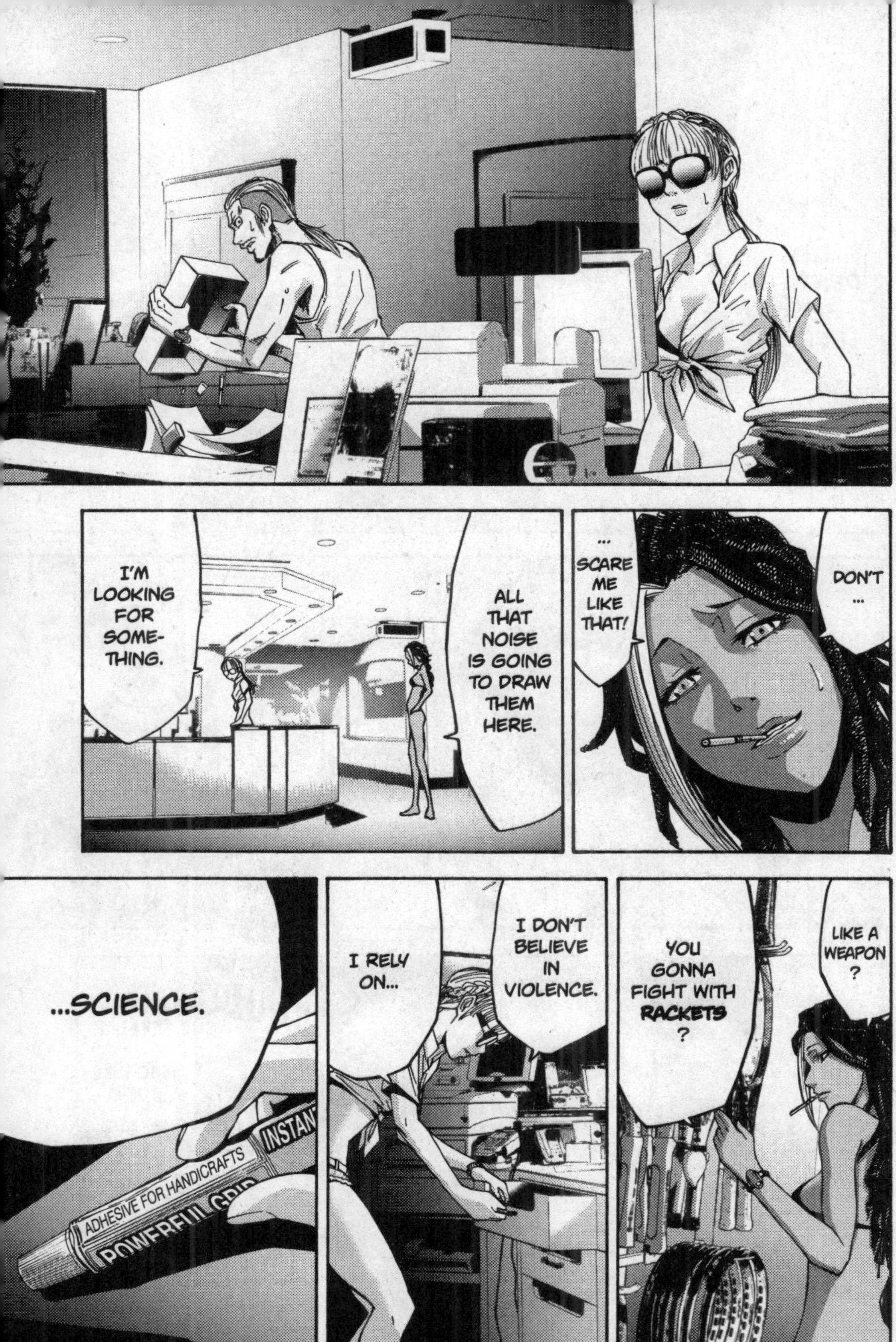
DON'T ...
... SCARE ME LIKE THAT!
ALL THAT NOISE IS GOING TO DRAW THEM HERE.
I'M LOOKING FOR SOME-THING.
LIKE A WEAPON?
YOU GONNA FIGHT WITH RACKETS?
I DON'T BELIEVE IN VIOLENCE.
I RELY ON...
...SCIENCE.
INSTANT
ADHESIVE FOR HANDICRAFTS
POWERFUL GRIP

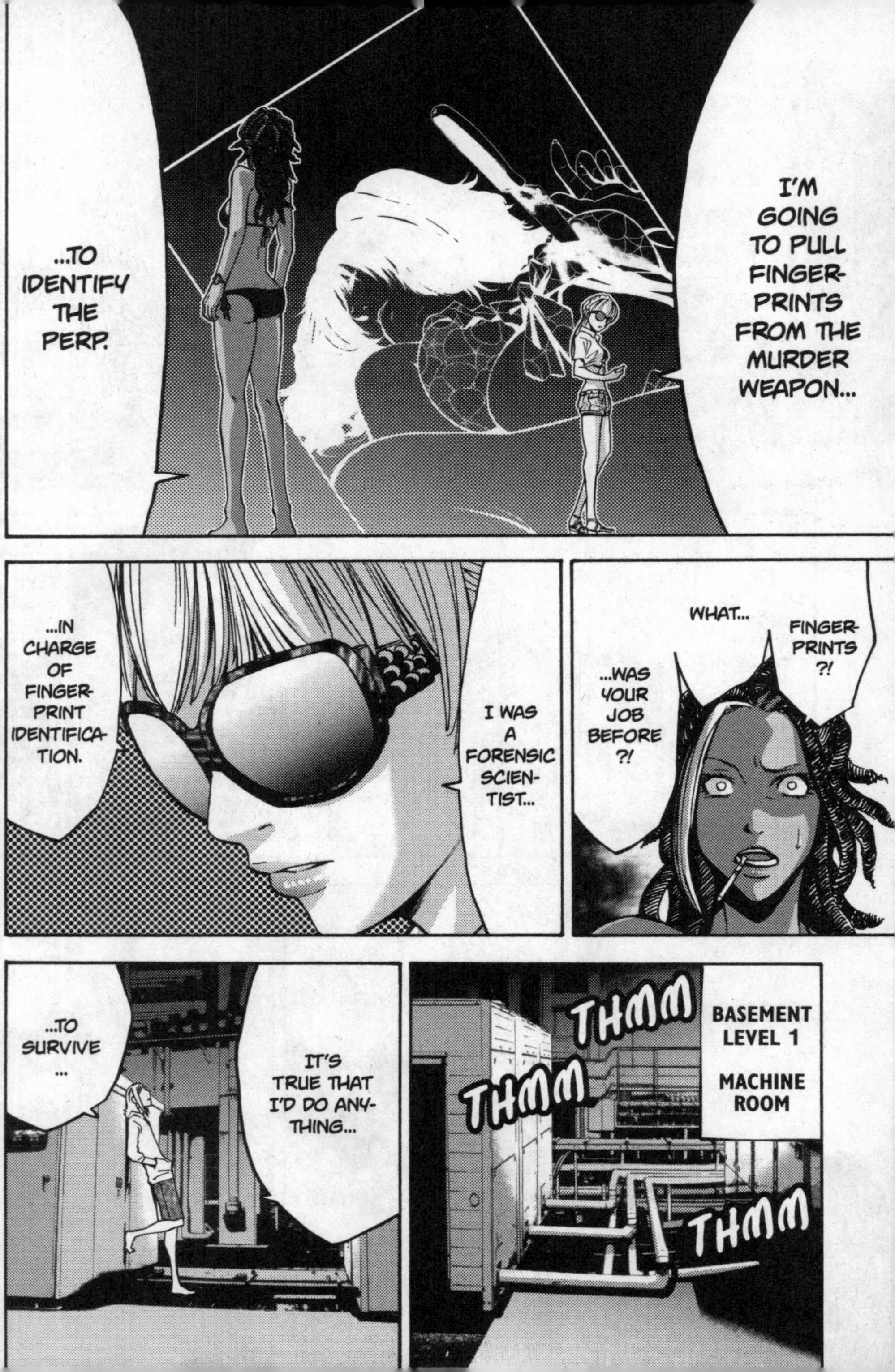
I'M GOING TO PULL FINGER-PRINTS FROM THE MURDER WEAPON...
...TO IDENTIFY THE PERP.
WHAT...
FINGER-PRINTS ?!
...WAS YOUR JOB BEFORE ?!
I WAS A FORENSIC SCIEN-TIST...
...IN CHARGE OF FINGER-PRINT IDENTIFICA-TION.
BASEMENT LEVEL 1
MACHINE ROOM
THMM
THMM
THMM
IT'S TRUE THAT I'D DO ANY-THING...
...TO SURVIVE ...

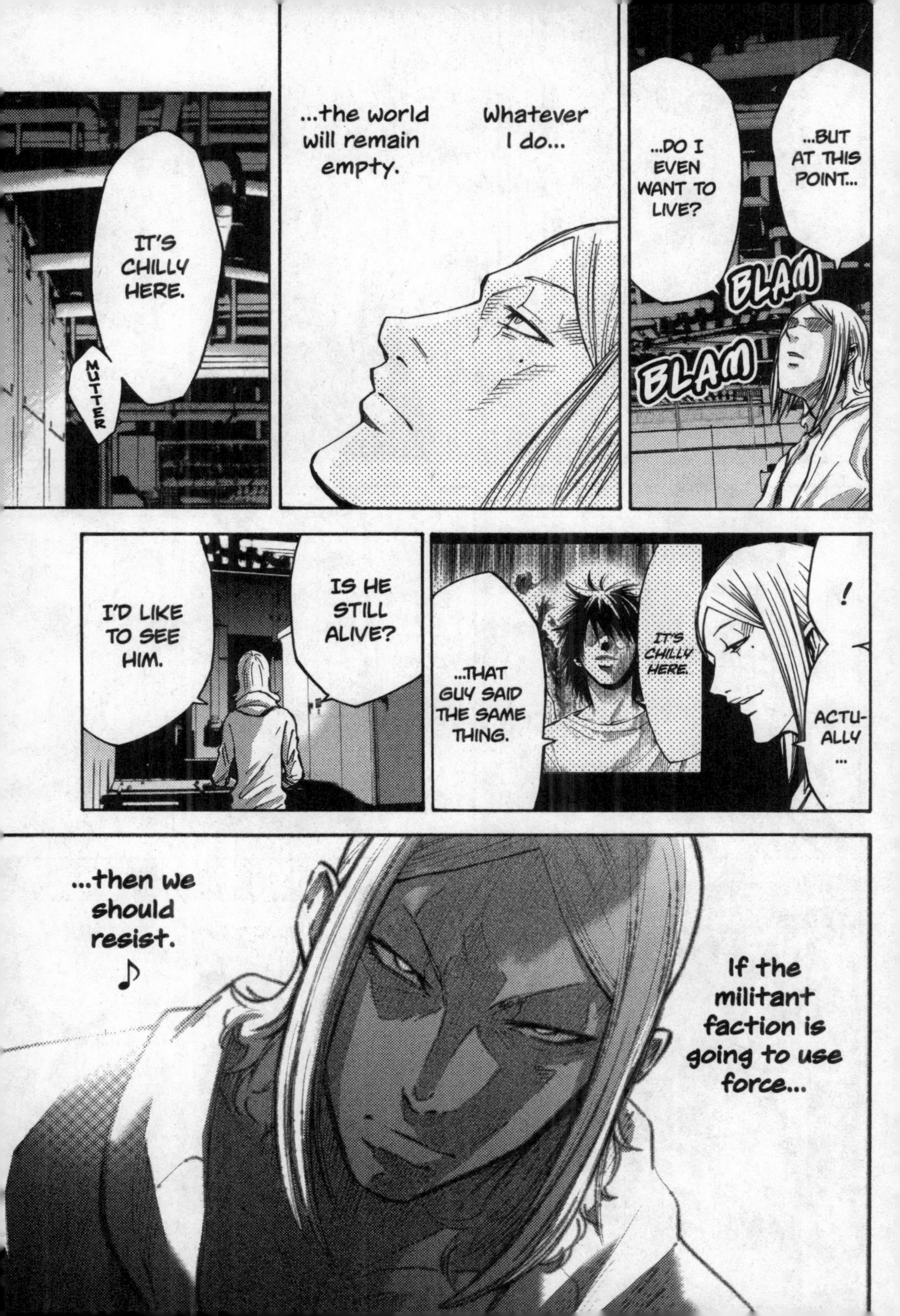
...BUT AT THIS POINT...
...DO I EVEN WANT TO LIVE?
BLAM
BLAM
Whatever I do...
...the world will remain empty.
IT'S CHILLY HERE.
MUTTER
!
ACTU-ALLY...
IT'S CHILLY HERE.
...THAT GUY SAID THE SAME THING.
IS HE STILL ALIVE?
I'D LIKE TO SEE HIM.
If the militant faction is going to use force...
...then we should resist. ♪

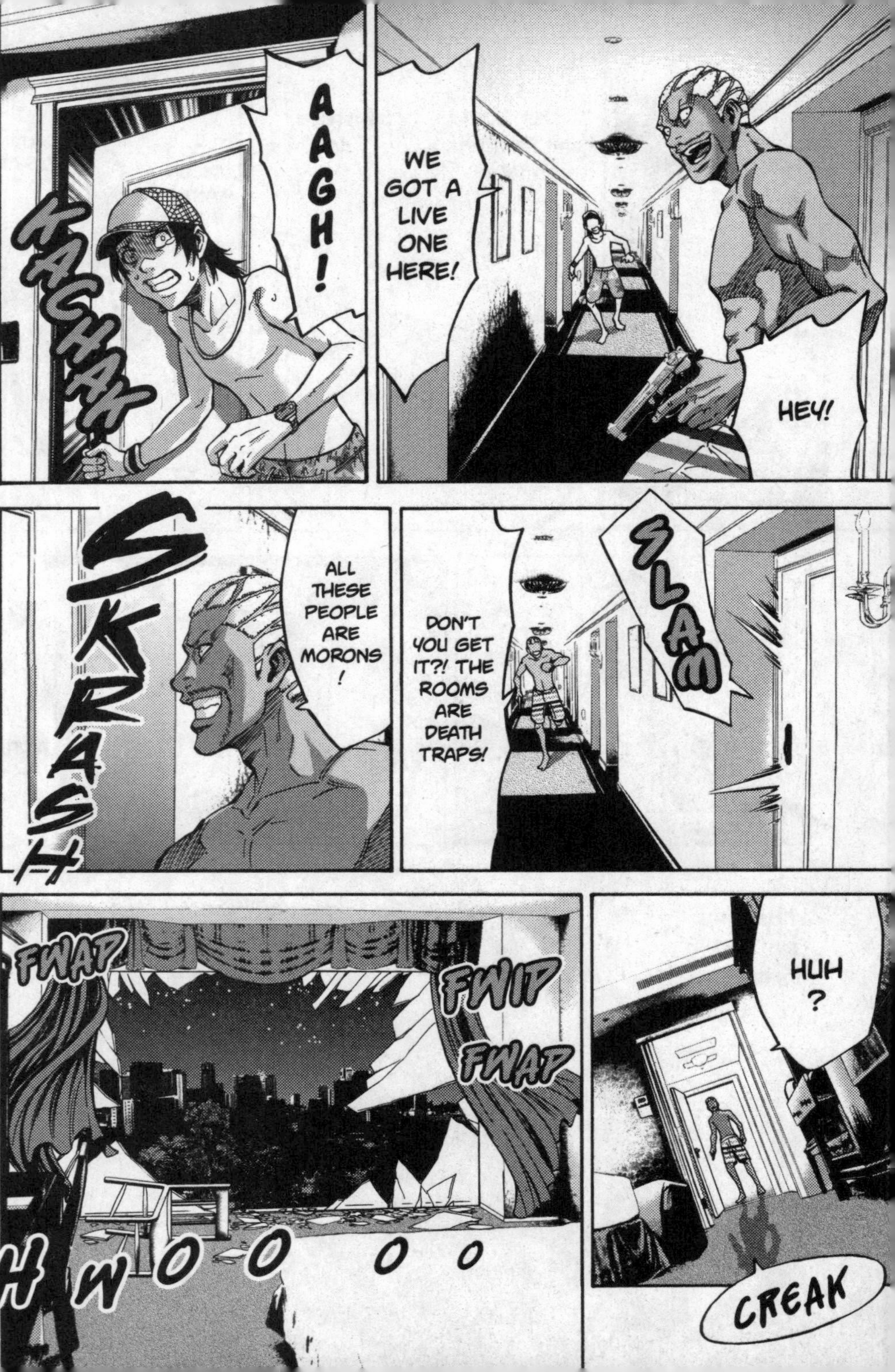
HEY!
WE GOT A LIVE ONE HERE!
AAGH!
KACHAK
SLAM
DON'T YOU GET IT?! THE ROOMS ARE DEATH TRAPS!
ALL THESE PEOPLE ARE MORONS!
SKRASH
HUH?
CREAK
FWIP
FWAP
FWAP
HWOOOOO

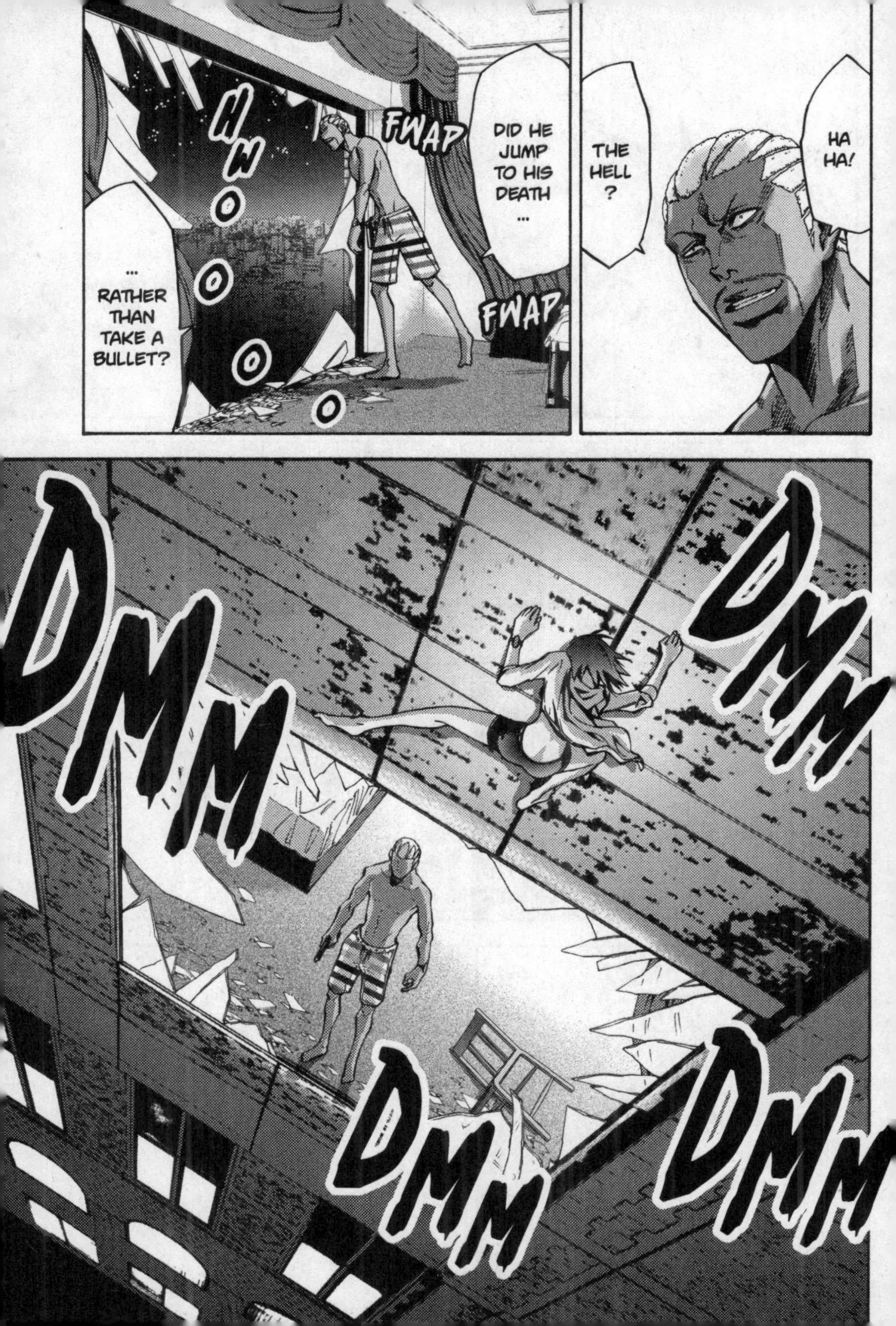
HA HA!
THE HELL ?
DID HE JUMP TO HIS DEATH ...
FWAP
HWOOOOO
... RATHER THAN TAKE A BULLET?
FWAP
DMM
DMM
DMM
DMM

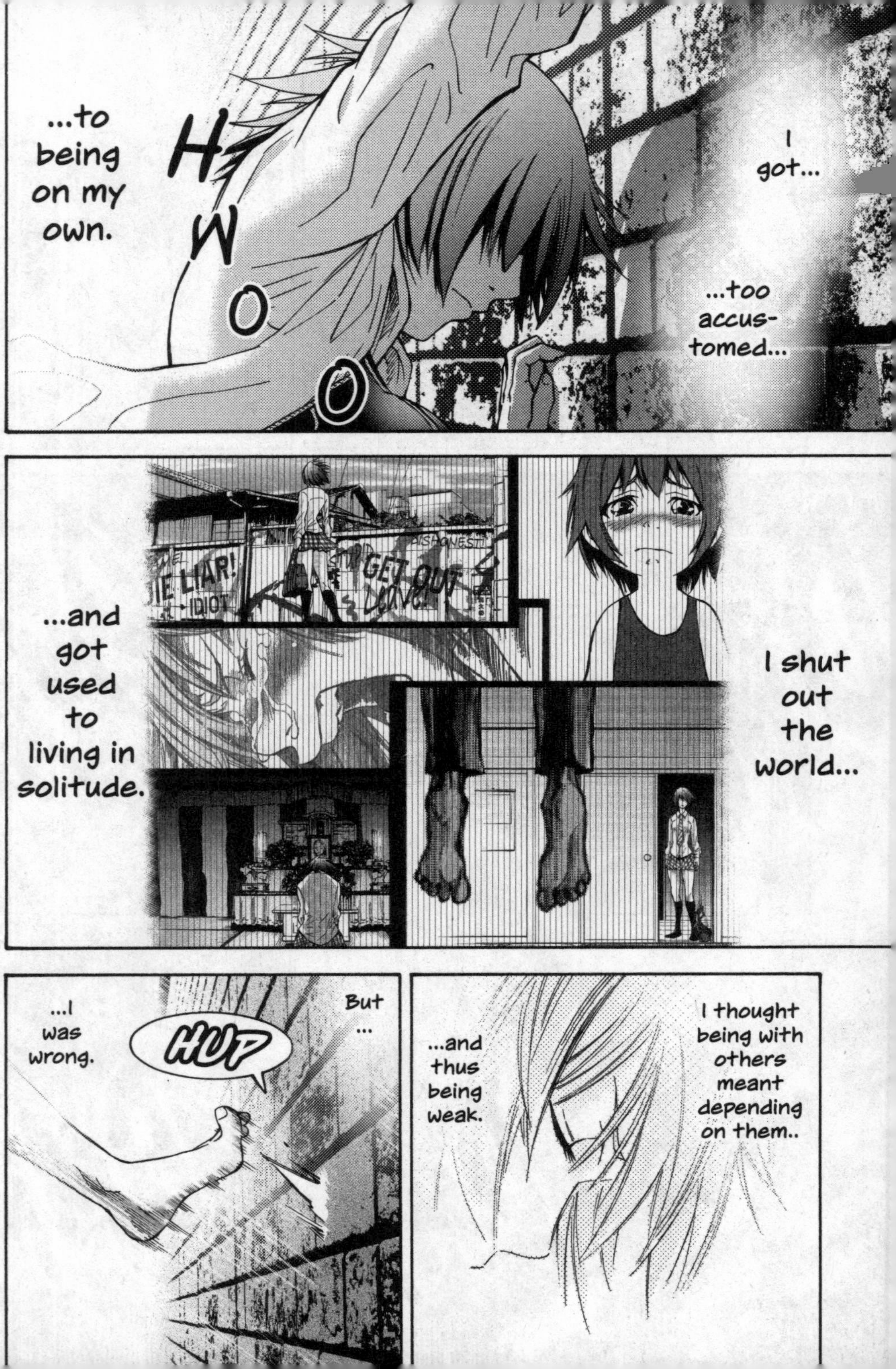
I got...
...too accus-tomed...
...to being on my own.
HWOO
I shut out the world...
LIAR!
IDIOT
GET OUT
LEAVE!
...and got used to living in solitude.
I thought being with others meant depending on them..
...and thus being weak.
But ...
HUP
...I was wrong.

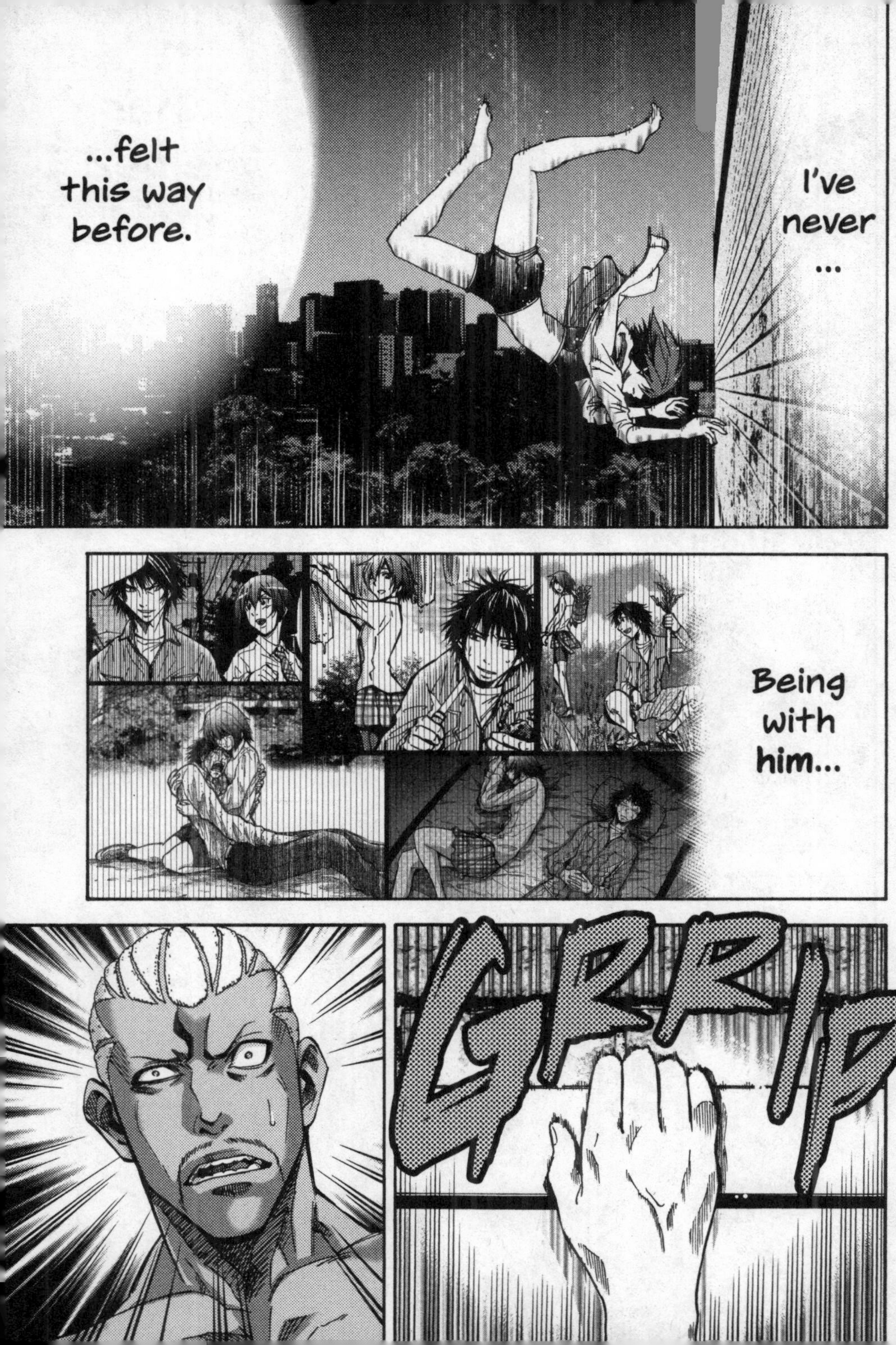
I've never ...
...felt this way before.
Being with him...
GRIP

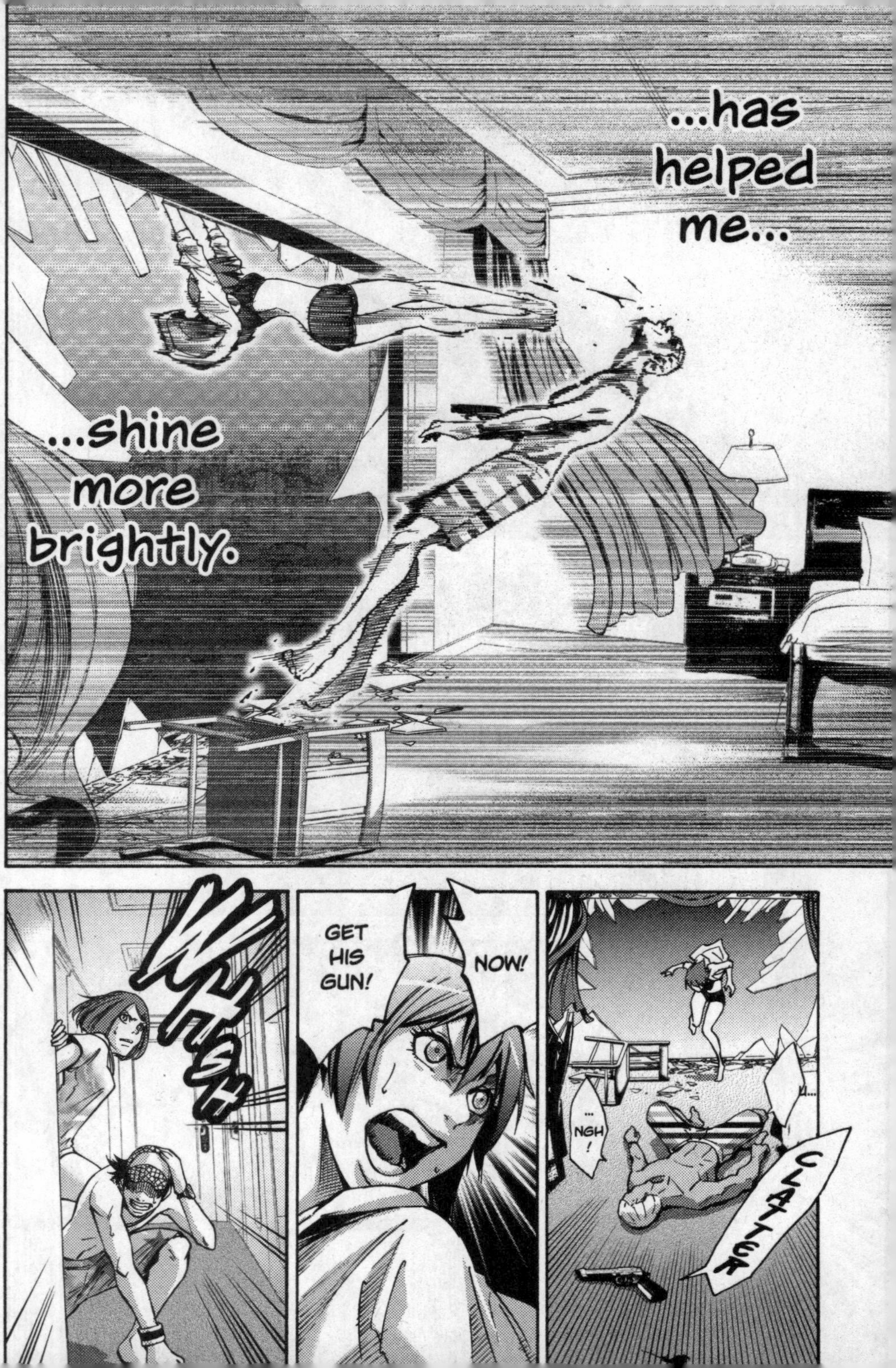
...has helped me...
...shine more brightly.
...NGH!
CLATTER
GET HIS GUN!
NOW!
WHSH

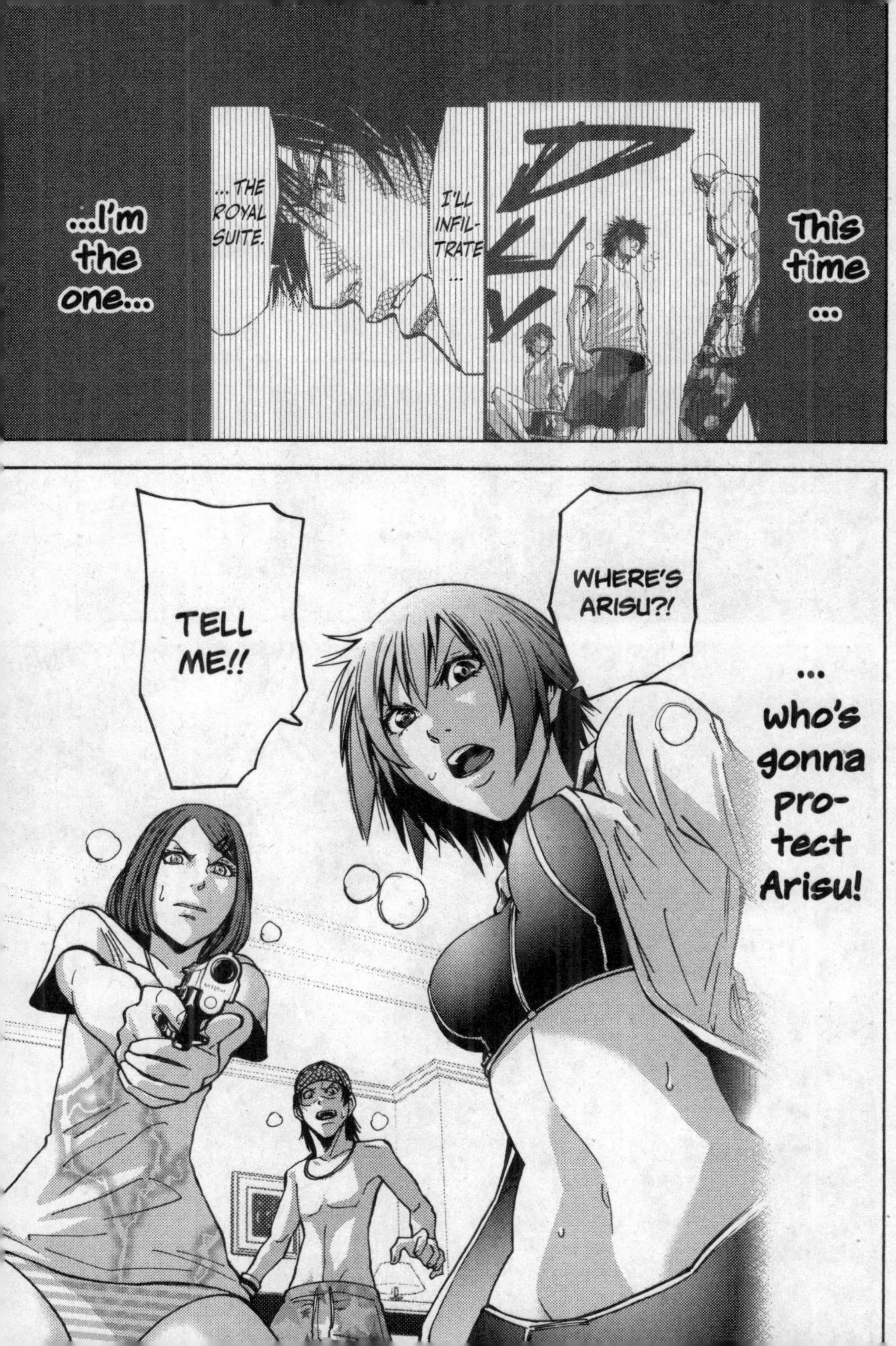
This time ...
I'LL INFILTRATE ...
... THE ROYAL SUITE.
...I'm the one...
... who's gonna protect Arisu!
WHERE'S ARISU?!
TELL ME!!

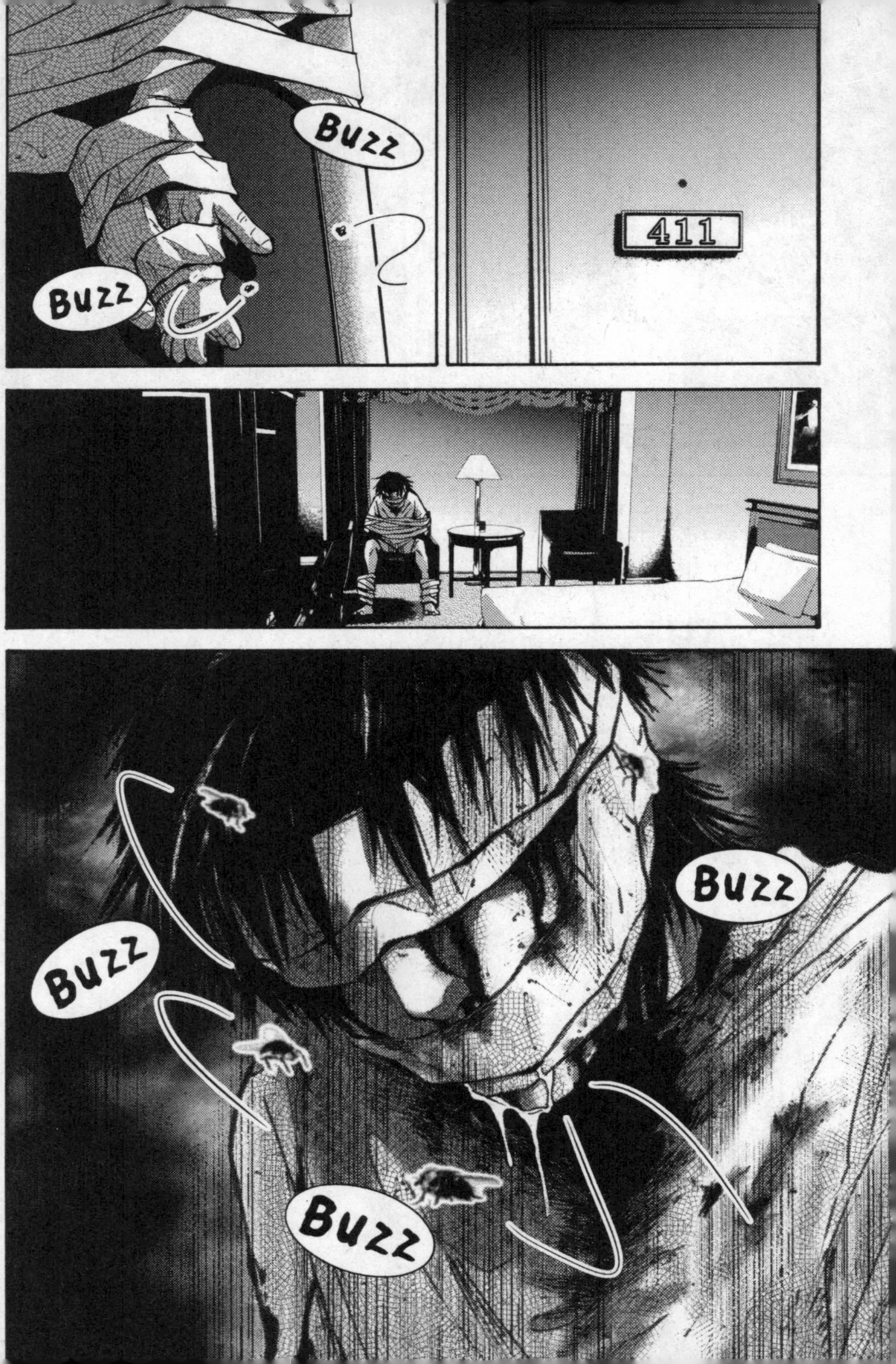
411
Buzz
Buzz
Buzz
Buzz
Buzz

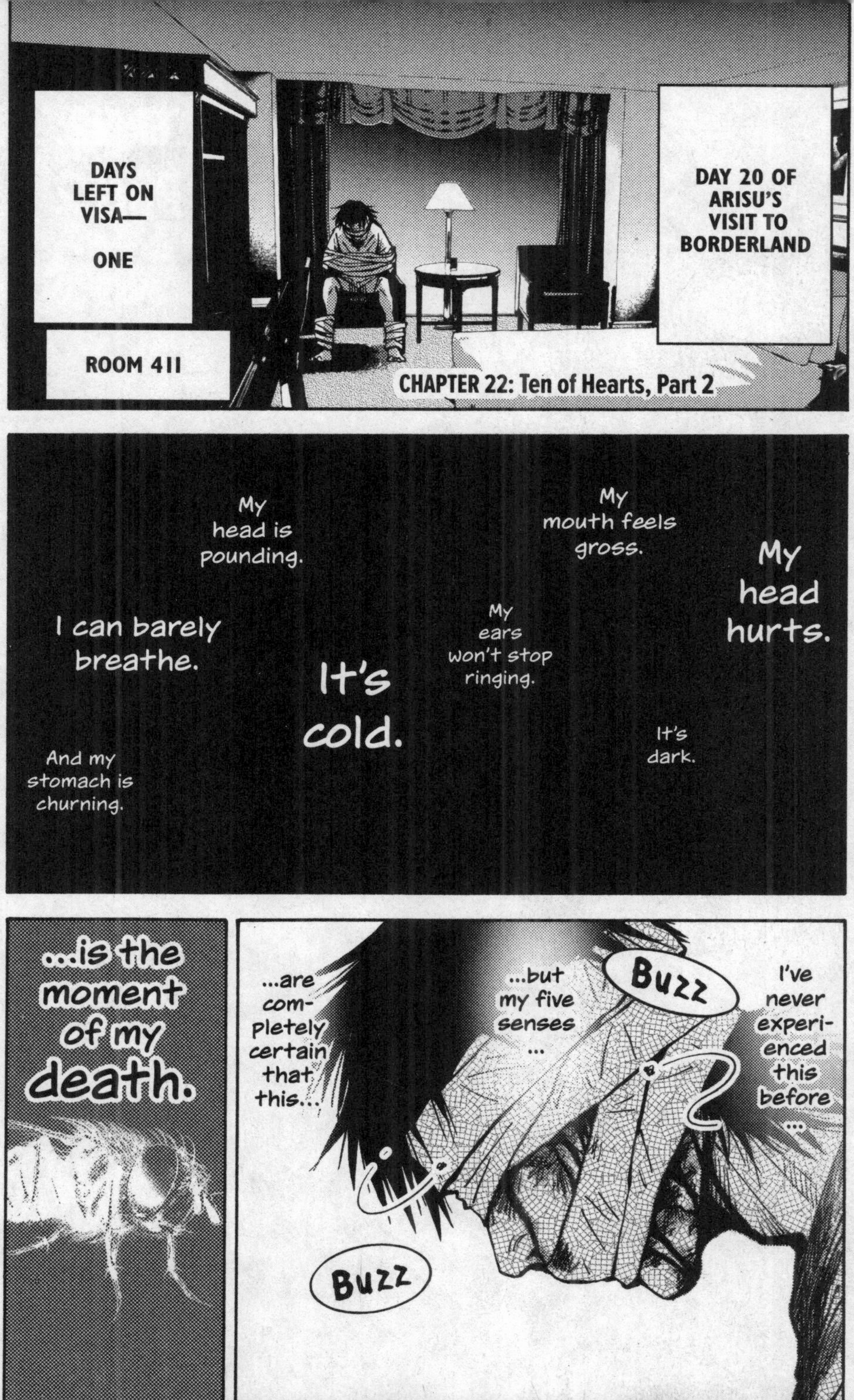
DAY 20 OF ARISU'S VISIT TO BORDERLAND
DAYS LEFT ON VISA— ONE
ROOM 411
CHAPTER 22: Ten of Hearts, Part 2
My head hurts.
My mouth feels gross.
My ears won't stop ringing.
It's dark.
My head is pounding.
It's cold.
I can barely breathe.
And my stomach is churning.
I've never experienced this before...
Buzz
...but my five senses...
...are completely certain that this...
Buzz
...is the moment of my death.

CHAPTER 22:
Ten of Hearts, Part 2

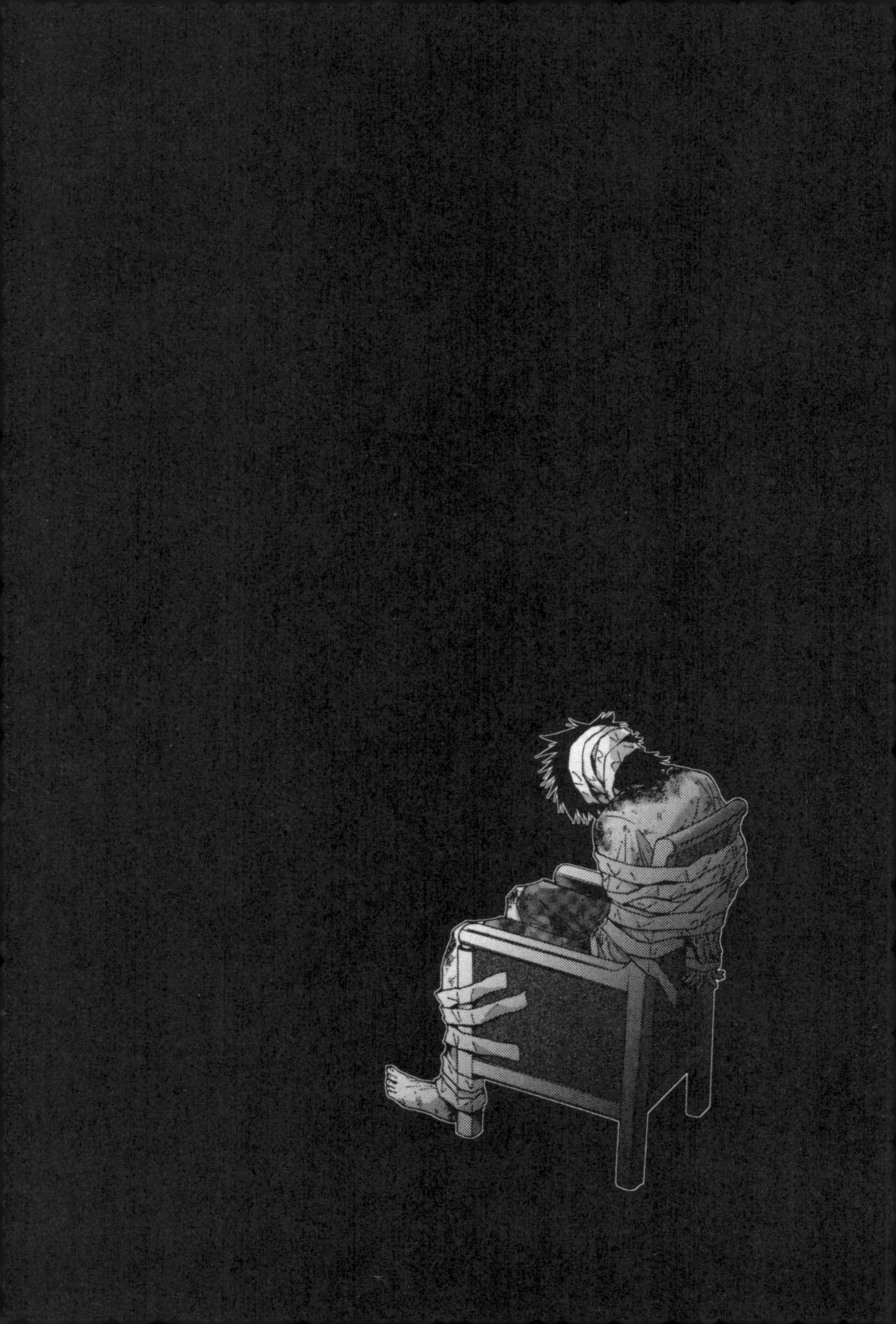

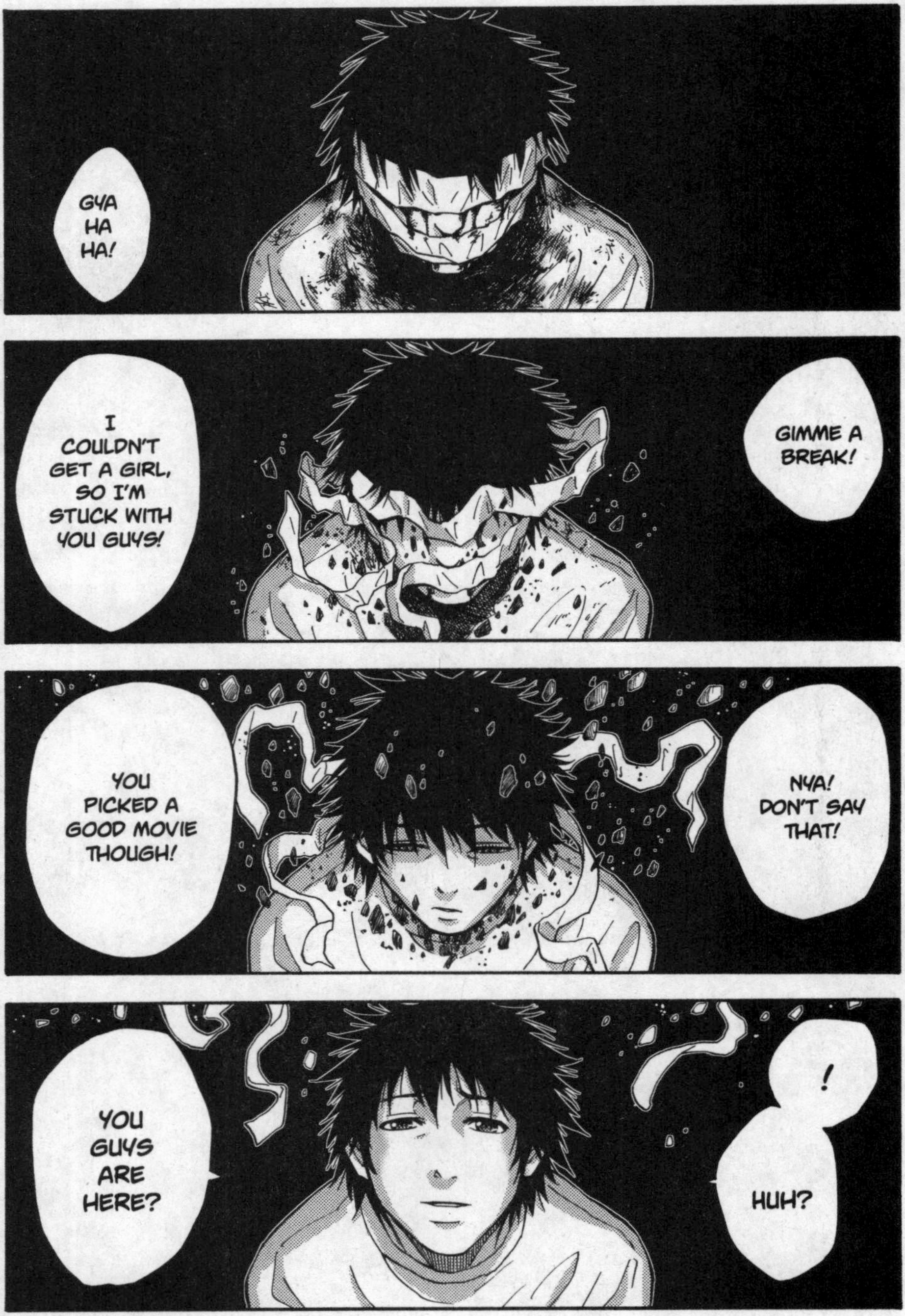
GYA HA HA!
GIMME A BREAK!
I COULDN'T GET A GIRL, SO I'M STUCK WITH YOU GUYS!
NYA! DON'T SAY THAT!
YOU PICKED A GOOD MOVIE THOUGH!
!
HUH?
YOU GUYS ARE HERE?

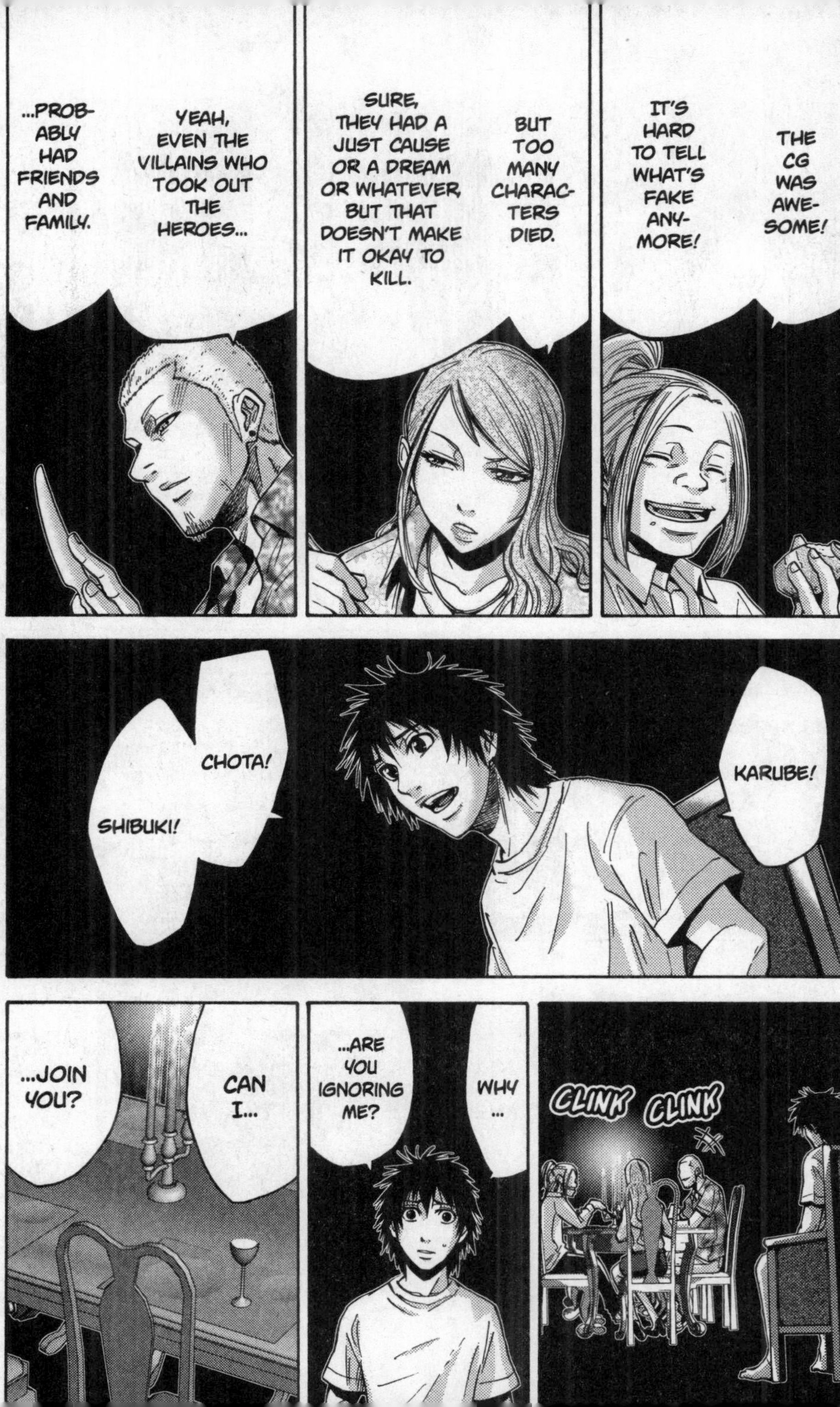
THE CG WAS AWESOME!
IT'S HARD TO TELL WHAT'S FAKE ANYMORE!
BUT TOO MANY CHARACTERS DIED.
SURE, THEY HAD A JUST CAUSE OR A DREAM OR WHATEVER, BUT THAT DOESN'T MAKE IT OKAY TO KILL.
YEAH, EVEN THE VILLAINS WHO TOOK OUT THE HEROES...
...PROBABLY HAD FRIENDS AND FAMILY.
KARUBE!
CHOTA!
SHIBUKI!
CLINK CLINK
WHY...
...ARE YOU IGNORING ME?
CAN I...
...JOIN YOU?

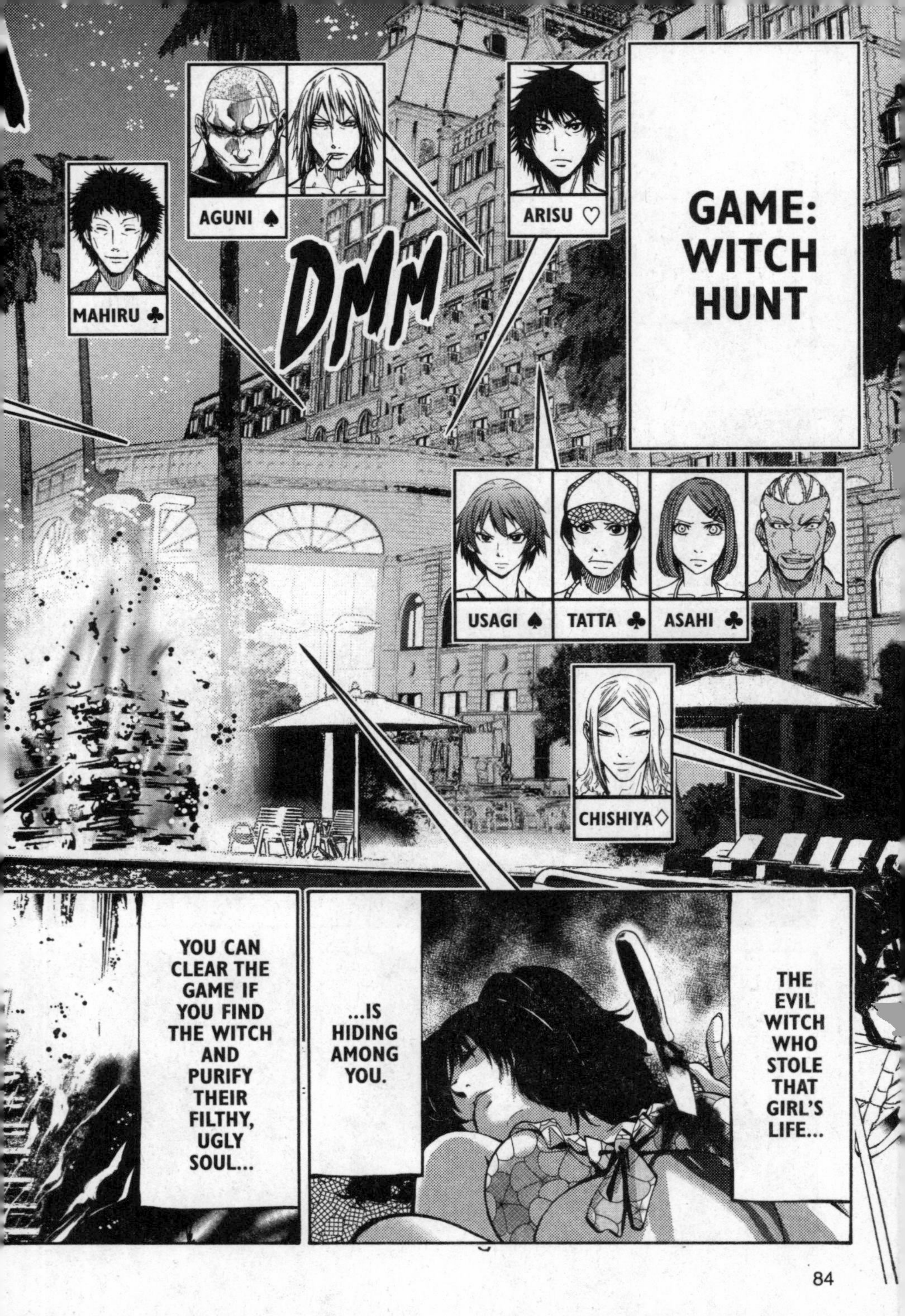
GAME: WITCH HUNT
ARISU ♡
AGUNI ♠
MAHIRU ♣
DMM
USAGI ♠
TATTA ♣
ASAHI ♣
CHISHIYA ♢
THE EVIL WITCH WHO STOLE THAT GIRL'S LIFE...
...IS HIDING AMONG YOU.
YOU CAN CLEAR THE GAME IF YOU FIND THE WITCH AND PURIFY THEIR FILTHY, UGLY SOUL...

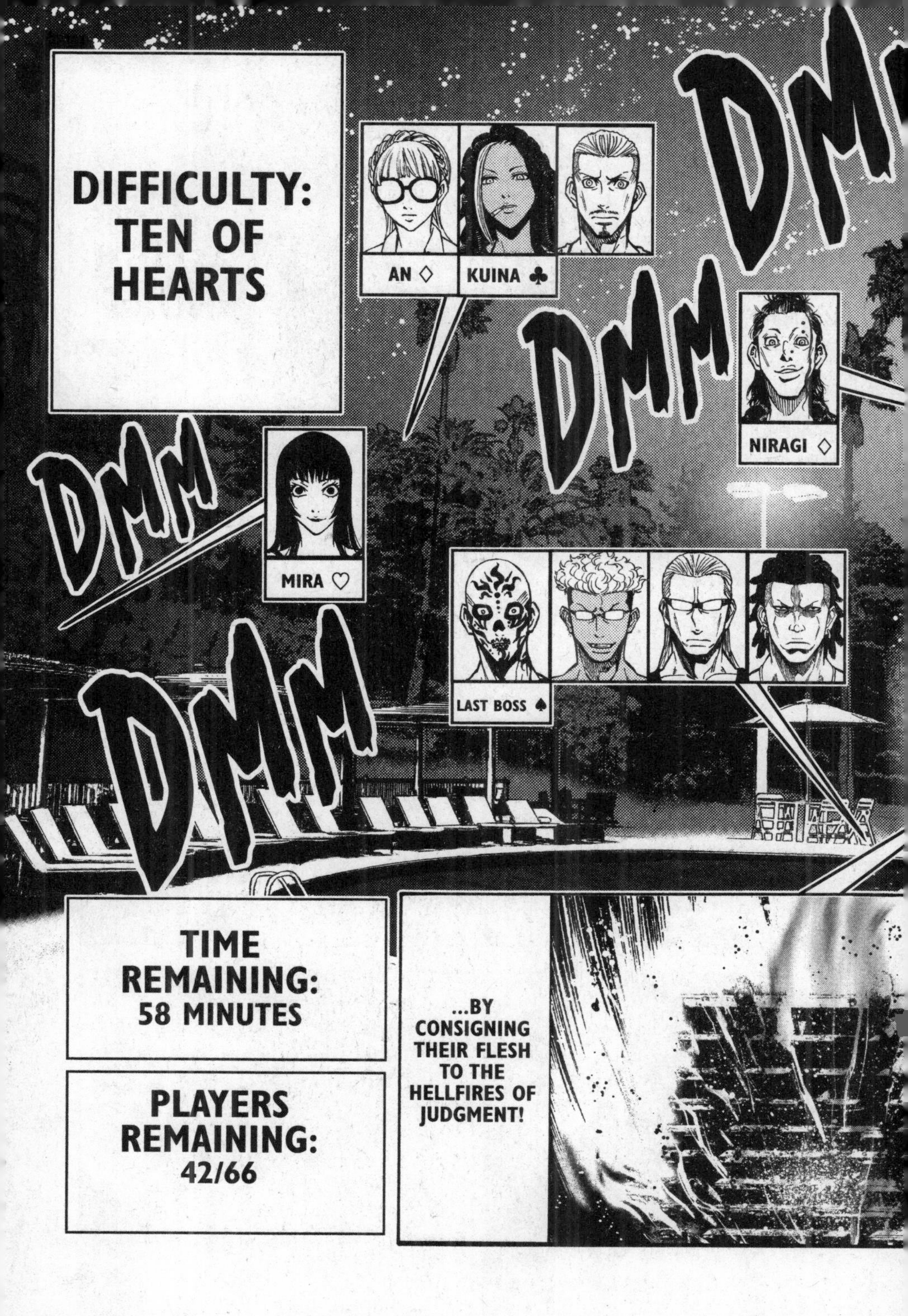
DMM DMM
KUINA ♣
AN ◇
NIRAGI ◇
DMM
DIFFICULTY: TEN OF HEARTS
LAST BOSS ♠
MIRA ♡
DMM
DMM
...BY CONSIGNING THEIR FLESH TO THE HELLFIRES OF JUDGMENT!
TIME REMAINING: 58 MINUTES
PLAYERS REMAINING: 42/66

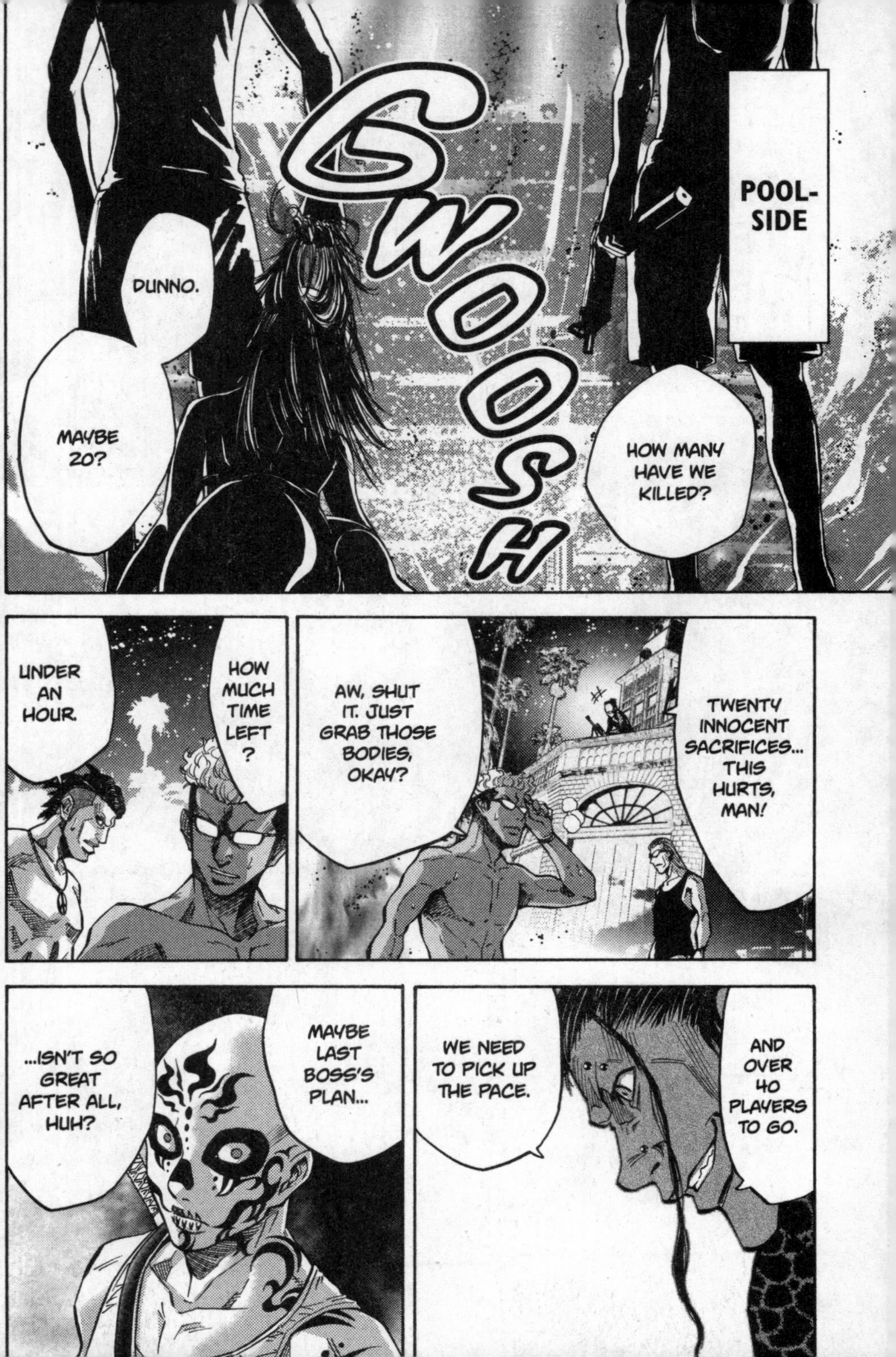
POOL-SIDE
HOW MANY HAVE WE KILLED?
GWOOSH
DUNNO.
MAYBE 20?
TWENTY INNOCENT SACRIFICES... THIS HURTS, MAN!
AW, SHUT IT. JUST GRAB THOSE BODIES, OKAY?
HOW MUCH TIME LEFT ?
UNDER AN HOUR.
AND OVER 40 PLAYERS TO GO.
WE NEED TO PICK UP THE PACE.
MAYBE LAST BOSS'S PLAN...
...ISN'T SO GREAT AFTER ALL, HUH?

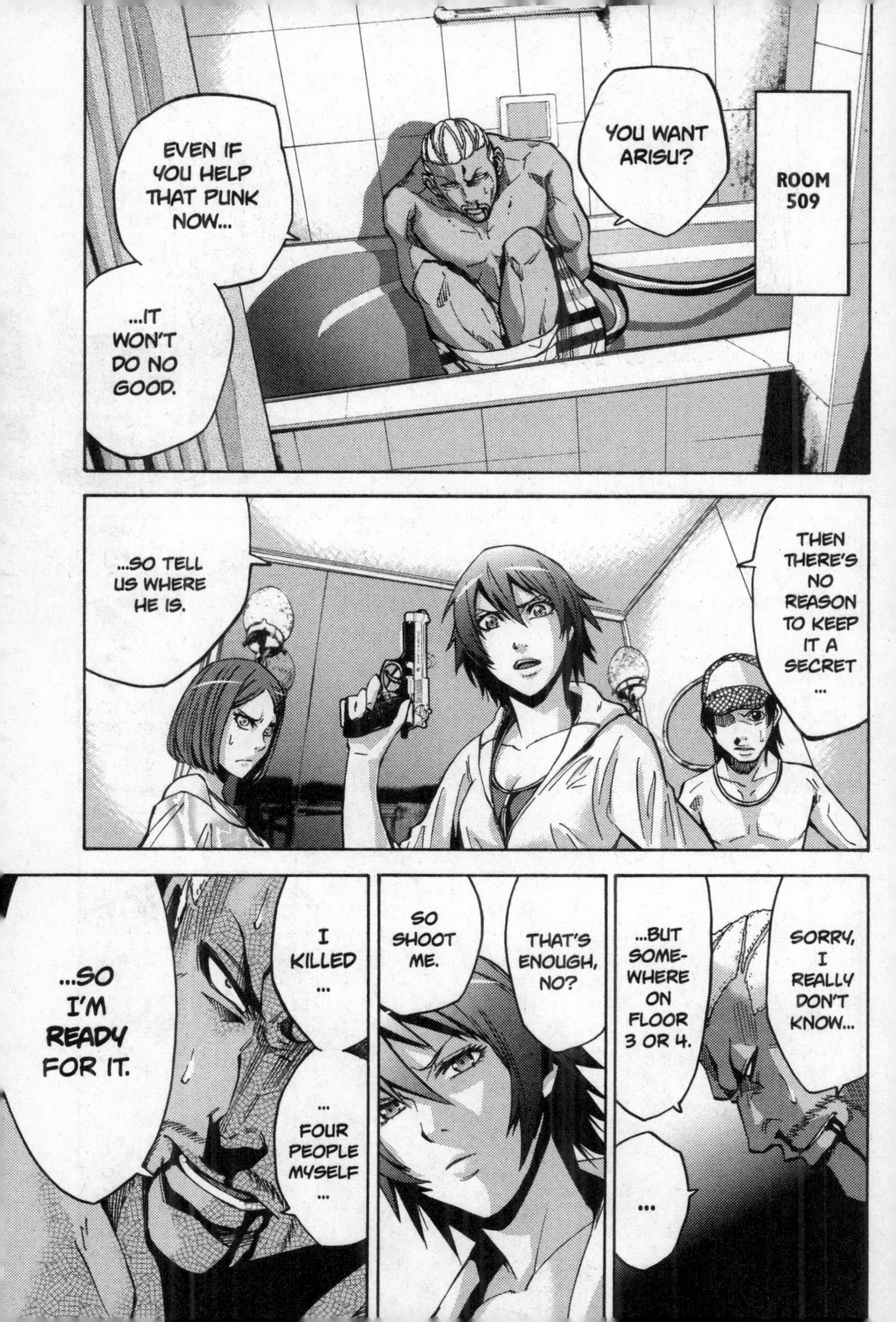
ROOM 509
YOU WANT ARISU?
EVEN IF YOU HELP THAT PUNK NOW...
...IT WON'T DO NO GOOD.
THEN THERE'S NO REASON TO KEEP IT A SECRET ...
...SO TELL US WHERE HE IS.
SORRY, I REALLY DON'T KNOW...
...BUT SOME-WHERE ON FLOOR 3 OR 4.
...
THAT'S ENOUGH, NO?
SO SHOOT ME.
I KILLED ...
... FOUR PEOPLE MYSELF ...
...SO I'M READY FOR IT.

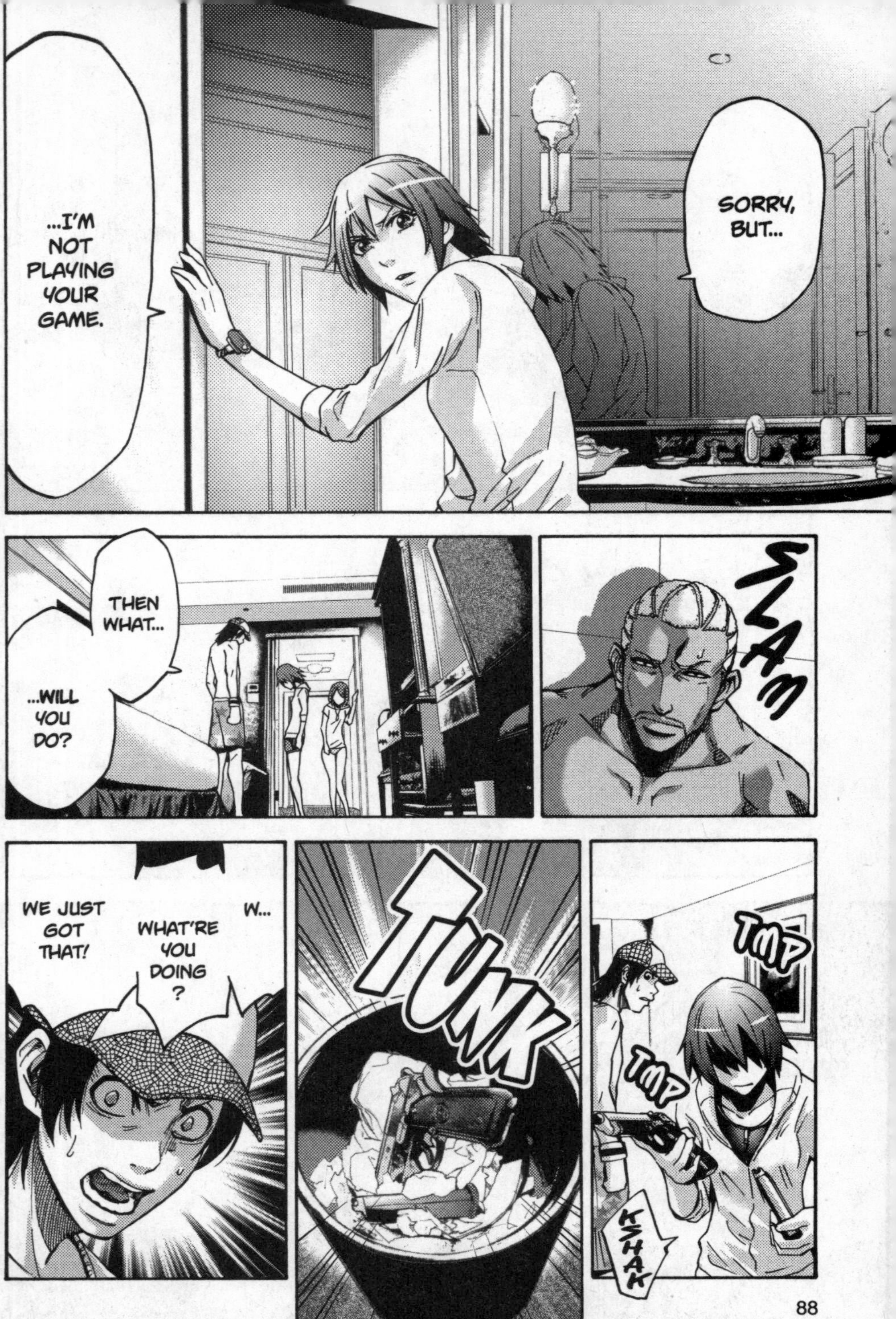
SORRY, BUT...
...I'M NOT PLAYING YOUR GAME.
SLAM
THEN WHAT...
...WILL YOU DO?
TMP
TMP
KSHAK
TUNK
W...
WHAT'RE YOU DOING?
WE JUST GOT THAT!

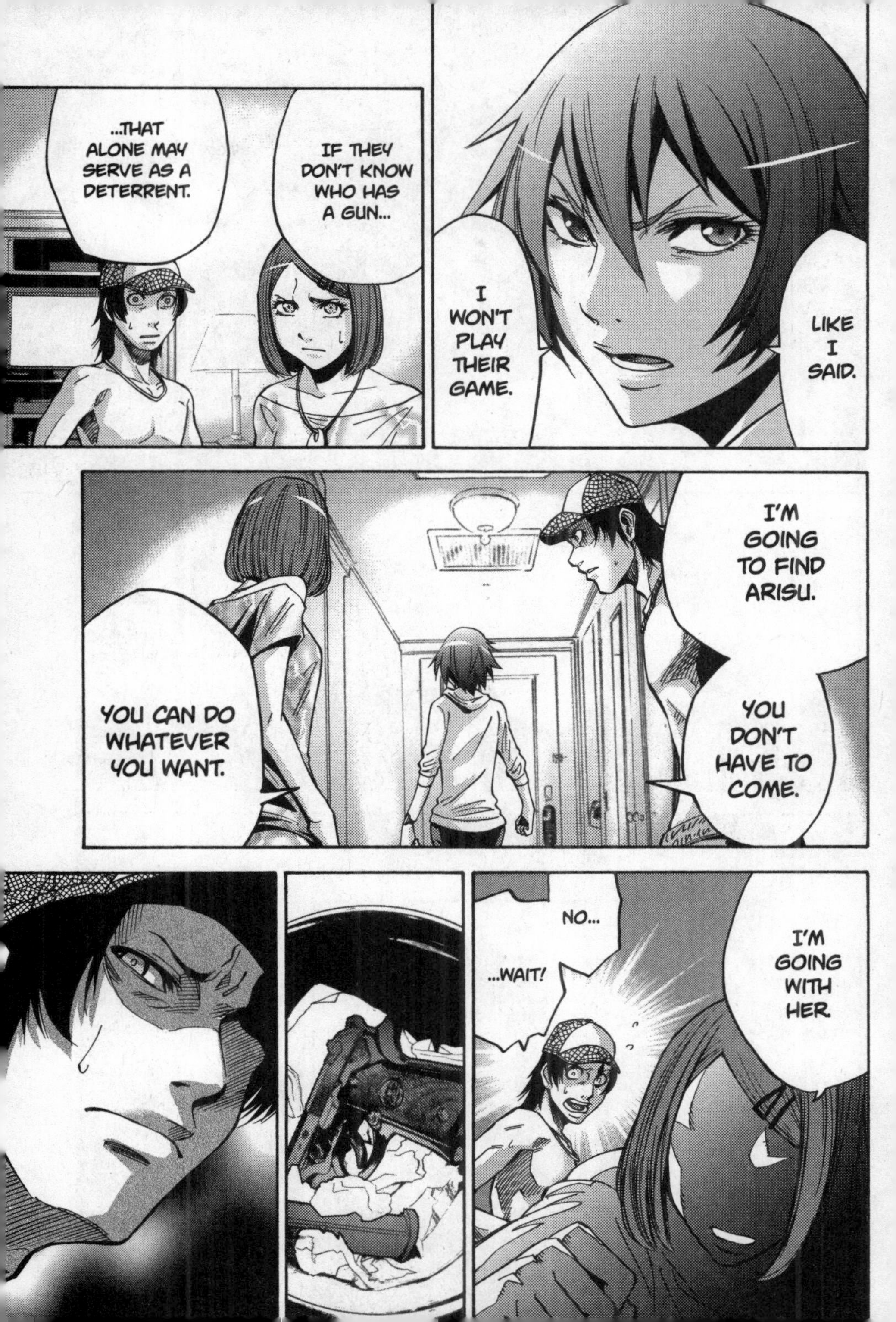
LIKE I SAID.
I WON'T PLAY THEIR GAME.
IF THEY DON'T KNOW WHO HAS A GUN...
...THAT ALONE MAY SERVE AS A DETERRENT.
I'M GOING TO FIND ARISU.
YOU DON'T HAVE TO COME.
YOU CAN DO WHATEVER YOU WANT.
I'M GOING WITH HER
NO...
...WAIT!

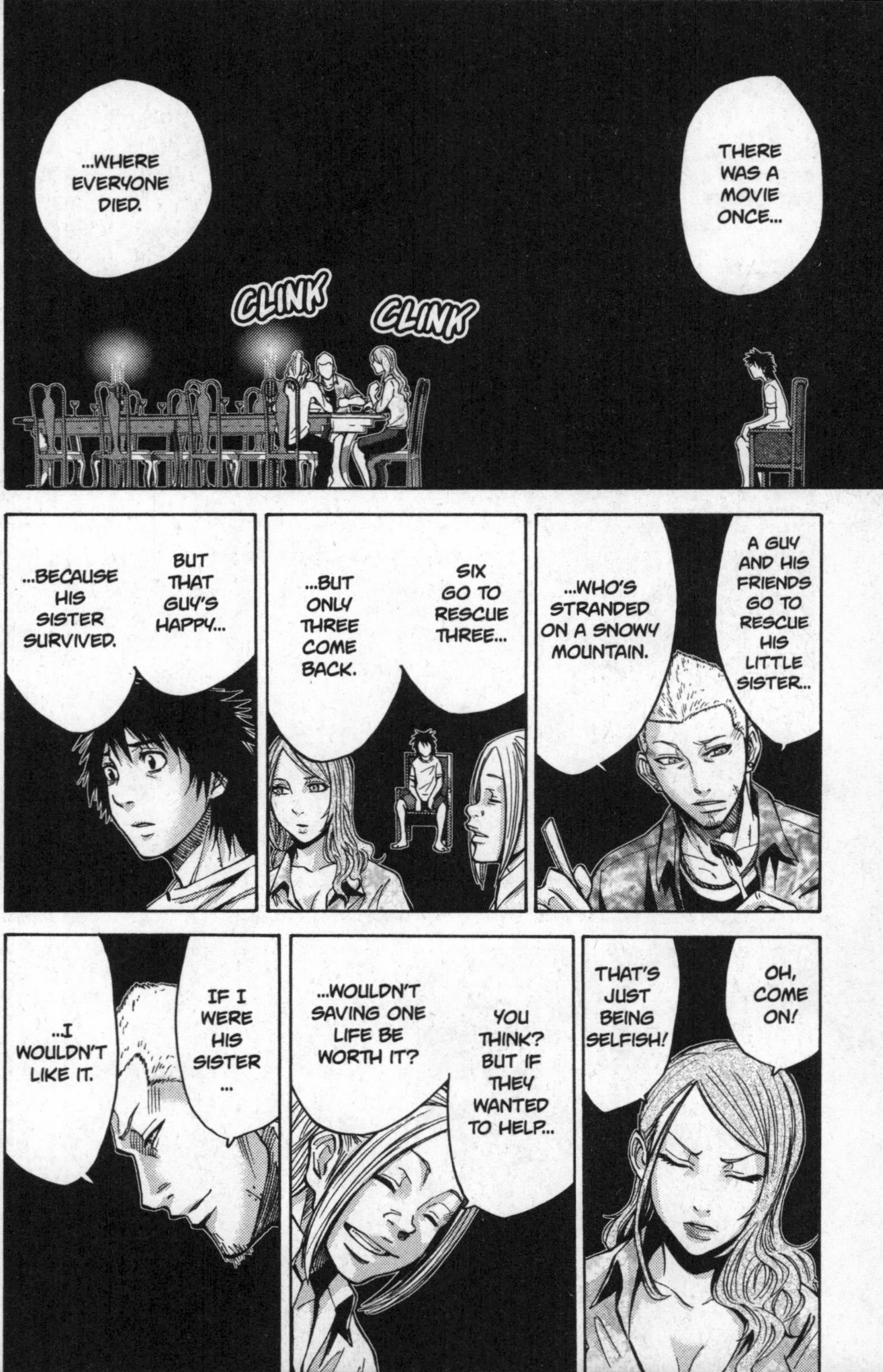
THERE WAS A MOVIE ONCE...
...WHERE EVERYONE DIED.
CLINK
CLINK
A GUY AND HIS FRIENDS GO TO RESCUE HIS LITTLE SISTER...
...WHO'S STRANDED ON A SNOWY MOUNTAIN.
SIX GO TO RESCUE THREE...
...BUT ONLY THREE COME BACK.
BUT THAT GUY'S HAPPY...
...BECAUSE HIS SISTER SURVIVED.
OH, COME ON!
THAT'S JUST BEING SELFISH!
YOU THINK? BUT IF THEY WANTED TO HELP...
...WOULDN'T SAVING ONE LIFE BE WORTH IT?
IF I WERE HIS SISTER ...
...I WOULDN'T LIKE IT.

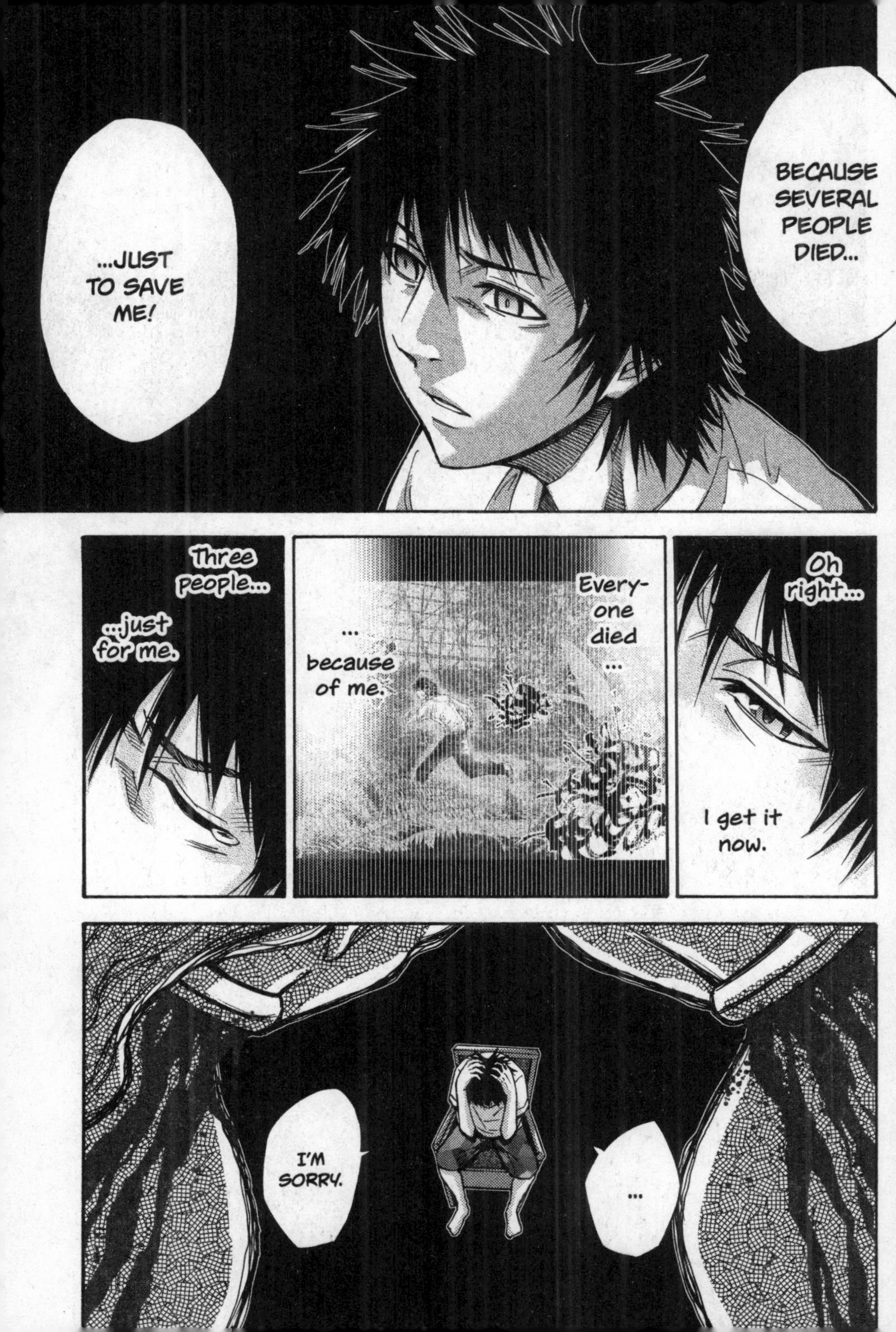

BECAUSE SEVERAL PEOPLE DIED...
...JUST TO SAVE ME!
Oh right...
I get it now.
Every-one died ...
... because of me.
Three people...
...just for me.
...
I'M SORRY.

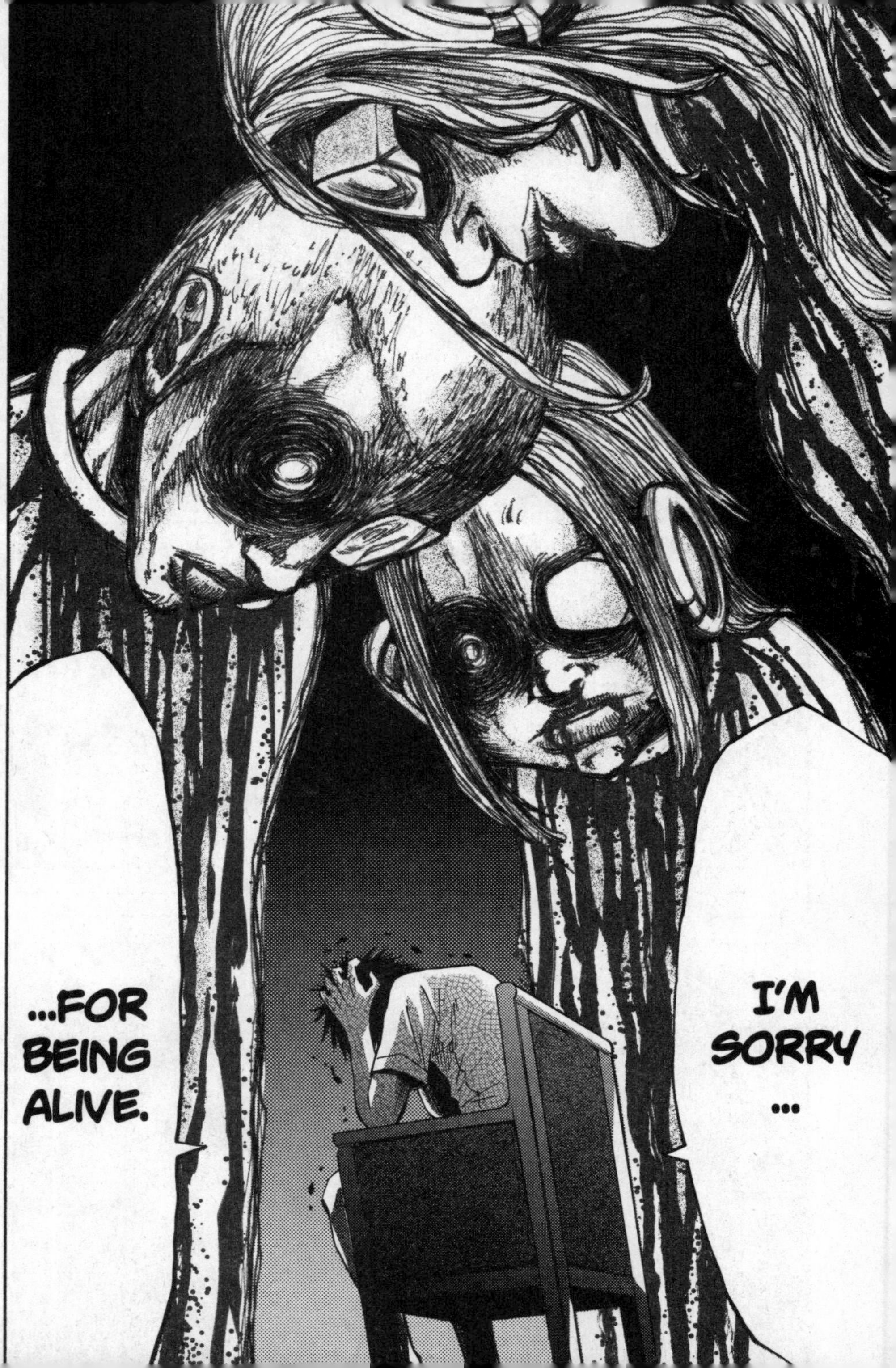
I'M SORRY ...
...FOR BEING ALIVE.

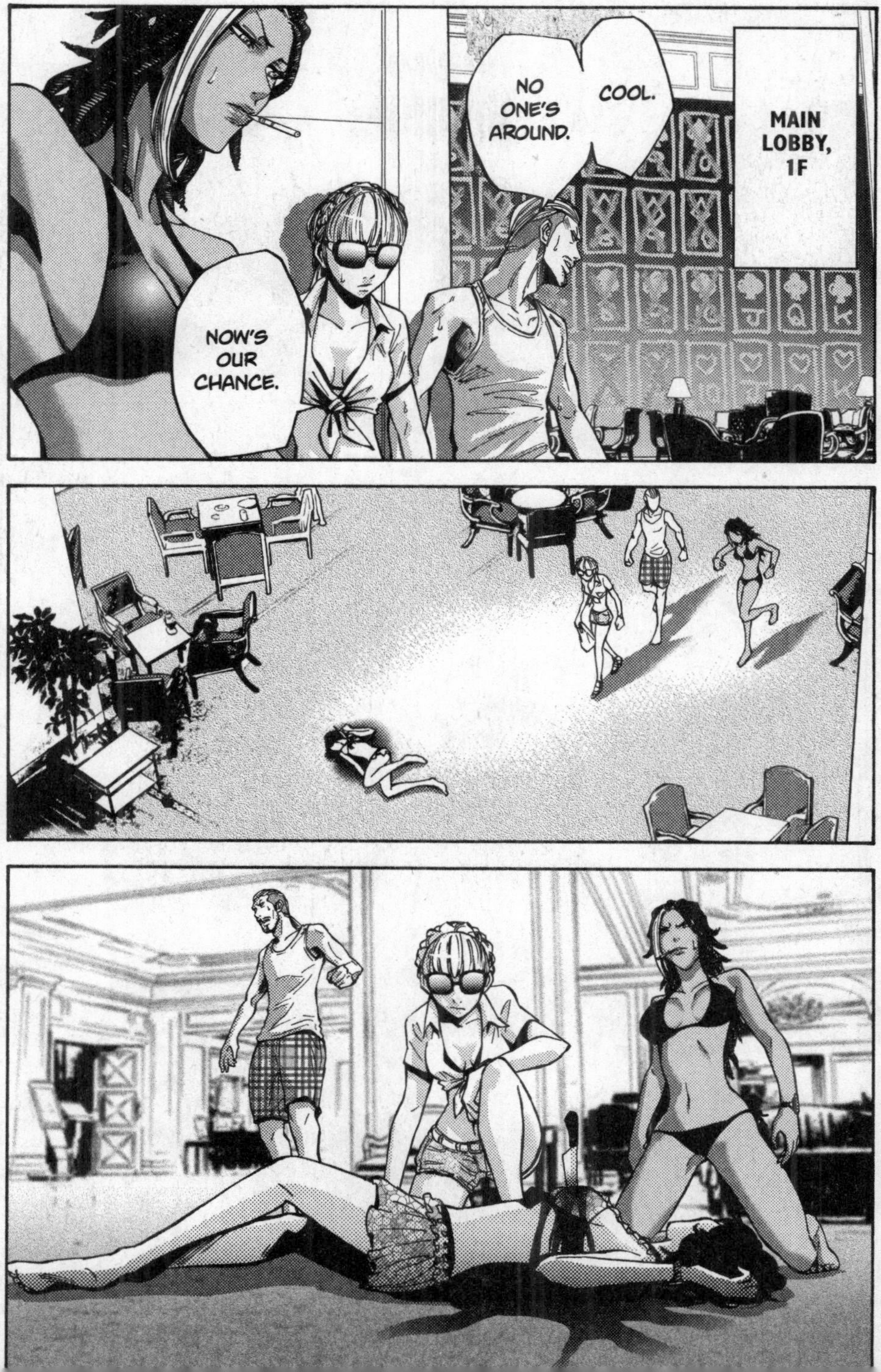
MAIN LOBBY, 1F
COOL.
NO ONE'S AROUND.
NOW'S OUR CHANCE.

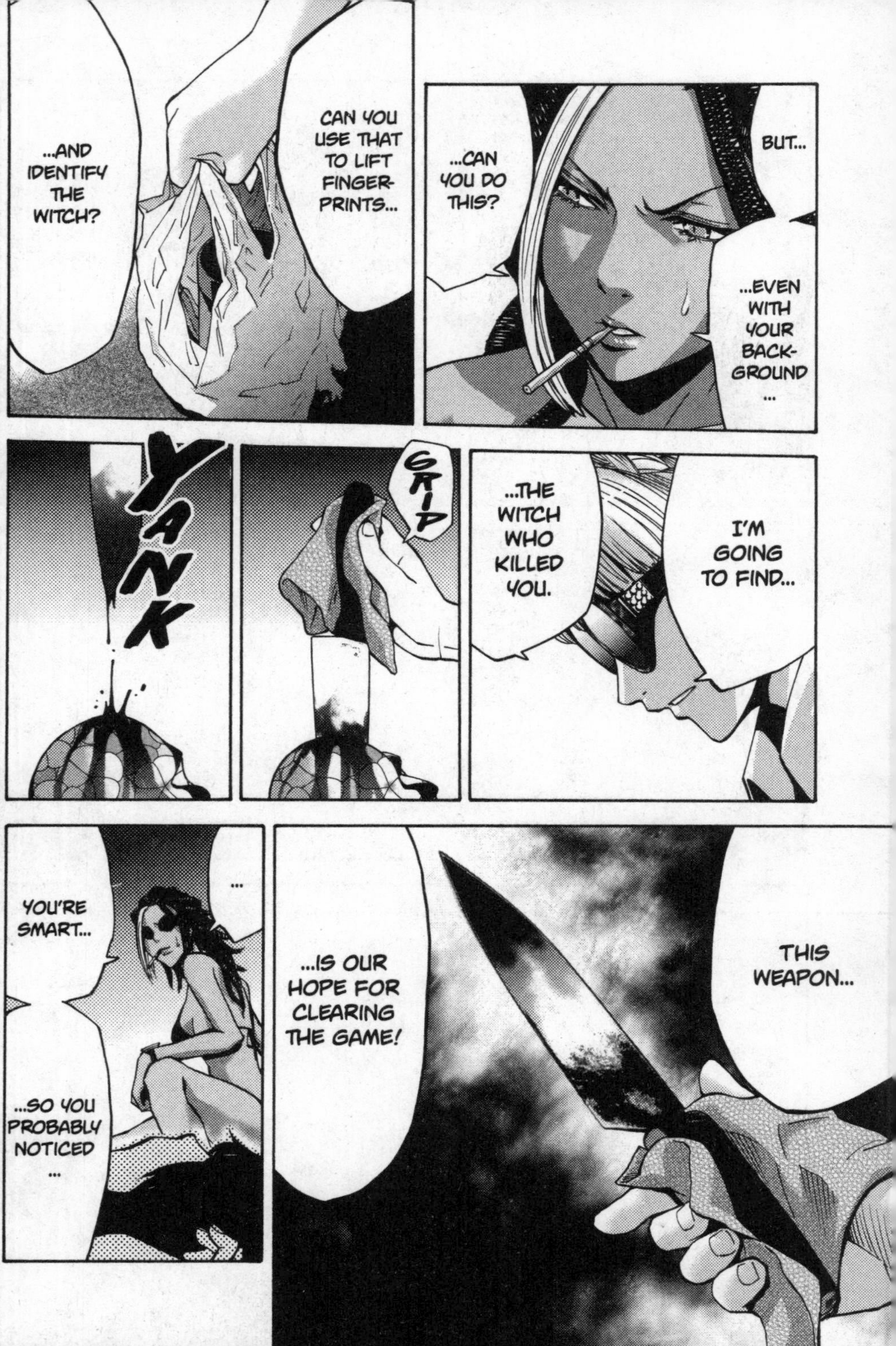
BUT...
...CAN YOU DO THIS?
...EVEN WITH YOUR BACKGROUND...
CAN YOU USE THAT TO LIFT FINGERPRINTS...
...AND IDENTIFY THE WITCH?
I'M GOING TO FIND...
...THE WITCH WHO KILLED YOU.
GRIP
YANK
THIS WEAPON...
...IS OUR HOPE FOR CLEARING THE GAME!
...
YOU'RE SMART...
...SO YOU PROBABLY NOTICED...

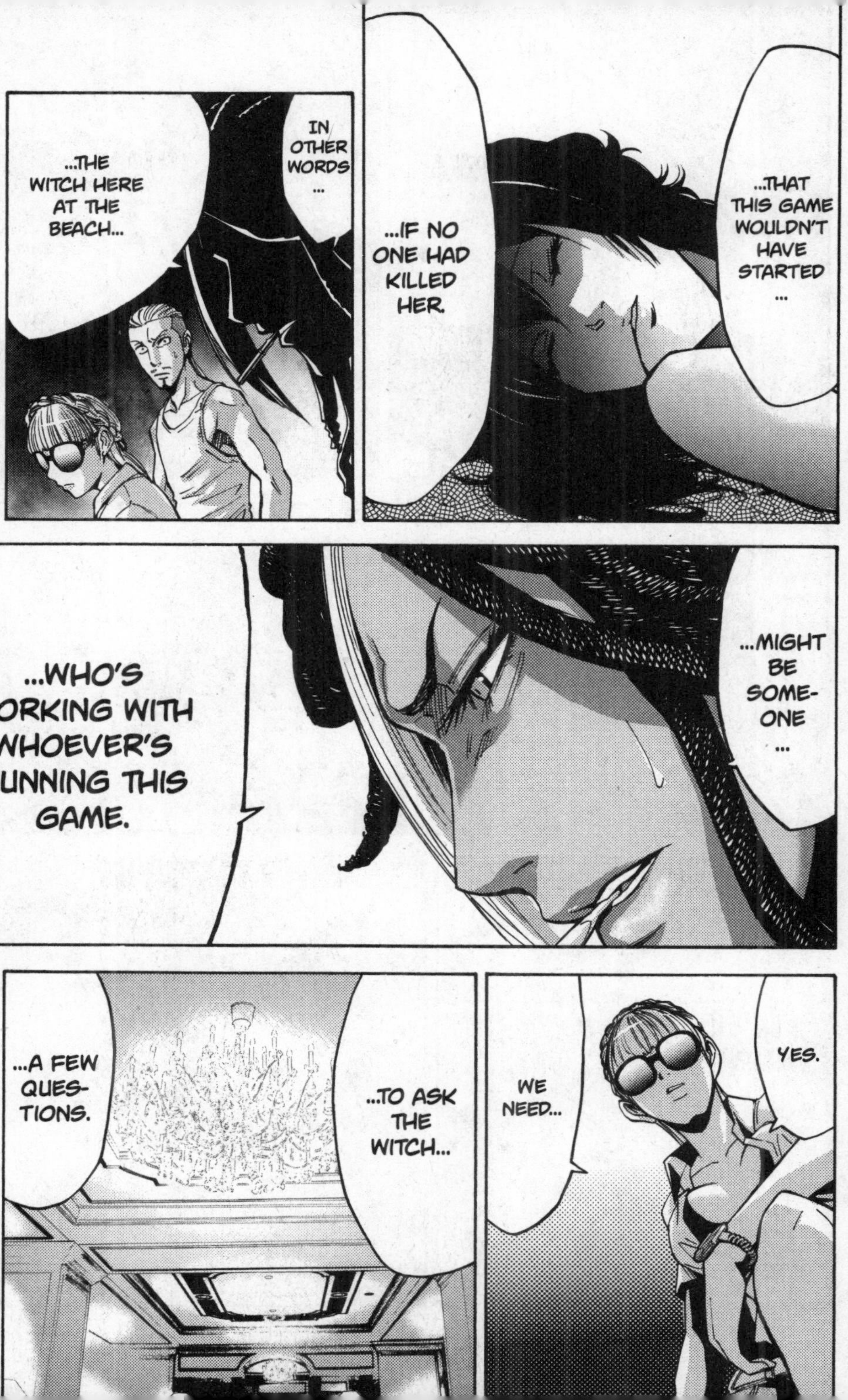
...THAT THIS GAME WOULDN'T HAVE STARTED ...
...IF NO ONE HAD KILLED HER.
IN OTHER WORDS ...
...THE WITCH HERE AT THE BEACH...
...MIGHT BE SOME-ONE ...
...WHO'S WORKING WITH WHOEVER'S RUNNING THIS GAME.
YES.
WE NEED...
...TO ASK THE WITCH...
...A FEW QUES-TIONS.

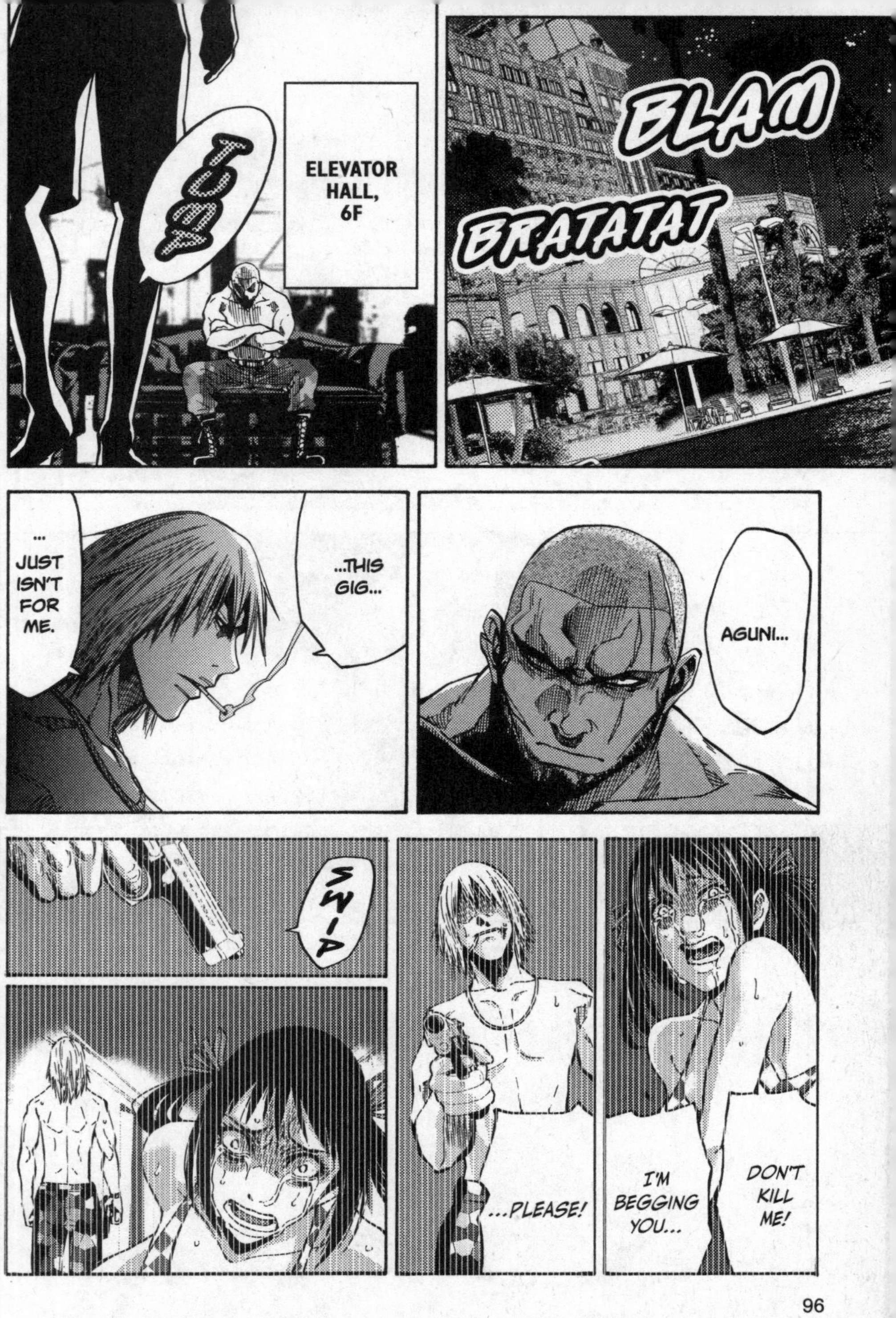
BLAM
BRATATAT
ELEVATOR HALL, 6F
AGUNI...
...THIS GIG...
... JUST ISN'T FOR ME.
DON'T KILL ME!
I'M BEGGING YOU...
...PLEASE!
SWIP

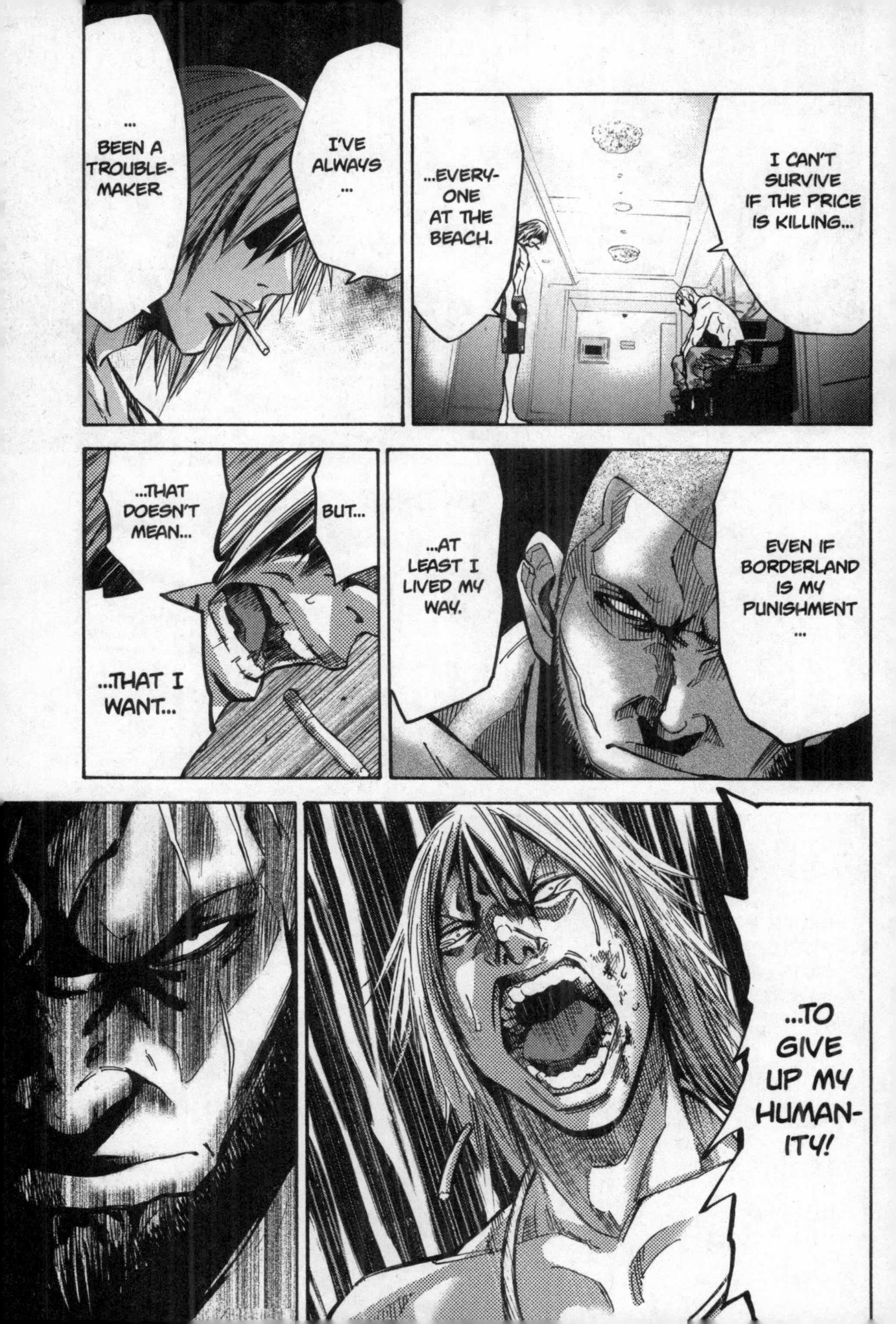
I CAN'T SURVIVE IF THE PRICE IS KILLING...
...EVERY-ONE AT THE BEACH.
I'VE ALWAYS ...
... BEEN A TROUBLE-MAKER.
EVEN IF BORDERLAND IS MY PUNISHMENT ...
...AT LEAST I LIVED MY WAY.
BUT...
...THAT DOESN'T MEAN...
...THAT I WANT...
...TO GIVE UP MY HUMAN-ITY!

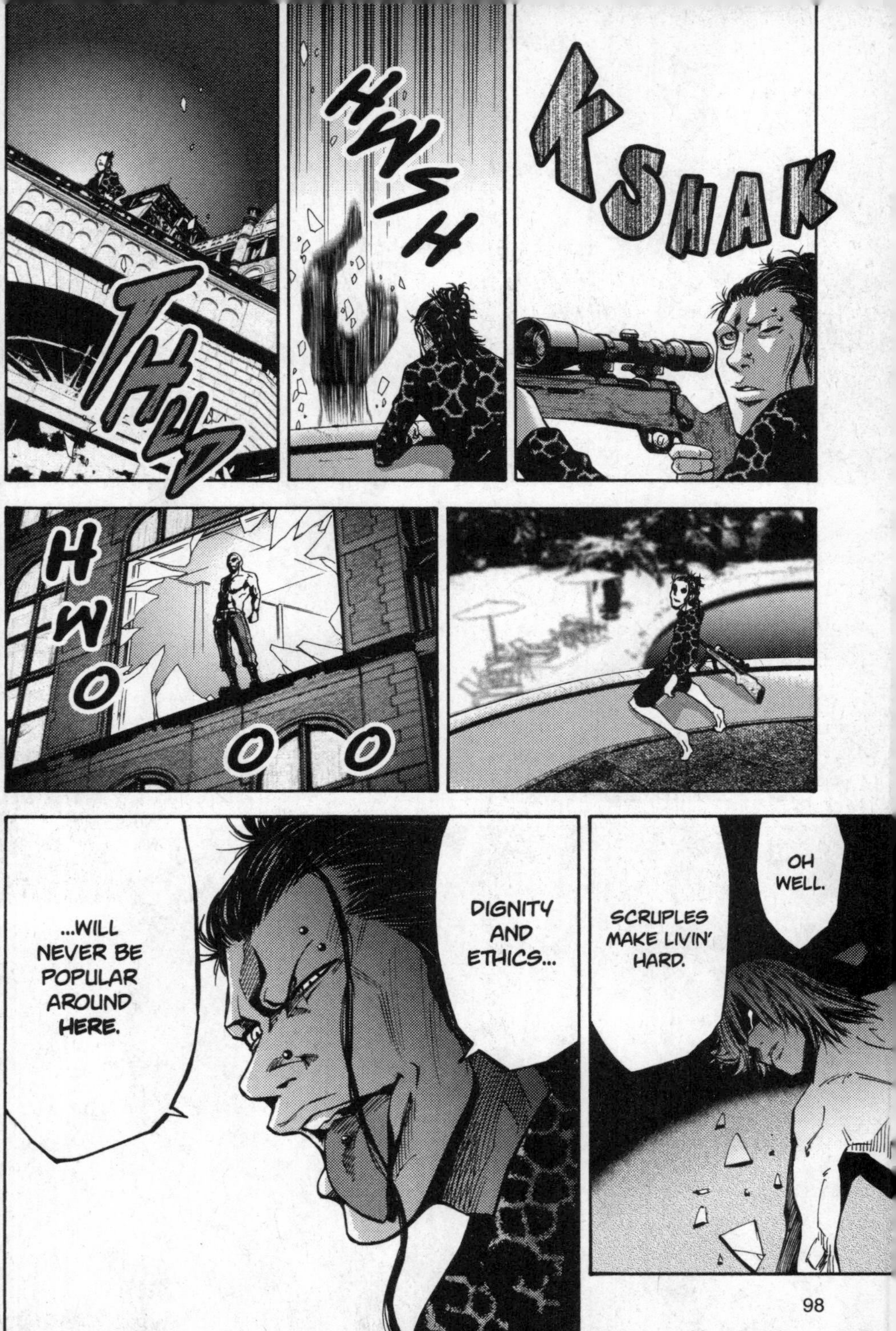
KSHAK
HWSH
THUD
HWOOO
OH WELL.
SCRUPLES MAKE LIVIN' HARD.
DIGNITY AND ETHICS...
...WILL NEVER BE POPULAR AROUND HERE.

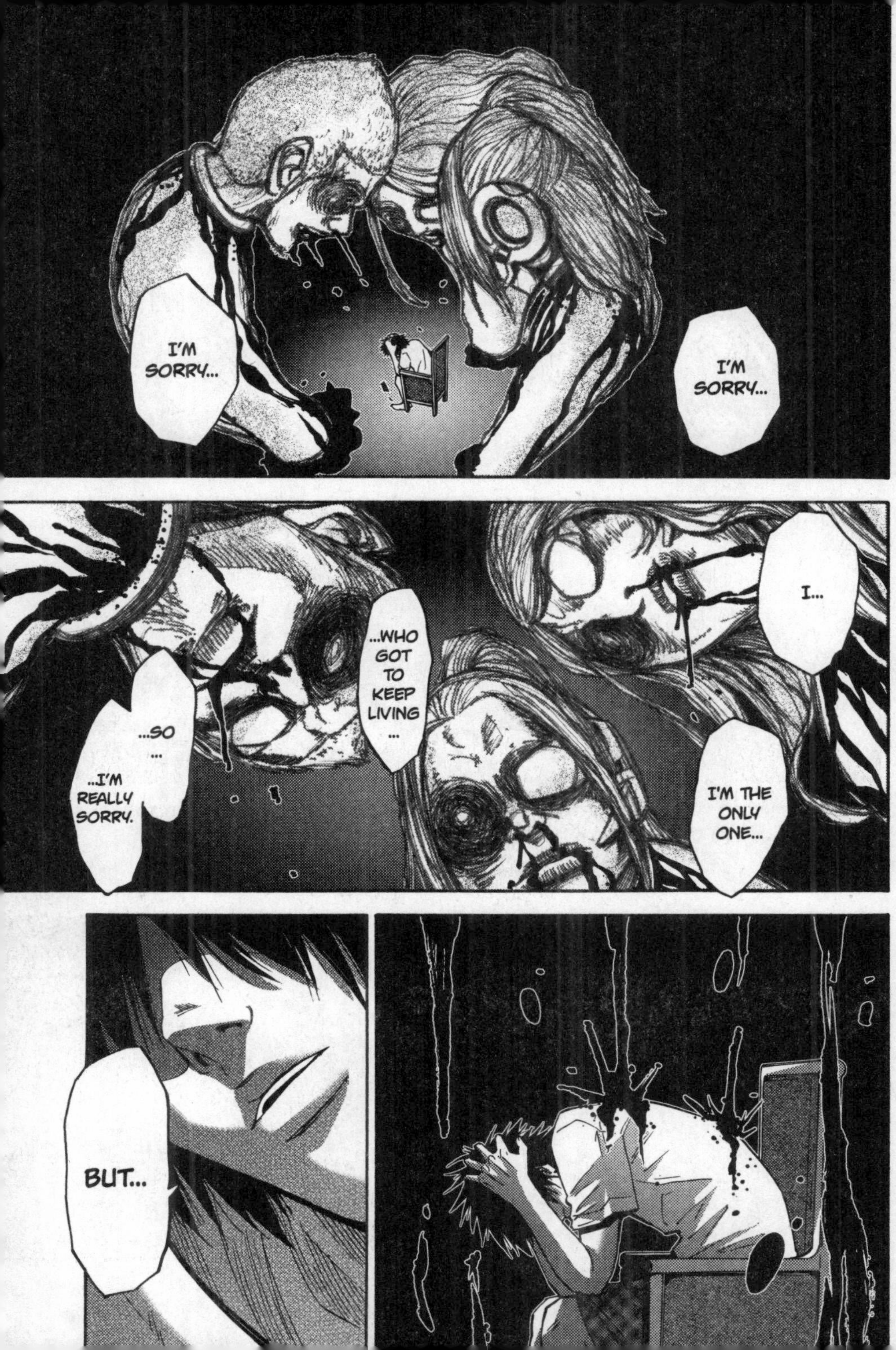
I'M SORRY...
I'M SORRY...
I...
I'M THE ONLY ONE...
...WHO GOT TO KEEP LIVING ...
...SO ... ...I'M REALLY SORRY.
BUT...

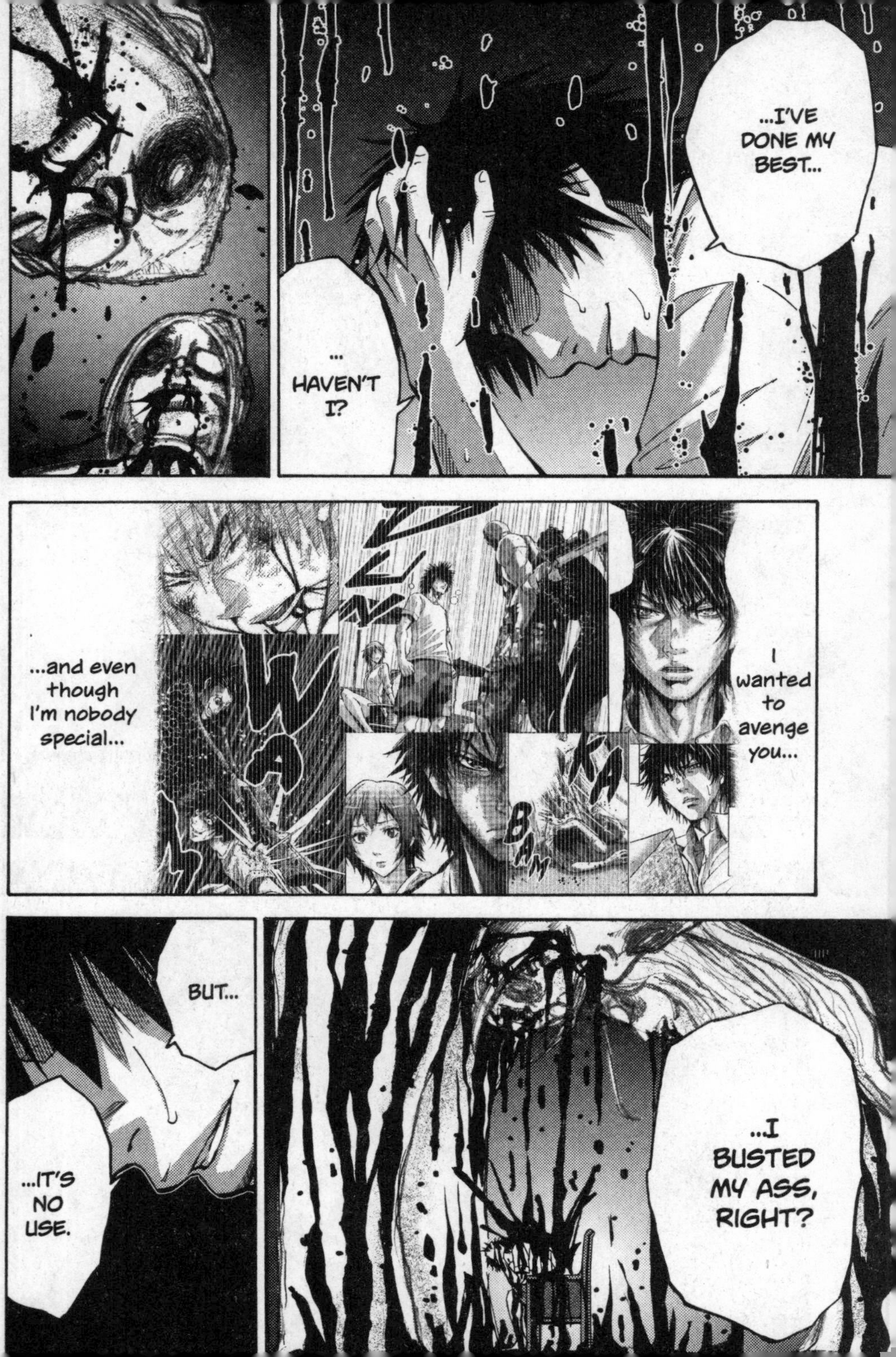
...I'VE DONE MY BEST...
... HAVEN'T I?
I wanted to avenge you...
...and even though I'm nobody special...
...I BUSTED MY ASS, RIGHT?
BUT...
...IT'S NO USE.

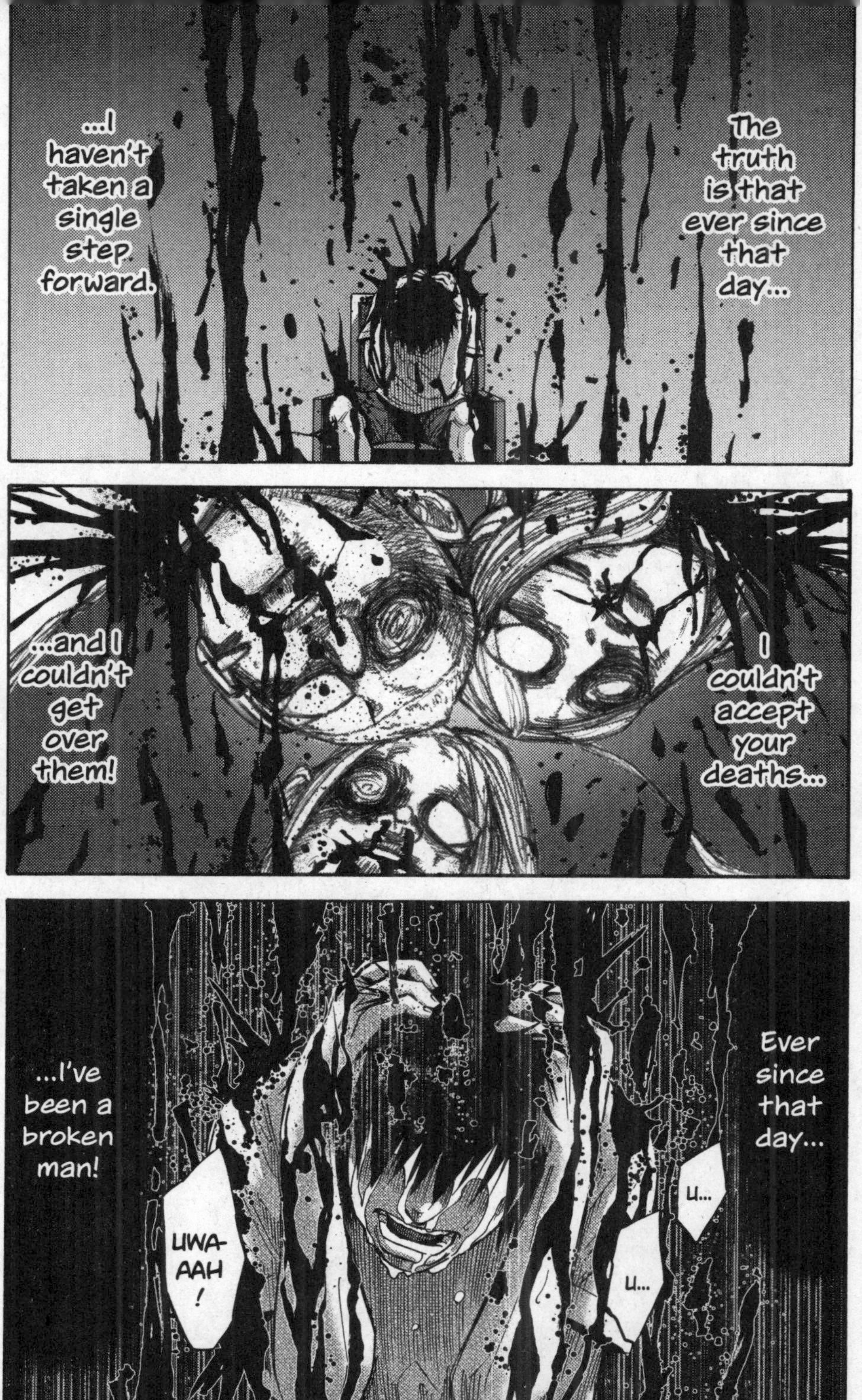
The truth is that ever since that day...
...I haven't taken a single step forward.
I couldn't accept your deaths...
...and I couldn't get over them!
Ever since that day...
...I've been a broken man!
U...
UWAAAH!
U...

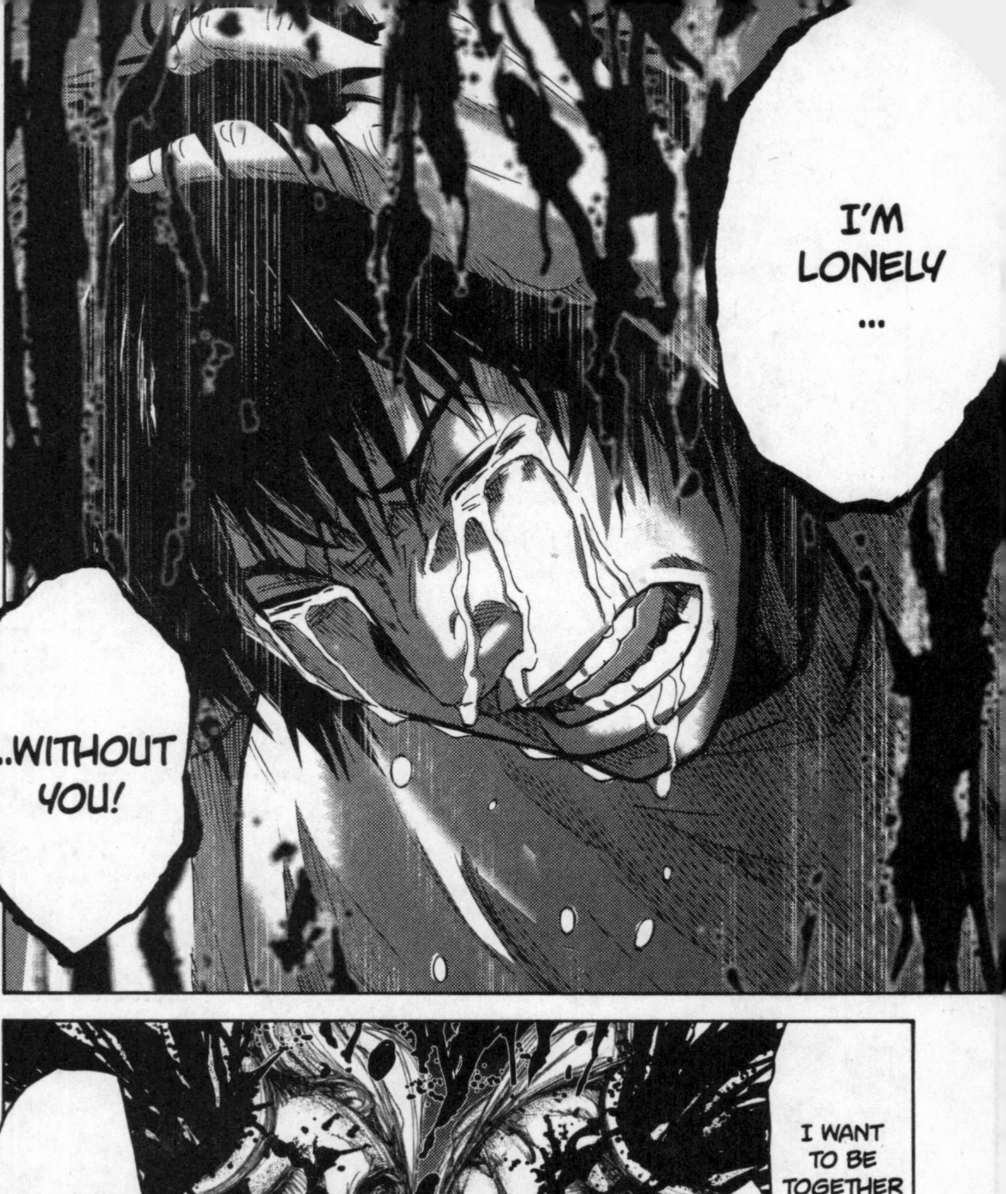
I'M LONELY ...
...WITHOUT YOU!

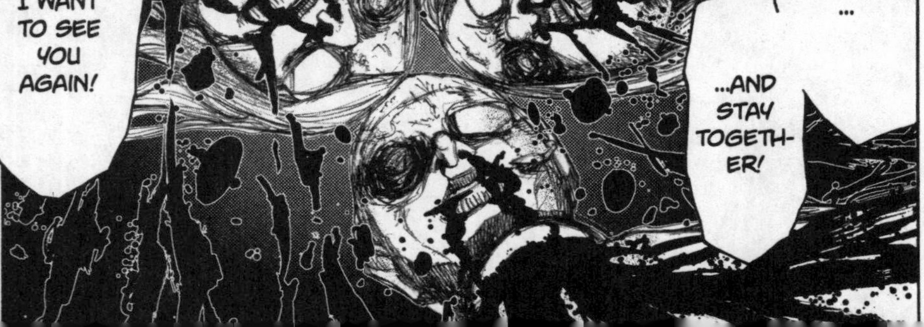
I WANT TO BE TOGETHER ...
...AND STAY TOGETH-ER!
I WANT TO SEE YOU AGAIN!

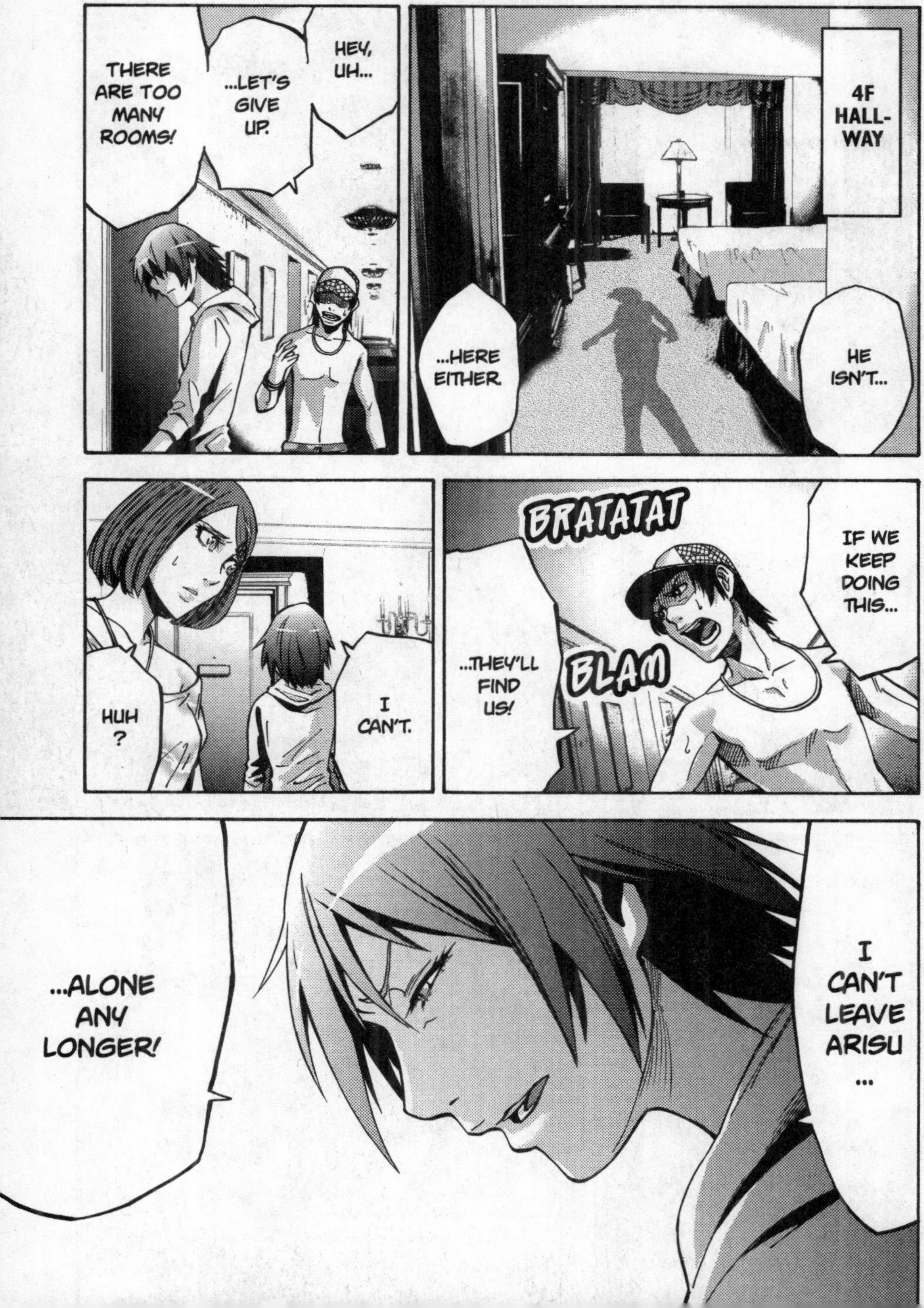
4F HALL-WAY
HE ISN'T...
...HERE EITHER.
HEY, UH...
...LET'S GIVE UP.
THERE ARE TOO MANY ROOMS!
BRATATAT
IF WE KEEP DOING THIS...
...THEY'LL FIND US!
BLAM
I CAN'T.
HUH?
I CAN'T LEAVE ARISU...
...ALONE ANY LONGER!

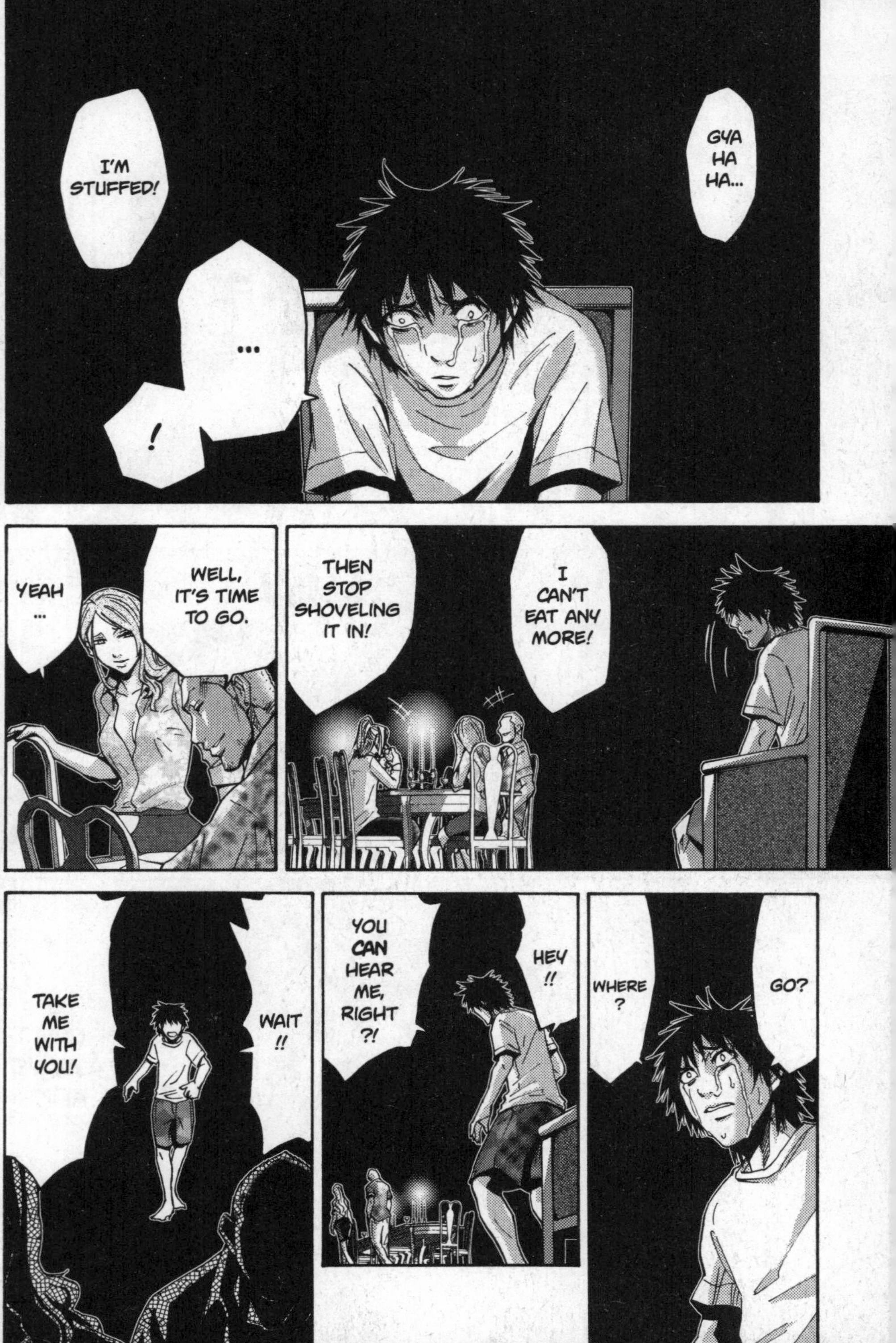
GYA HA HA...
I'M STUFFED!
...
!
I CAN'T EAT ANY MORE!
THEN STOP SHOVELING IT IN!
WELL, IT'S TIME TO GO.
YEAH ...
GO?
WHERE ?
HEY !!
YOU CAN HEAR ME, RIGHT ?!
WAIT !!
TAKE ME WITH YOU!

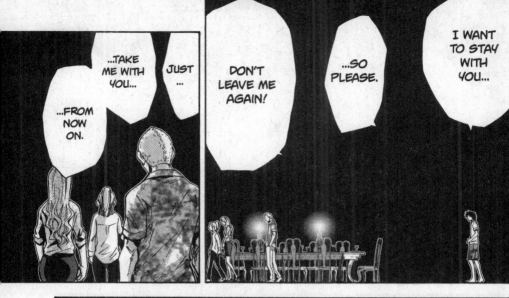

I WANT TO STAY WITH YOU...
...SO PLEASE.
DON'T LEAVE ME AGAIN!
JUST ...
...TAKE ME WITH YOU...
...FROM NOW ON.
...
HEY, UM...
...WE'RE ...
...STILL ...
... FRIENDS, RIGHT?

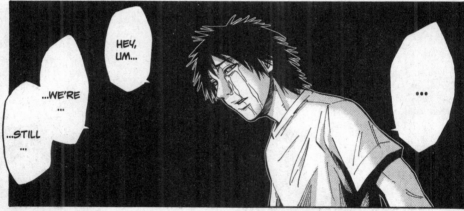

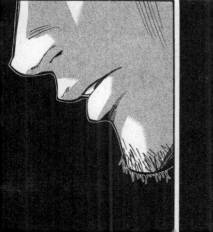

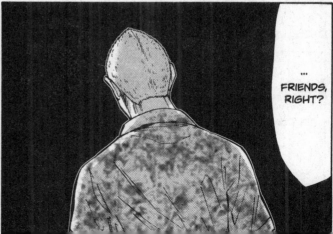

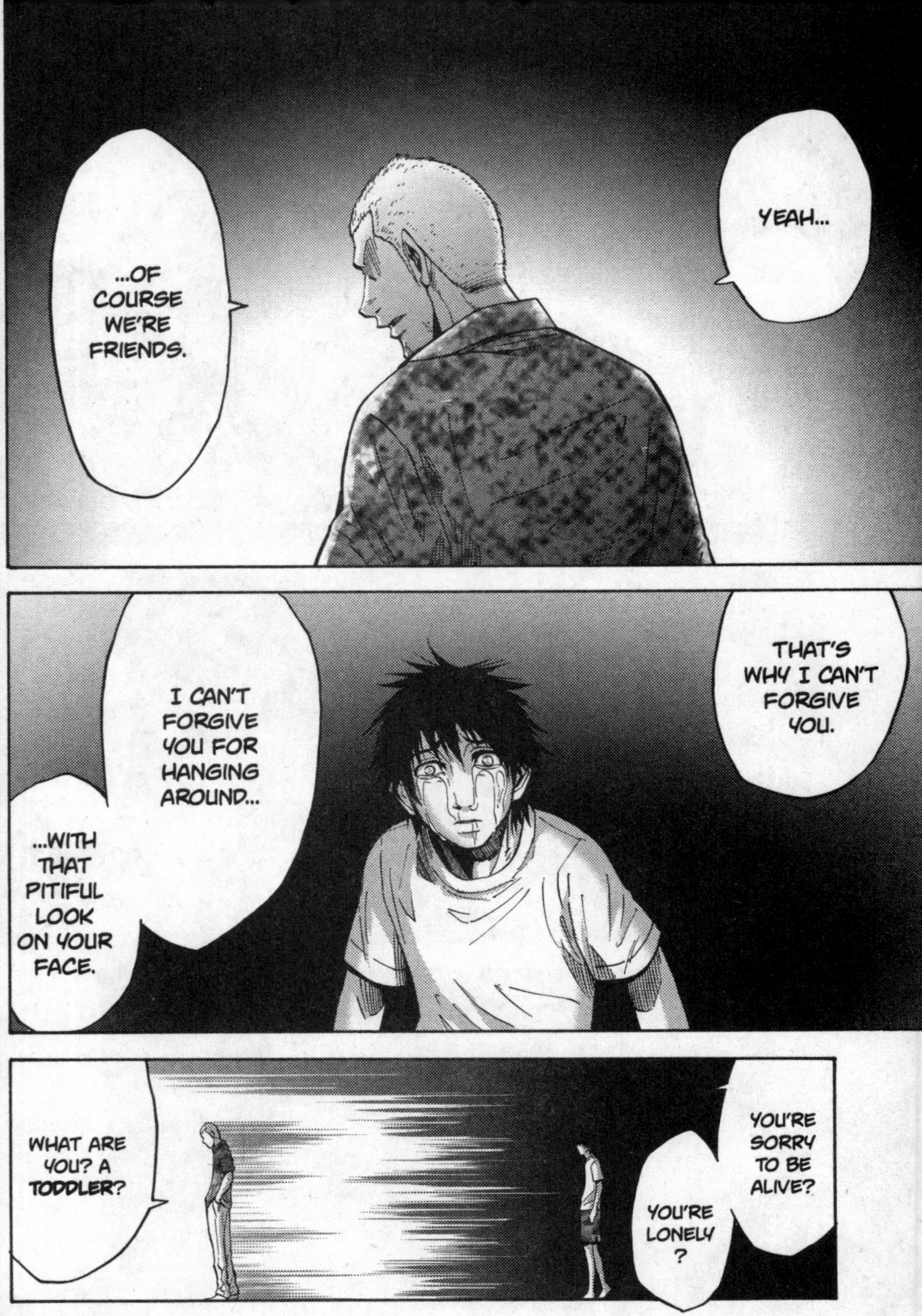
YEAH...
...OF COURSE WE'RE FRIENDS.
THAT'S WHY I CAN'T FORGIVE YOU.
I CAN'T FORGIVE YOU FOR HANGING AROUND...
...WITH THAT PITIFUL LOOK ON YOUR FACE.
YOU'RE SORRY TO BE ALIVE?
YOU'RE LONELY ?
WHAT ARE YOU? A **TODDLER**?

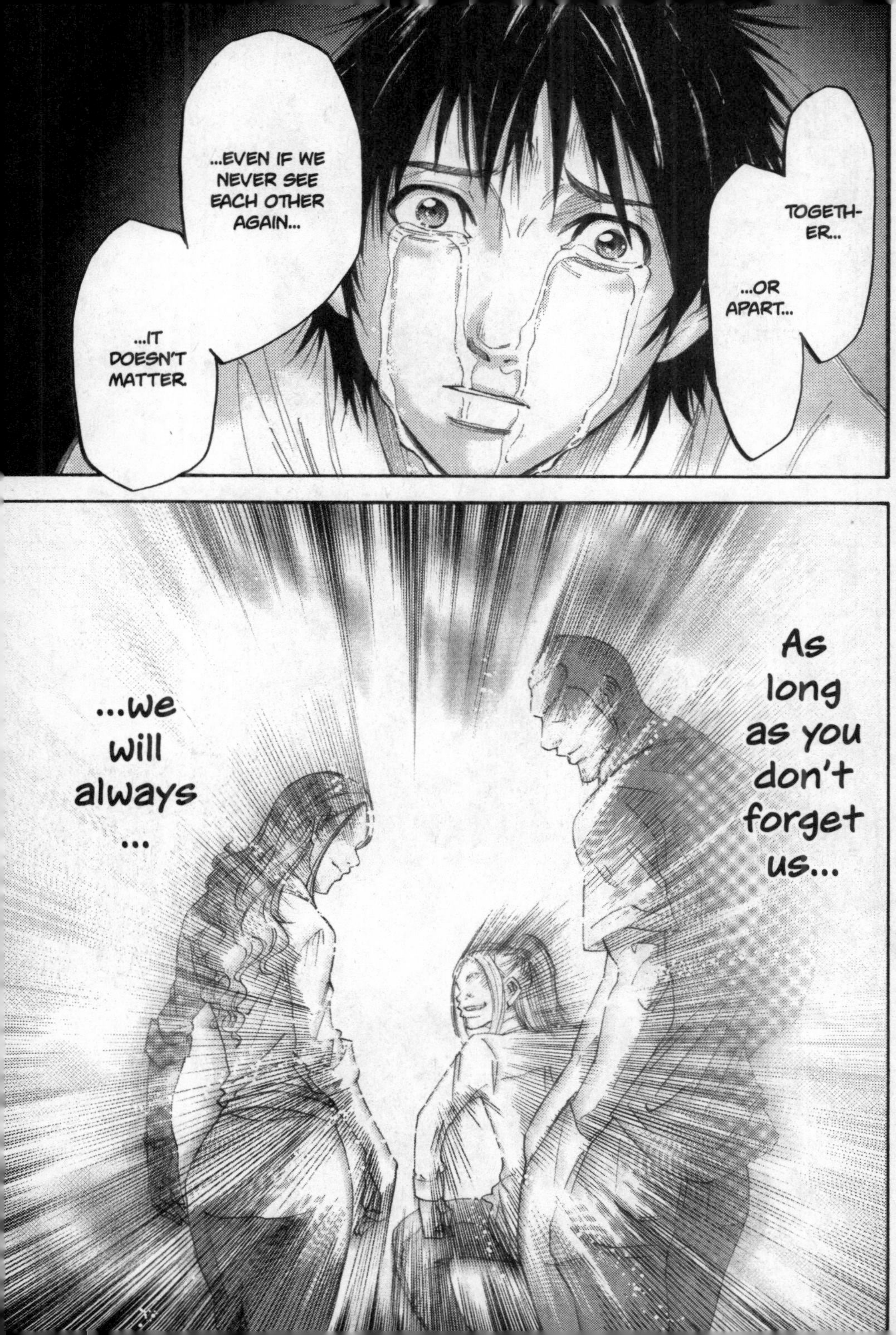
TOGETH-ER...
...OR APART...
...EVEN IF WE NEVER SEE EACH OTHER AGAIN...
...IT DOESN'T MATTER.
As long as you don't forget us...
...we will always ...

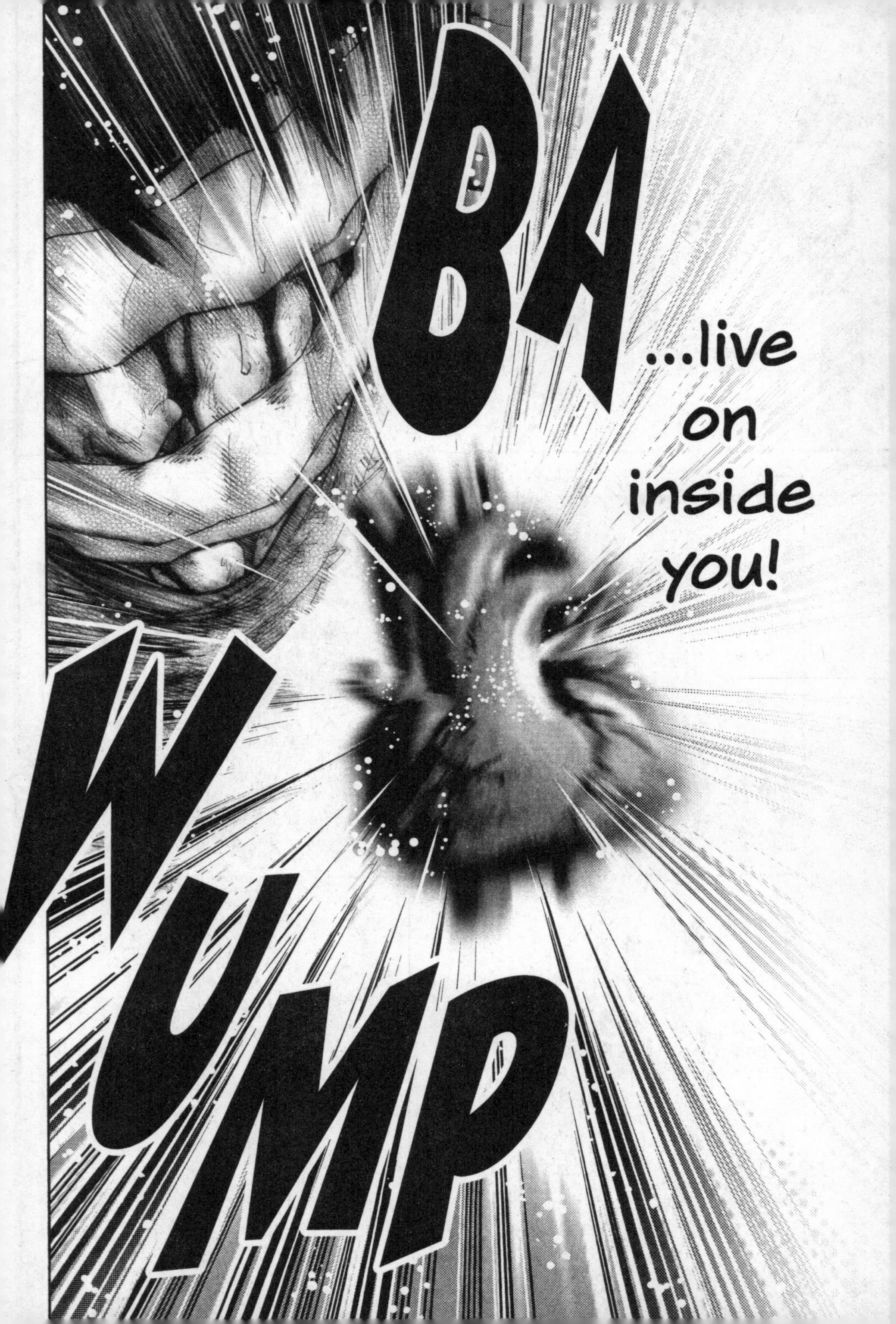
BA
...live on inside you!
WUMP

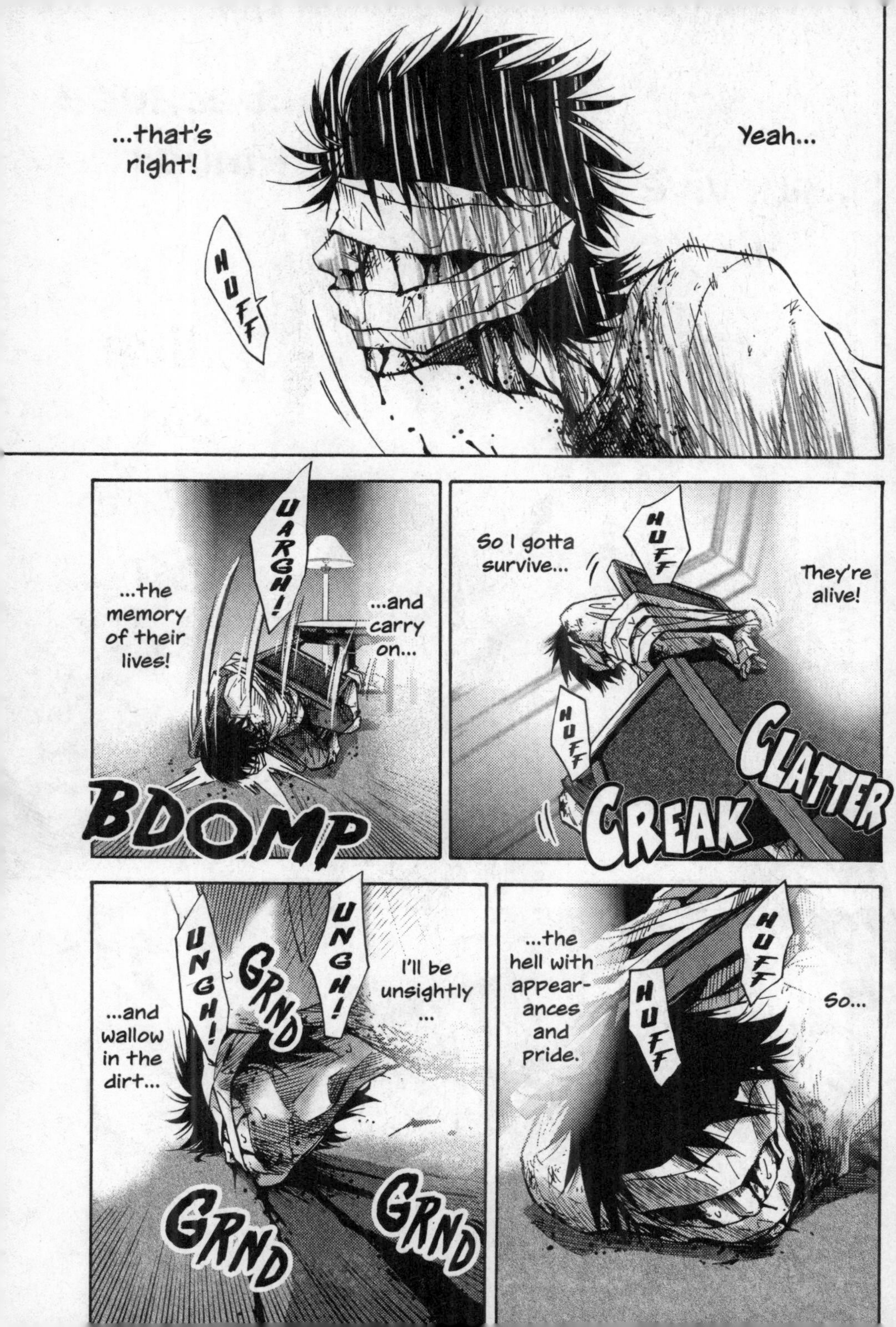
Yeah...
...that's right!
HUFF
They're alive!
HUFF
So I gotta survive...
HUFF
CLATTER
CREAK
...and carry on...
UARGH!
...the memory of their lives!
BDOMP
So...
HUFF
HUFF
...the hell with appearances and pride.
I'll be unsightly ...
UNGH!
GRND
UNGH!
...and wallow in the dirt...
GRND
GRND

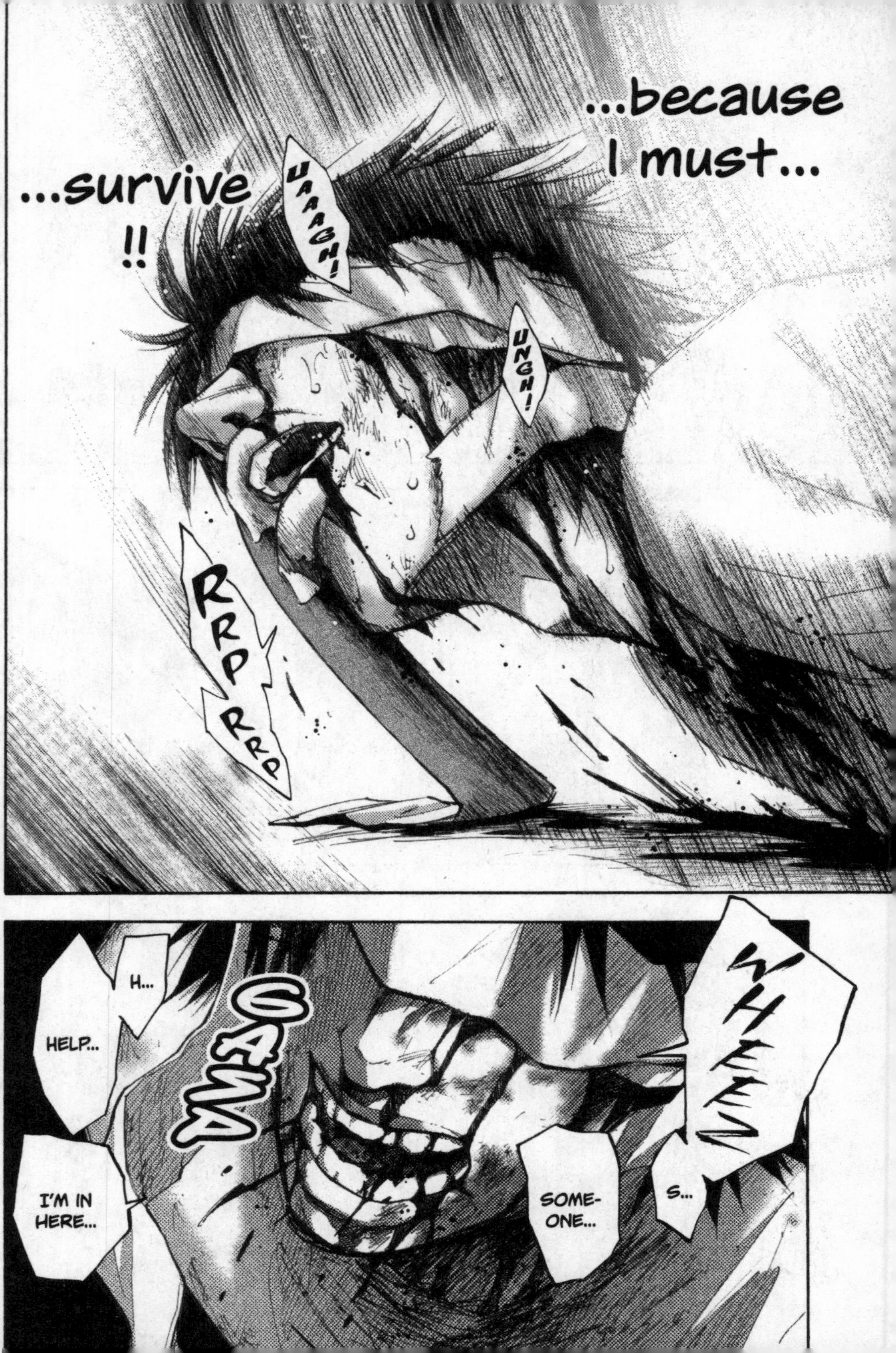
...because I must...
...survive !!
UAAAGH!
UNGH!
RRP RRRP
WHEEZ
S...
SOME-ONE...
GASP
H...
HELP...
I'M IN HERE...

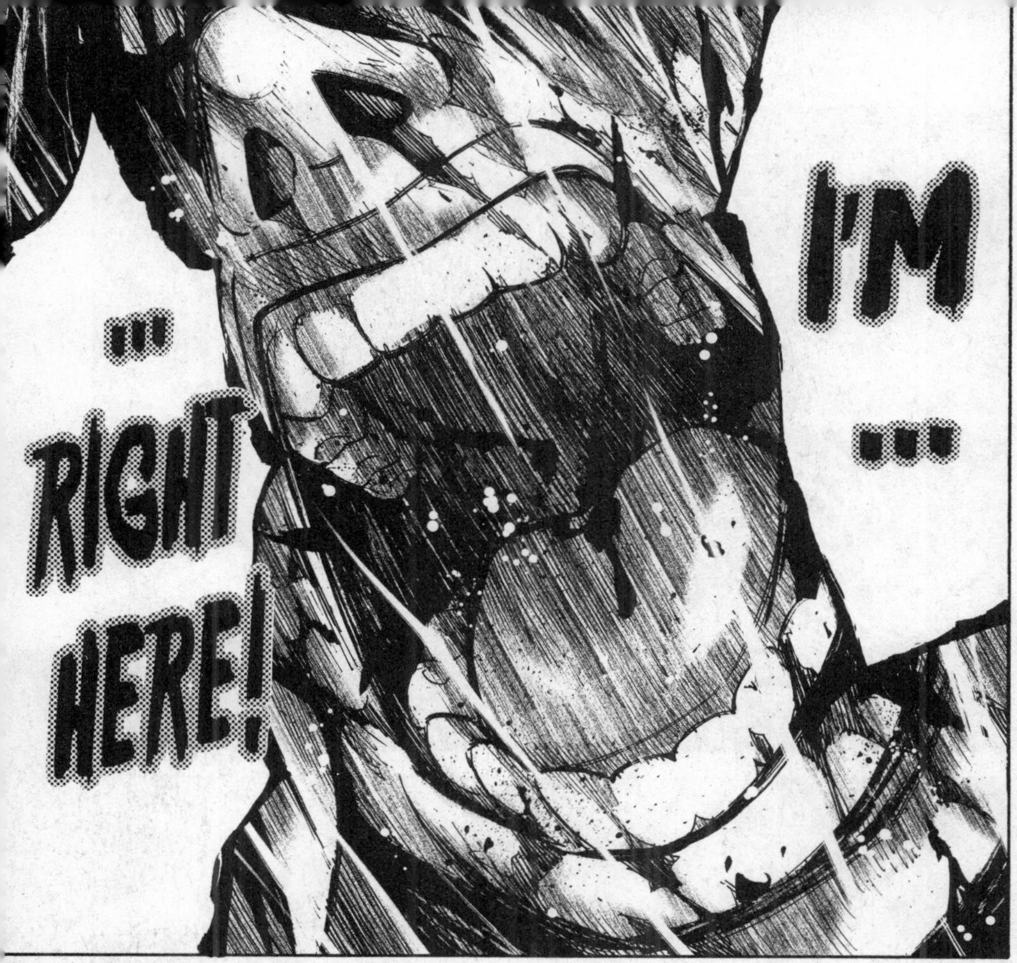
I'M ...
... RIGHT HERE!
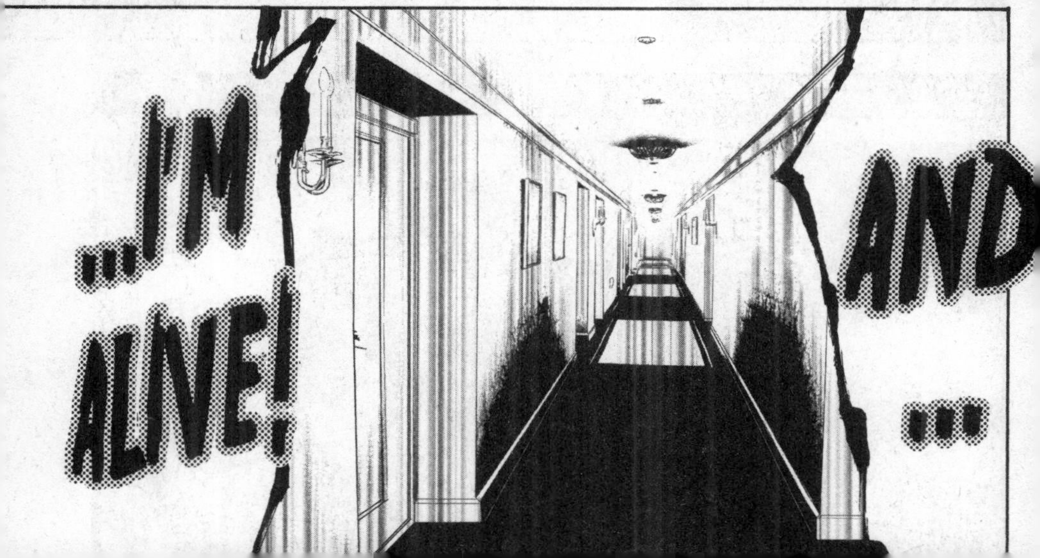
AND ...
...I'M ALIVE!

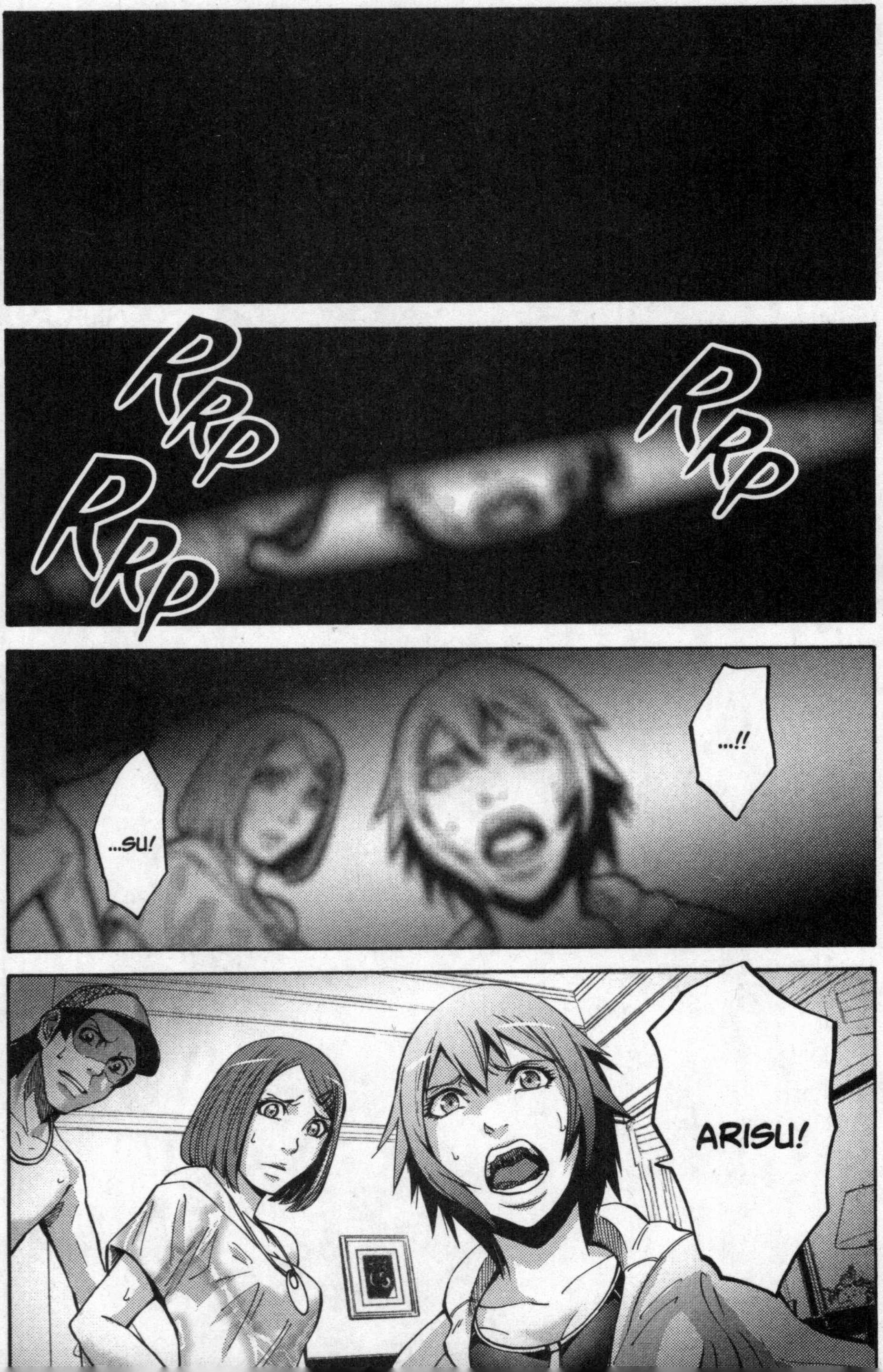
RRP
RRP
RRP
...!!
...SU!
ARISU!

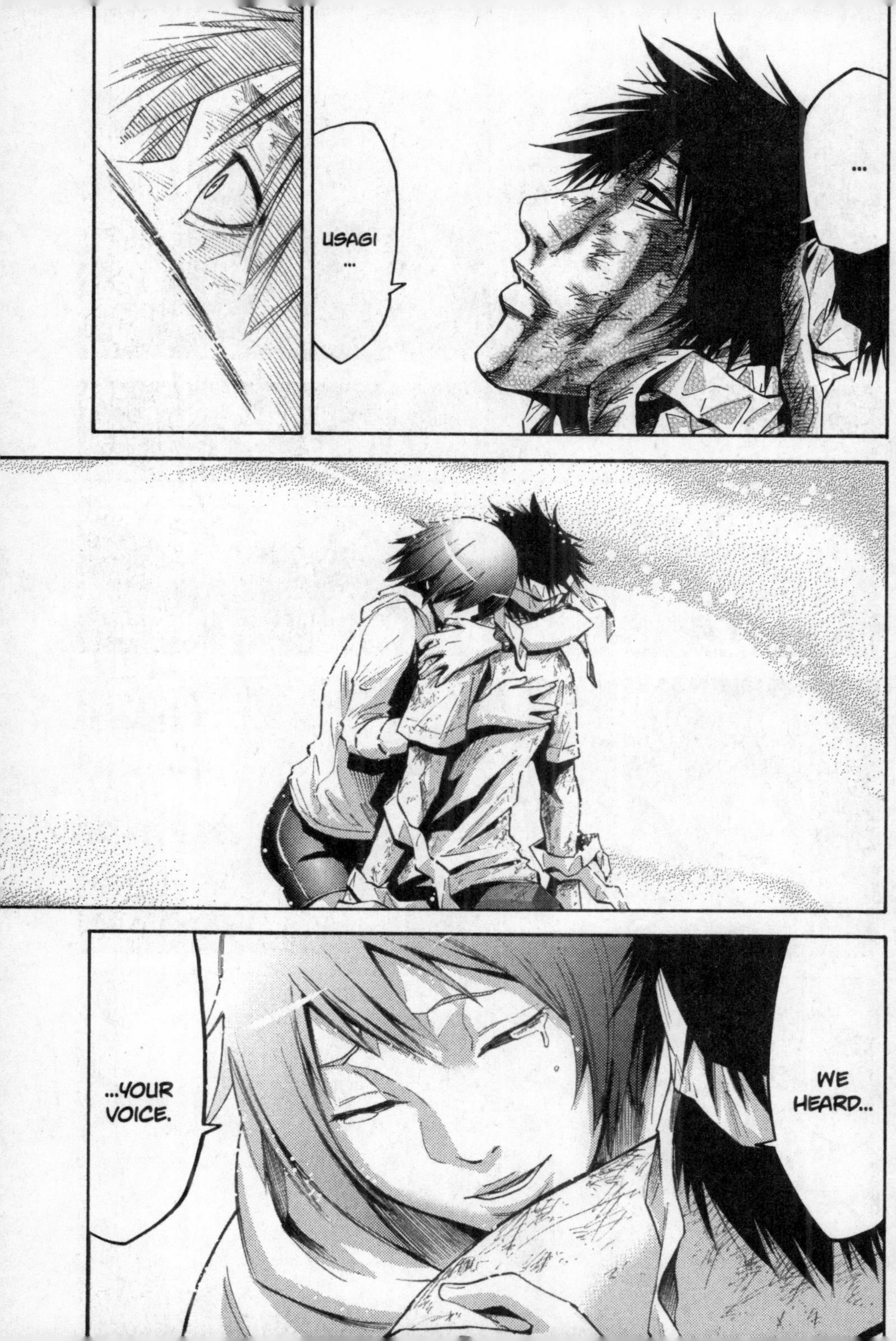
...
USAGI ...
WE HEARD...
...YOUR VOICE.

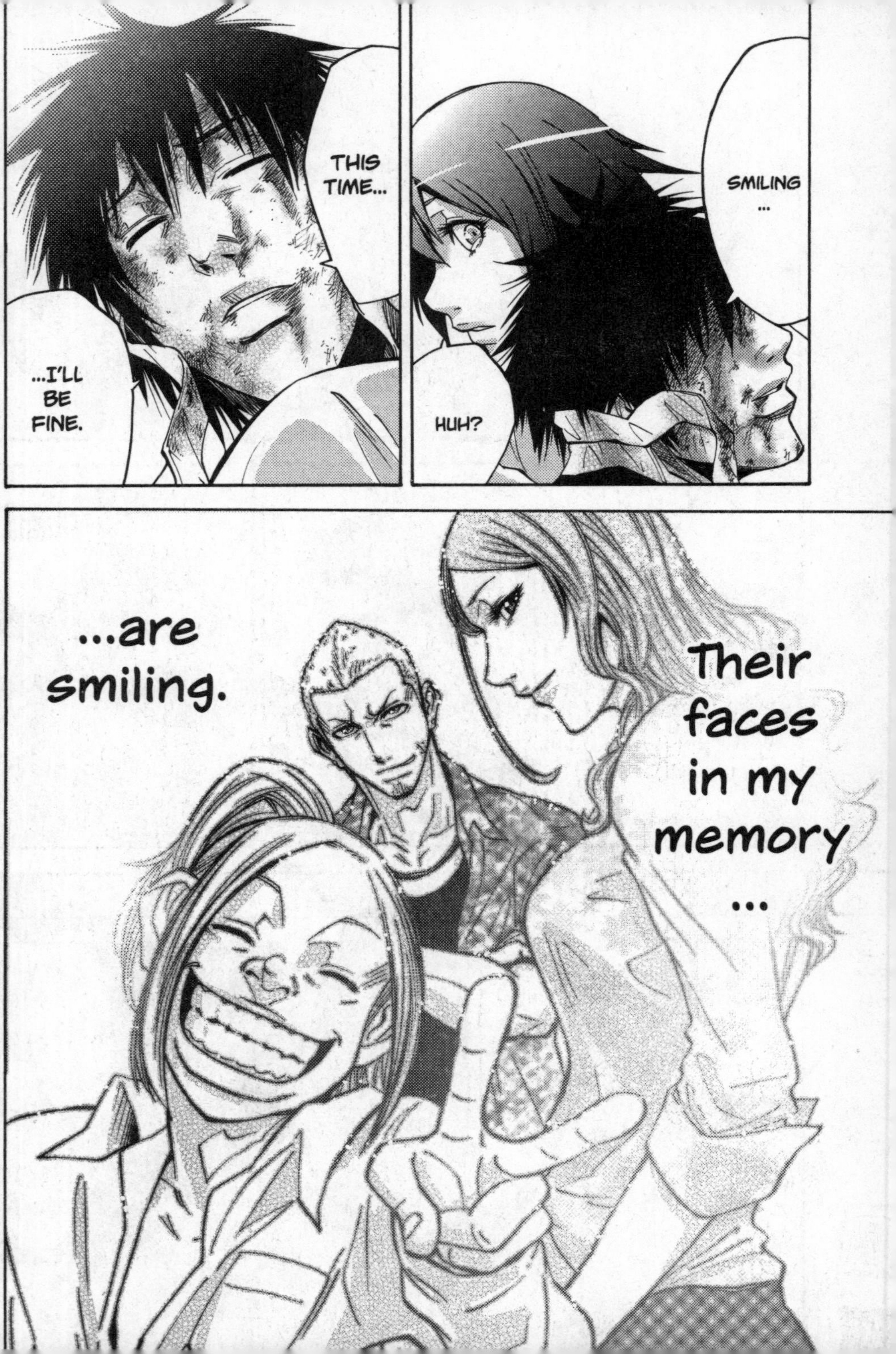
SMILING ...
HUH?
THIS TIME...
...I'LL BE FINE.
Their faces in my memory ...
...are smiling.

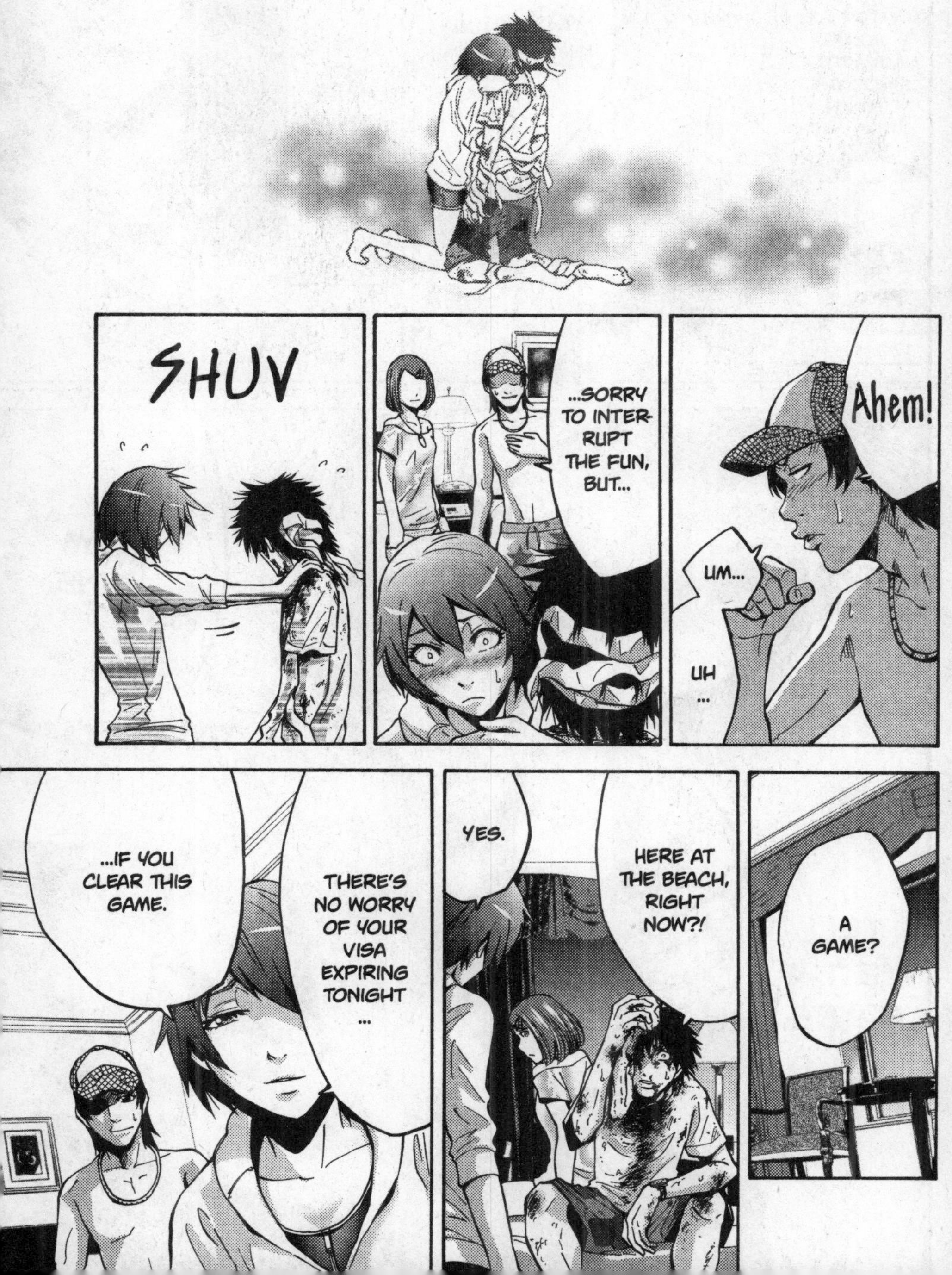
Ahem!
UM...
UH ...
...SORRY TO INTER-RUPT THE FUN, BUT...
SHUV
A GAME?
HERE AT THE BEACH, RIGHT NOW?!
YES.
THERE'S NO WORRY OF YOUR VISA EXPIRING TONIGHT ...
...IF YOU CLEAR THIS GAME.

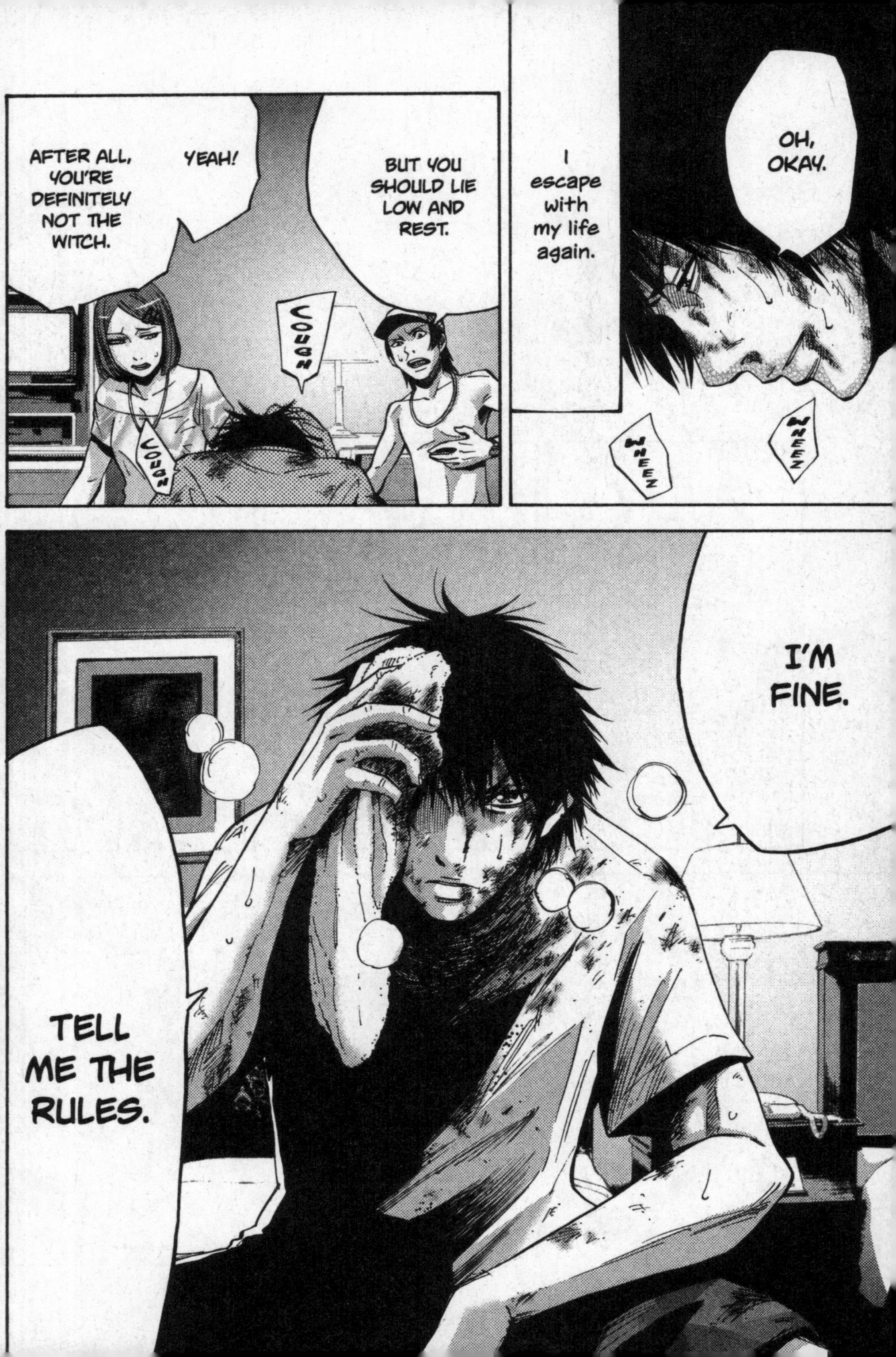
OH, OKAY.
WHEEZ
WHEEZ
I escape with my life again.
BUT YOU SHOULD LIE LOW AND REST.
YEAH!
AFTER ALL, YOU'RE DEFINITELY NOT THE WITCH.
COUGH
COUGH
I'M FINE.
TELL ME THE RULES.

THE MAIN STORY WILL RESUME ON PAGE 239

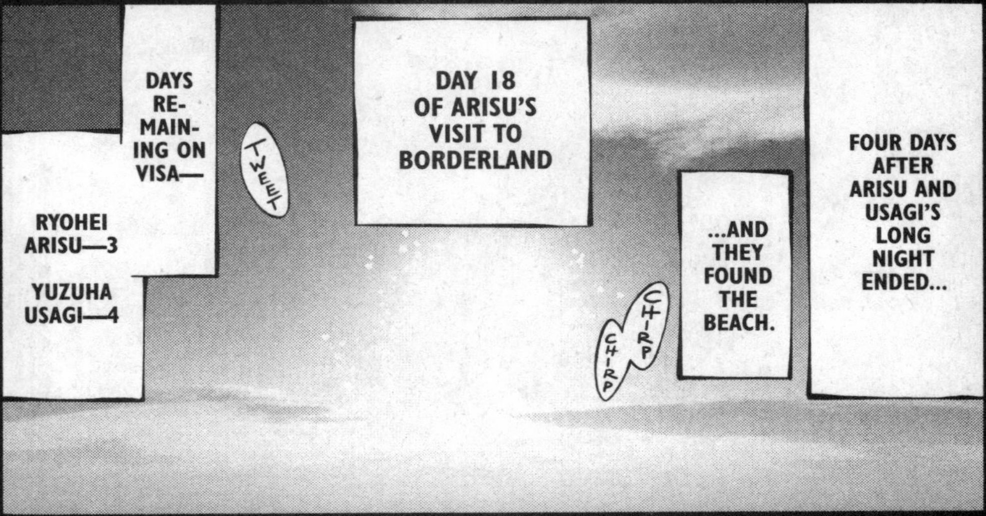
FOUR DAYS AFTER ARISU AND USAGI'S LONG NIGHT ENDED...
...AND THEY FOUND THE BEACH.
CHIRP
CHIRP
DAY 18 OF ARISU'S VISIT TO BORDERLAND
TWEET
DAYS REMAINING ON VISA—
RYOHEI ARISU—3
YUZUHA USAGI—4

THIS SIDE STORY...

...INVOLVES EVENTS THAT OCCURED DURING THE FOUR BLANK DAYS...

...AFTER ARISU ARRIVED AT THE BEACH.

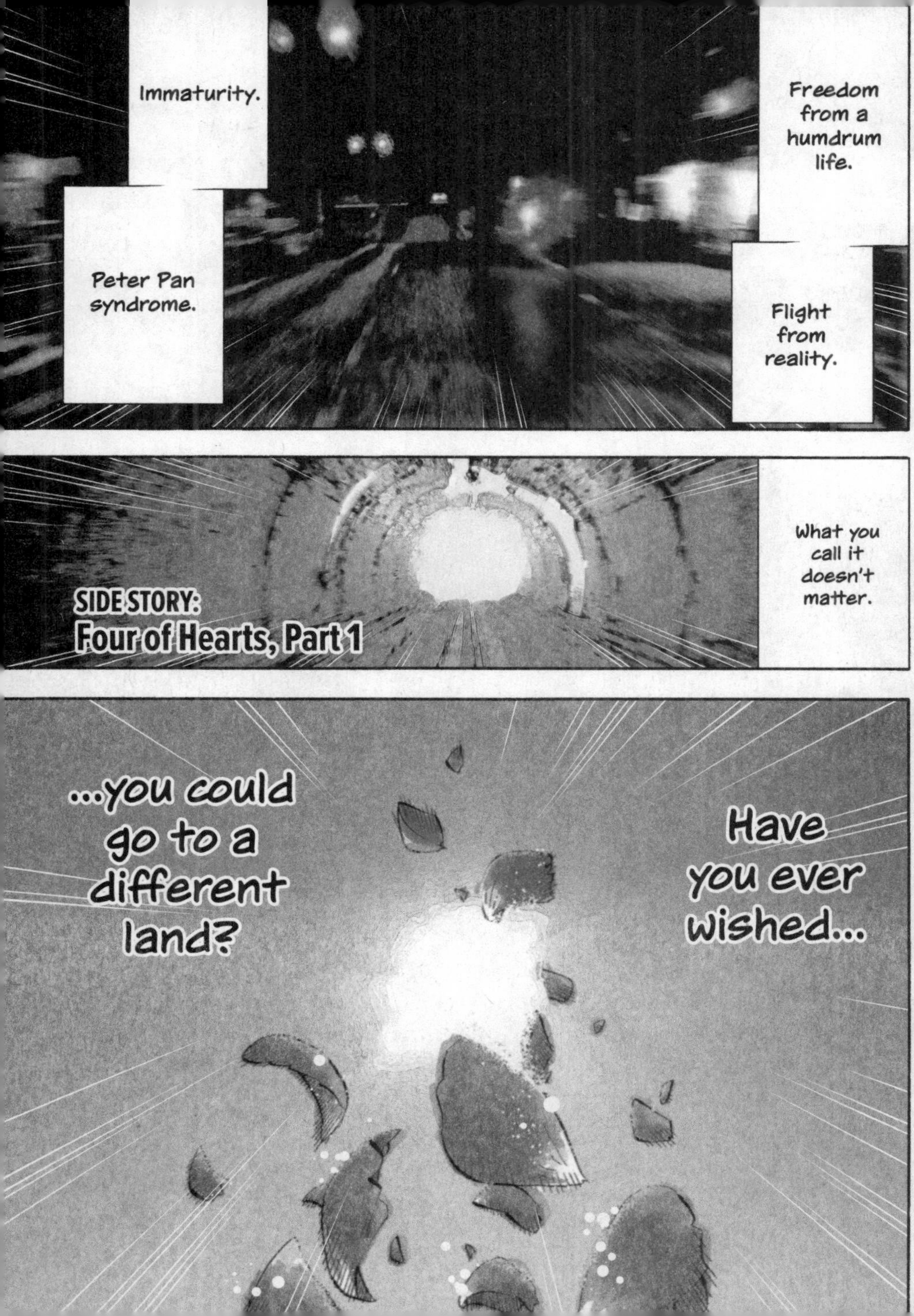
Freedom from a humdrum life.
Flight from reality.
Immaturity.
Peter Pan syndrome.
What you call it doesn't matter.
SIDE STORY:
Four of Hearts, Part 1
Have you ever wished...
...you could go to a different land?

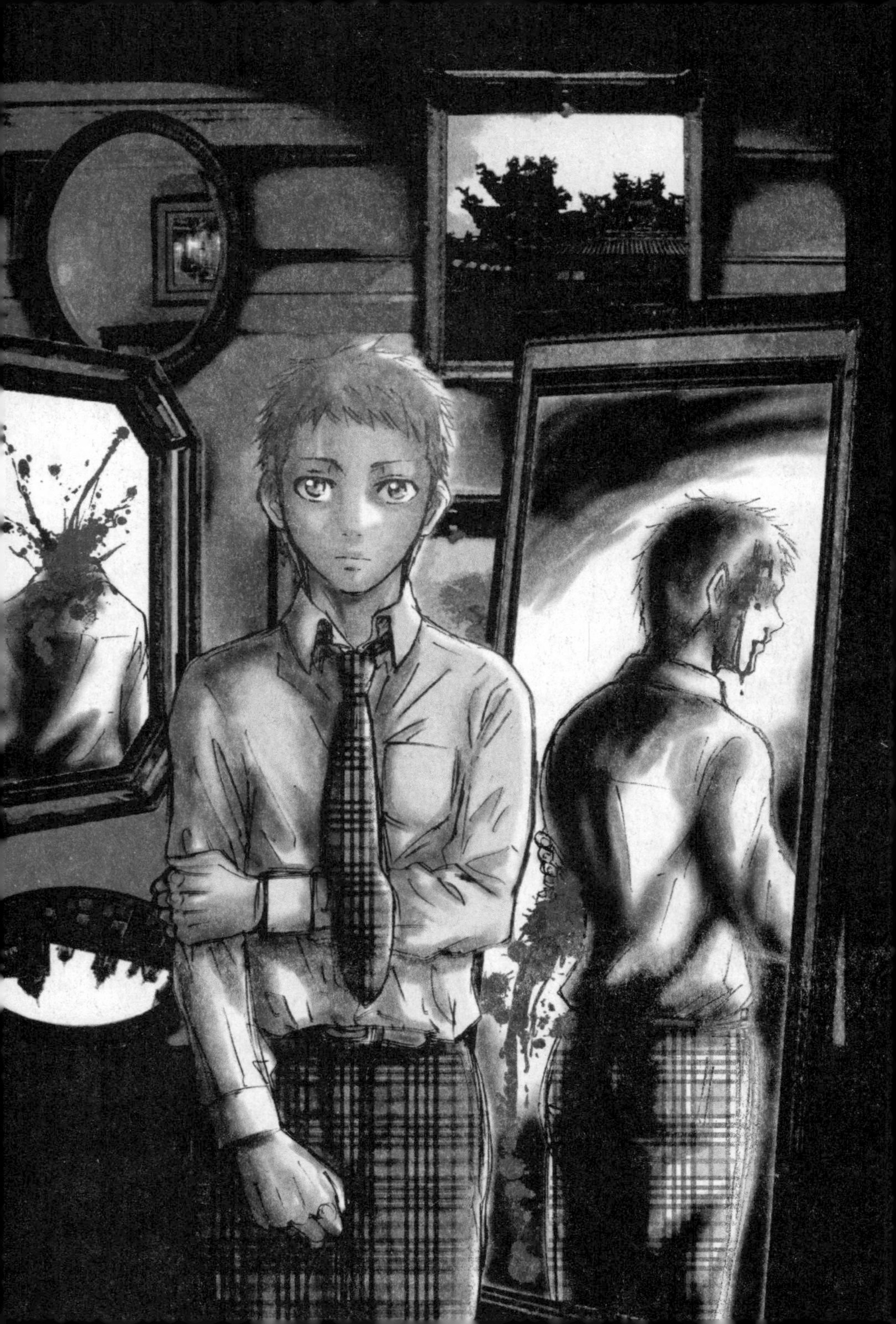

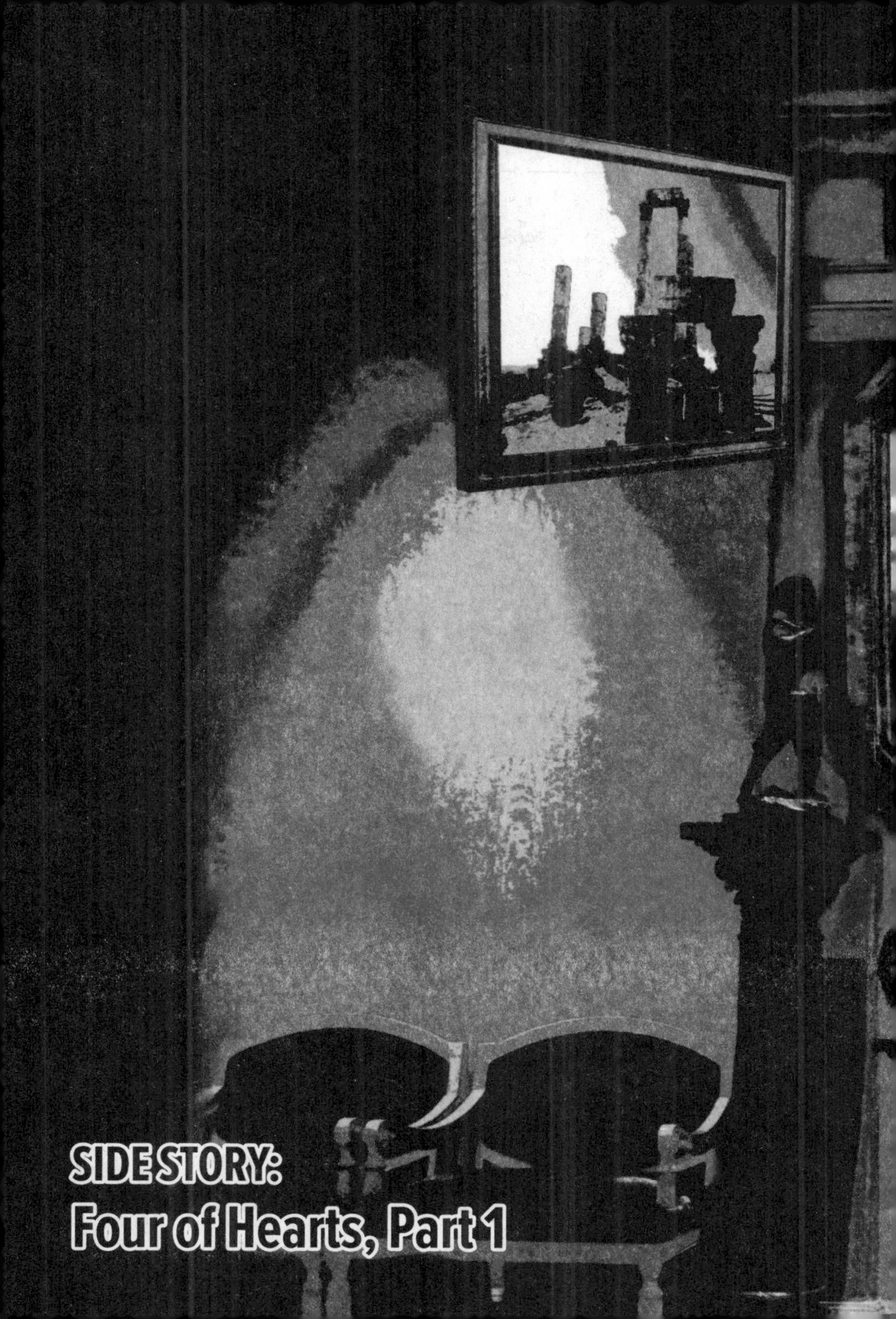

SIDE STORY:
Four of Hearts, Part 1

ALICE IN BORDERLAND

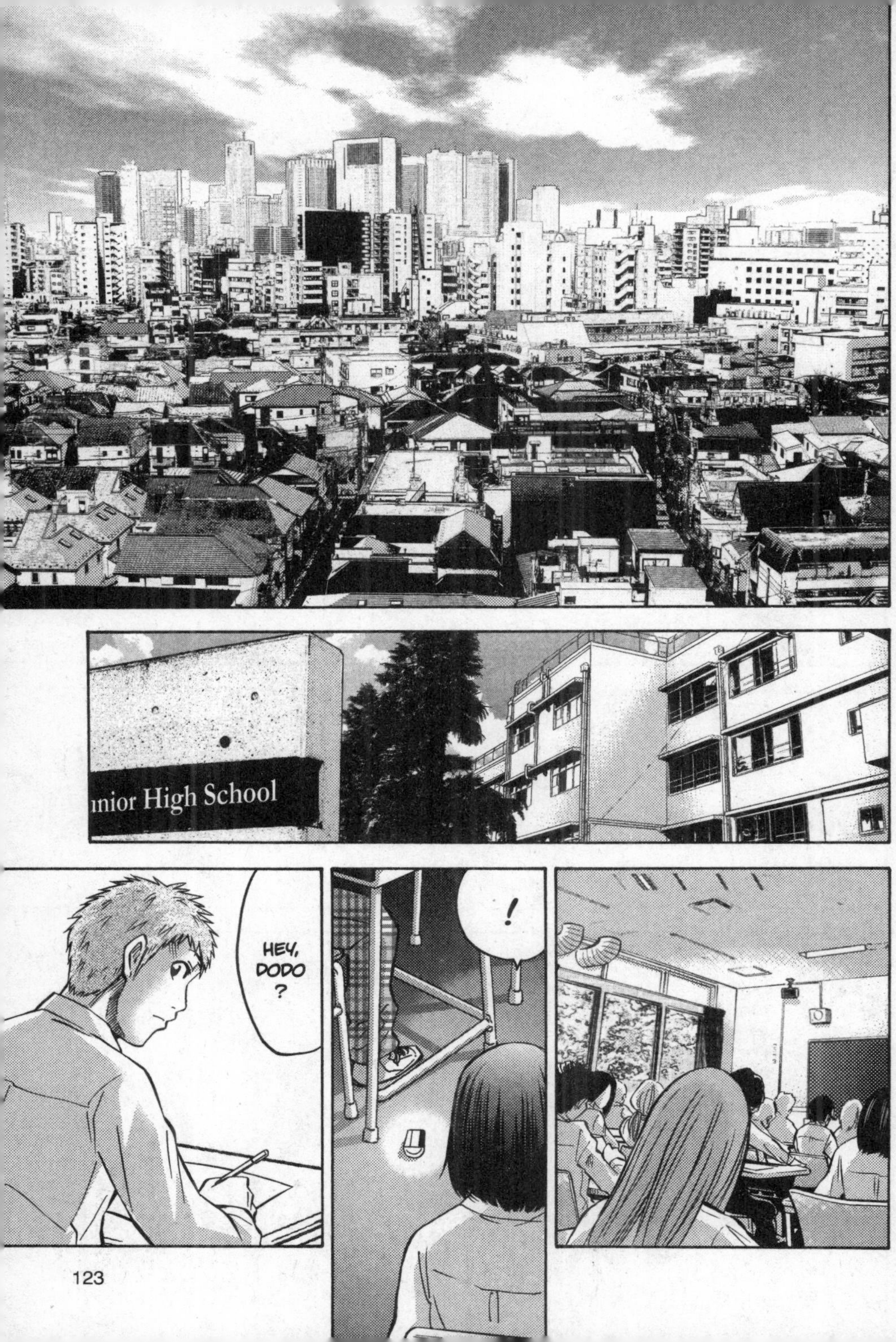
unior High School
!
HEY, DODO?

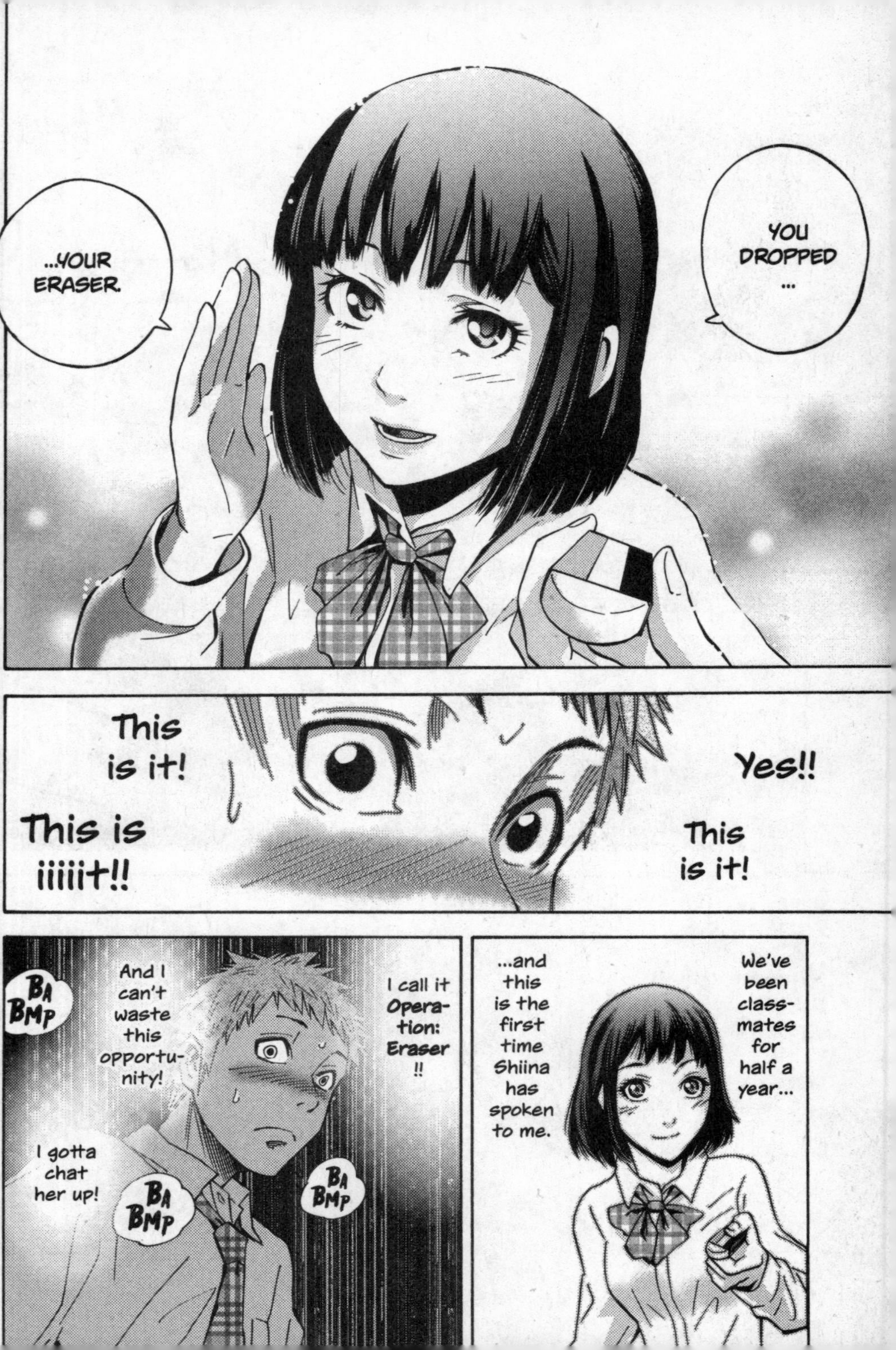
YOU DROPPED ...
...YOUR ERASER.
Yes!!
This is it!
This is it!
This is iiiiit!!
We've been classmates for half a year...
...and this is the first time Shiina has spoken to me.
I call it Operation: Eraser!!
And I can't waste this opportunity!
BA BMP
BA BMP
I gotta chat her up!
BA BMP

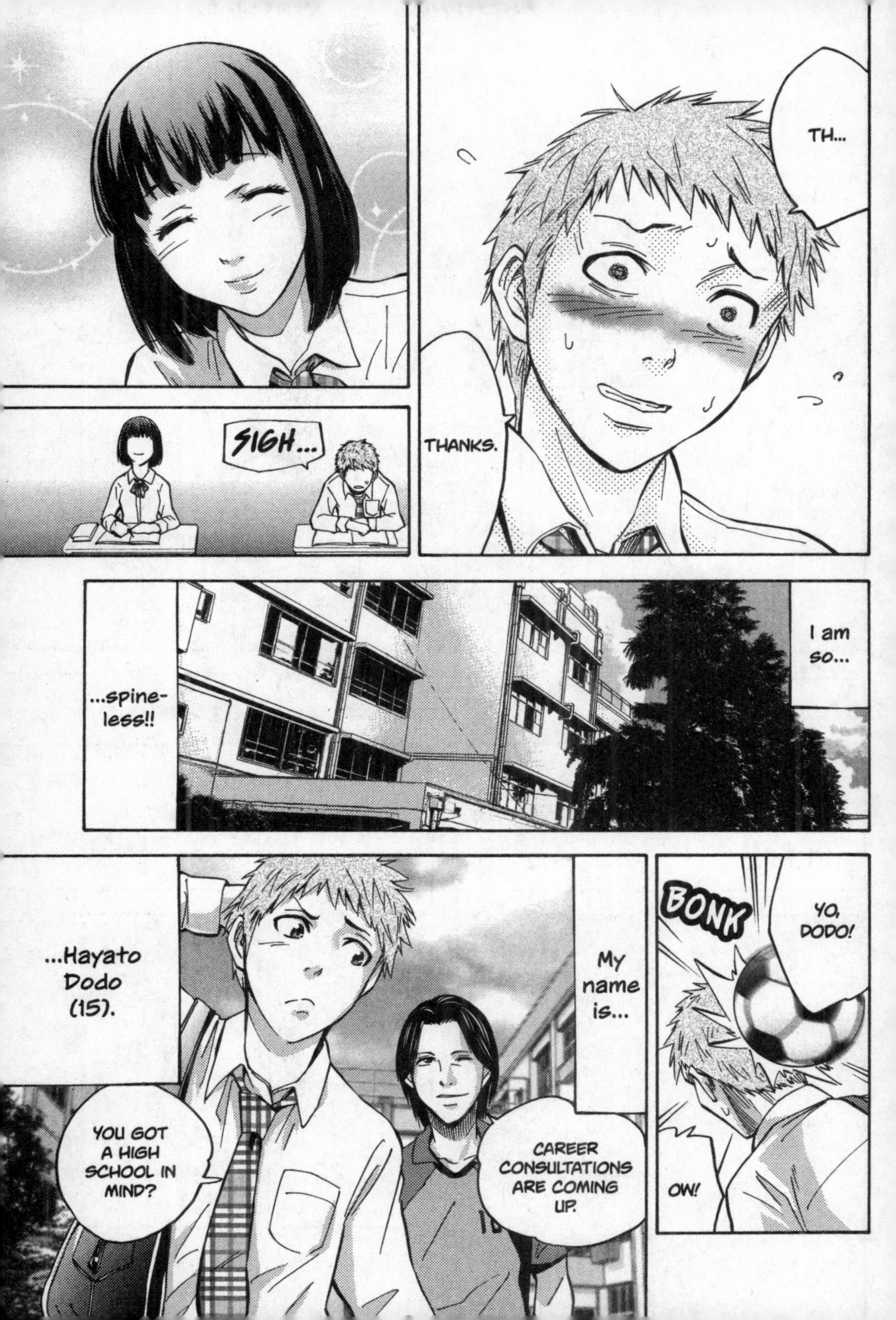
TH...
THANKS.
SIGH...
I am so...
...spine-less!!
BONK
YO, DODO!
OW!
My name is...
...Hayato Dodo (15).
CAREER CONSULTATIONS ARE COMING UP.
YOU GOT A HIGH SCHOOL IN MIND?

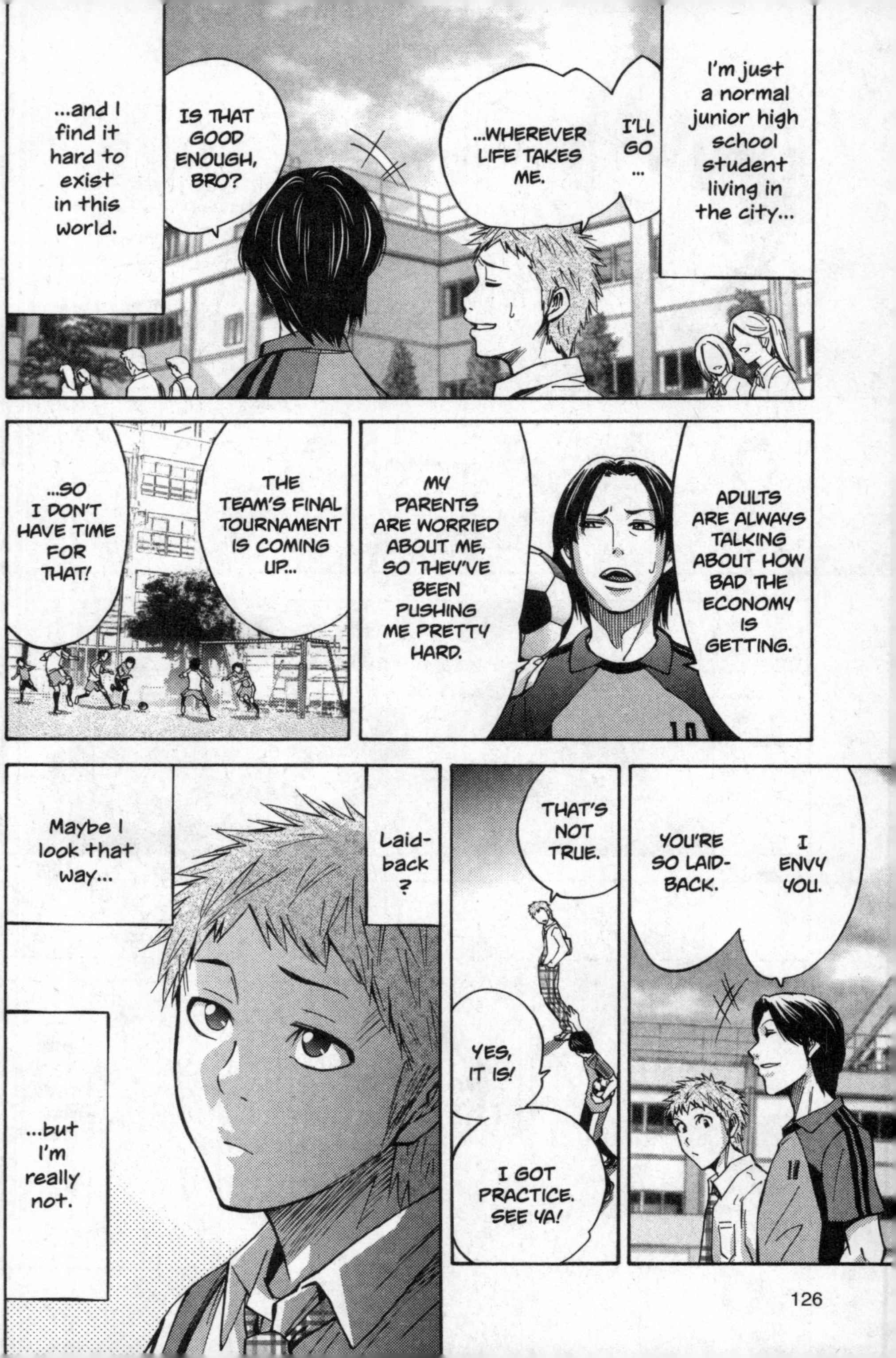
I'm just a normal junior high school student living in the city...
I'LL GO ...
...WHEREVER LIFE TAKES ME.
IS THAT GOOD ENOUGH, BRO?
...and I find it hard to exist in this world.
ADULTS ARE ALWAYS TALKING ABOUT HOW BAD THE ECONOMY IS GETTING.
MY PARENTS ARE WORRIED ABOUT ME, SO THEY'VE BEEN PUSHING ME PRETTY HARD.
THE TEAM'S FINAL TOURNAMENT IS COMING UP...
...SO I DON'T HAVE TIME FOR THAT!
I ENVY YOU.
YOU'RE SO LAID-BACK.
THAT'S NOT TRUE.
YES, IT IS!
I GOT PRACTICE. SEE YA!
Laid-back?
Maybe I look that way...
...but I'm really not.

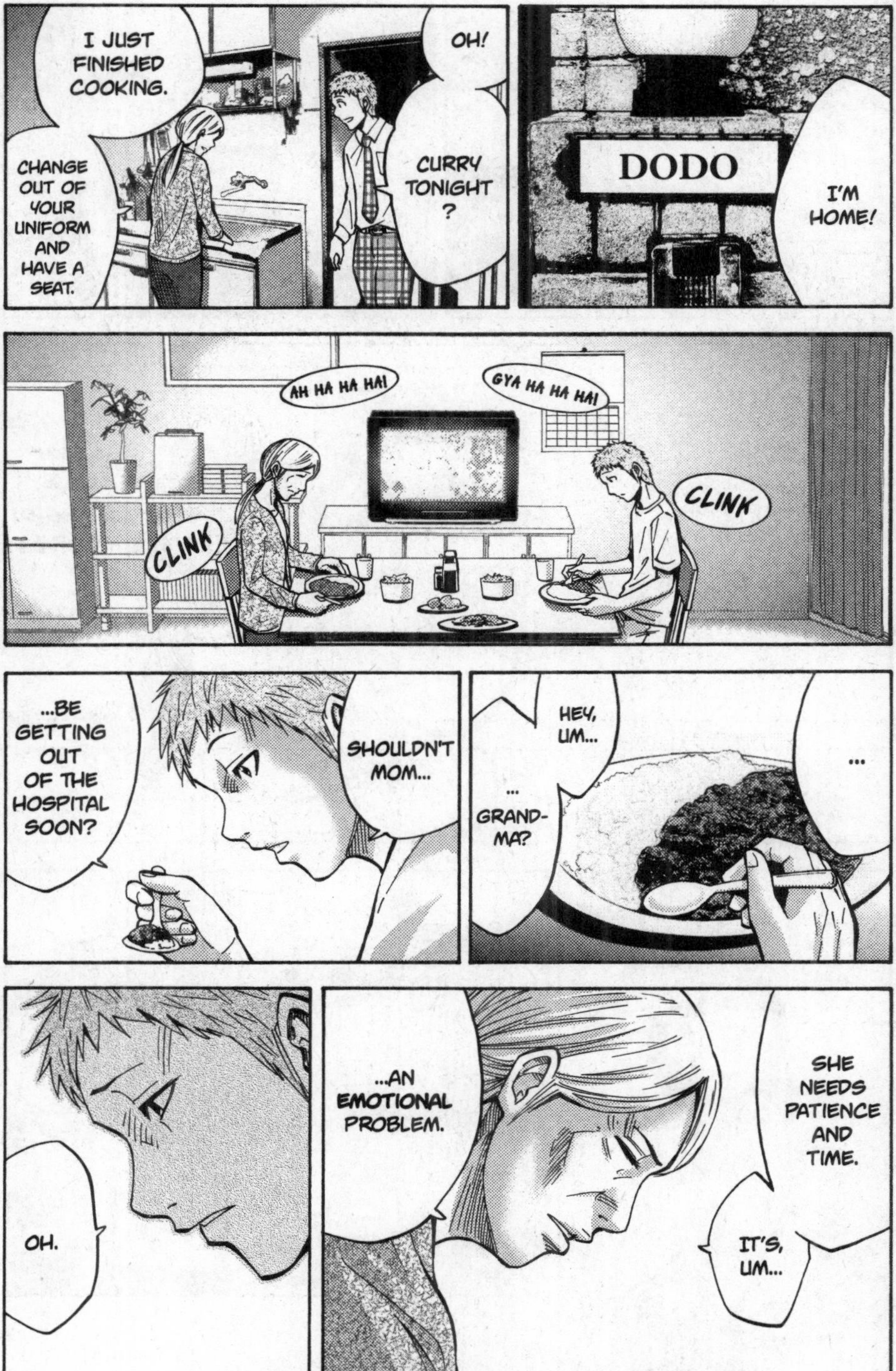
DODO
I'M HOME!
OH!
CURRY TONIGHT?
I JUST FINISHED COOKING.
CHANGE OUT OF YOUR UNIFORM AND HAVE A SEAT.
GYA HA HA HA!
AH HA HA HA!
CLINK
CLINK
...
HEY, UM...
... GRANDMA?
SHOULDN'T MOM...
...BE GETTING OUT OF THE HOSPITAL SOON?
IT'S, UM...
...AN EMOTIONAL PROBLEM.
SHE NEEDS PATIENCE AND TIME.
OH.

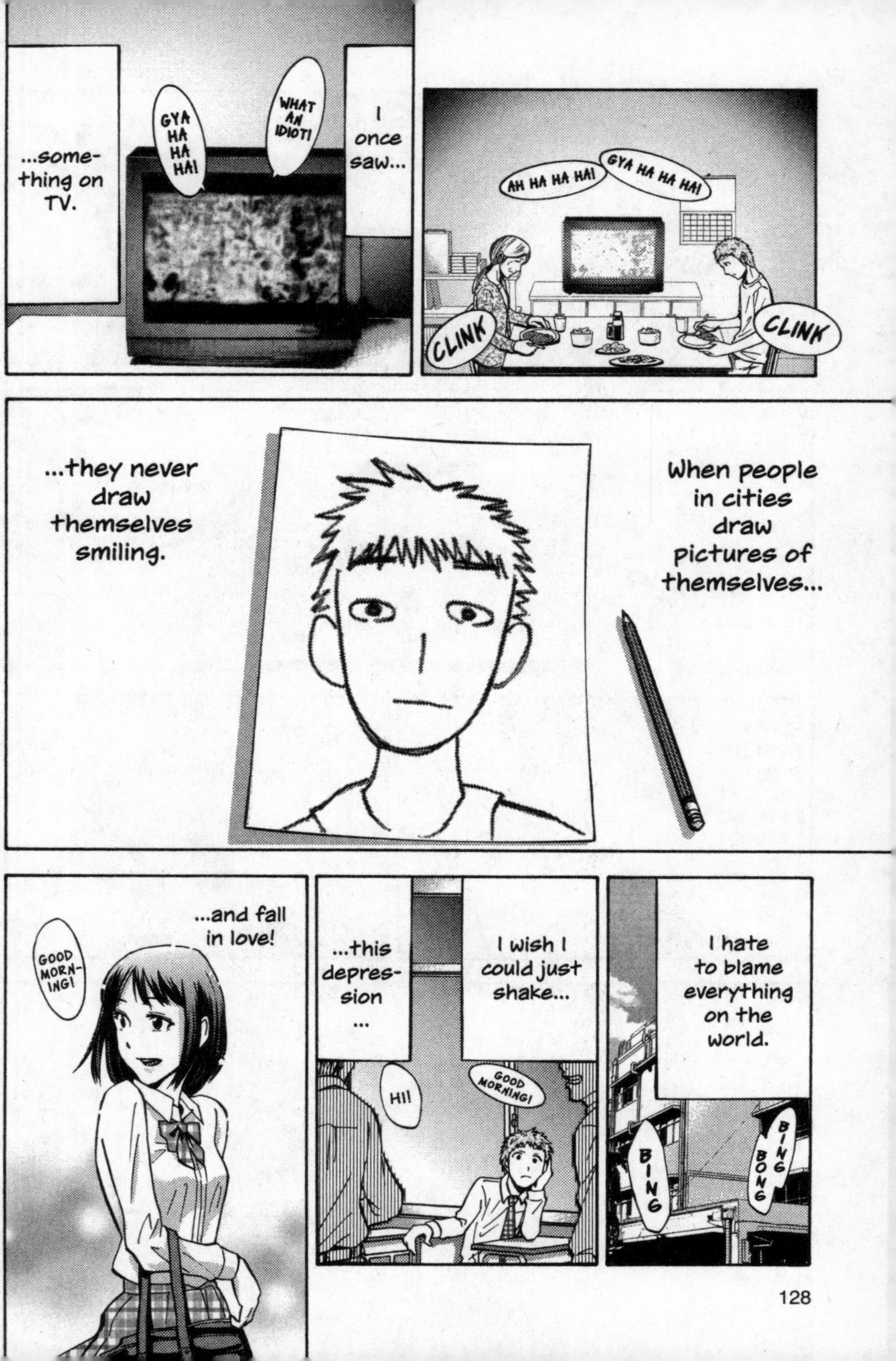
GYA HA HA HA!
AH HA HA HA!
CLINK
CLINK
I once saw...
WHAT AN IDIOT!
GYA HA HA HA!
...something on TV.
When people in cities draw pictures of themselves...
...they never draw themselves smiling.
I hate to blame everything on the world.
BING BONG
BING
I wish I could just shake...
...this depression...
GOOD MORNING!
HI!
...and fall in love!
GOOD MORNING!

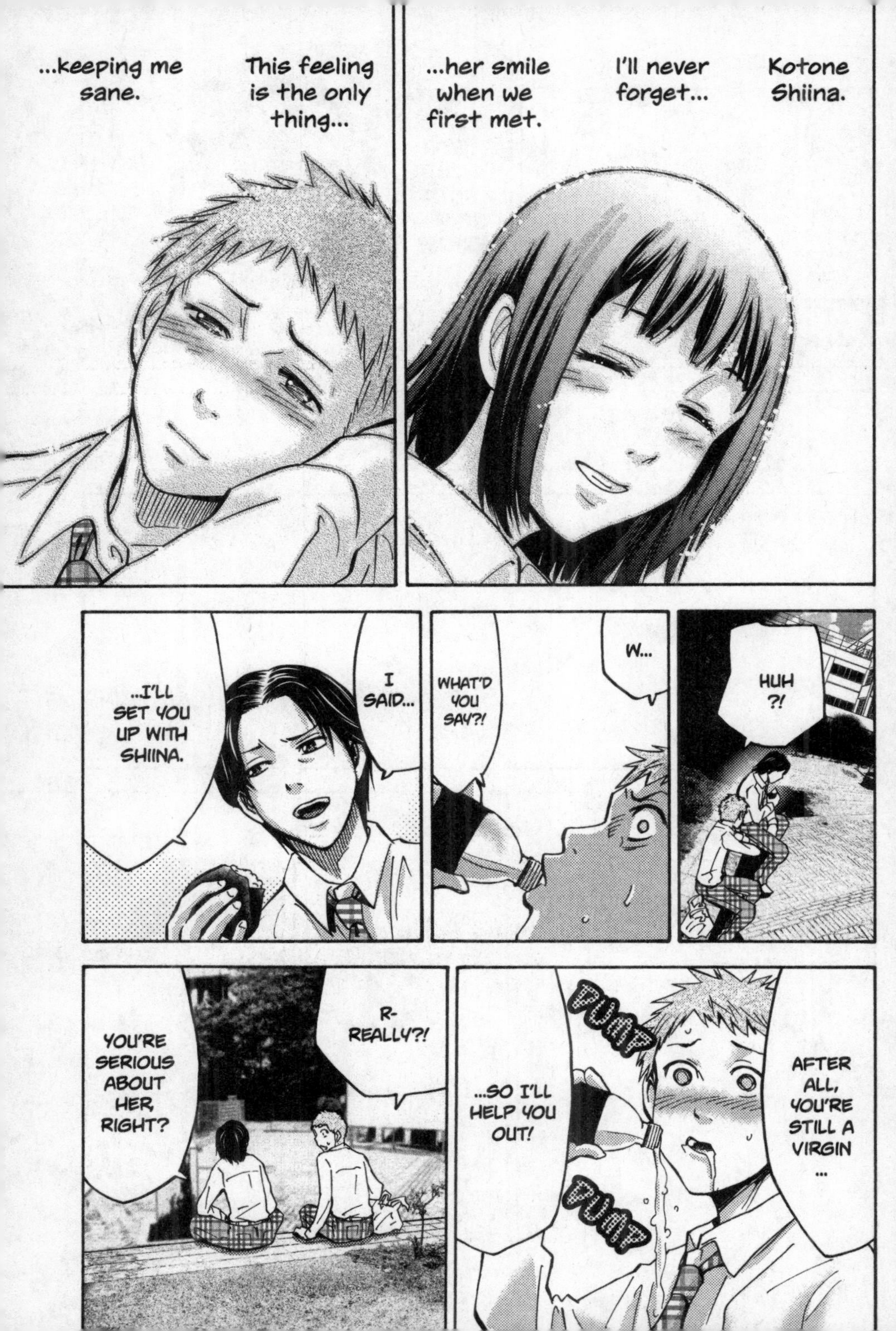
Kotone Shiina.
I'll never forget...
...her smile when we first met.
This feeling is the only thing...
...keeping me sane.
HUH ?!
W...
WHAT'D YOU SAY?!
I SAID...
...I'LL SET YOU UP WITH SHIINA.
AFTER ALL, YOU'RE STILL A VIRGIN ...
PUMP
PUMP
...SO I'LL HELP YOU OUT!
R-REALLY?!
YOU'RE SERIOUS ABOUT HER, RIGHT?

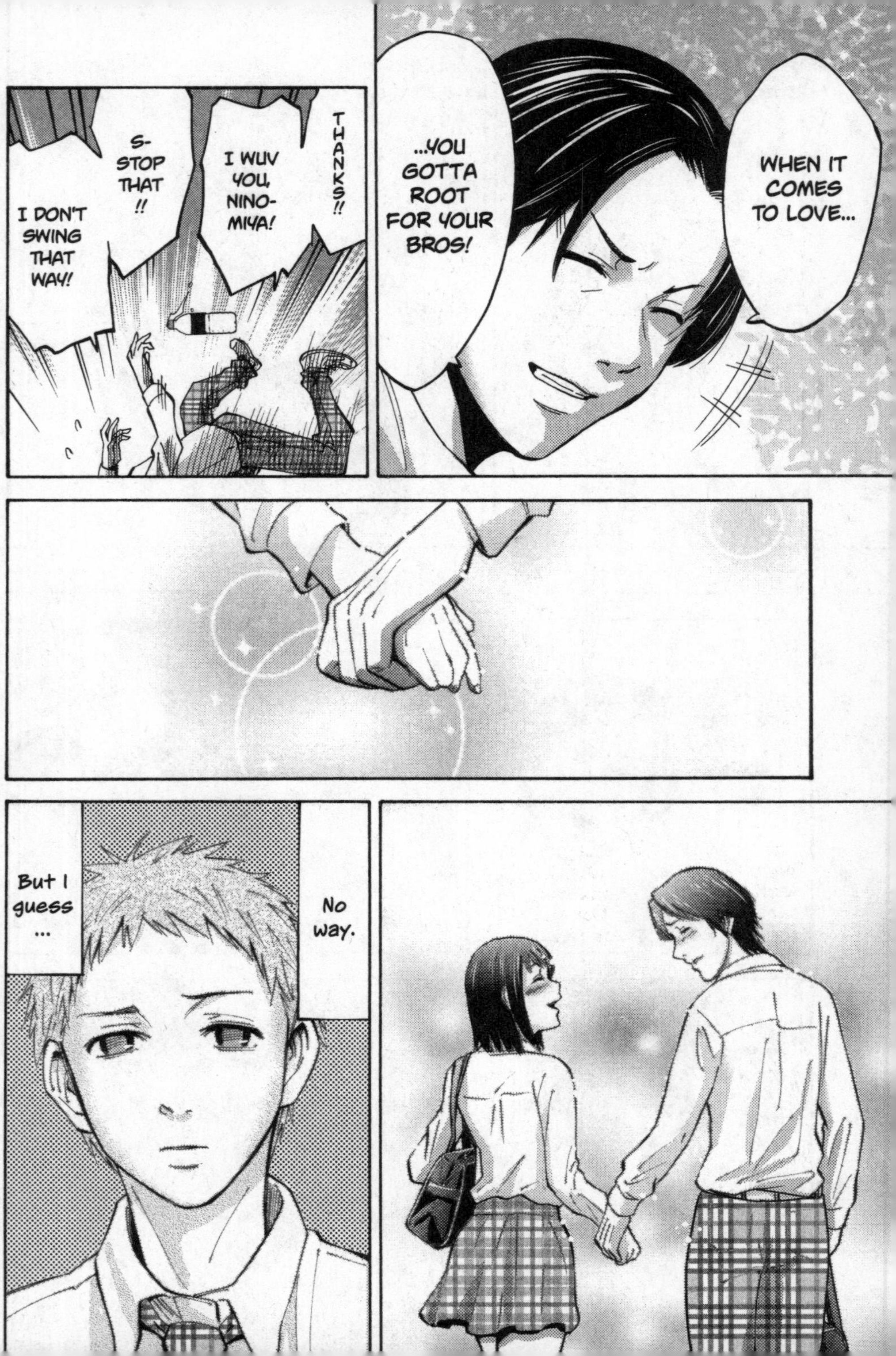
WHEN IT COMES TO LOVE...
...YOU GOTTA ROOT FOR YOUR BROS!
THANKS!!
I WUV YOU, NINO-MIYA!
S-STOP THAT!!
I DON'T SWING THAT WAY!
No way.
But I guess ...

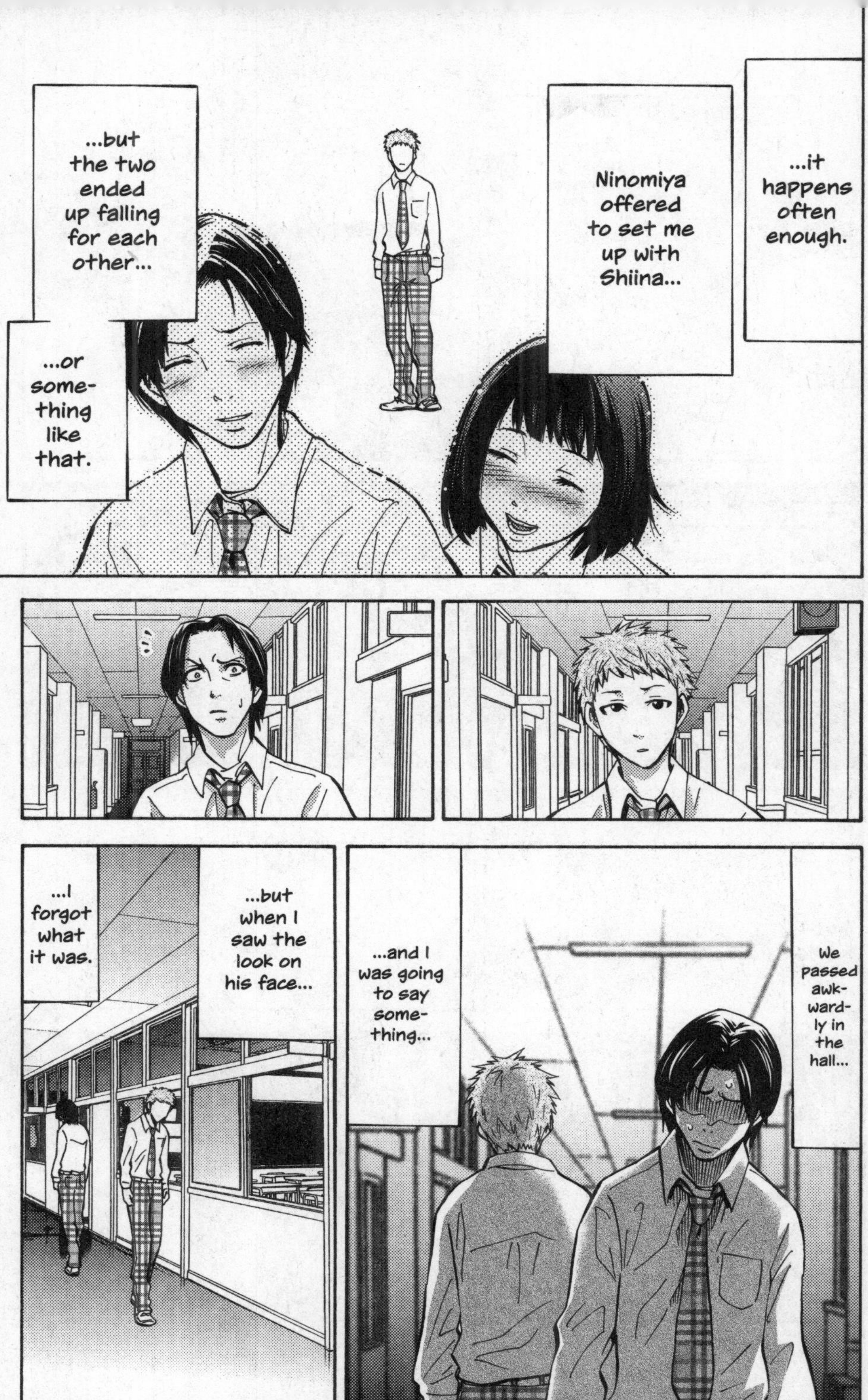
...it happens often enough.
Ninomiya offered to set me up with Shiina...
...but the two ended up falling for each other...
...or some-thing like that.
We passed awk-ward-ly in the hall...
...and I was going to say some-thing...
...but when I saw the look on his face...
...I forgot what it was.

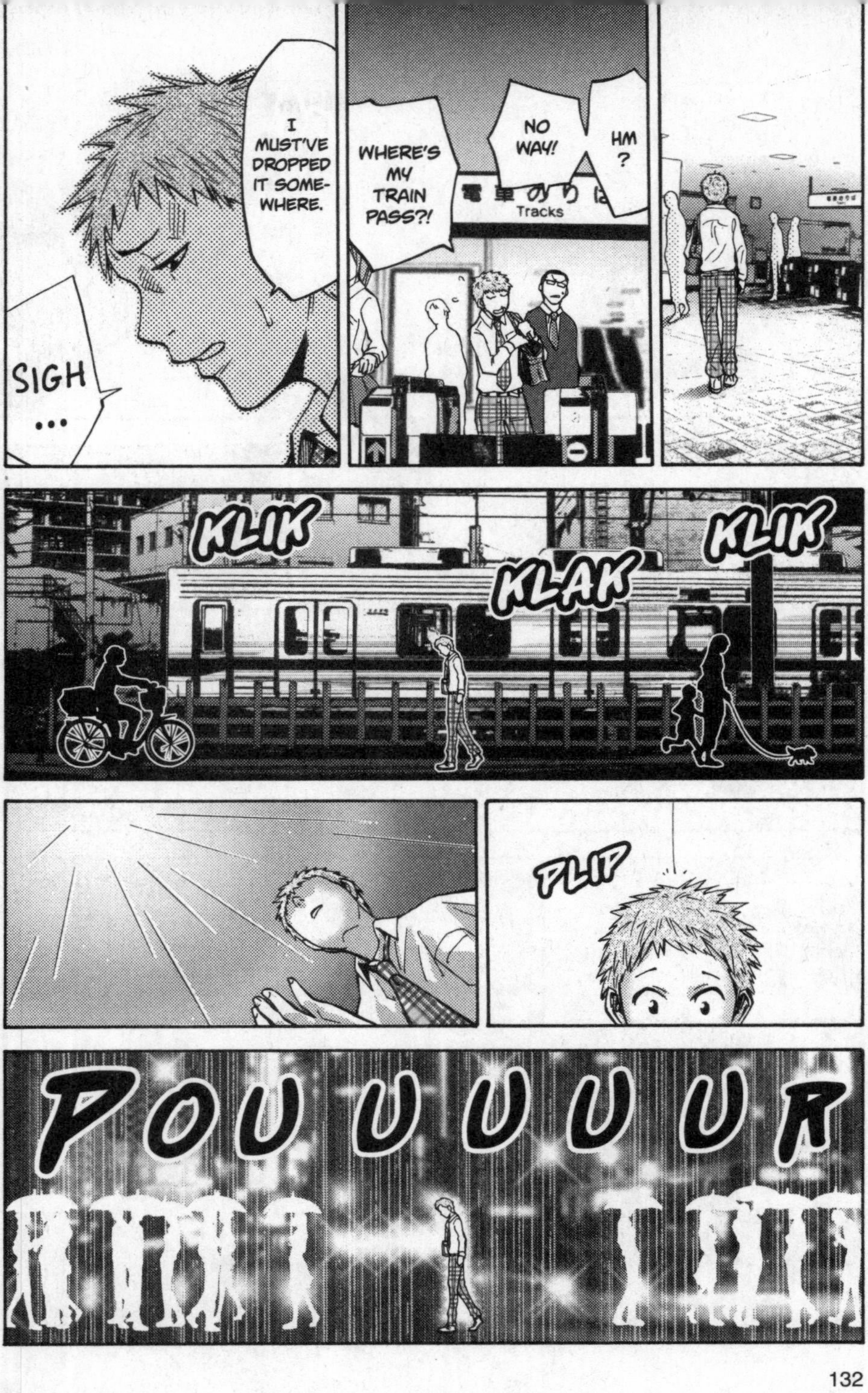
HM ?
NO WAY!
WHERE'S MY TRAIN PASS?!
電車のりば
Tracks
I MUST'VE DROPPED IT SOMEWHERE.
SIGH ...
KLIK
KLAK
KLIK
PLIP
POUUUUUR

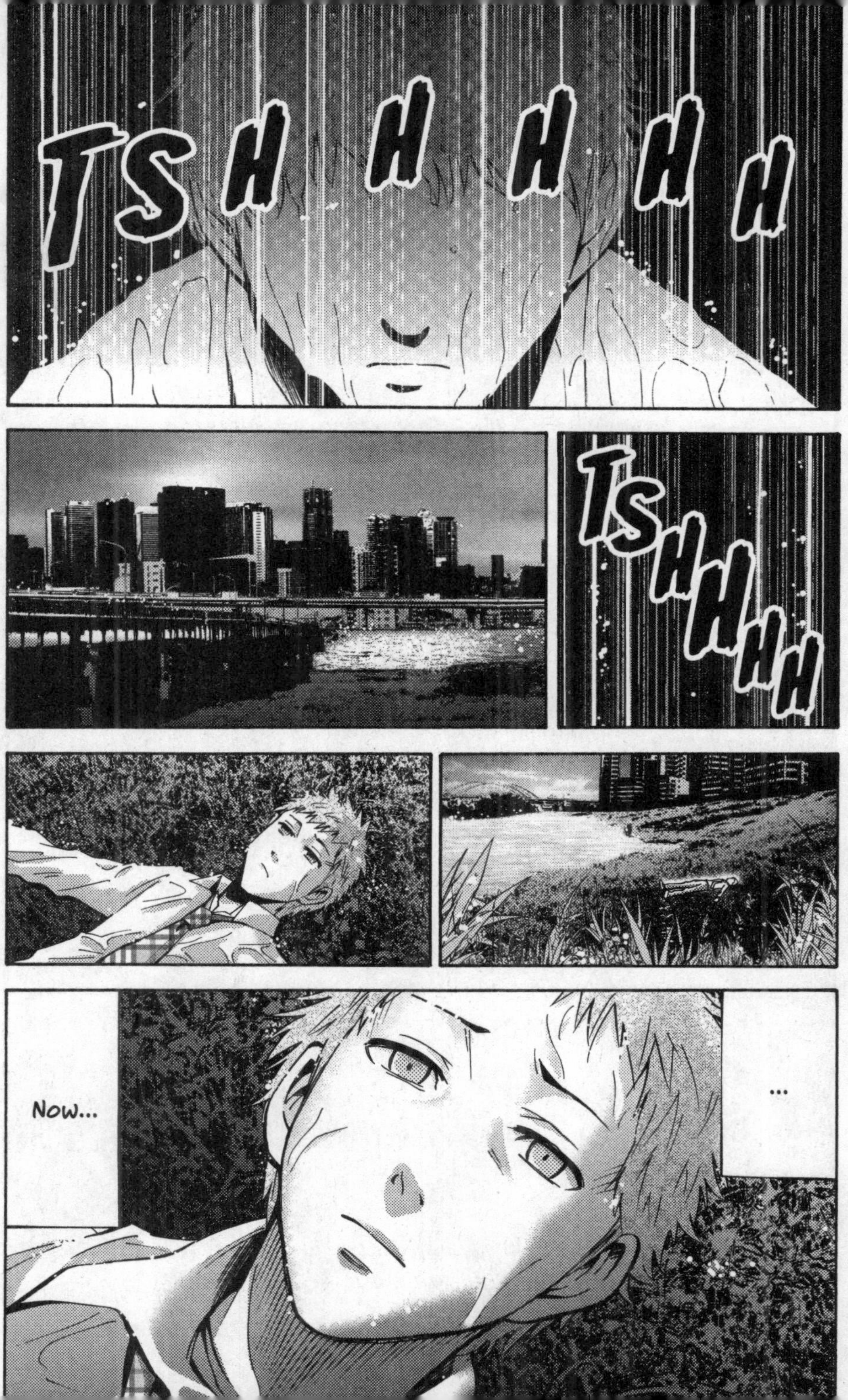
TSHHHHH
TSHHHHH
...
Now...

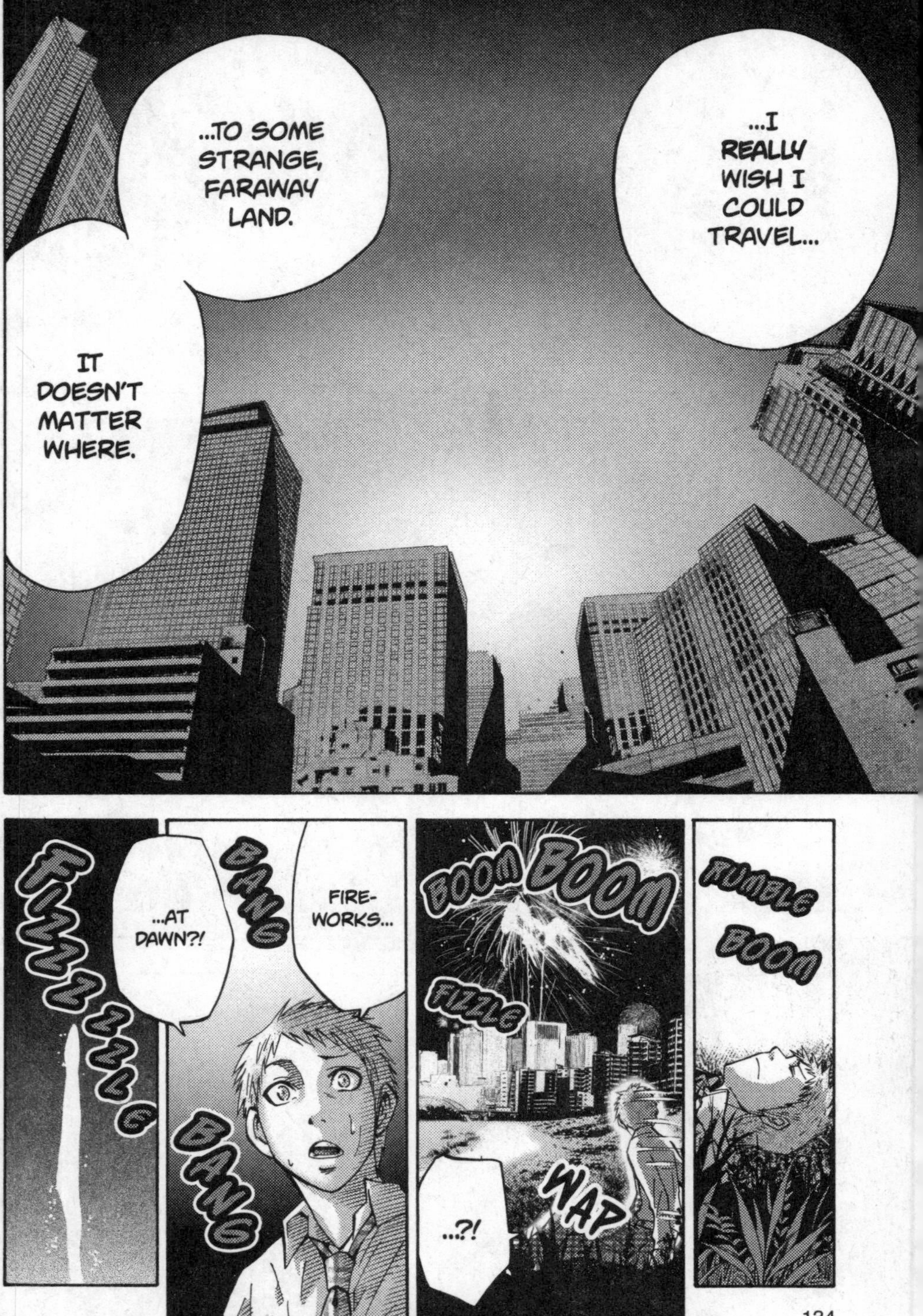
...I REALLY WISH I COULD TRAVEL...
...TO SOME STRANGE, FARAWAY LAND.
IT DOESN'T MATTER WHERE.
TUMBLE
BOOM
BOOM BOOM
FIZZLE
WAP
...?!
FIRE-WORKS...
BANG
...AT DAWN?!
BANG
FIZZZZZLE

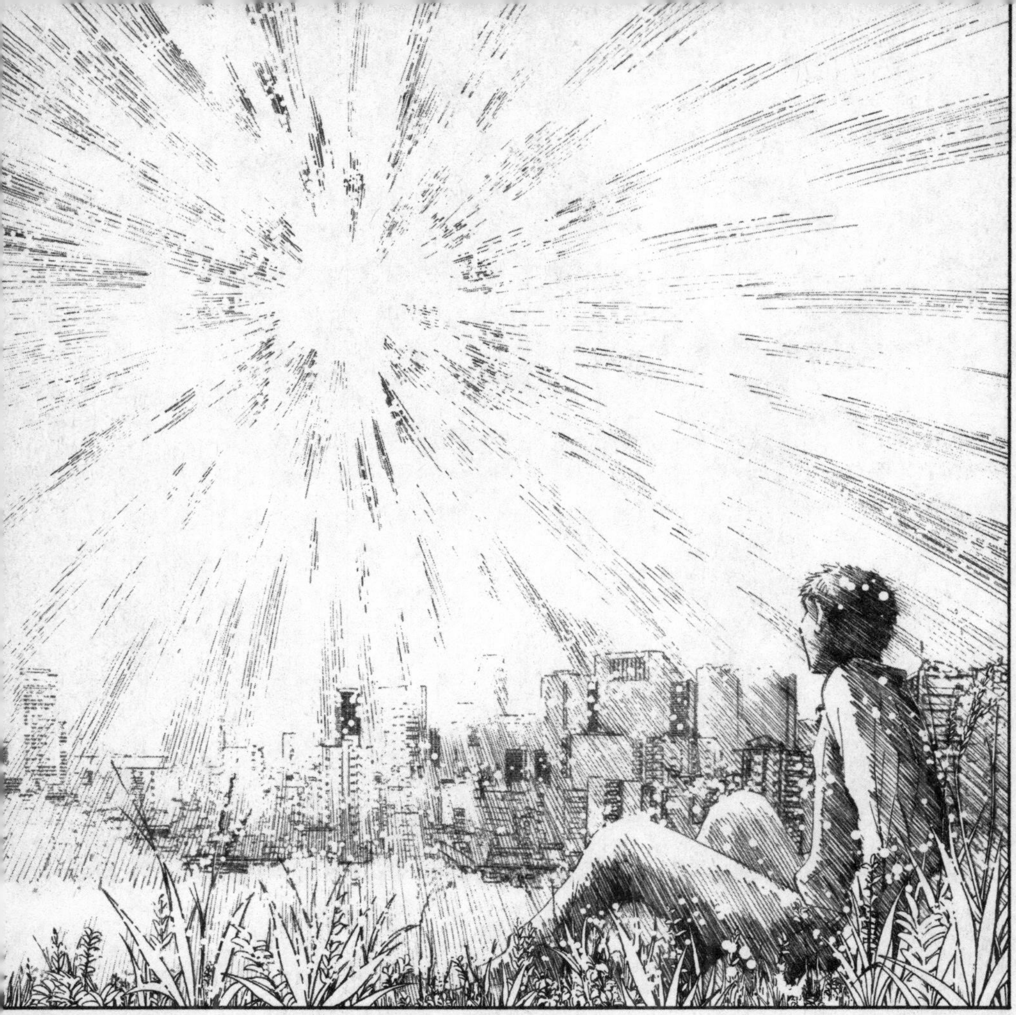
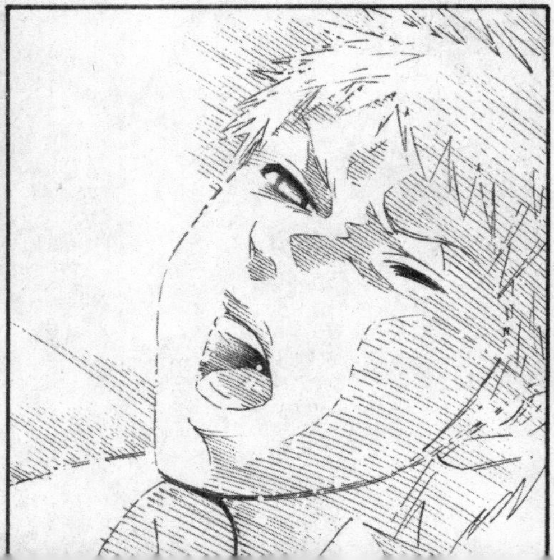
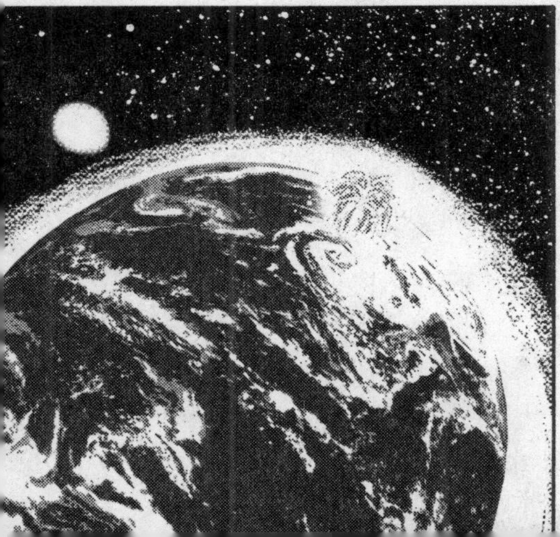

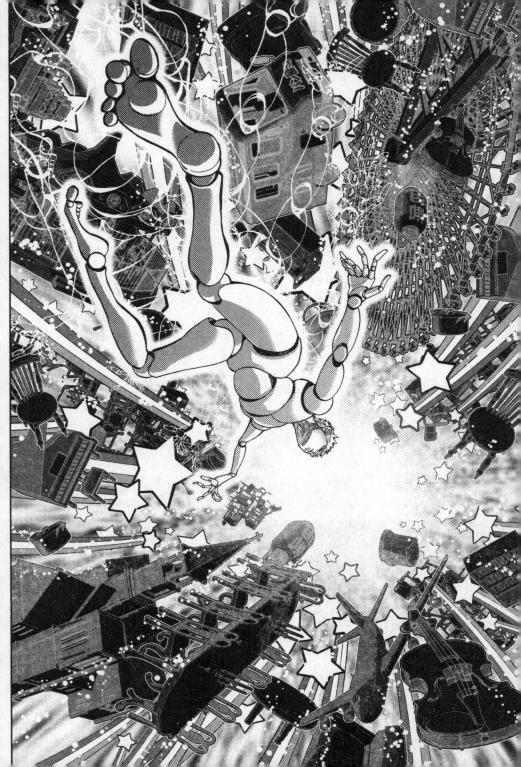

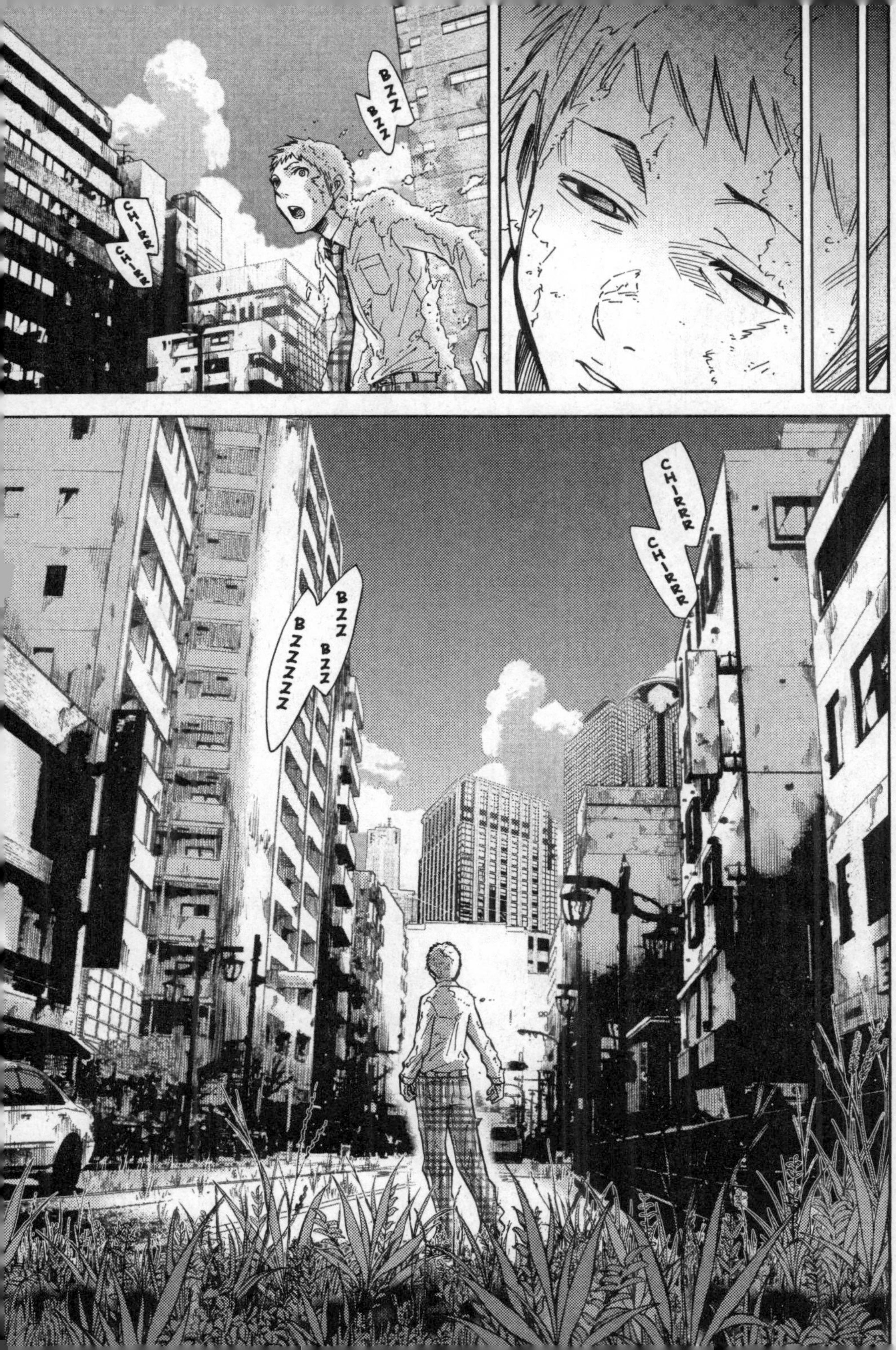
BZZ BZZ
CHIRR CHIRR
CHIRRR CHIRRR
BZZ BZZ BZZZZZZ

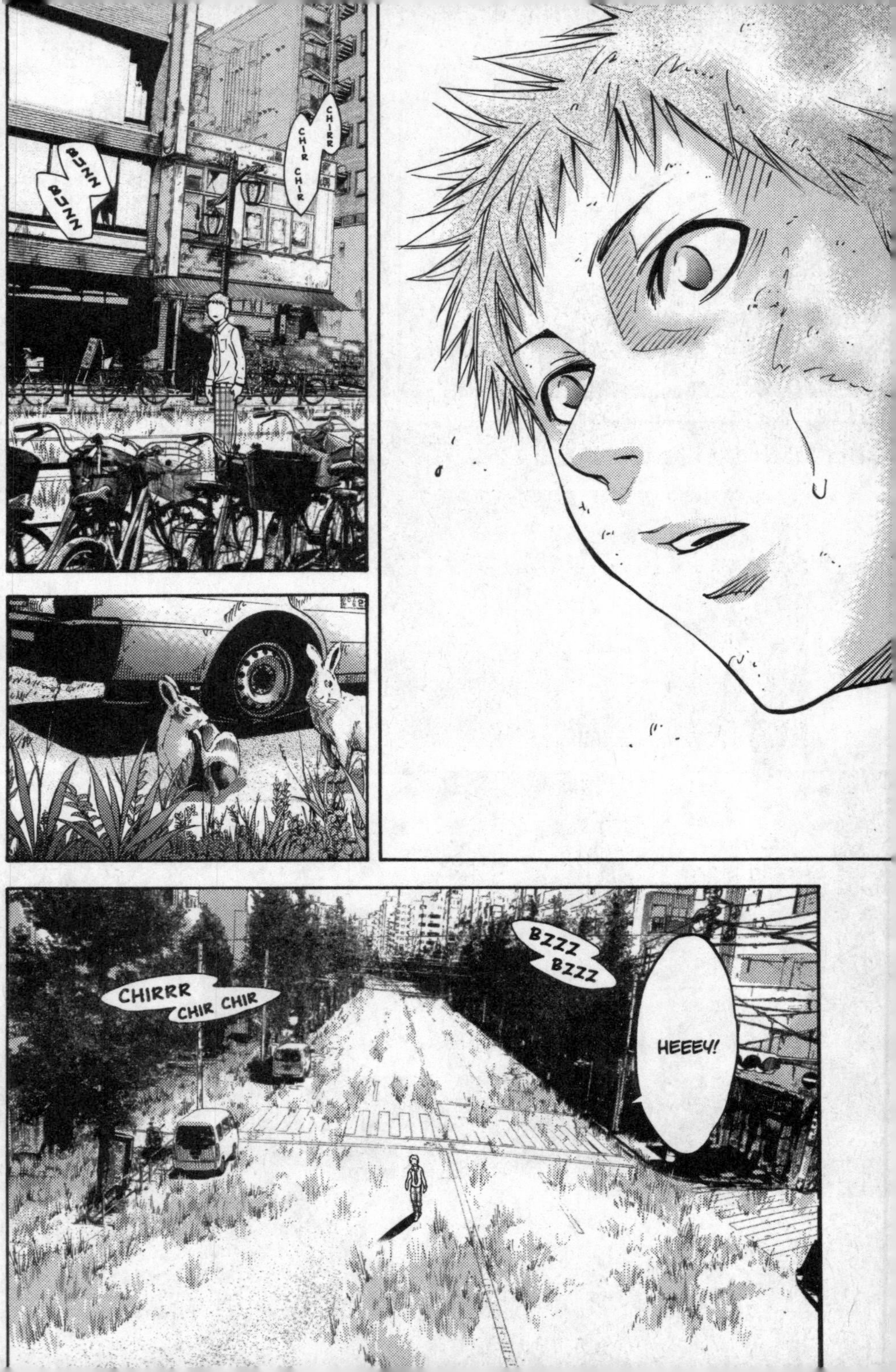
CHIRR CHIR CHIR
BUNN BUNN
HEEEY!
BZZZ BZZZ
CHIRRR CHIR CHIR

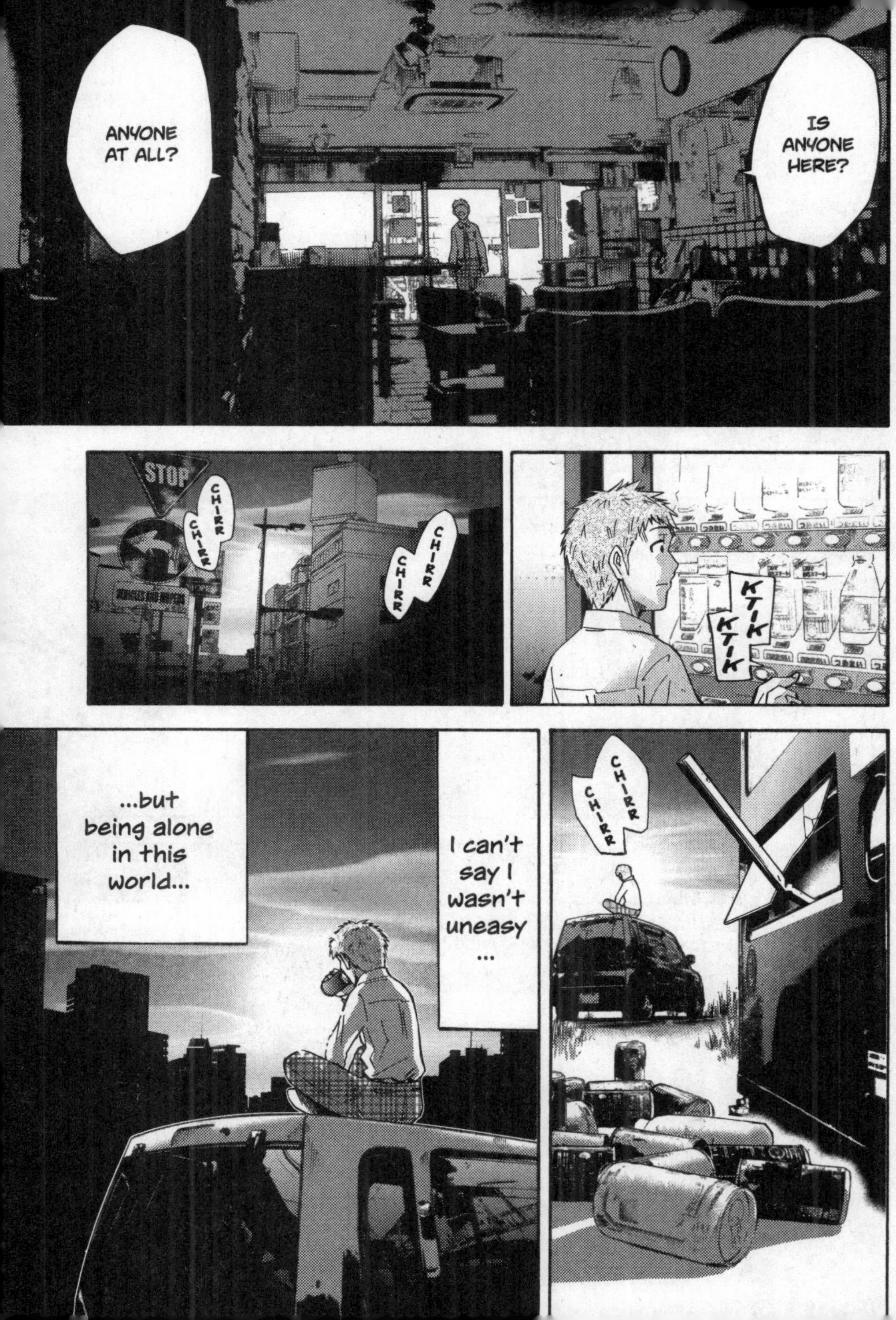
IS ANYONE HERE?
ANYONE AT ALL?
KTIK KTIK
CHIRR CHIRR
STOP
CHIRR CHIRR
CHIRR CHIRR
I can't say I wasn't uneasy...
...but being alone in this world...

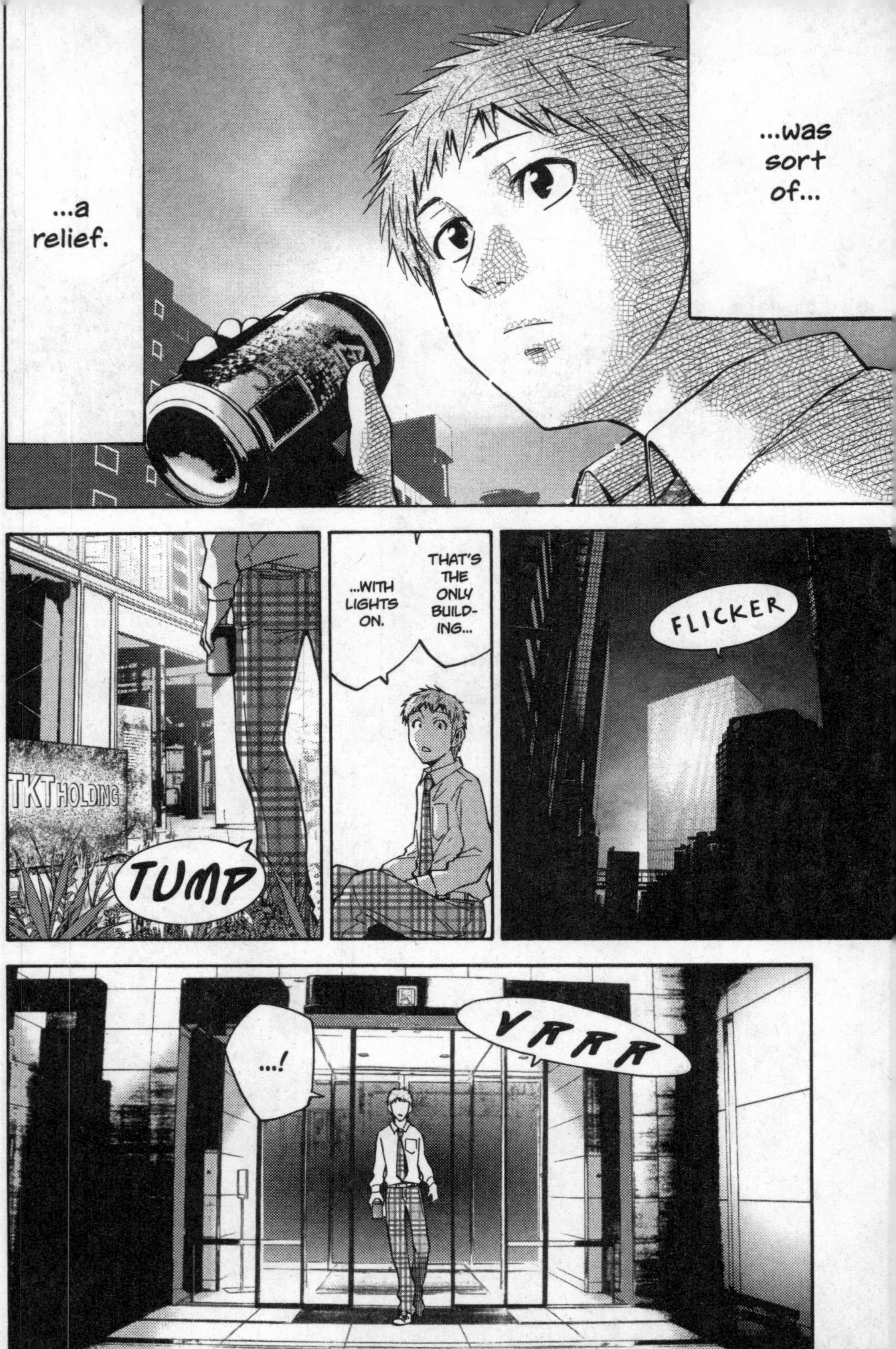
...was sort of...
...a relief.
FLICKER
THAT'S THE ONLY BUILD-ING...
...WITH LIGHTS ON.
TKT HOLDING
TUMP
VRRR
...!

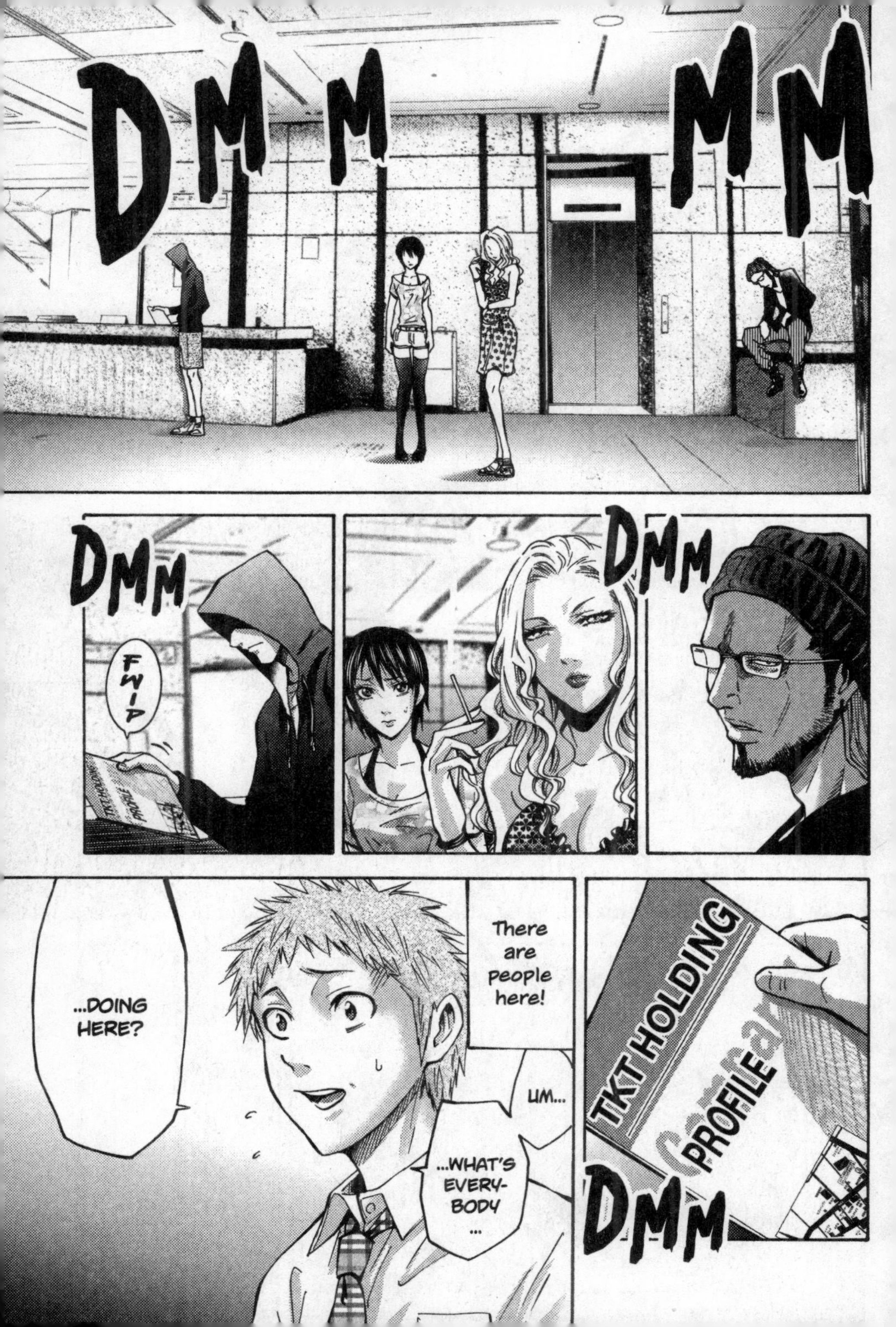
DMM
MM
DMM
DMM
TKT HOLDING
PROFILE
FWIP
TKT HOLDING
Company
PROFILE
DMM
There are people here!
UM...
...WHAT'S EVERY-BODY ...
...DOING HERE?

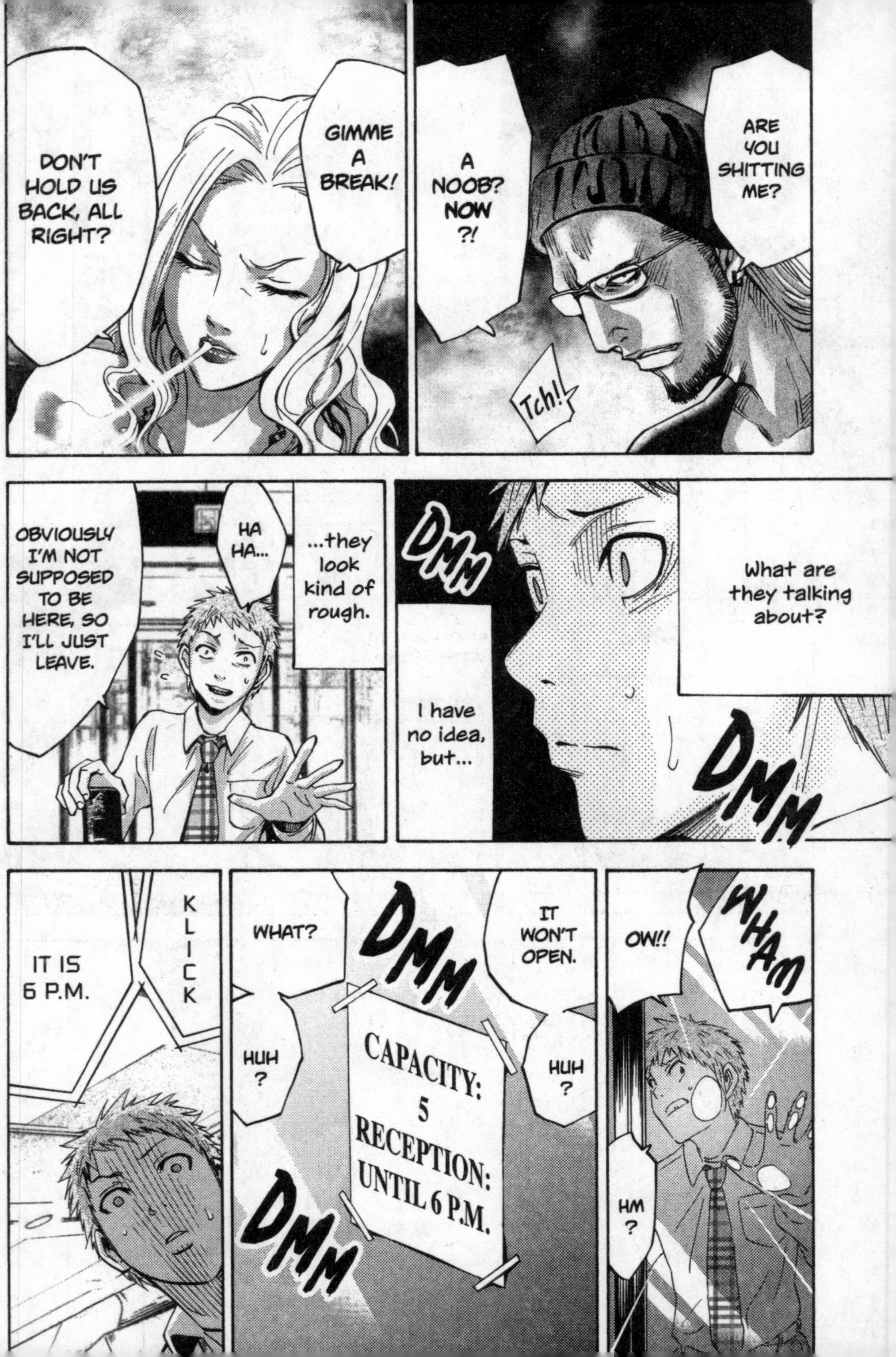
ARE YOU SHITTING ME?
A NOOB? NOW ?!
Tch!!
GIMME A BREAK!
DON'T HOLD US BACK, ALL RIGHT?
What are they talking about?
DMM
I have no idea, but...
DMM
...they look kind of rough.
HA HA...
OBVIOUSLY I'M NOT SUPPOSED TO BE HERE, SO I'LL JUST LEAVE.
WHAM
OW!!
HM ?
IT WON'T OPEN.
HUH ?
DMM
WHAT?
HUH ?
CAPACITY: 5 RECEPTION: UNTIL 6 P.M.
DMM
KLICK
IT IS 6 P.M.

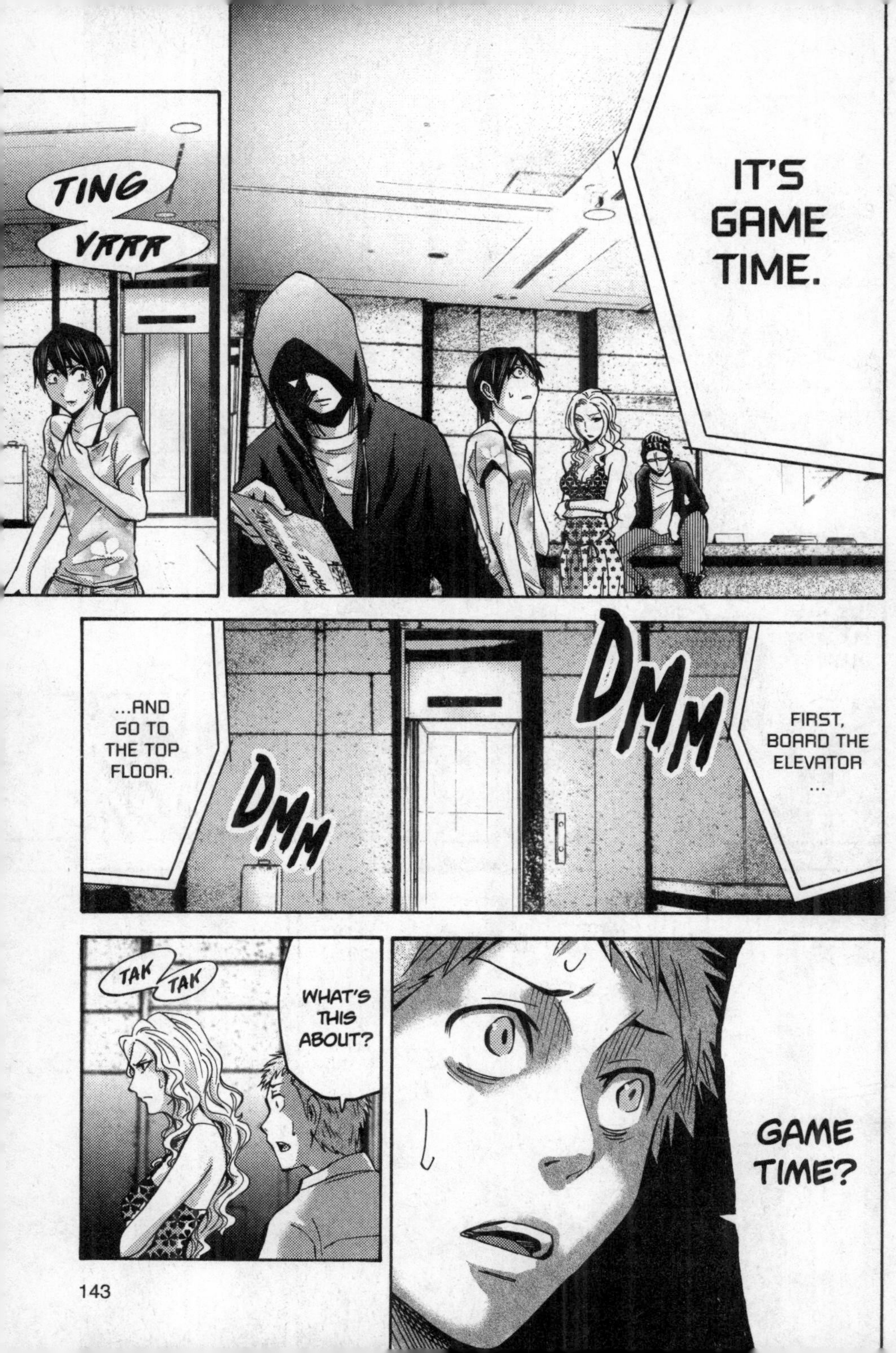
IT'S GAME TIME.
TING
VRRR
FIRST, BOARD THE ELEVATOR ...
DMM
DMM
...AND GO TO THE TOP FLOOR.
GAME TIME?
WHAT'S THIS ABOUT?
TAK TAK

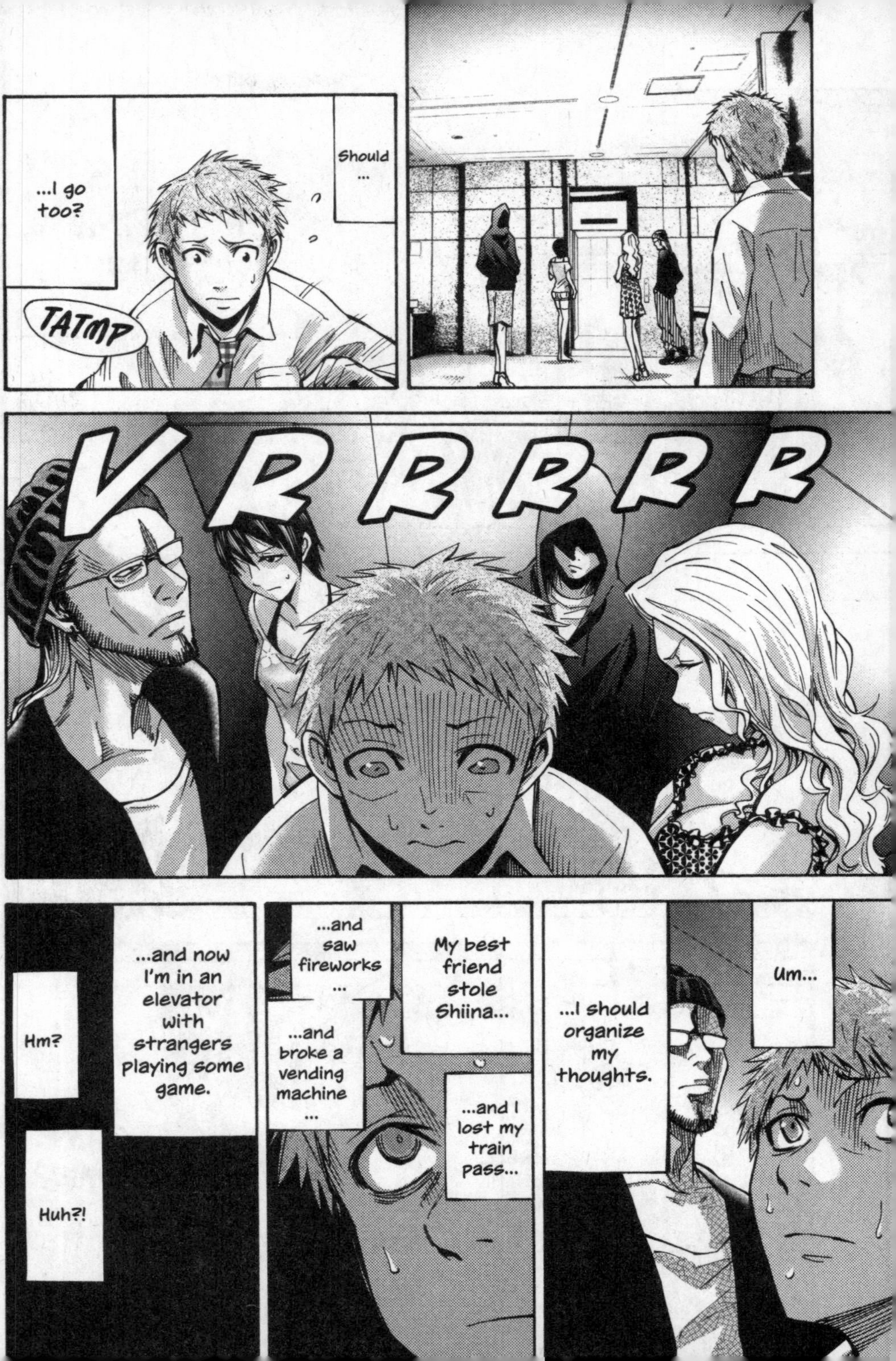
Should ...
...I go too?
TATMP
VRRRRR
Um...
...I should organize my thoughts.
My best friend stole Shiina...
...and saw fireworks ...
...and broke a vending machine ...
...and I lost my train pass...
...and now I'm in an elevator with strangers playing some game.
Hm?
Huh?!

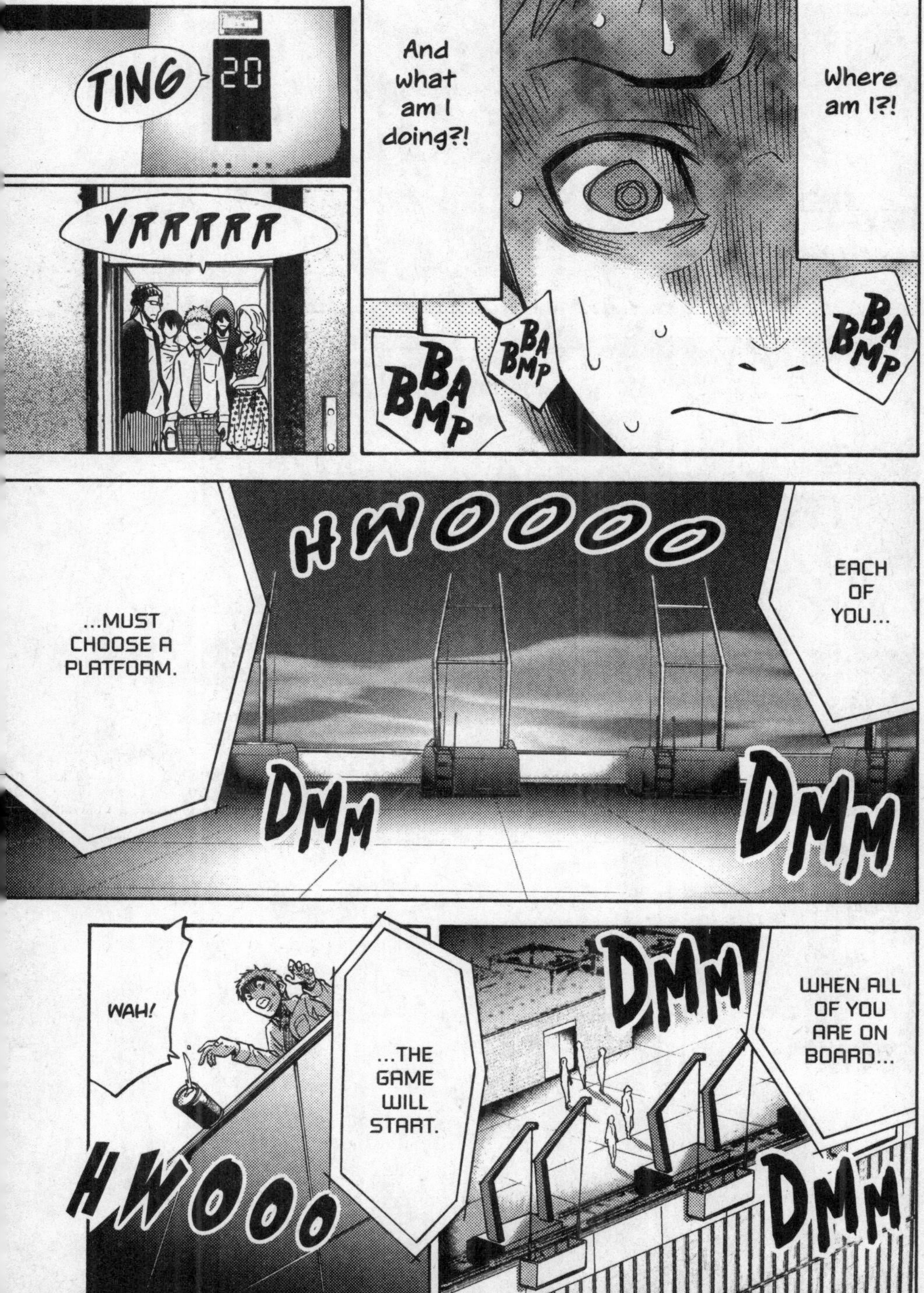
Where am I?!
And what am I doing?!
BABMP
BABMP
BABMP
TING
20
VRRRRR
EACH OF YOU...
HWOOOO
...MUST CHOOSE A PLATFORM.
DMM
DMM
DMM
WHEN ALL OF YOU ARE ON BOARD...
DMM
...THE GAME WILL START.
WAH!
HWOOO

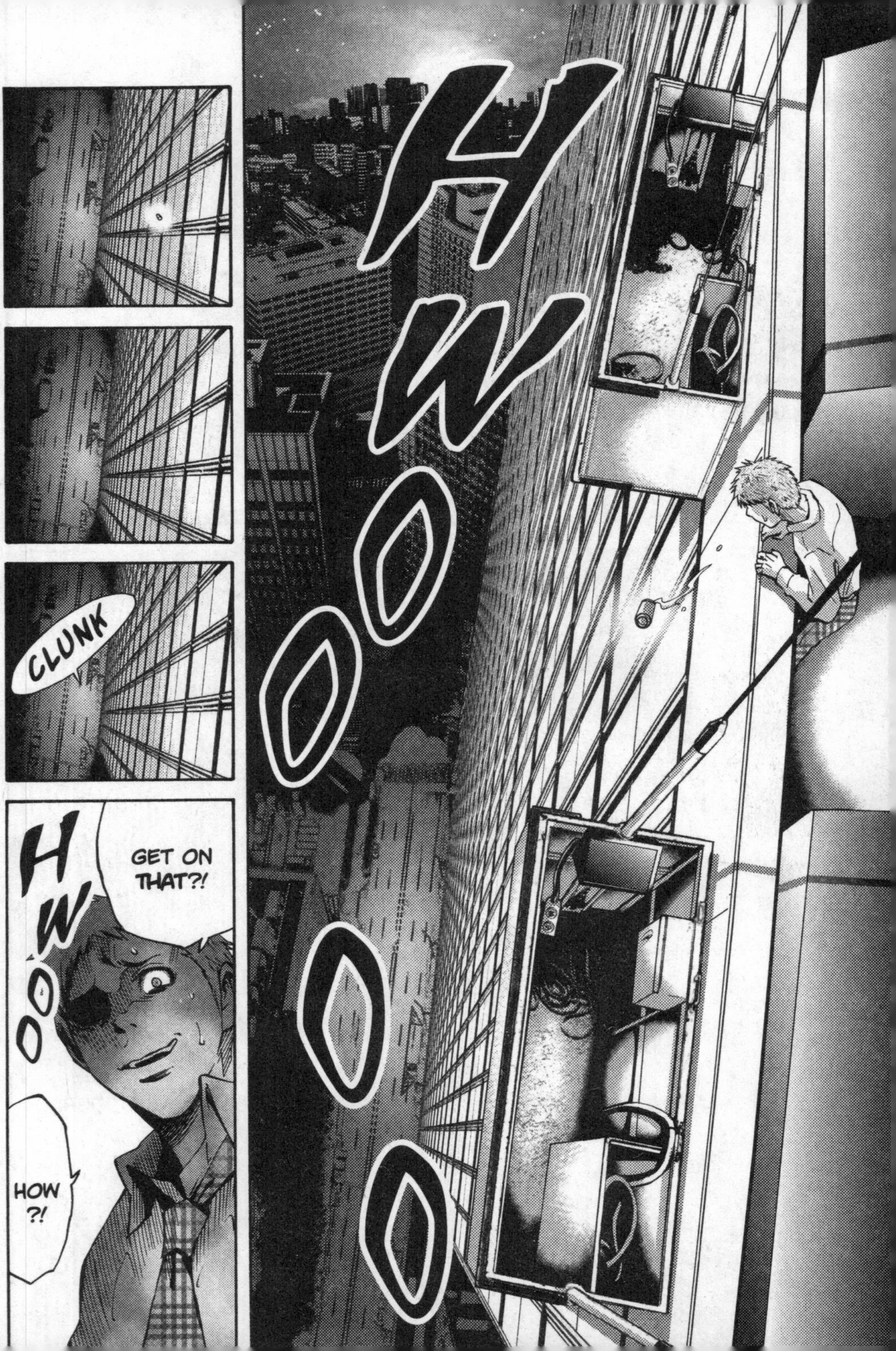
HWOOOOO
CLUNK
HWOOO
GET ON THAT?!
HOW ?!

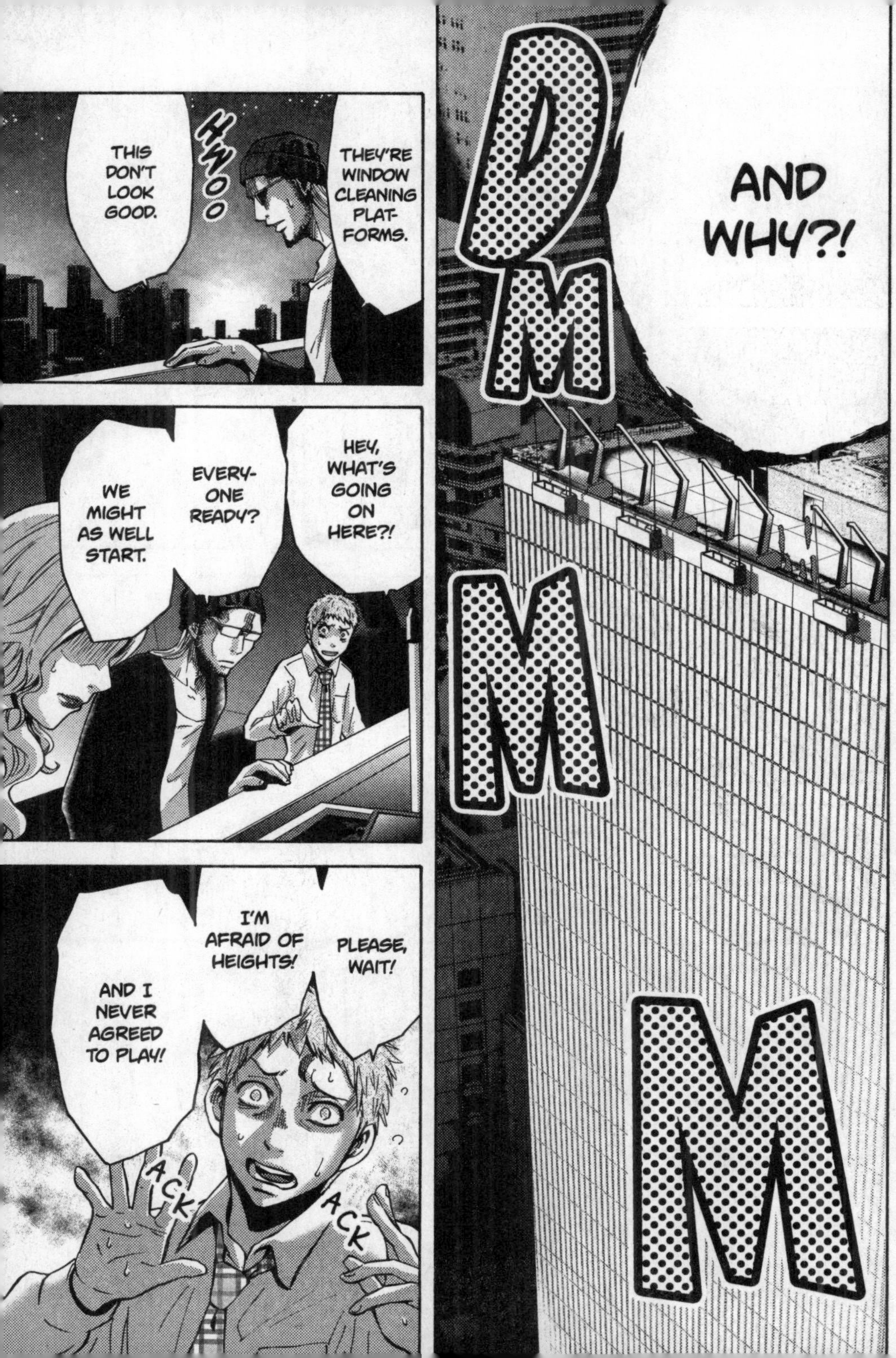
DMMM
AND WHY?!
THEY'RE WINDOW CLEANING PLATFORMS.
HWOO
THIS DON'T LOOK GOOD.
HEY, WHAT'S GOING ON HERE?!
EVERYONE READY?
WE MIGHT AS WELL START.
PLEASE, WAIT!
I'M AFRAID OF HEIGHTS!
AND I NEVER AGREED TO PLAY!
ACK
ACK

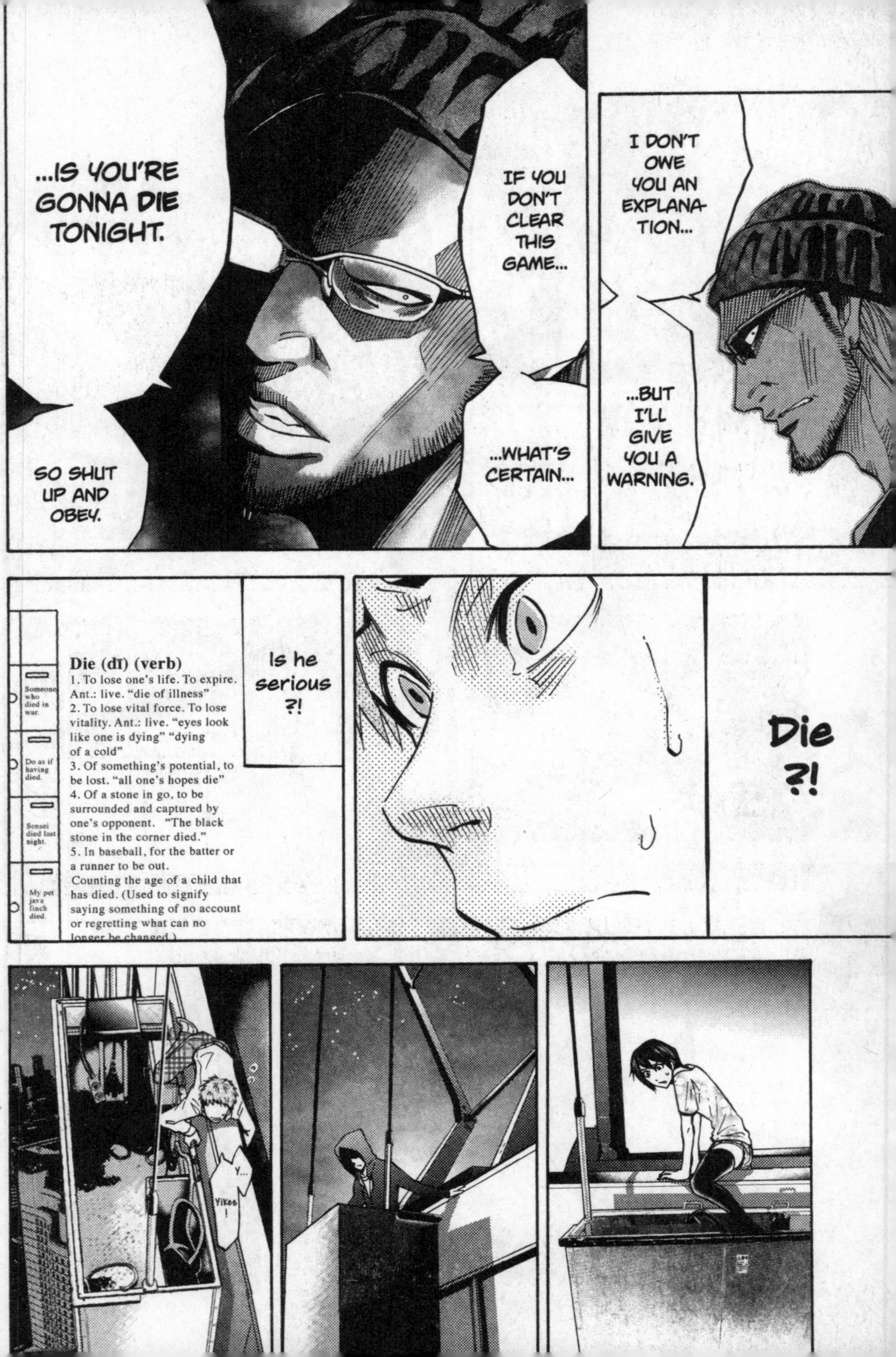
I DON'T OWE YOU AN EXPLANATION...
...BUT I'LL GIVE YOU A WARNING.
IF YOU DON'T CLEAR THIS GAME...
...WHAT'S CERTAIN...
...IS YOU'RE GONNA DIE TONIGHT.
SO SHUT UP AND OBEY.
Die ?!
Is he serious ?!
Die (dī) (verb)
1. To lose one's life. To expire. Ant.: live. "die of illness"
2. To lose vital force. To lose vitality. Ant.: live. "eyes look like one is dying" "dying of a cold"
3. Of something's potential, to be lost. "all one's hopes die"
4. Of a stone in go, to be surrounded and captured by one's opponent. "The black stone in the corner died."
5. In baseball, for the batter or a runner to be out.
Counting the age of a child that has died. (Used to signify saying something of no account or regretting what can no longer be changed.)
Someone who died in war.
Do as if having died.
Sensei died last night.
My pet java finch died.
Y...
Yikes !

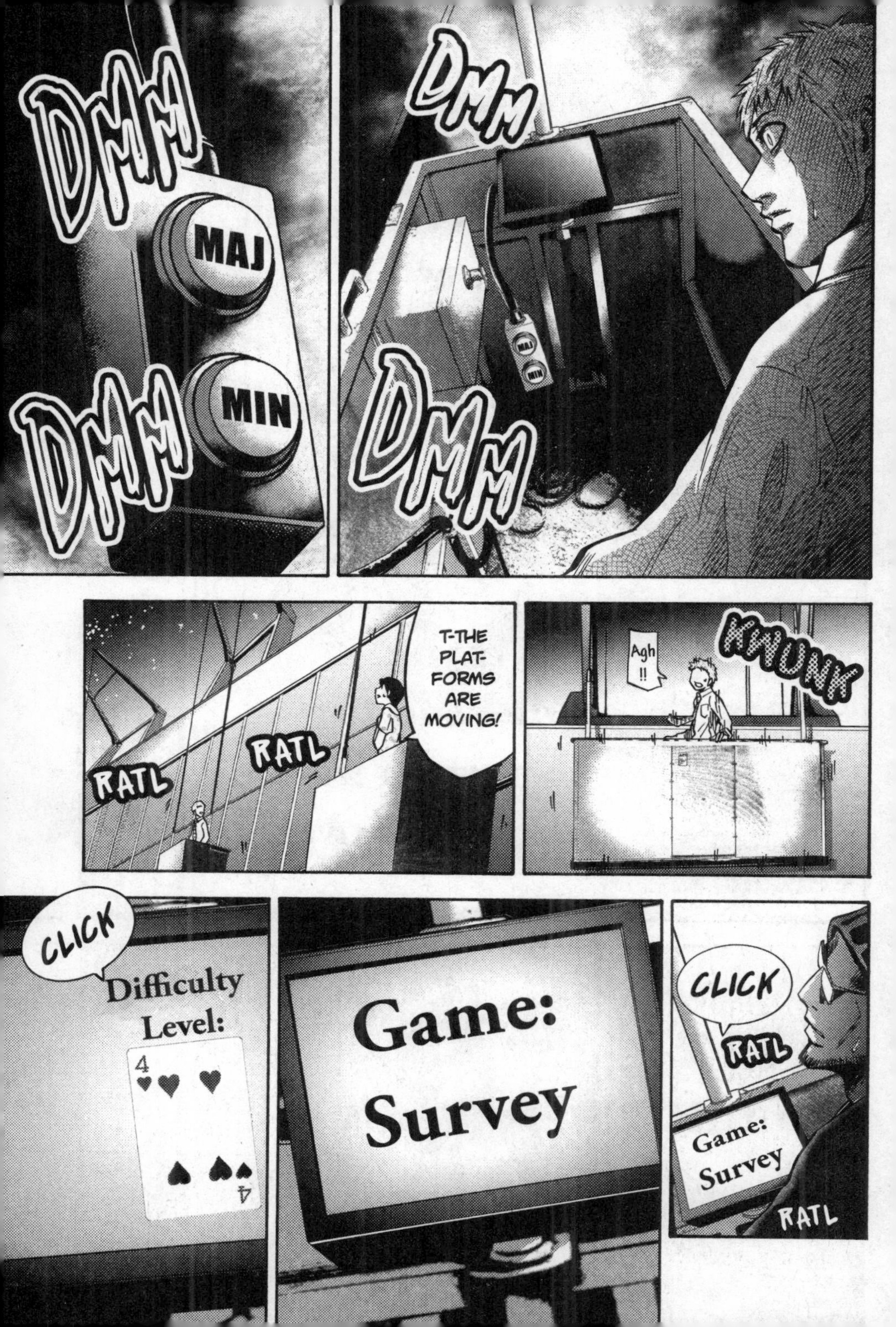
DMM
MAJ
MIN
DMM
DMM
MAJ
DMM
MIN
Agh!!
KWUNK
T-THE PLAT-FORMS ARE MOVING!
RATL
RATL
CLICK
RATL
Game: Survey
RATL
Game: Survey
CLICK
Difficulty Level:
4

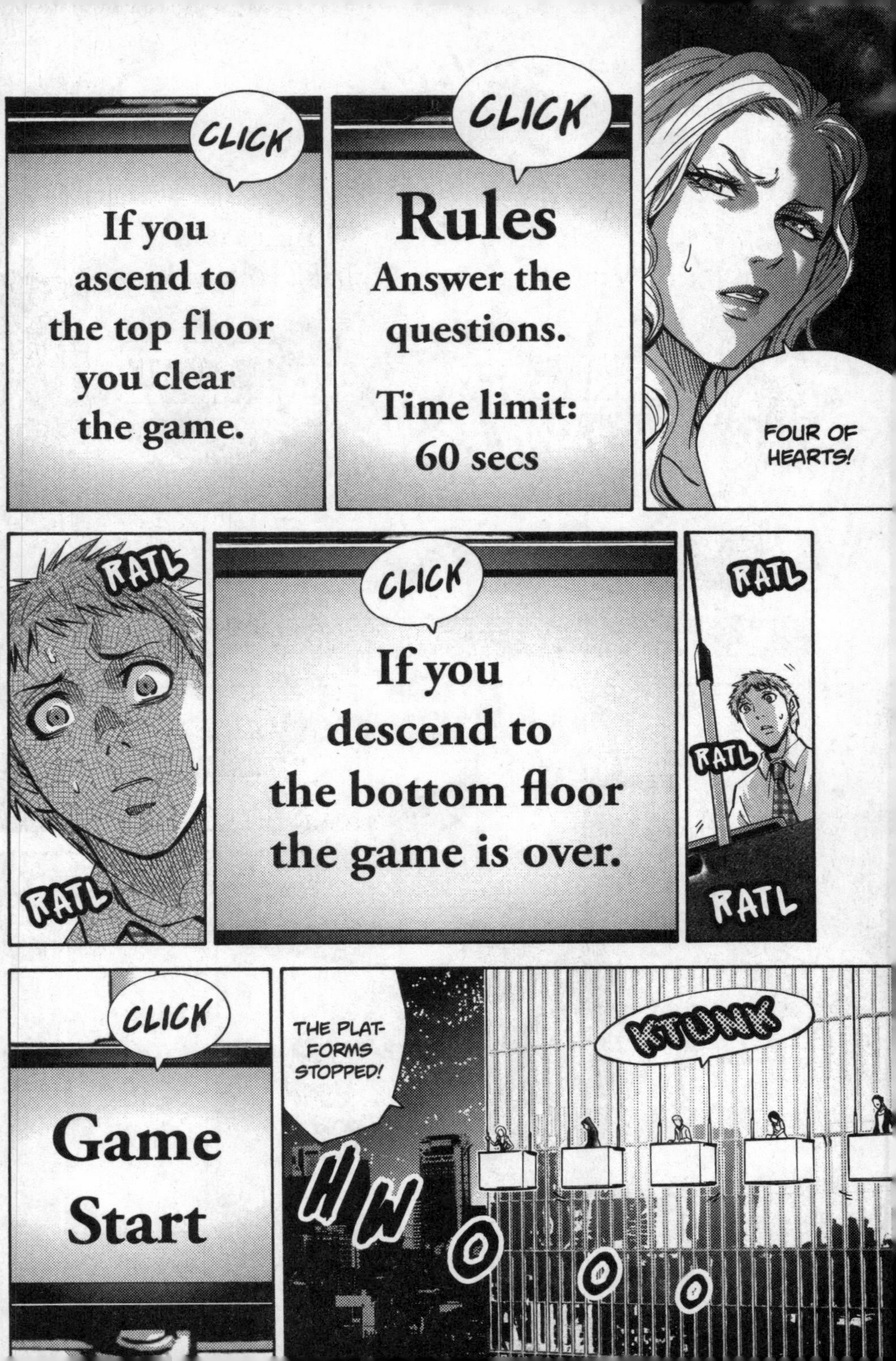
FOUR OF HEARTS!
CLICK
Rules
Answer the questions.
Time limit: 60 secs
CLICK
If you ascend to the top floor you clear the game.
RATL
RATL
RATL
CLICK
If you descend to the bottom floor the game is over.
RATL
RATL
KTONK
THE PLAT-FORMS STOPPED!
HWOOO
CLICK
Game Start

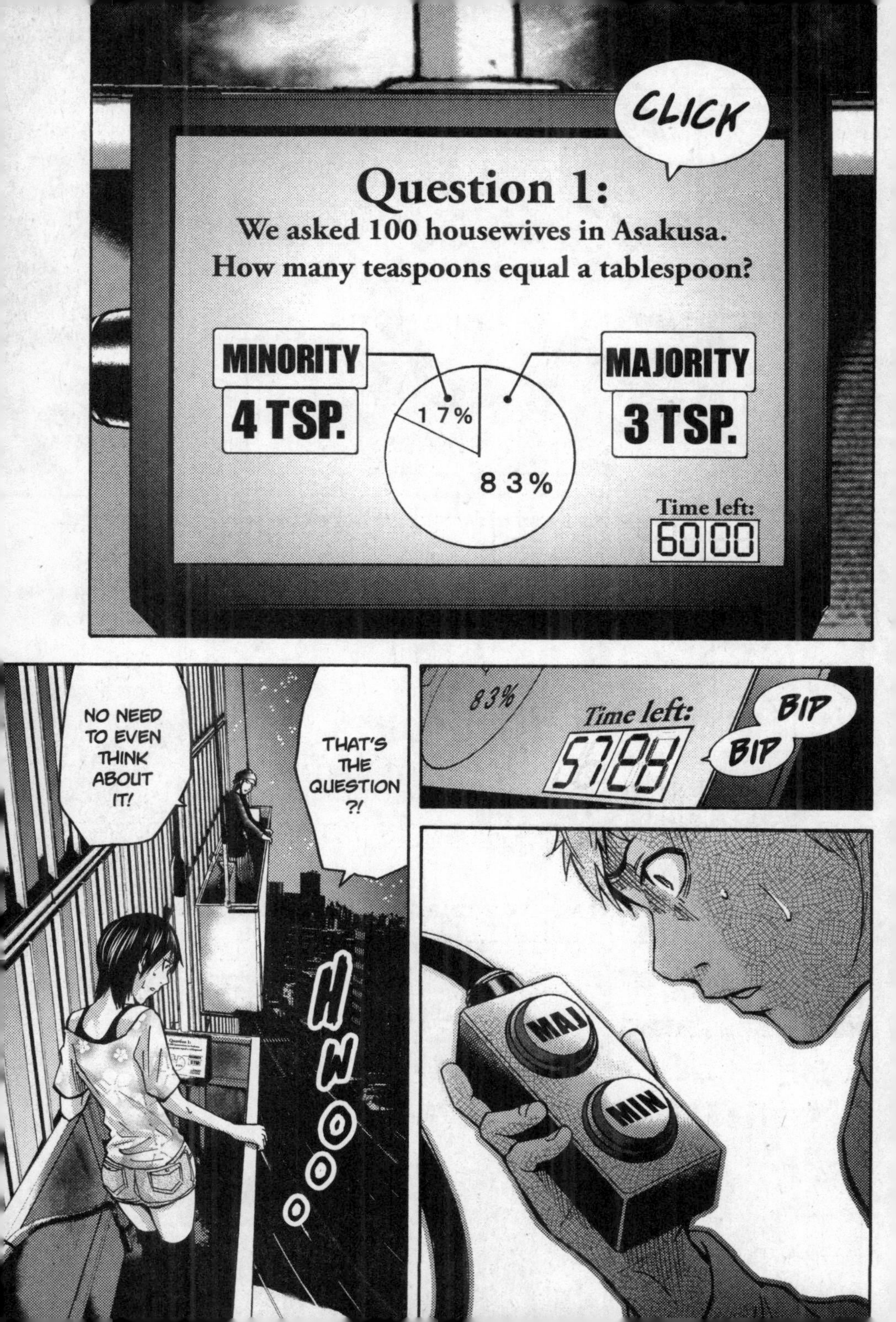
CLICK
Question 1:
We asked 100 housewives in Asakusa.
How many teaspoons equal a tablespoon?
MINORITY
4 TSP.
17%
MAJORITY
3 TSP.
83%
Time left:
60 00
83%
Time left:
57 28
BIP
BIP
MAJ
MIN
THAT'S THE QUESTION?!
NO NEED TO EVEN THINK ABOUT IT!
HWOOOOO

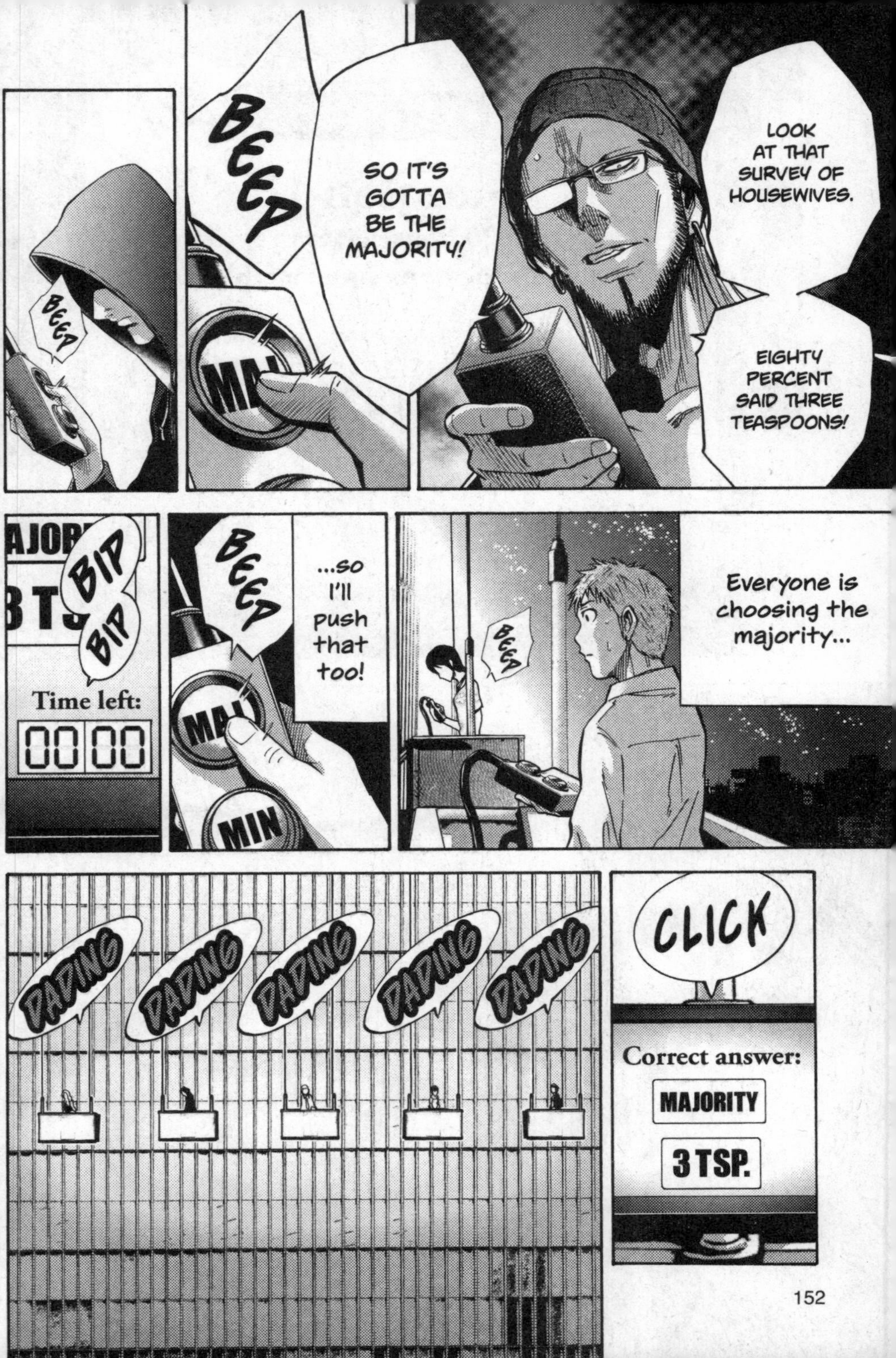
LOOK AT THAT SURVEY OF HOUSEWIVES.
EIGHTY PERCENT SAID THREE TEASPOONS!
BEEP
SO IT'S GOTTA BE THE MAJORITY!
BEEP
Everyone is choosing the majority...
BEEP
BEEP
...so I'll push that too!
MIN
BIP
BIP
Time left:
00 00
CLICK
Correct answer:
MAJORITY
3 TSP.
DADING
DADING
DADING
DADING
DADING

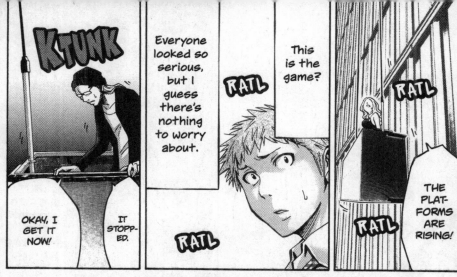

RATL
RATL
THE PLATFORMS ARE RISING!
This is the game?
RATL
Everyone looked so serious, but I guess there's nothing to worry about.
RATL
KTUNK
IT STOPPED.
OKAY, I GET IT NOW!
This office building has 20 floors and we started in the center on the tenth floor.
20F
GAME CLEAR
10F
1 F
GAME OVER
CORRECT
1 FLOOR UP
1 FLOOR DOWN
INCORRECT
I bet we go up one floor for a correct answer and go down one floor for an incorrect answer!
CLICK
Question 2:
We asked 100 mahjong parlor employees in Shinjuku.
How many points is the next call worth?
Self-draw
MINORITY
2000PTS
21%
79%
MAJORITY
2600PTS
Time left:
60:00

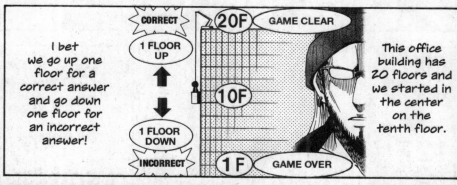

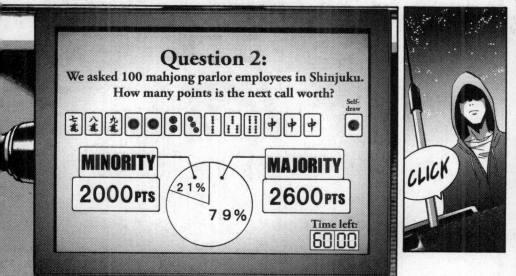

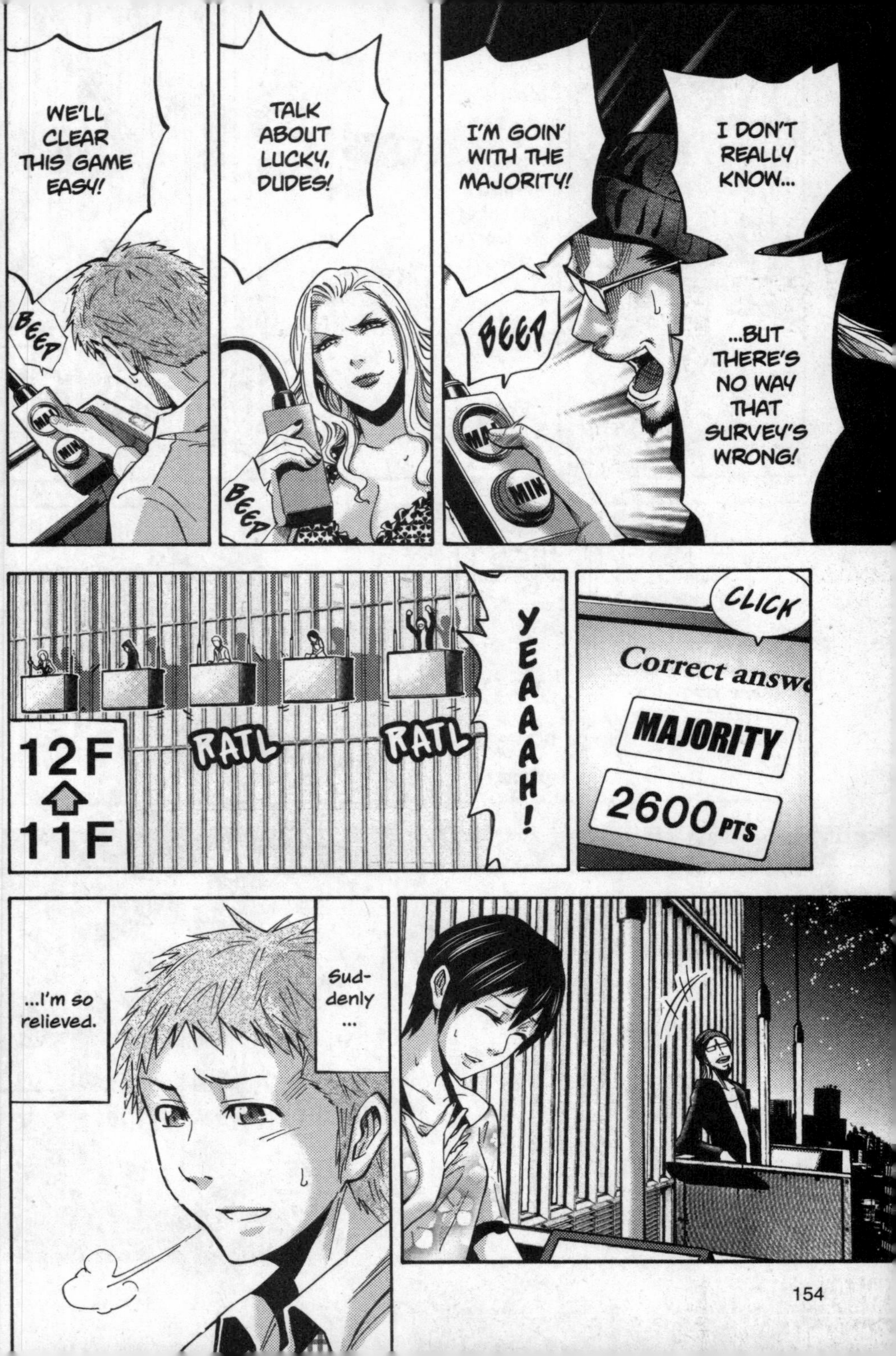
I DON'T REALLY KNOW...
...BUT THERE'S NO WAY THAT SURVEY'S WRONG!
I'M GOIN' WITH THE MAJORITY!
BEEP
TALK ABOUT LUCKY, DUDES!
BEEP
BEEP
WE'LL CLEAR THIS GAME EASY!
BEEP
CLICK
Correct answ
MAJORITY
2600 PTS
YEAAAAH!
RATL
RATL
12F
11F
Sud- denly ...
...I'm so relieved.

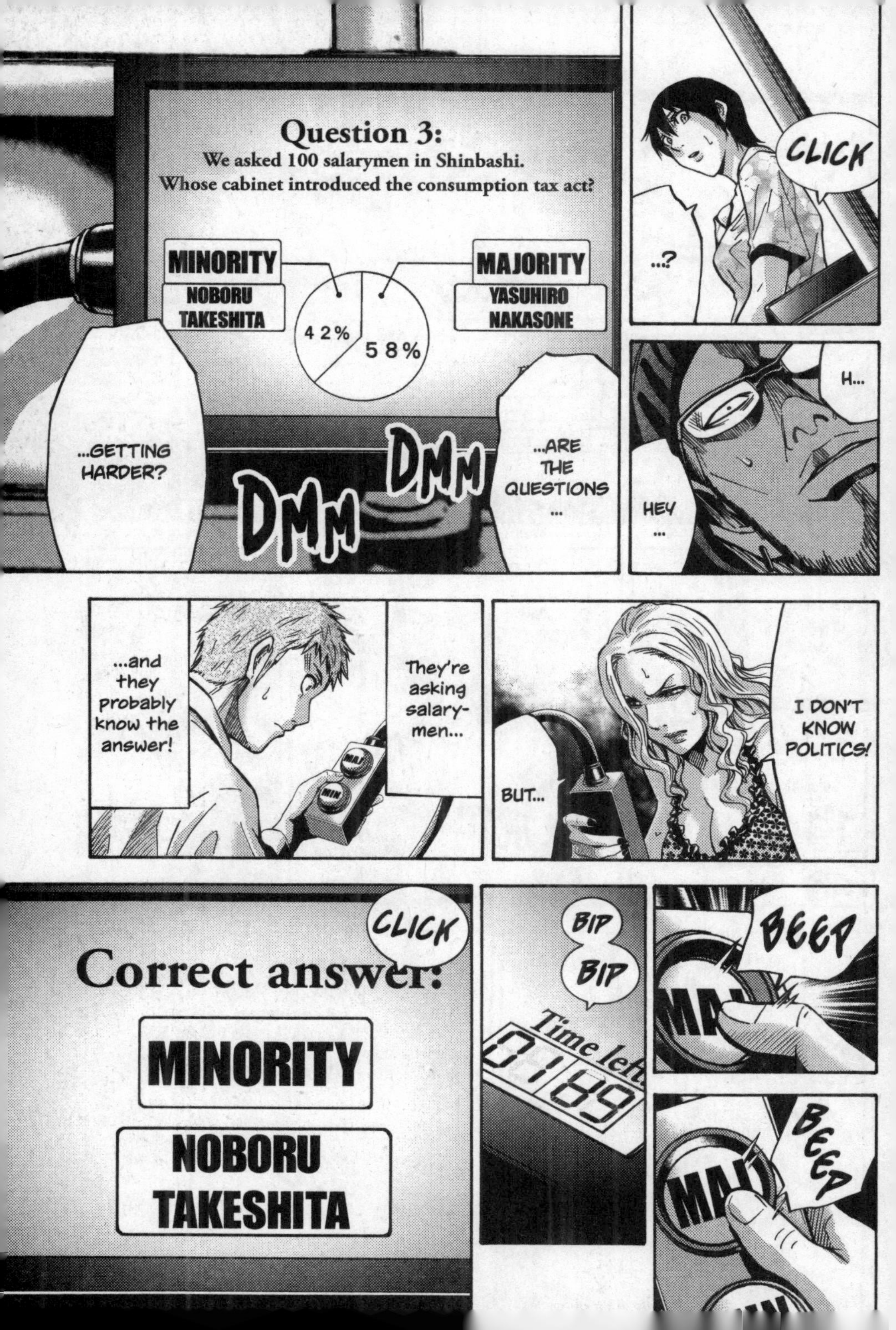
CLICK
...?
H...
HEY ...
Question 3:
We asked 100 salarymen in Shinbashi.
Whose cabinet introduced the consumption tax act?
MAJORITY
YASUHIRO NAKASONE
58%
MINORITY
NOBORU TAKESHITA
42%
...ARE THE QUESTIONS ...
...GETTING HARDER?
DMM
DMM
I DON'T KNOW POLITICS!
BUT...
They're asking salary-men...
...and they probably know the answer!
BEEP
MAJ
BEEP
MAJ
BIP
BIP
Time left
01 89
CLICK
Correct answer:
MINORITY
NOBORU TAKESHITA

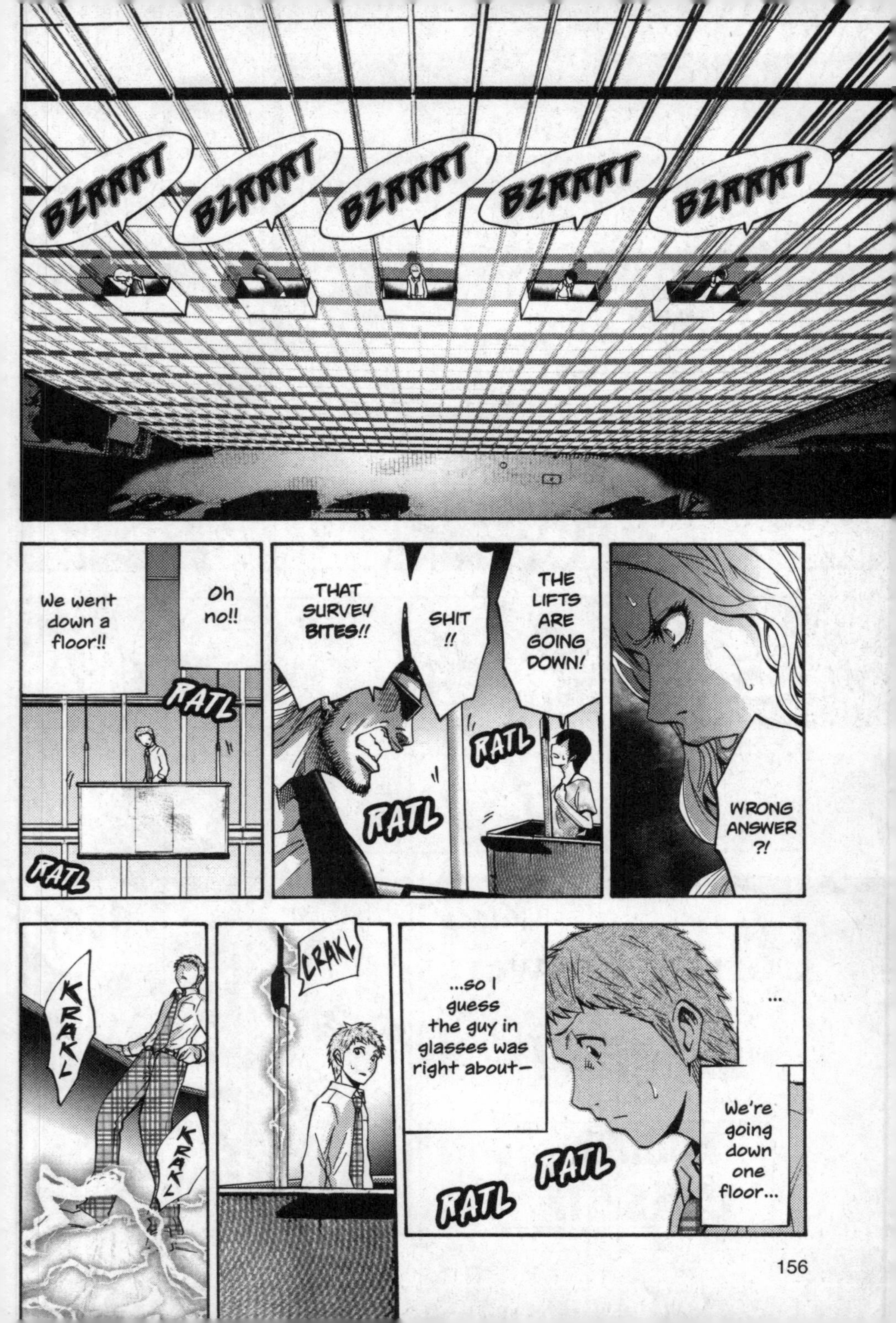
BZRRRT
BZRRRT
BZRRRT
BZRRRT
BZRRRT
WRONG ANSWER?!
THE LIFTS ARE GOING DOWN!
SHIT!!
THAT SURVEY BITES!!
RATL
RATL
Oh no!!
We went down a floor!!
RATL
RATL
...
...so I guess the guy in glasses was right about—
We're going down one floor...
RATL
RATL
CRAK!
KRAK!
KRAK!

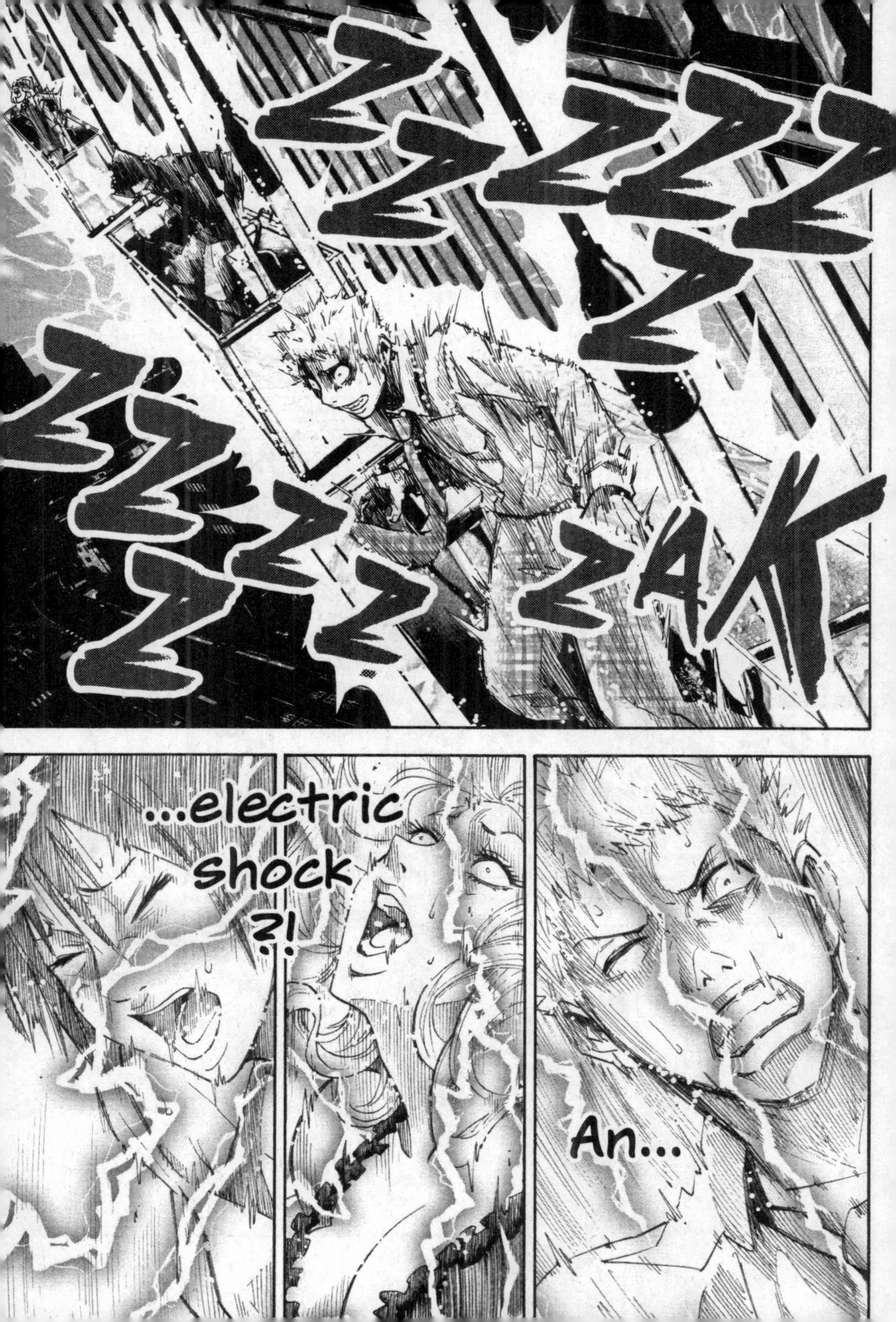
ZZZZZZ
ZZZZZZ
ZAK
An...
...electric shock?!

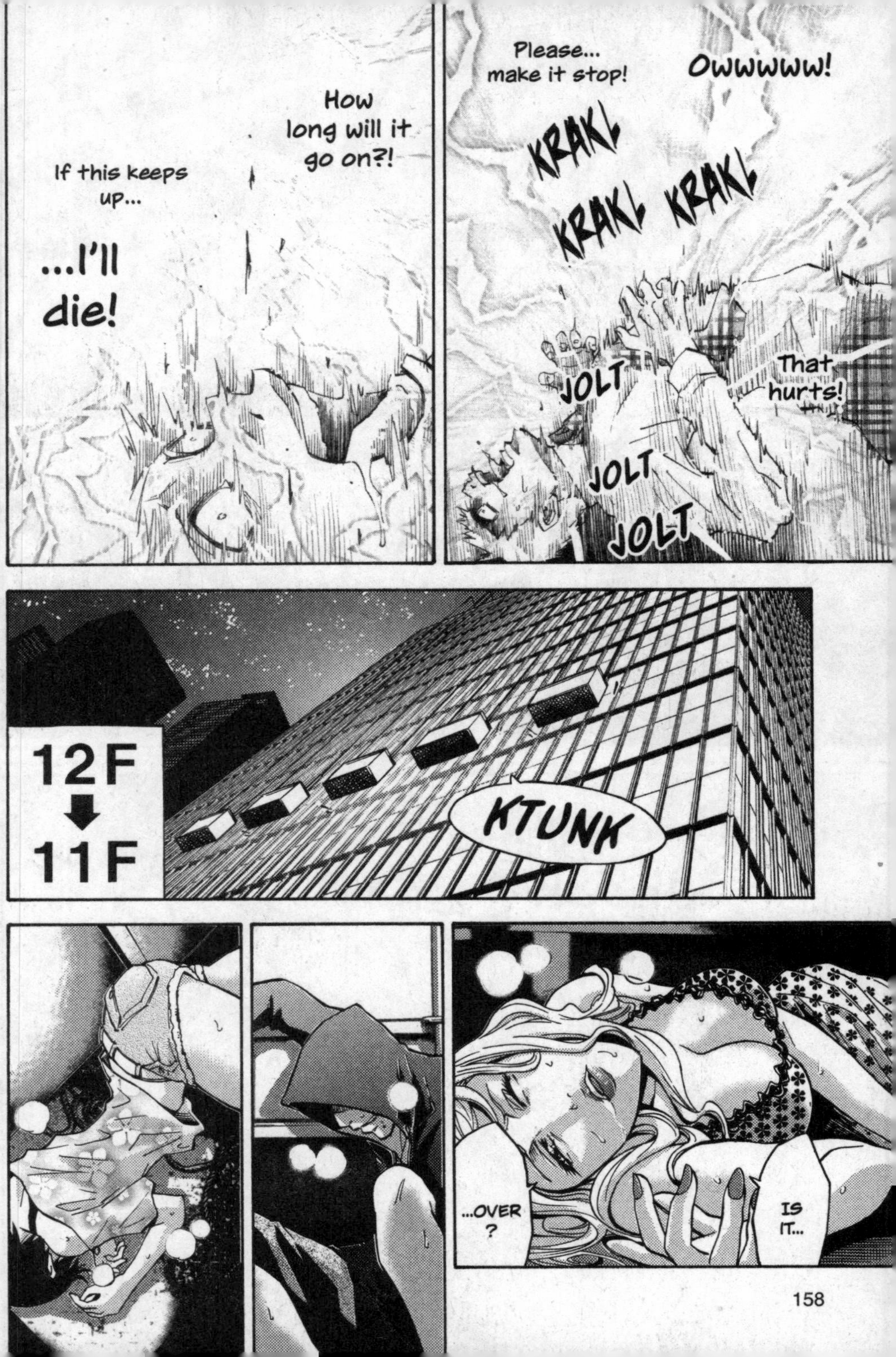
Owwwww!
Please... make it stop!
KRAK! KRAK! KRAK!
That hurts!
JOLT
JOLT
JOLT
How long will it go on?!
If this keeps up...
...I'll die!
KTUNK
12F ↓ 11F
IS IT...
...OVER?

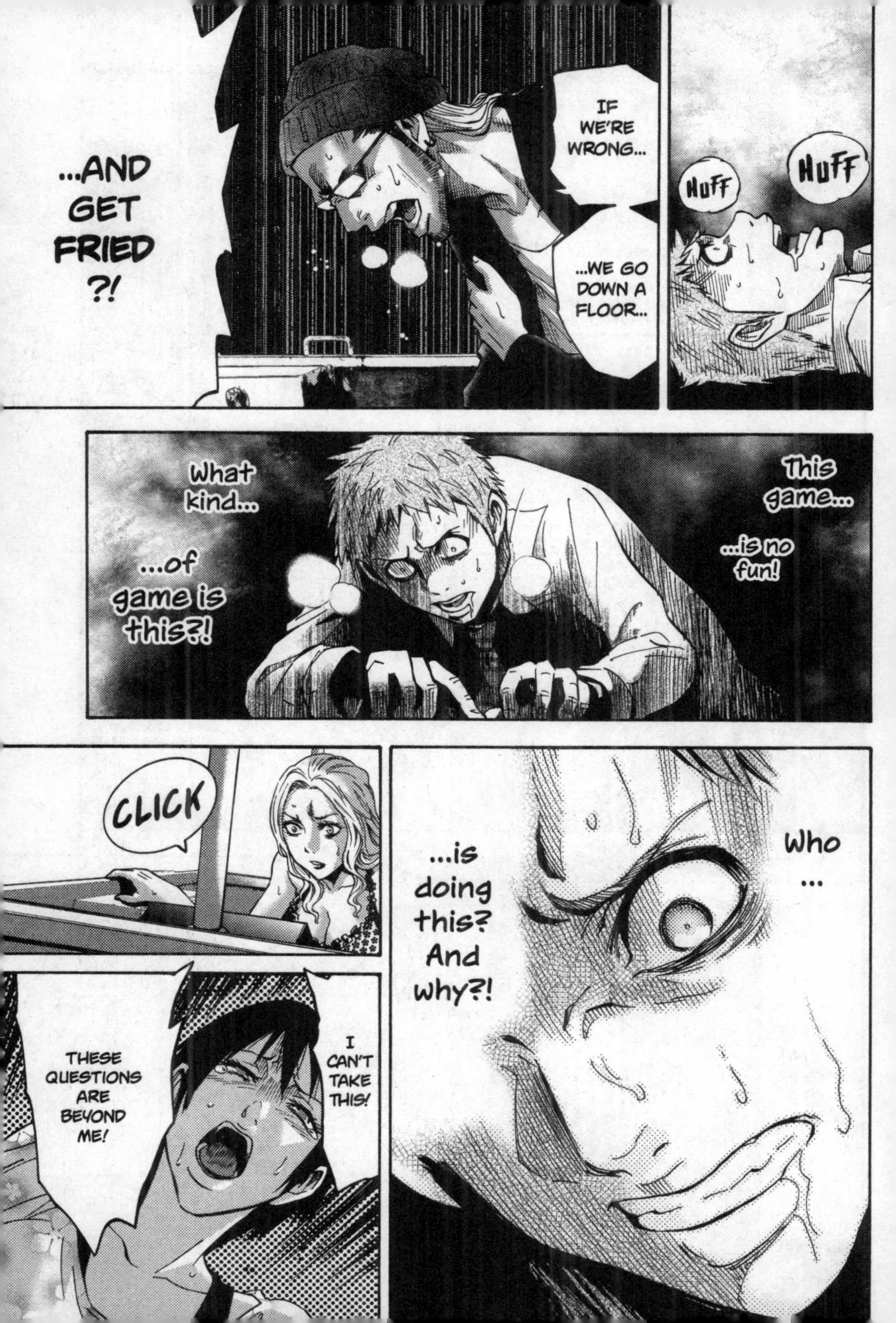
HUFF
HUFF
IF WE'RE WRONG...
...WE GO DOWN A FLOOR...
...AND GET FRIED?!
This game...
...is no fun!
What kind...
...of game is this?!
Who...
...is doing this? And why?!
CLICK
I CAN'T TAKE THIS!
THESE QUESTIONS ARE BEYOND ME!

Question 4:
We asked 100 music conservatory students in Ueno. Which romantic composer is known for such works as "Mazeppa" and "Feux follets"?
MAJORITY
FRANZ LISZT
55%
MINORITY
FELIX MENDELSSOHN
45%
Time left:
BIP
BIP
No matter what...
...I don't want...
... another shock!
TRMBL
TRMBL
I'd rather die...
...than suffer that pain again!
TRMBL
TRMBL
Which is it?!
MAJ
FR
55%
45%
Which one...
MAJ
MIN
...is the correct answer?!

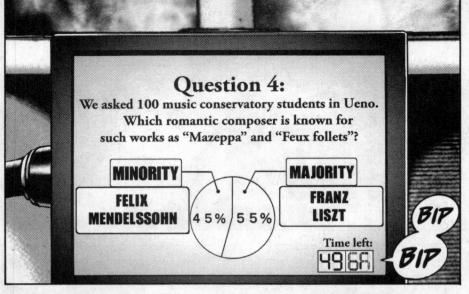

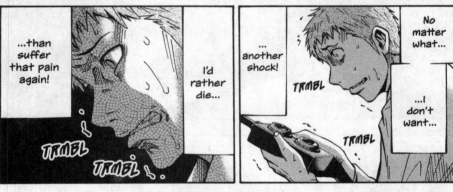

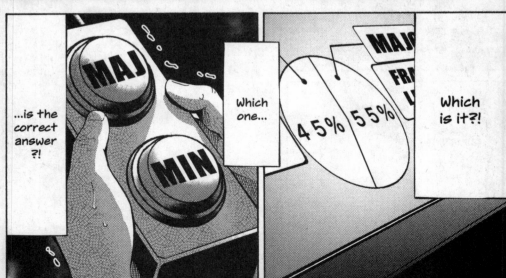

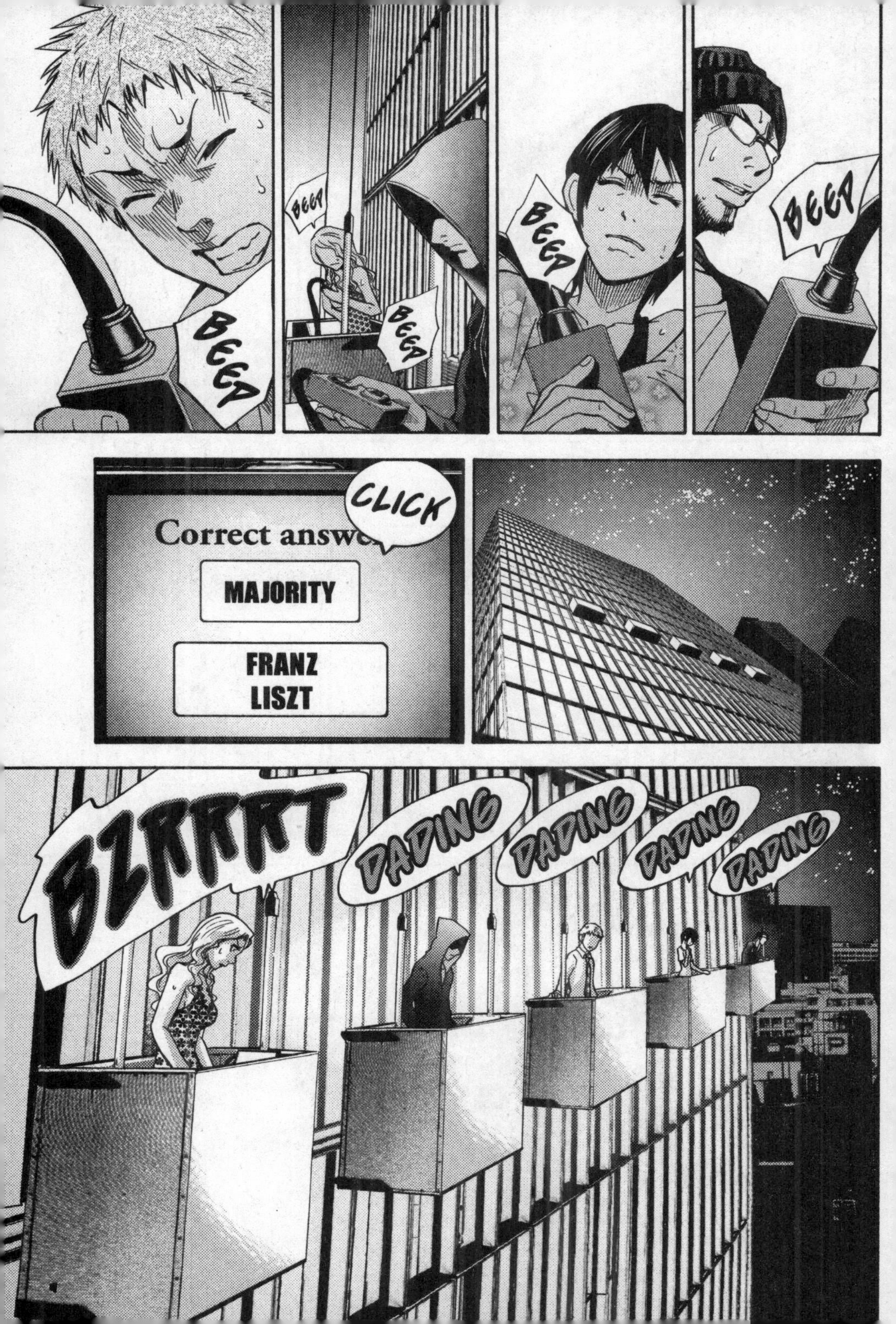
BEEP
BEEP
BEEP
BEEP
BEEP
CLICK
Correct answ
MAJORITY
FRANZ LISZT
BZRRRT
DADING
DADING
DADING
DADING

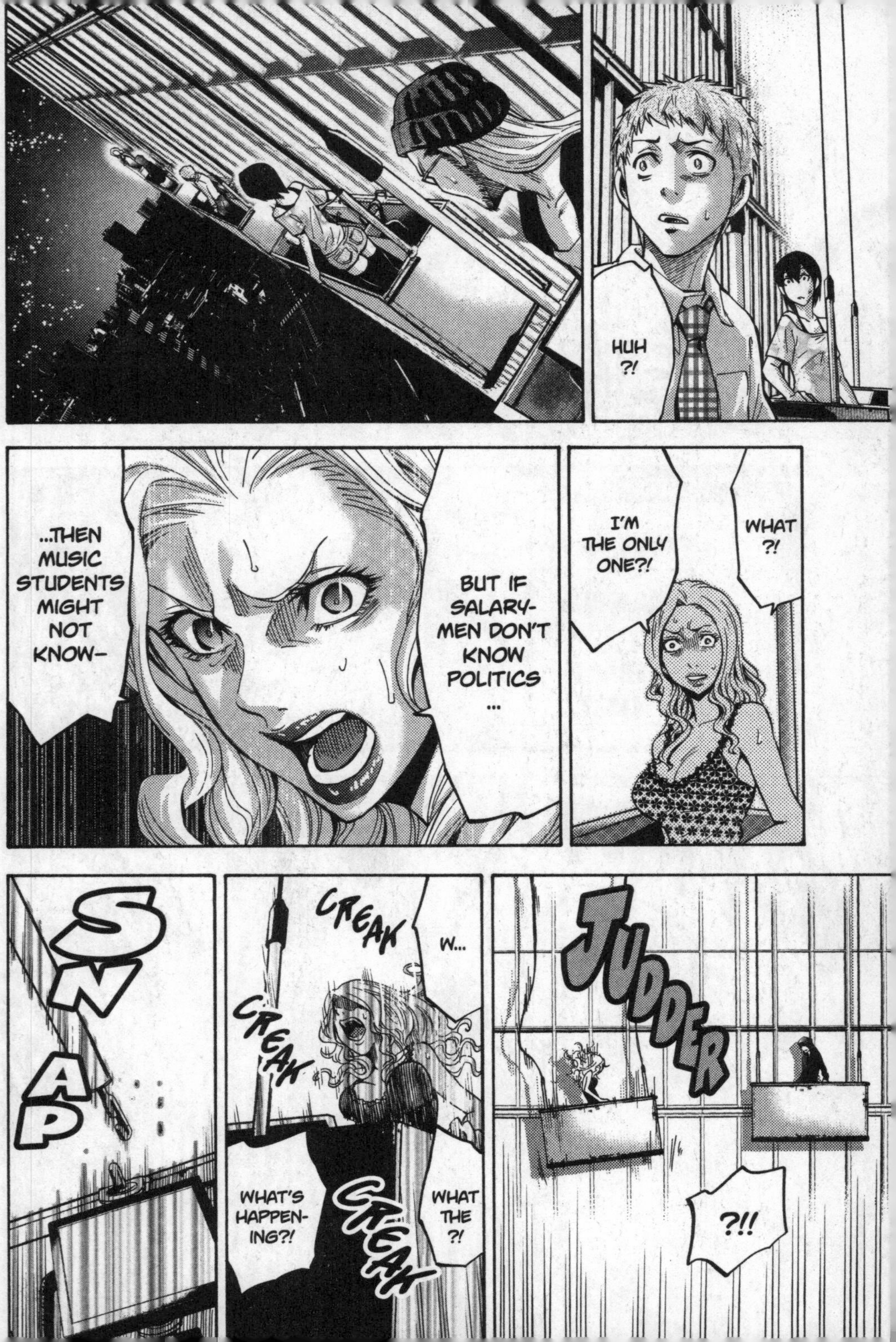
HUH ?!
WHAT ?!
I'M THE ONLY ONE?!
BUT IF SALARY-MEN DON'T KNOW POLITICS ...
...THEN MUSIC STUDENTS MIGHT NOT KNOW-
JUDDER
?!!
CREAK
W...
CREAK
WHAT THE ?!
WHAT'S HAPPEN-ING?!
CREAK
SNAP

KLATTER
KLATTER
KLATTER
KLATTER
KLATTER
KLATTER
KYAAA...
KLATTER
BANG
KLANG
KLANK
...AHHH!

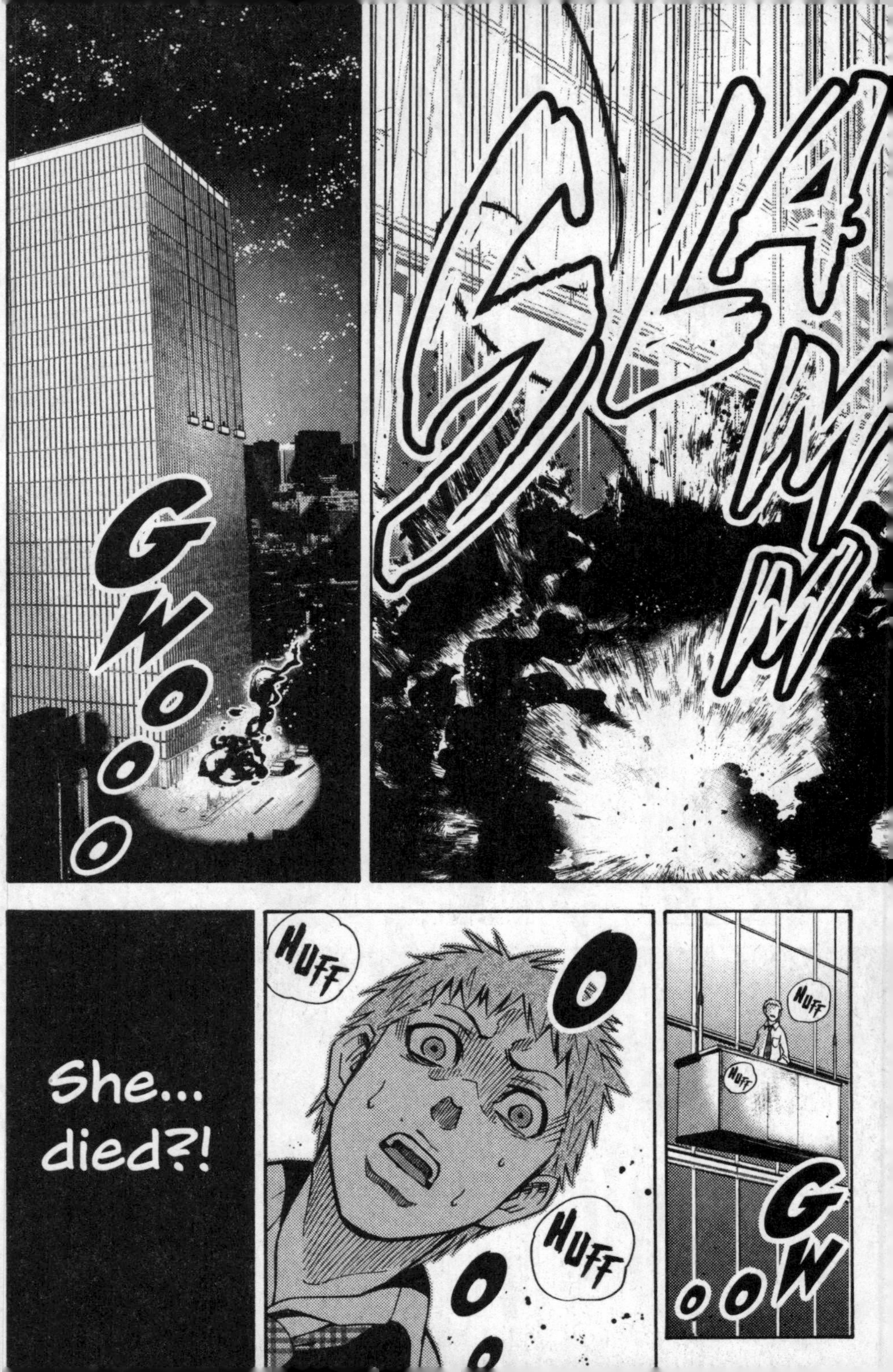
GLAMMM
GWOOOO
GWOO
HUFF
HUFF
HUFF
O
HUFF
O
She... died?!

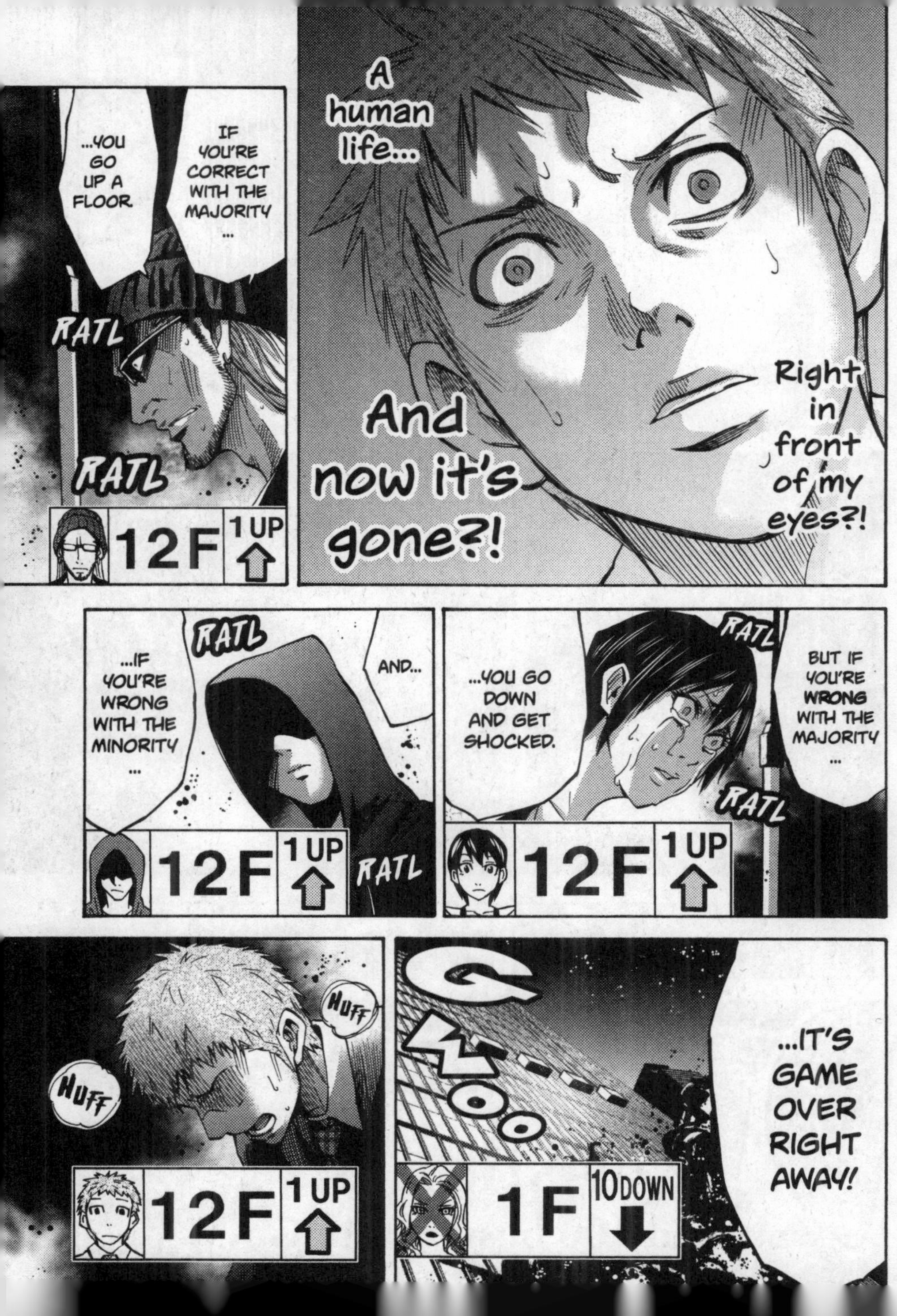
A human life...
And now it's gone?!
Right in front of my eyes?!
IF YOU'RE CORRECT WITH THE MAJORITY ...
...YOU GO UP A FLOOR
RATL
RATL
12F
1 UP
BUT IF YOU'RE WRONG WITH THE MAJORITY ...
...YOU GO DOWN AND GET SHOCKED.
RATL
RATL
12F
1 UP
AND...
...IF YOU'RE WRONG WITH THE MINORITY ...
RATL
RATL
12F
1 UP
...IT'S GAME OVER RIGHT AWAY!
GWOO
1F
10 DOWN
HUFF
HUFF
12F
1 UP

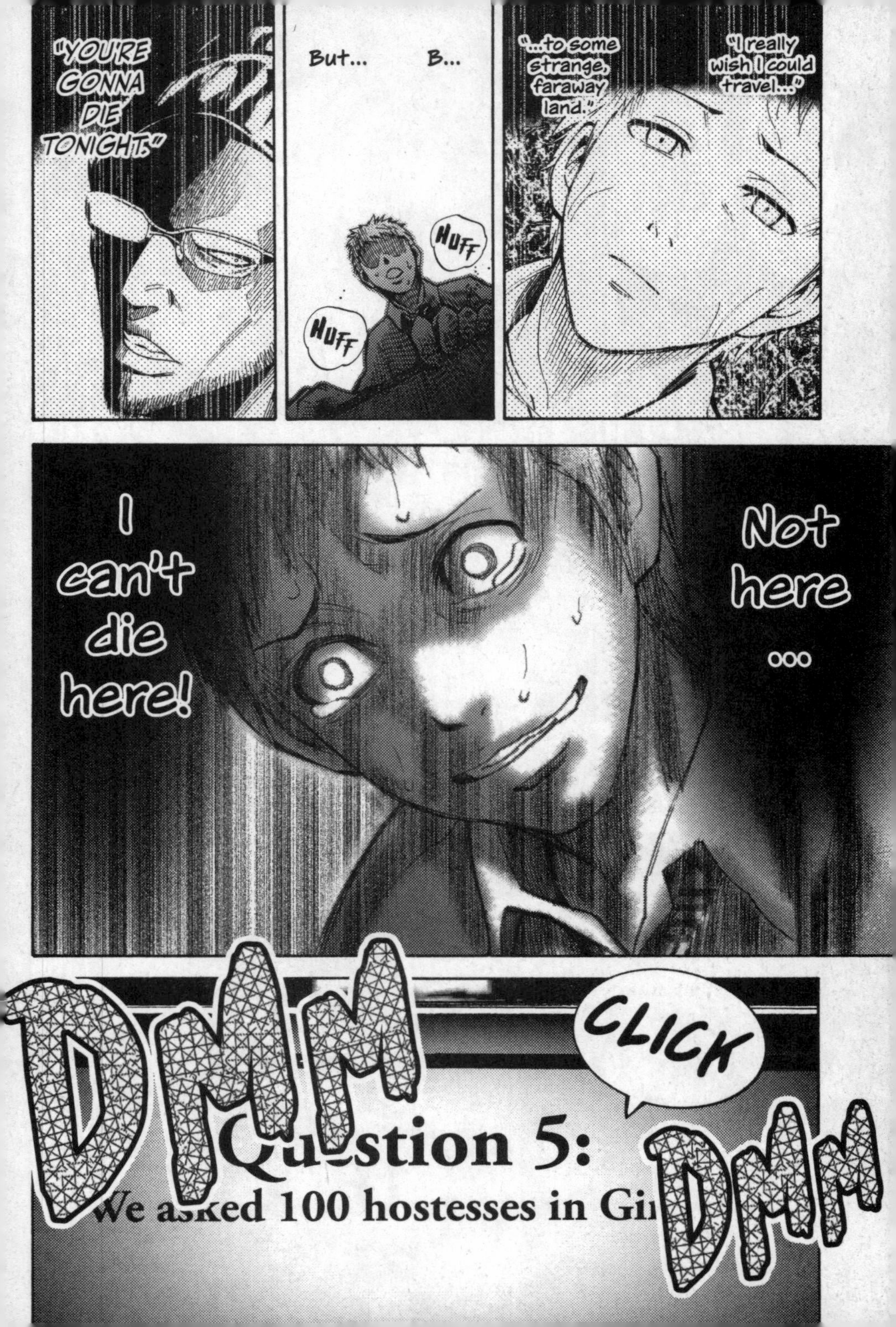
"I really wish I could travel..."
"...to some strange, faraway land."
But...
B...
HUFF
HUFF
"YOU'RE GONNA DIE TONIGHT."
Not here ...
I can't die here!
CLICK
DMM
DMM
Question 5:
We asked 100 hostesses in Gi

I was traveling in Asia and as I was leaving a village where I had stayed, someone who had looked after me said, "Don't forget us." To them, dying didn't mean physical death. It meant disappearing from memory.

Do you occasionally recall the people who were important to you?

— HARO ASO

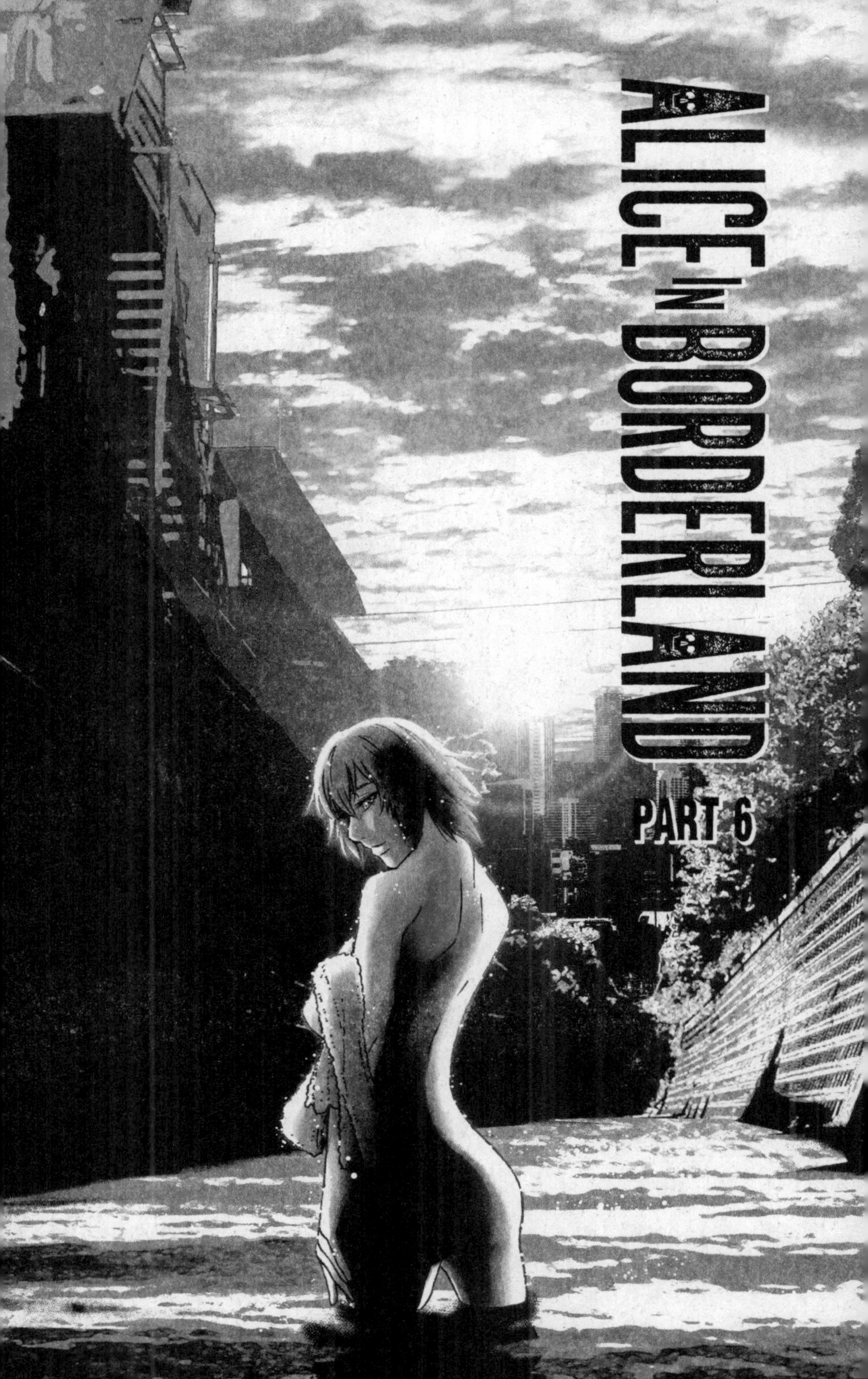
ALICE IN BORDERLAND
PART 6

ALICE IN BORDERLAND

PART 6

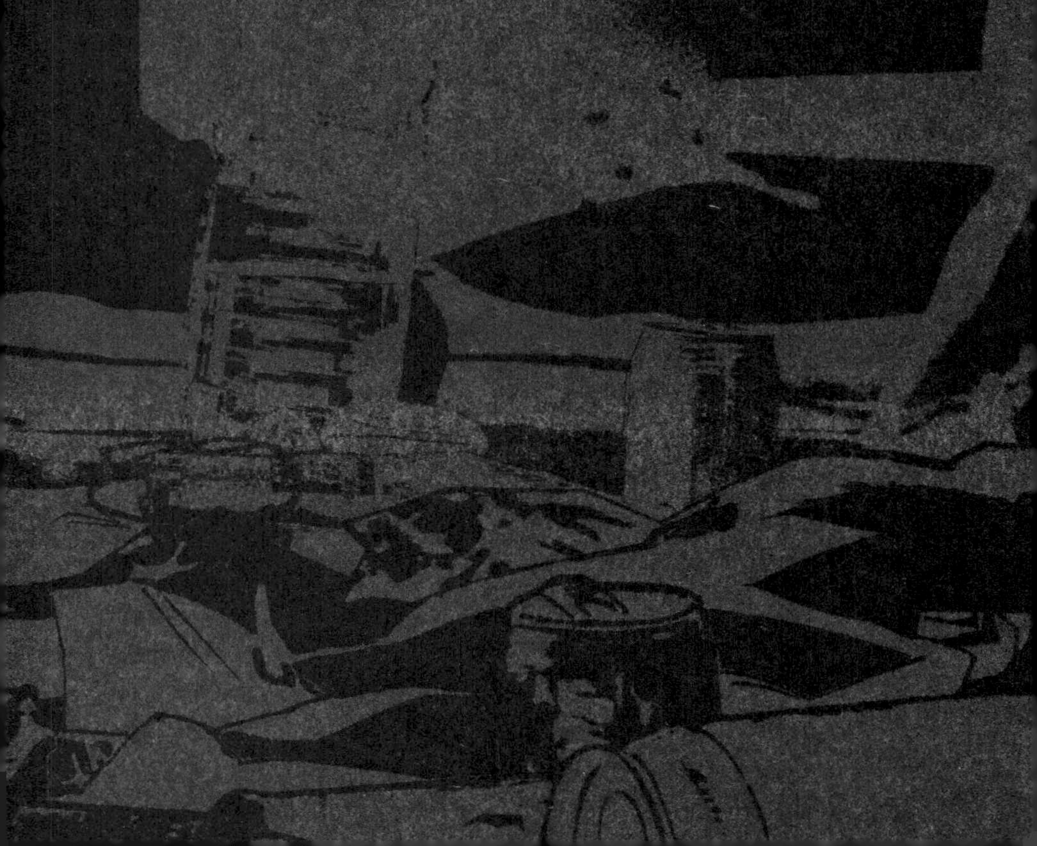

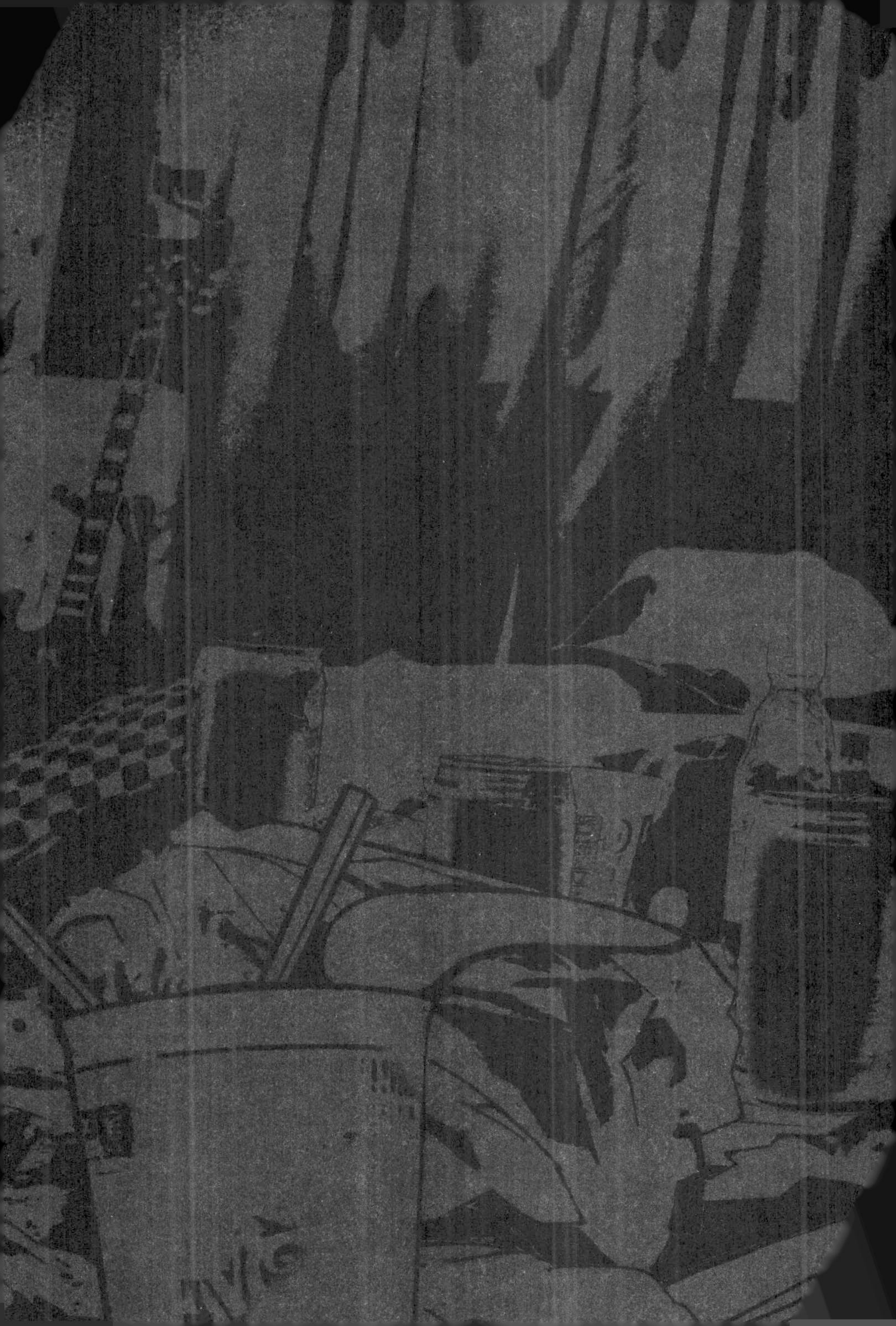

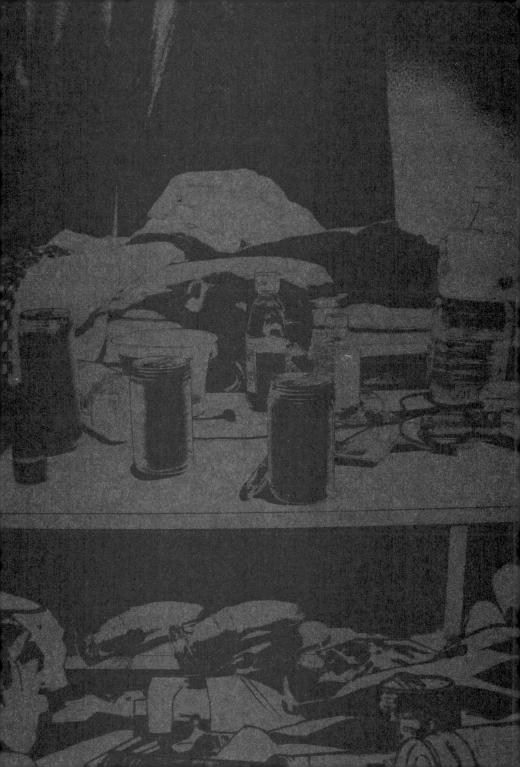

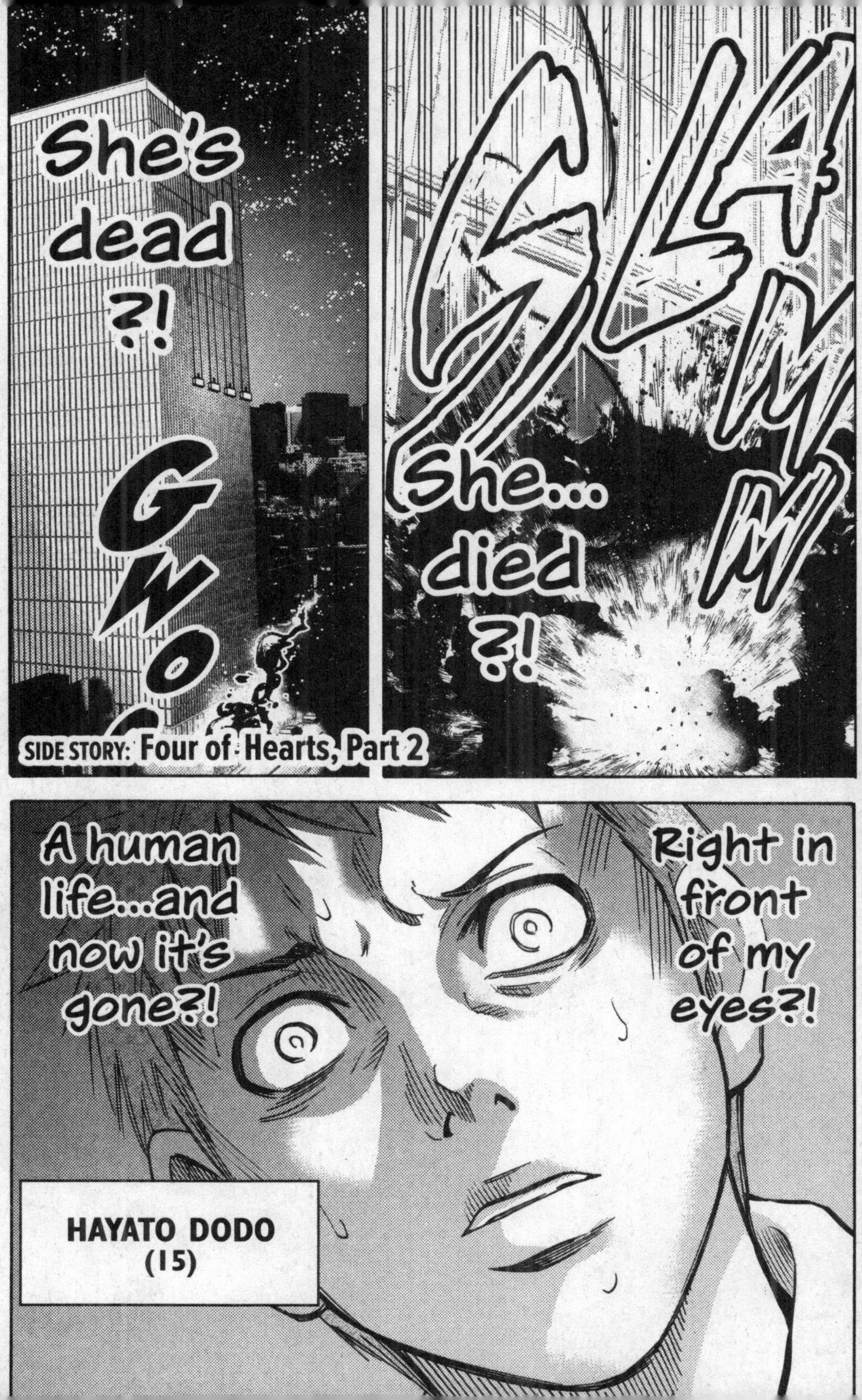
GLAMMM
She... died ?!
She's dead ?!
GWO
SIDE STORY: Four of Hearts, Part 2
Right in front of my eyes?!
A human life...and now it's gone?!
HAYATO DODO (15)

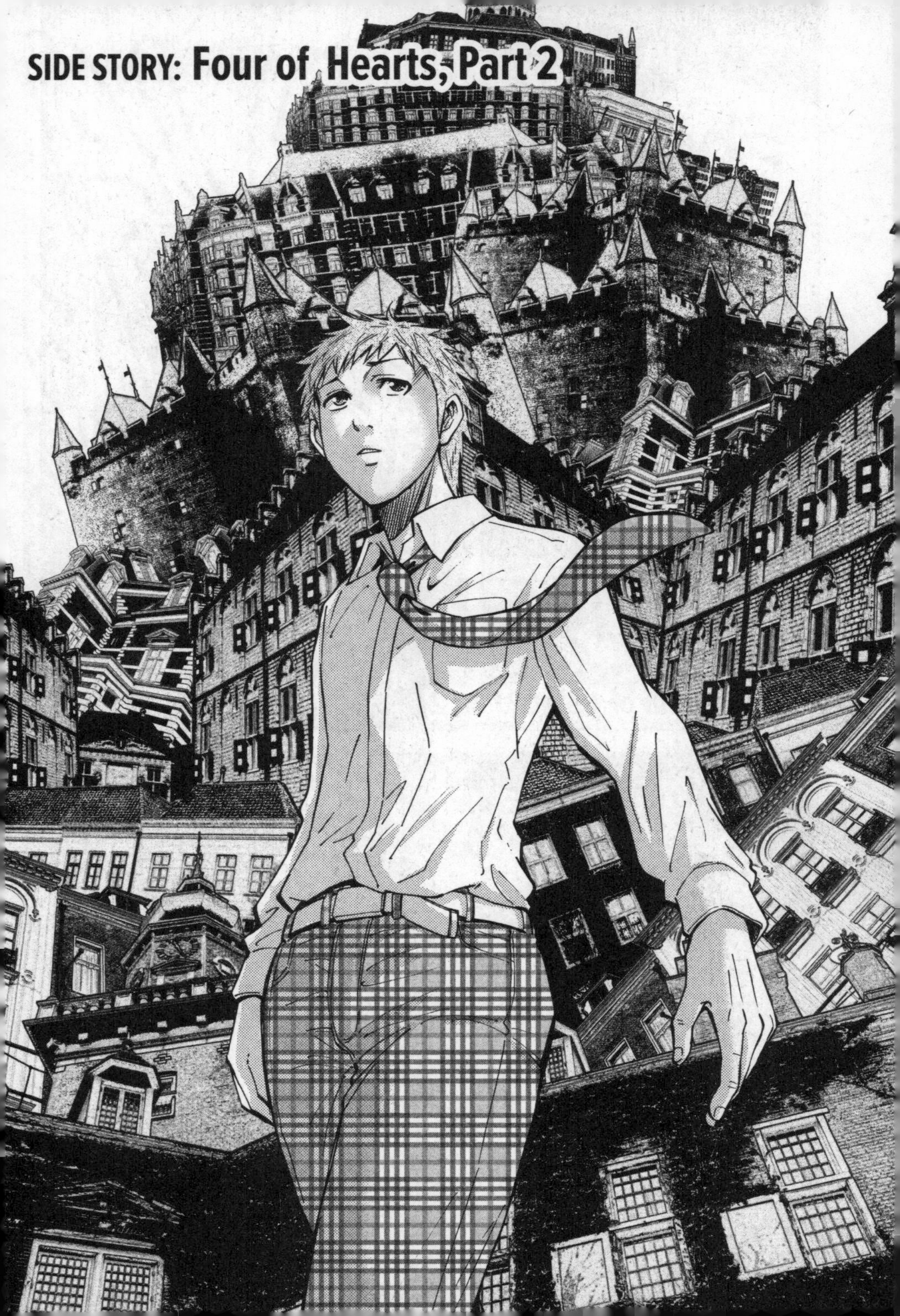
SIDE STORY: Four of Hearts, Part 2

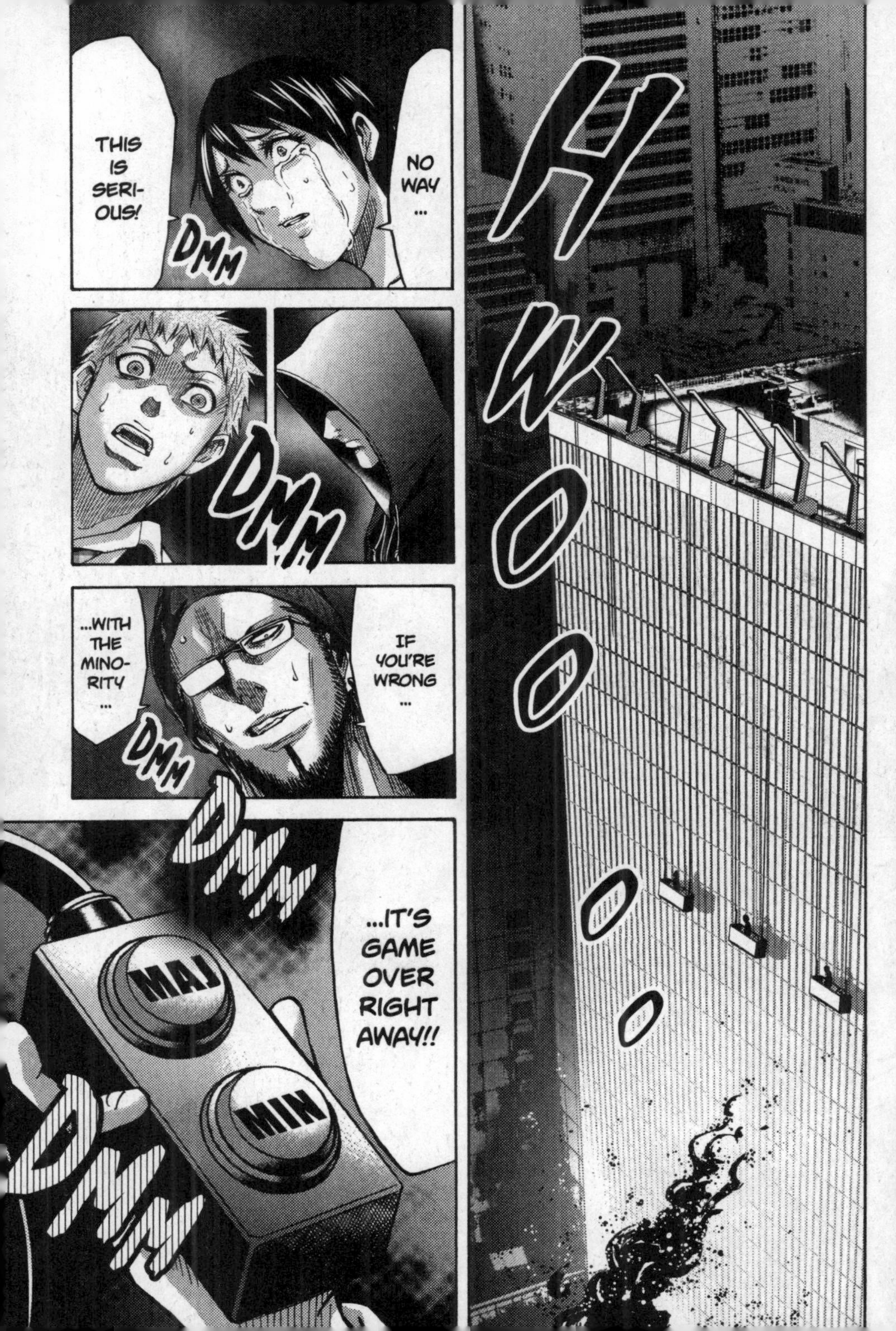
HWOOOOO
NO WAY ...
THIS IS SERI-OUS!
DMM
DMM
IF YOU'RE WRONG ...
...WITH THE MINO-RITY ...
DMM
...IT'S GAME OVER RIGHT AWAY!!
DMM
MAJ
MIN
DMM

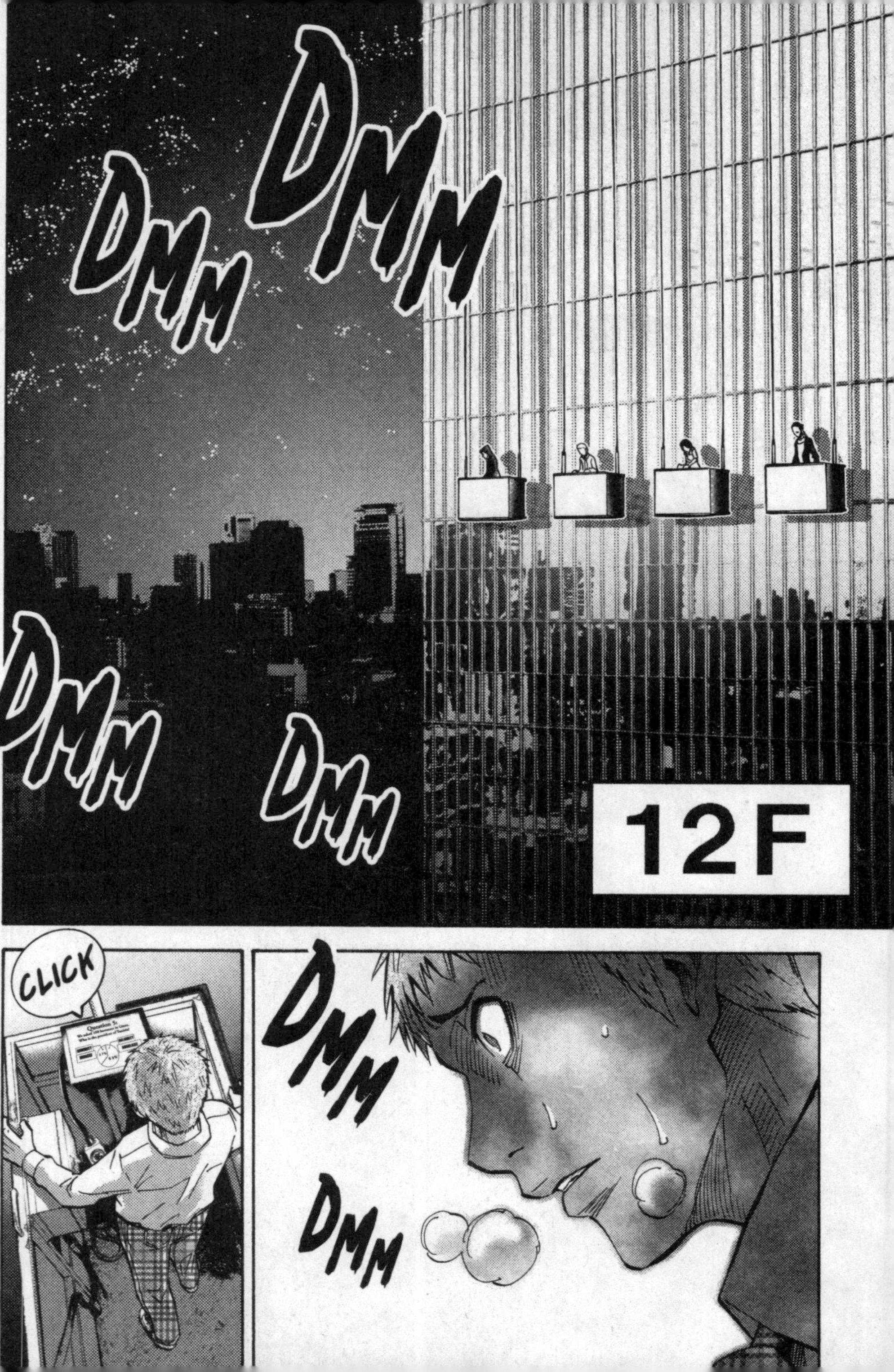
DMM
DMM
DMM
DMM
12F
DMM
DMM
CLICK

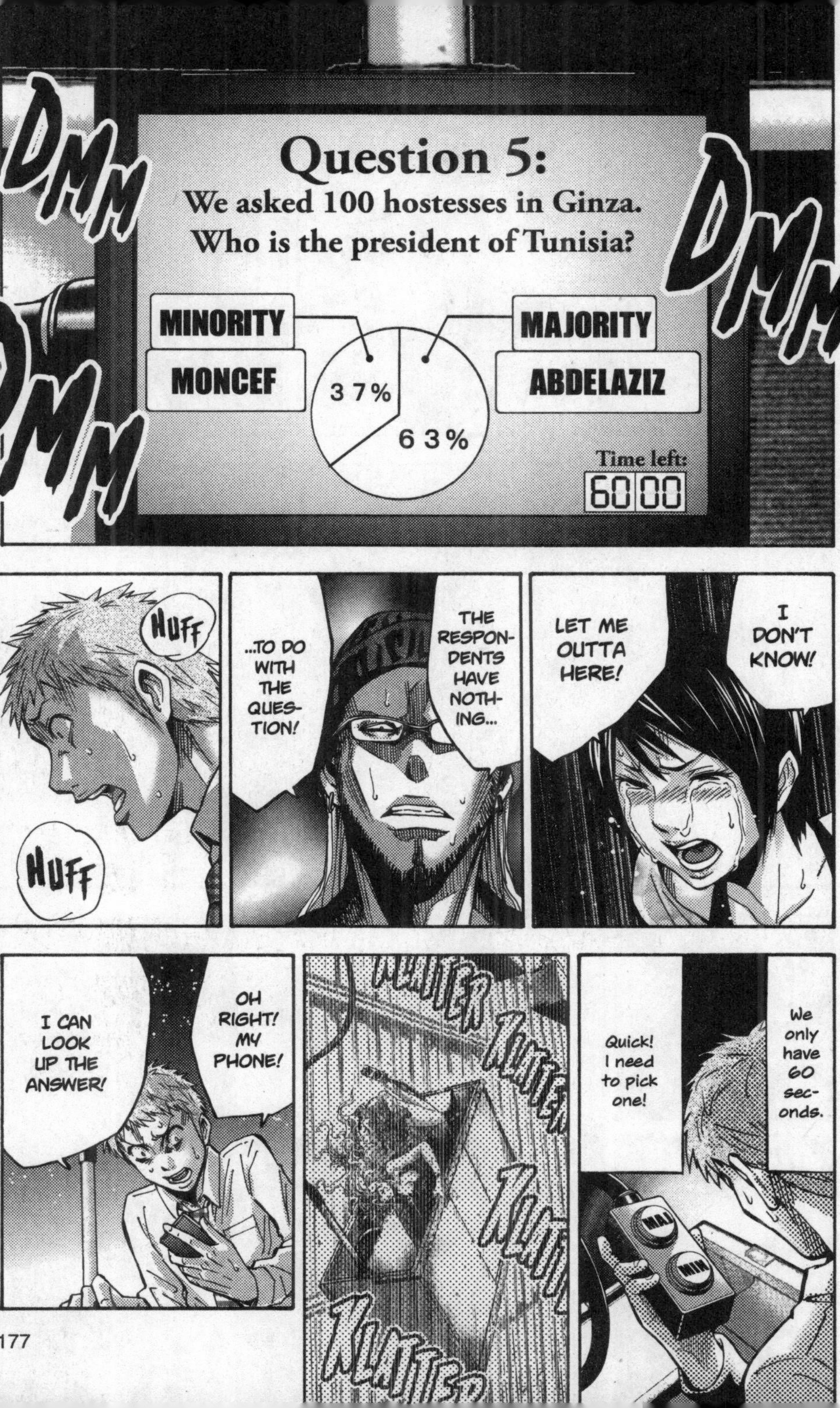
DMM
DMM
Question 5:
We asked 100 hostesses in Ginza.
Who is the president of Tunisia?
MAJORITY
ABDELAZIZ
MINORITY
MONCEF
37%
63%
Time left:
60 00
DMM
I DON'T KNOW!
LET ME OUTTA HERE!
THE RESPONDENTS HAVE NOTHING...
...TO DO WITH THE QUESTION!
HUFF
HUFF
We only have 60 seconds.
Quick! I need to pick one!
MAJ
MIN
OH RIGHT! MY PHONE!
I CAN LOOK UP THE ANSWER!

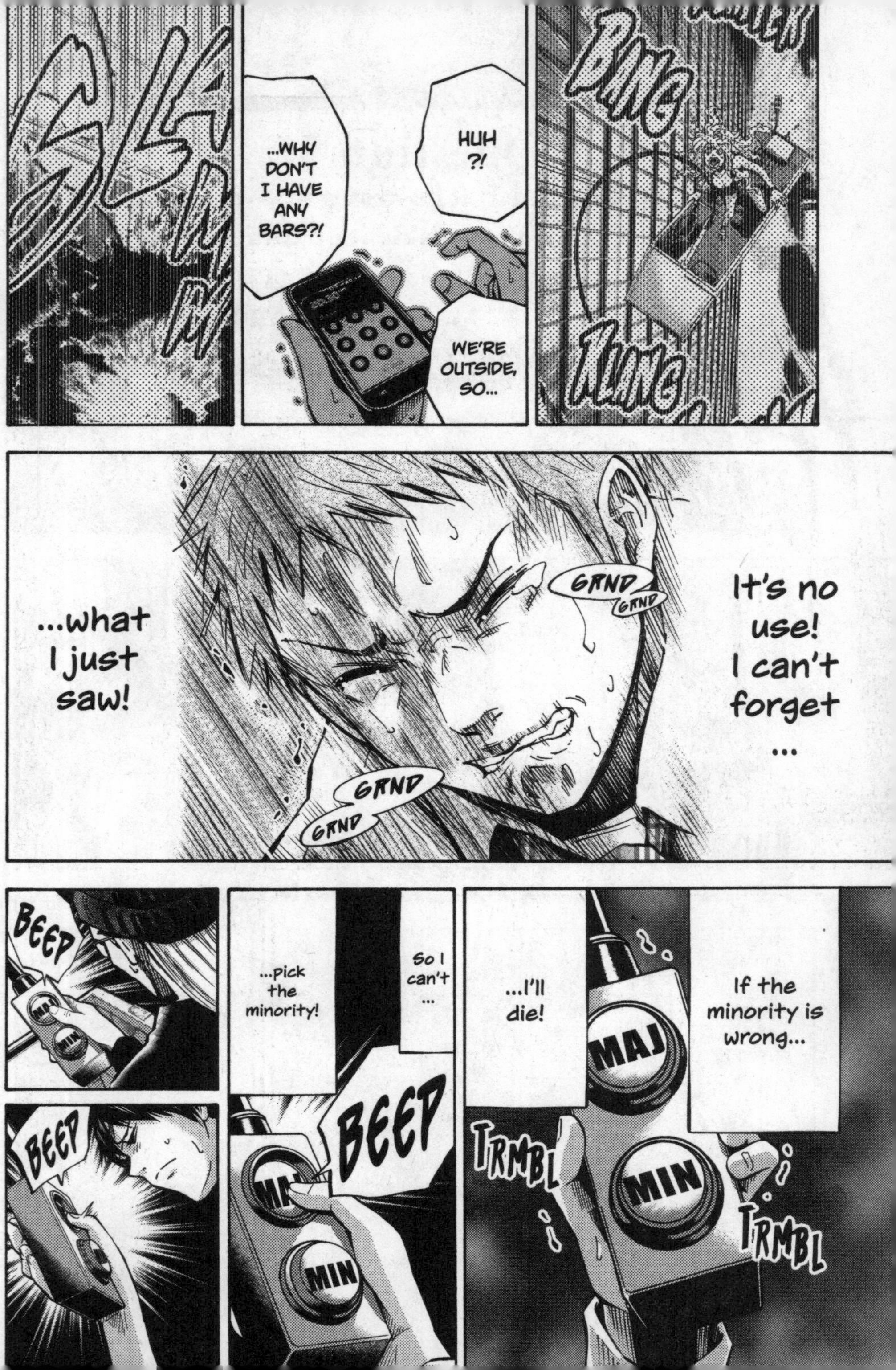
BANG
CLANG
HUH ?!
...WHY DON'T I HAVE ANY BARS?!
WE'RE OUTSIDE, SO...
It's no use! I can't forget ...
GRND
GRND
...what I just saw!
GRND
GRND
If the minority is wrong...
...I'll die!
MAJ
MIN
TRMBL
TRMBL
So I can't ...
...pick the minority!
BEEP
MIN
BEEP
BEEP

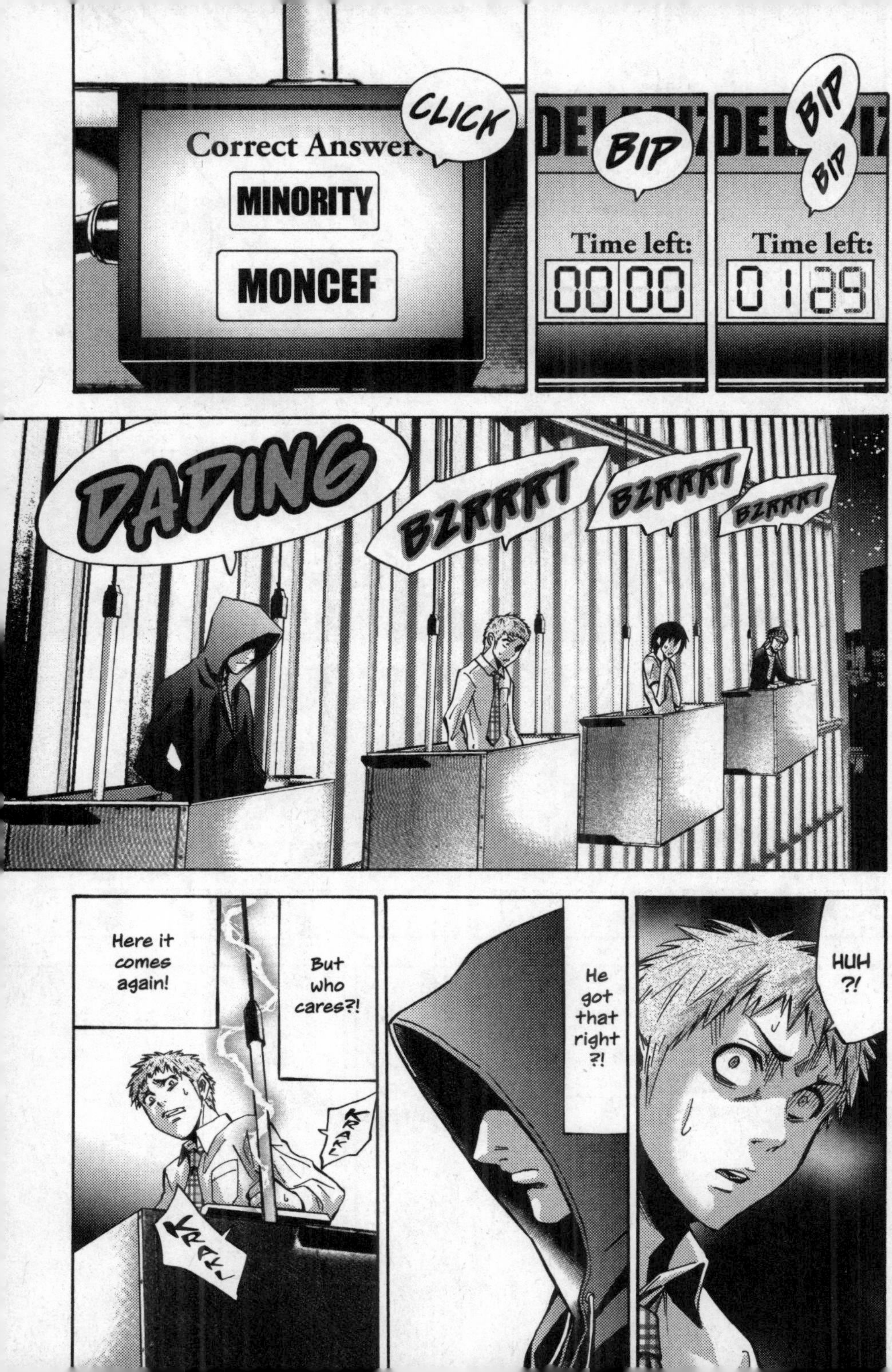
BIP
BIP
Time left:
01 29
BIP
Time left:
00 00
CLICK
Correct Answer:
MINORITY
MONCEF
BZRRRT
BZRRRT
BZRRRT
DADING
HUH ?!
He got that right ?!
Here it comes again!
But who cares?!
KRAK
KRAK

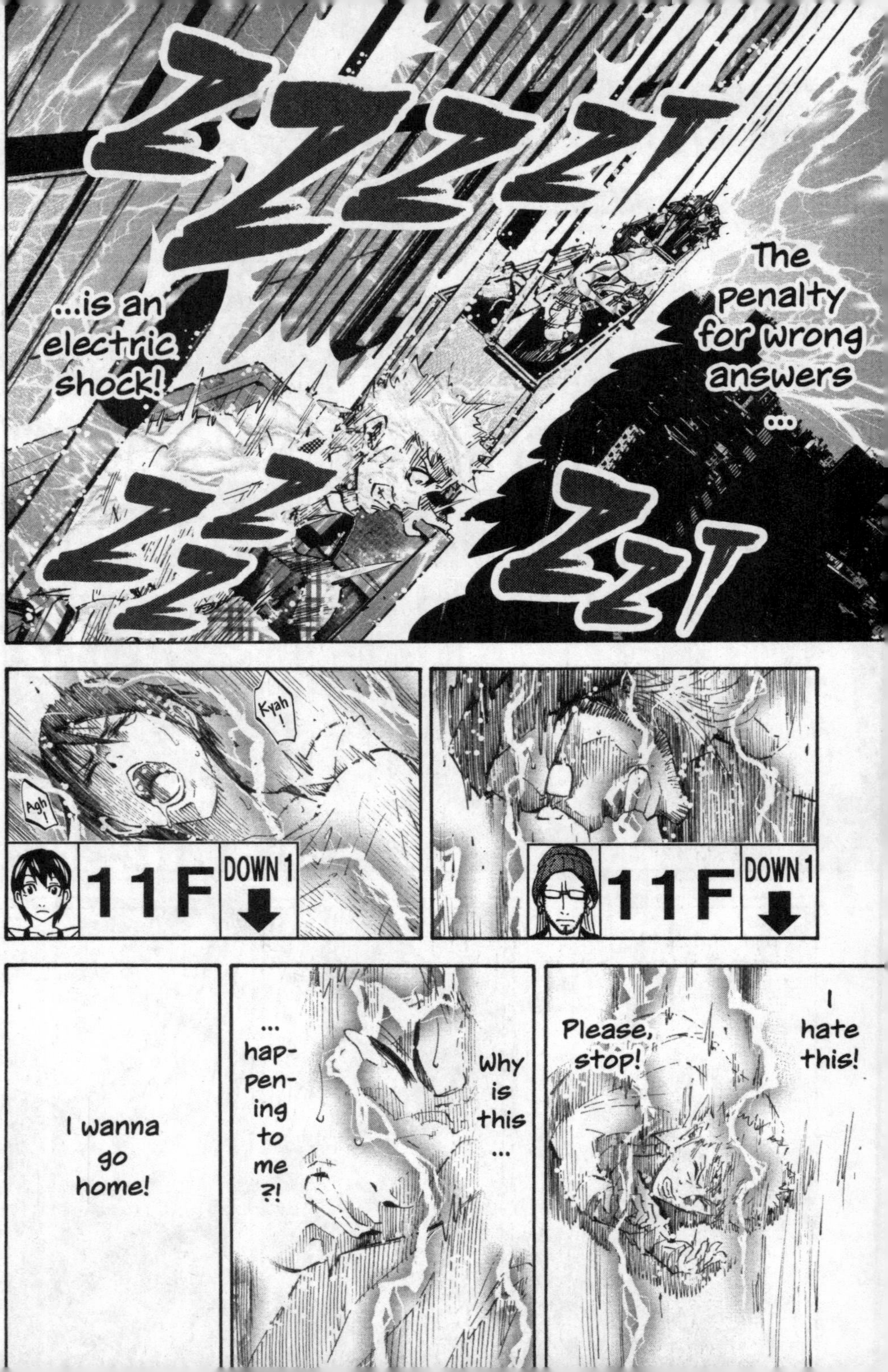
ZZZZT
The penalty for wrong answers ...
...is an electric shock!
ZZT
ZZZ
11F
DOWN 1
Kyah!
Agh!
11F
DOWN 1
I hate this!
Please, stop!
Why is this ...
... hap-pen-ing to me?!
I wanna go home!

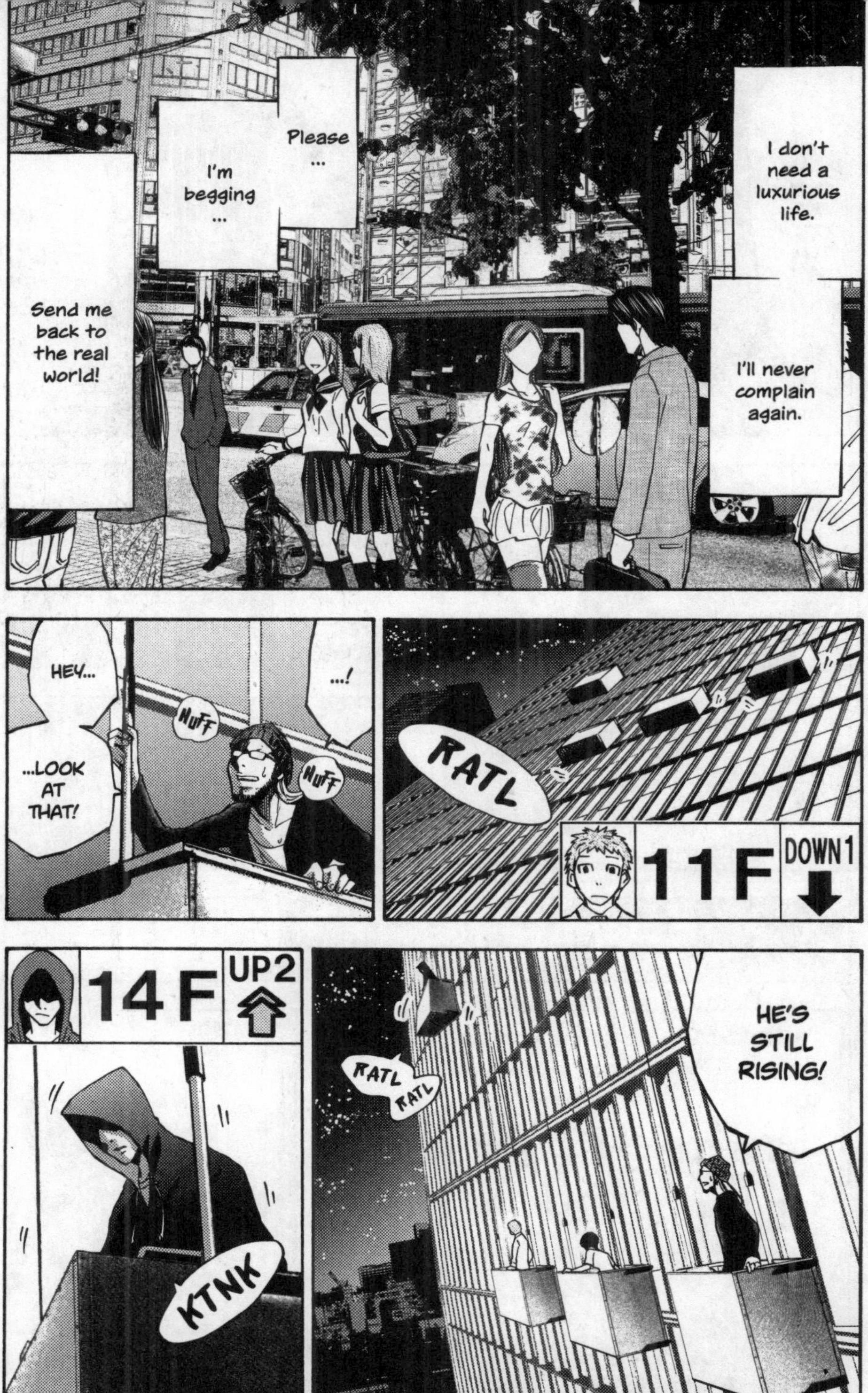
I don't need a luxurious life.
I'll never complain again.
Please ...
I'm begging ...
Send me back to the real world!
RATL
11F
DOWN1
...!
HEY...
NUFF
NUFF
...LOOK AT THAT!
HE'S STILL RISING!
RATL RATL
14F
UP2
KTNK

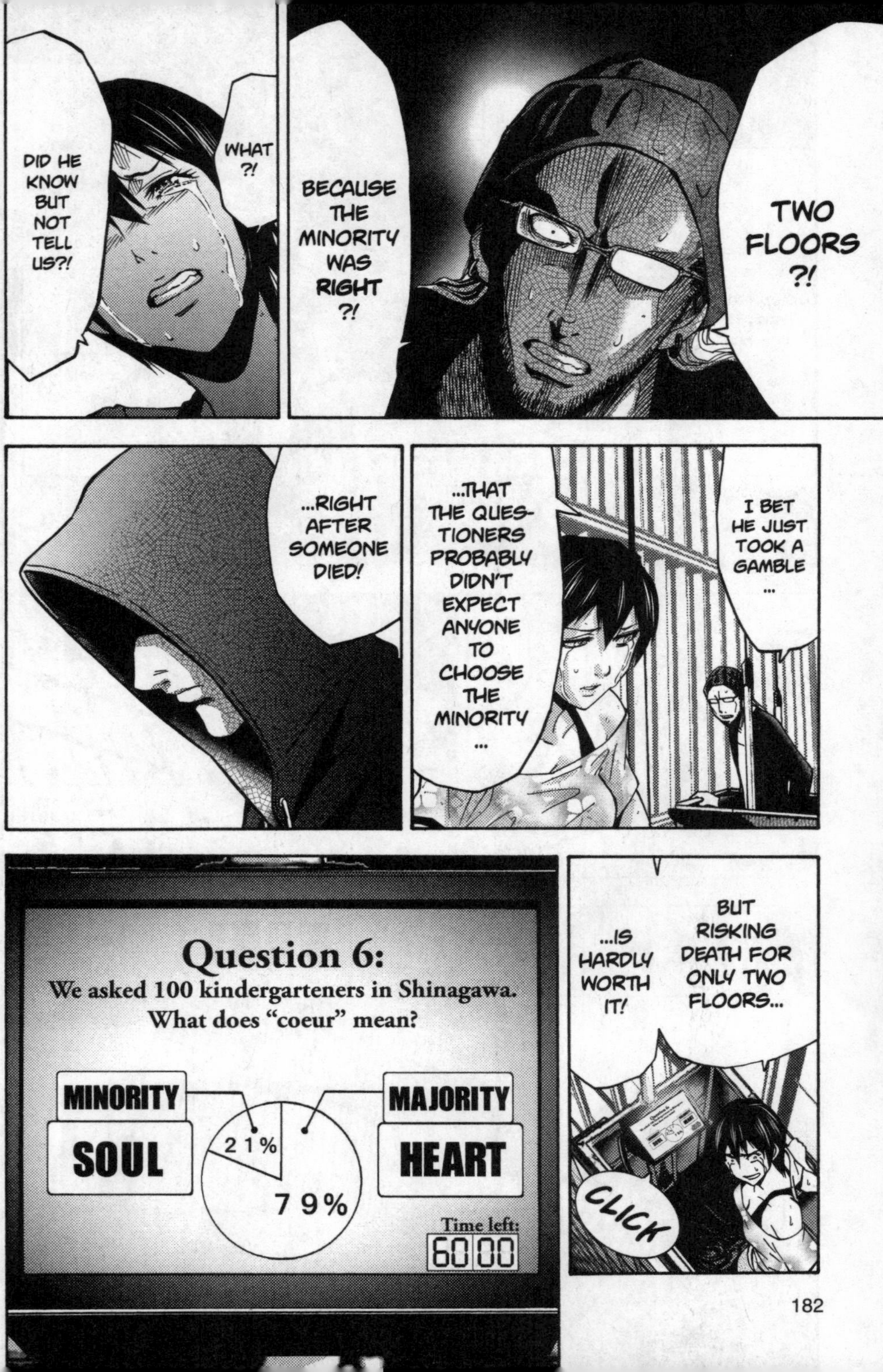
TWO FLOORS ?!
BECAUSE THE MINORITY WAS RIGHT ?!
WHAT ?!
DID HE KNOW BUT NOT TELL US?!
I BET HE JUST TOOK A GAMBLE ...
...THAT THE QUES-TIONERS PROBABLY DIDN'T EXPECT ANYONE TO CHOOSE THE MINORITY ...
...RIGHT AFTER SOMEONE DIED!
BUT RISKING DEATH FOR ONLY TWO FLOORS...
...IS HARDLY WORTH IT!
CLICK
Question 6:
We asked 100 kindergarteners in Shinagawa.
What does "coeur" mean?
MINORITY
SOUL
21%
79%
MAJORITY
HEART
Time left:
60 00

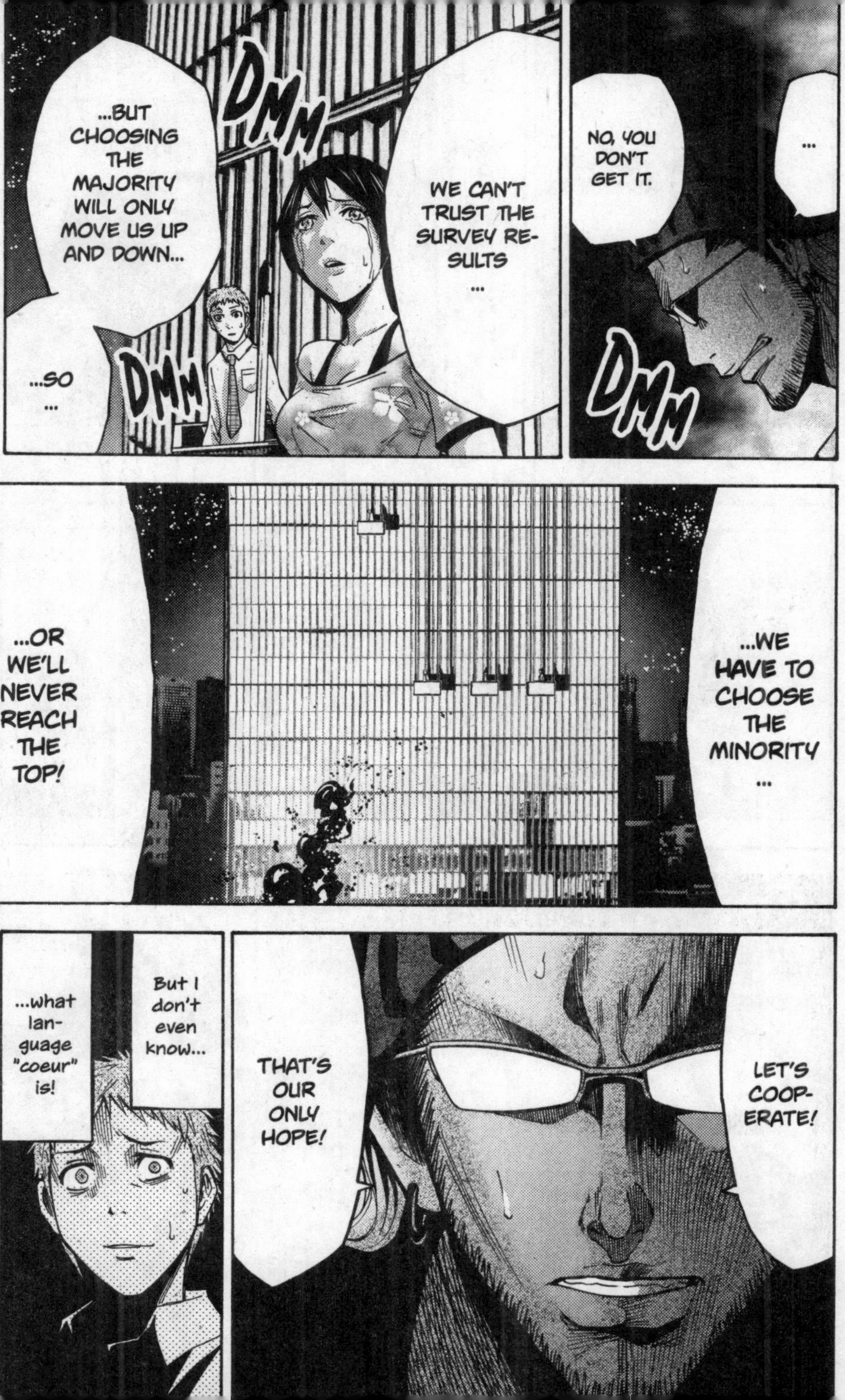
...
NO, YOU DON'T GET IT.
DMM
WE CAN'T TRUST THE SURVEY RESULTS ...
DMM
...BUT CHOOSING THE MAJORITY WILL ONLY MOVE US UP AND DOWN...
DMM
...SO ...
...WE HAVE TO CHOOSE THE MINORITY ...
...OR WE'LL NEVER REACH THE TOP!
LET'S COOPERATE!
THAT'S OUR ONLY HOPE!
But I don't even know...
...what language "coeur" is!

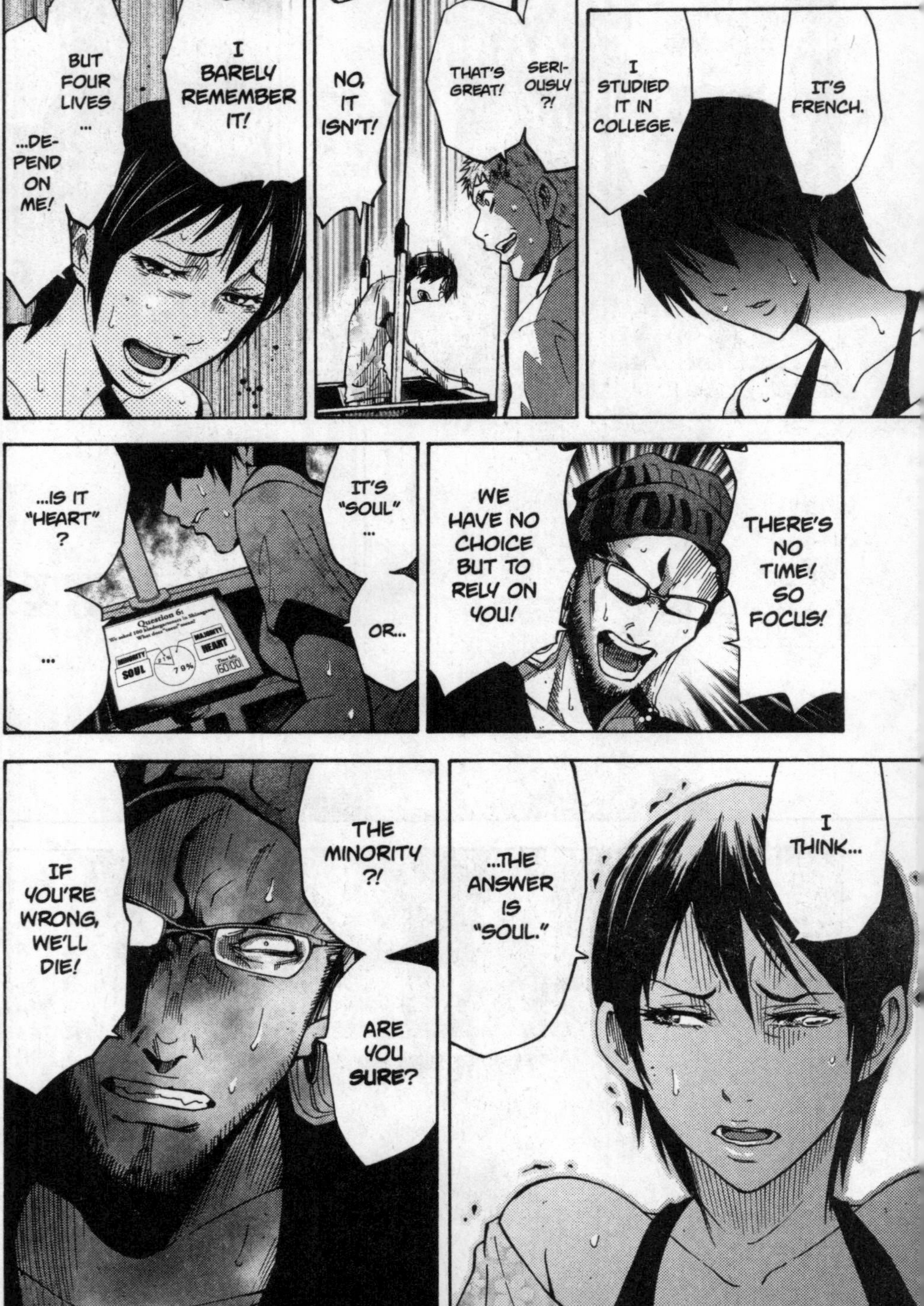
IT'S FRENCH.
I STUDIED IT IN COLLEGE.
SERIOUSLY?!
THAT'S GREAT!
NO, IT ISN'T!
I BARELY REMEMBER IT!
BUT FOUR LIVES ...
...DEPEND ON ME!
THERE'S NO TIME! SO FOCUS!
WE HAVE NO CHOICE BUT TO RELY ON YOU!
IT'S "SOUL" ...
OR...
...IS IT "HEART" ?
...
Question 6:
MINORITY
SOUL
MAJORITY
HEART
79%
I THINK...
...THE ANSWER IS "SOUL."
THE MINORITY ?!
ARE YOU SURE?
IF YOU'RE WRONG, WE'LL DIE!

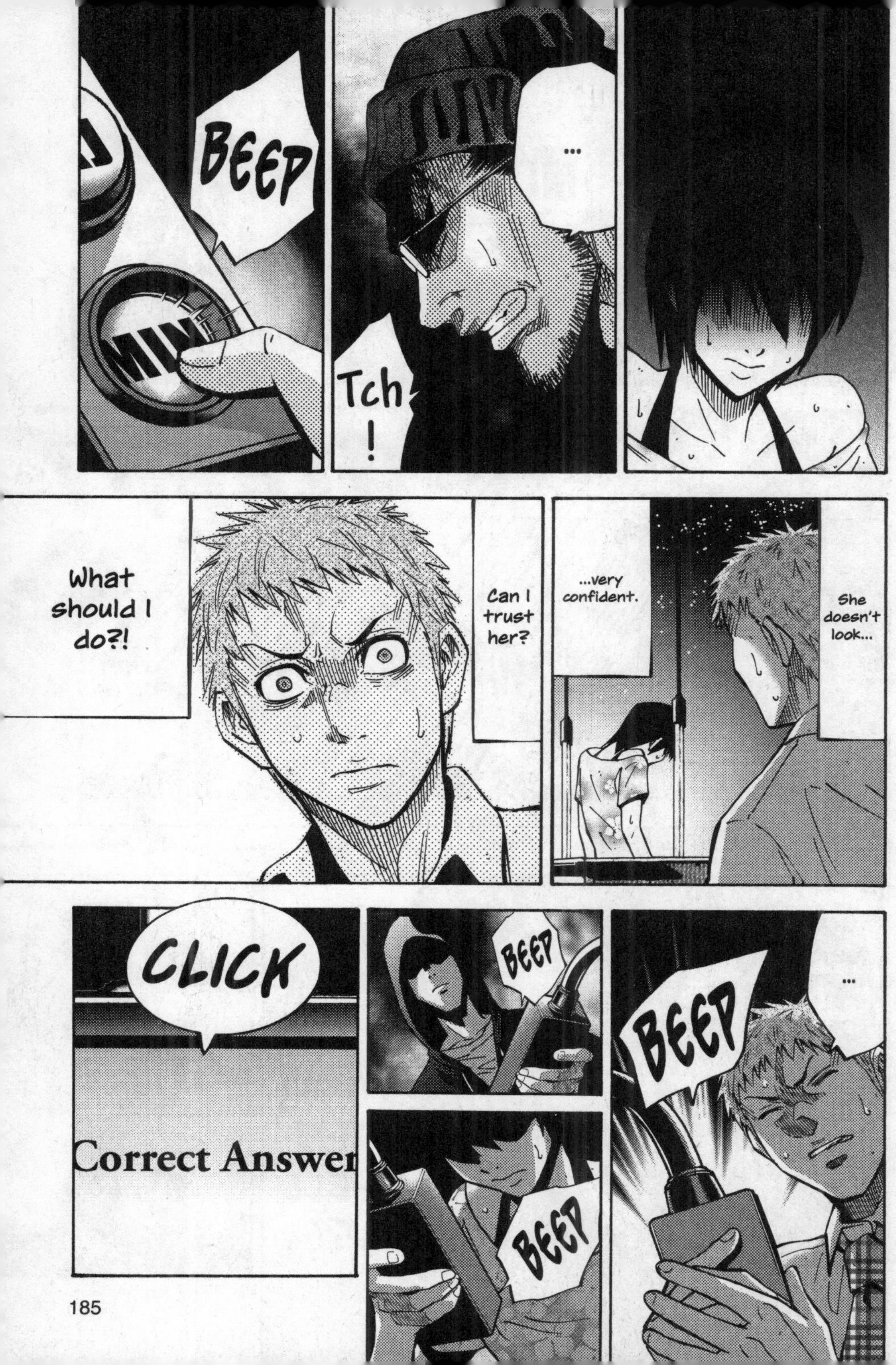
...
Tch!
BEEP
She doesn't look...
...very confident.
Can I trust her?
What should I do?!
...
BEEP
BEEP
BEEP
CLICK
Correct Answer

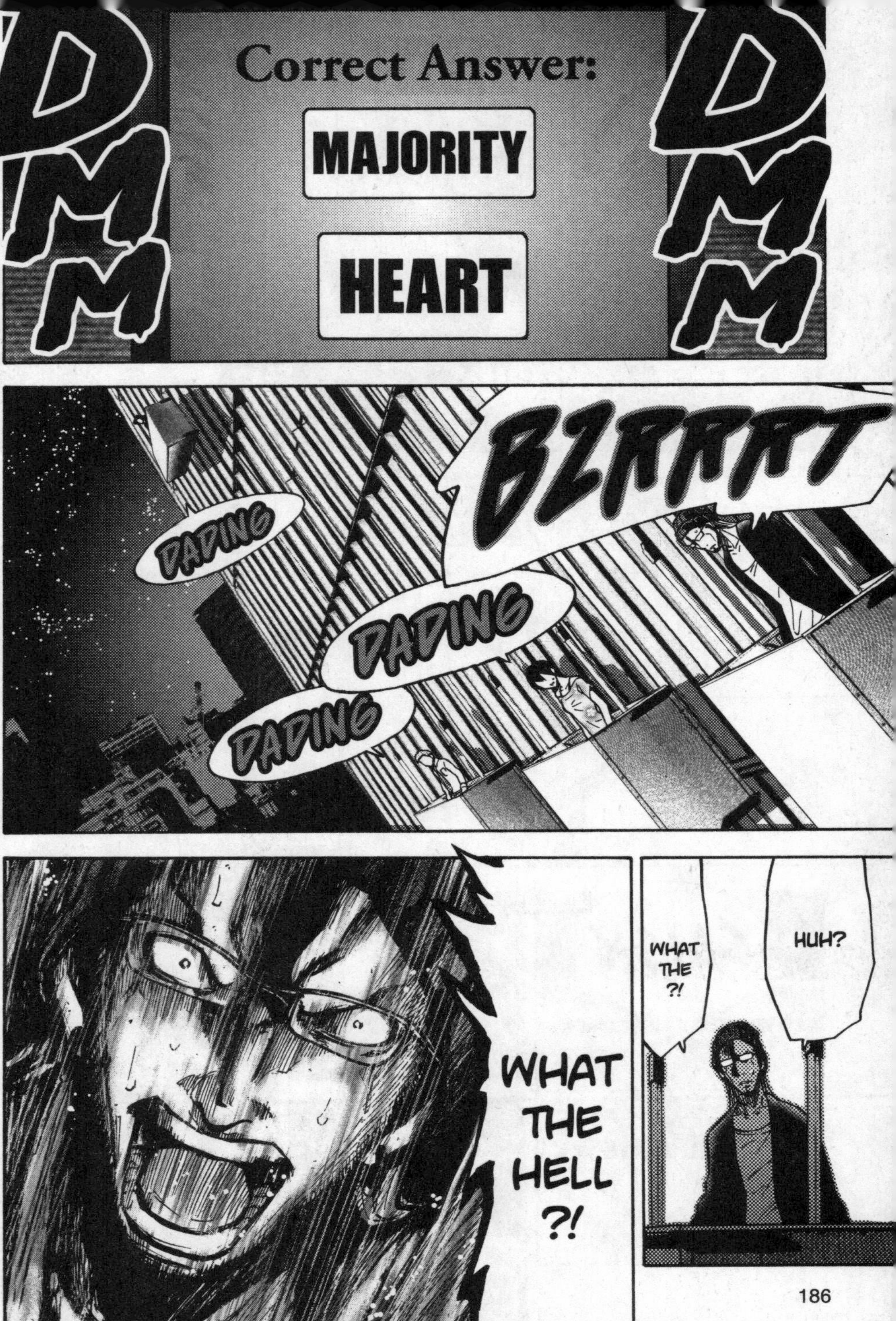
DMM
Correct Answer:
MAJORITY
HEART
DMM
BZRRRT
DADING
DADING
DADING
HUH?
WHAT THE ?!
WHAT THE HELL ?!

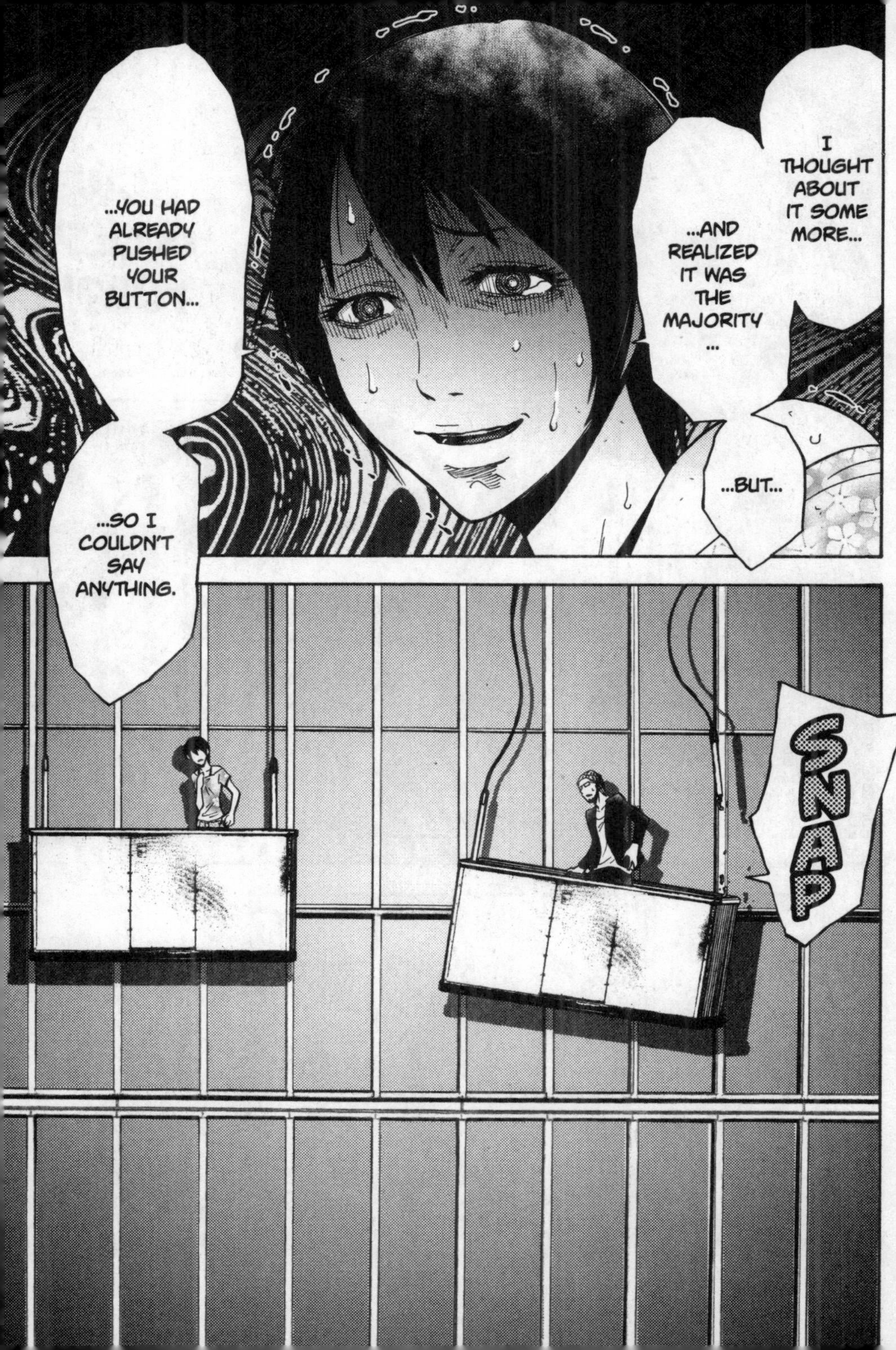
I THOUGHT ABOUT IT SOME MORE...
...AND REALIZED IT WAS THE MAJORITY...
...BUT...
...YOU HAD ALREADY PUSHED YOUR BUTTON...
...SO I COULDN'T SAY ANYTHING.
SNAP

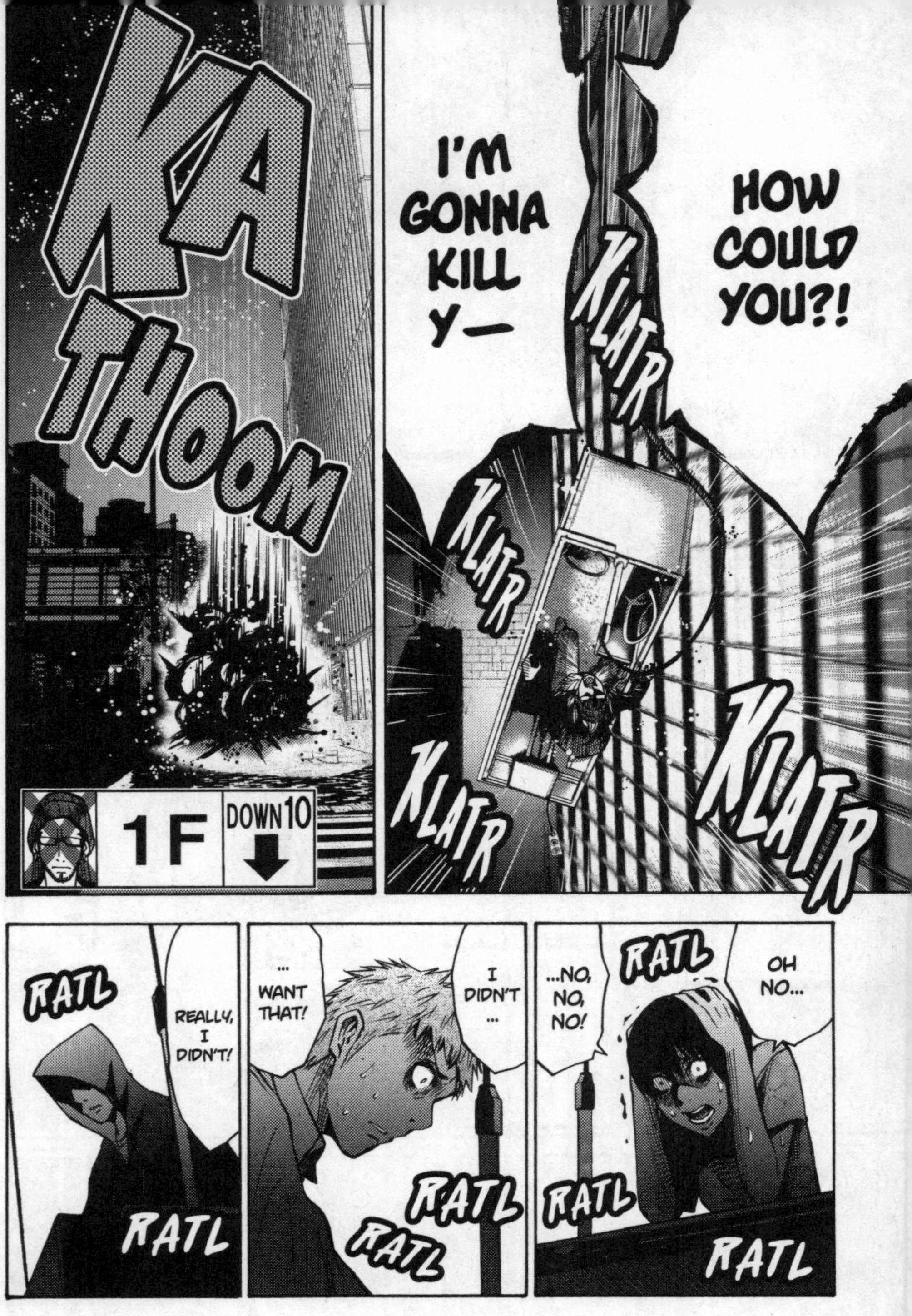
HOW COULD YOU?!
I'M GONNA KILL Y—
KLATR
KLATR
KLATR
KLATR
KLATR
KA THOOM
1F
DOWN 10
OH NO...
RATL
...NO, NO, NO!
RATL
RATL
I DIDN'T ...
... WANT THAT!
RATL
RATL
REALLY, I DIDN'T!
RATL
RATL

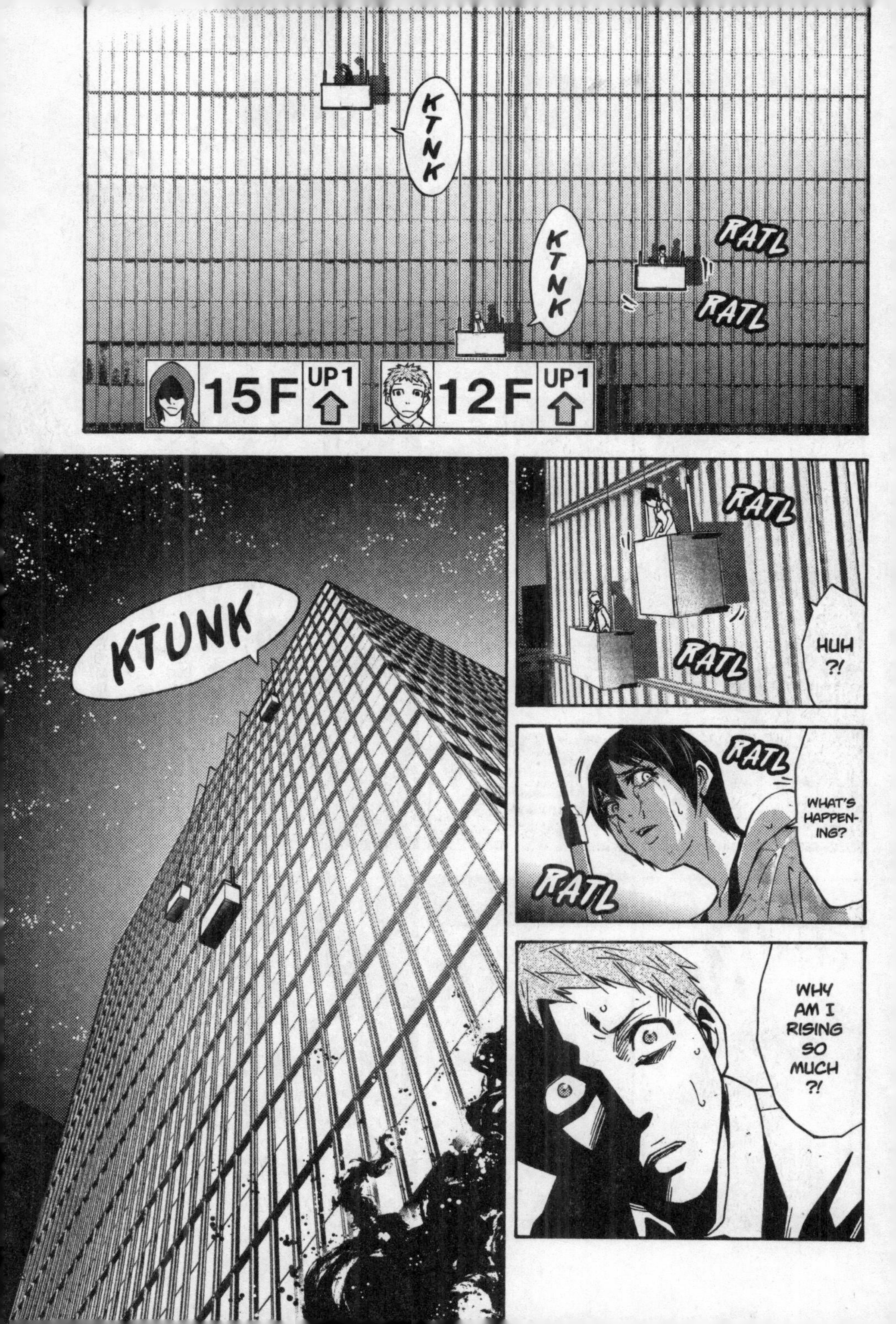
RATL
RATL
KTNK
KTNK
15F UP1
12F UP1
RATL
RATL
HUH ?!
RATL
WHAT'S HAPPEN-ING?
RATL
WHY AM I RISING SO MUCH ?!
KTUNK

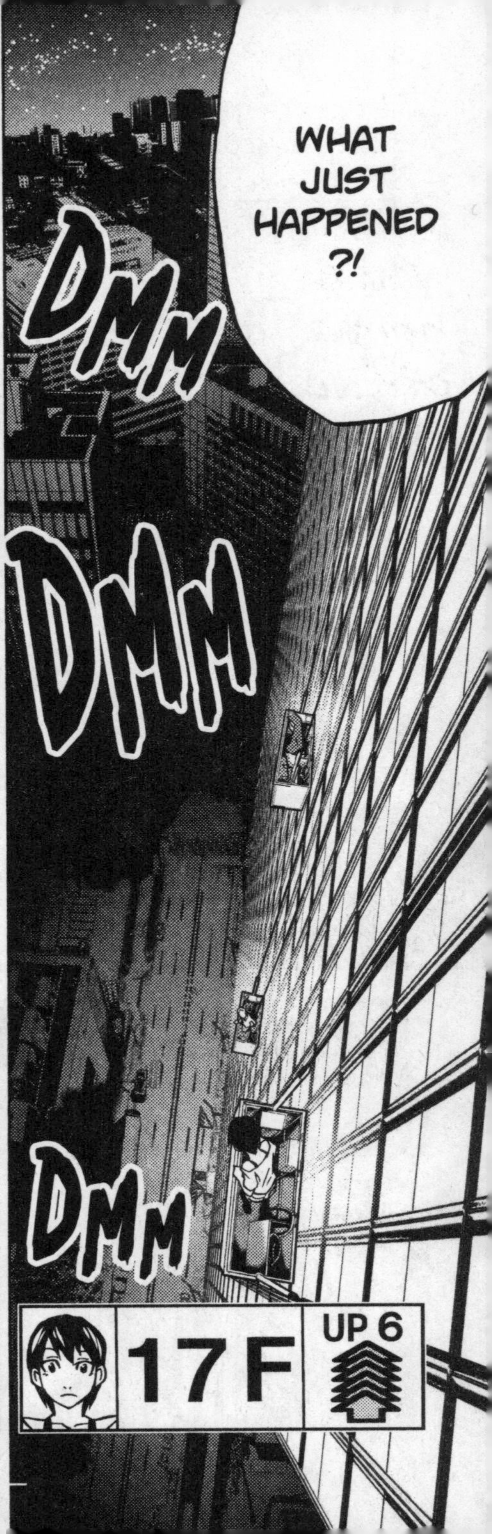
WHAT JUST HAPPENED ?!
DMM
DMM
DMM
17 F
UP 6
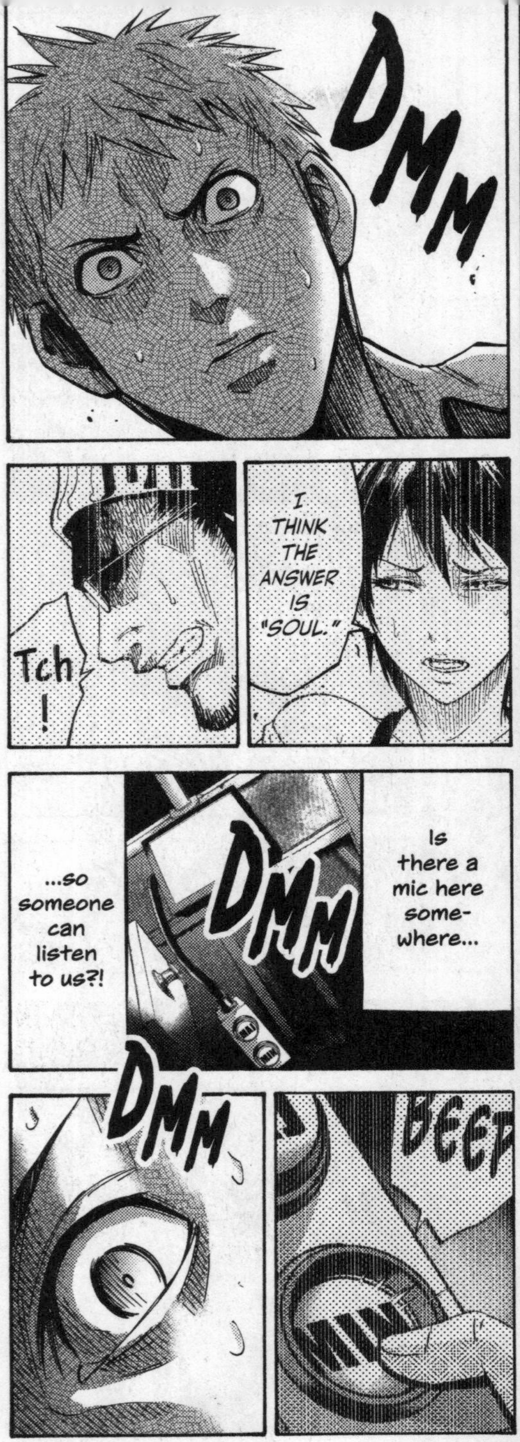
DMM
I THINK THE ANSWER IS "SOUL."
Tch !
Is there a mic here some-where...
DMM
...so someone can listen to us?!
BEEP
DMM

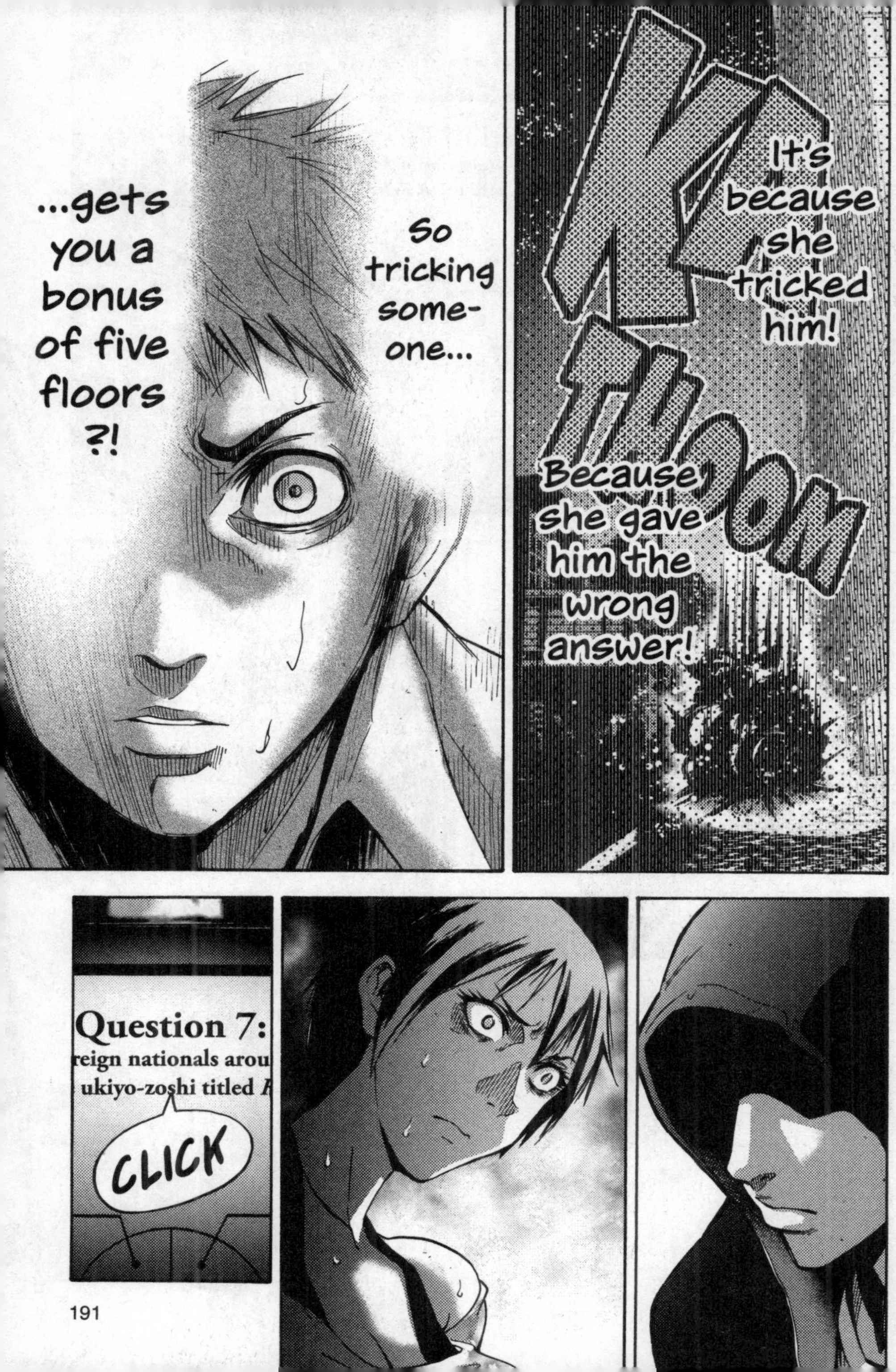
KTHOOM
It's because she tricked him!
Because she gave him the wrong answer!
So tricking someone...
...gets you a bonus of five floors?!
Question 7:
reign nationals arou
ukiyo-zoshi titled
CLICK

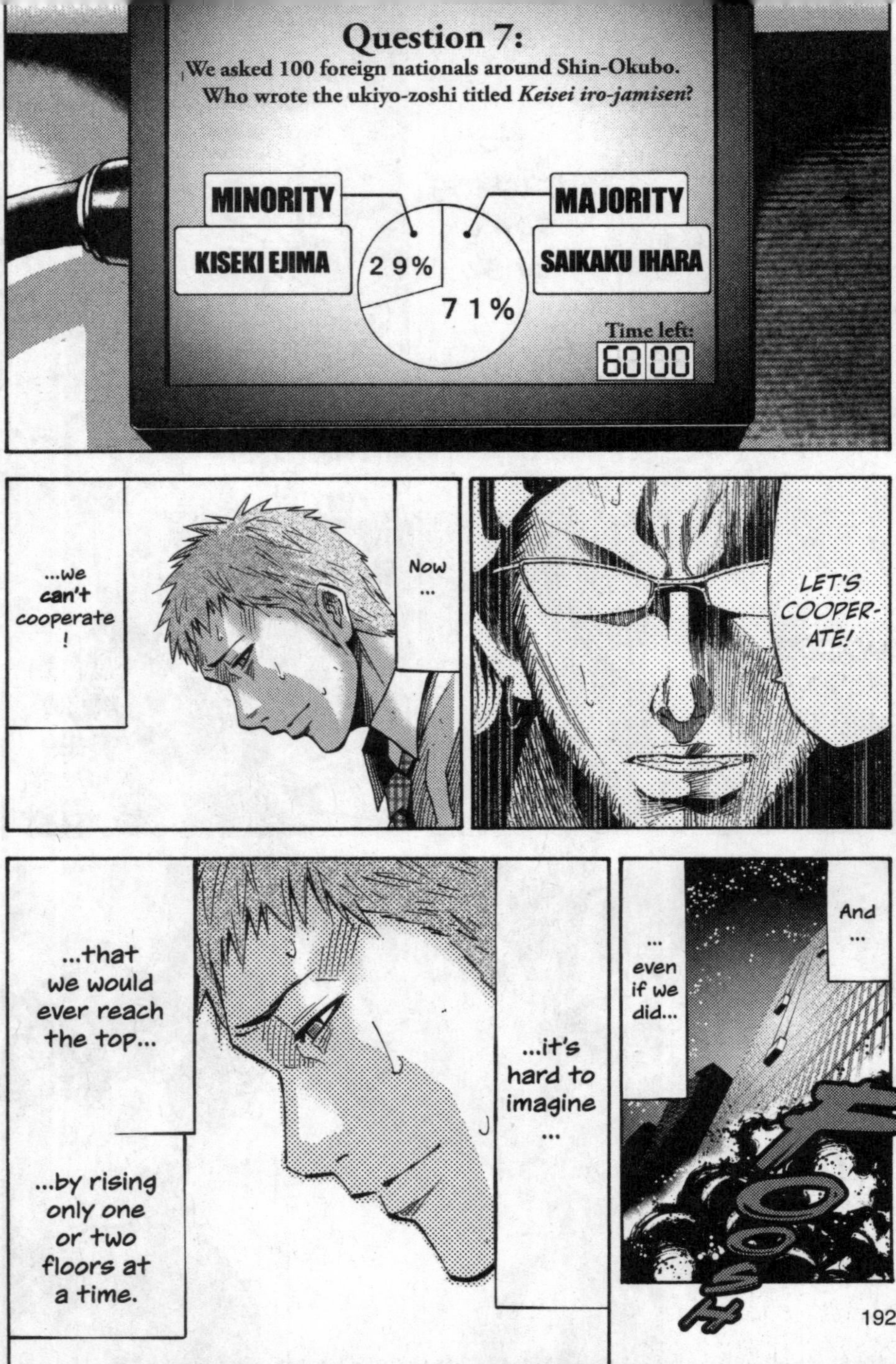
Question 7:
We asked 100 foreign nationals around Shin-Okubo. Who wrote the ukiyo-zoshi titled *Keisei iro-jamisen*?
MAJORITY
SAIKAKU IHARA
MINORITY
KISEKI EJIMA
29%
71%
Time left:
60 00
LET'S COOPER-ATE!
Now...
...we can't cooperate!
And...
...even if we did...
FWOOSH
...it's hard to imagine...
...that we would ever reach the top...
...by rising only one or two floors at a time.

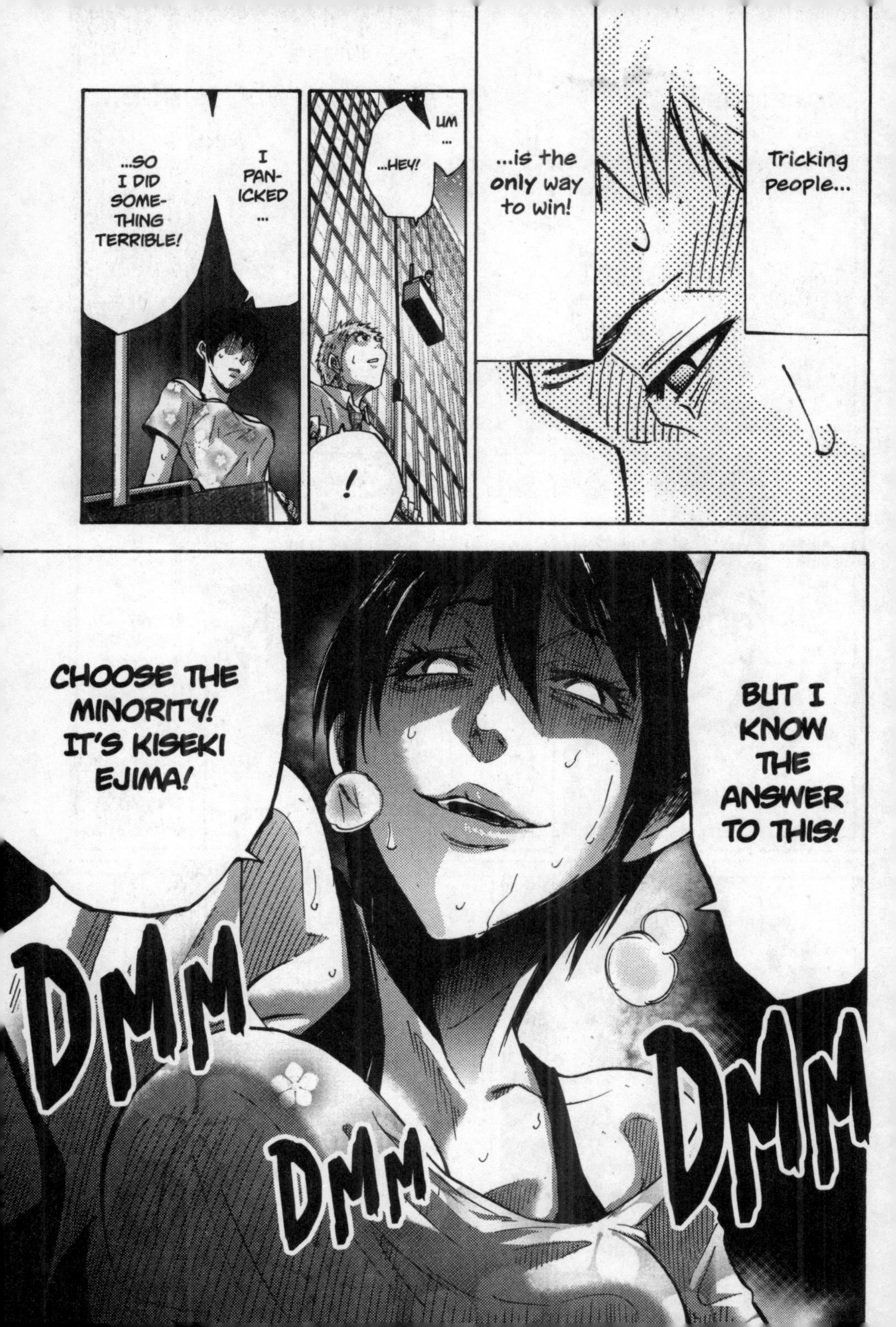
Tricking people...
...is the only way to win!
UM ...
...HEY!
!
I PAN-ICKED ...
...SO I DID SOME-THING TERRIBLE!
BUT I KNOW THE ANSWER TO THIS!
CHOOSE THE MINORITY! IT'S KISEKI EJIMA!
DMM
DMM
DMM

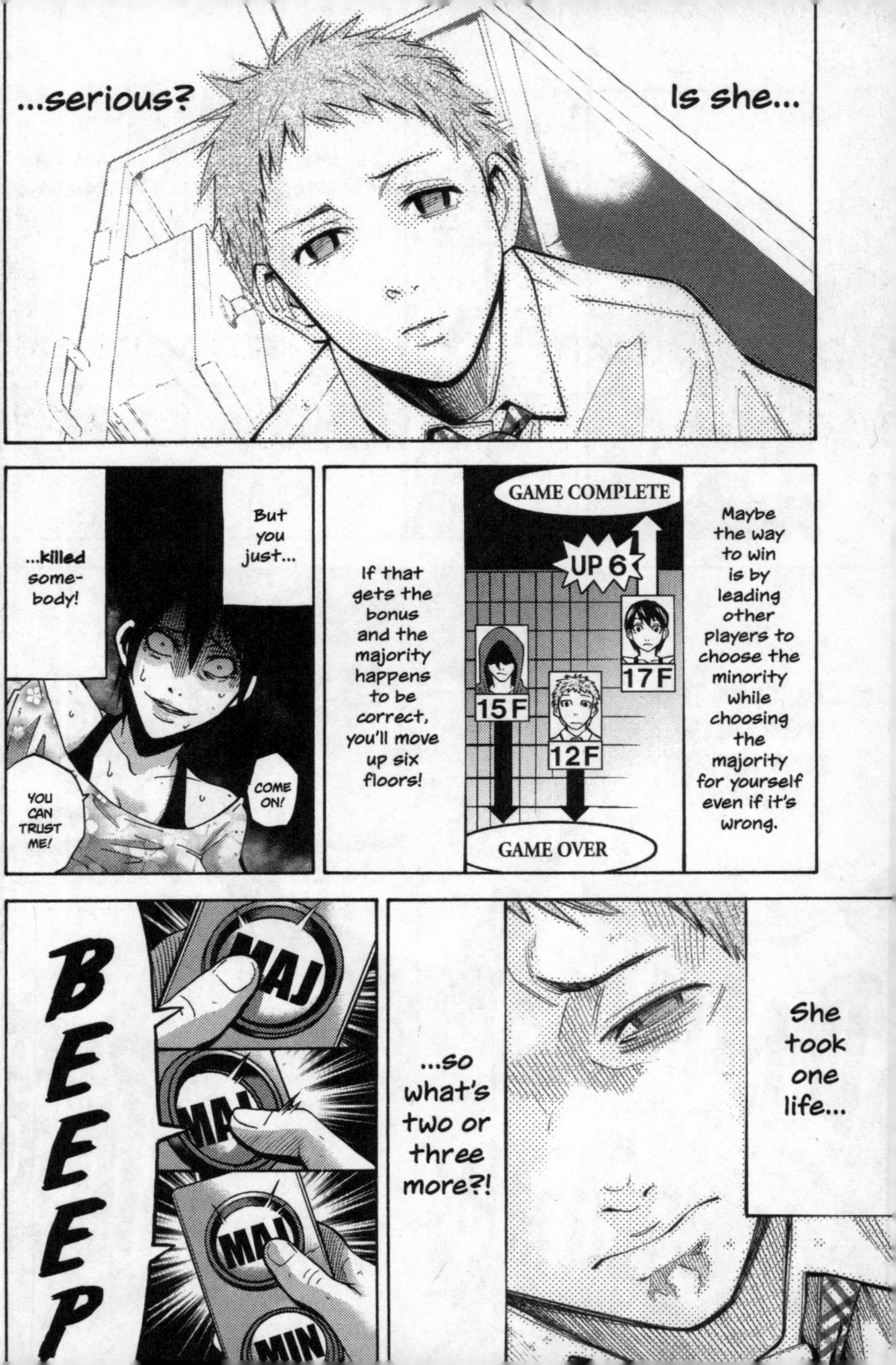
Is she...
...serious?
Maybe the way to win is by leading other players to choose the minority while choosing the majority for yourself even if it's wrong.
GAME COMPLETE
UP 6
17F
15F
12F
GAME OVER
If that gets the bonus and the majority happens to be correct, you'll move up six floors!
But you just...
...killed somebody!
COME ON!
YOU CAN TRUST ME!
She took one life...
...so what's two or three more?!
MAJ
MAJ
MAJ
MIN
BEEEEP

BZRRT

BZRRT

BZRRRT

CLICK

Correct Answer:

MINORITY

KISEKI EJIMA

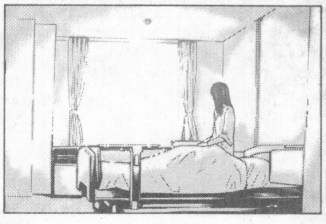

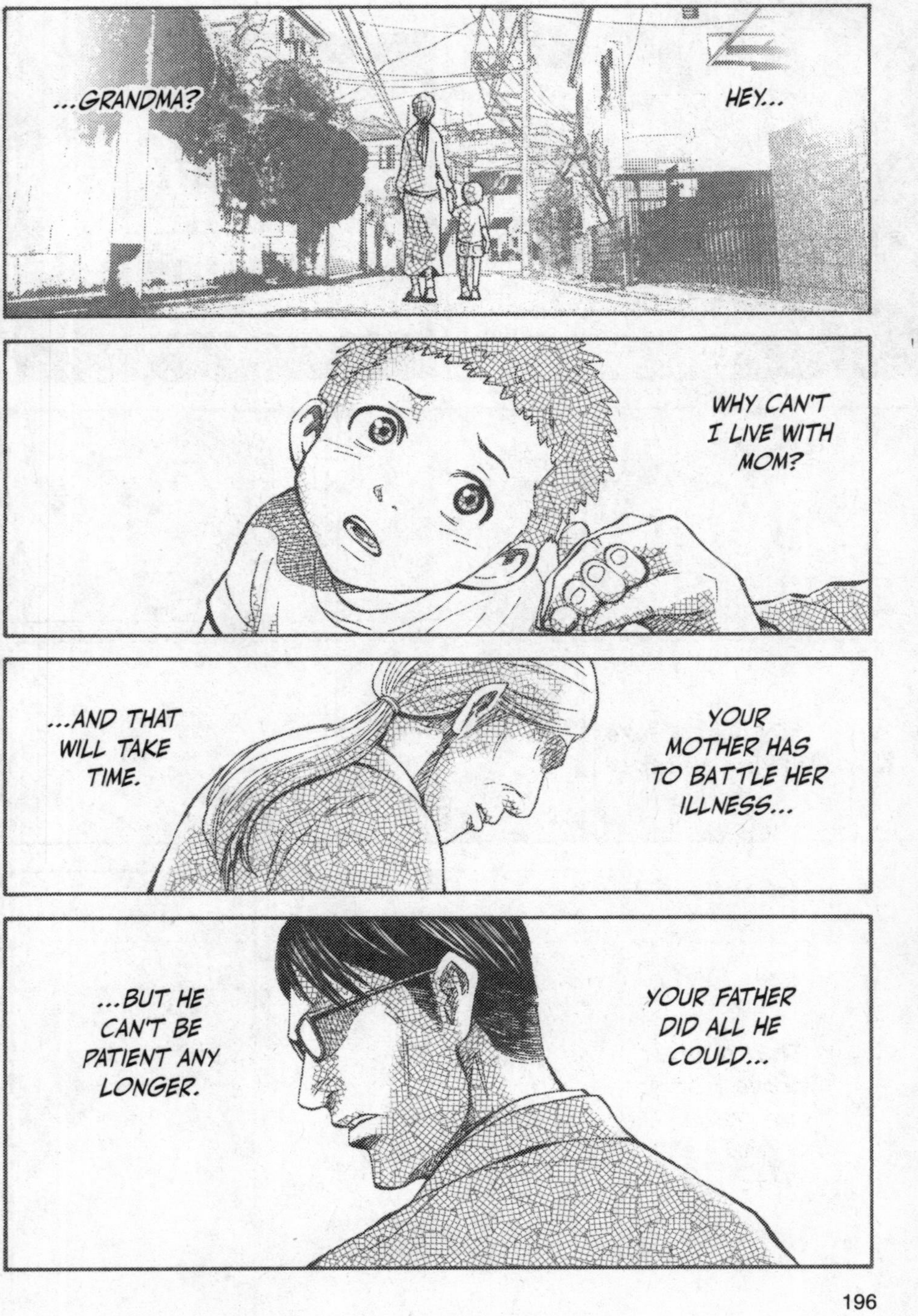
HEY...
...GRANDMA?
WHY CAN'T I LIVE WITH MOM?
YOUR MOTHER HAS TO BATTLE HER ILLNESS...
...AND THAT WILL TAKE TIME.
YOUR FATHER DID ALL HE COULD...
...BUT HE CAN'T BE PATIENT ANY LONGER.

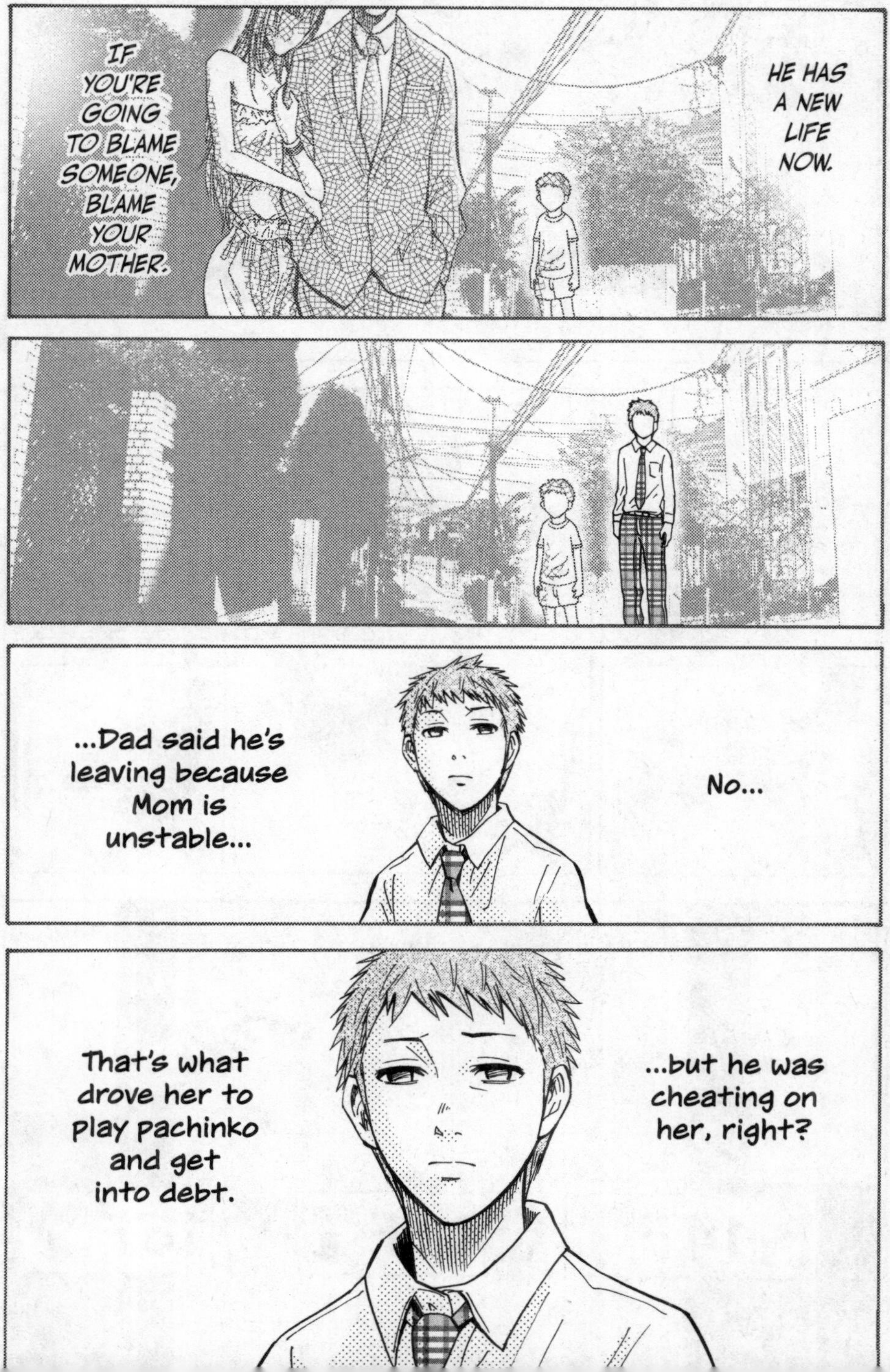
HE HAS A NEW LIFE NOW.
IF YOU'RE GOING TO BLAME SOMEONE, BLAME YOUR MOTHER.
No...
...Dad said he's leaving because Mom is unstable...
...but he was cheating on her, right?
That's what drove her to play pachinko and get into debt.

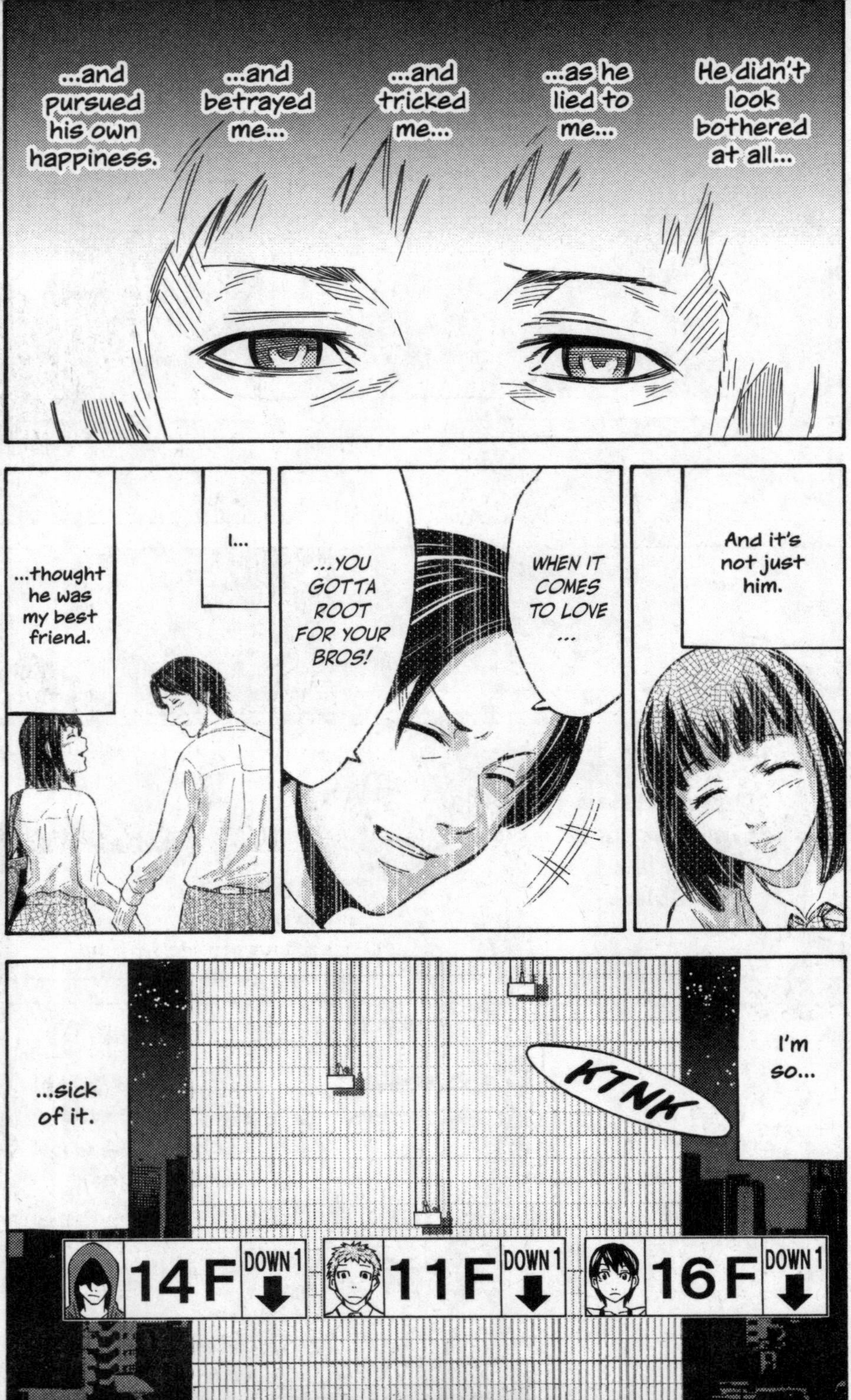

He didn't look bothered at all...
...as he lied to me...
...and tricked me...
...and betrayed me...
...and pursued his own happiness.
And it's not just him.
WHEN IT COMES TO LOVE ...
...YOU GOTTA ROOT FOR YOUR BROS!
I...
...thought he was my best friend.
I'm so...
KTNK
...sick of it.
16F DOWN 1
11F DOWN 1
14F DOWN 1

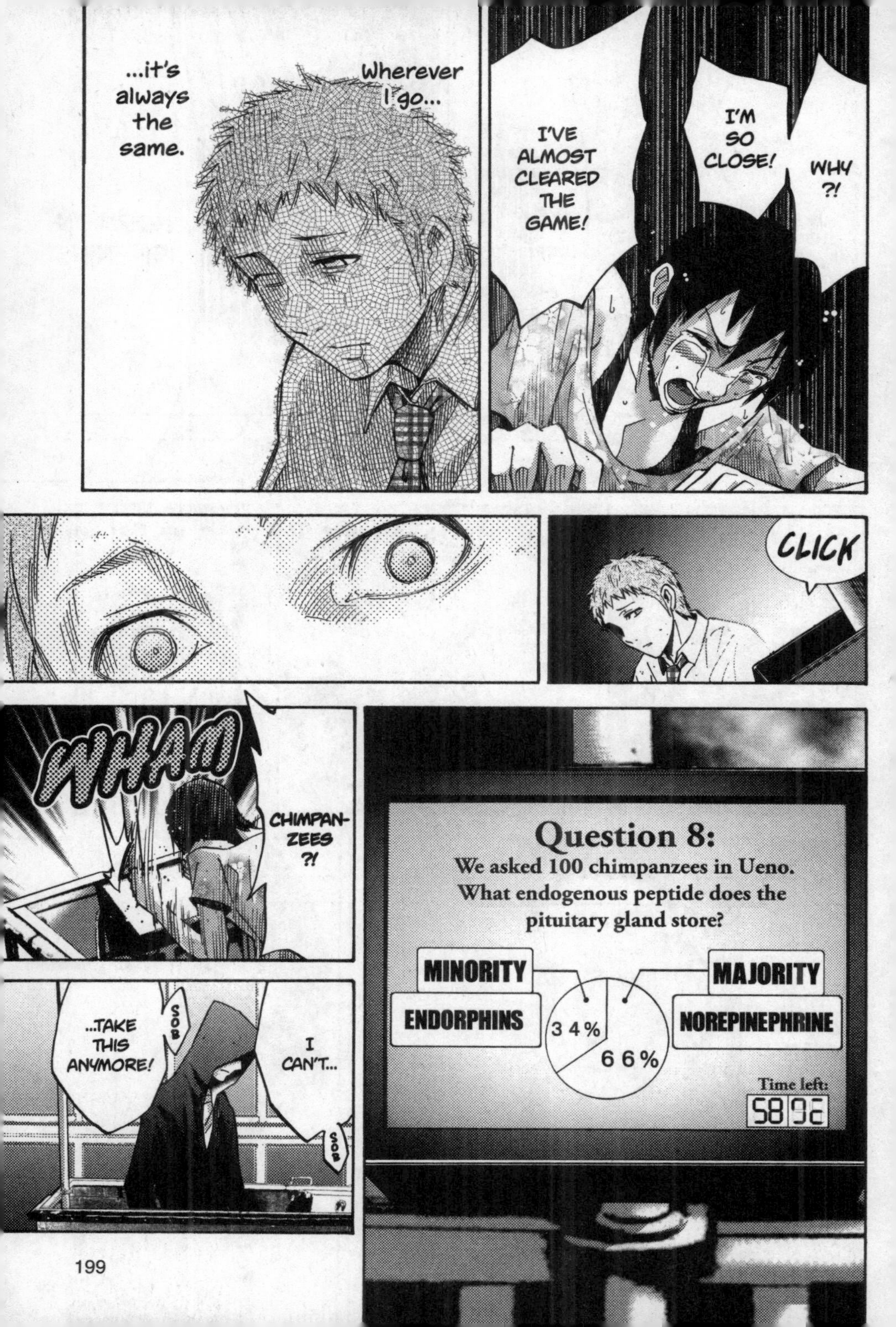
WHY ?!
I'M SO CLOSE!
I'VE ALMOST CLEARED THE GAME!
Wherever I go...
...it's always the same.
CLICK
Question 8:
We asked 100 chimpanzees in Ueno. What endogenous peptide does the pituitary gland store?
MAJORITY
NOREPINEPHRINE
MINORITY
ENDORPHINS
34%
66%
Time left:
58 96
WHAM
CHIMPANZEES ?!
I CAN'T...
SOB
...TAKE THIS ANYMORE!
SOB

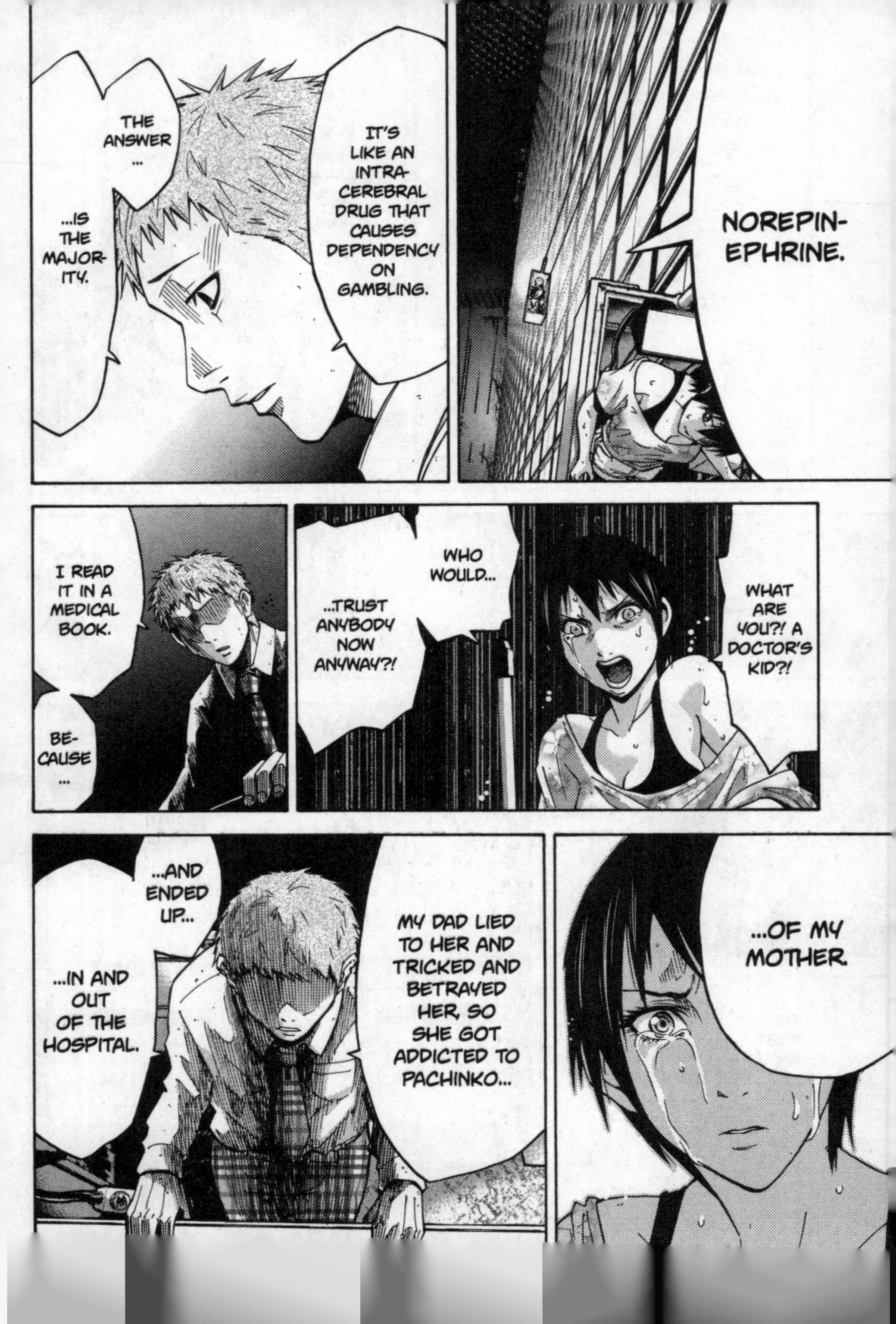
NOREPIN-EPHRINE.
IT'S LIKE AN INTRA-CEREBRAL DRUG THAT CAUSES DEPENDENCY ON GAMBLING.
THE ANSWER ...
...IS THE MAJOR-ITY.
WHAT ARE YOU?! A DOCTOR'S KID?!
WHO WOULD...
...TRUST ANYBODY NOW ANYWAY?!
I READ IT IN A MEDICAL BOOK.
BE-CAUSE ...
...OF MY MOTHER.
MY DAD LIED TO HER AND TRICKED AND BETRAYED HER, SO SHE GOT ADDICTED TO PACHINKO...
...AND ENDED UP...
...IN AND OUT OF THE HOSPITAL.

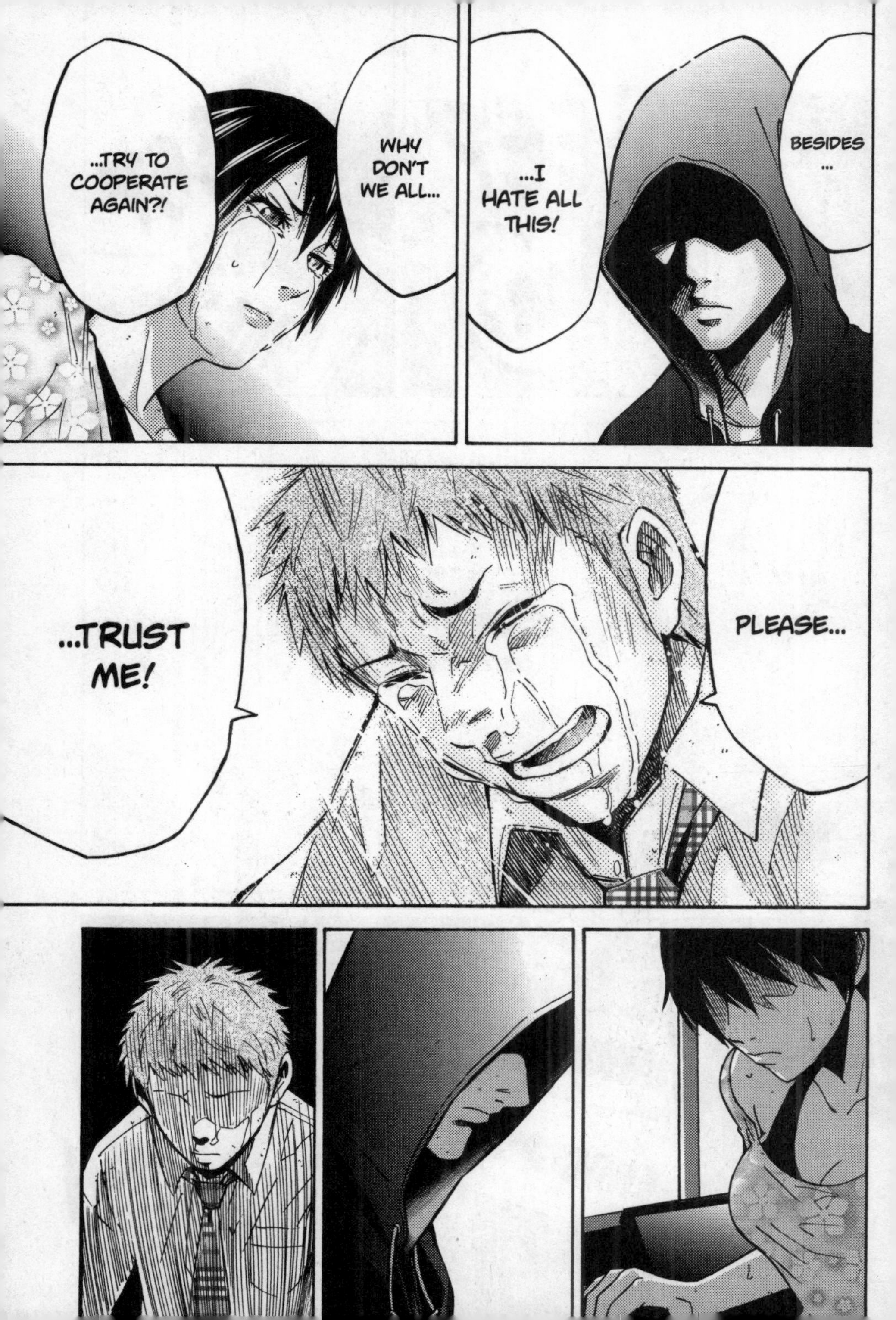
BESIDES ...
...I HATE ALL THIS!
WHY DON'T WE ALL...
...TRY TO COOPERATE AGAIN?!
PLEASE...
...TRUST ME!

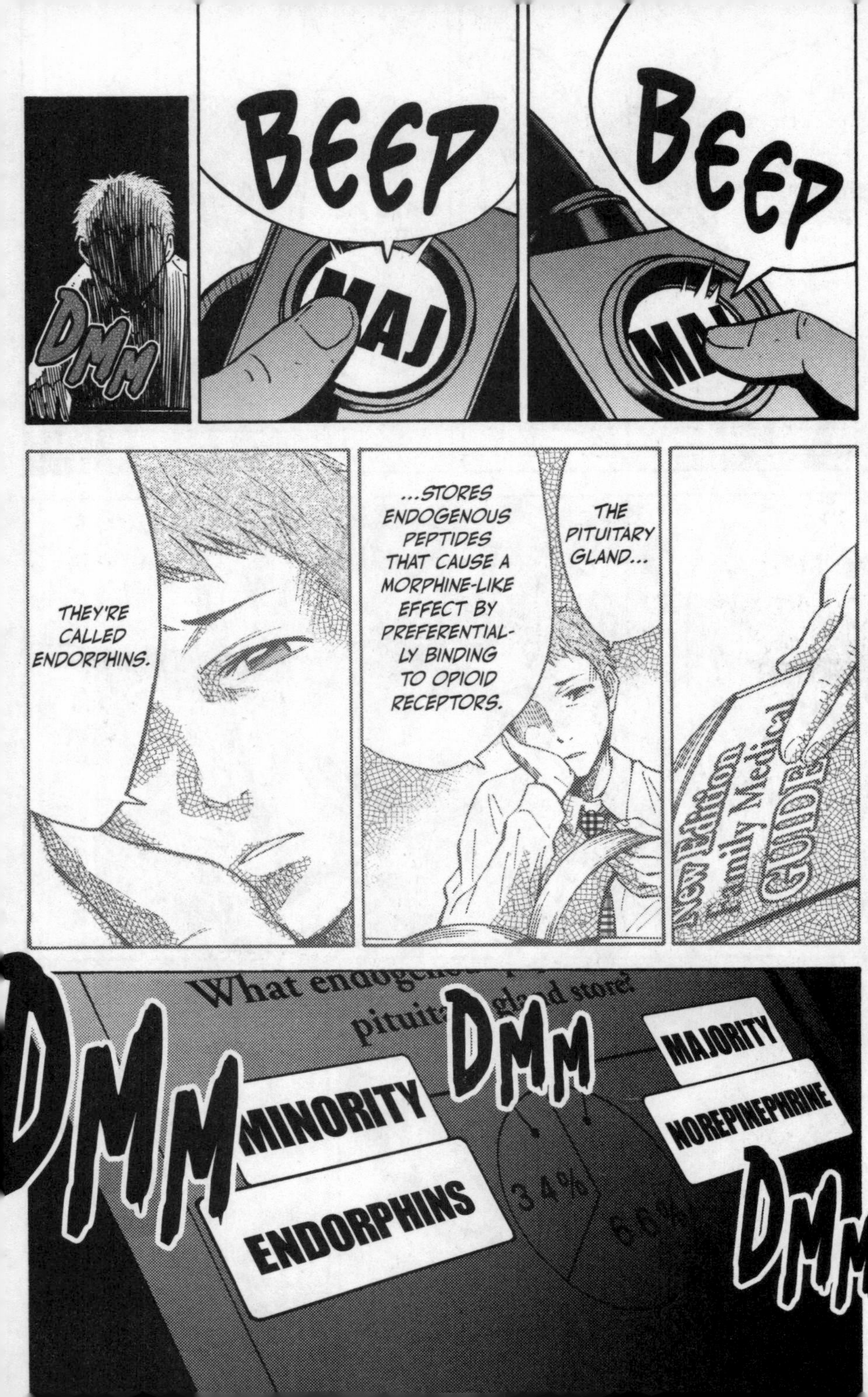
BEEP
MA
BEEP
MAJ
DMM
New Edition
Family Medical
GUIDE
THE PITUITARY GLAND...
...STORES ENDOGENOUS PEPTIDES THAT CAUSE A MORPHINE-LIKE EFFECT BY PREFERENTIALLY BINDING TO OPIOID RECEPTORS.
THEY'RE CALLED ENDORPHINS.
DMM
MAJORITY
NOREPINEPHRINE
DMM
DMM
MINORITY
ENDORPHINS
34%
66%
DMM

You're all just selfish!

That's right...

And betray!

And trick!

...as you-lie!

You don't look bothered at all...

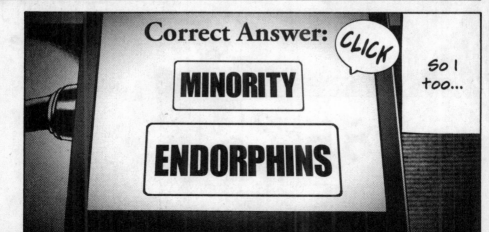

Correct Answer:

CLICK

MINORITY

ENDORPHINS

So I too...

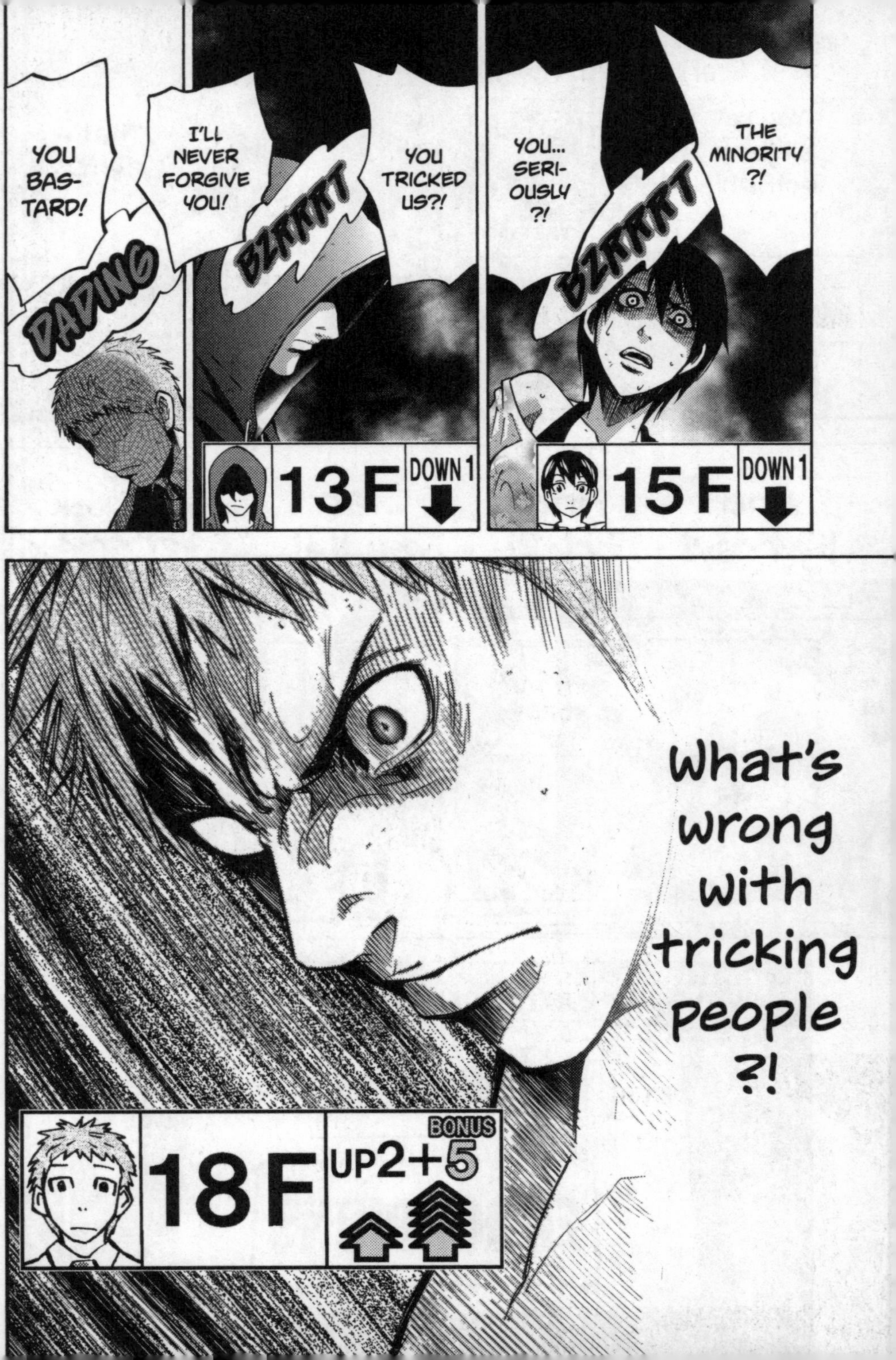
THE MINORITY ?!
YOU... SERI-OUSLY ?!
BZRRRT
15 F
DOWN 1
YOU TRICKED US?!
I'LL NEVER FORGIVE YOU!
BZRRRT
13 F
DOWN 1
YOU BAS-TARD!
DADING
What's wrong with tricking people ?!
18 F
UP2+5
BONUS

SIDE STORY:
Four of Hearts, Part 3

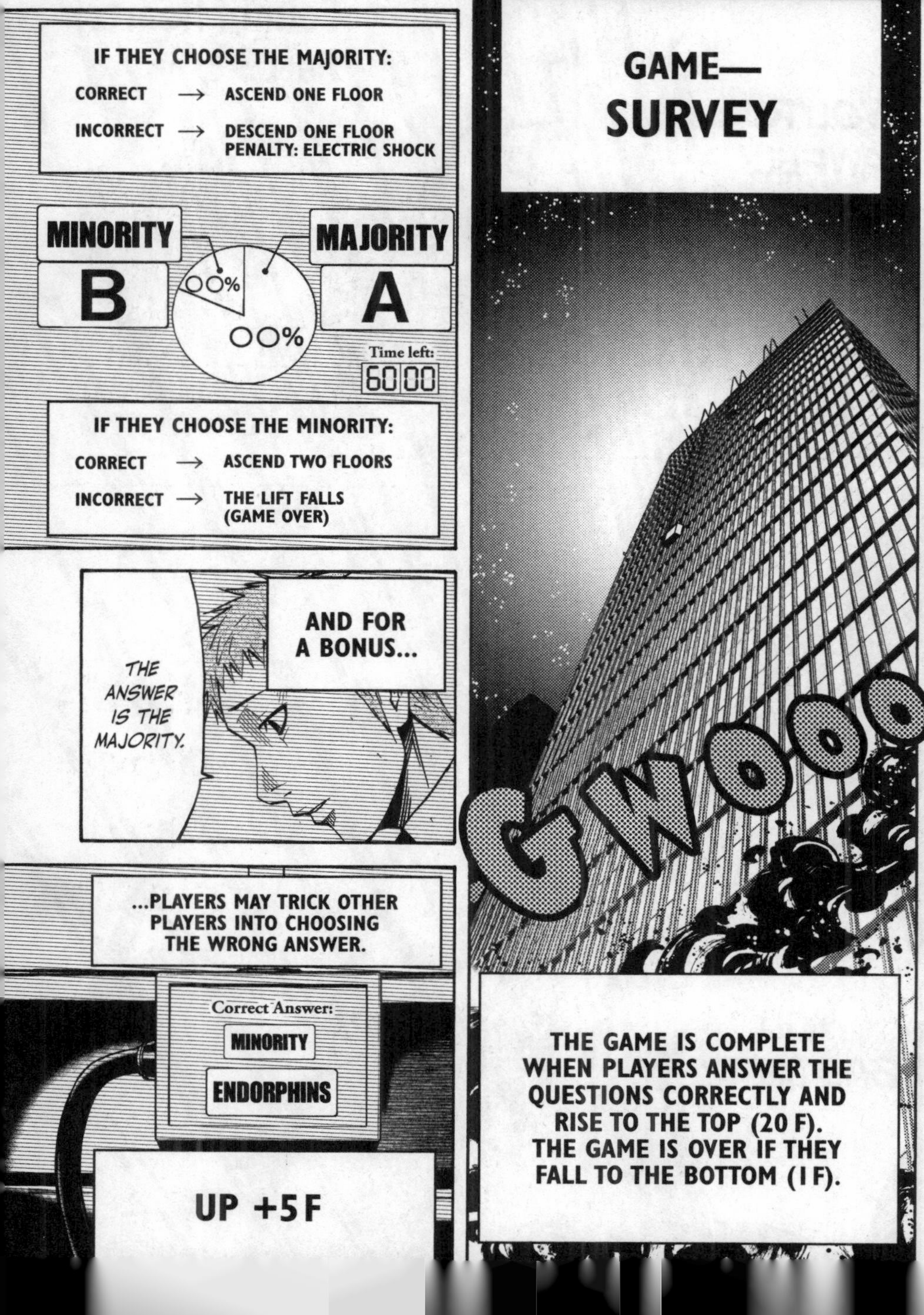
GAME—
SURVEY
GWOOO
THE GAME IS COMPLETE WHEN PLAYERS ANSWER THE QUESTIONS CORRECTLY AND RISE TO THE TOP (20 F). THE GAME IS OVER IF THEY FALL TO THE BOTTOM (1 F).
IF THEY CHOOSE THE MAJORITY:
CORRECT → ASCEND ONE FLOOR
INCORRECT → DESCEND ONE FLOOR PENALTY: ELECTRIC SHOCK
MAJORITY
A
MINORITY
B
OO%
OO%
Time left:
60:00
IF THEY CHOOSE THE MINORITY:
CORRECT → ASCEND TWO FLOORS
INCORRECT → THE LIFT FALLS (GAME OVER)
AND FOR A BONUS...
THE ANSWER IS THE MAJORITY.
...PLAYERS MAY TRICK OTHER PLAYERS INTO CHOOSING THE WRONG ANSWER.
Correct Answer:
MINORITY
ENDORPHINS
UP +5 F

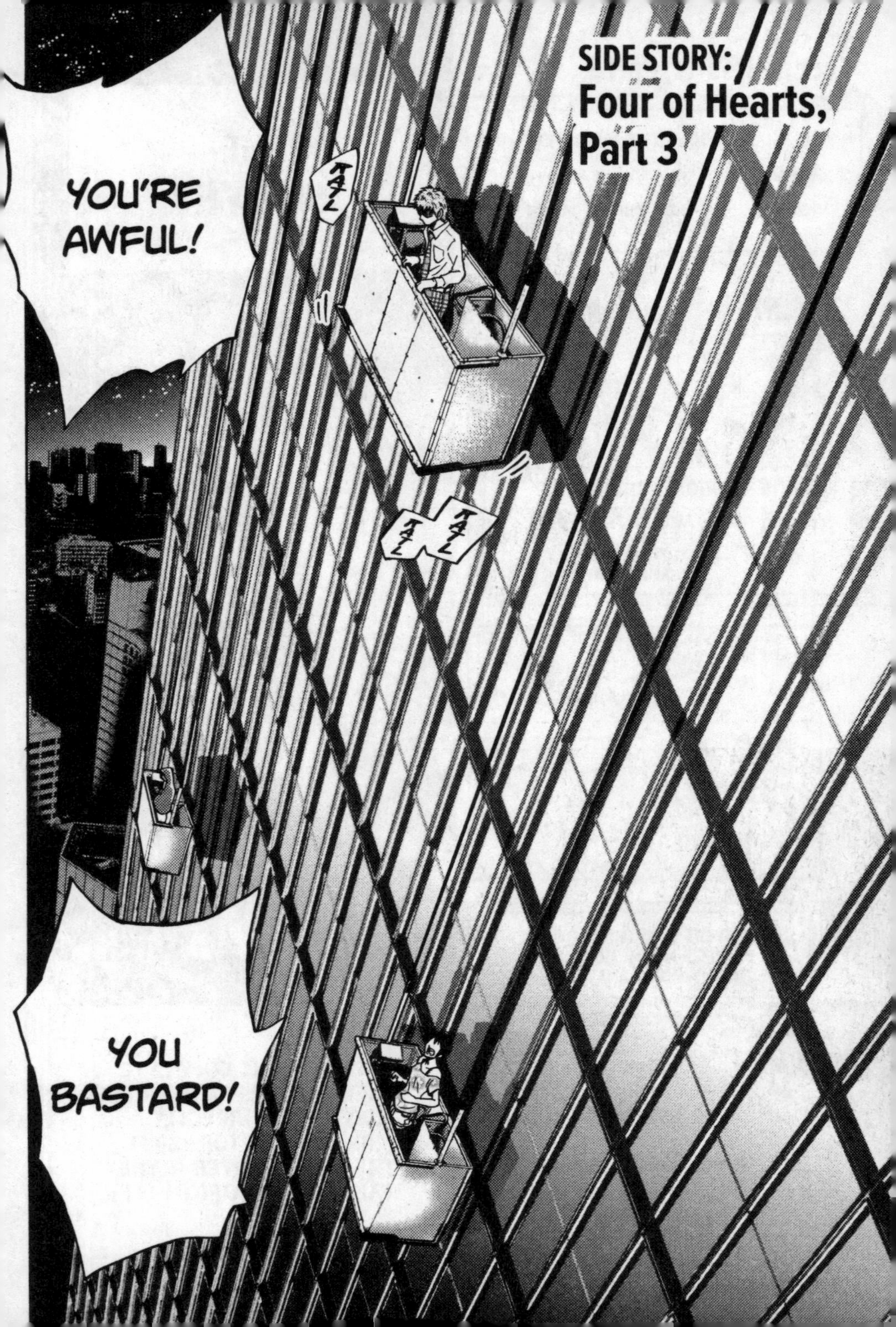
SIDE STORY:
Four of Hearts,
Part 3
YOU'RE AWFUL!
TATL
TATL
TATL
YOU BASTARD!

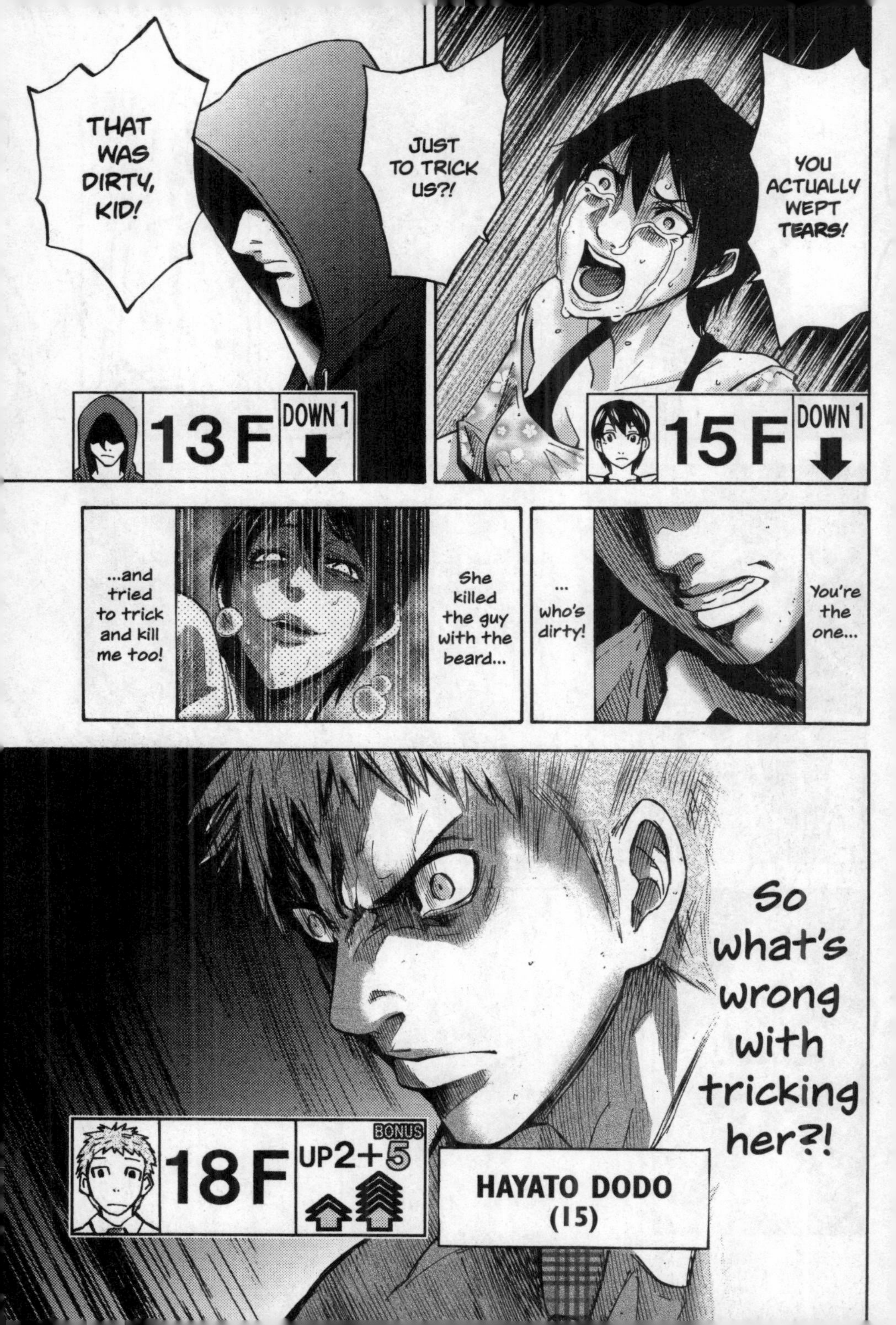
YOU ACTUALLY WEPT TEARS!
JUST TO TRICK US?!
15 F
DOWN 1
THAT WAS DIRTY, KID!
13 F
DOWN 1
You're the one...
... who's dirty!
She killed the guy with the beard...
...and tried to trick and kill me too!
So what's wrong with tricking her?!
HAYATO DODO
(15)
18 F
BONUS
UP2+5

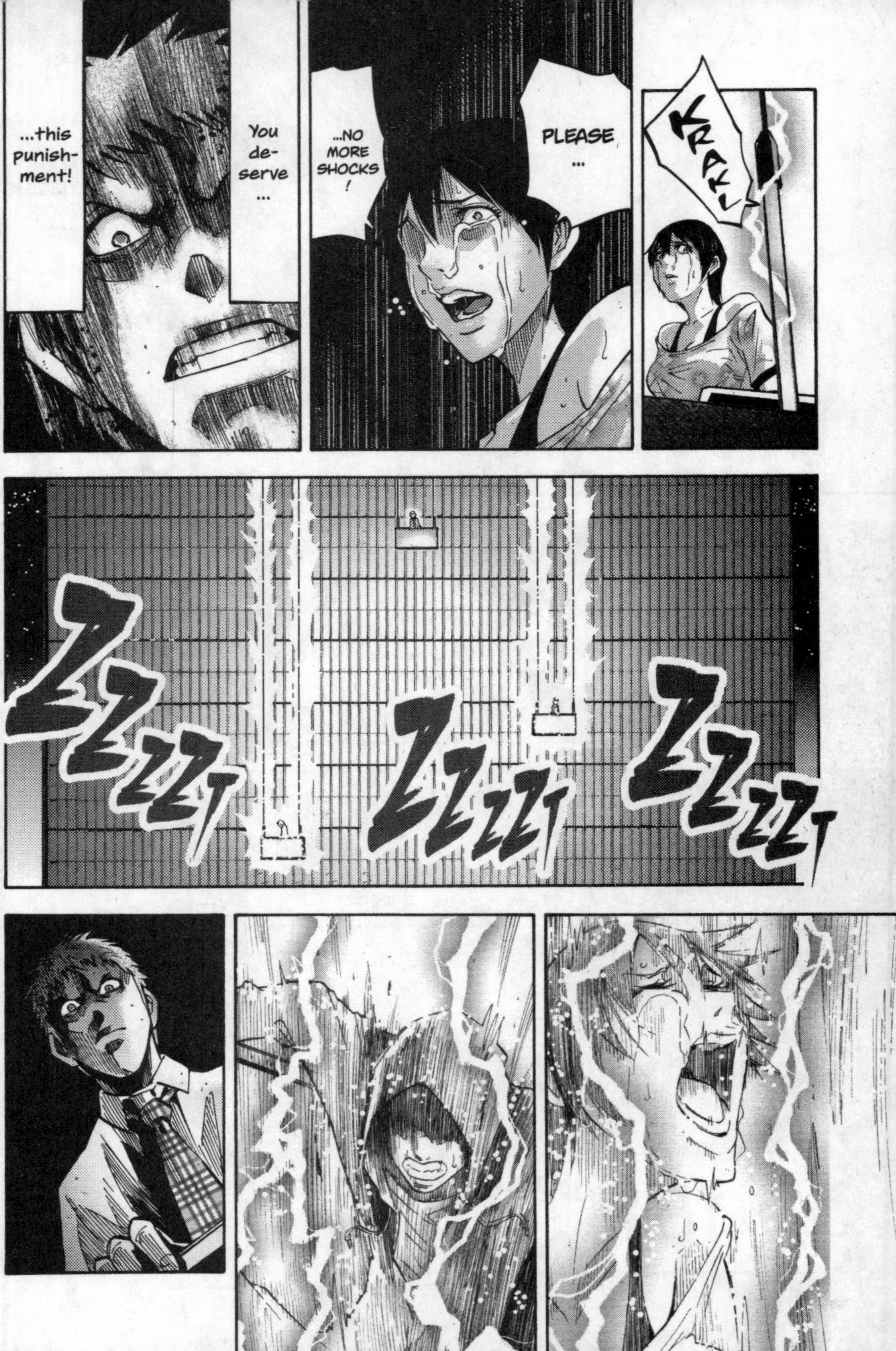
KRAKL
PLEASE...
...NO MORE SHOCKS!
You deserve...
...this punishment!
ZZZZZT
ZZZZZT
ZZZZZT

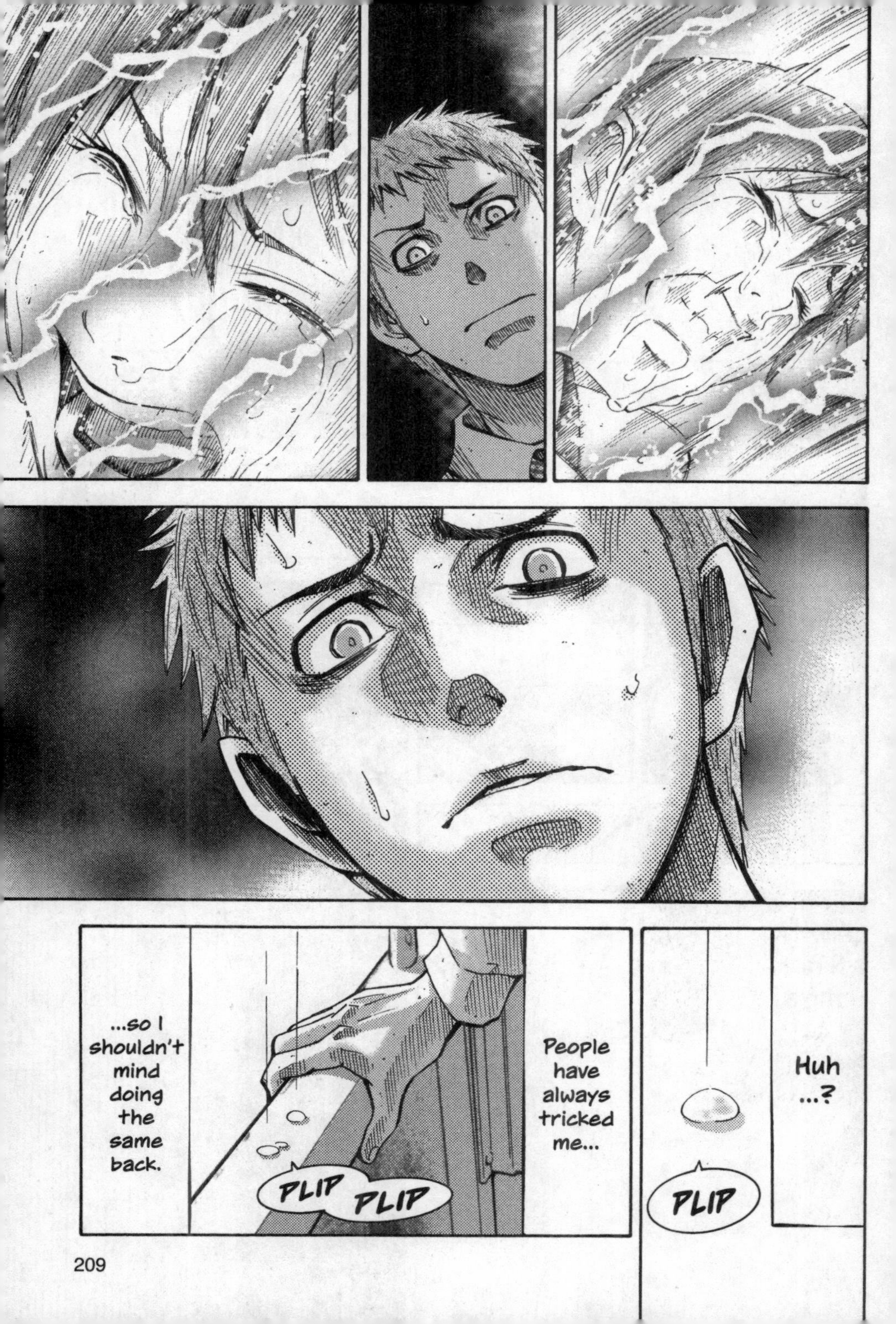
Huh ...?
PLIP
People have always tricked me...
...so I shouldn't mind doing the same back.
PLIP
PLIP

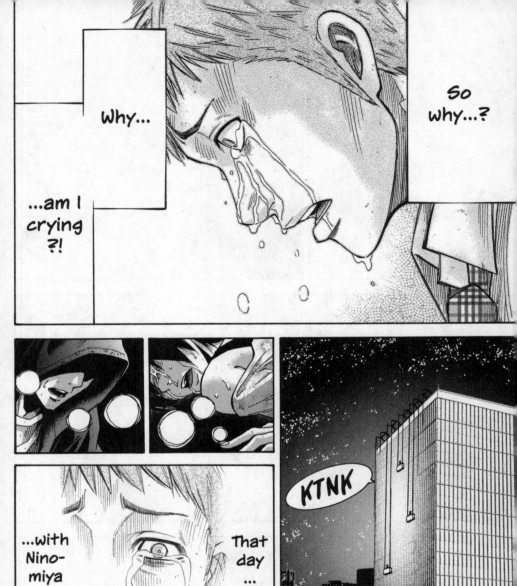

Why...

So why...?

...am I crying ?!

...with Nino-miya...

That day...

KTNK

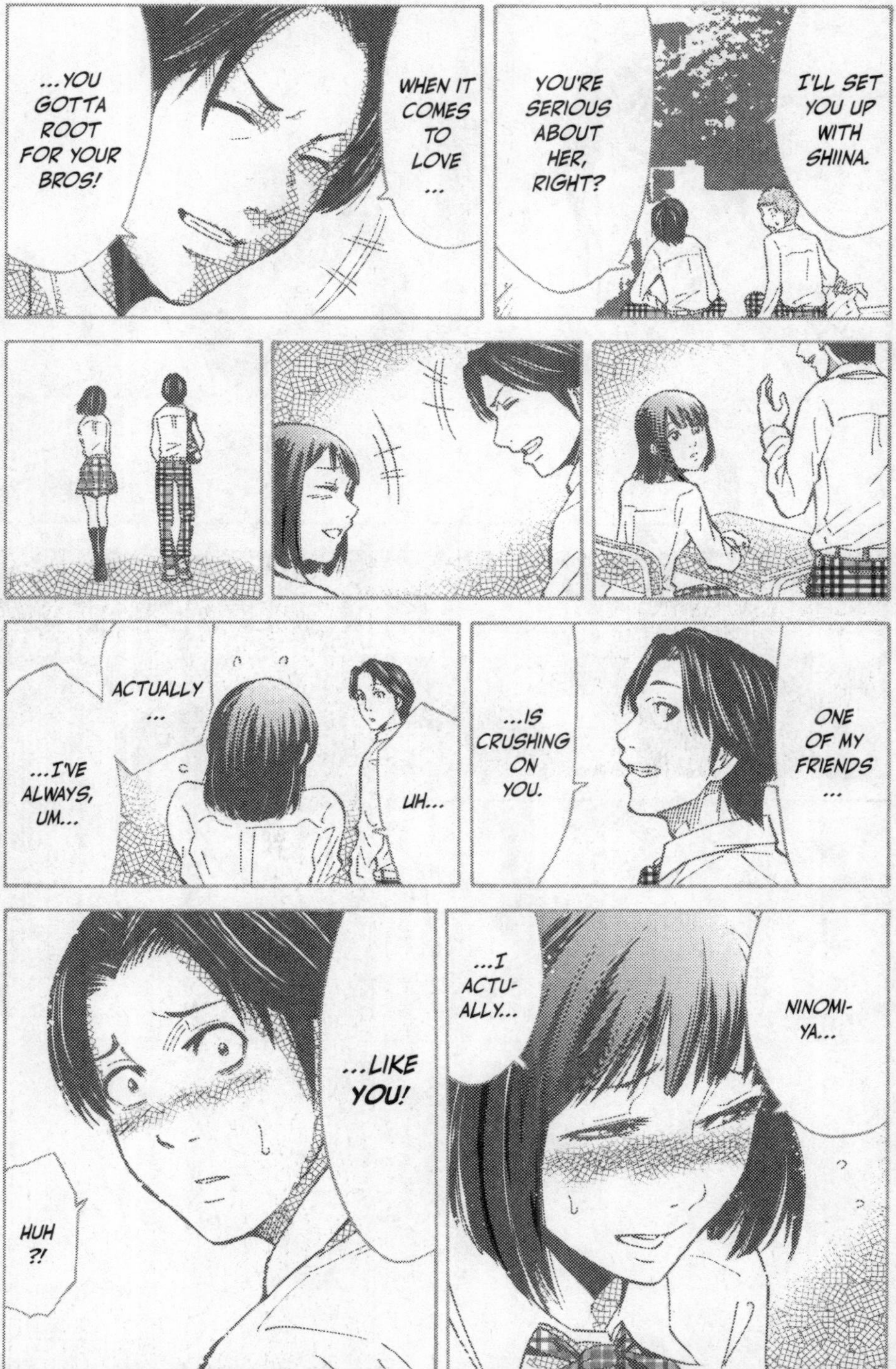
I'LL SET YOU UP WITH SHIINA.
YOU'RE SERIOUS ABOUT HER, RIGHT?
WHEN IT COMES TO LOVE...
...YOU GOTTA ROOT FOR YOUR BROS!
ONE OF MY FRIENDS...
...IS CRUSHING ON YOU.
ACTUALLY...
...I'VE ALWAYS, UM...
UH...
NINOMI-YA...
...I ACTU-ALLY...
...LIKE YOU!
HUH?!

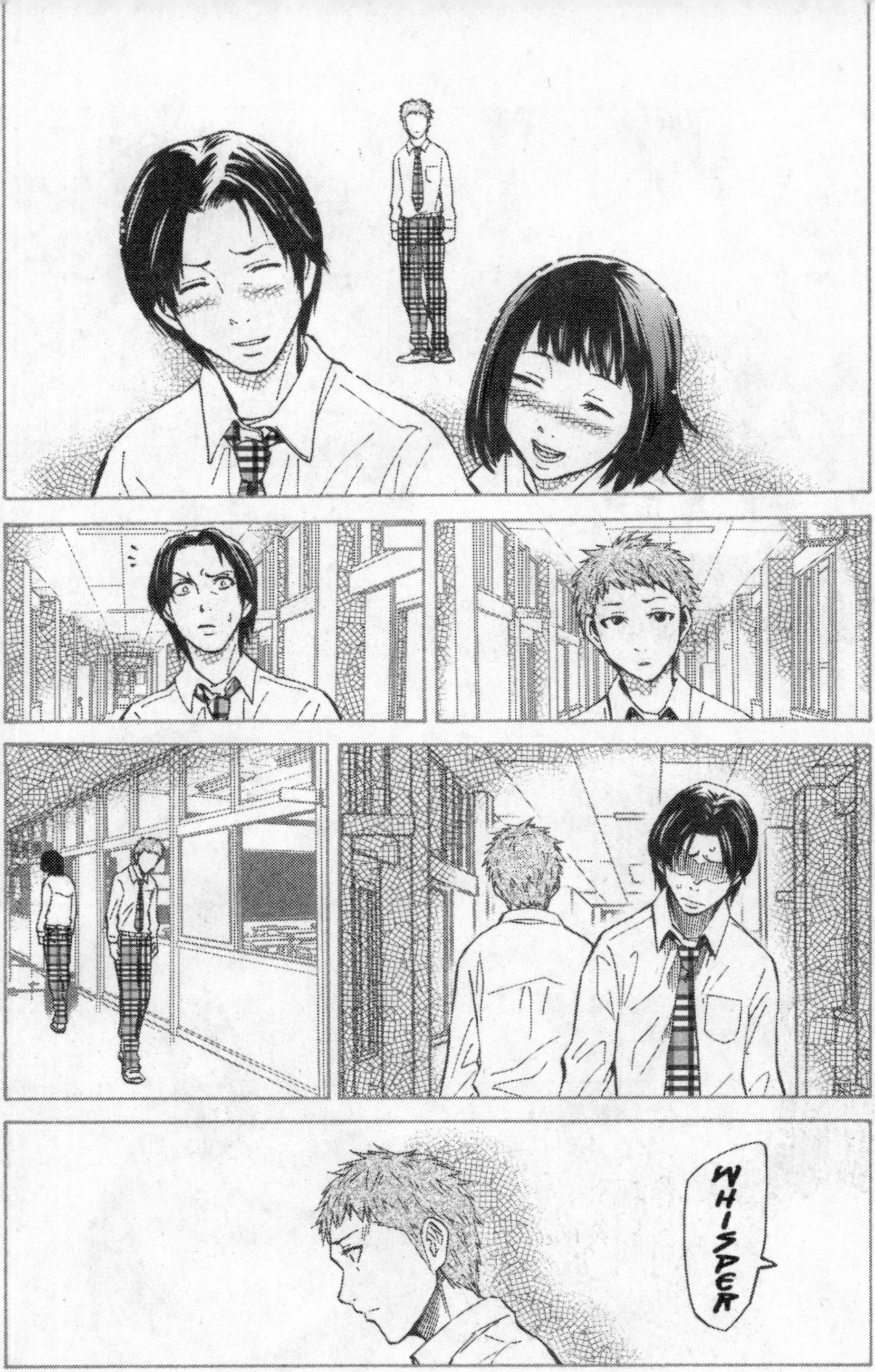
WHISPER

I'M SORRY.

...he apolo-gized.

That day...

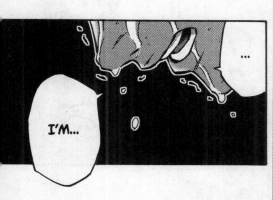

...

I'M...

I'M SORRY!

I REALLY AM!

...

I'M SORRY!

I'M ...

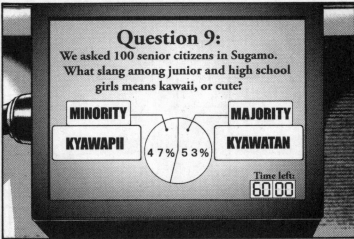

Question 9:
We asked 100 senior citizens in Sugamo. What slang among junior and high school girls means kawaii, or cute?

MINORITY

KYAWAPII

47% 53%

MAJORITY

KYAWATAN

Time left:
60 00

CLICK

THE ANSWER IS THE MAJORITY!

IT'S KYAWA TAN!

THAT'S SO KYAWA-TAN! ♪

214

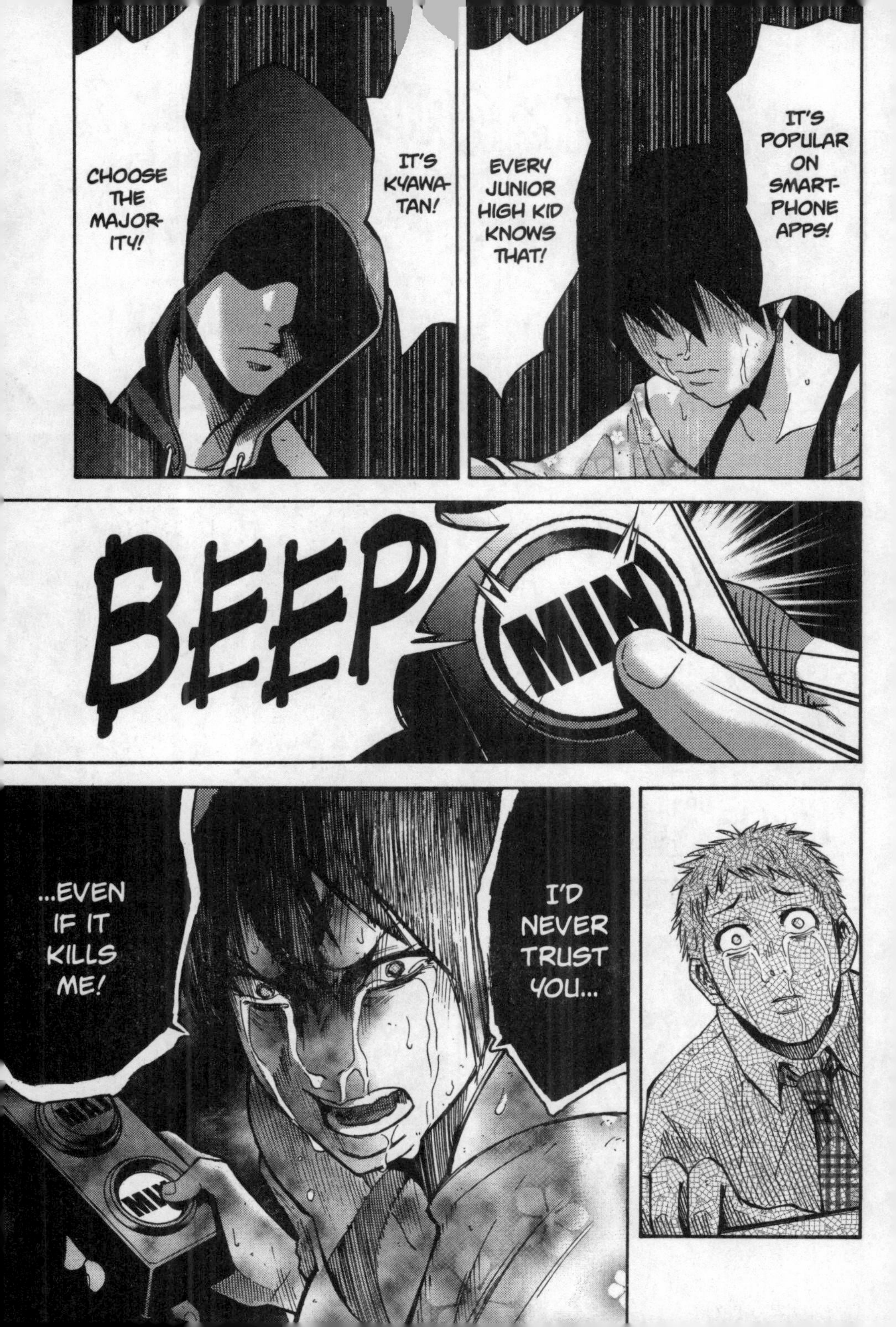
IT'S POPULAR ON SMART-PHONE APPS!
EVERY JUNIOR HIGH KID KNOWS THAT!
IT'S KYAWA-TAN!
CHOOSE THE MAJOR-ITY!
BEEP
MIN
I'D NEVER TRUST YOU...
...EVEN IF IT KILLS ME!

BZRRRT

DADING

DADING

CLICK

Correct Answer

MAJORITY

KYAWATAN

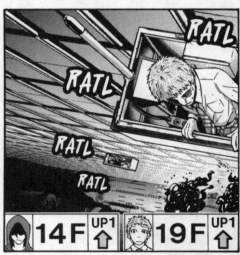

RATL

RATL

RATL

RATL

14 F UP1

19 F UP1

KLATR
KLATR
KLA
TR
KLATR

GWO OM

1 F DOWN 14

...much better...

It's...

SHUMP

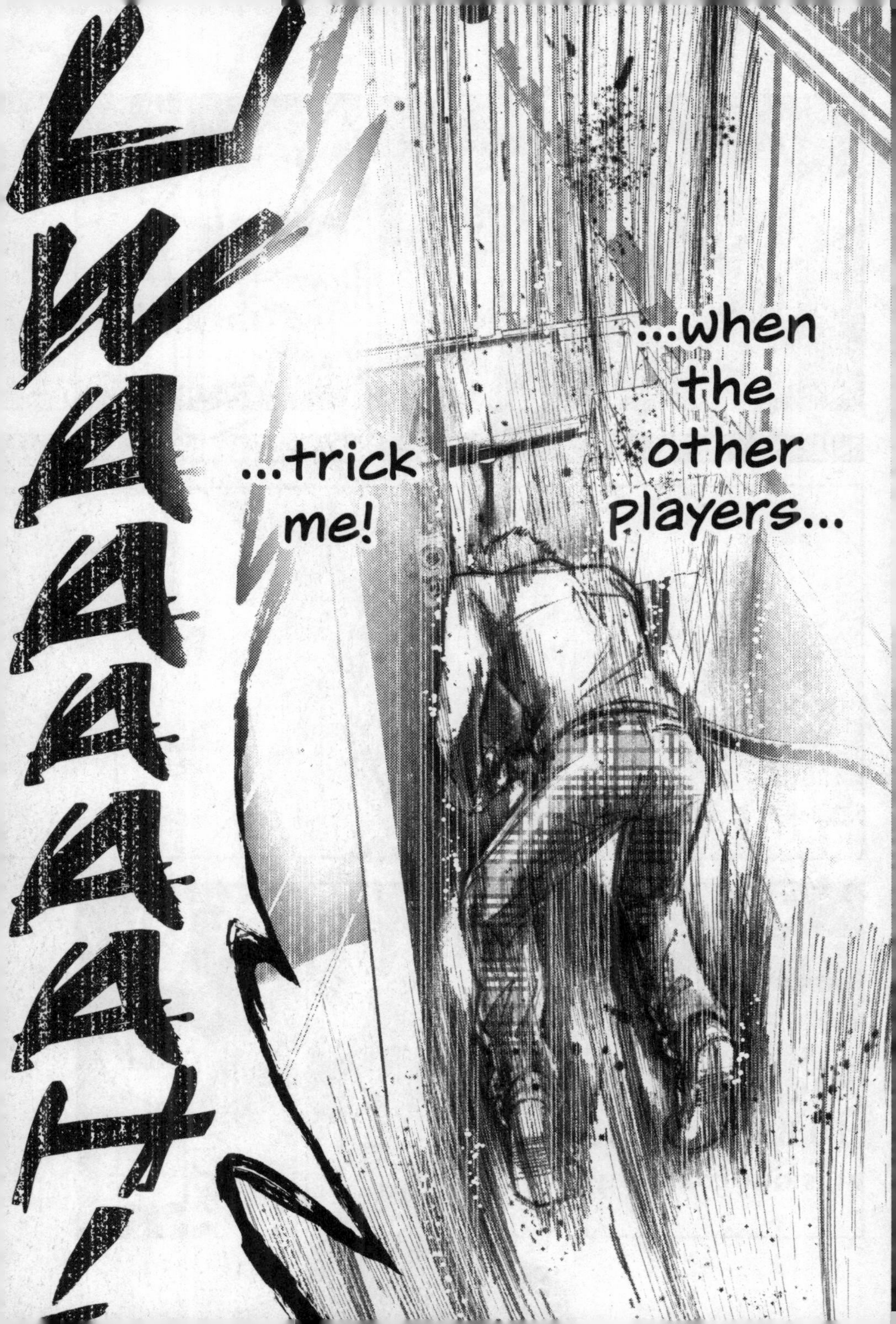
...when the other players...
...trick me!

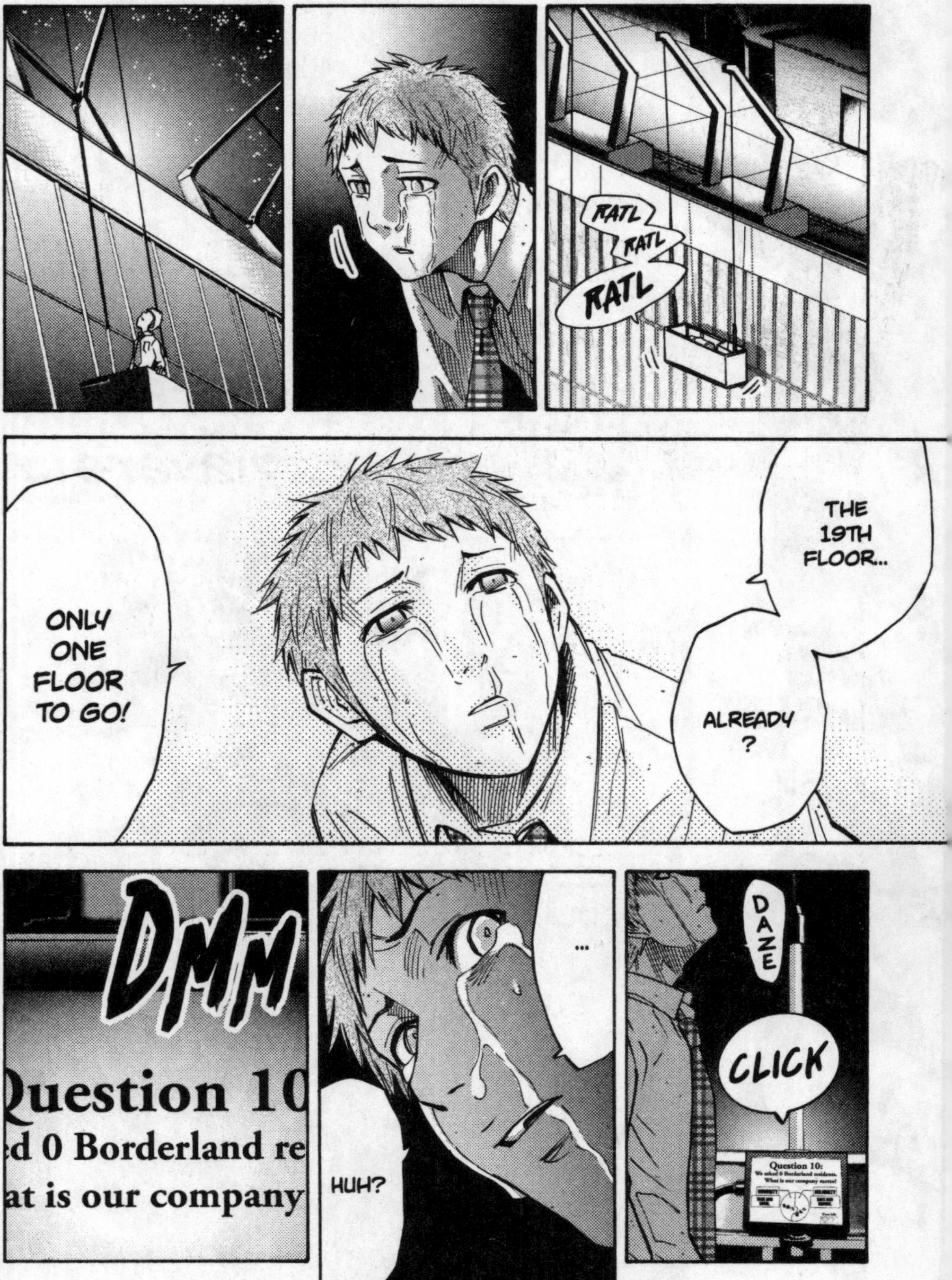
RATL
RATL
RATL
THE 19TH FLOOR...
ALREADY ?
ONLY ONE FLOOR TO GO!
DAZE
CLICK
Question 10:
...
HUH?
DMM
Question 10
ed 0 Borderland re
at is our company

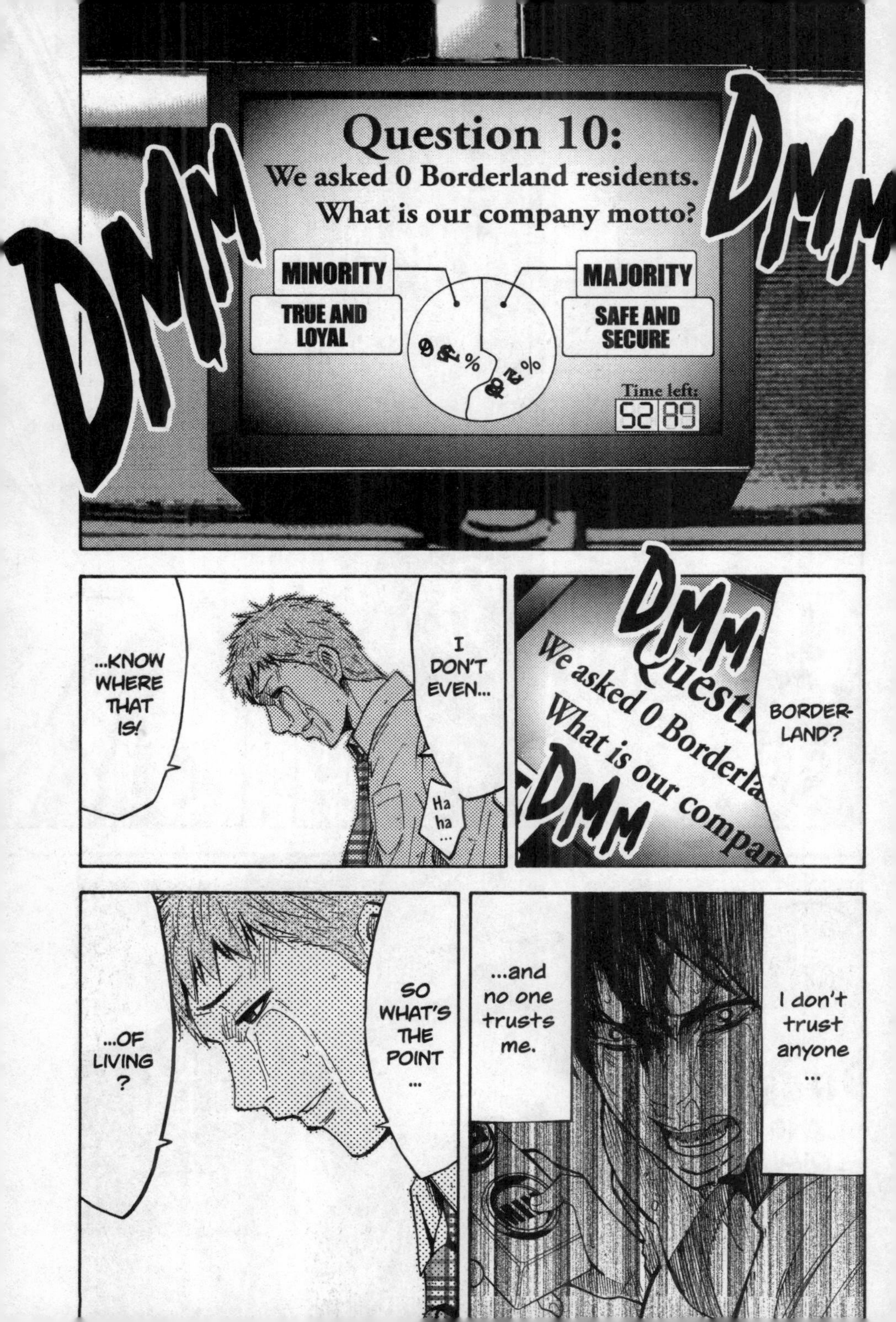
DMM
DMM
Question 10:
We asked 0 Borderland residents.
What is our company motto?
MINORITY
TRUE AND LOYAL
MAJORITY
SAFE AND SECURE
Time left:
DMM
Question
We asked 0 Borderla
What is our compan
DMM
BORDER-LAND?
I DON'T EVEN...
Ha ha...
...KNOW WHERE THAT IS!
I don't trust anyone...
...and no one trusts me.
SO WHAT'S THE POINT...
...OF LIVING?

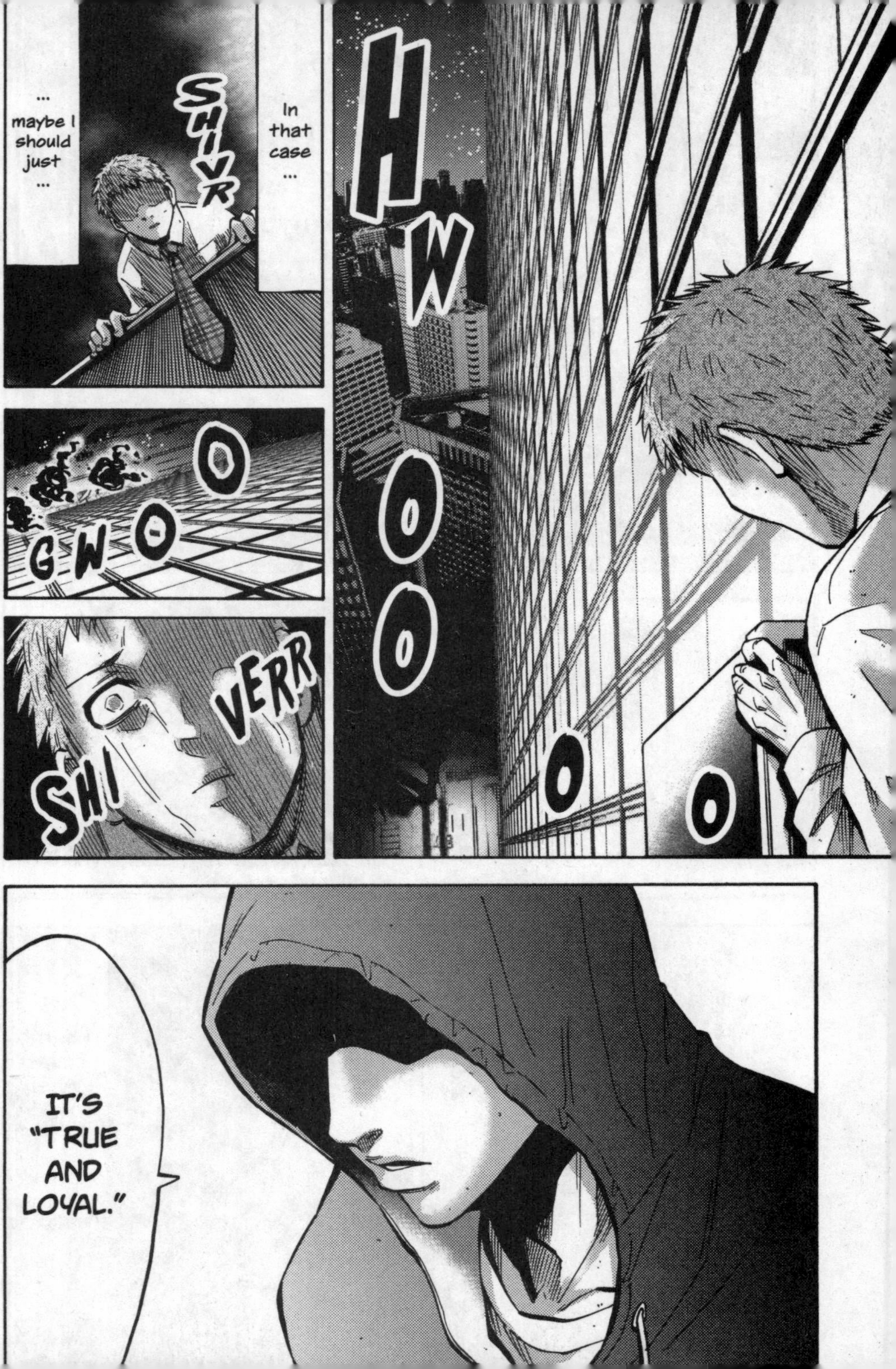
HWOOOOO
In that case ...
... maybe I should just ...
SHIVR
GWO-O
SHIVERR
IT'S "TRUE AND LOYAL."

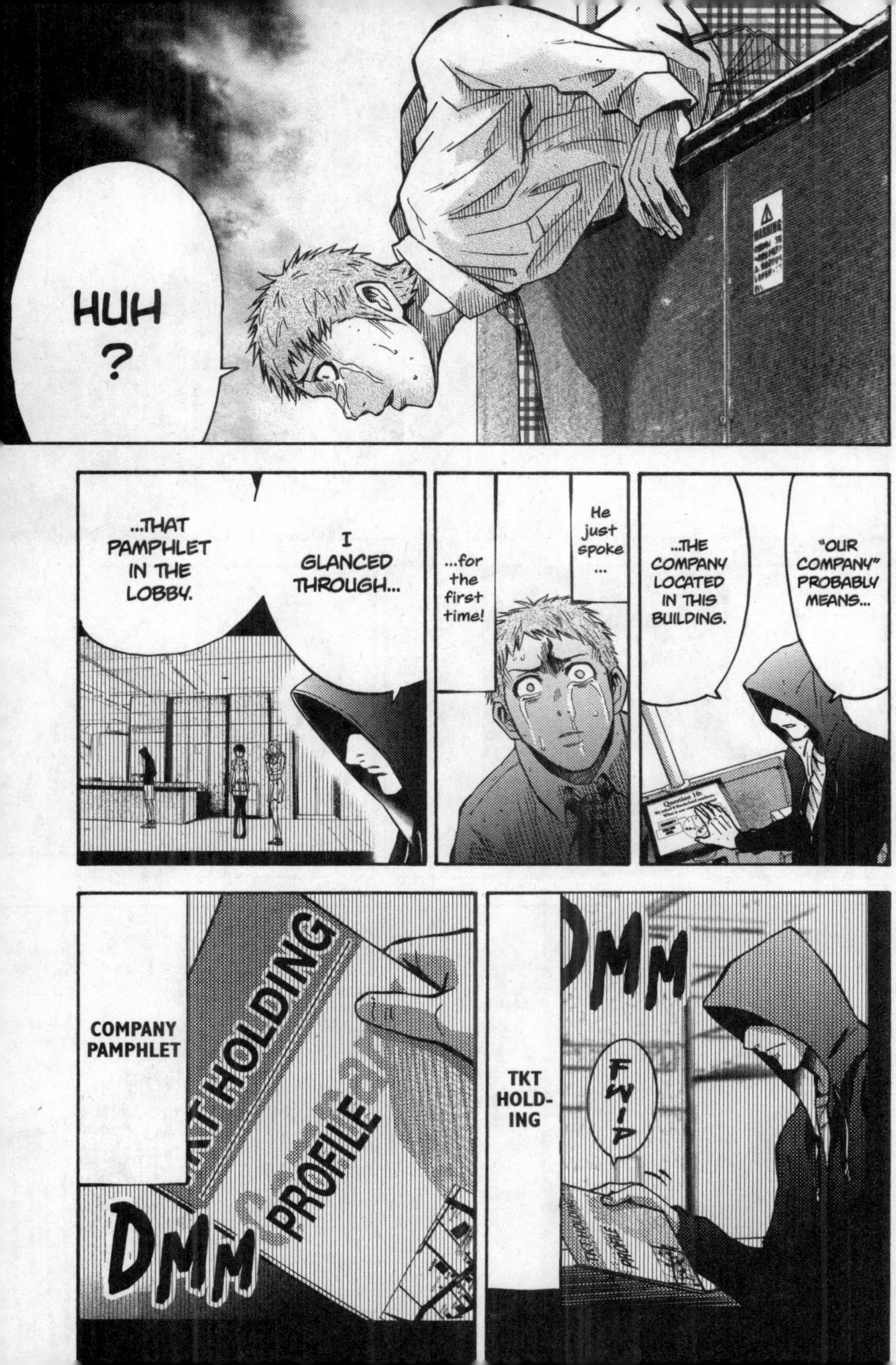
HUH?
"OUR COMPANY" PROBABLY MEANS...
...THE COMPANY LOCATED IN THIS BUILDING.
Question 10:
He just spoke...
...for the first time!
I GLANCED THROUGH...
...THAT PAMPHLET IN THE LOBBY.
DMM
FWIP
TKT HOLDING
COMPANY PAMPHLET
TKT HOLDING
PROFILE
DMM

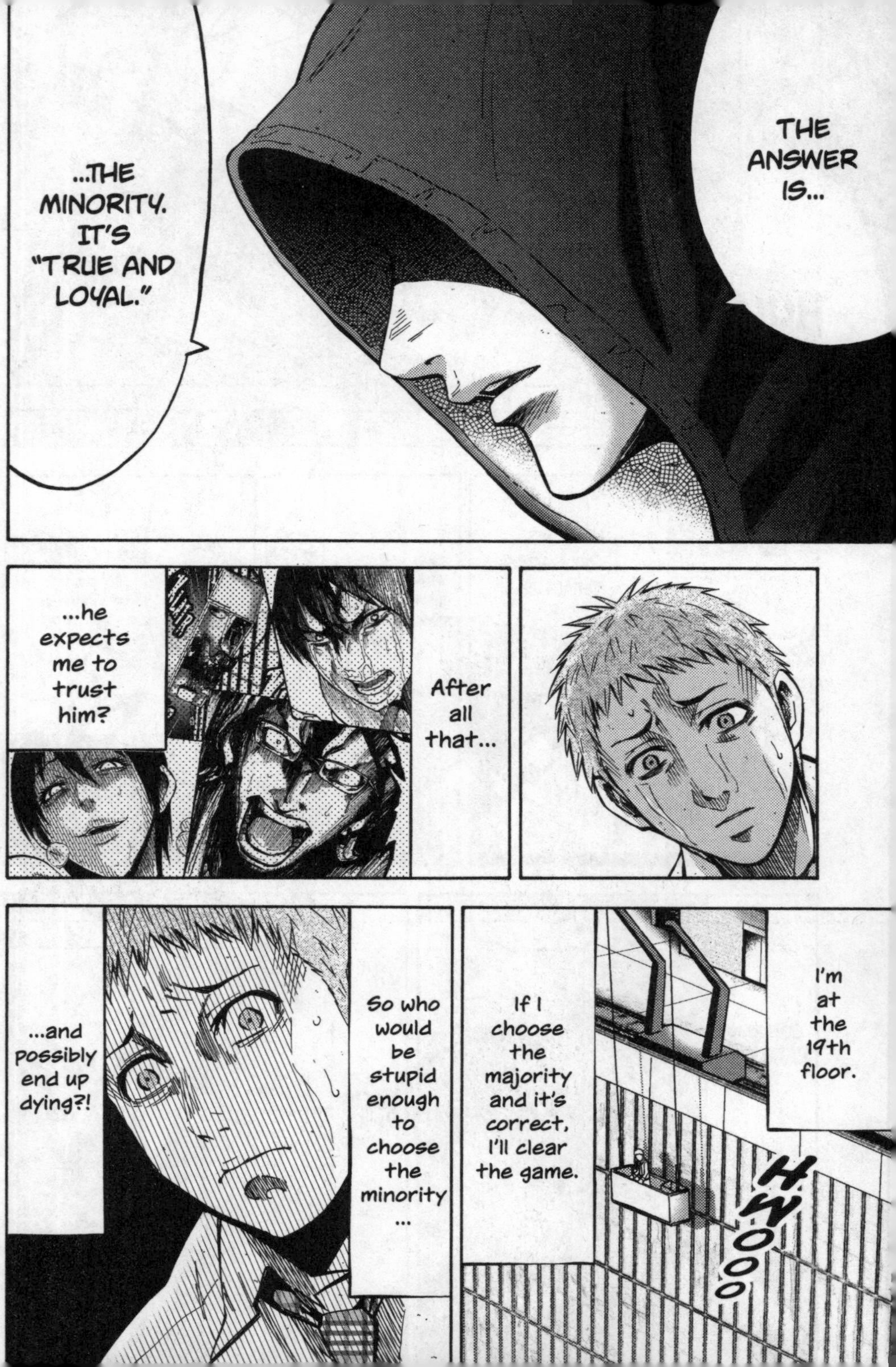
THE ANSWER IS...
...THE MINORITY. IT'S "TRUE AND LOYAL."
After all that...
...he expects me to trust him?
I'm at the 19th floor.
HWOOO
If I choose the majority and it's correct, I'll clear the game.
So who would be stupid enough to choose the minority...
...and possibly end up dying?!

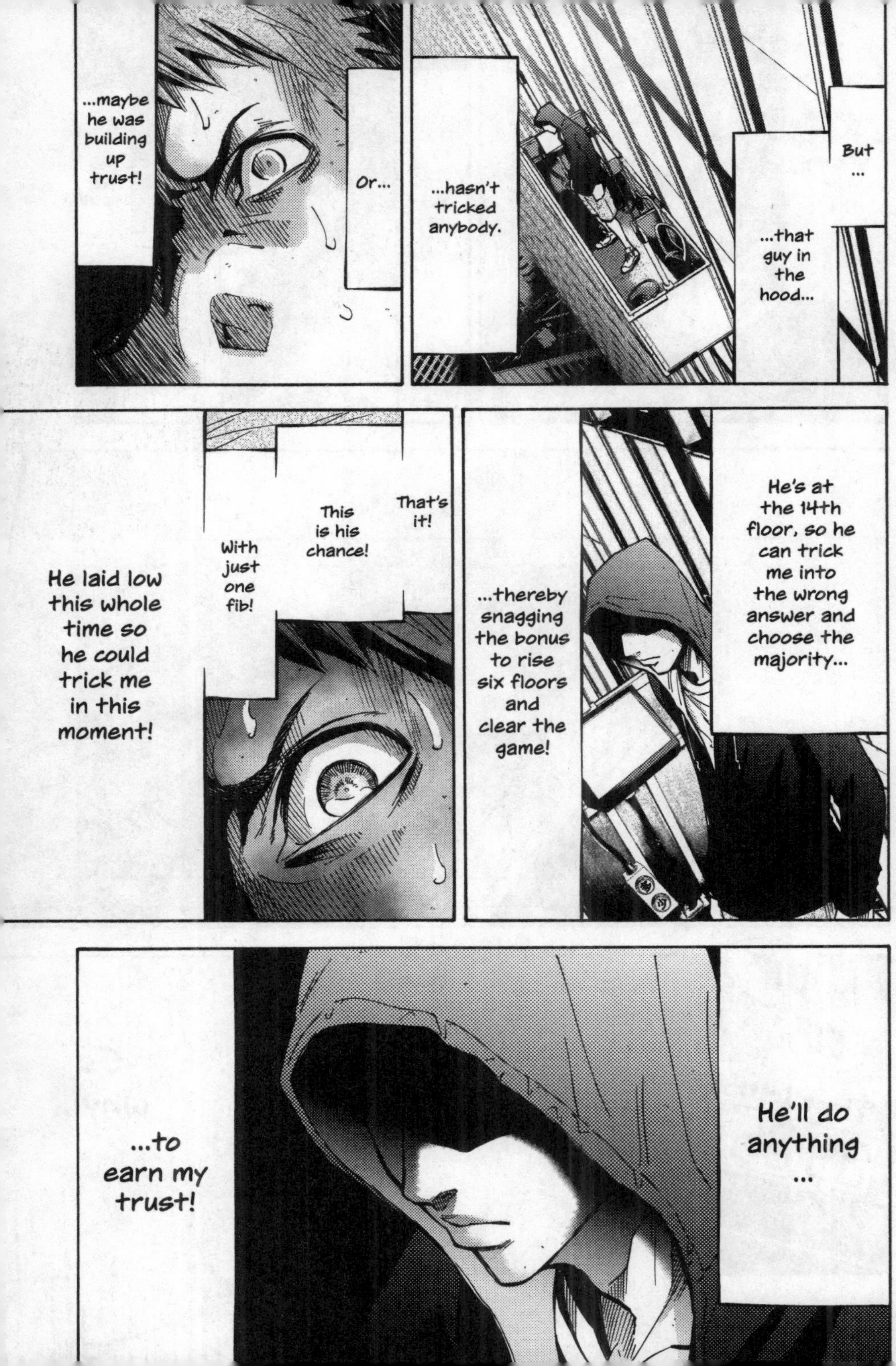
But ...
...that guy in the hood...
...hasn't tricked anybody.
Or...
...maybe he was building up trust!
He's at the 14th floor, so he can trick me into the wrong answer and choose the majority...
...thereby snagging the bonus to rise six floors and clear the game!
That's it!
This is his chance!
With just one fib!
He laid low this whole time so he could trick me in this moment!
He'll do anything ...
...to earn my trust!

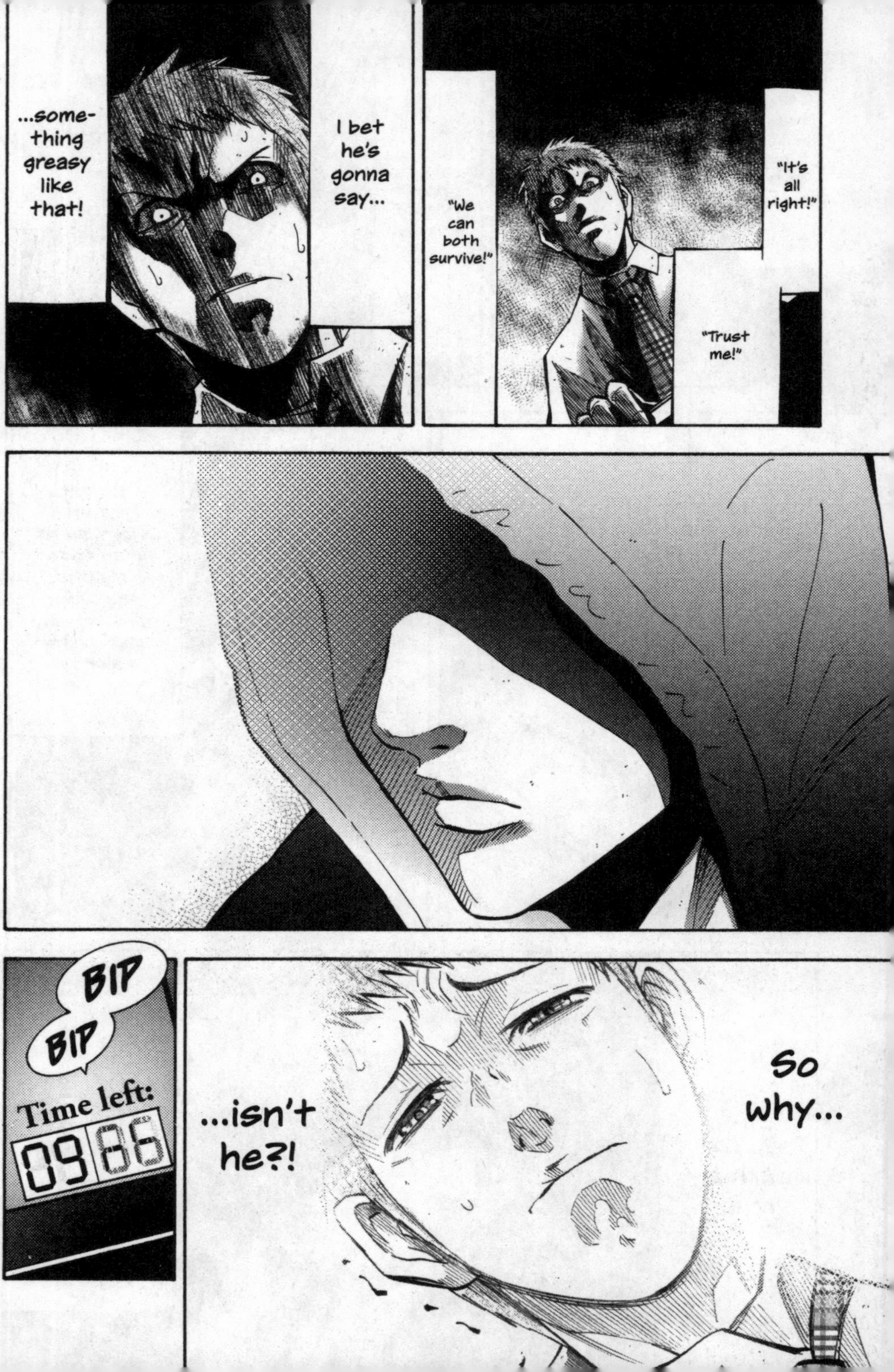
"It's all right!"
"We can both survive!"
"Trust me!"
I bet he's gonna say...
...some-thing greasy like that!
So why...
...isn't he?!
BIP
BIP
Time left:
09 66

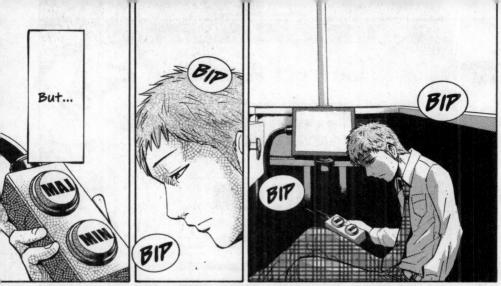

But...

BIP

BIP

BIP

BIP

BIP

Time left:

0189

...without trust?

...how can I live...

MIN

BEEP

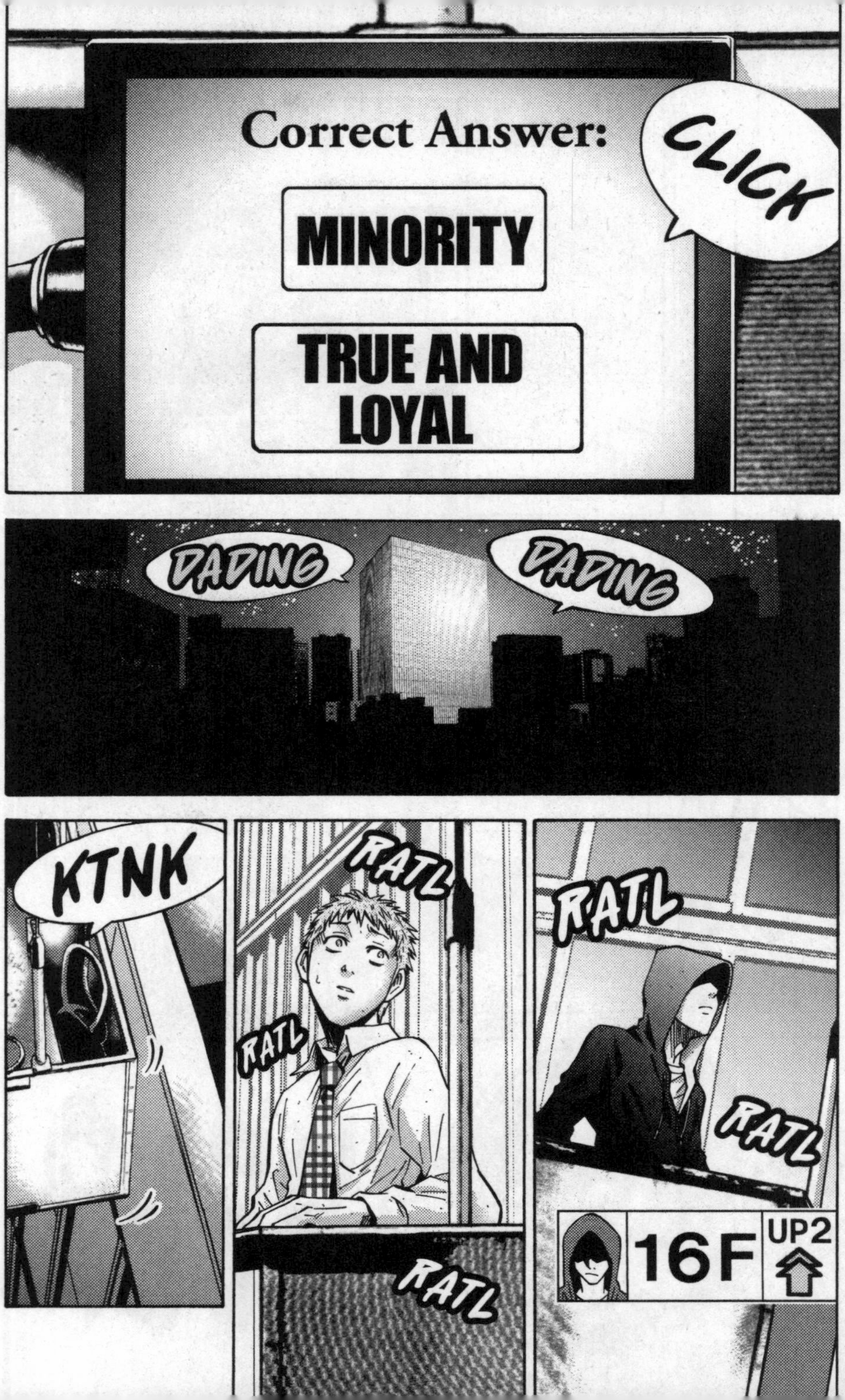
Correct Answer:
MINORITY
TRUE AND LOYAL
CLICK
DADING
DADING
RATL
RATL
16F
UP2
RATL
RATL
RATL
KTNK

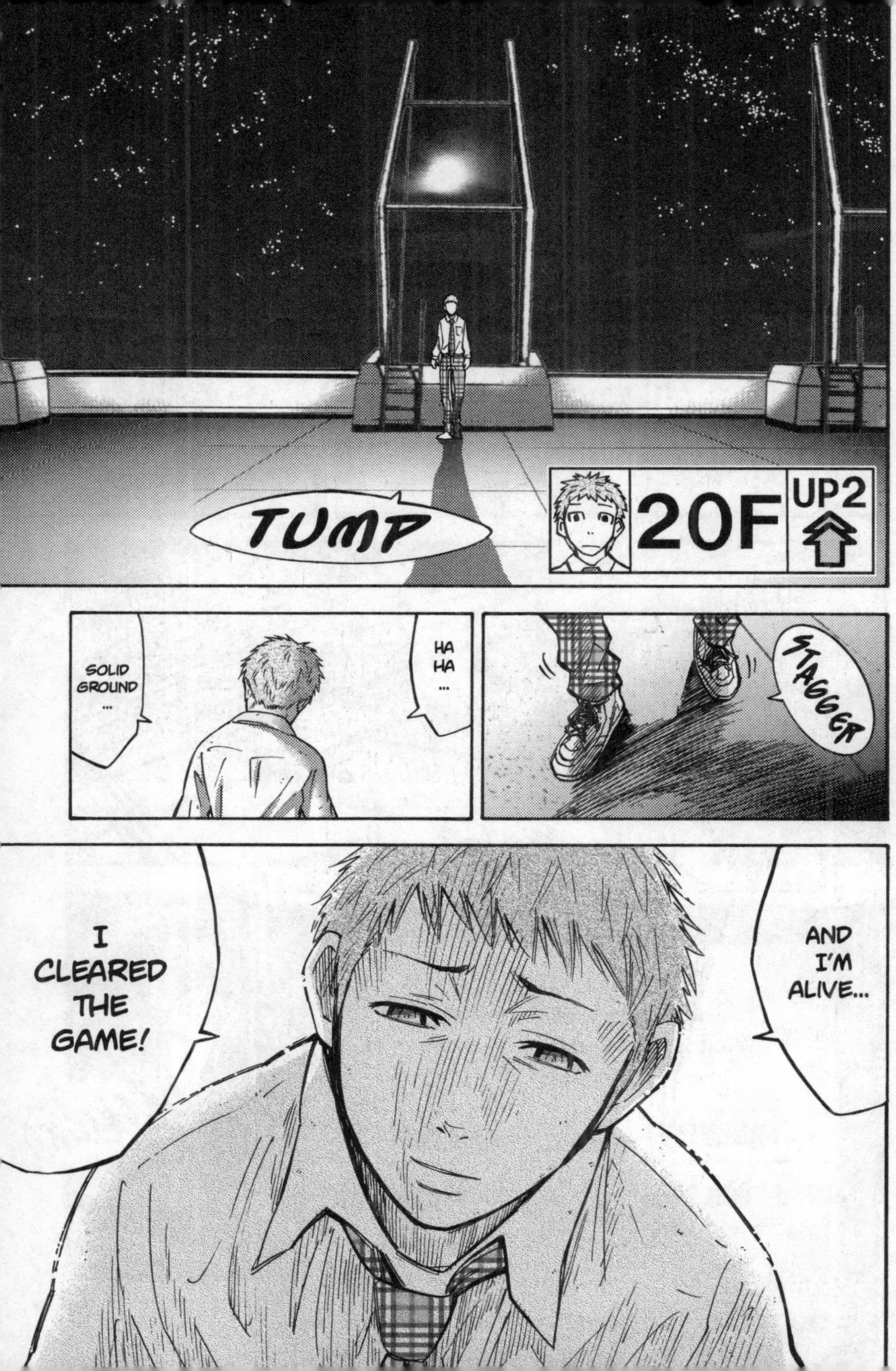
TUMP
20F
UP2
STAGGER
HA HA ...
SOLID GROUND ...
AND I'M ALIVE...
I CLEARED THE GAME!

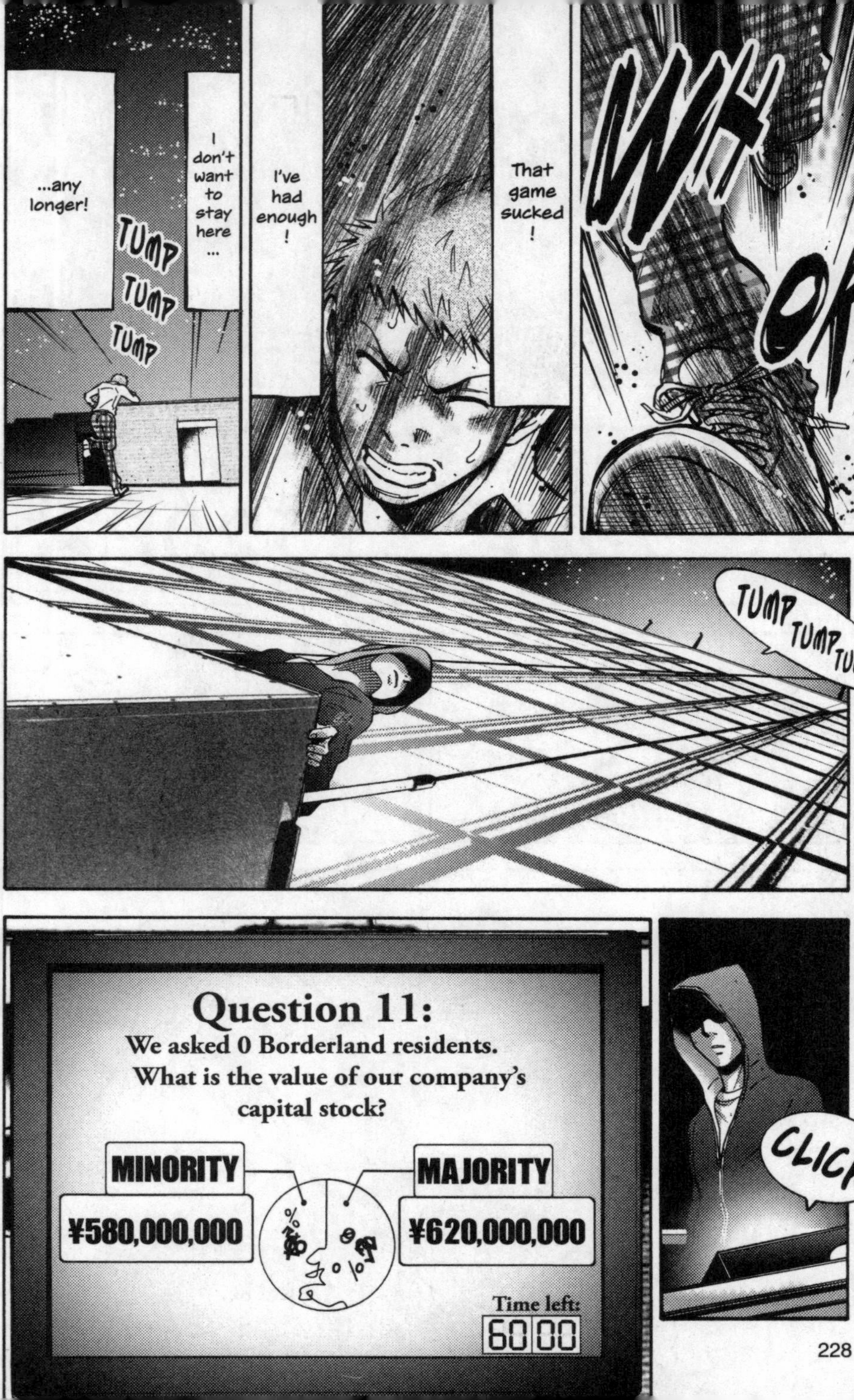
WHOK
That game sucked!
I've had enough!
I don't want to stay here...
...any longer!
TUMP
TUMP
TUMP
TUMP TUMP TUMP
CLICK
Question 11:
We asked 0 Borderland residents.
What is the value of our company's capital stock?
MINORITY
¥580,000,000
MAJORITY
¥620,000,000
Time left:
60:00

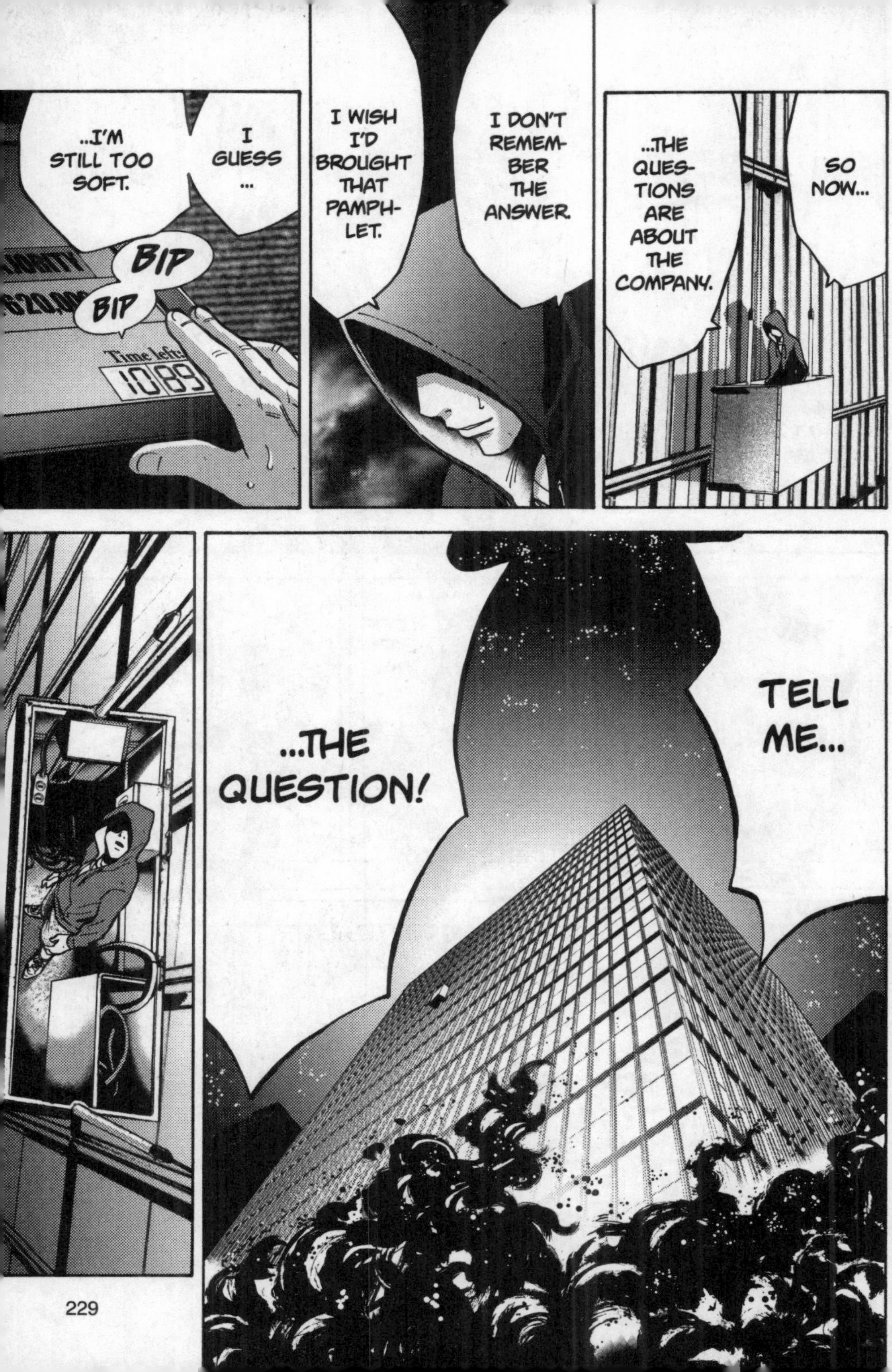
SO NOW...
...THE QUES-TIONS ARE ABOUT THE COMPANY.
I DON'T REMEM-BER THE ANSWER.
I WISH I'D BROUGHT THAT PAMPH-LET.
I GUESS ...
...I'M STILL TOO SOFT.
BIP
BIP
Time left:
TELL ME...
...THE QUESTION!

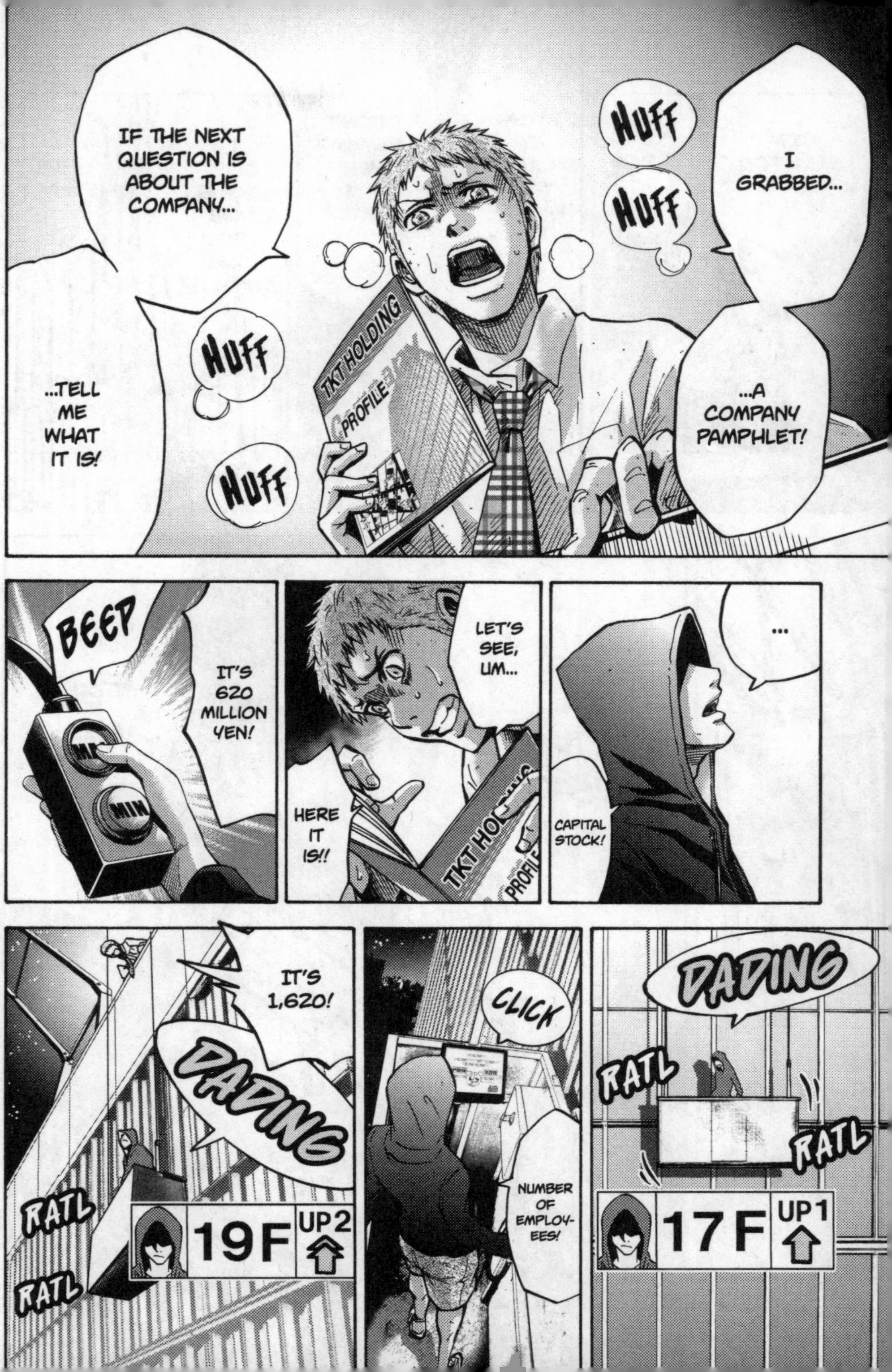
HUFF
HUFF
I GRABBED...
...A COMPANY PAMPHLET!
TKT HOLDING PROFILE
IF THE NEXT QUESTION IS ABOUT THE COMPANY...
HUFF
HUFF
...TELL ME WHAT IT IS!
...
CAPITAL STOCK!
LET'S SEE, UM...
TKT HOLDING PROFILE
HERE IT IS!!
BEEP
IT'S 620 MILLION YEN!
MIN
DADING
RATL
RATL
17 F
UP 1
CLICK
NUMBER OF EMPLOY-EES!
IT'S 1,620!
DADING
19 F
UP 2
RATL
RATL

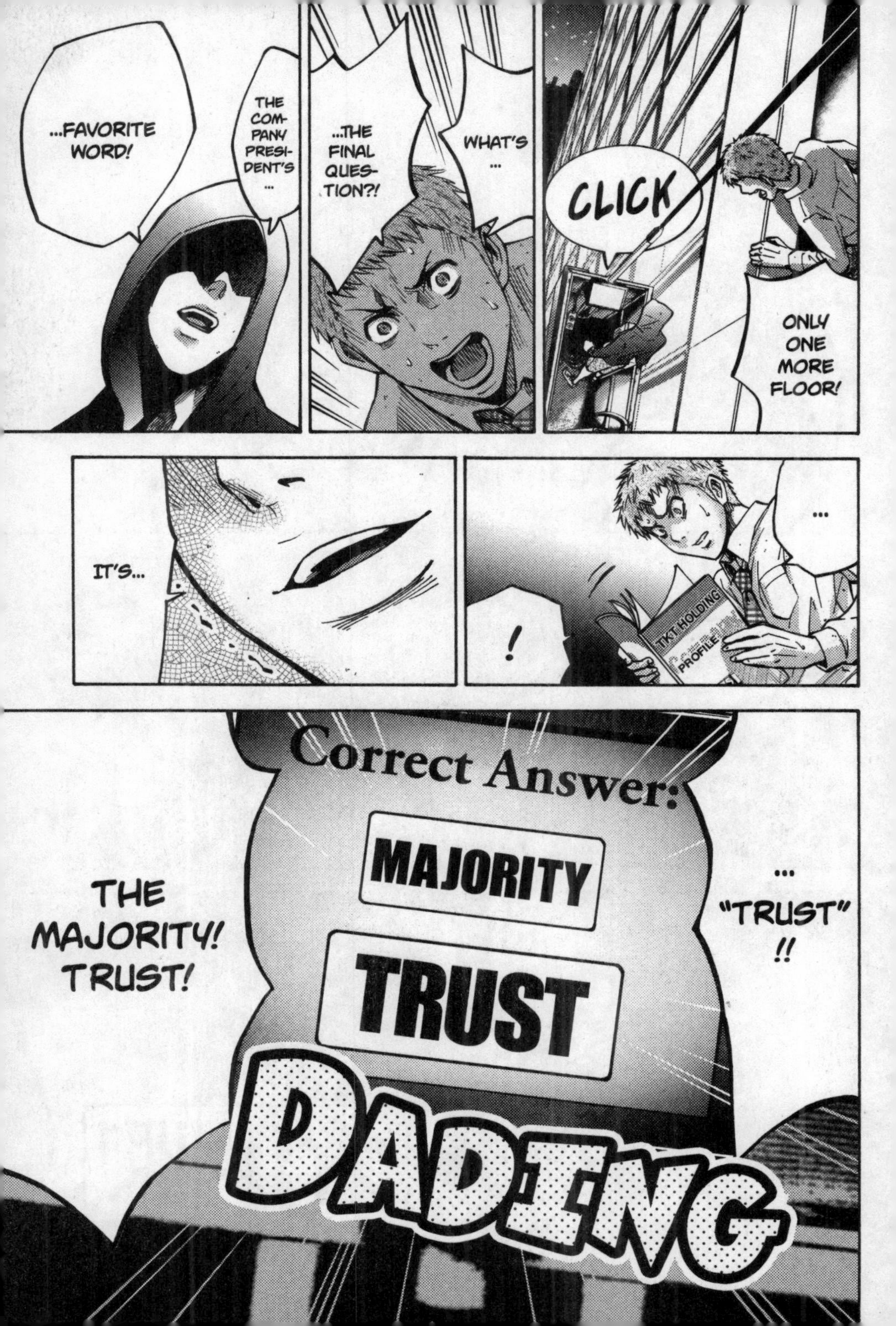
CLICK
ONLY ONE MORE FLOOR!
WHAT'S ...
...THE FINAL QUES-TION?!
THE COM-PANY PRESI-DENT'S ...
...FAVORITE WORD!
...
TKT HOLDING
PROFILE
!
IT'S...
Correct Answer:
MAJORITY
TRUST
... "TRUST" !!
THE MAJORITY! TRUST!
DADING

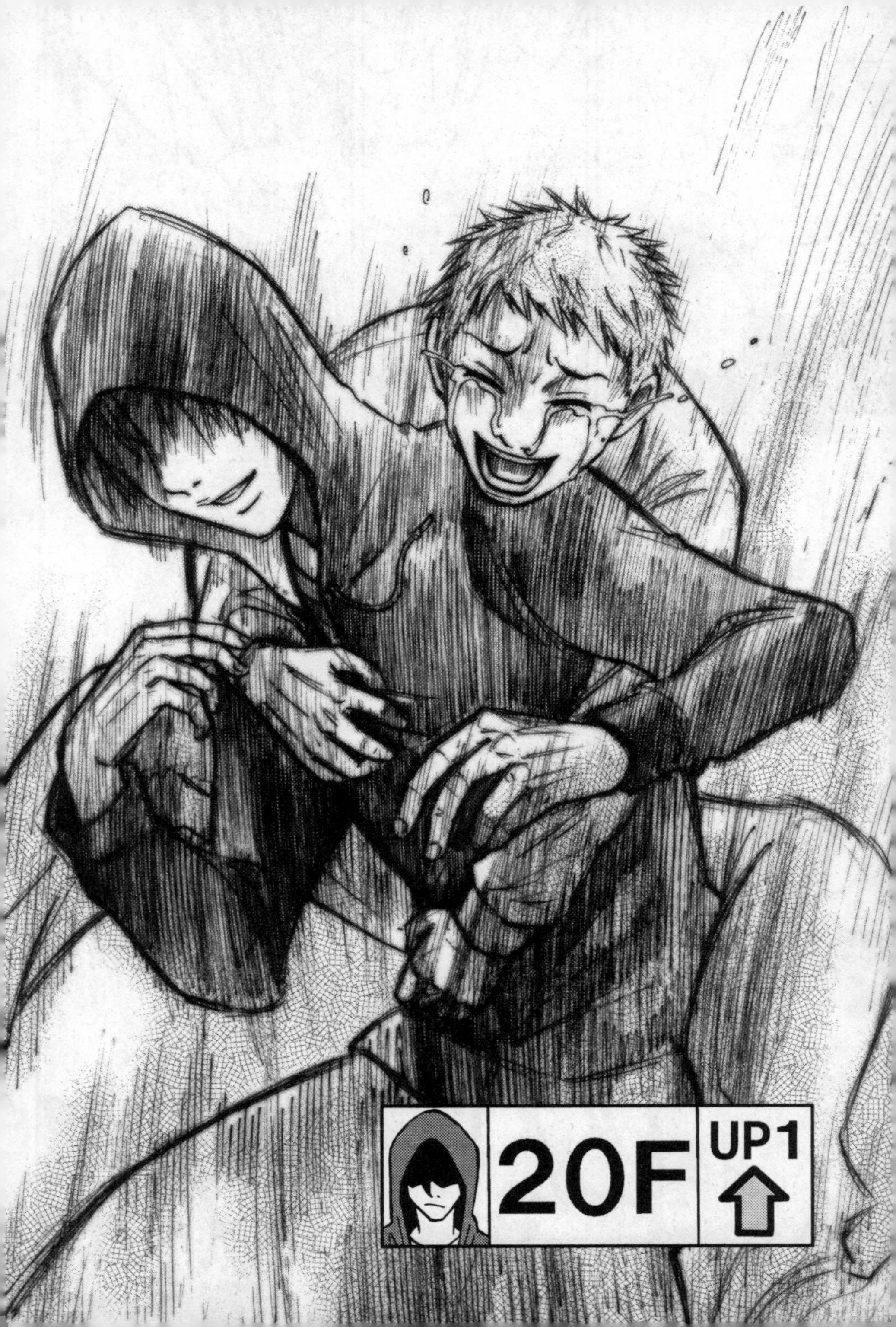
20F
UP1

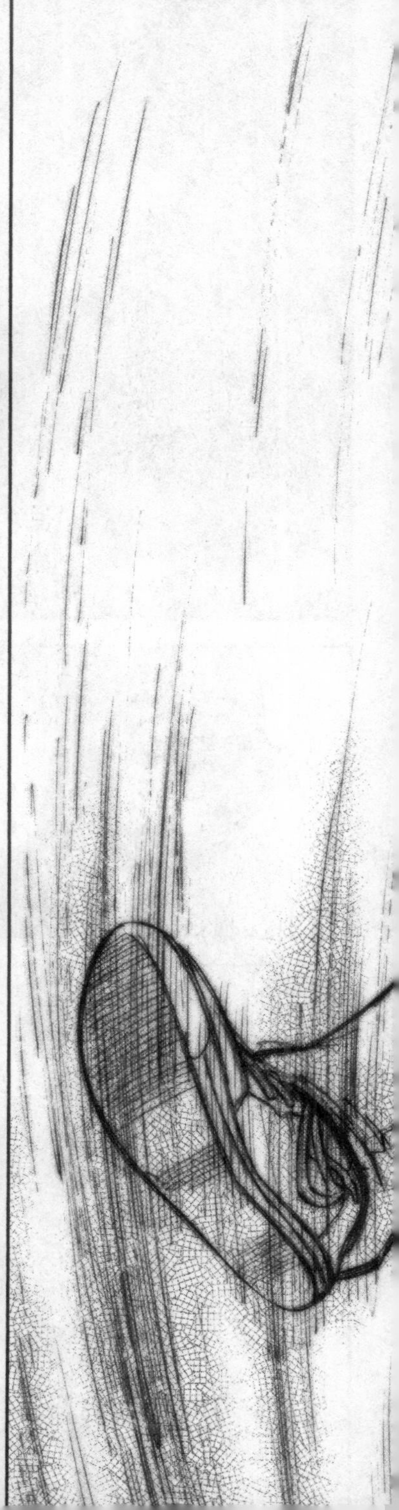

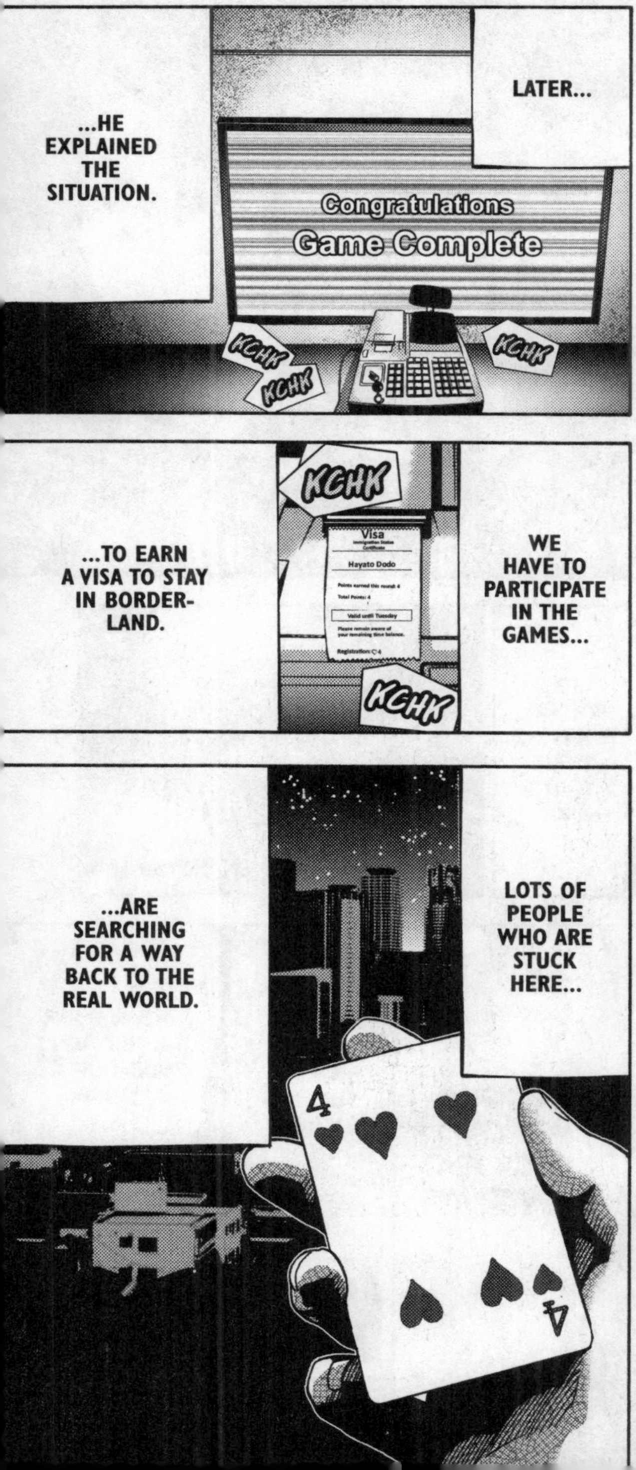
LATER...
Congratulations
Game Complete
KCHK
KCHK
KCHK
...HE EXPLAINED THE SITUATION.
WE HAVE TO PARTICIPATE IN THE GAMES...
KCHK
Visa
Hayato Dodo
Points earned this round: 4
Total Points: 4
Valid until Tuesday
Please remain aware of your remaining time balance.
Registration: ♡4
KCHK
...TO EARN A VISA TO STAY IN BORDER-LAND.
LOTS OF PEOPLE WHO ARE STUCK HERE...
...ARE SEARCHING FOR A WAY BACK TO THE REAL WORLD.

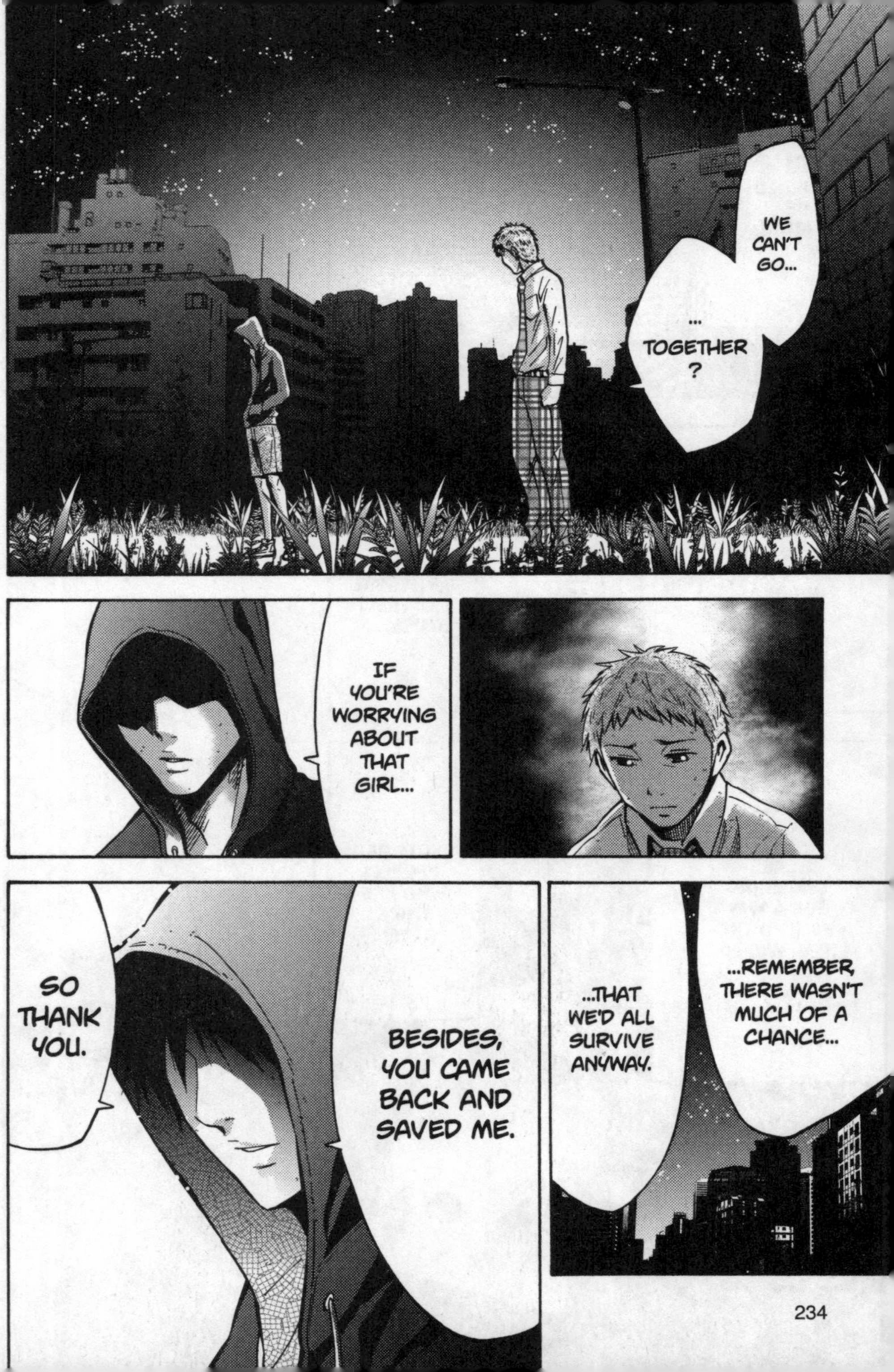
WE CAN'T GO...
...TOGETHER?
IF YOU'RE WORRYING ABOUT THAT GIRL...
...REMEMBER, THERE WASN'T MUCH OF A CHANCE...
...THAT WE'D ALL SURVIVE ANYWAY.
BESIDES, YOU CAME BACK AND SAVED ME.
SO THANK YOU.

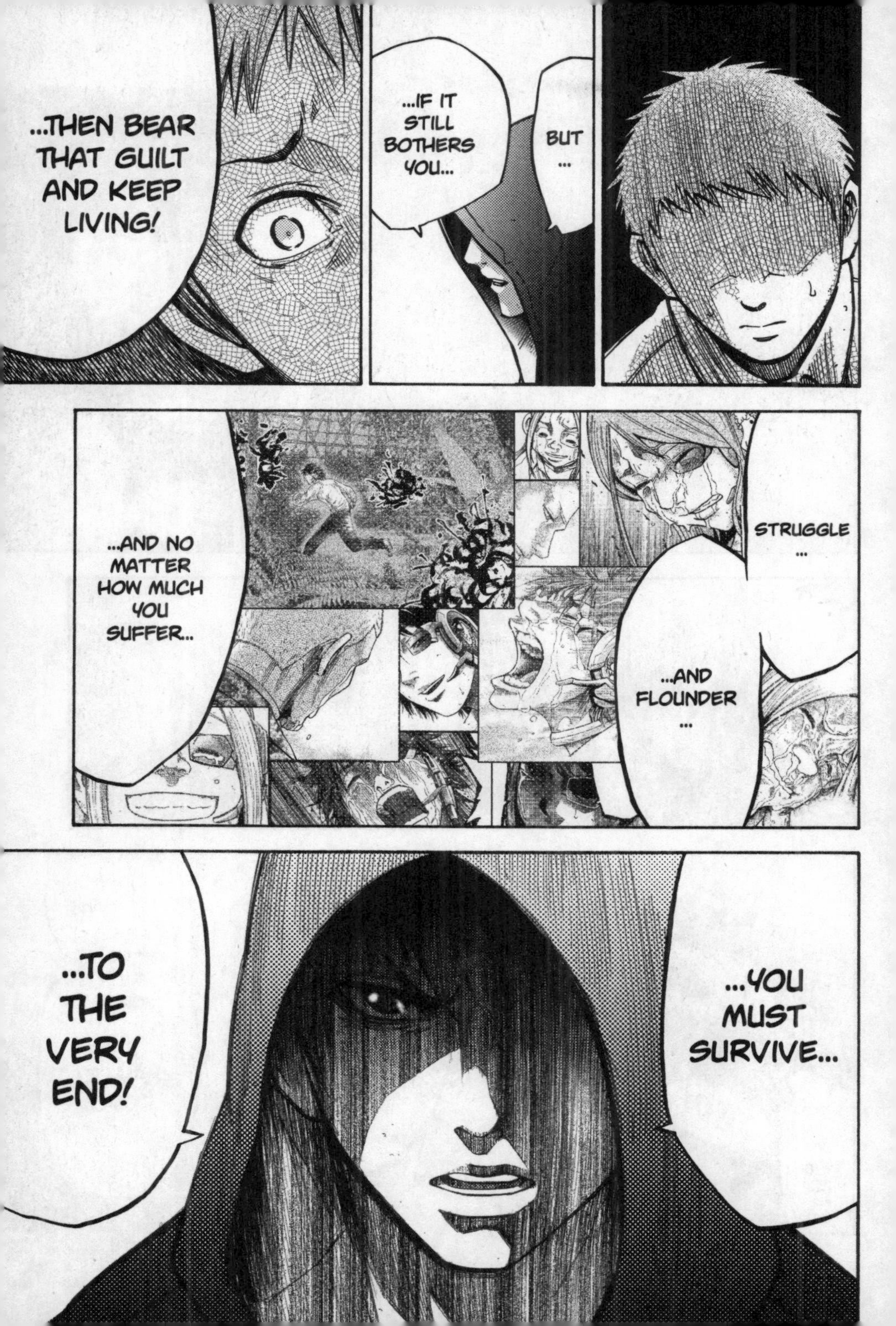
BUT ...
...IF IT STILL BOTHERS YOU...
...THEN BEAR THAT GUILT AND KEEP LIVING!
STRUGGLE ...
...AND FLOUNDER ...
...AND NO MATTER HOW MUCH YOU SUFFER...
...YOU MUST SURVIVE...
...TO THE VERY END!

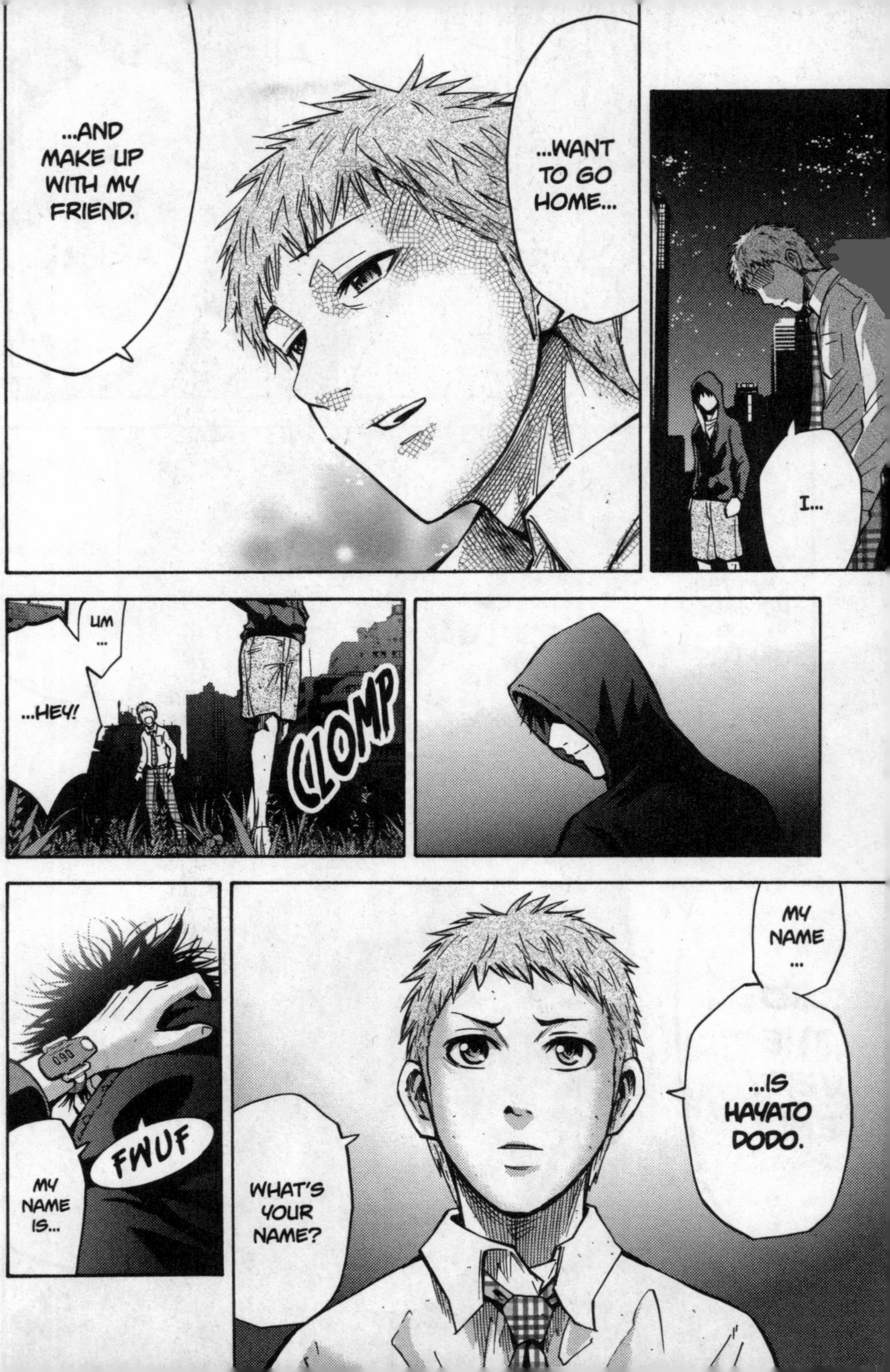
I...
...WANT TO GO HOME...
...AND MAKE UP WITH MY FRIEND.
UM ...
...HEY!
CLOMP
MY NAME ...
...IS HAYATO DODO.
WHAT'S YOUR NAME?
FWUF
MY NAME IS...

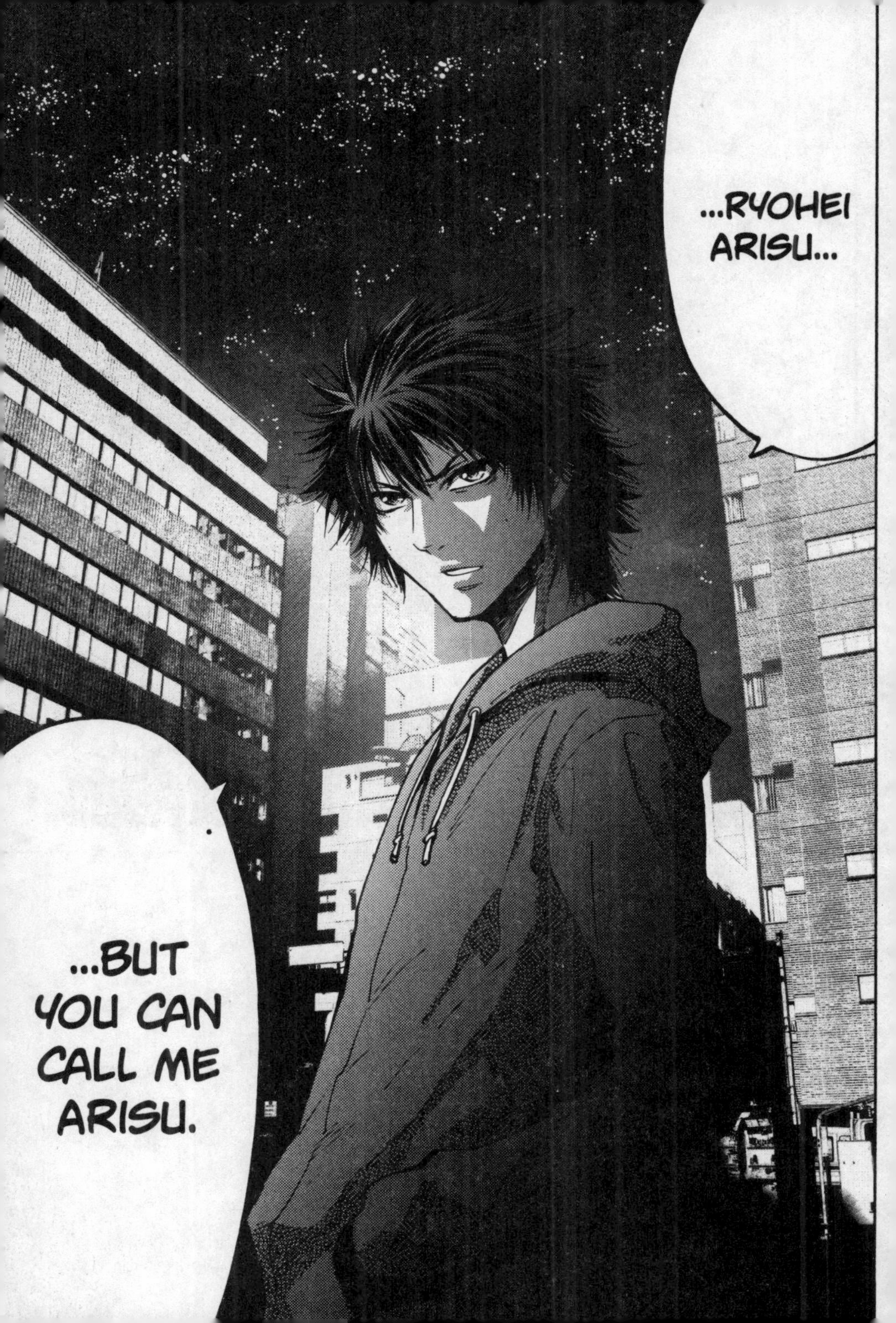
...RYOHEI ARISU...
...BUT YOU CAN CALL ME ARISU.

NOW WE
RETURN TO
THE MAIN
STORY.

CHAPTER 23: Ten of Hearts, Part 3

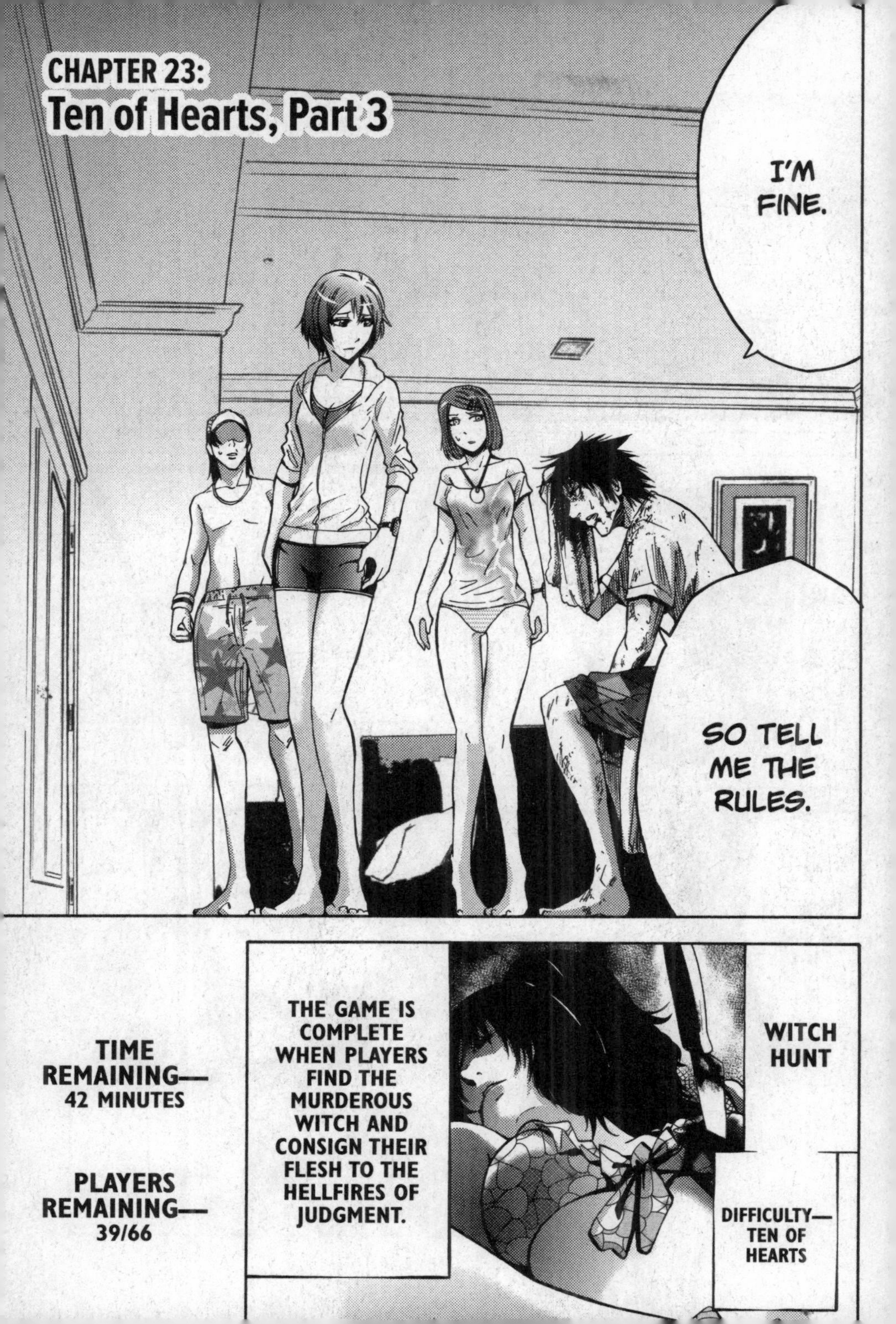
I'M FINE.
SO TELL ME THE RULES.
WITCH HUNT
DIFFICULTY—TEN OF HEARTS
THE GAME IS COMPLETE WHEN PLAYERS FIND THE MURDEROUS WITCH AND CONSIGN THEIR FLESH TO THE HELLFIRES OF JUDGMENT.
TIME REMAINING—42 MINUTES
PLAYERS REMAINING—39/66

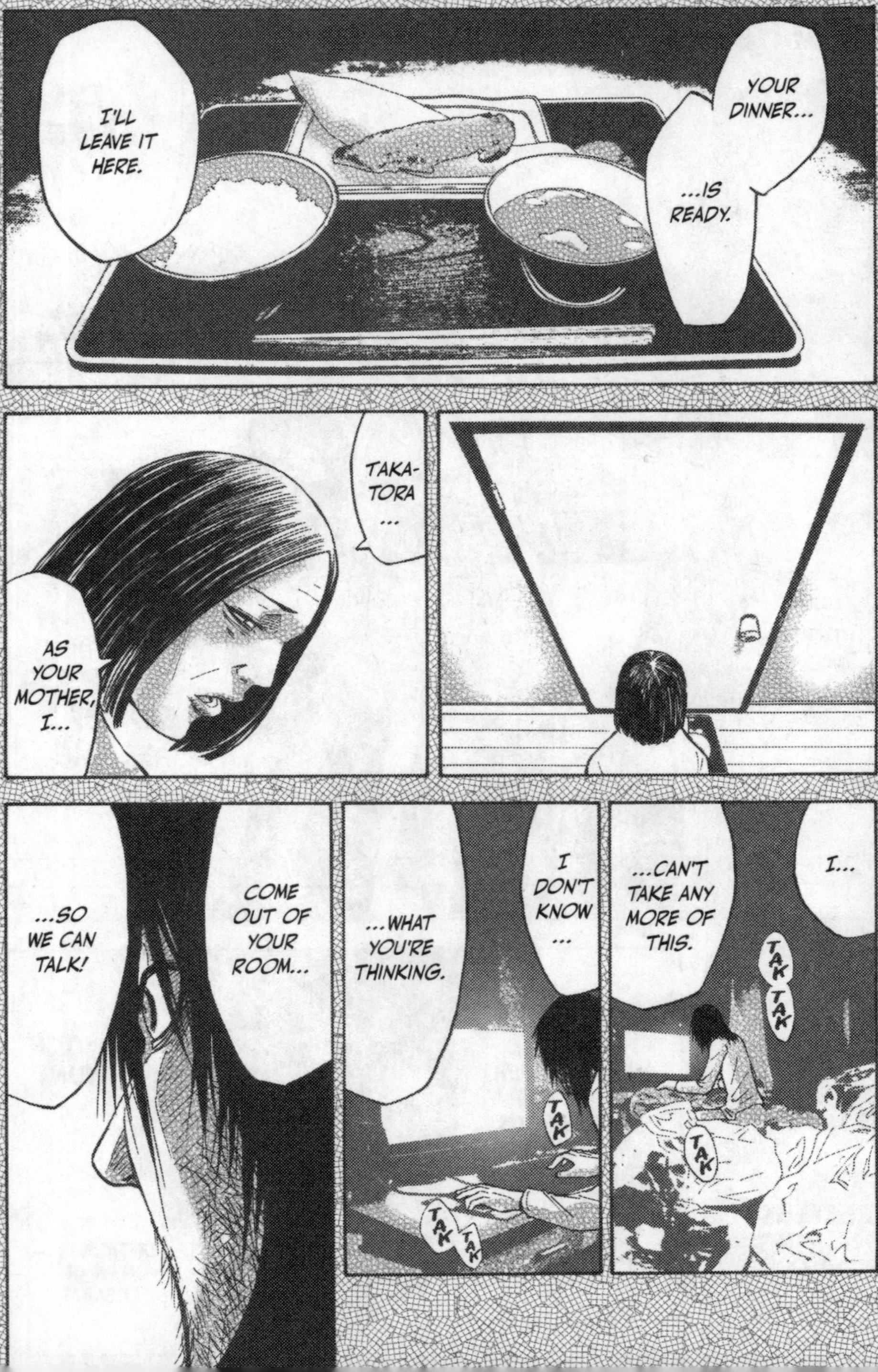
YOUR DINNER...
...IS READY.
I'LL LEAVE IT HERE.
TAKATORA...
AS YOUR MOTHER, I...
I...
...CAN'T TAKE ANY MORE OF THIS.
TAK TAK TAK
TAK
I DON'T KNOW...
...WHAT YOU'RE THINKING.
TAK
TAK TAK
COME OUT OF YOUR ROOM...
...SO WE CAN TALK!

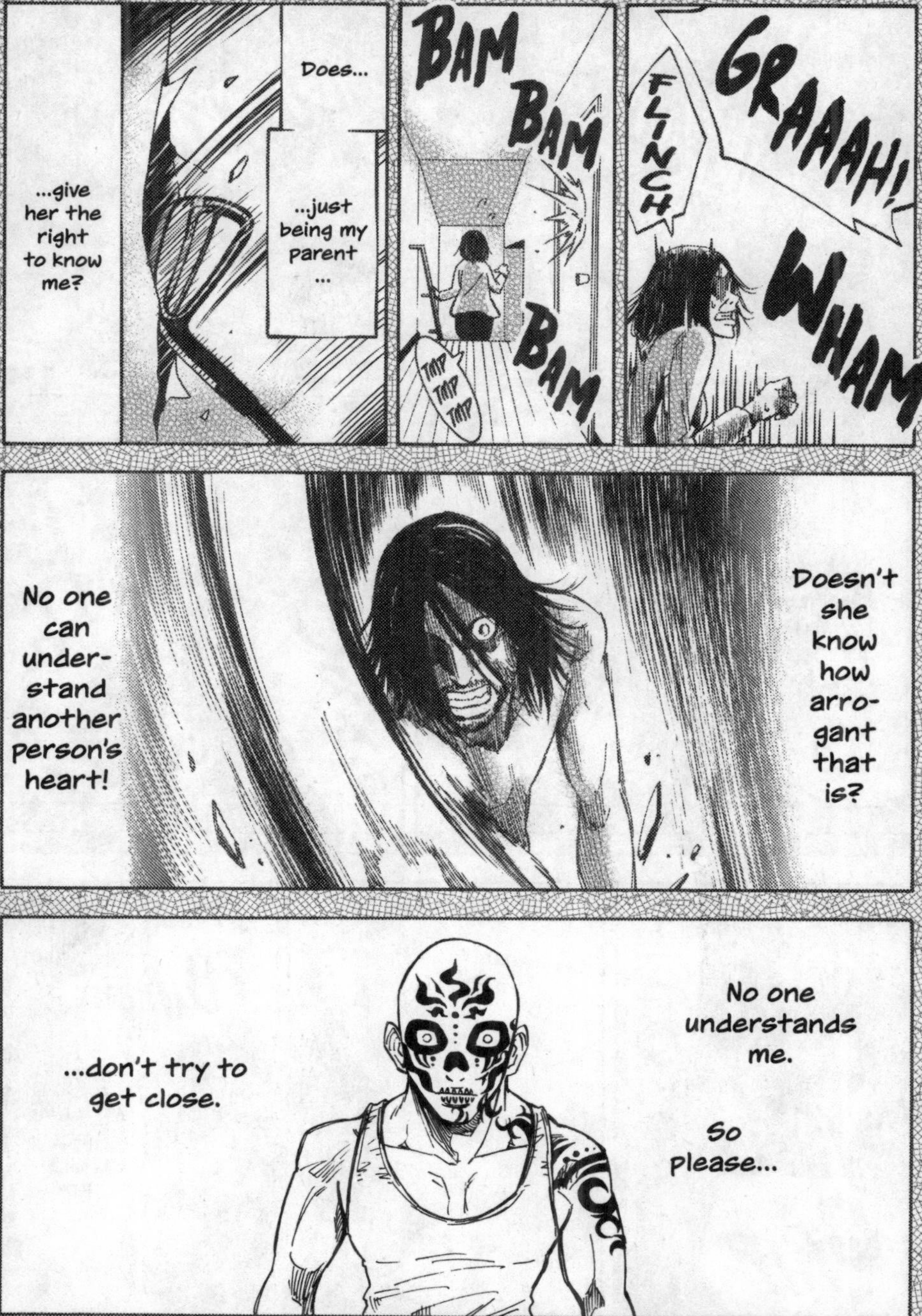
GRAAAH!
FLINCH
WHAM
BAM
BAM
BAM
TMP TMP TMP
Does...
...just being my parent ...
...give her the right to know me?
Doesn't she know how arrogant that is?
No one can understand another person's heart!
No one understands me.
So please...
...don't try to get close.

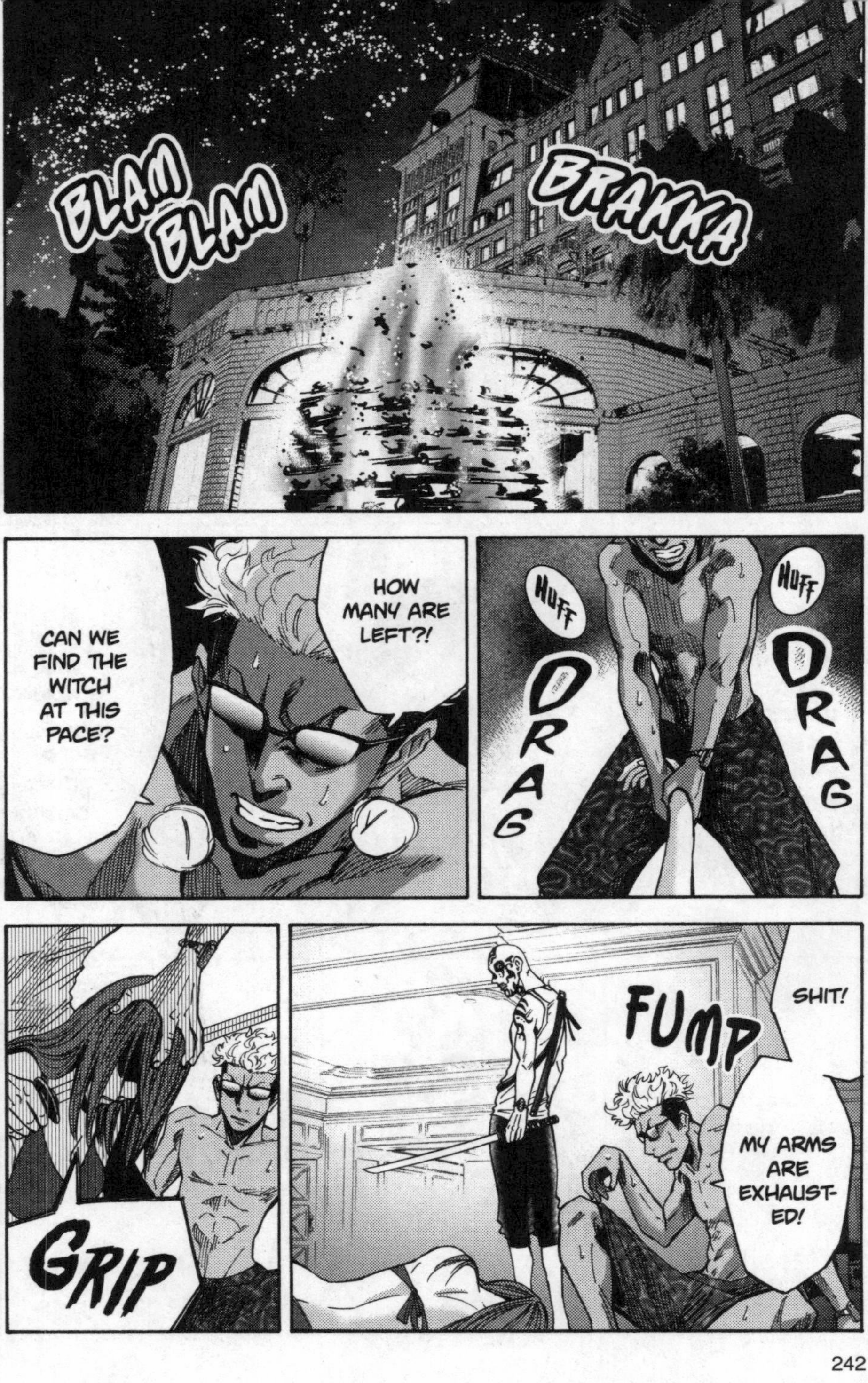
BRAKKA
BLAM BLAM
HUFF
HUFF
DRAG DRAG
HOW MANY ARE LEFT?!
CAN WE FIND THE WITCH AT THIS PACE?
SHIT!
FUMP
MY ARMS ARE EXHAUST-ED!
GRIP

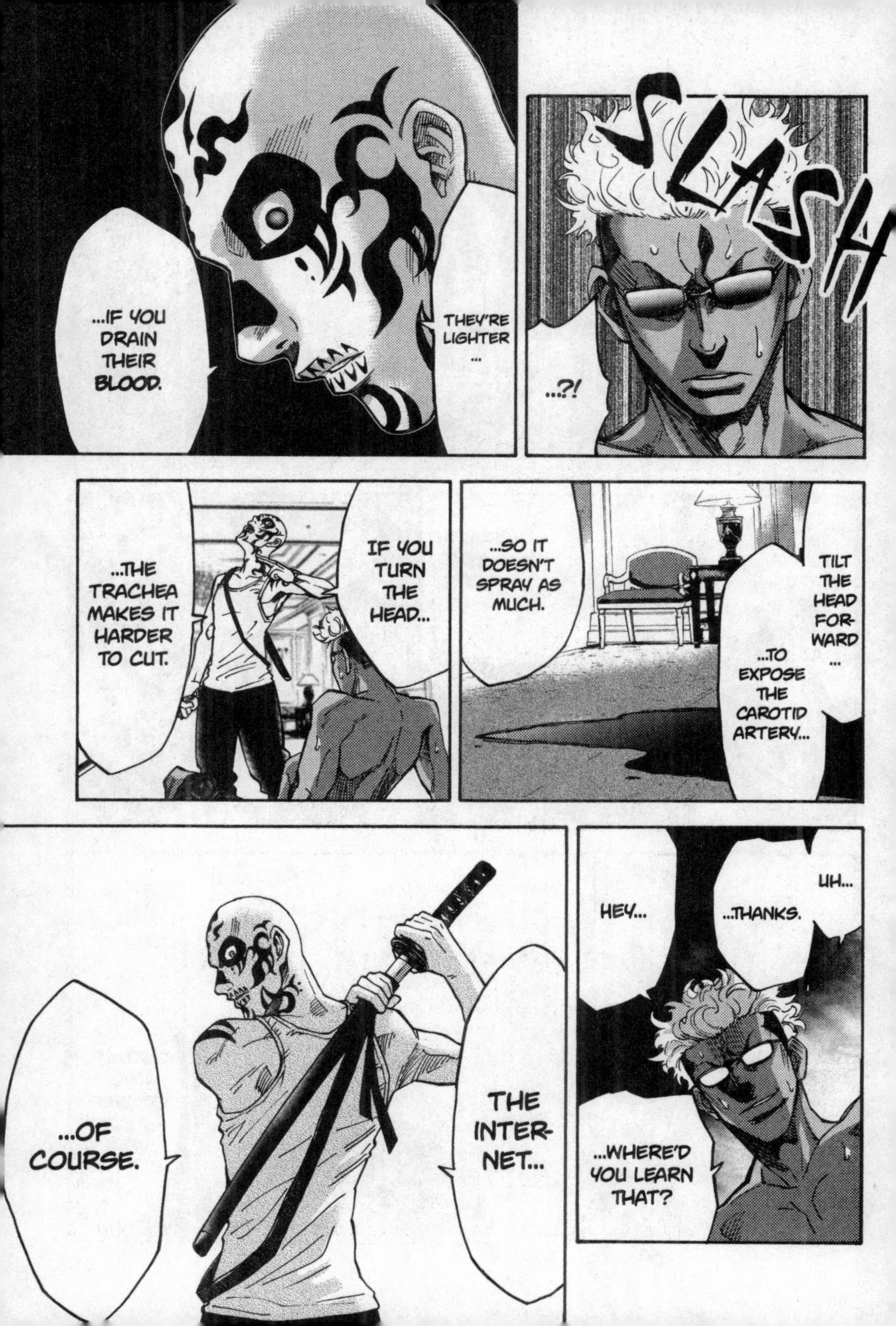
SLASH
...?!
THEY'RE LIGHTER...
...IF YOU DRAIN THEIR BLOOD.
TILT THE HEAD FORWARD...
...TO EXPOSE THE CAROTID ARTERY...
...SO IT DOESN'T SPRAY AS MUCH.
IF YOU TURN THE HEAD...
...THE TRACHEA MAKES IT HARDER TO CUT.
UH...
...THANKS.
HEY...
...WHERE'D YOU LEARN THAT?
THE INTERNET...
...OF COURSE.

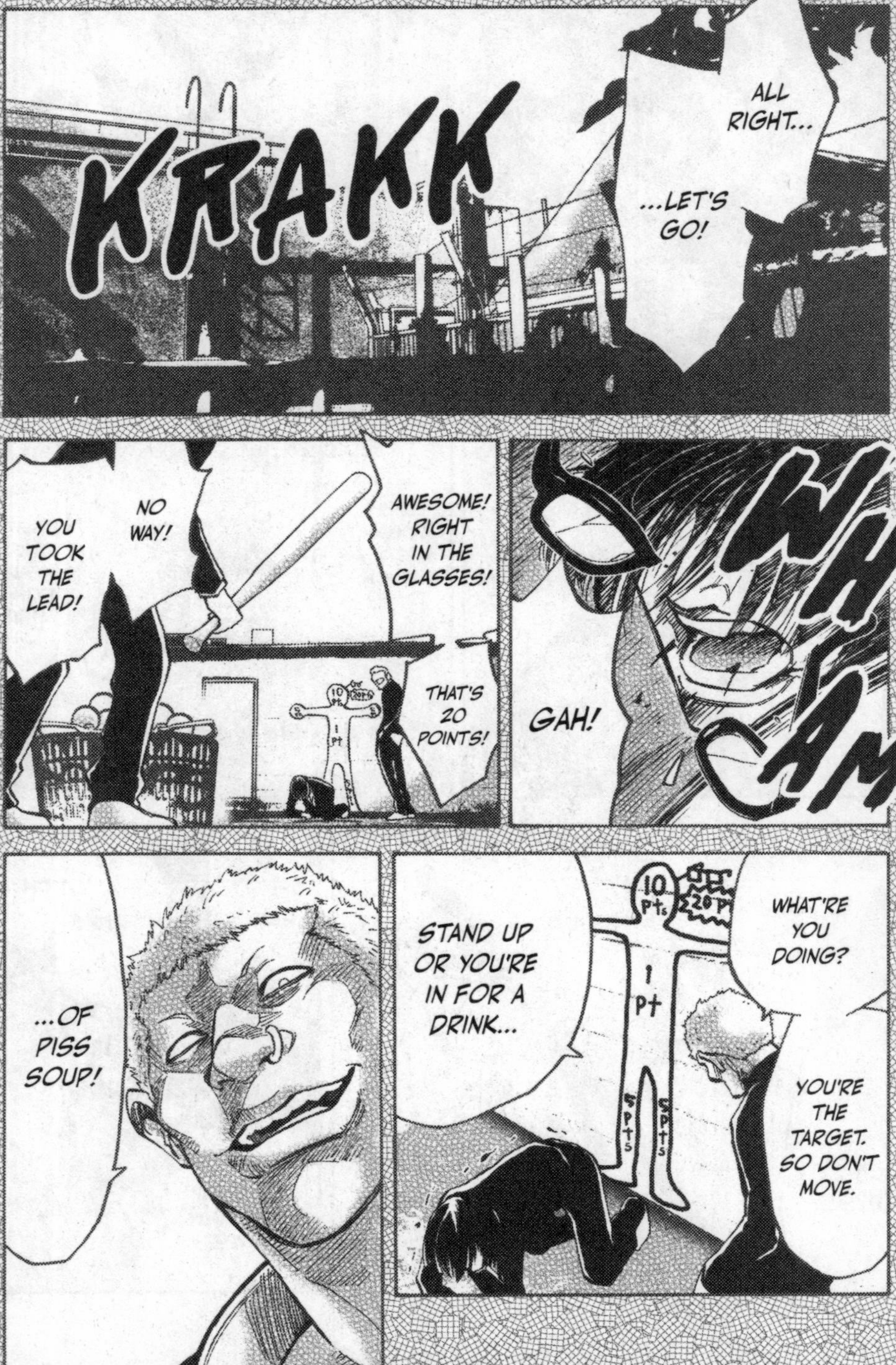
ALL RIGHT...
...LET'S GO!
KRAKK
WHAM
GAH!
AWESOME! RIGHT IN THE GLASSES!
THAT'S 20 POINTS!
NO WAY!
YOU TOOK THE LEAD!
WHAT'RE YOU DOING?
10 pts
20 pts
1 pt
5 pts
5 pts
YOU'RE THE TARGET. SO DON'T MOVE.
STAND UP OR YOU'RE IN FOR A DRINK...
...OF PISS SOUP!

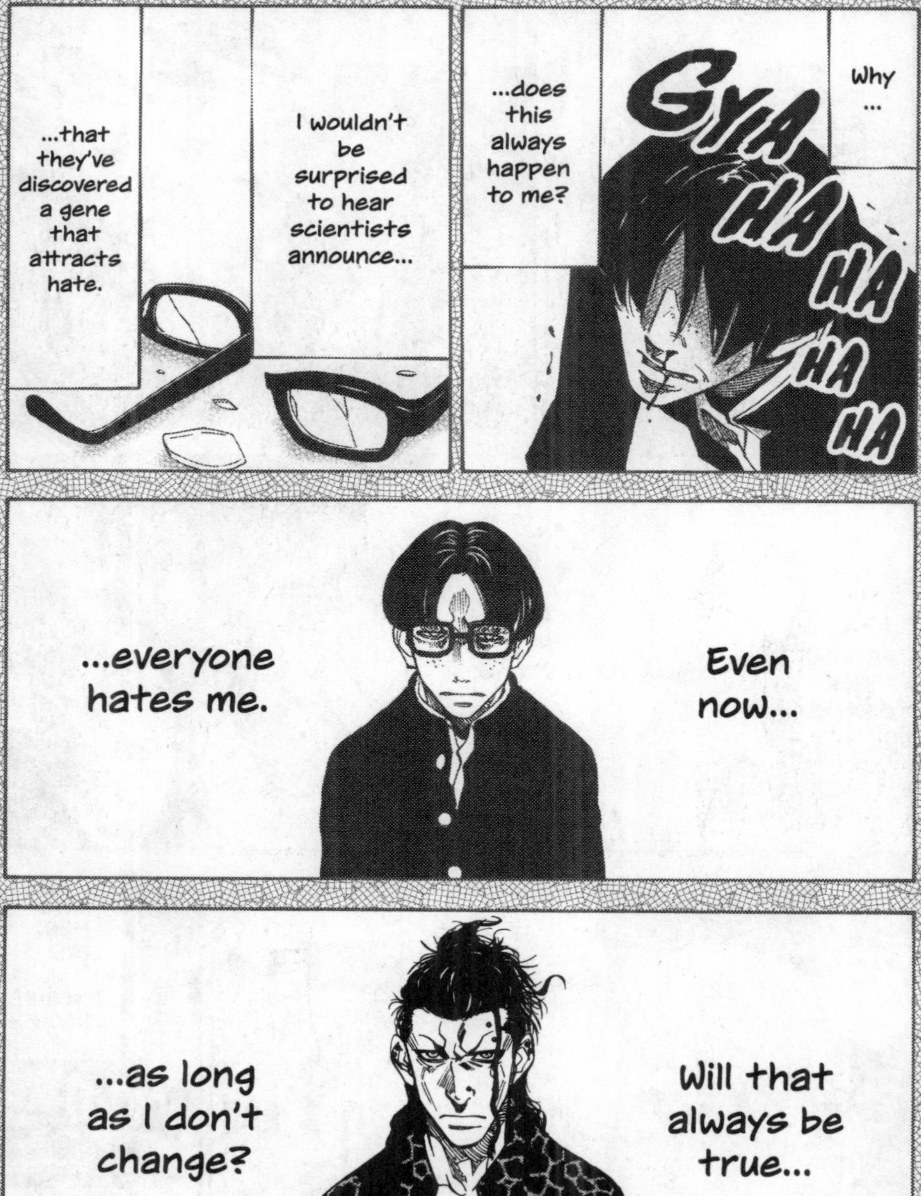
Why ...
...does this always happen to me?
GYA HA HA HA HA HA
I wouldn't be surprised to hear scientists announce...
...that they've discovered a gene that attracts hate.
Even now...
...everyone hates me.
Will that always be true...
...as long as I don't change?

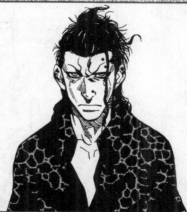

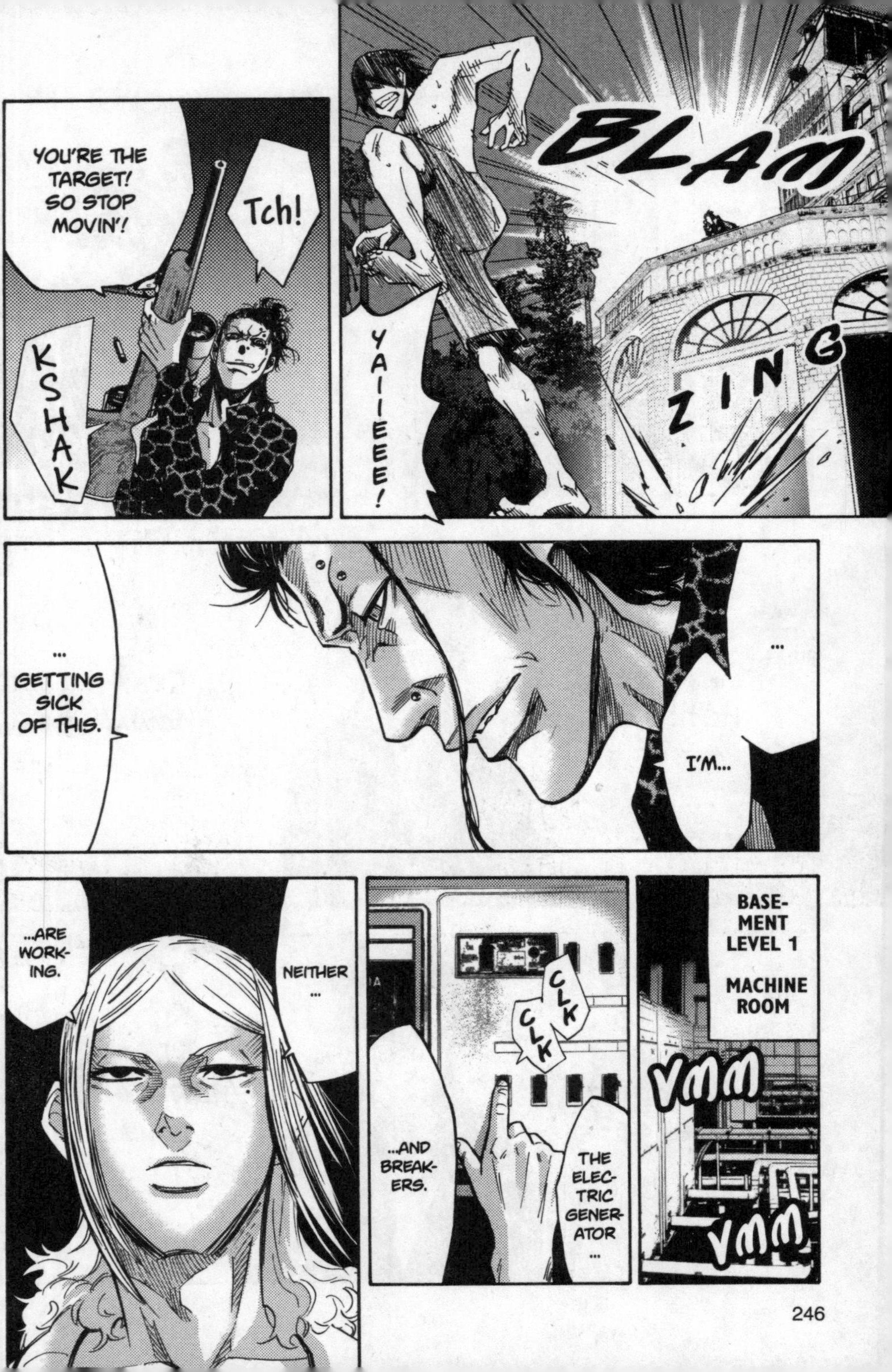
BLAM
ZING
YAIIEEE!
Tch!
YOU'RE THE TARGET! SO STOP MOVIN'!
KSHAK
... I'M...
... GETTING SICK OF THIS.
BASEMENT LEVEL 1
MACHINE ROOM
VMM
VMM
CLK
CLK
THE ELECTRIC GENERATOR...
...AND BREAKERS.
NEITHER...
...ARE WORKING.

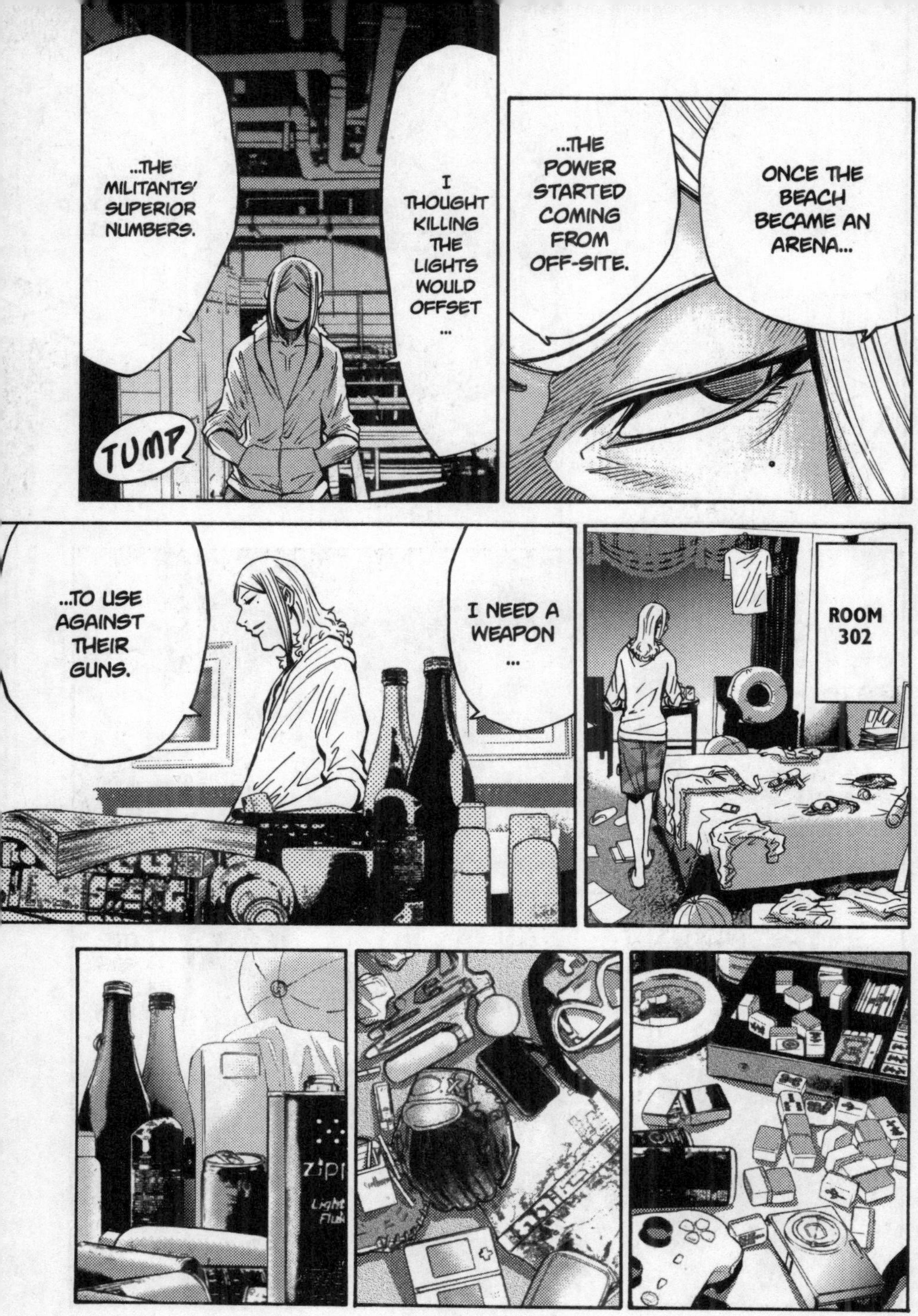
ONCE THE BEACH BECAME AN ARENA...
...THE POWER STARTED COMING FROM OFF-SITE.
I THOUGHT KILLING THE LIGHTS WOULD OFFSET ...
...THE MILITANTS' SUPERIOR NUMBERS.
TUMP
ROOM 302
I NEED A WEAPON ...
...TO USE AGAINST THEIR GUNS.

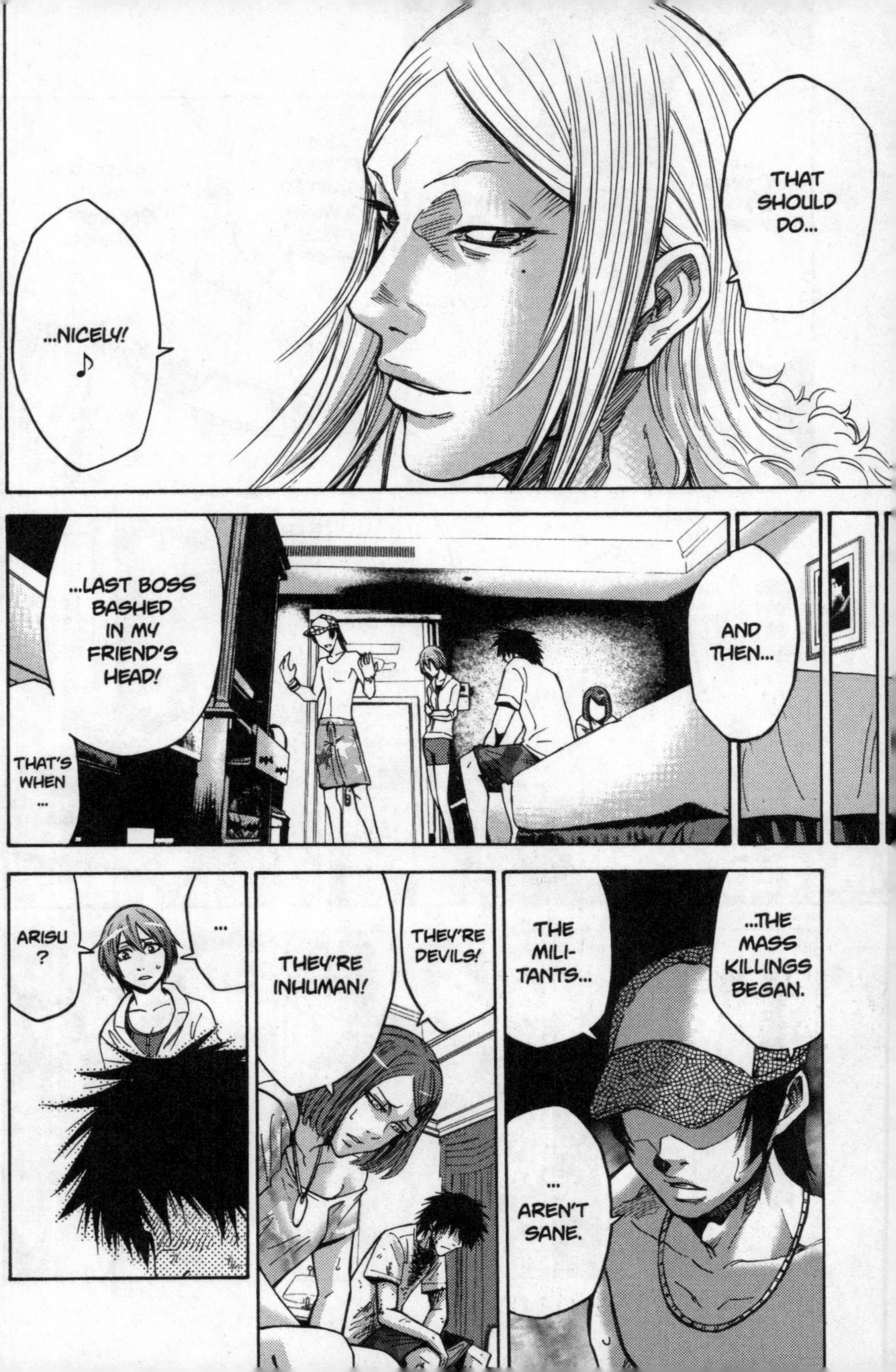
THAT SHOULD DO...
...NICELY! ♪
AND THEN...
...LAST BOSS BASHED IN MY FRIEND'S HEAD!
THAT'S WHEN ...
...THE MASS KILLINGS BEGAN.
THE MILI- TANTS...
... AREN'T SANE.
THEY'RE DEVILS!
THEY'RE INHUMAN!
...
ARISU ?

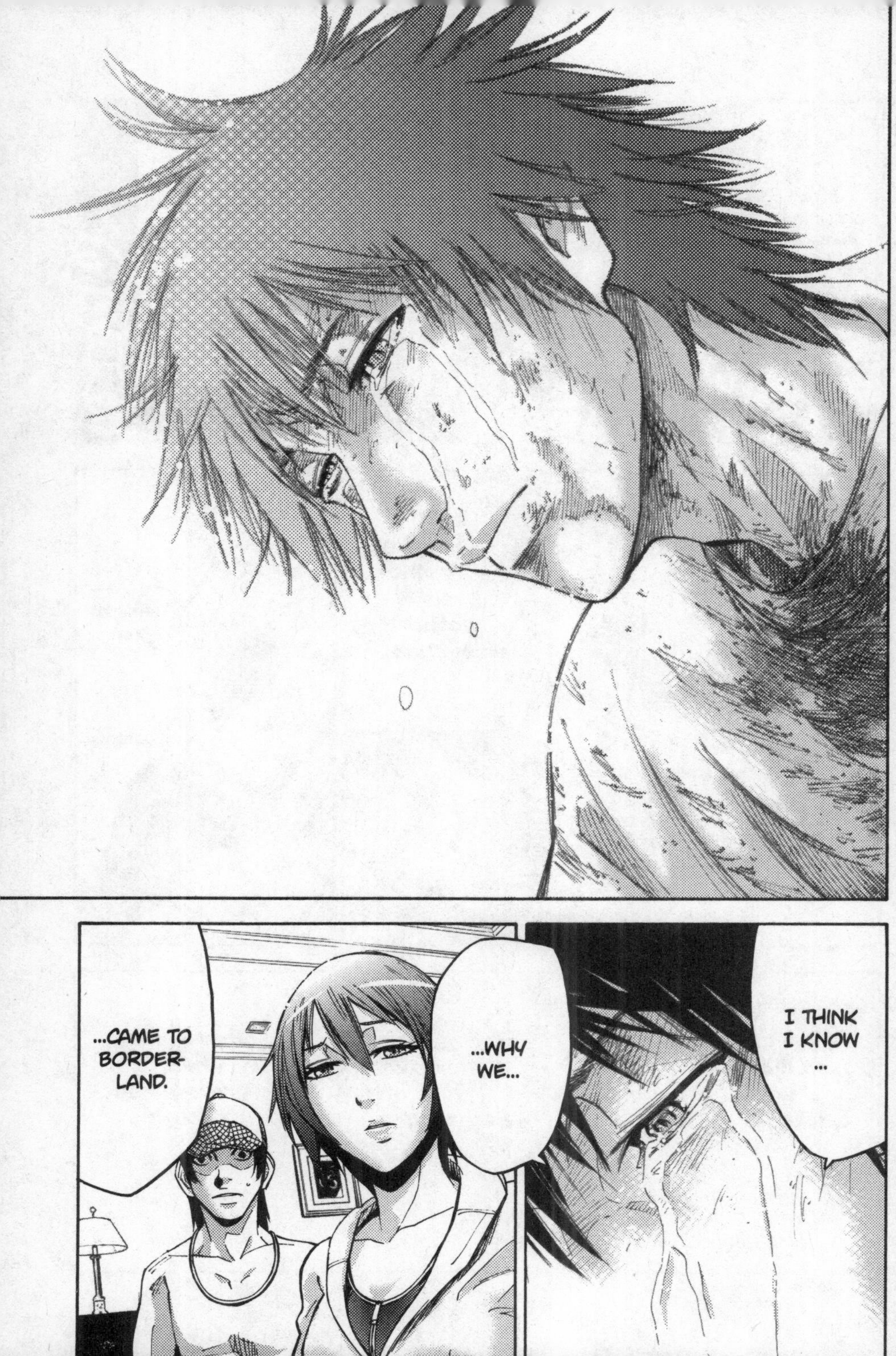
I THINK I KNOW ...
...WHY WE...
...CAME TO BORDER-LAND.

Even now, I flinch at that sound...
CREAK
The sound of my old man climb-ing the stairs...
CREAK
CREAK
...after drowning himself in alcohol.
He was useless scum...
...clinging to what little authority he had...
...and I cowered in fear of him.
Sometimes I had to provoke him, though...
...so he wouldn't turn on my mom.
But she left anyway...
...and so did I, when I was 12.

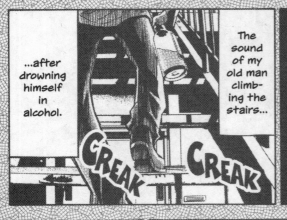

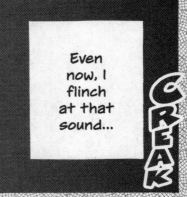

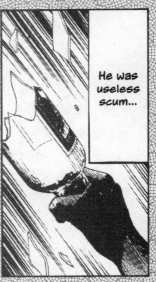

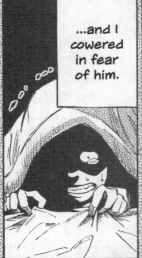

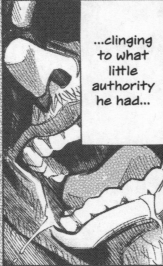

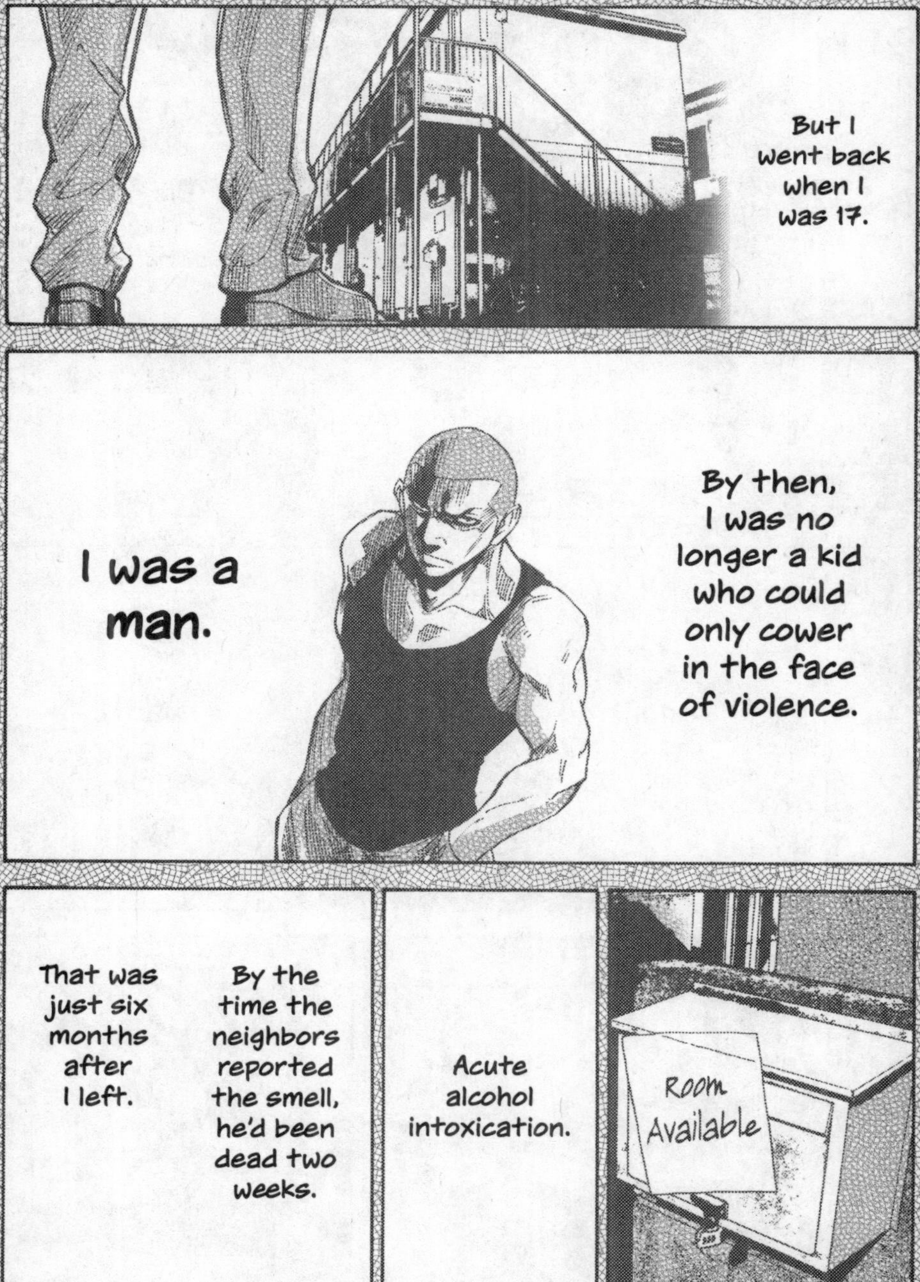
But I went back when I was 17.
By then, I was no longer a kid who could only cower in the face of violence.
I was a man.
Room Available
Acute alcohol intoxication.
By the time the neighbors reported the smell, he'd been dead two weeks.
That was just six months after I left.

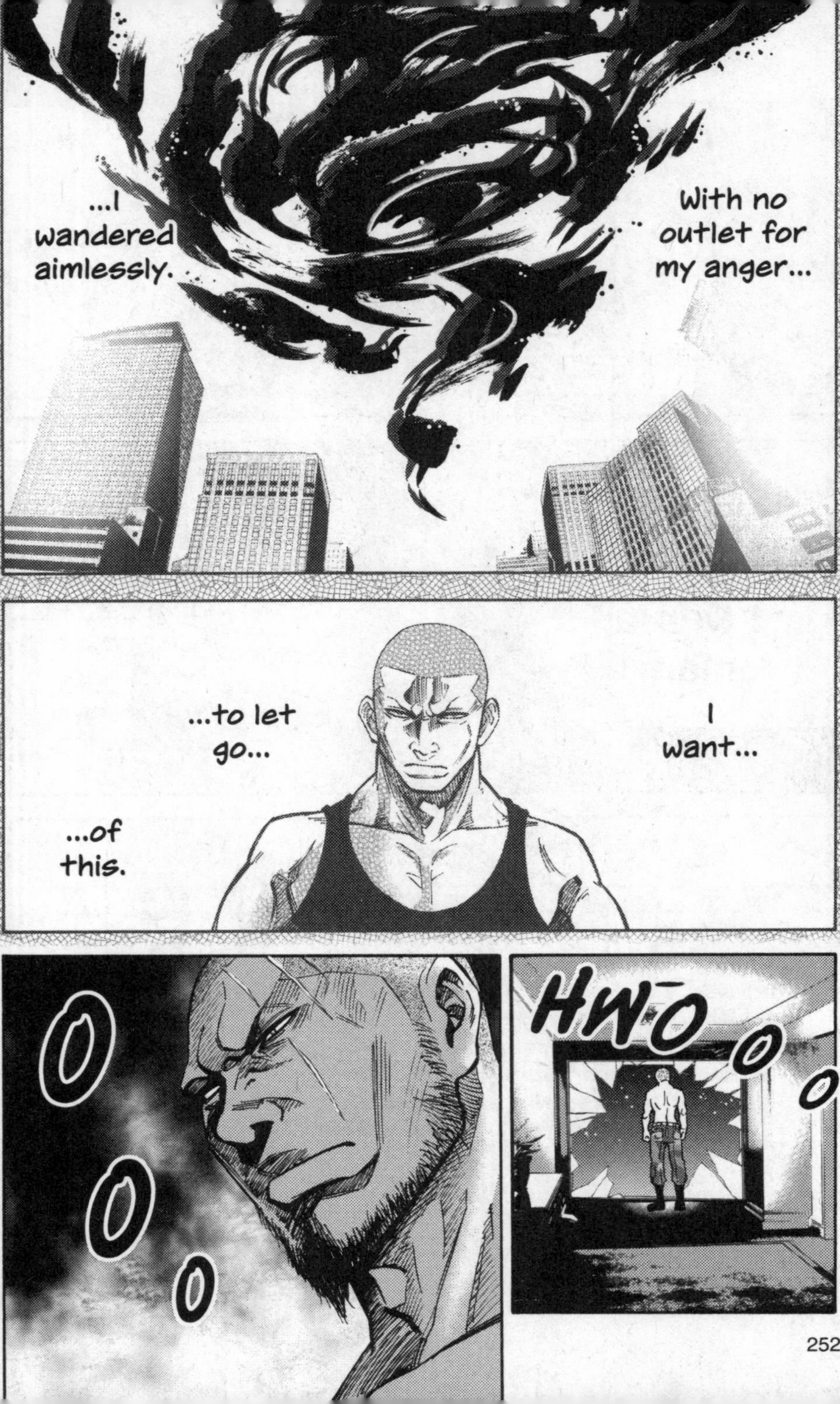
With no outlet for my anger...
...I wandered aimlessly.
I want...
...to let go...
...of this.
HWOooo
OOO

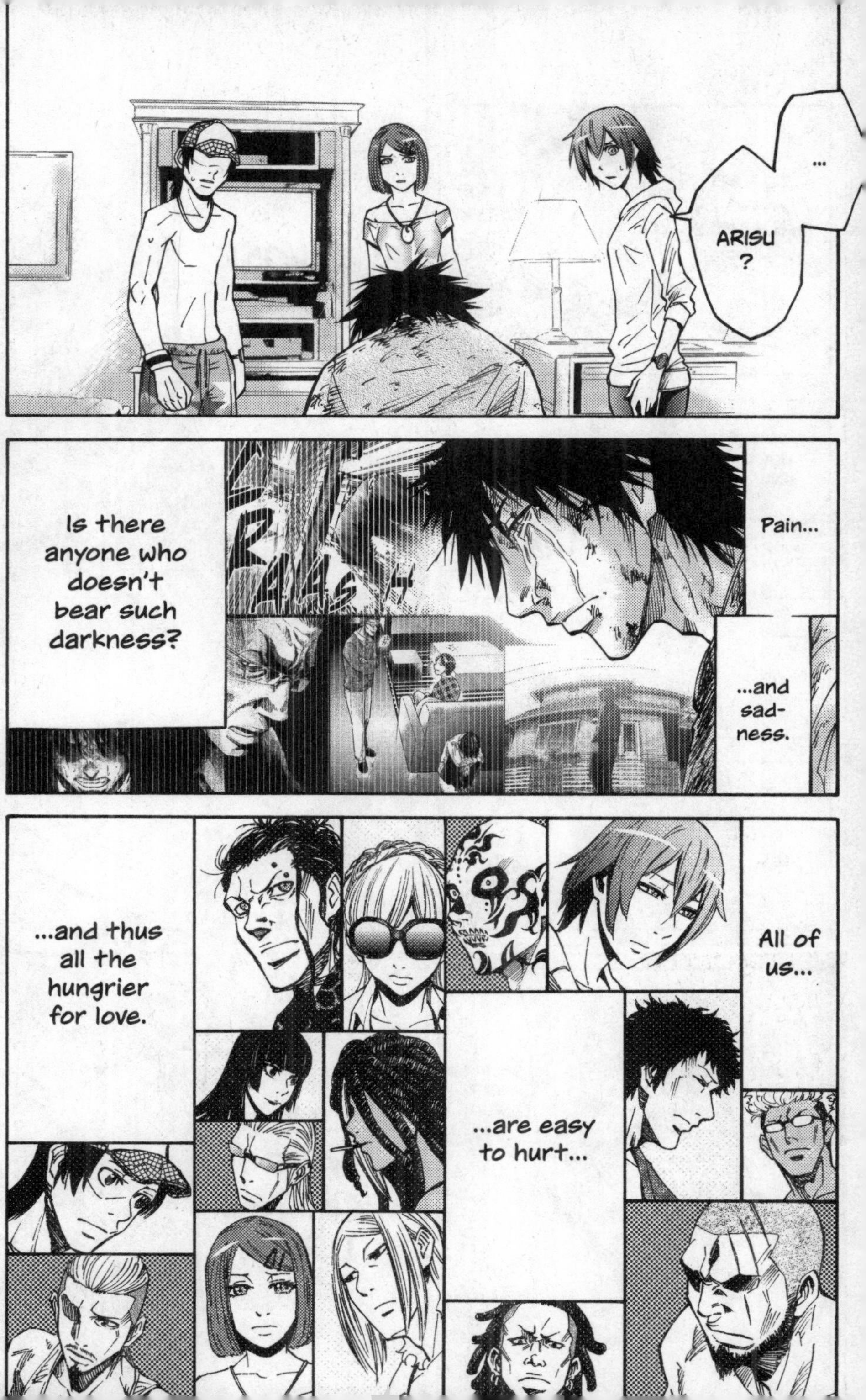
...
ARISU
?
Pain...
...and
sad-
ness.
Is there
anyone who
doesn't
bear such
darkness?
All of
us...
...are easy
to hurt...
...and thus
all the
hungrier
for love.

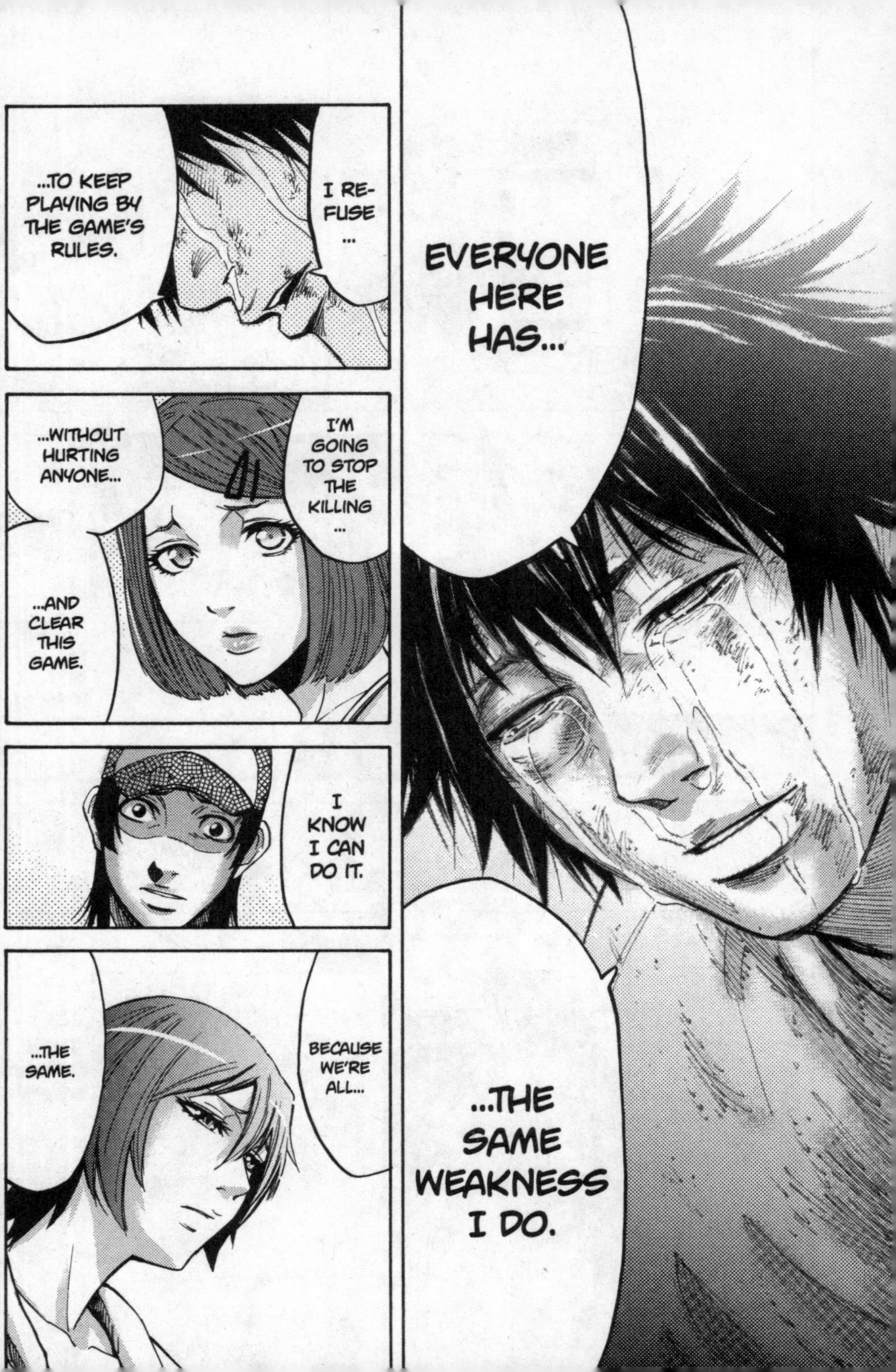
EVERYONE HERE HAS...
...THE SAME WEAKNESS I DO.
I RE-FUSE ...
...TO KEEP PLAYING BY THE GAME'S RULES.
I'M GOING TO STOP THE KILLING ...
...WITHOUT HURTING ANYONE...
...AND CLEAR THIS GAME.
I KNOW I CAN DO IT.
BECAUSE WE'RE ALL...
...THE SAME.

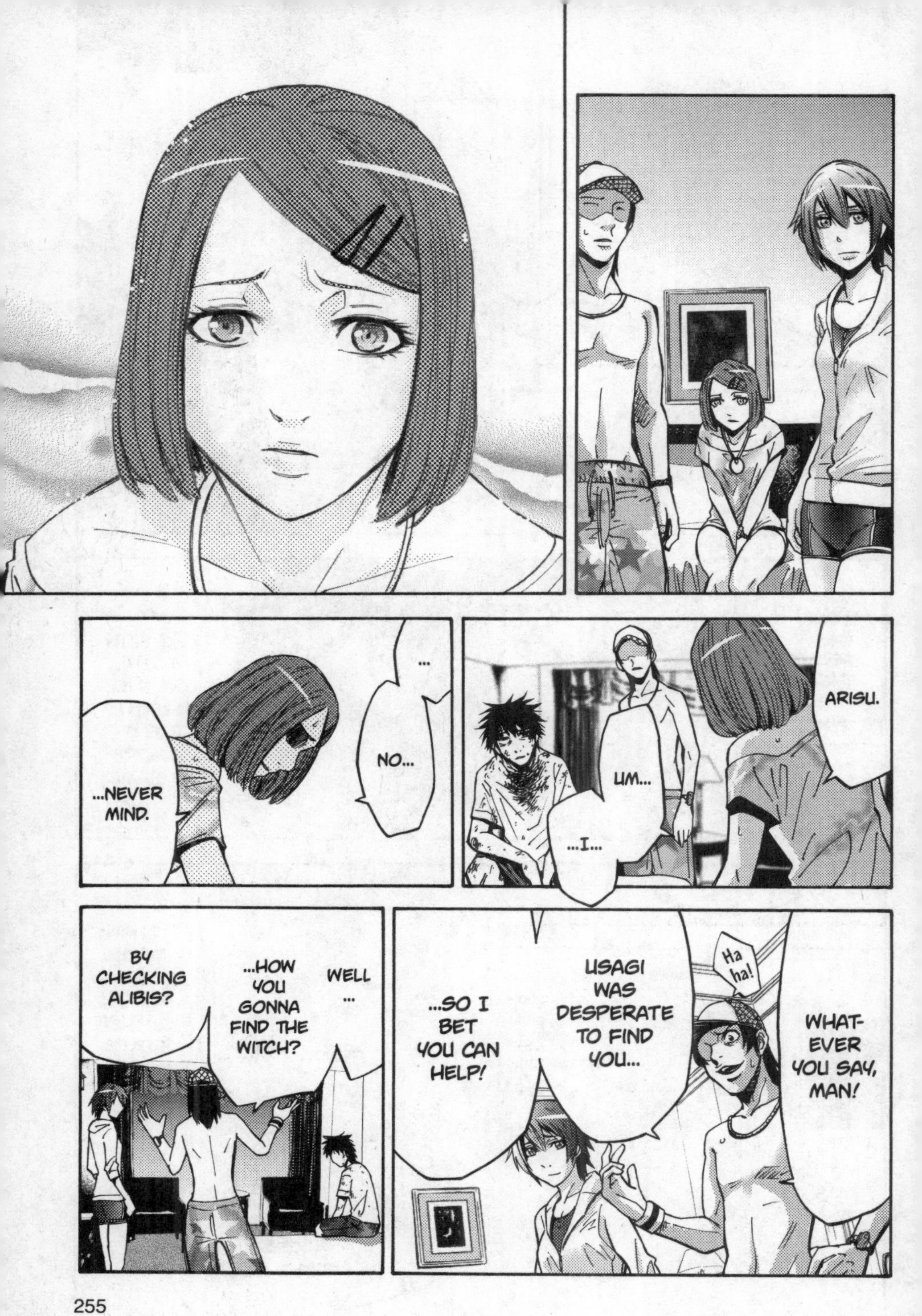
ARISU.
UM...
...I...
...
NO...
...NEVER MIND.
WHAT-EVER YOU SAY, MAN!
Ha ha!
USAGI WAS DESPERATE TO FIND YOU...
...SO I BET YOU CAN HELP!
WELL ...
...HOW YOU GONNA FIND THE WITCH?
BY CHECKING ALIBIS?

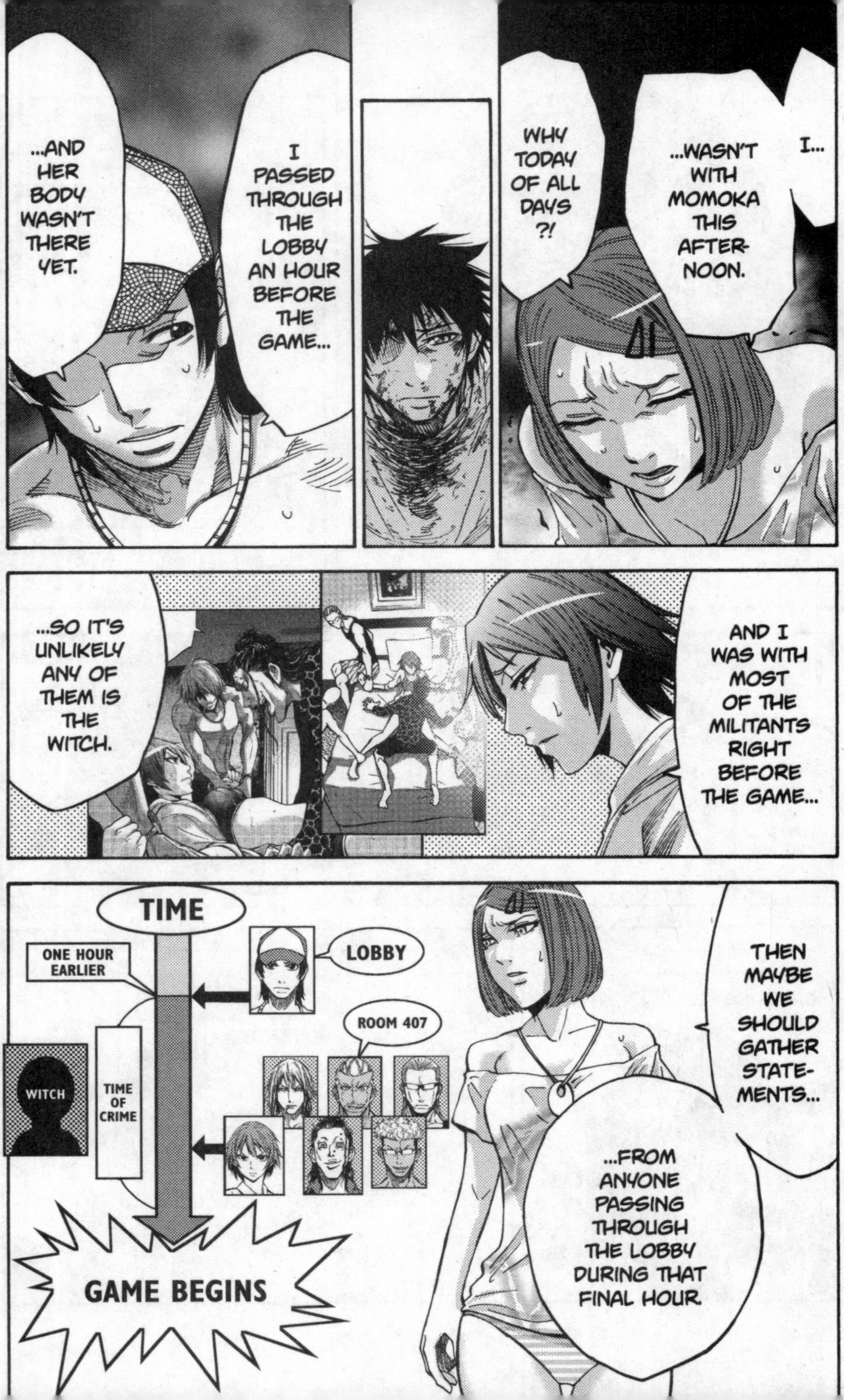
I...
...WASN'T WITH MOMOKA THIS AFTER-NOON.
WHY TODAY OF ALL DAYS ?!
I PASSED THROUGH THE LOBBY AN HOUR BEFORE THE GAME...
...AND HER BODY WASN'T THERE YET.
AND I WAS WITH MOST OF THE MILITANTS RIGHT BEFORE THE GAME...
...SO IT'S UNLIKELY ANY OF THEM IS THE WITCH.
THEN MAYBE WE SHOULD GATHER STATE-MENTS...
...FROM ANYONE PASSING THROUGH THE LOBBY DURING THAT FINAL HOUR.
TIME
ONE HOUR EARLIER
LOBBY
ROOM 407
WITCH
TIME OF CRIME
GAME BEGINS

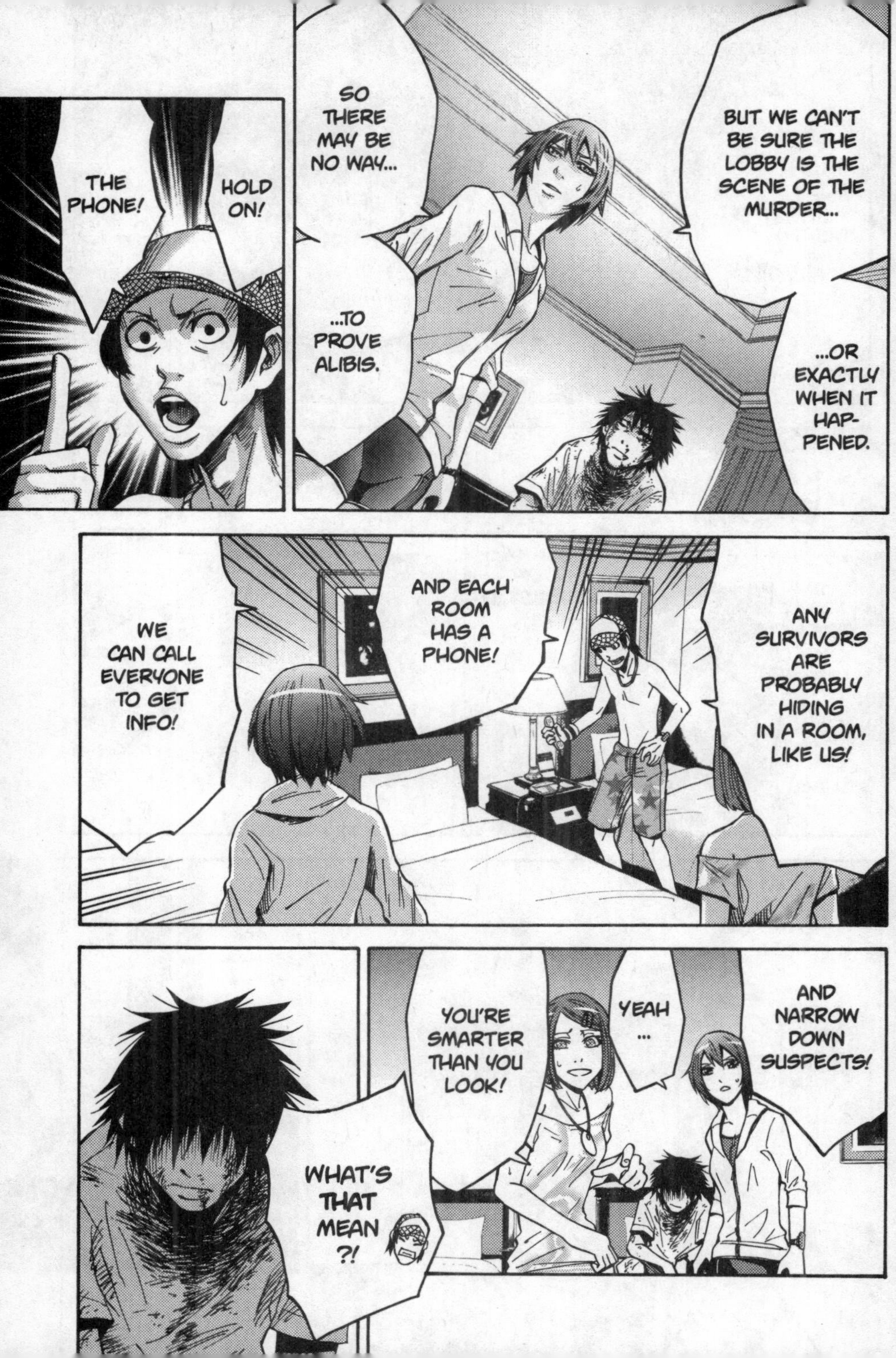
BUT WE CAN'T BE SURE THE LOBBY IS THE SCENE OF THE MURDER...
...OR EXACTLY WHEN IT HAP-PENED.
SO THERE MAY BE NO WAY...
...TO PROVE ALIBIS.
HOLD ON!
THE PHONE!
ANY SURVIVORS ARE PROBABLY HIDING IN A ROOM, LIKE US!
AND EACH ROOM HAS A PHONE!
WE CAN CALL EVERYONE TO GET INFO!
AND NARROW DOWN SUSPECTS!
YEAH ...
YOU'RE SMARTER THAN YOU LOOK!
WHAT'S THAT MEAN ?!

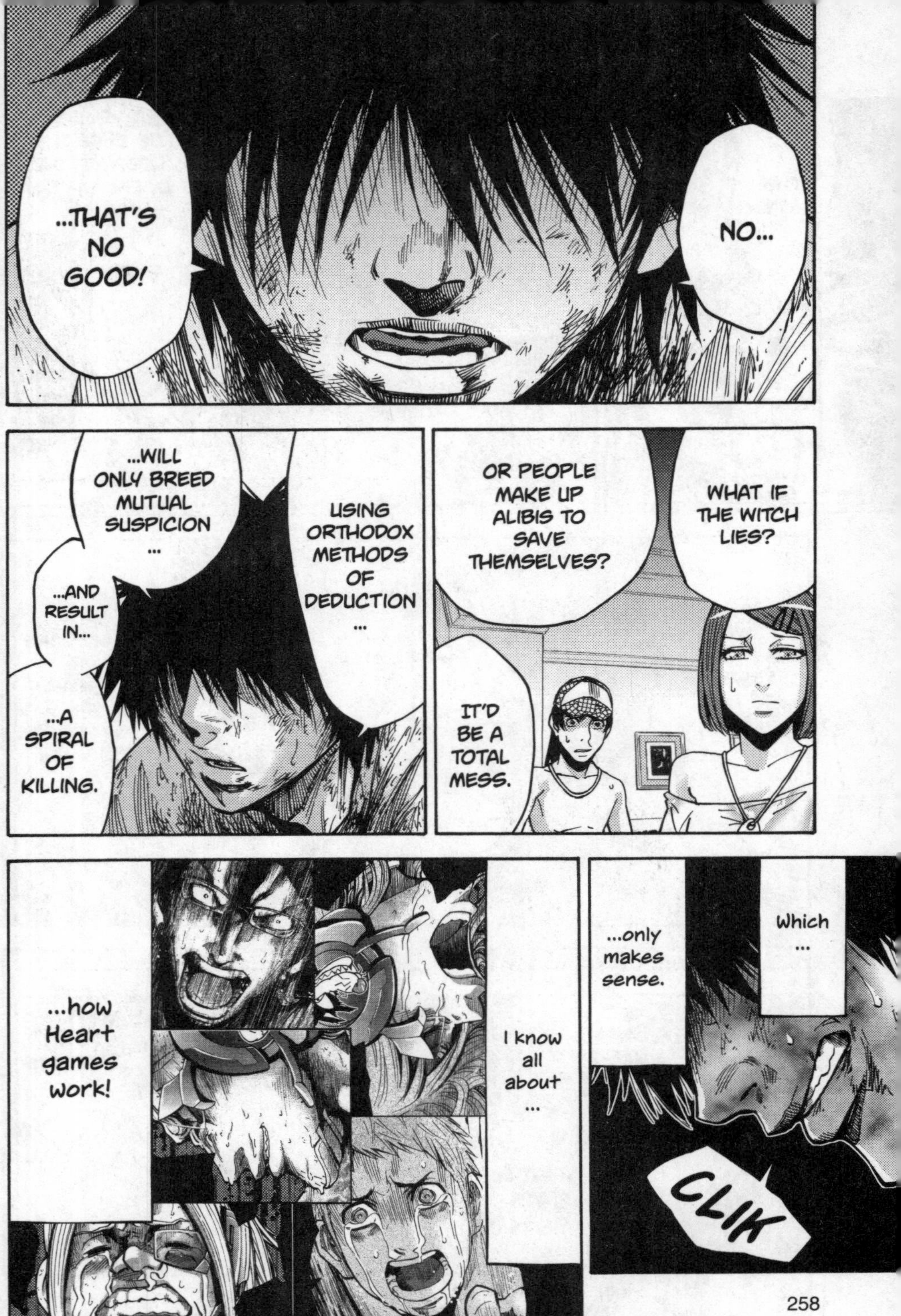
NO...
...THAT'S NO GOOD!
WHAT IF THE WITCH LIES?
OR PEOPLE MAKE UP ALIBIS TO SAVE THEMSELVES?
IT'D BE A TOTAL MESS.
USING ORTHODOX METHODS OF DEDUCTION ...
...WILL ONLY BREED MUTUAL SUSPICION ...
...AND RESULT IN...
...A SPIRAL OF KILLING.
Which ...
...only makes sense.
CLIK
I know all about ...
...how Heart games work!

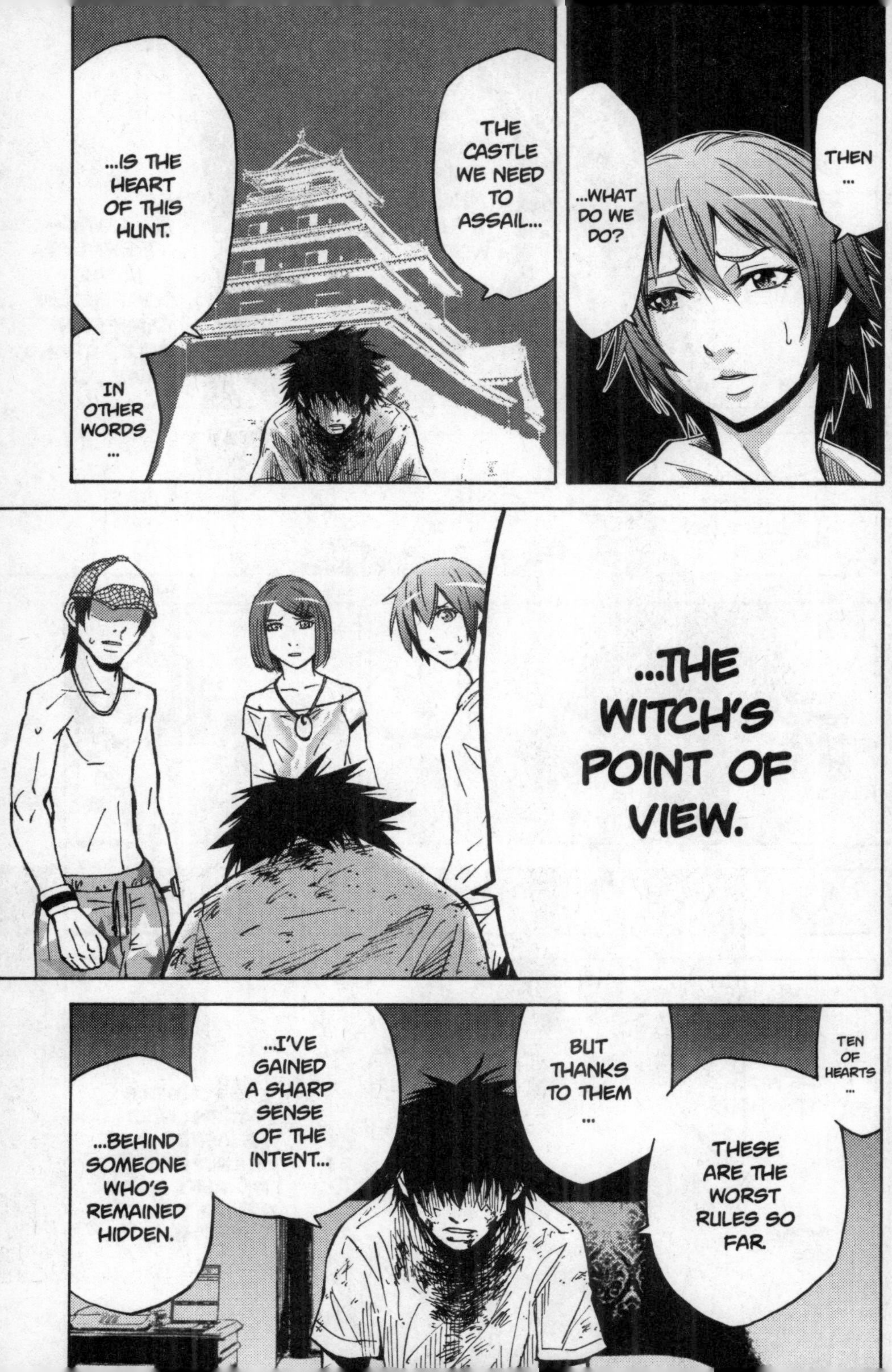
THEN ...
...WHAT DO WE DO?
THE CASTLE WE NEED TO ASSAIL...
...IS THE HEART OF THIS HUNT.
IN OTHER WORDS ...
...THE WITCH'S POINT OF VIEW.
TEN OF HEARTS ...
THESE ARE THE WORST RULES SO FAR.
BUT THANKS TO THEM ...
...I'VE GAINED A SHARP SENSE OF THE INTENT...
...BEHIND SOMEONE WHO'S REMAINED HIDDEN.

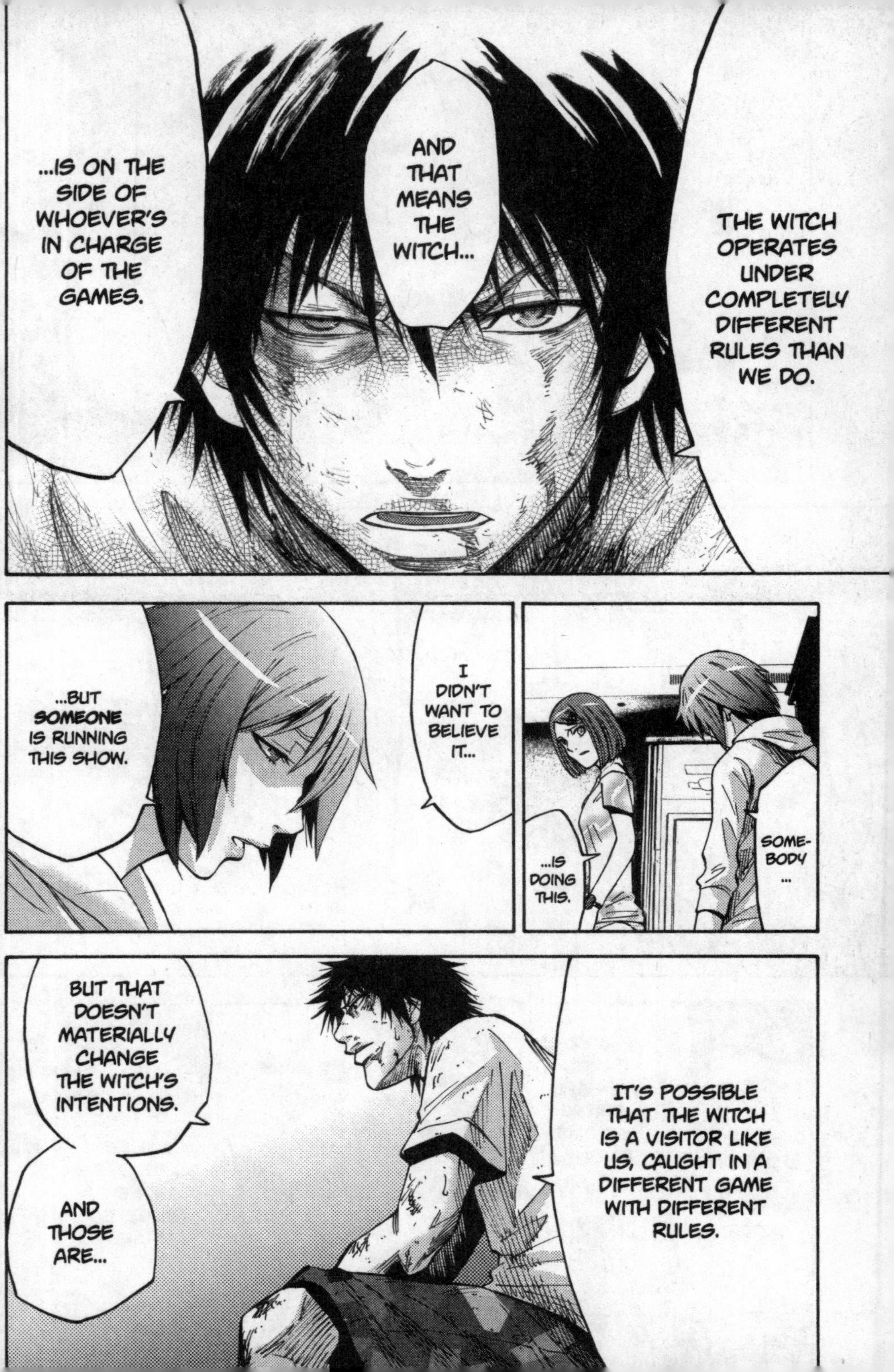
THE WITCH OPERATES UNDER COMPLETELY DIFFERENT RULES THAN WE DO.
AND THAT MEANS THE WITCH...
...IS ON THE SIDE OF WHOEVER'S IN CHARGE OF THE GAMES.
SOME-BODY...
...IS DOING THIS.
I DIDN'T WANT TO BELIEVE IT...
...BUT SOMEONE IS RUNNING THIS SHOW.
IT'S POSSIBLE THAT THE WITCH IS A VISITOR LIKE US, CAUGHT IN A DIFFERENT GAME WITH DIFFERENT RULES.
BUT THAT DOESN'T MATERIALLY CHANGE THE WITCH'S INTENTIONS.
AND THOSE ARE...

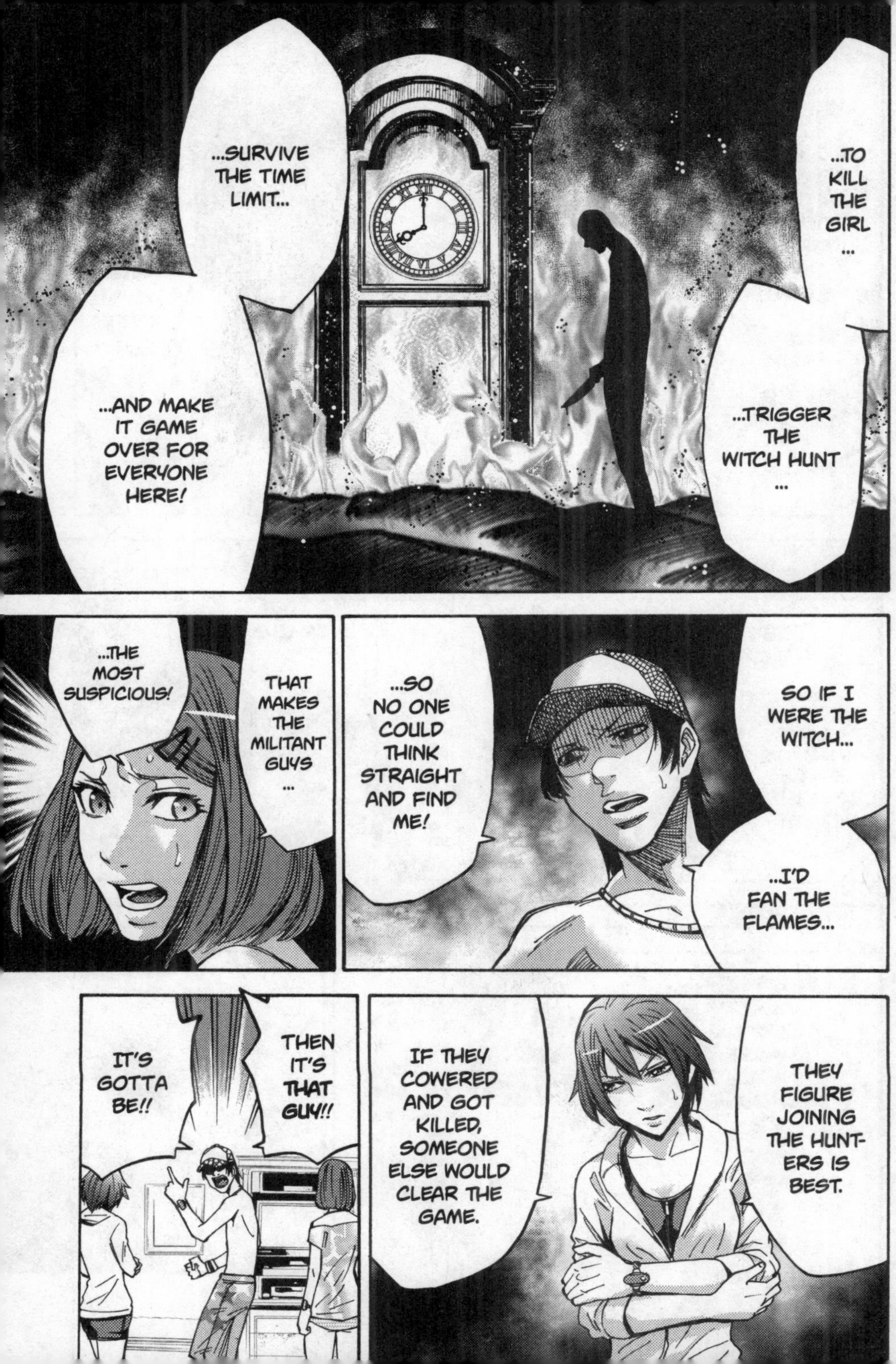
...TO KILL THE GIRL ...
...TRIGGER THE WITCH HUNT ...
...SURVIVE THE TIME LIMIT...
...AND MAKE IT GAME OVER FOR EVERYONE HERE!
SO IF I WERE THE WITCH...
...I'D FAN THE FLAMES...
...SO NO ONE COULD THINK STRAIGHT AND FIND ME!
THAT MAKES THE MILITANT GUYS ...
...THE MOST SUSPICIOUS!
THEY FIGURE JOINING THE HUNTERS IS BEST.
IF THEY COWERED AND GOT KILLED, SOMEONE ELSE WOULD CLEAR THE GAME.
THEN IT'S THAT GUY!!
IT'S GOTTA BE!!

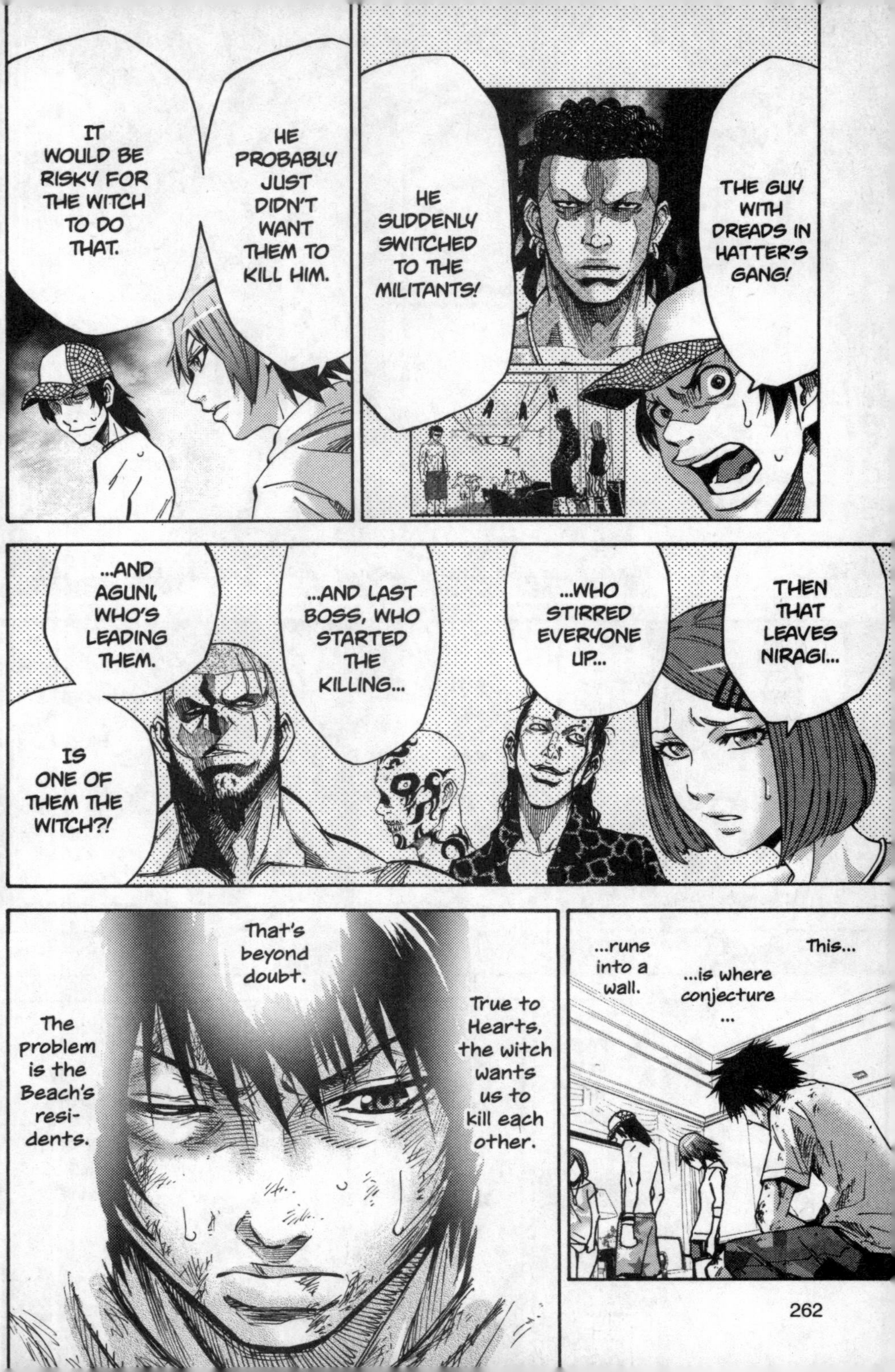
THE GUY WITH DREADS IN HATTER'S GANG!
HE SUDDENLY SWITCHED TO THE MILITANTS!
HE PROBABLY JUST DIDN'T WANT THEM TO KILL HIM.
IT WOULD BE RISKY FOR THE WITCH TO DO THAT.
THEN THAT LEAVES NIRAGI...
...WHO STIRRED EVERYONE UP...
...AND LAST BOSS, WHO STARTED THE KILLING...
...AND AGUNI, WHO'S LEADING THEM.
IS ONE OF THEM THE WITCH?!
This...
...is where conjecture ...
...runs into a wall.
True to Hearts, the witch wants us to kill each other.
That's beyond doubt.
The problem is the Beach's resi-dents.

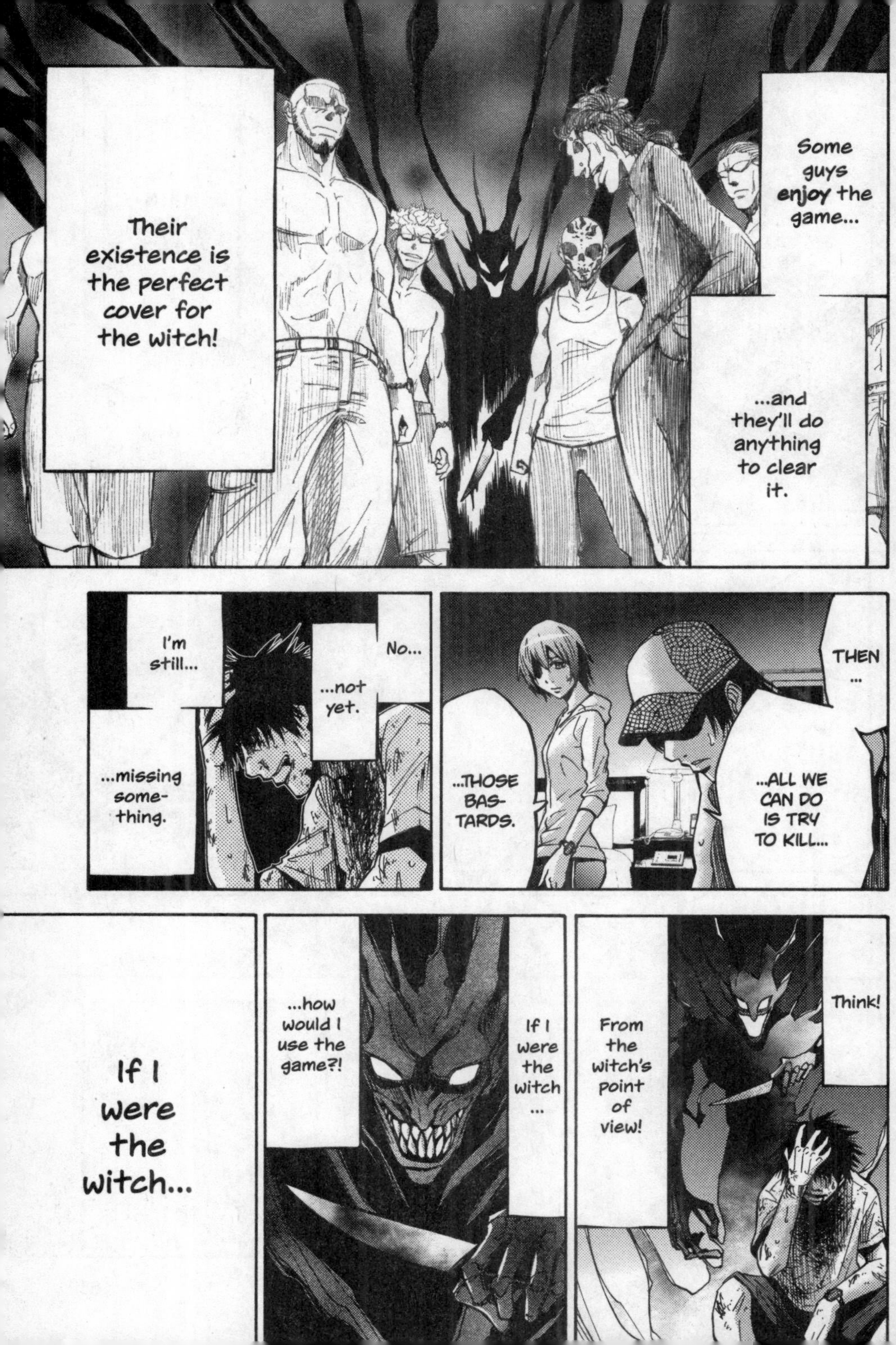
Some guys enjoy the game...
...and they'll do anything to clear it.
Their existence is the perfect cover for the witch!
THEN...
...ALL WE CAN DO IS TRY TO KILL...
...THOSE BAS-TARDS.
No...
...not yet.
I'm still...
...missing some-thing.
Think!
From the witch's point of view!
If I were the witch...
...how would I use the game?!
If I were the witch...

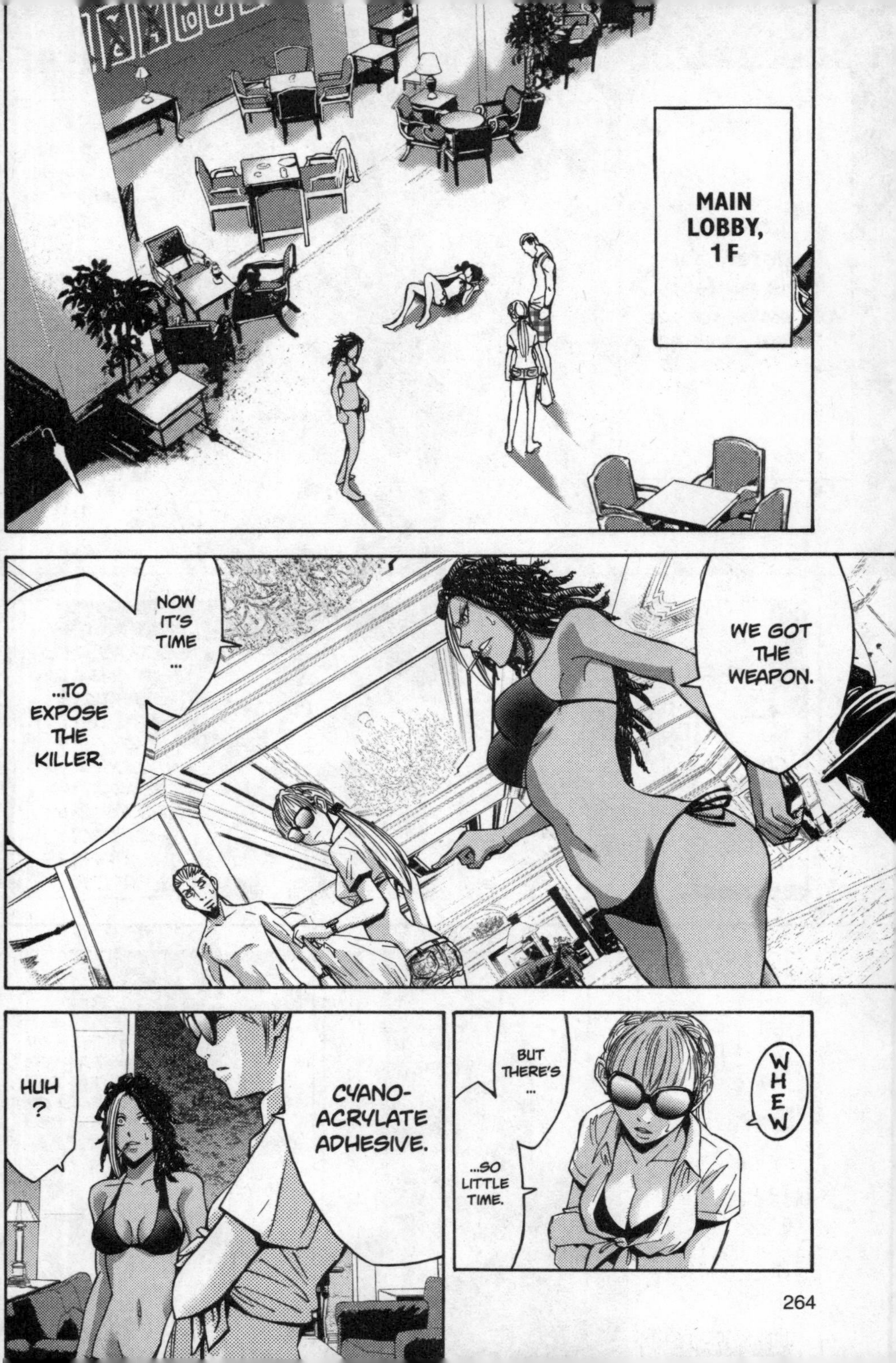
MAIN LOBBY, 1F
WE GOT THE WEAPON.
NOW IT'S TIME ...
...TO EXPOSE THE KILLER.
WHEW
BUT THERE'S ...
...SO LITTLE TIME.
CYANO-ACRYLATE ADHESIVE.
HUH ?

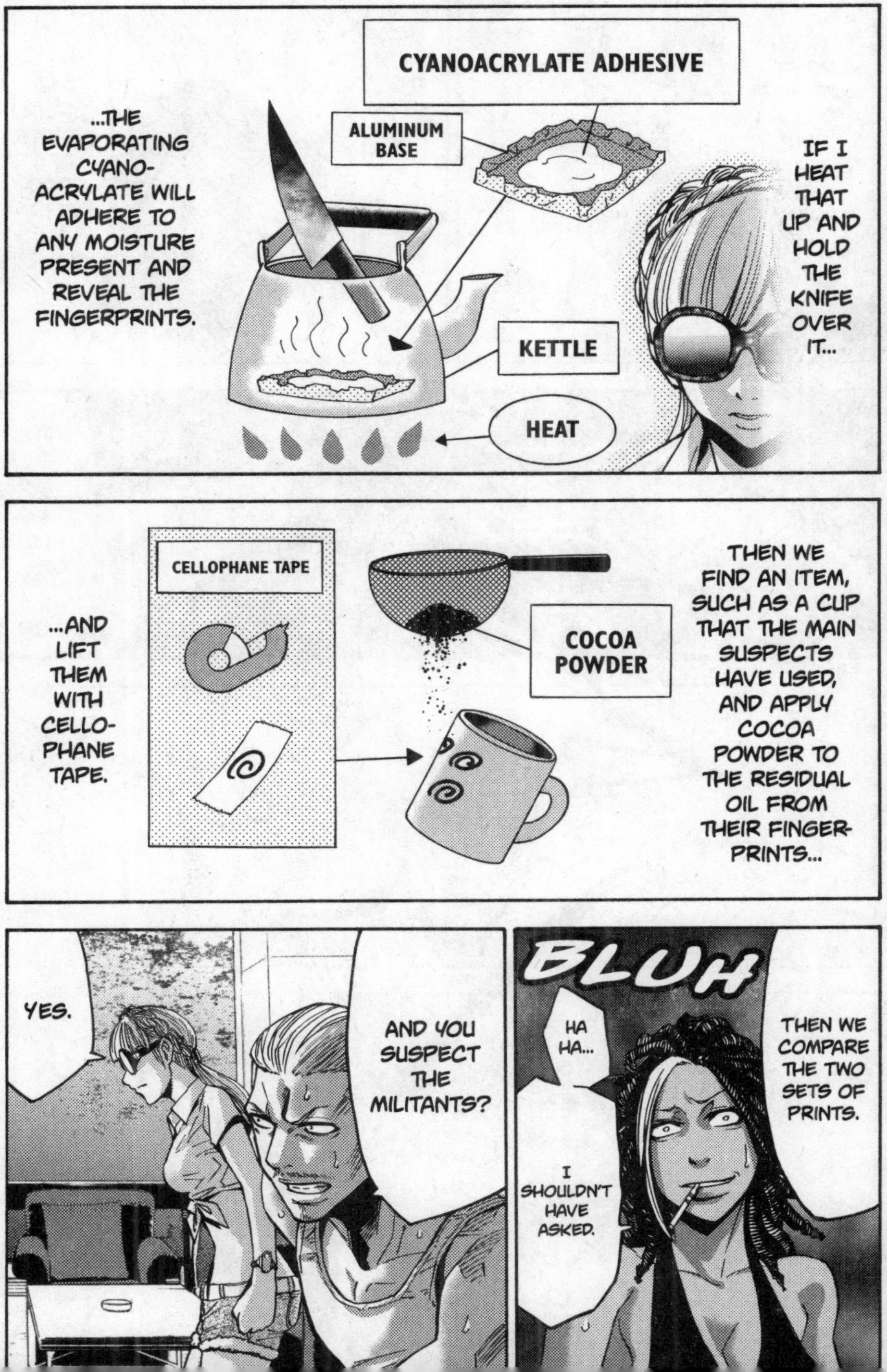
IF I HEAT THAT UP AND HOLD THE KNIFE OVER IT...
CYANOACRYLATE ADHESIVE
ALUMINUM BASE
KETTLE
HEAT
...THE EVAPORATING CYANO-ACRYLATE WILL ADHERE TO ANY MOISTURE PRESENT AND REVEAL THE FINGERPRINTS.
THEN WE FIND AN ITEM, SUCH AS A CUP THAT THE MAIN SUSPECTS HAVE USED, AND APPLY COCOA POWDER TO THE RESIDUAL OIL FROM THEIR FINGER-PRINTS...
COCOA POWDER
CELLOPHANE TAPE
...AND LIFT THEM WITH CELLO-PHANE TAPE.
BLUH
THEN WE COMPARE THE TWO SETS OF PRINTS.
HA HA...
I SHOULDN'T HAVE ASKED.
AND YOU SUSPECT THE MILITANTS?
YES.

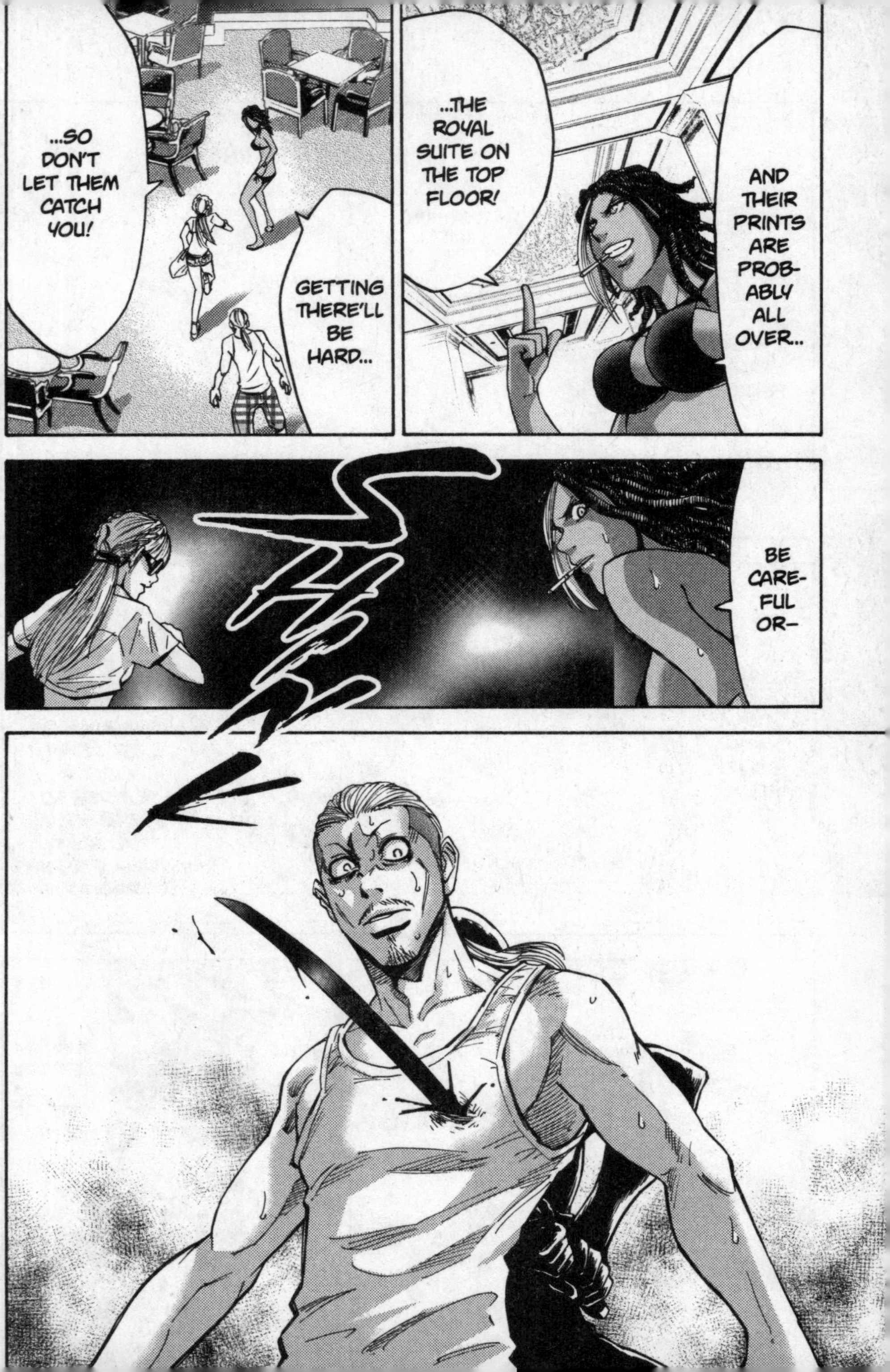
AND THEIR PRINTS ARE PROB-ABLY ALL OVER...
...THE ROYAL SUITE ON THE TOP FLOOR!
GETTING THERE'LL BE HARD...
...SO DON'T LET THEM CATCH YOU!
BE CARE-FUL OR–

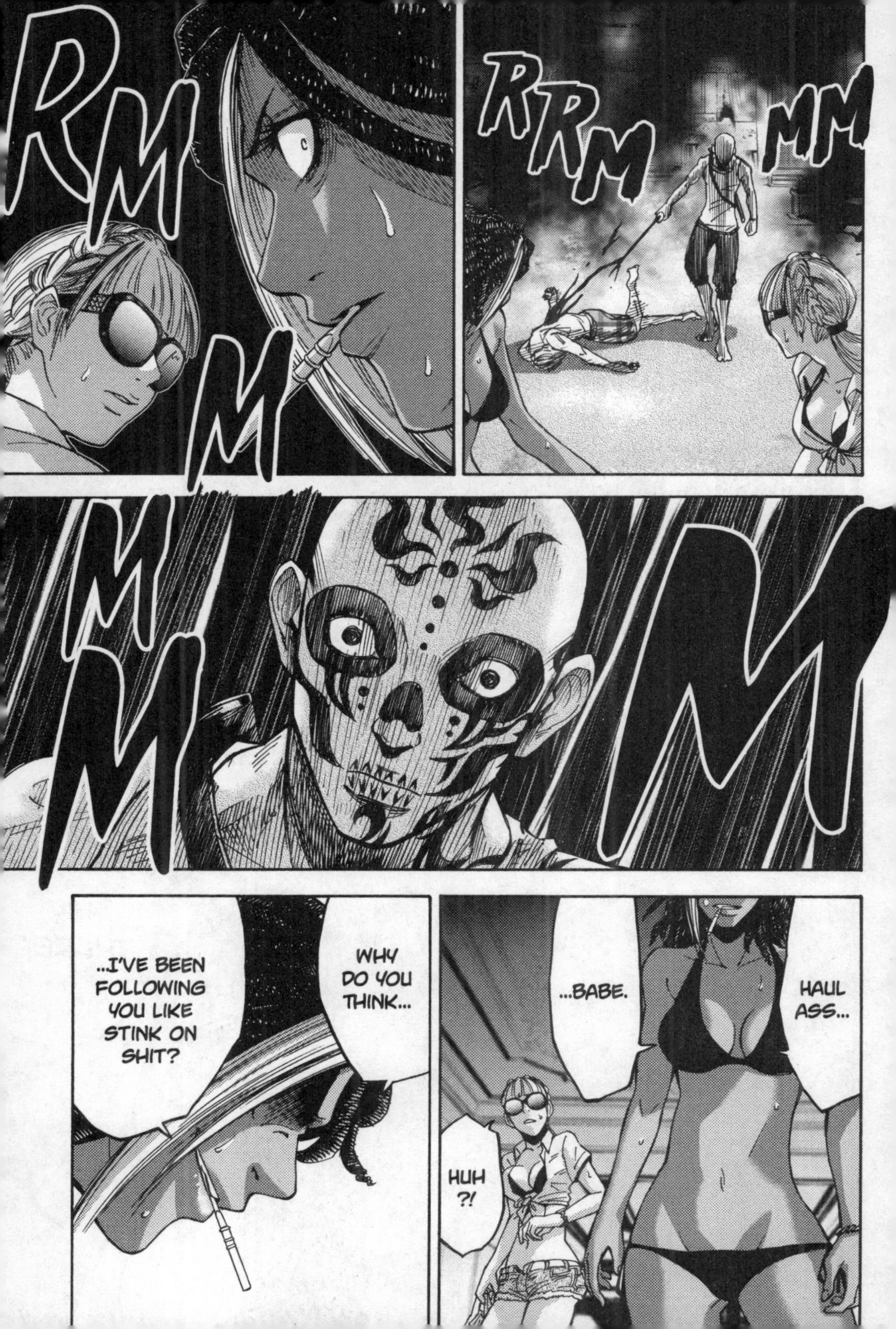
RRRM
MMM
RM
MM
MMM
M
HAUL ASS...
...BABE.
HUH ?!
WHY DO YOU THINK...
...I'VE BEEN FOLLOWING YOU LIKE STINK ON SHIT?

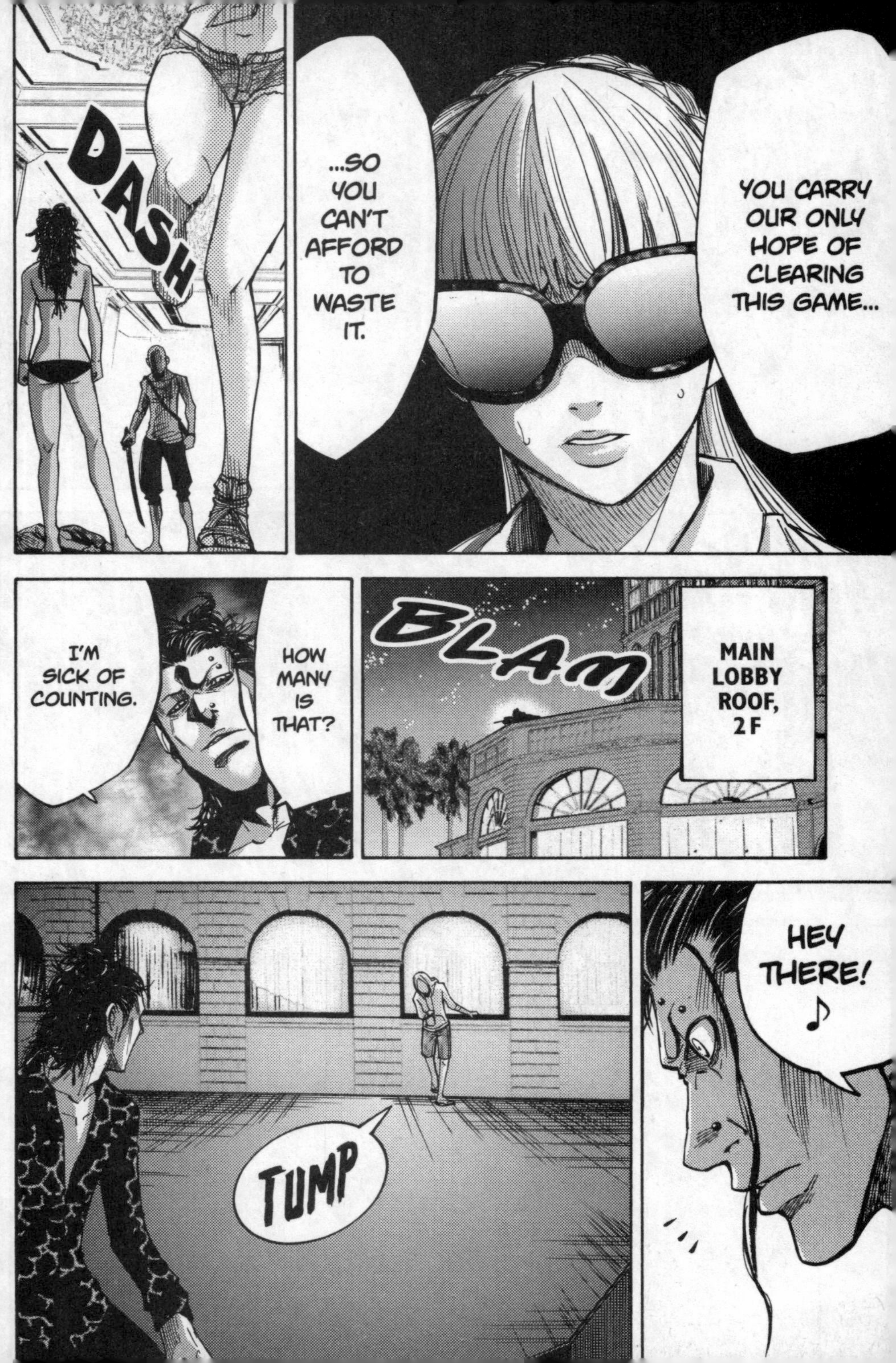
YOU CARRY OUR ONLY HOPE OF CLEARING THIS GAME...
...SO YOU CAN'T AFFORD TO WASTE IT.
DASH
MAIN LOBBY ROOF, 2F
BLAM
HOW MANY IS THAT?
I'M SICK OF COUNTING.
HEY THERE! ♪
TUMP

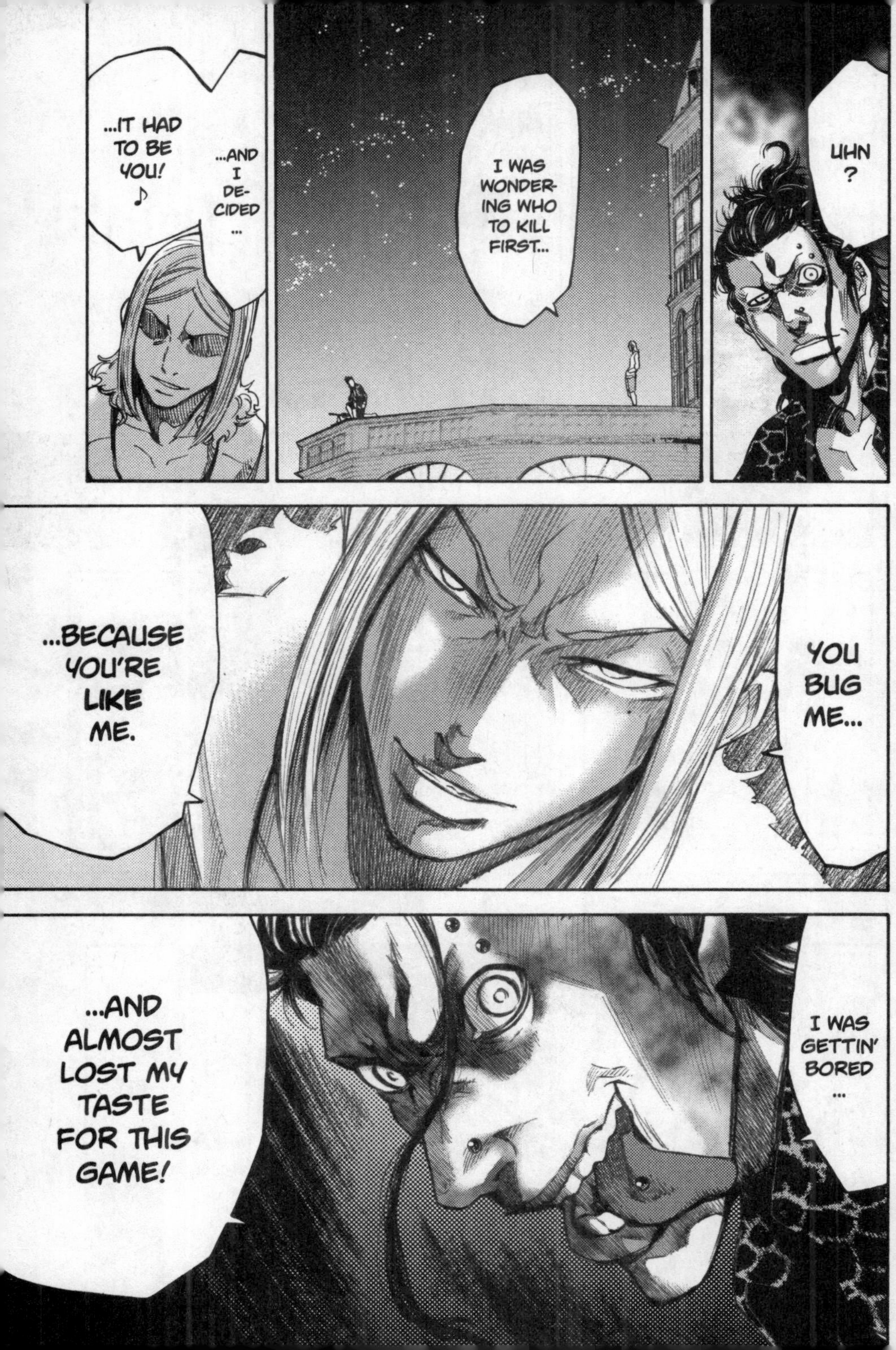
UHN ?
I WAS WONDERING WHO TO KILL FIRST...
...AND I DECIDED...
...IT HAD TO BE YOU! ♪
YOU BUG ME...
...BECAUSE YOU'RE LIKE ME.
I WAS GETTIN' BORED...
...AND ALMOST LOST MY TASTE FOR THIS GAME!

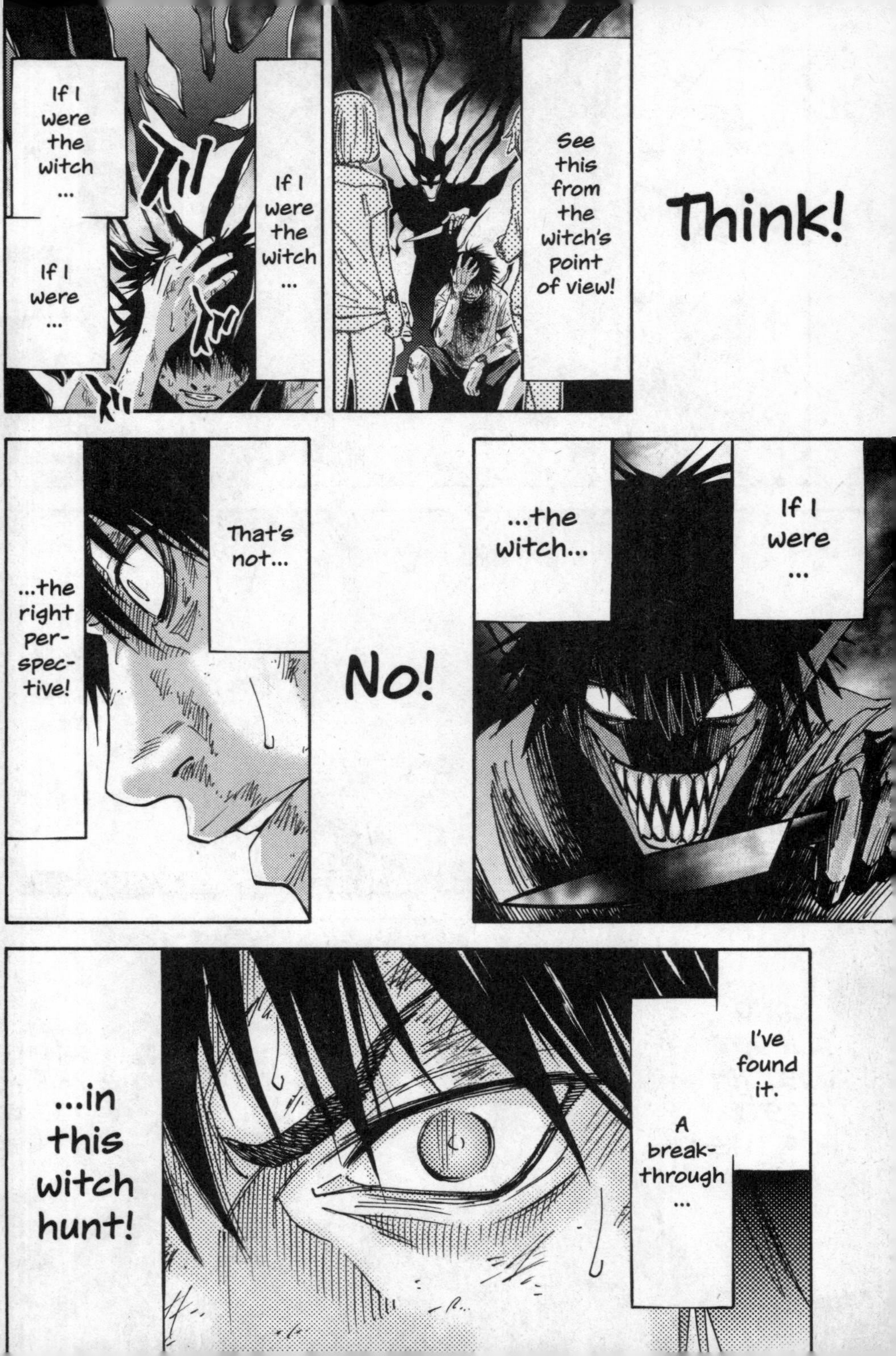
Think!
See this from the witch's point of view!
If I were the witch ...
If I were the witch ...
If I were ...
If I were ...
...the witch...
No!
That's not...
...the right per-spec-tive!
I've found it.
A break-through ...
...in this witch hunt!

CHAPTER 24:
Ten of Hearts, Part 4

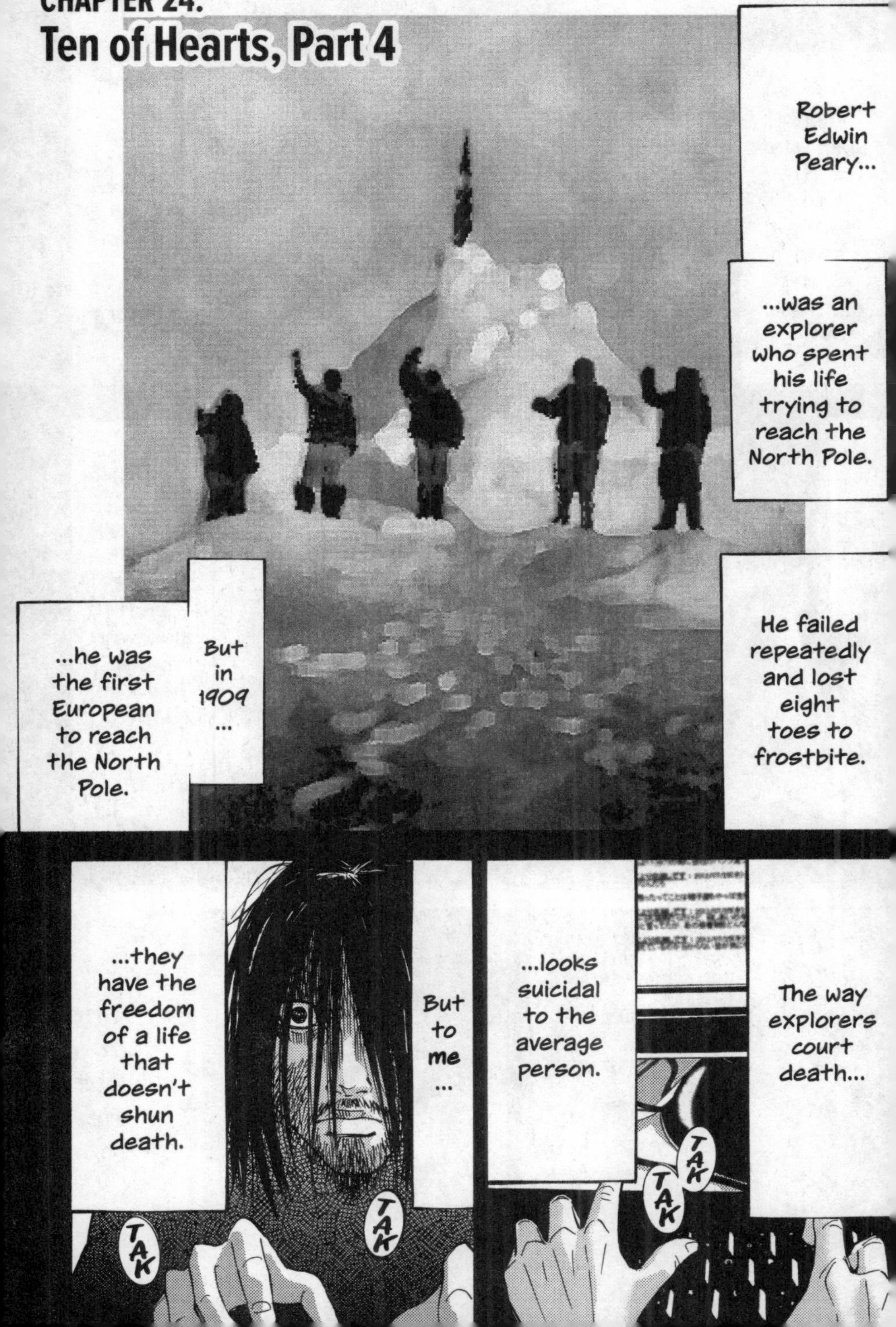
Robert Edwin Peary...
...was an explorer who spent his life trying to reach the North Pole.
He failed repeatedly and lost eight toes to frostbite.
But in 1909...
...he was the first European to reach the North Pole.
The way explorers court death...
...looks suicidal to the average person.
TAK
TAK
But to me...
...they have the freedom of a life that doesn't shun death.
TAK
TAK

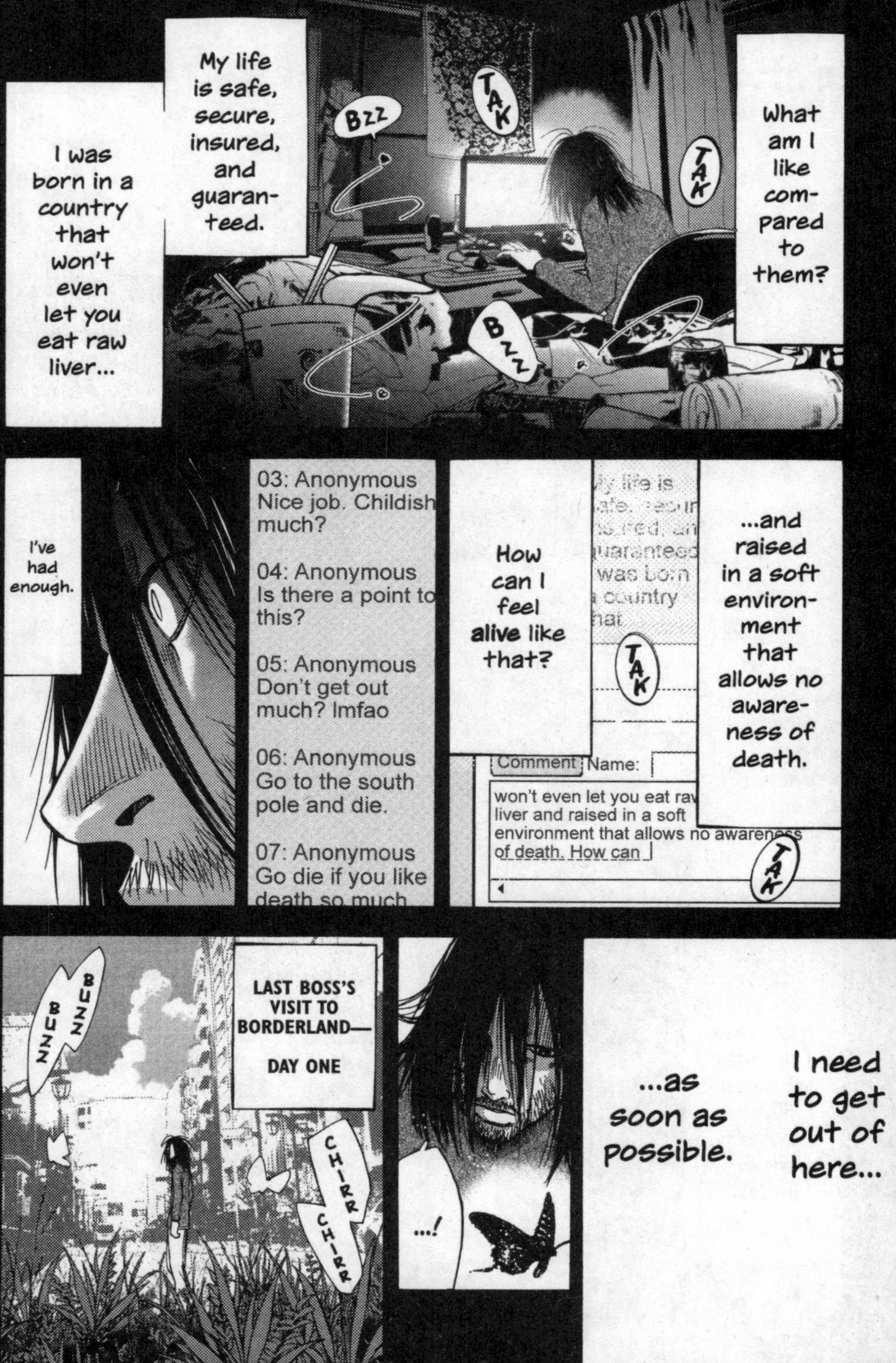

What am I like compared to them?
TAK
TAK
My life is safe, secure, insured, and guaranteed.
Bzz
I was born in a country that won't even let you eat raw liver...
Bzz
...and raised in a soft environment that allows no awareness of death.
TAK
How can I feel alive like that?
Comment
Name:
won't even let you eat raw liver and raised in a soft environment that allows no awareness of death. How can
TAK
03: Anonymous
Nice job. Childish much?
04: Anonymous
Is there a point to this?
05: Anonymous
Don't get out much? lmfao
06: Anonymous
Go to the south pole and die.
07: Anonymous
Go die if you like death so much
I've had enough.
I need to get out of here...
...as soon as possible.
...!
LAST BOSS'S VISIT TO BORDERLAND—
DAY ONE
BUZZ
BUZZ
CHIRR
CHIRR

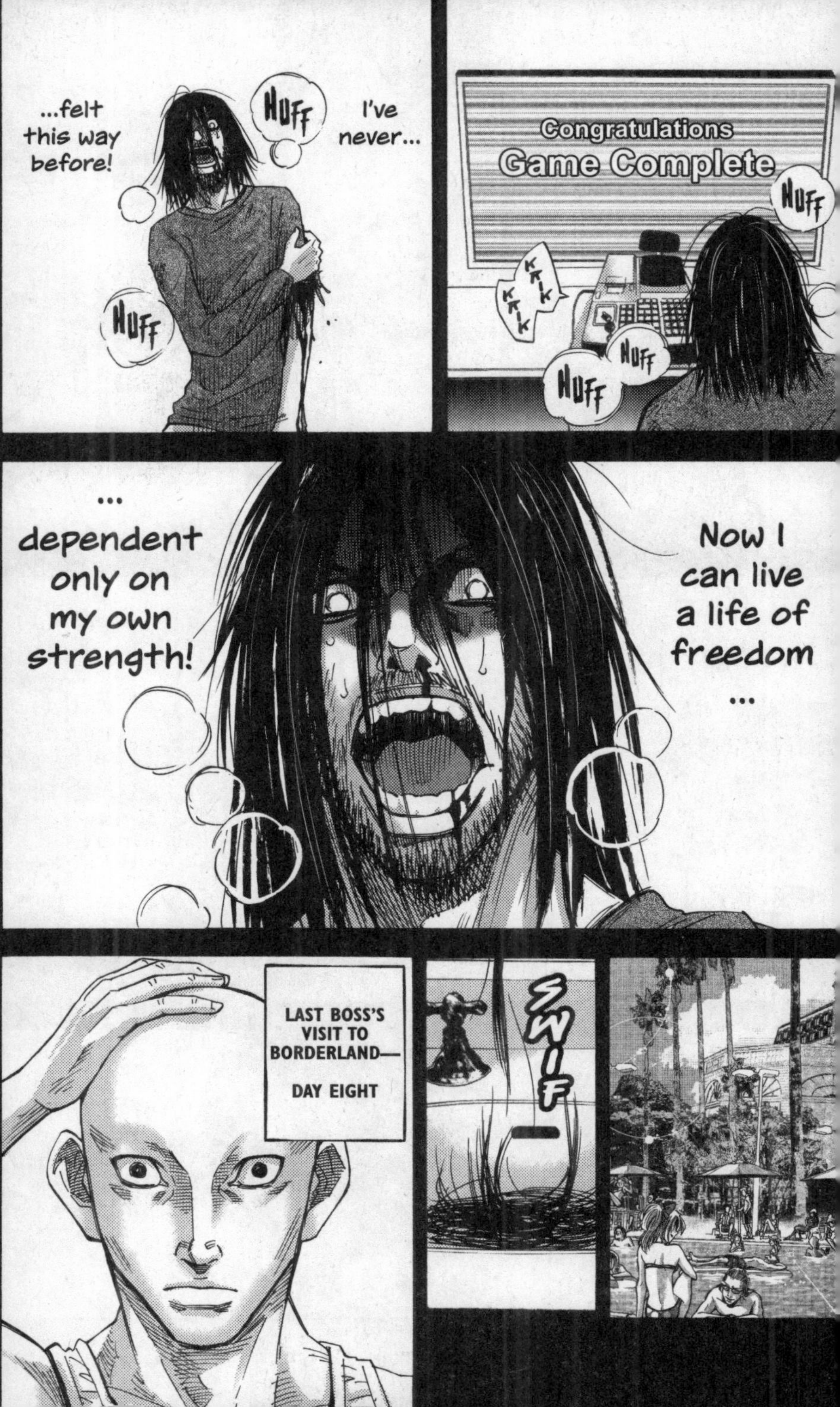
Congratulations
Game Complete
HUFF
KRIK KRIK
HUFF
HUFF
I've never...
...felt this way before!
HUFF
HUFF
Now I can live a life of freedom ...
... dependent only on my own strength!
SWIF
LAST BOSS'S VISIT TO BORDERLAND— DAY EIGHT

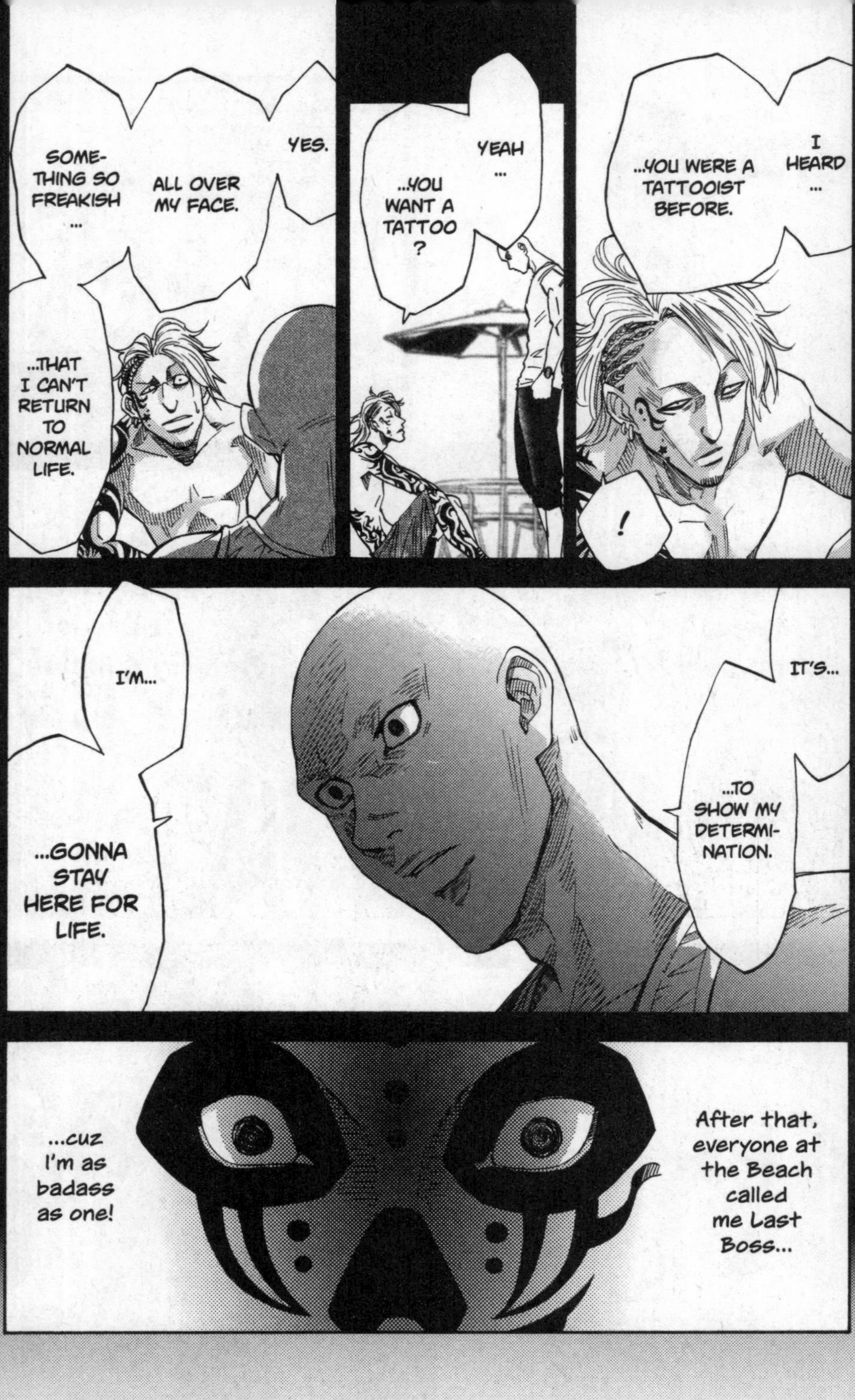
I HEARD...
...YOU WERE A TATTOOIST BEFORE.
!
YEAH...
...YOU WANT A TATTOO?
YES.
ALL OVER MY FACE.
SOMETHING SO FREAKISH...
...THAT I CAN'T RETURN TO NORMAL LIFE.
IT'S...
...TO SHOW MY DETERMINATION.
I'M...
...GONNA STAY HERE FOR LIFE.
After that, everyone at the Beach called me Last Boss...
...cuz I'm as badass as one!

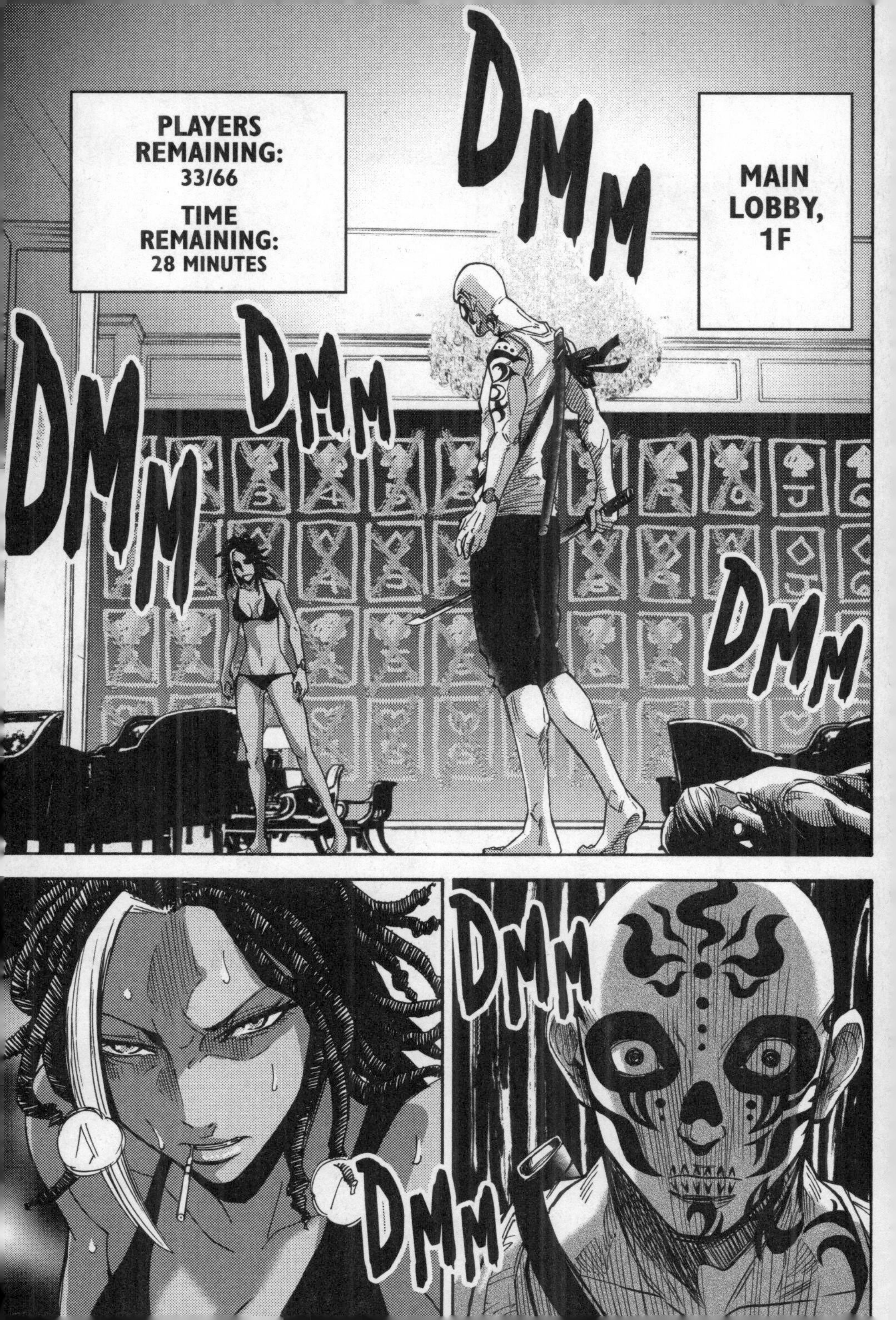
MAIN LOBBY, 1F
DMM
PLAYERS REMAINING: 33/66
TIME REMAINING: 28 MINUTES
DMM
DMM
DMM
DMM
DMM

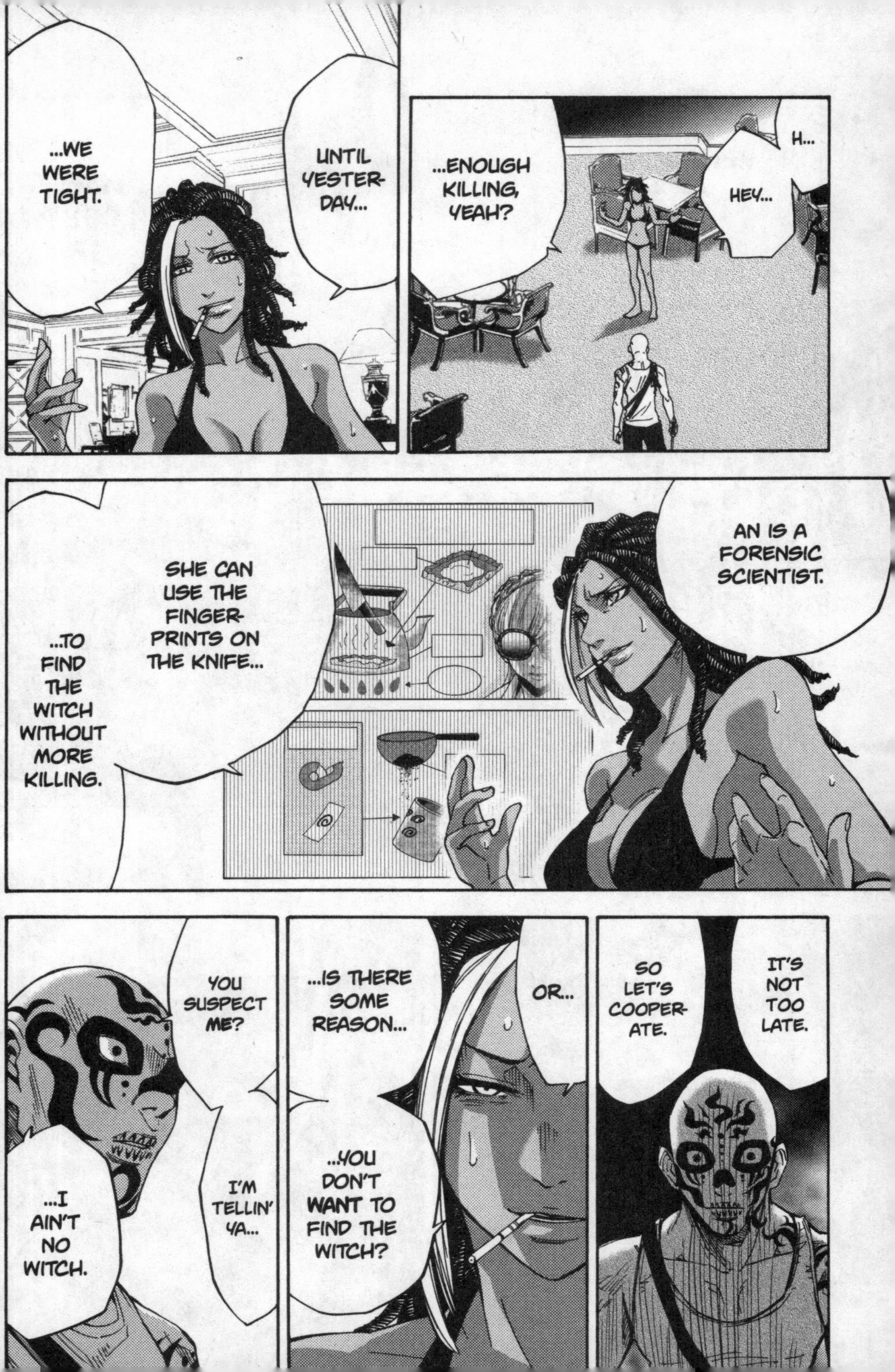
H...
HEY...
...ENOUGH KILLING, YEAH?
UNTIL YESTERDAY...
...WE WERE TIGHT.
AN IS A FORENSIC SCIENTIST.
SHE CAN USE THE FINGERPRINTS ON THE KNIFE...
...TO FIND THE WITCH WITHOUT MORE KILLING.
IT'S NOT TOO LATE.
SO LET'S COOPERATE.
OR...
...IS THERE SOME REASON...
...YOU DON'T WANT TO FIND THE WITCH?
YOU SUSPECT ME?
I'M TELLIN' YA...
...I AIN'T NO WITCH.

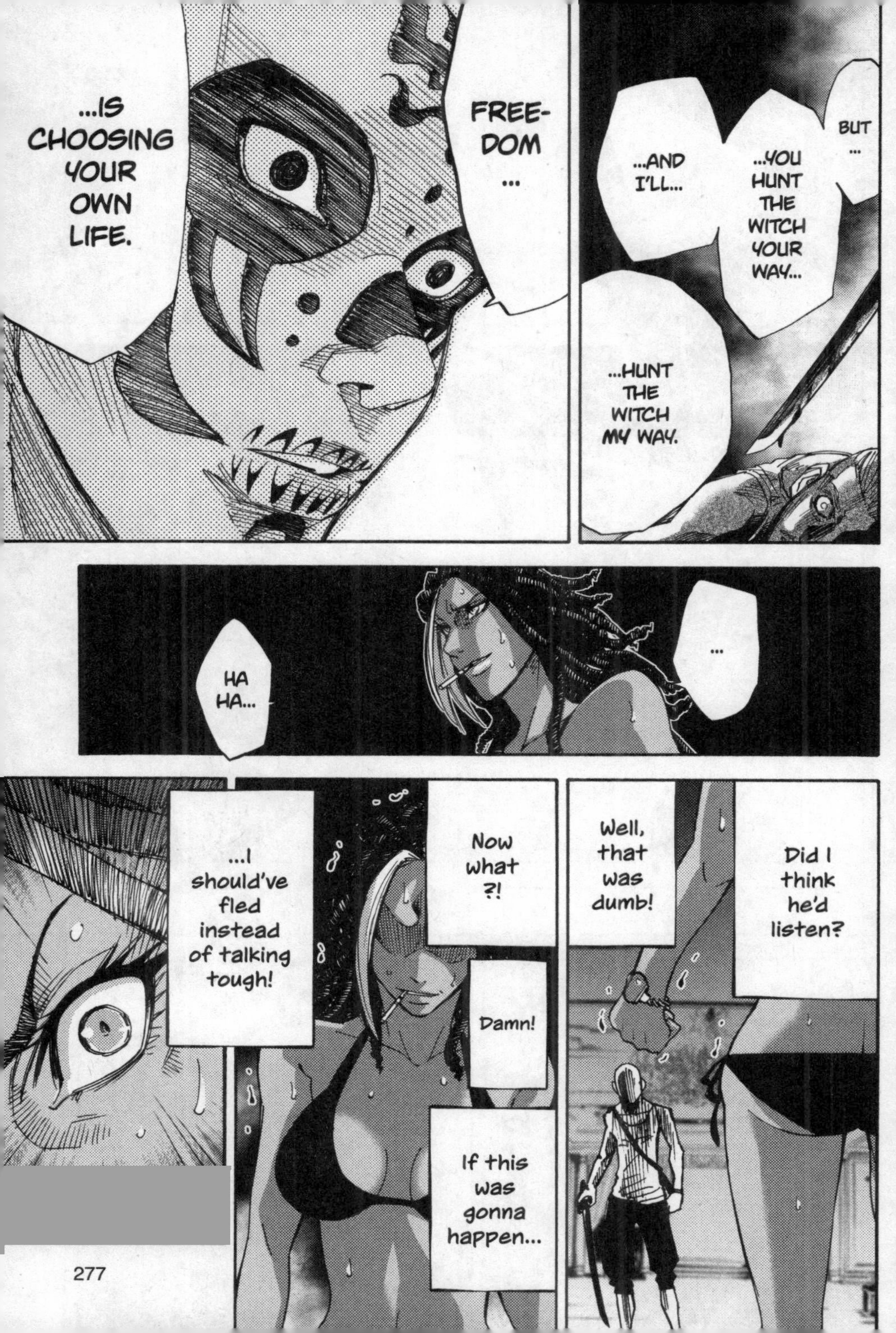
BUT ...
...YOU HUNT THE WITCH YOUR WAY...
...AND I'LL...
...HUNT THE WITCH MY WAY.
FREE-DOM ...
...IS CHOOSING YOUR OWN LIFE.
...
HA HA...
Did I think he'd listen?
Well, that was dumb!
Now what ?!
Damn!
If this was gonna happen...
...I should've fled instead of talking tough!

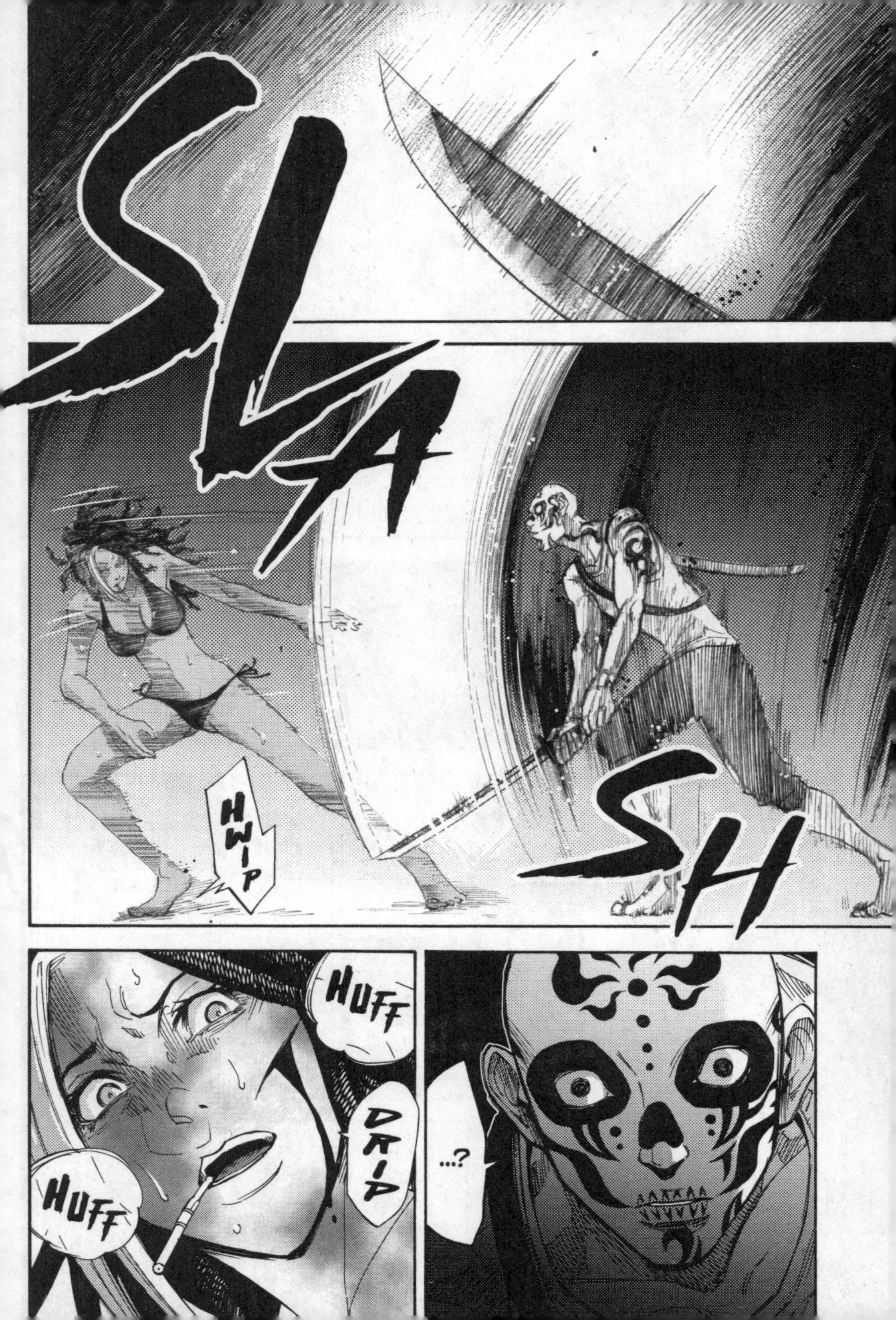
SLASH
HWIP
...?
HUFF
DRIP
HUFF

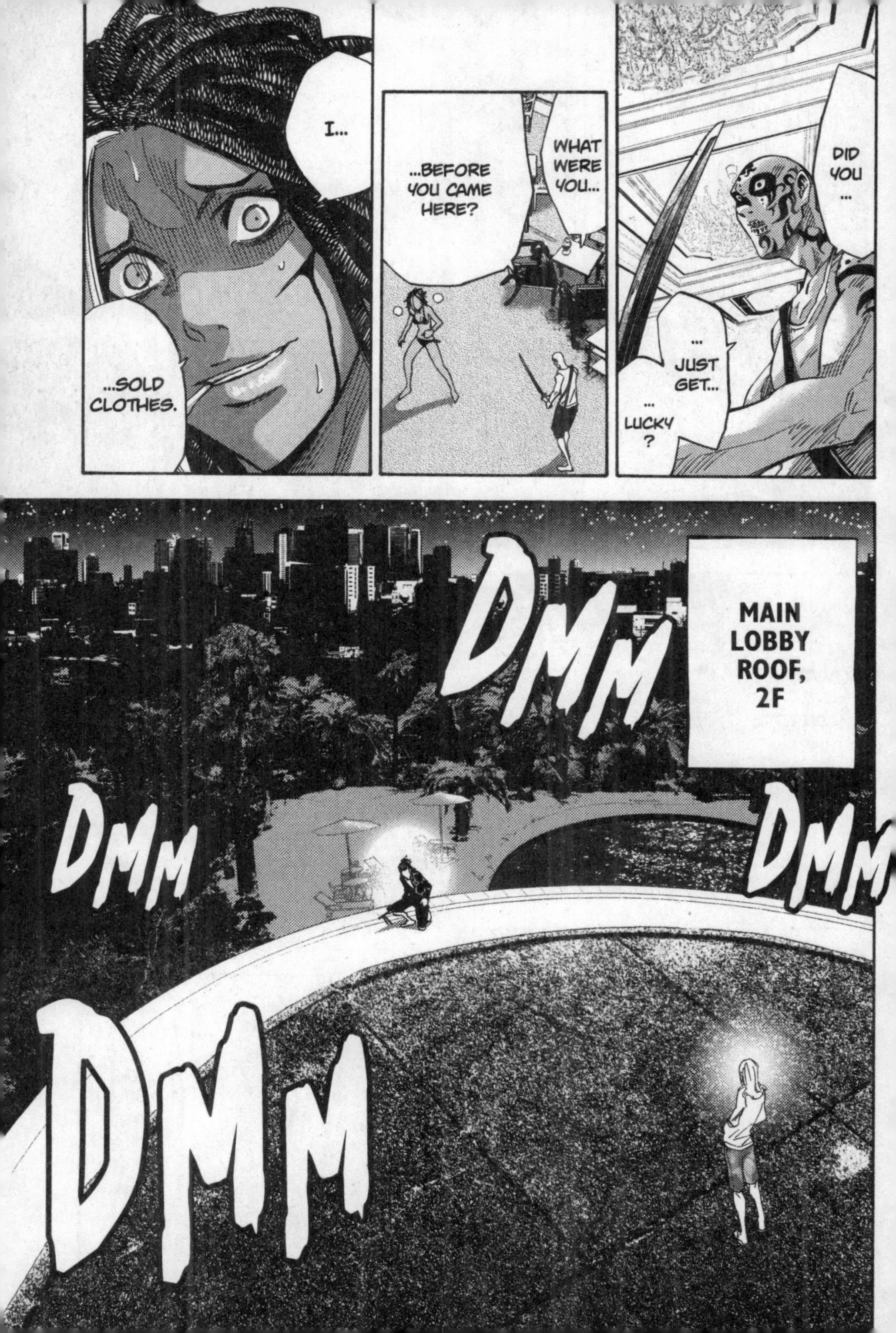
DID YOU ...
... JUST GET...
... LUCKY ?
WHAT WERE YOU...
...BEFORE YOU CAME HERE?
I...
...SOLD CLOTHES.
MAIN LOBBY ROOF, 2F
DMM
DMM
DMM
DMM

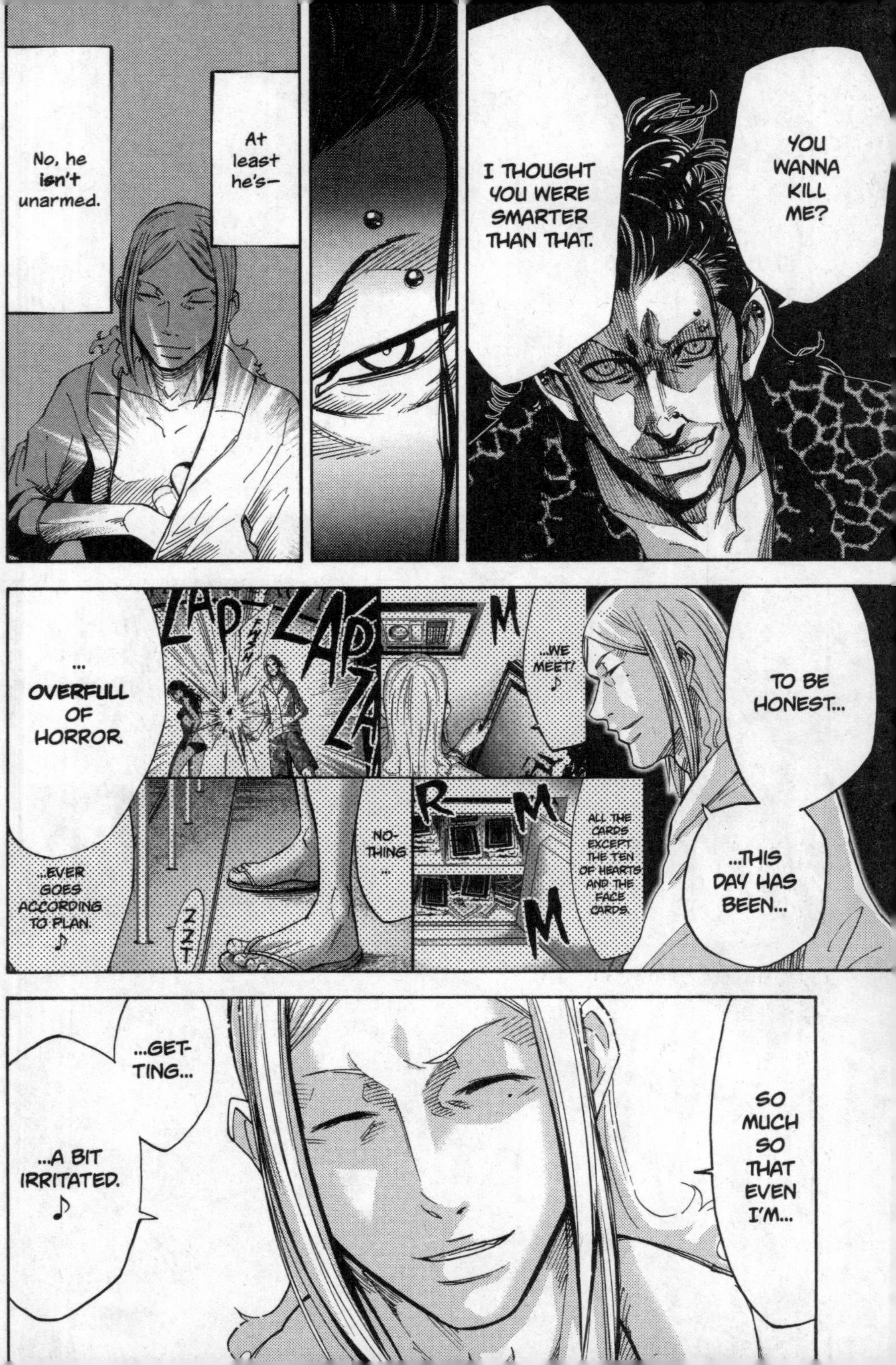
YOU WANNA KILL ME?
I THOUGHT YOU WERE SMARTER THAN THAT.
At least he's—
No, he isn't unarmed.
TO BE HONEST...
...THIS DAY HAS BEEN...
M
...WE MEET! ♪
ZAP ZAP
FWSH
... OVERFULL OF HORROR.
R—M M M
ALL THE CARDS EXCEPT THE TEN OF HEARTS AND THE FACE CARDS.
NO-THING...
ZZT
...EVER GOES ACCORDING TO PLAN. ♪
SO MUCH SO THAT EVEN I'M...
...GET-TING...
...A BIT IRRITATED. ♪

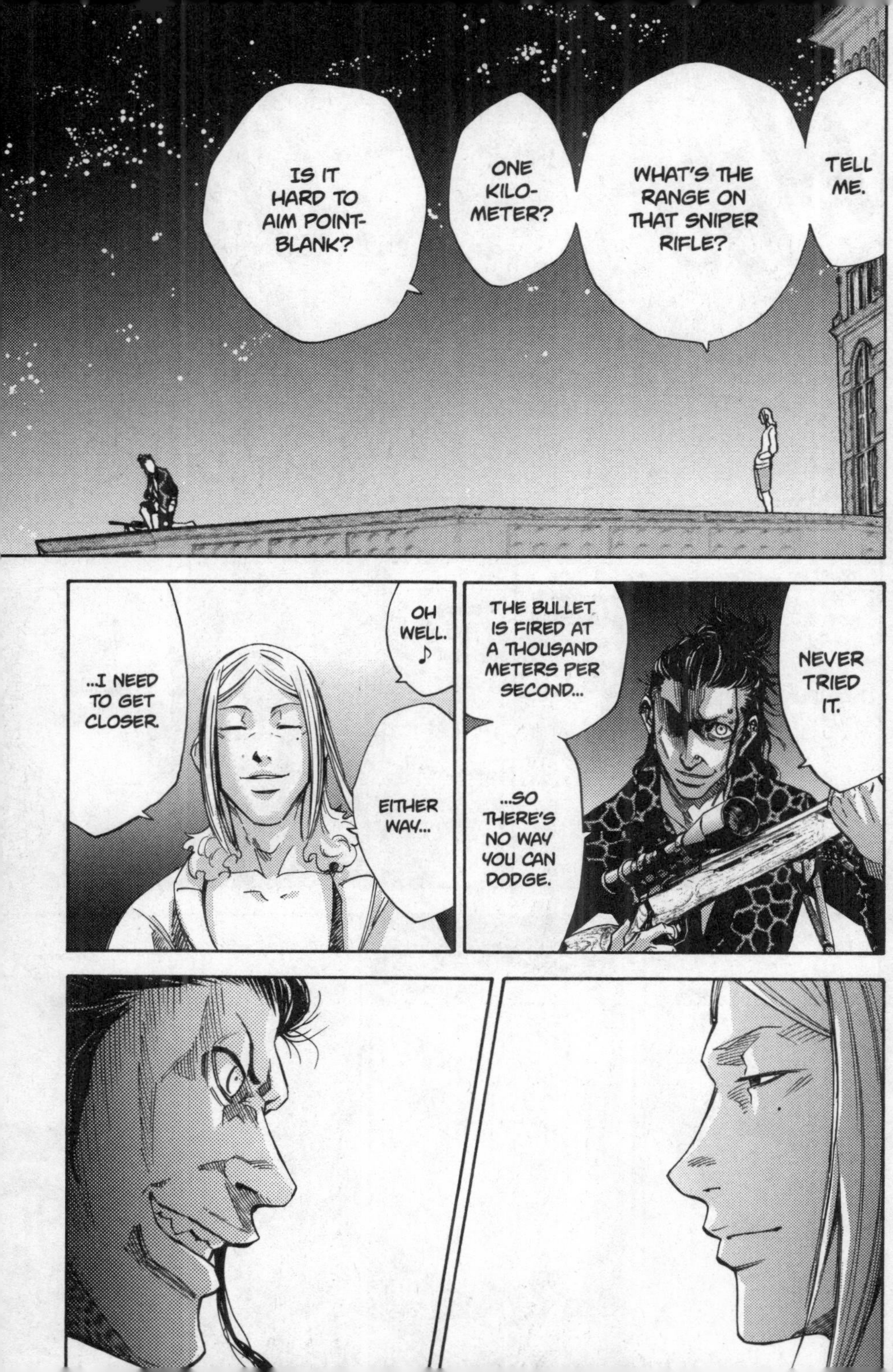
TELL ME.
WHAT'S THE RANGE ON THAT SNIPER RIFLE?
ONE KILO-METER?
IS IT HARD TO AIM POINT-BLANK?
NEVER TRIED IT.
THE BULLET IS FIRED AT A THOUSAND METERS PER SECOND...
...SO THERE'S NO WAY YOU CAN DODGE.
OH WELL. ♪
EITHER WAY...
...I NEED TO GET CLOSER.

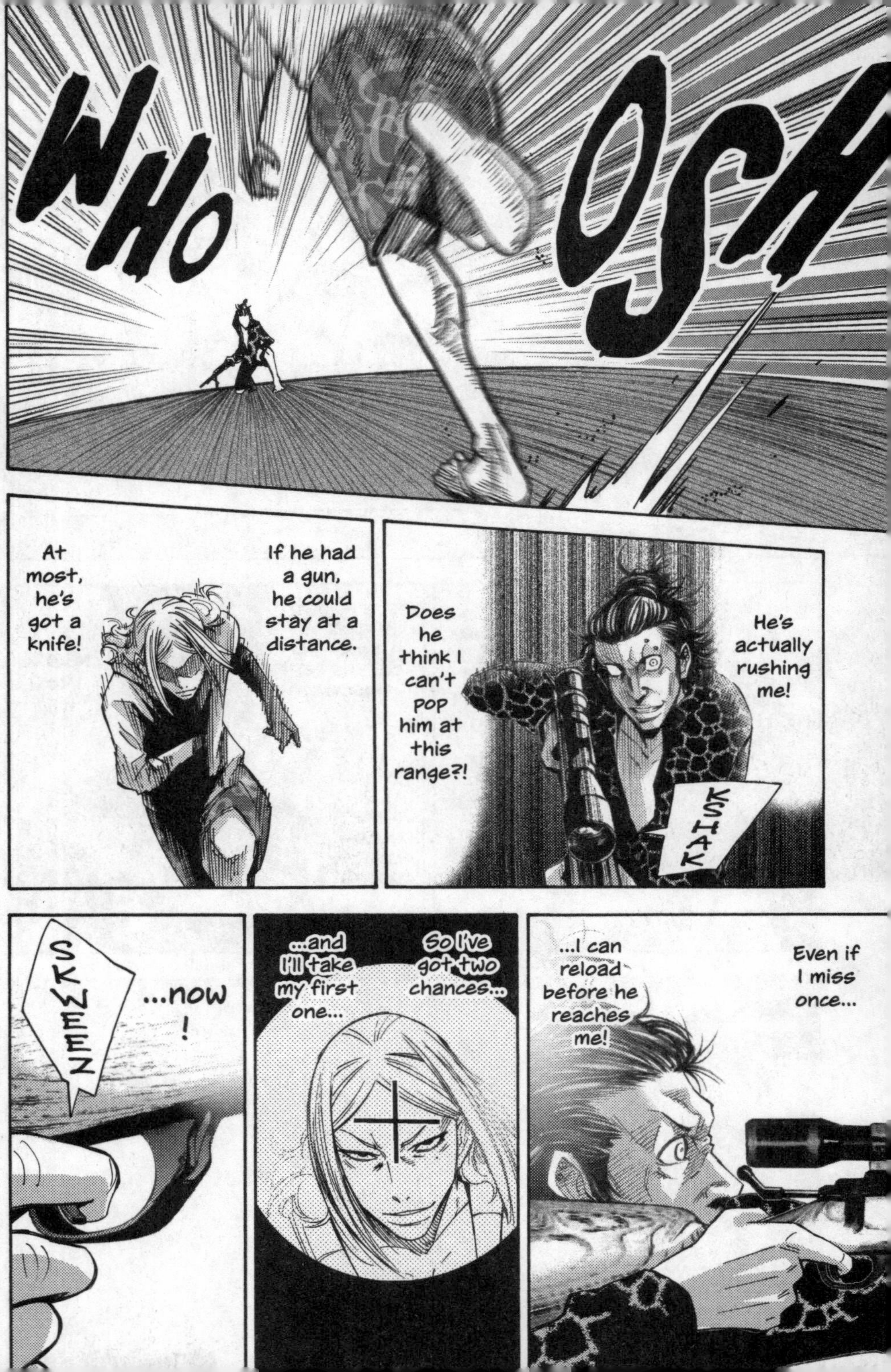
WHOOSH
He's actually rushing me!
Does he think I can't pop him at this range?!
KSHAK
If he had a gun, he could stay at a distance.
At most, he's got a knife!
Even if I miss once...
...I can reload before he reaches me!
So I've got two chances...
...and I'll take my first one...
SKWEEZ
...now!

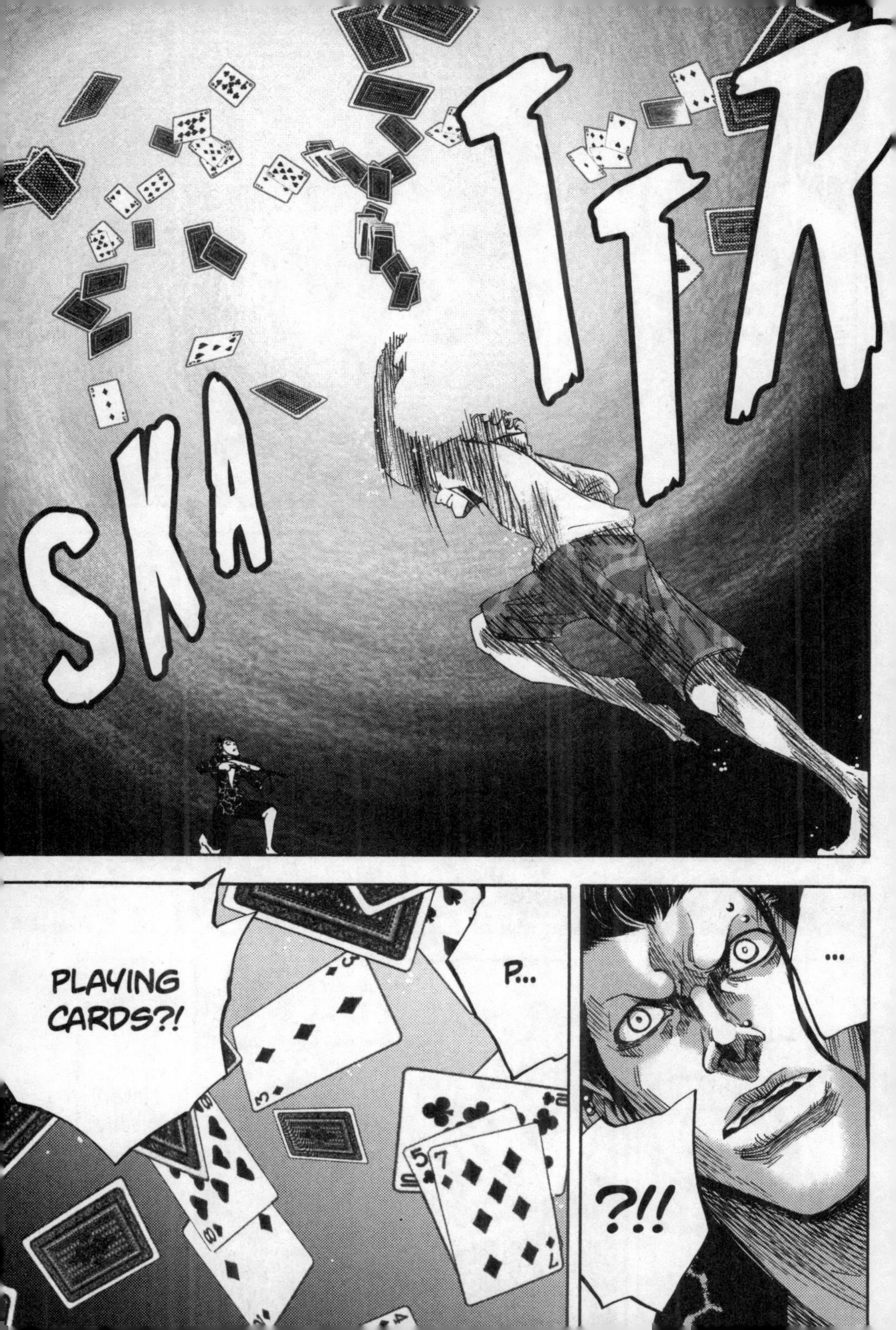
SKATTR
...
?!!
P...
PLAYING CARDS?!

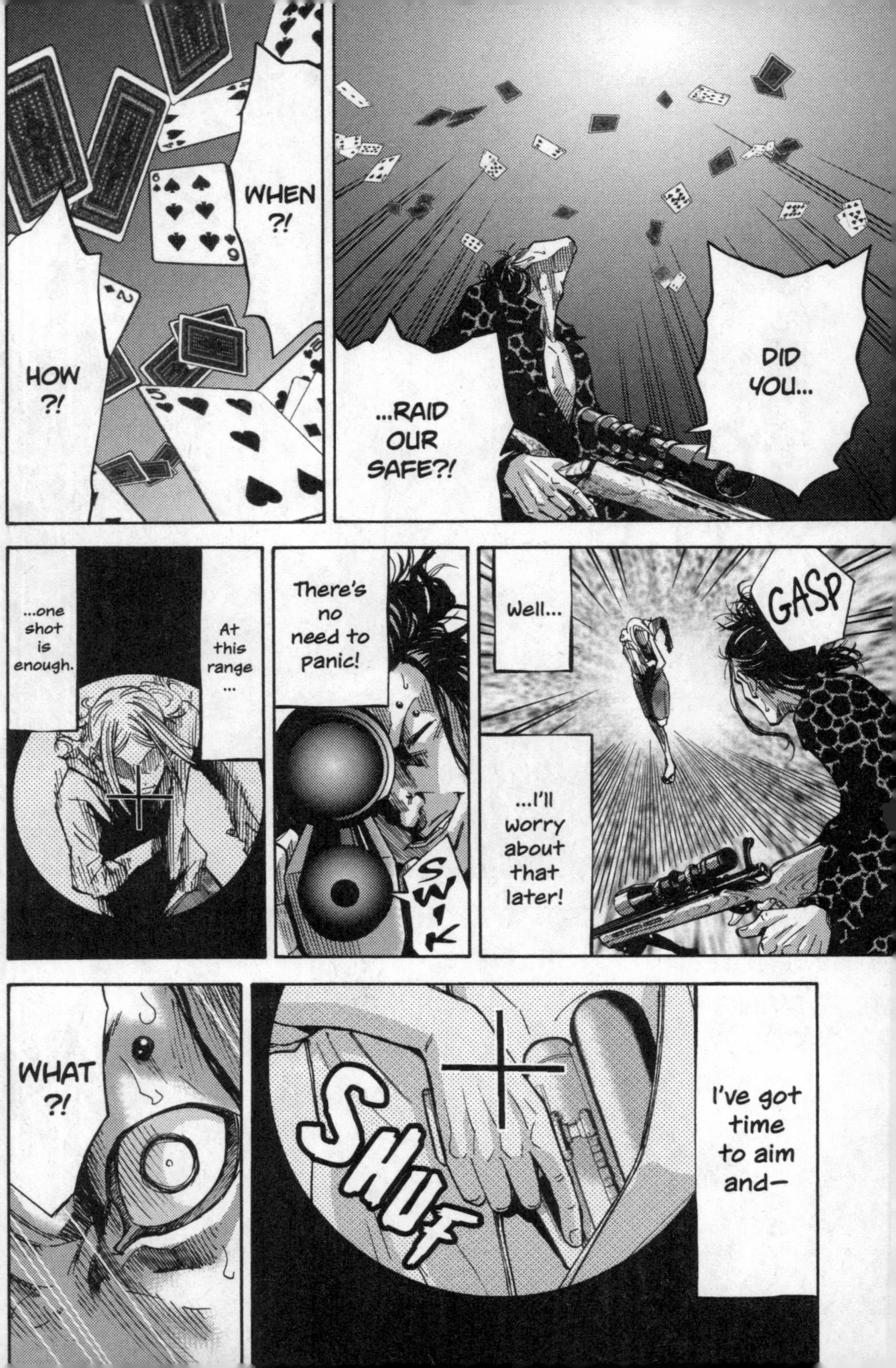
DID YOU...
...RAID OUR SAFE?!
WHEN ?!
HOW ?!
GASP
Well...
...I'll worry about that later!
There's no need to panic!
SWIK
At this range ...
...one shot is enough.
I've got time to aim and–
SHUF
WHAT ?!

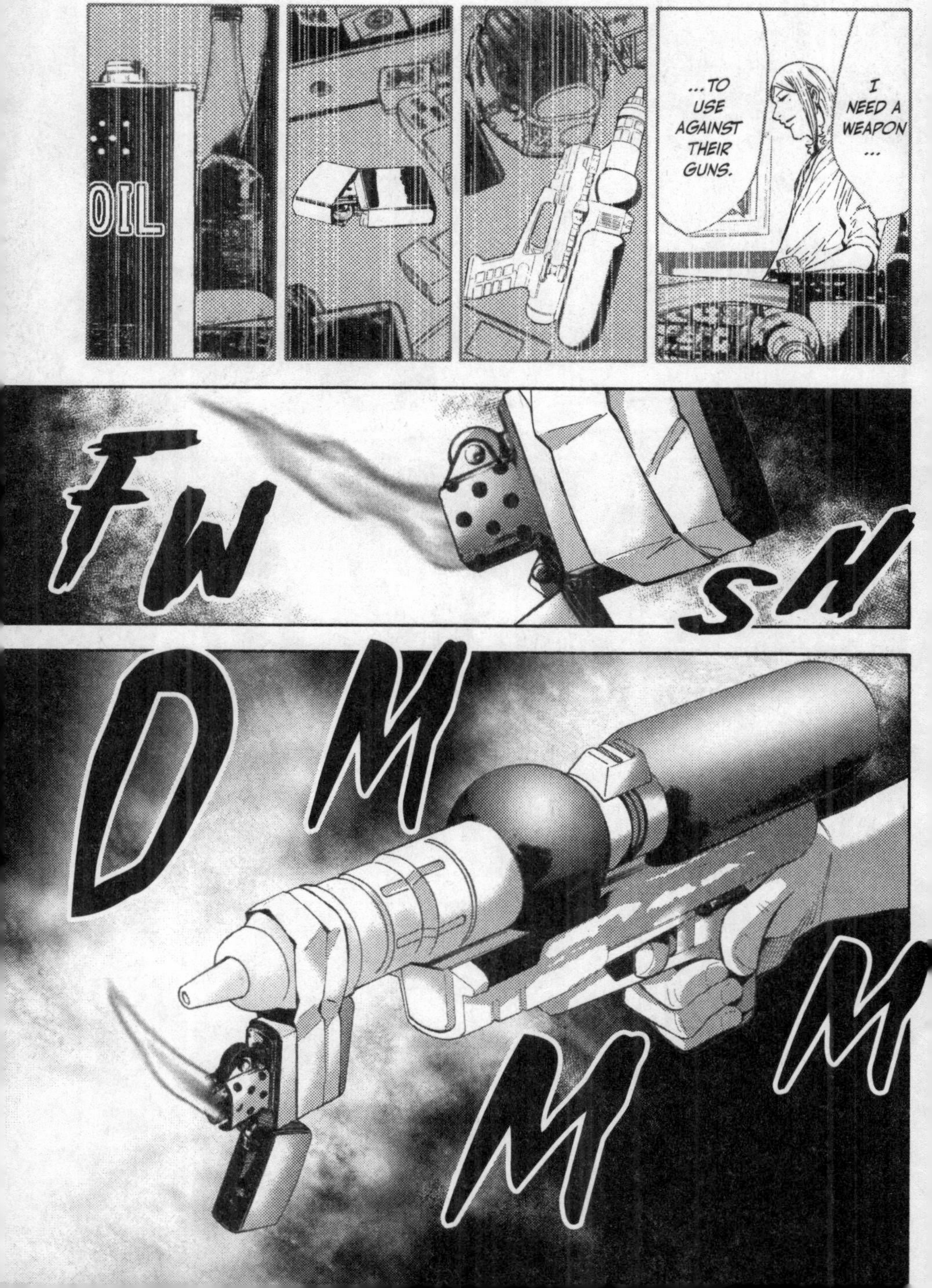
I NEED A WEAPON ...
...TO USE AGAINST THEIR GUNS.
FWSH
DMMMM

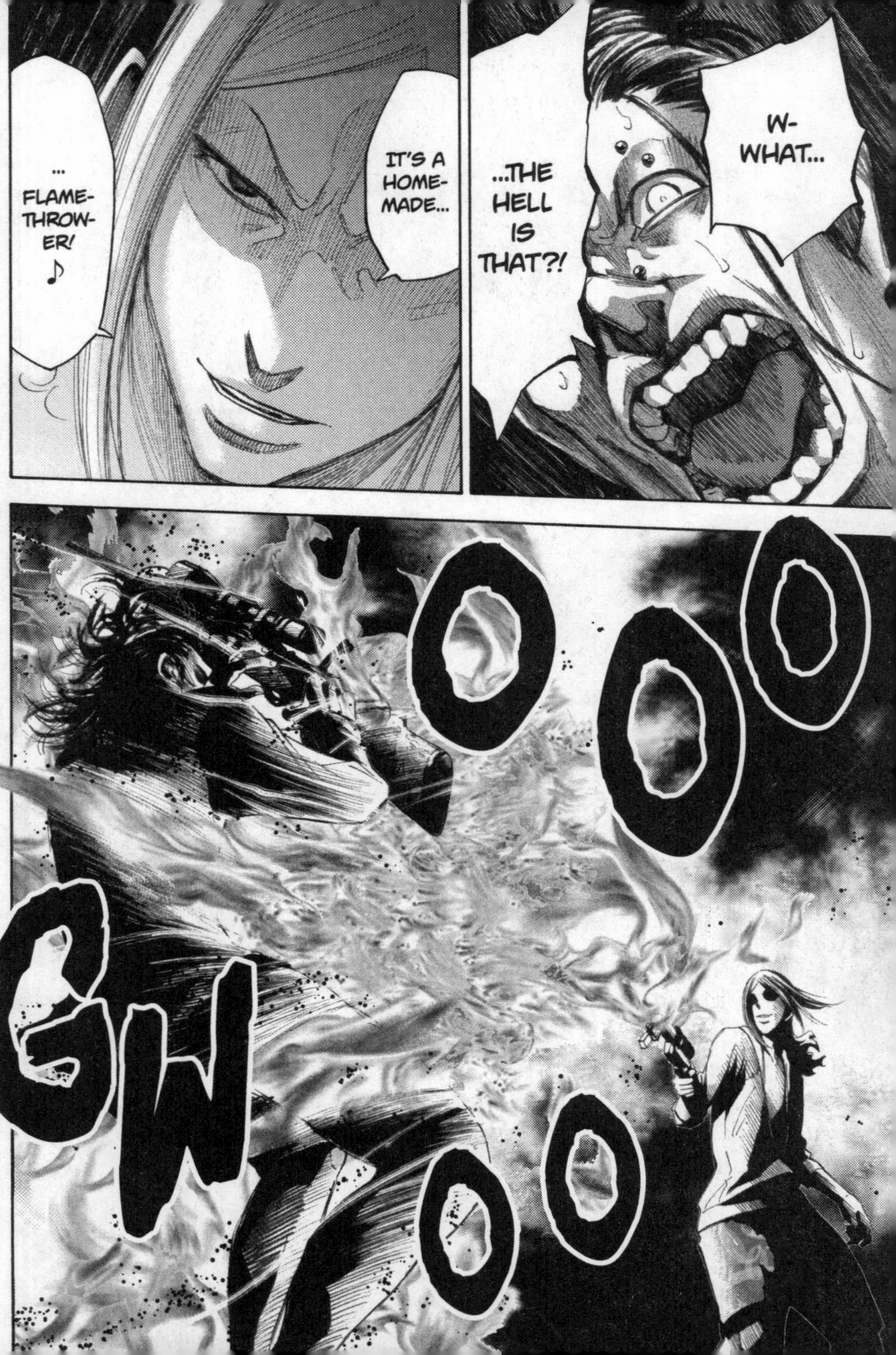
W-WHAT...
...THE HELL IS THAT?!
IT'S A HOMEMADE...
...FLAMETHROWER! ♪
GWOOOOOOO

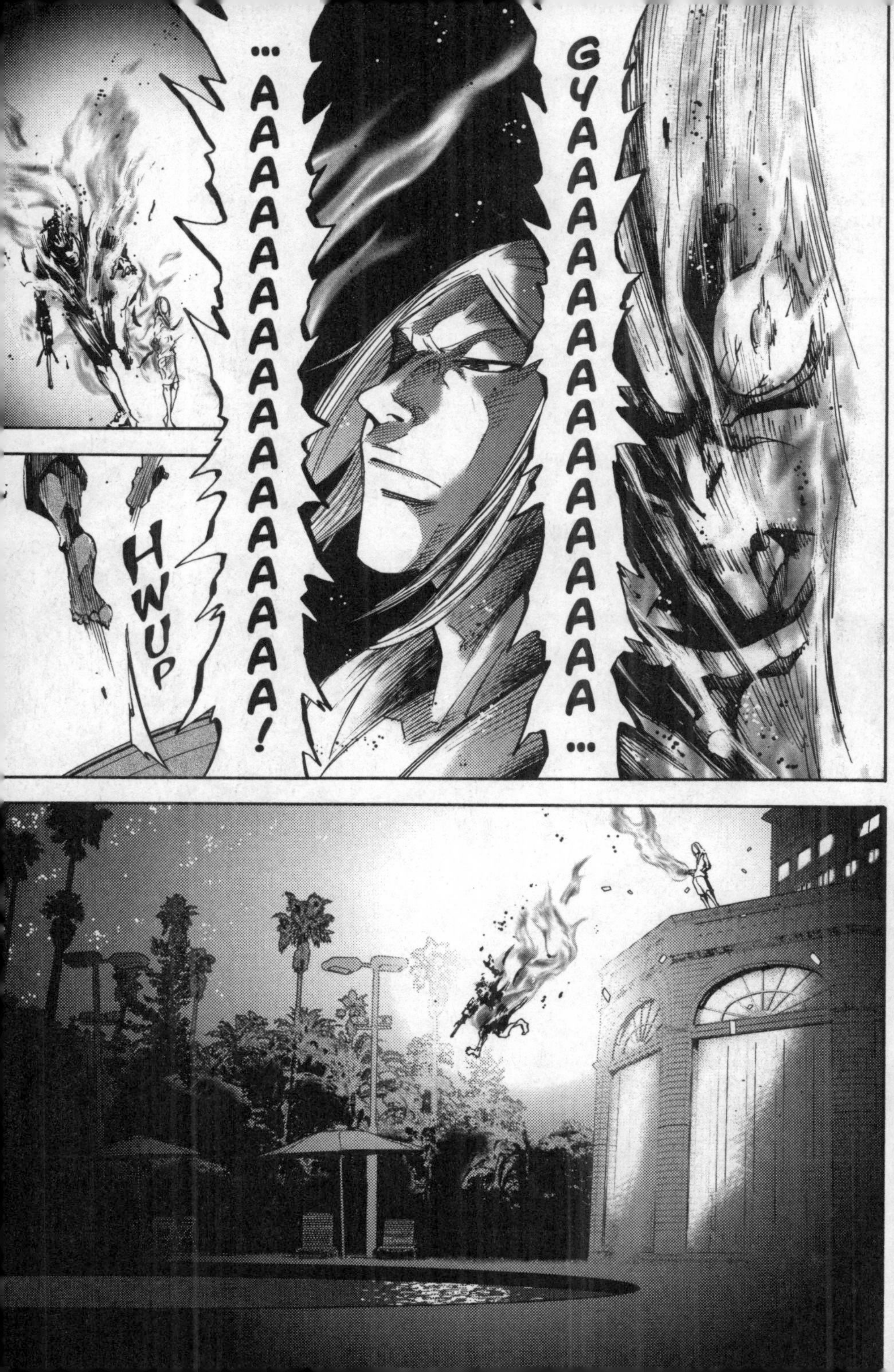
GYAAAAAAAAAAAAAAAA...
...AAAAAAAAAAAAAAAAAA!
HWUP

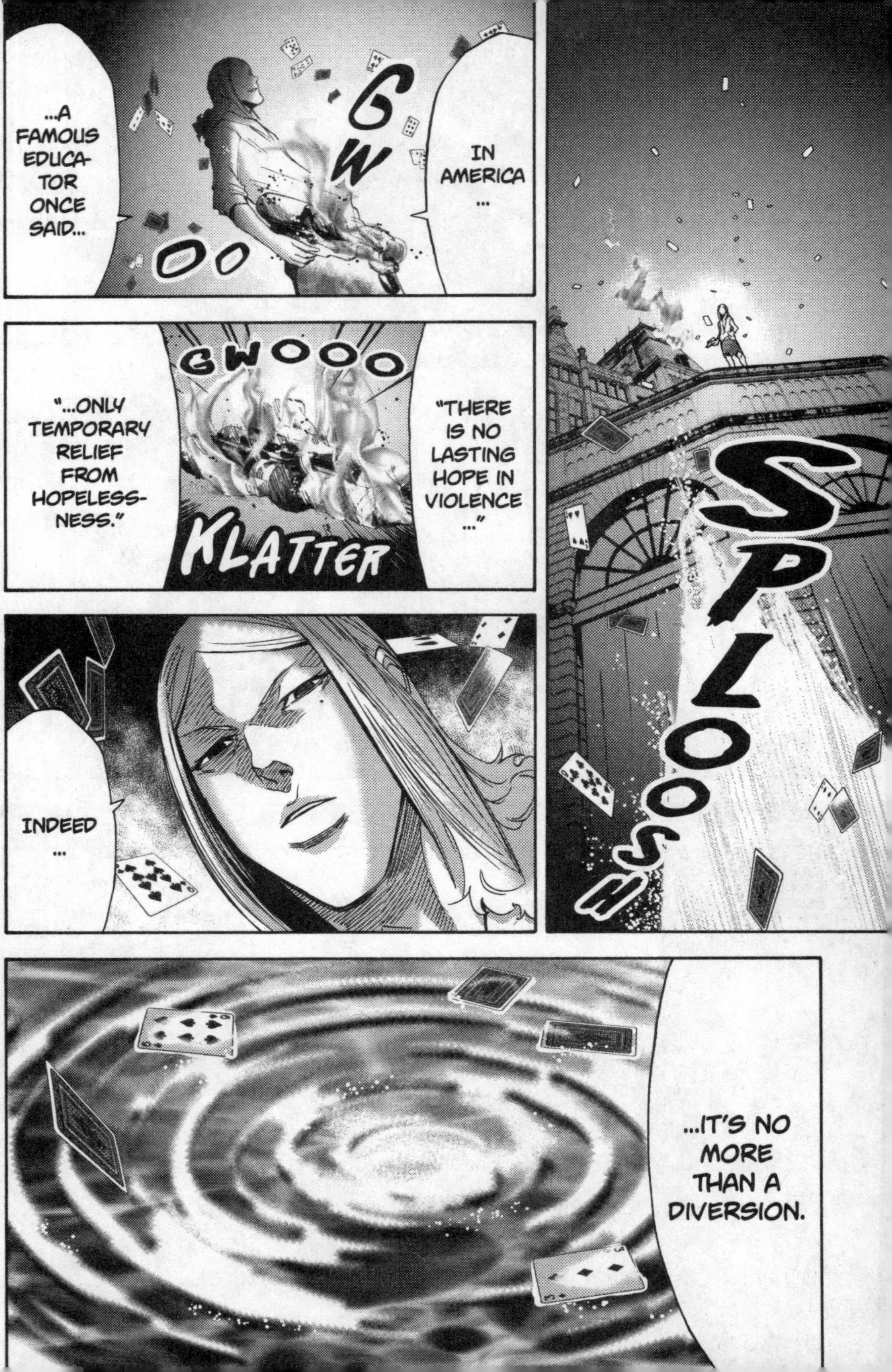
SPLOOSH
IN AMERICA ...
GWOO
...A FAMOUS EDUCATOR ONCE SAID...
GWOOO
"THERE IS NO LASTING HOPE IN VIOLENCE ..."
"...ONLY TEMPORARY RELIEF FROM HOPELESSNESS."
KLATTER
INDEED ...
...IT'S NO MORE THAN A DIVERSION.

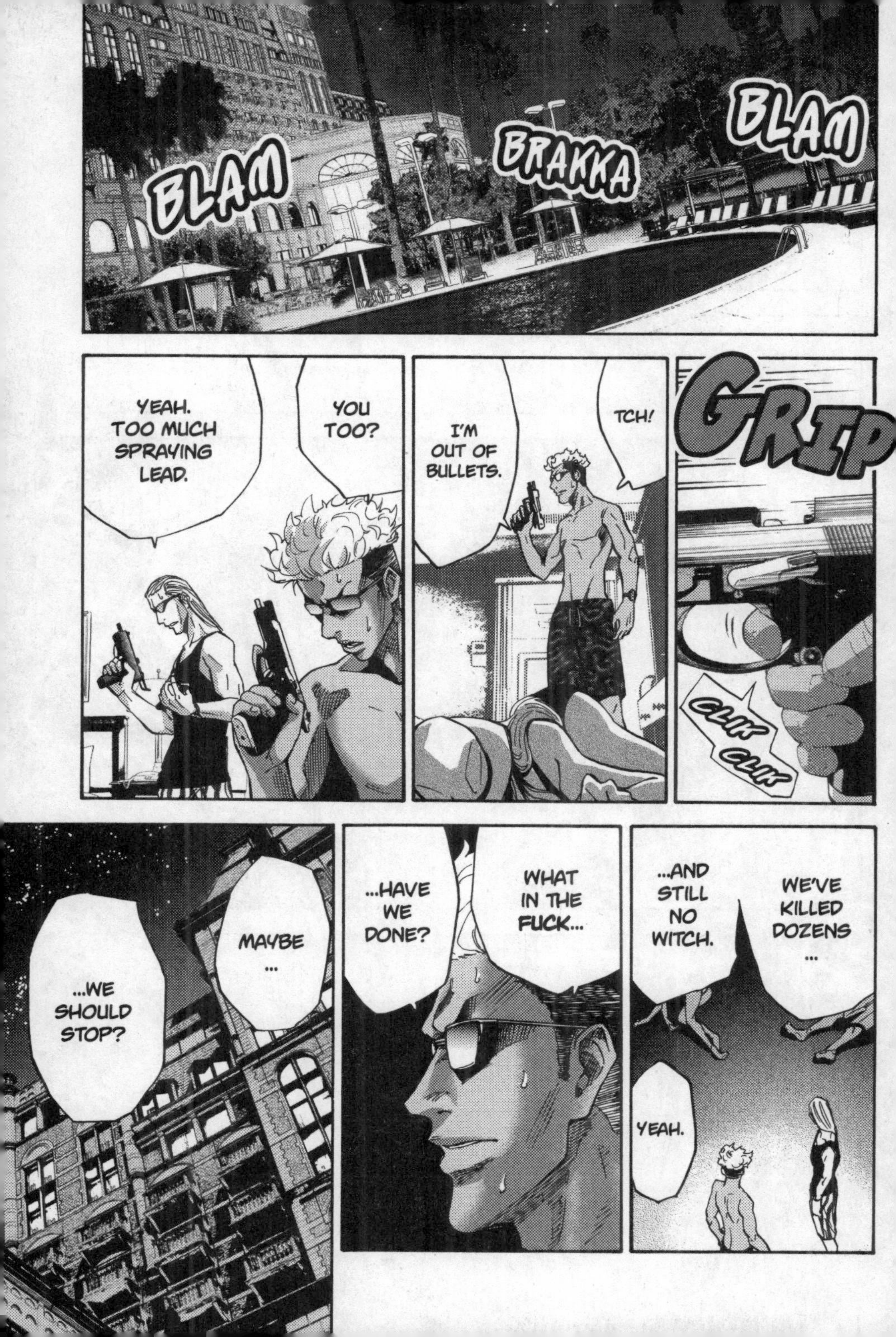
BLAM
BRAKKA
BLAM
GRIP
CLIK
CLIK
TCH!
I'M OUT OF BULLETS.
YOU TOO?
YEAH. TOO MUCH SPRAYING LEAD.
WE'VE KILLED DOZENS ...
...AND STILL NO WITCH.
YEAH.
WHAT IN THE FUCK...
...HAVE WE DONE?
MAYBE ...
...WE SHOULD STOP?

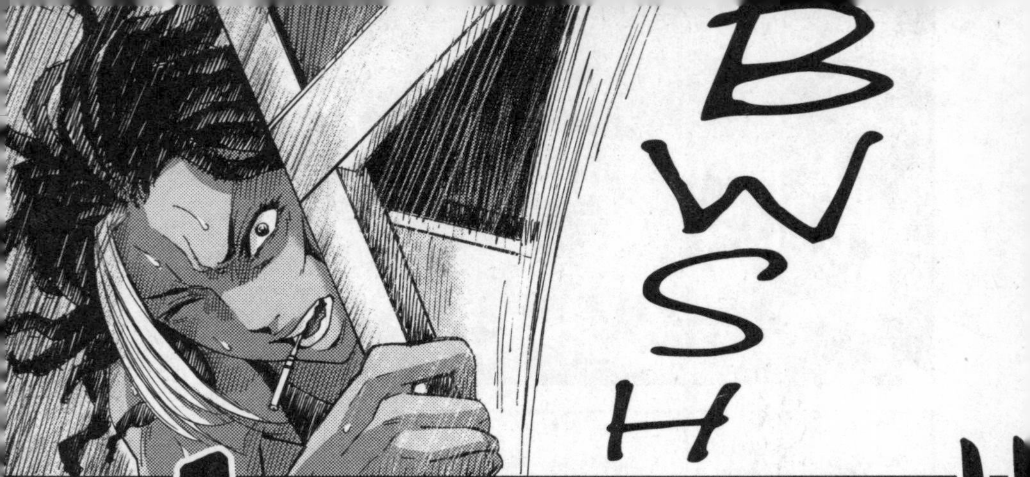
BWSH
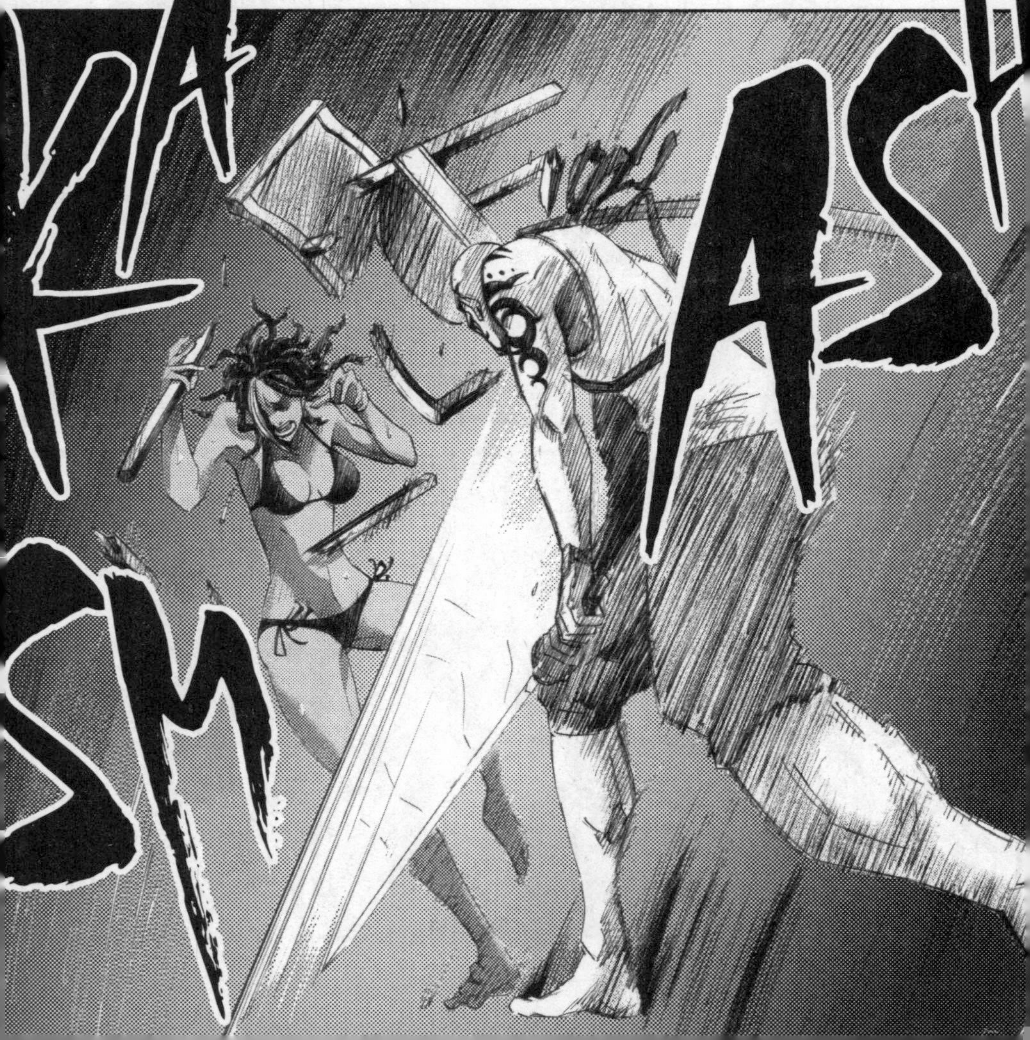
SMASH

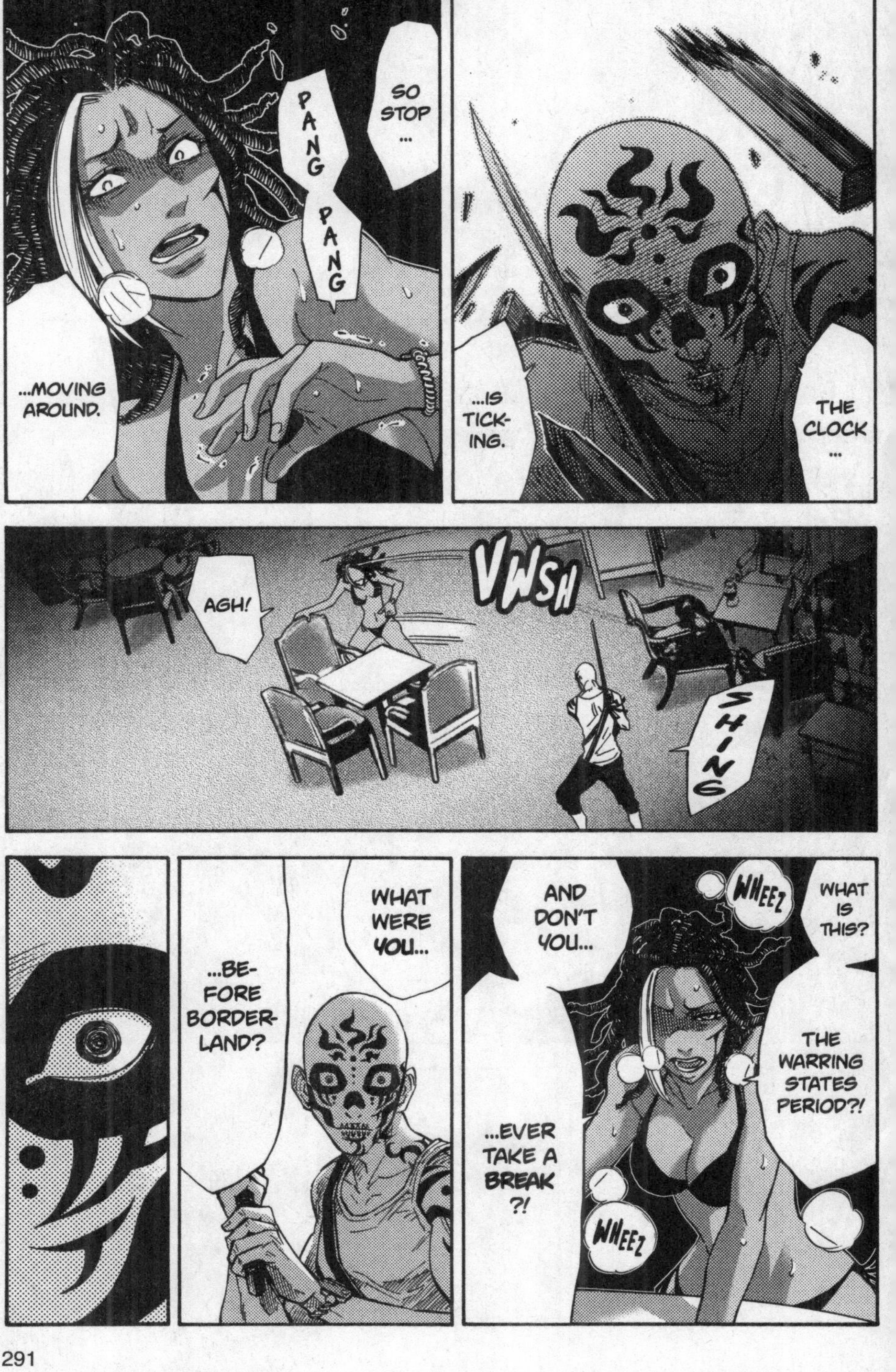
THE CLOCK ...
...IS TICKING.
SO STOP ...
PANG PANG
...MOVING AROUND.
SHING
VWSH
AGH!
WHAT IS THIS?
WHEEZ
THE WARRING STATES PERIOD?!
AND DON'T YOU...
...EVER TAKE A BREAK ?!
WHEEZ
WHAT WERE YOU...
...BEFORE BORDERLAND?

I WAS NOTHING BEFORE. I AIN'T GOT A PAST.

ME ?

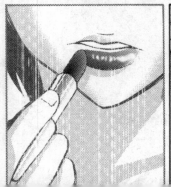

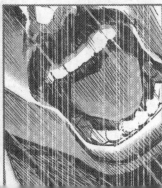

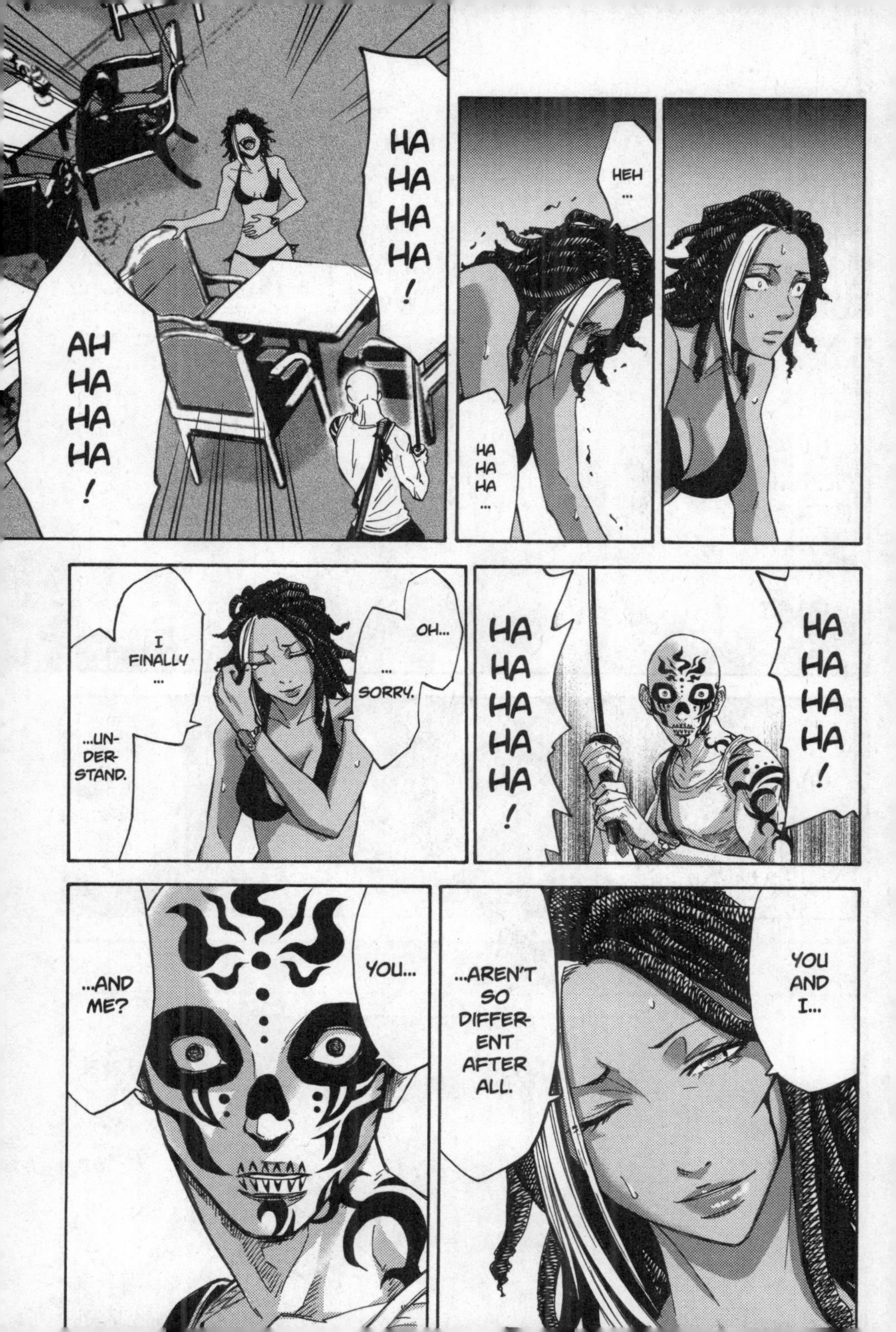
HEH...
HA HA HA...
HA HA HA HA!
AH HA HA HA!
HA HA HA HA!
HA HA HA HA HA!
OH... ...SORRY.
I FINALLY... ...UNDER-STAND.
YOU AND I...
...AREN'T SO DIFFER-ENT AFTER ALL.
YOU...
...AND ME?

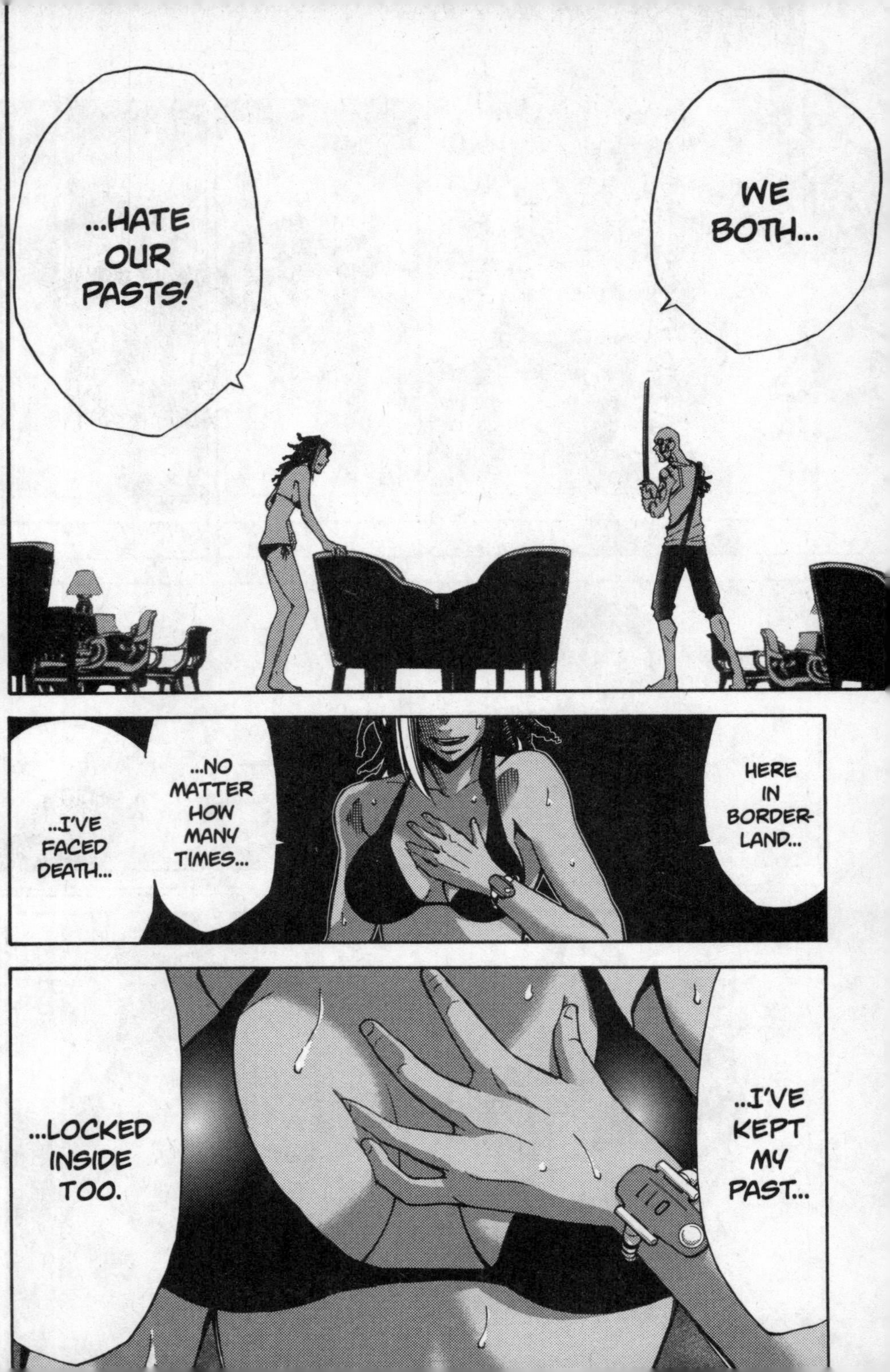
WE BOTH...
...HATE OUR PASTS!
HERE IN BORDER-LAND...
...NO MATTER HOW MANY TIMES...
...I'VE FACED DEATH...
...I'VE KEPT MY PAST...
...LOCKED INSIDE TOO.

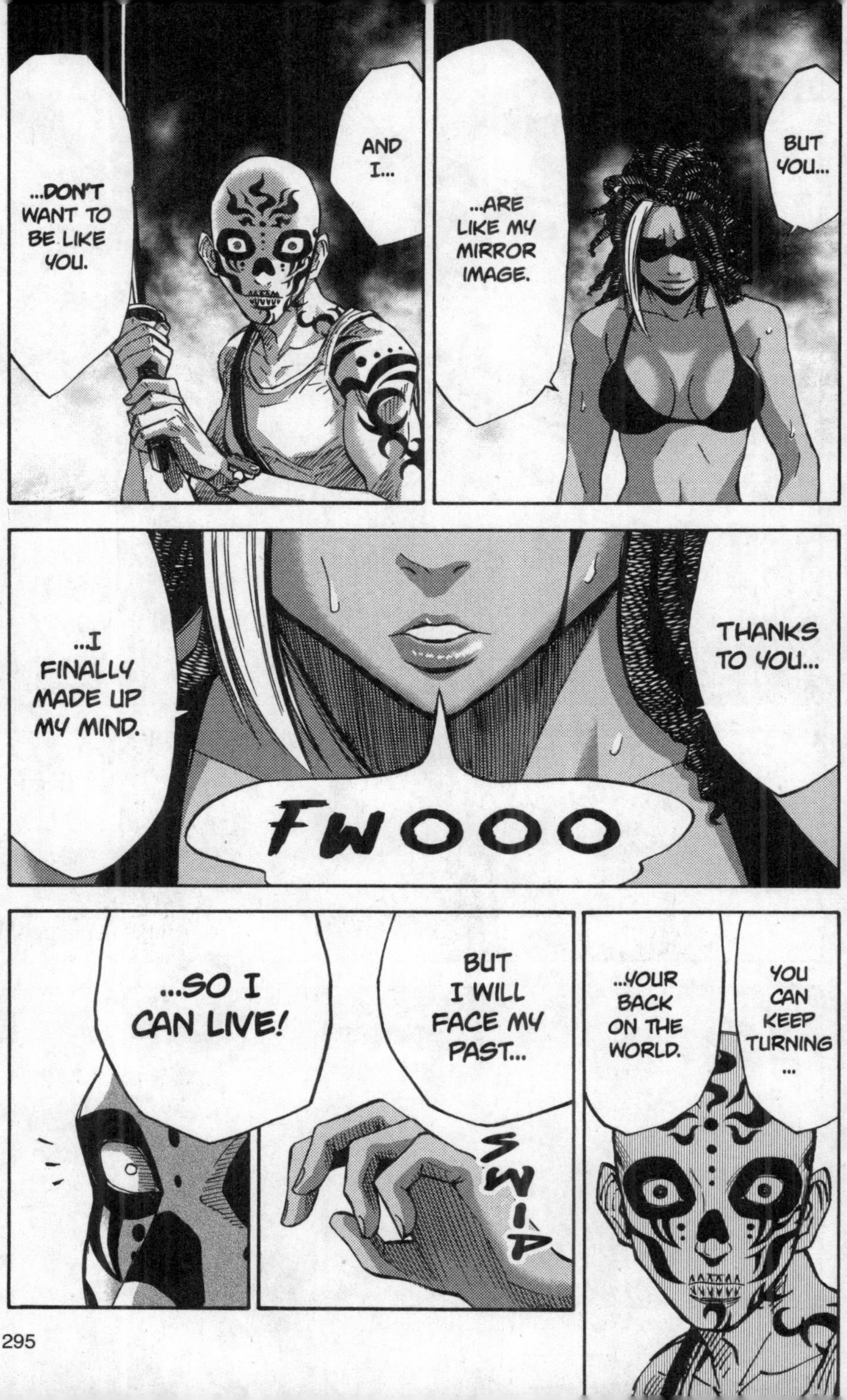
BUT YOU...
...ARE LIKE MY MIRROR IMAGE.
AND I...
...DON'T WANT TO BE LIKE YOU.
THANKS TO YOU...
...I FINALLY MADE UP MY MIND.
FWOOO
YOU CAN KEEP TURNING ...
...YOUR BACK ON THE WORLD.
BUT I WILL FACE MY PAST...
SWIP
...SO I CAN LIVE!

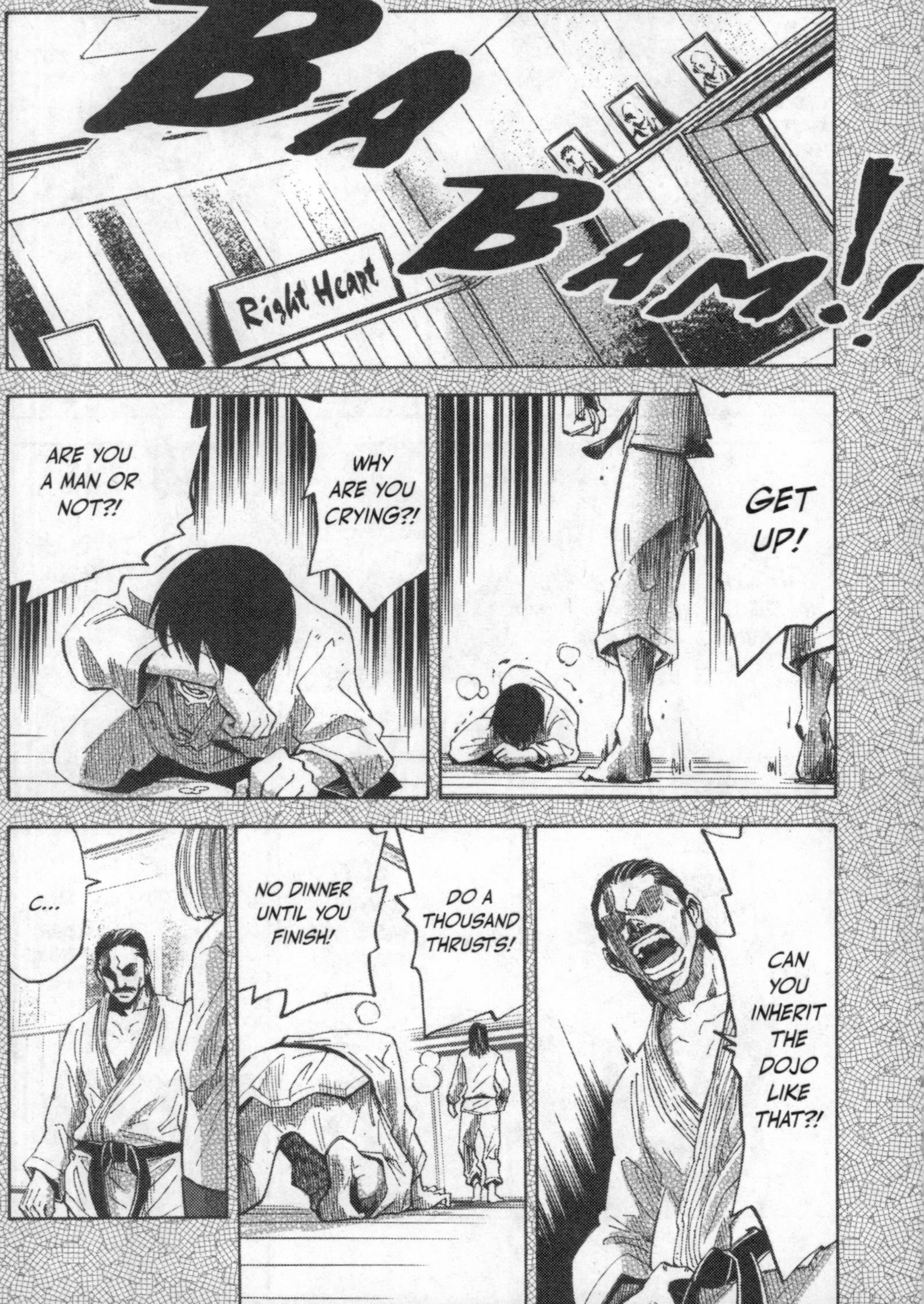
BA-BAM!!
Right Heart
GET UP!
WHY ARE YOU CRYING?!
ARE YOU A MAN OR NOT?!
CAN YOU INHERIT THE DOJO LIKE THAT?!
DO A THOUSAND THRUSTS!
NO DINNER UNTIL YOU FINISH!
C...

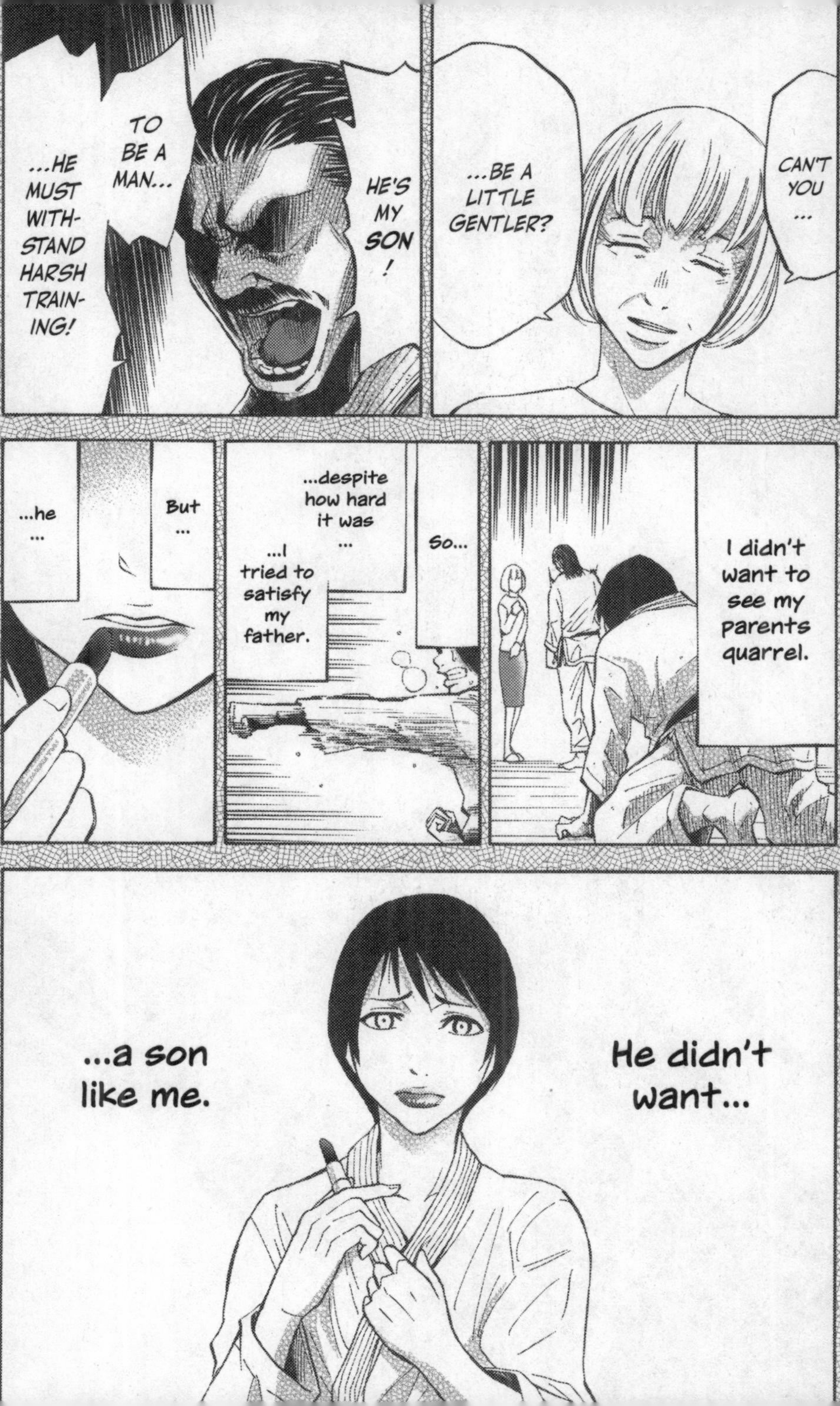
CAN'T YOU ...
...BE A LITTLE GENTLER?
HE'S MY SON!
TO BE A MAN...
...HE MUST WITHSTAND HARSH TRAINING!
I didn't want to see my parents quarrel.
So...
...despite how hard it was ...
...I tried to satisfy my father.
But ...
...he ...
He didn't want...
...a son like me.

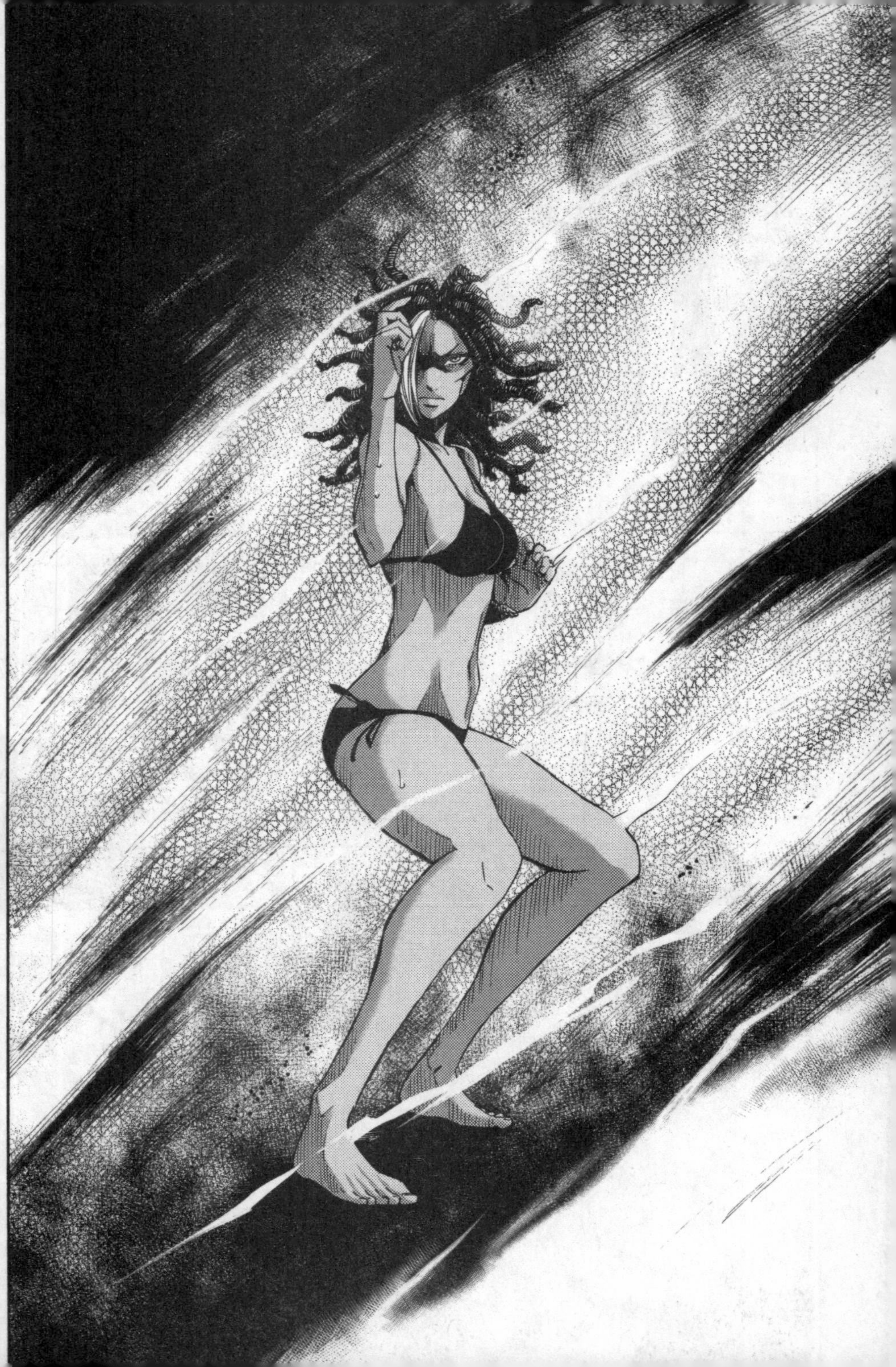

I SEE NOW ...

THAT'S YOUR PAST!

THOSE EYES...

ARE YOU... A DUDE?

WE HAVE ...

...THE SAME EYES.

IRONIC ...

...INNIT?

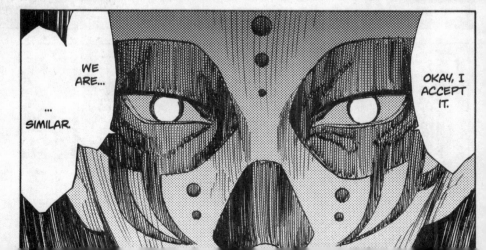

WE ARE...

...SIMILAR.

OKAY, I ACCEPT IT.

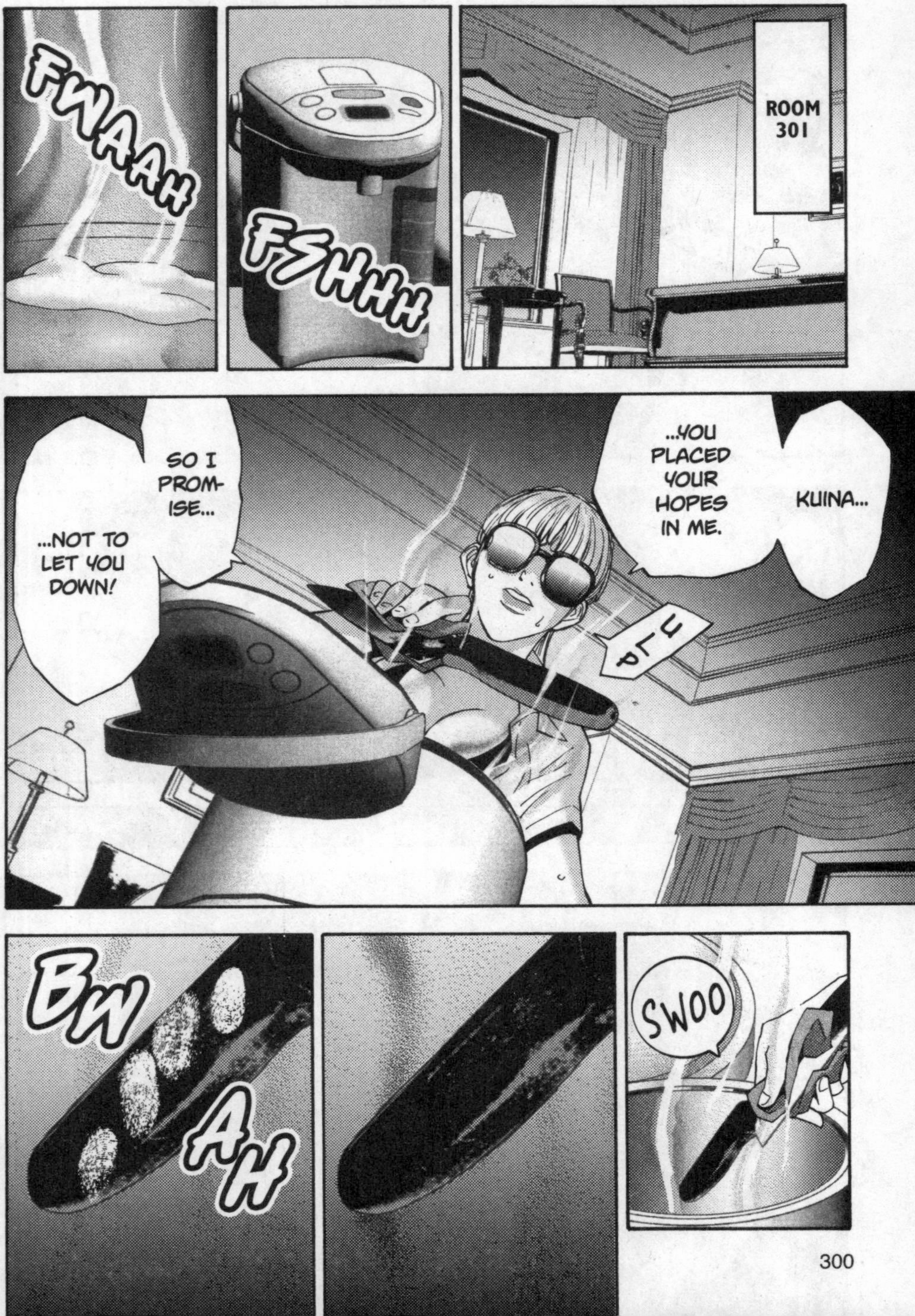
ROOM 301
FSHHH
FWAAAH
KUINA...
...YOU PLACED YOUR HOPES IN ME.
ULP
SO I PROMISE...
...NOT TO LET YOU DOWN!
SWOO
BWAH

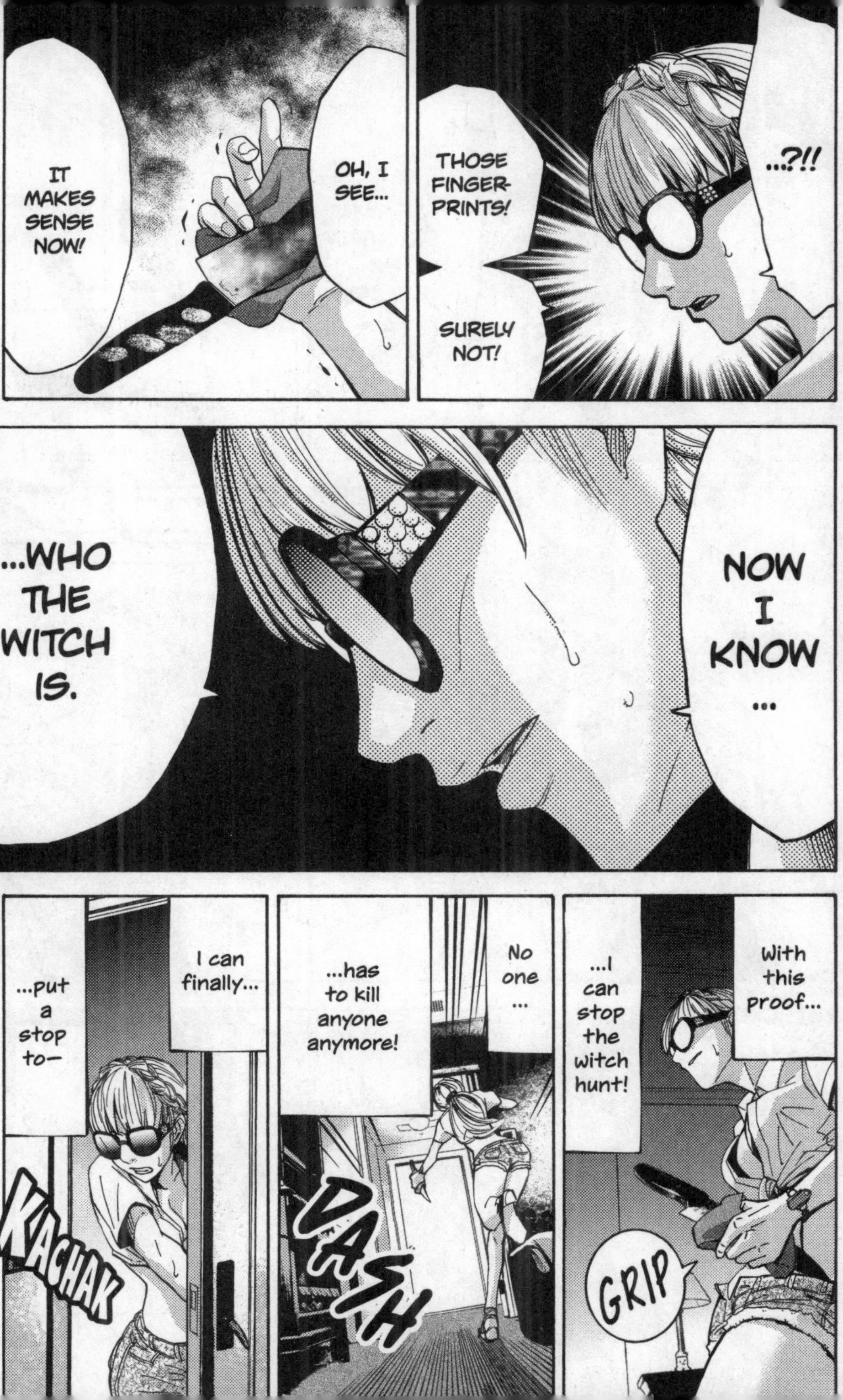
...?!!
THOSE FINGER-PRINTS!
SURELY NOT!
OH, I SEE...
IT MAKES SENSE NOW!
NOW I KNOW...
...WHO THE WITCH IS.
With this proof...
...I can stop the witch hunt!
GRIP
No one...
...has to kill anyone anymore!
DASH
I can finally...
...put a stop to—
KACHAK

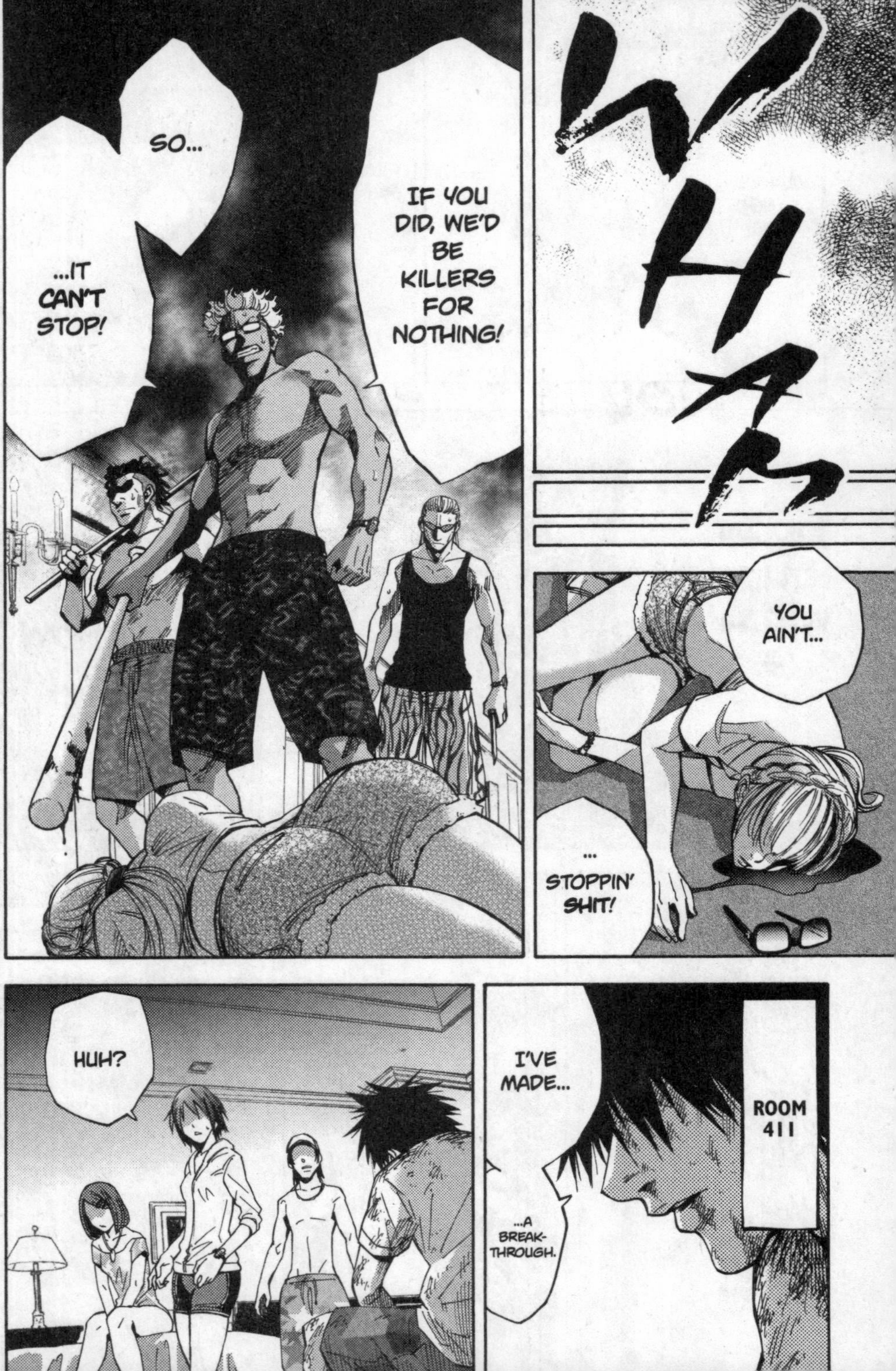
WHAM
IF YOU DID, WE'D BE KILLERS FOR NOTHING!
SO...
...IT CAN'T STOP!
YOU AIN'T...
...STOPPIN' SHIT!
ROOM 411
I'VE MADE...
...A BREAK-THROUGH.
HUH?

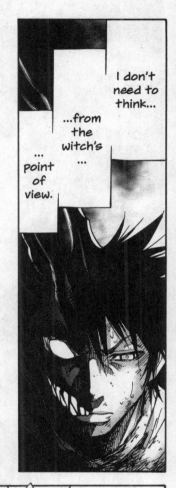

I don't need to think...
...from the witch's ...
... point of view.

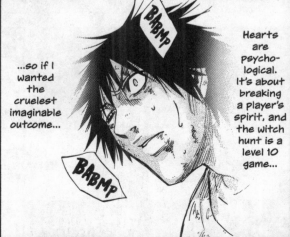

How would the game master view it?!

Hearts are psycho-logical. It's about breaking a player's spirit, and the witch hunt is a level 10 game...
BABMP
...so if I wanted the cruelest imaginable outcome...
BABMP

BABMP
...what would I do?
BABMP

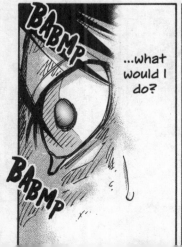

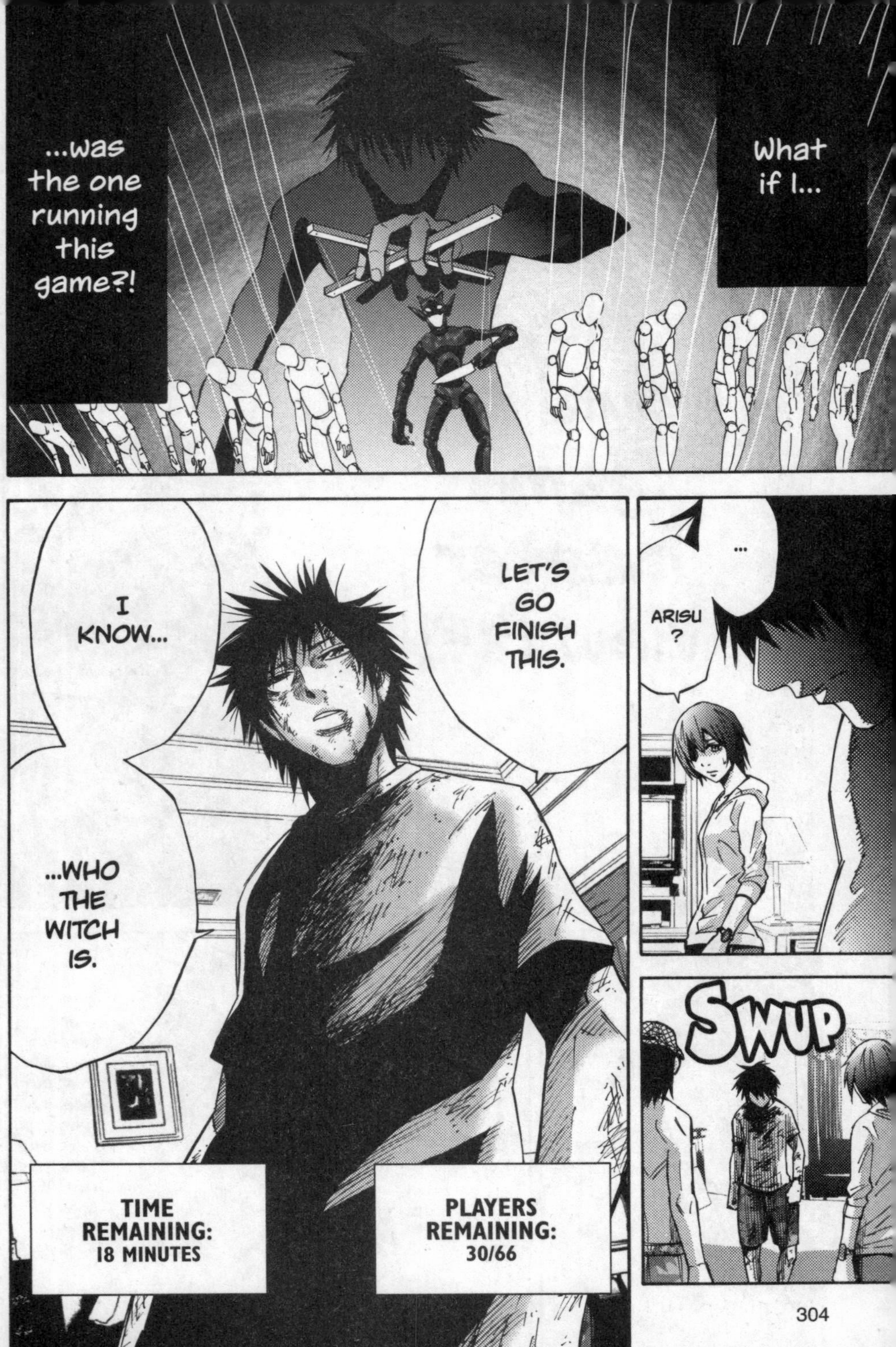
What if I...
...was the one running this game?!
...
ARISU ?
SWUP
LET'S GO FINISH THIS.
I KNOW...
...WHO THE WITCH IS.
PLAYERS REMAINING: 30/66
TIME REMAINING: 18 MINUTES

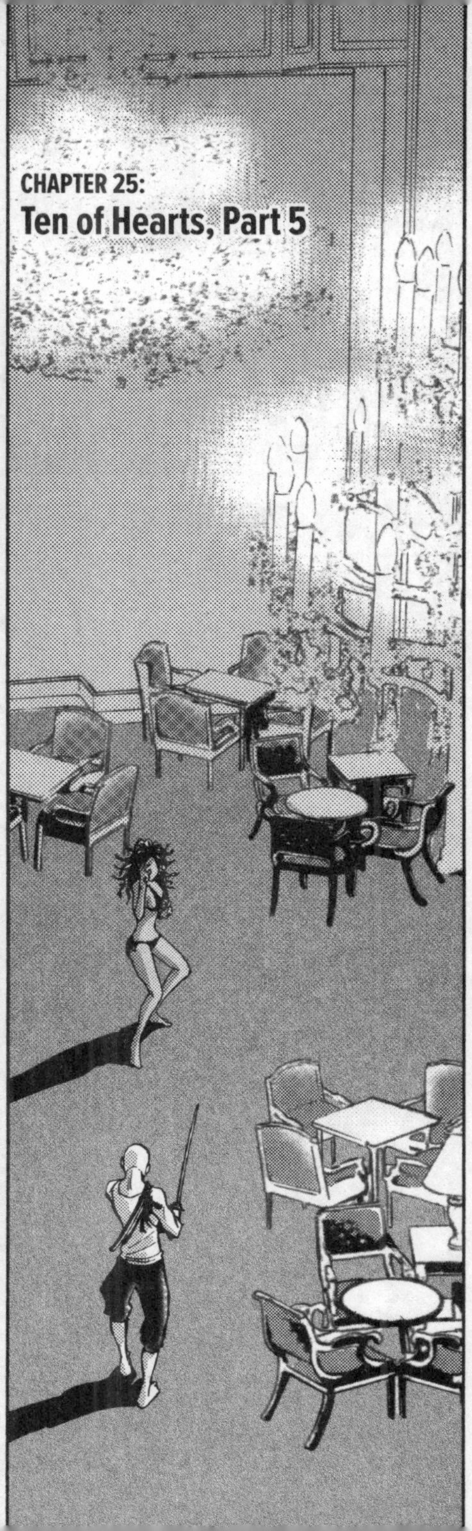
CHAPTER 25:
Ten of Hearts, Part 5

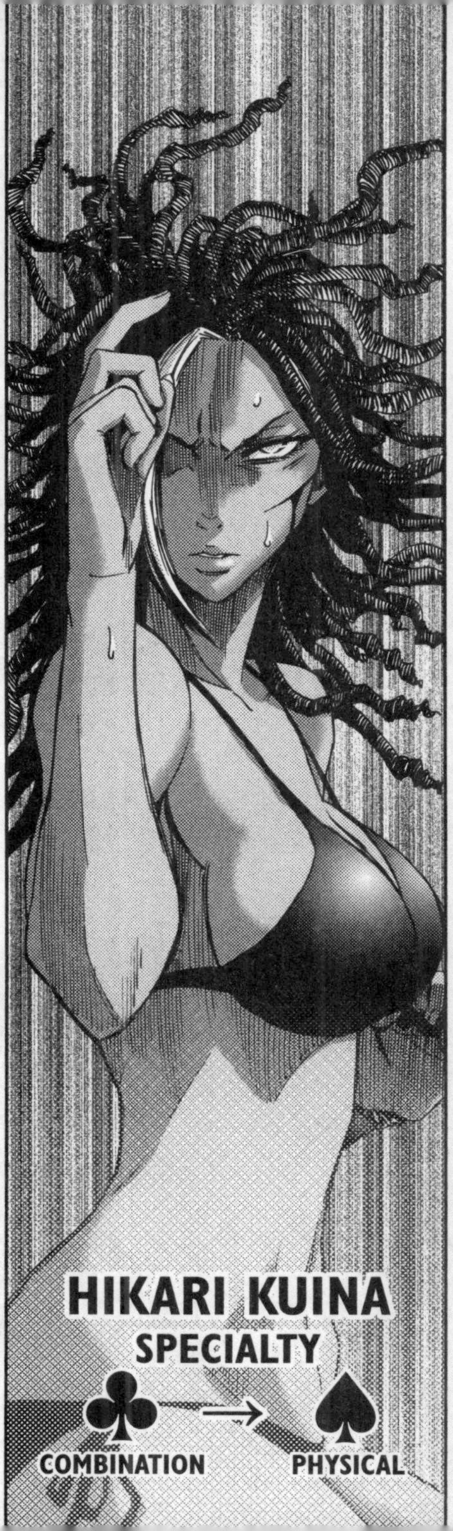
HIKARI KUINA
SPECIALTY
COMBINATION → PHYSICAL

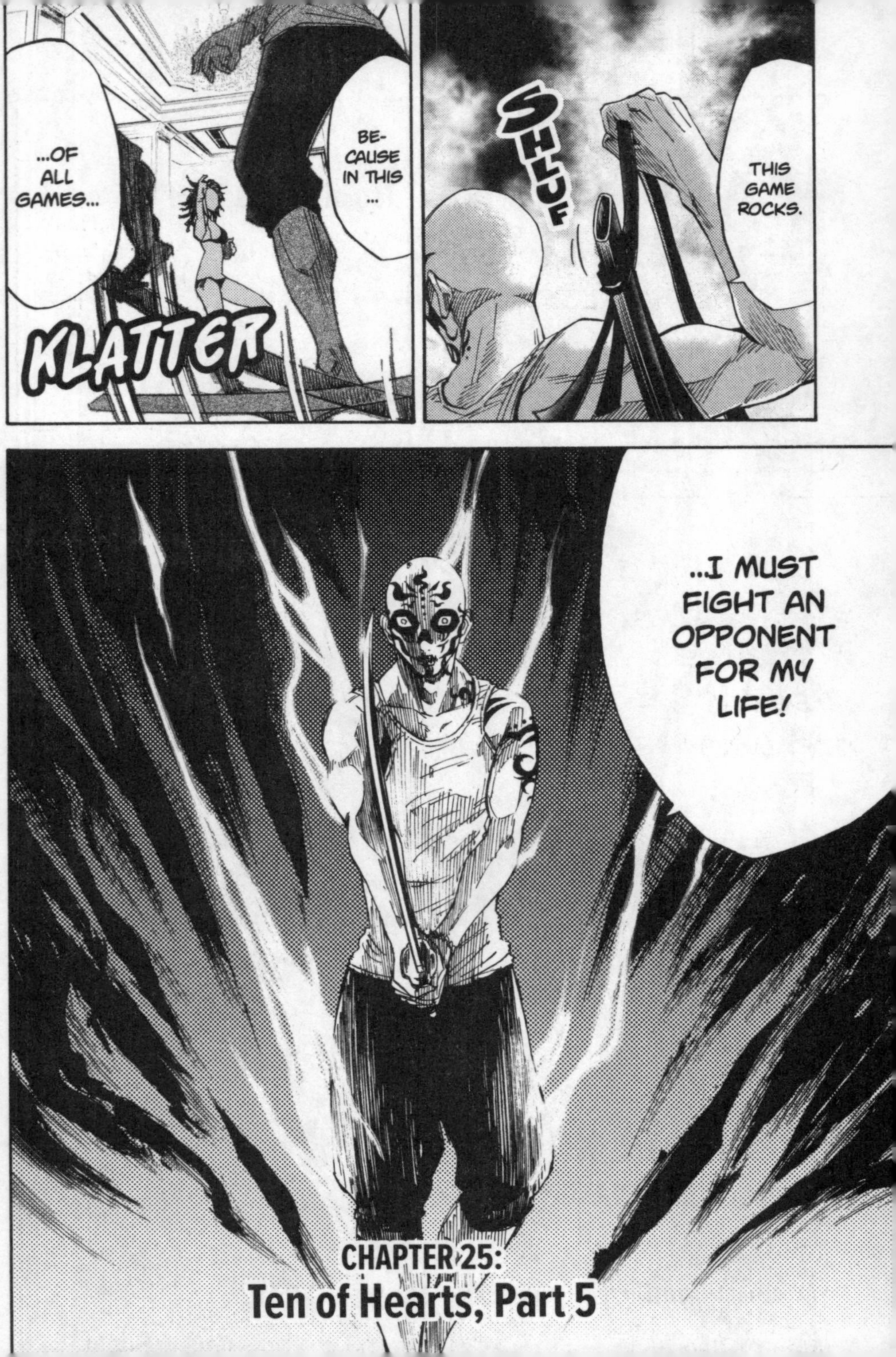
THIS GAME ROCKS.
SHLUF
BE-CAUSE IN THIS ...
...OF ALL GAMES...
KLATTER
...I MUST FIGHT AN OPPONENT FOR MY LIFE!
CHAPTER 25:
Ten of Hearts, Part 5

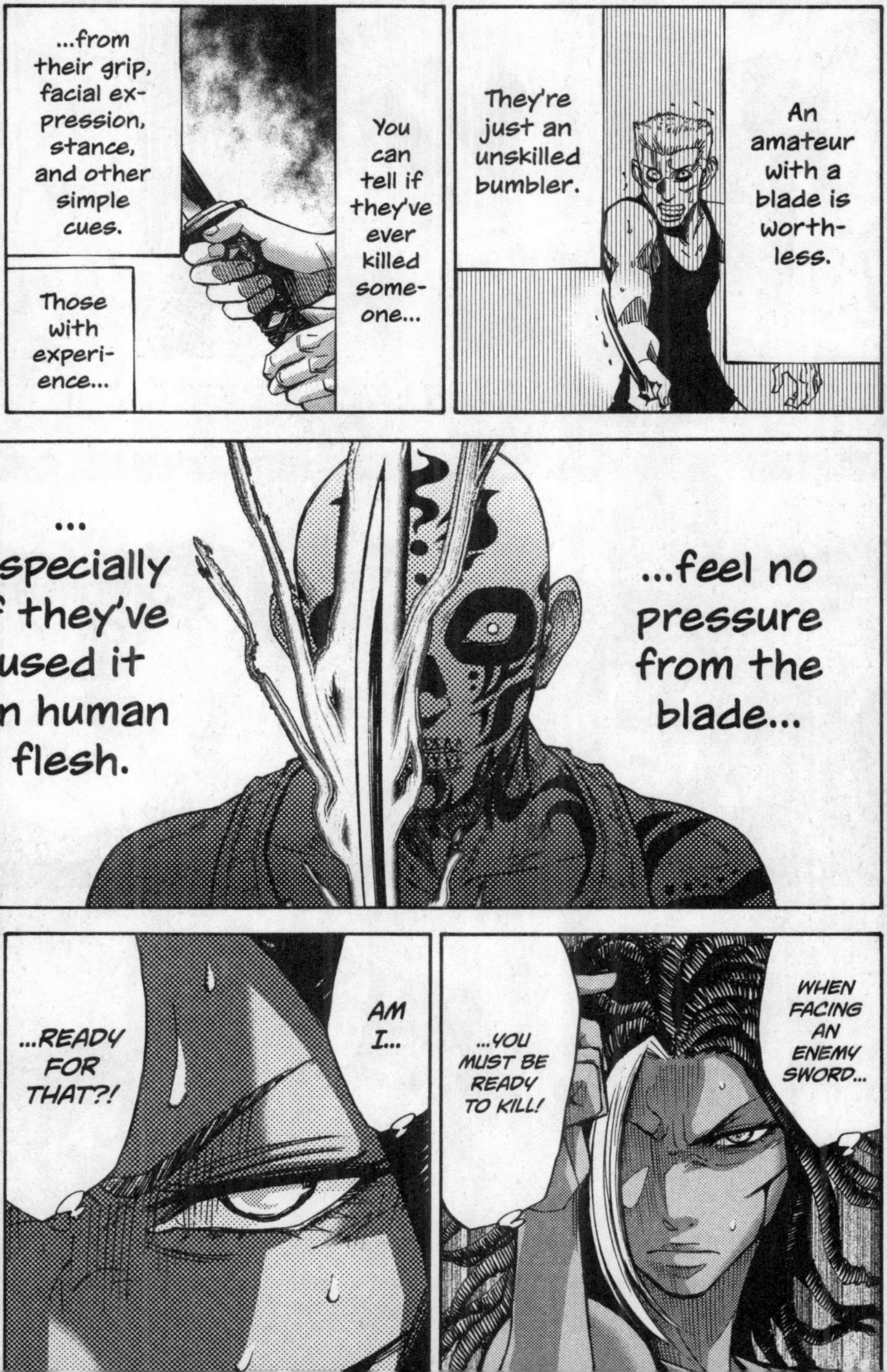
An amateur with a blade is worthless.
They're just an unskilled bumbler.
You can tell if they've ever killed someone...
...from their grip, facial expression, stance, and other simple cues.
Those with experience...
...feel no pressure from the blade...
... especially if they've used it on human flesh.
WHEN FACING AN ENEMY SWORD...
...YOU MUST BE READY TO KILL!
AM I...
...READY FOR THAT?!

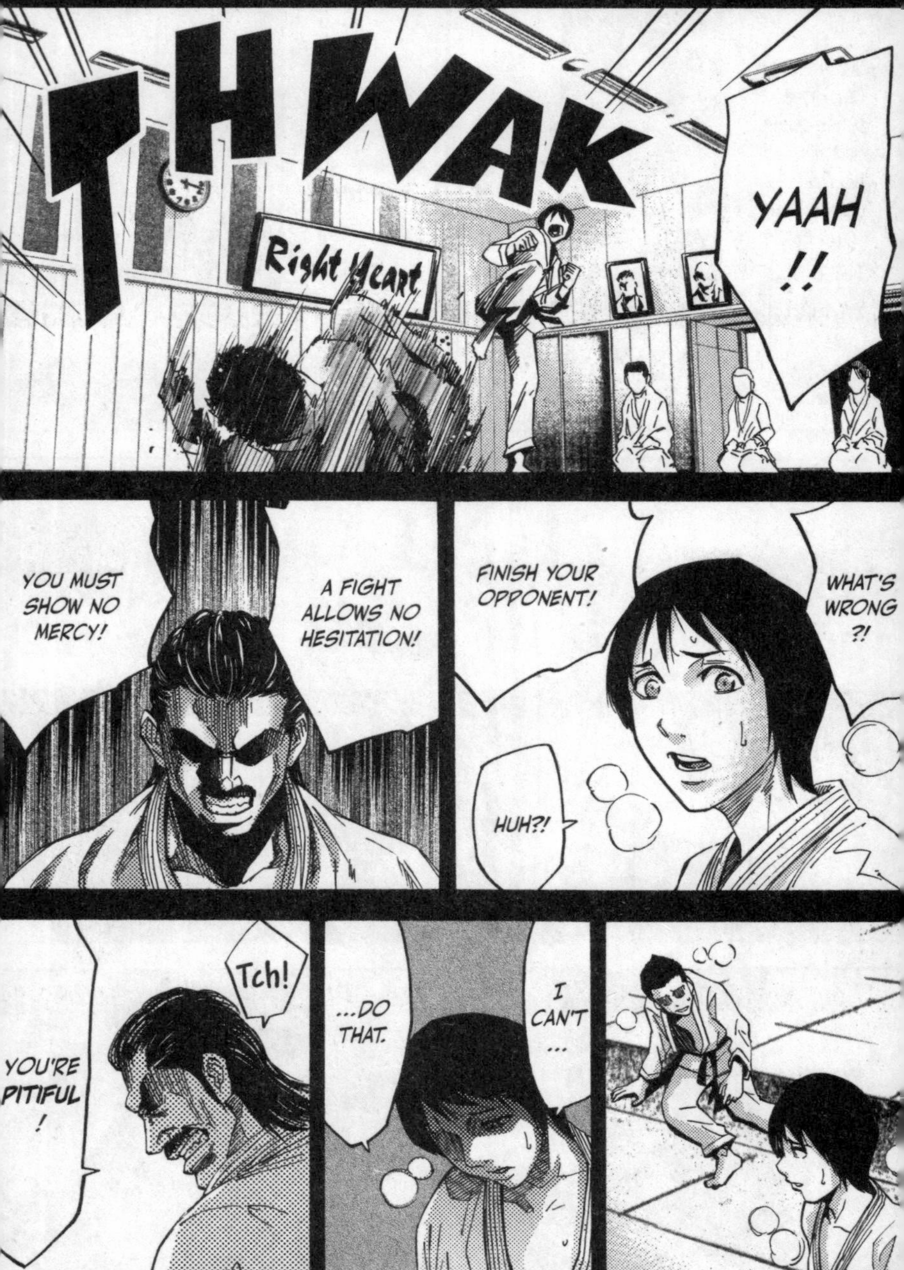
YAAH !!
THWAK
Right Heart
WHAT'S WRONG ?!
FINISH YOUR OPPONENT!
HUH?!
A FIGHT ALLOWS NO HESITATION!
YOU MUST SHOW NO MERCY!
I CAN'T ...
...DO THAT.
Tch!
YOU'RE PITIFUL !

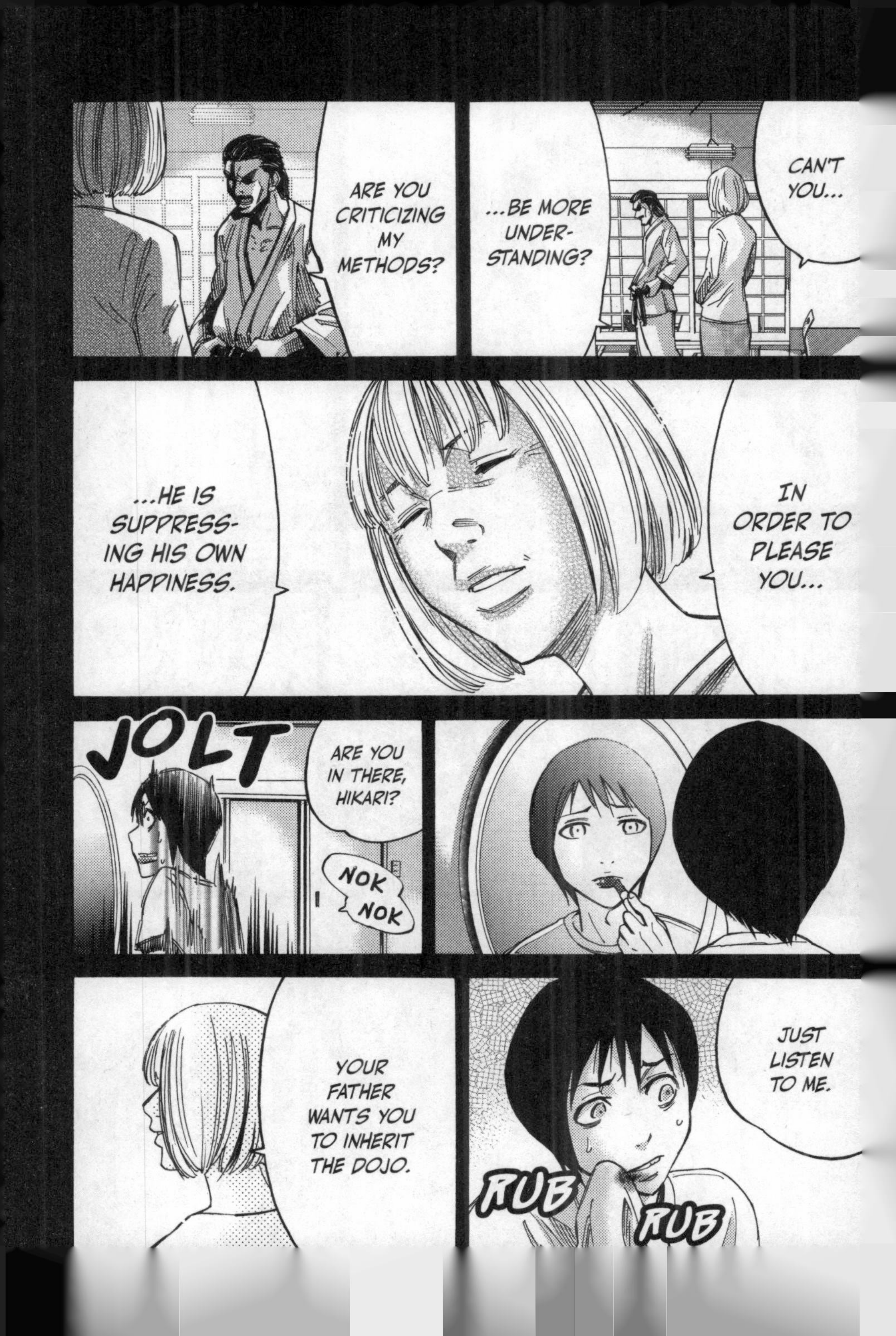
CAN'T YOU...
...BE MORE UNDER-STANDING?
ARE YOU CRITICIZING MY METHODS?
IN ORDER TO PLEASE YOU...
...HE IS SUPPRESS-ING HIS OWN HAPPINESS.
ARE YOU IN THERE, HIKARI?
JOLT
NOK NOK
JUST LISTEN TO ME.
RUB RUB
YOUR FATHER WANTS YOU TO INHERIT THE DOJO.

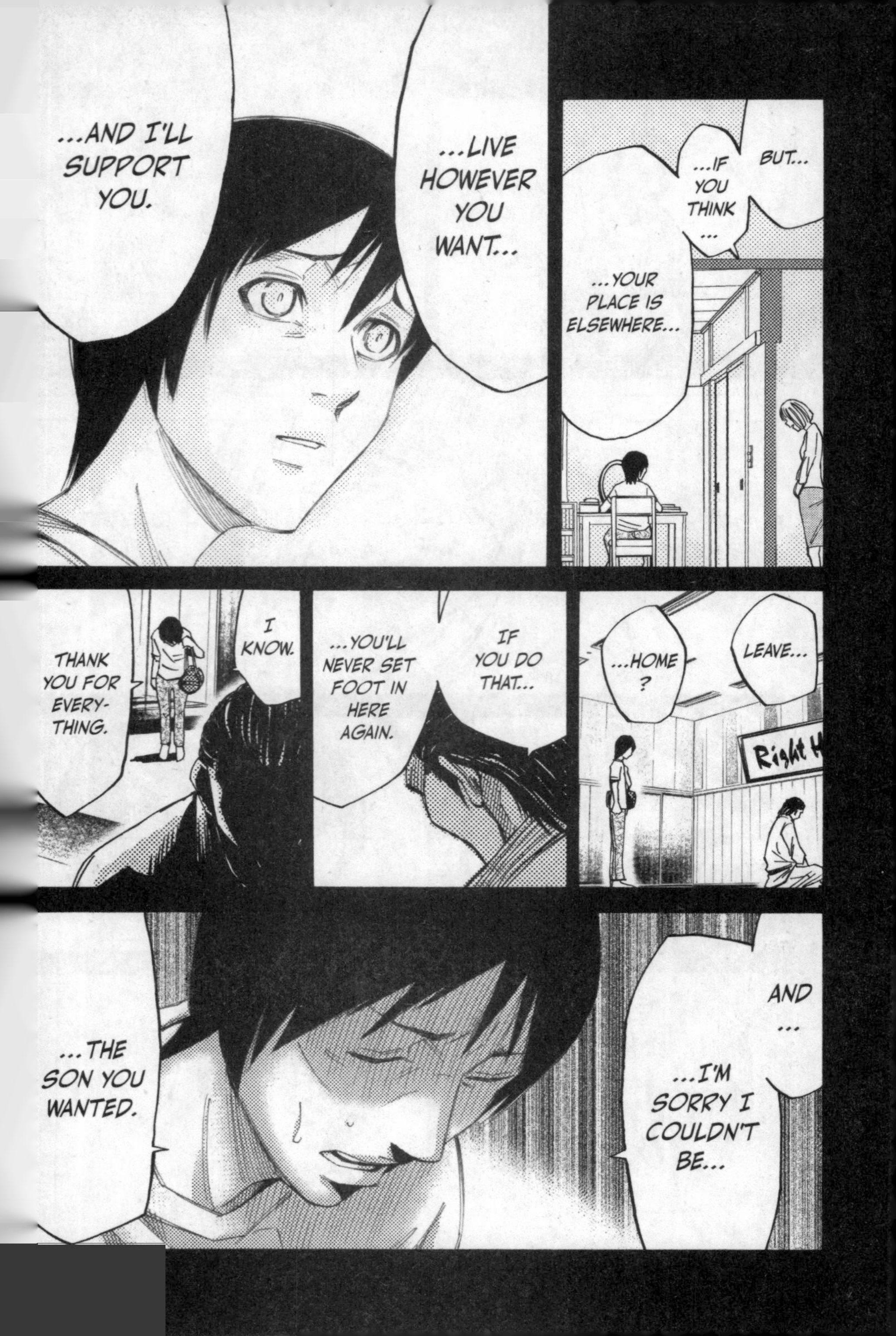
BUT...
...IF YOU THINK...
...YOUR PLACE IS ELSEWHERE...
...LIVE HOWEVER YOU WANT...
...AND I'LL SUPPORT YOU.
LEAVE...
...HOME?
IF YOU DO THAT...
...YOU'LL NEVER SET FOOT IN HERE AGAIN.
I KNOW.
THANK YOU FOR EVERY-THING.
AND...
...I'M SORRY I COULDN'T BE...
...THE SON YOU WANTED.

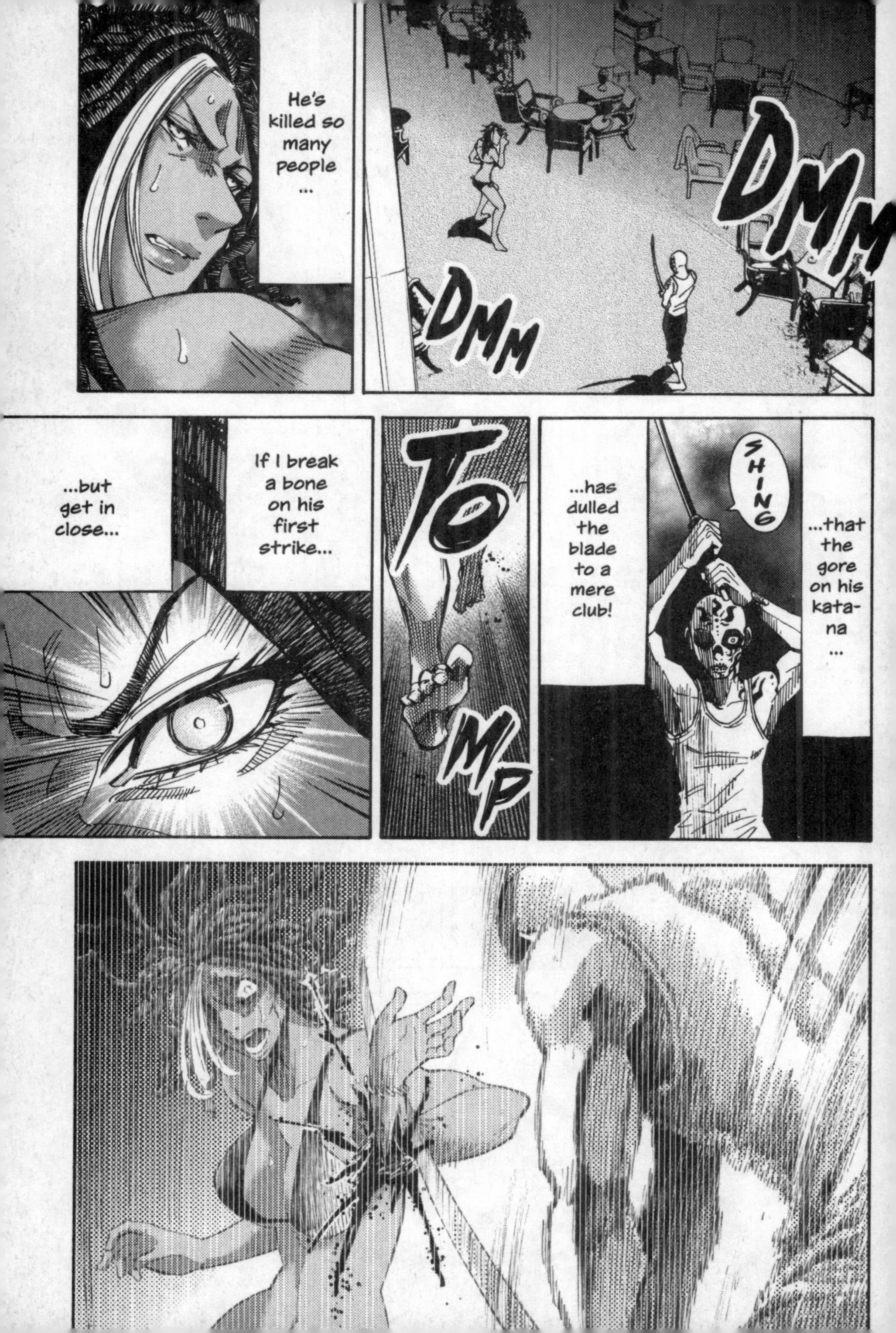
DMM
DMM
He's killed so many people ...
...that the gore on his katana ...
SHING
...has dulled the blade to a mere club!
TOMP
If I break a bone on his first strike...
...but get in close...

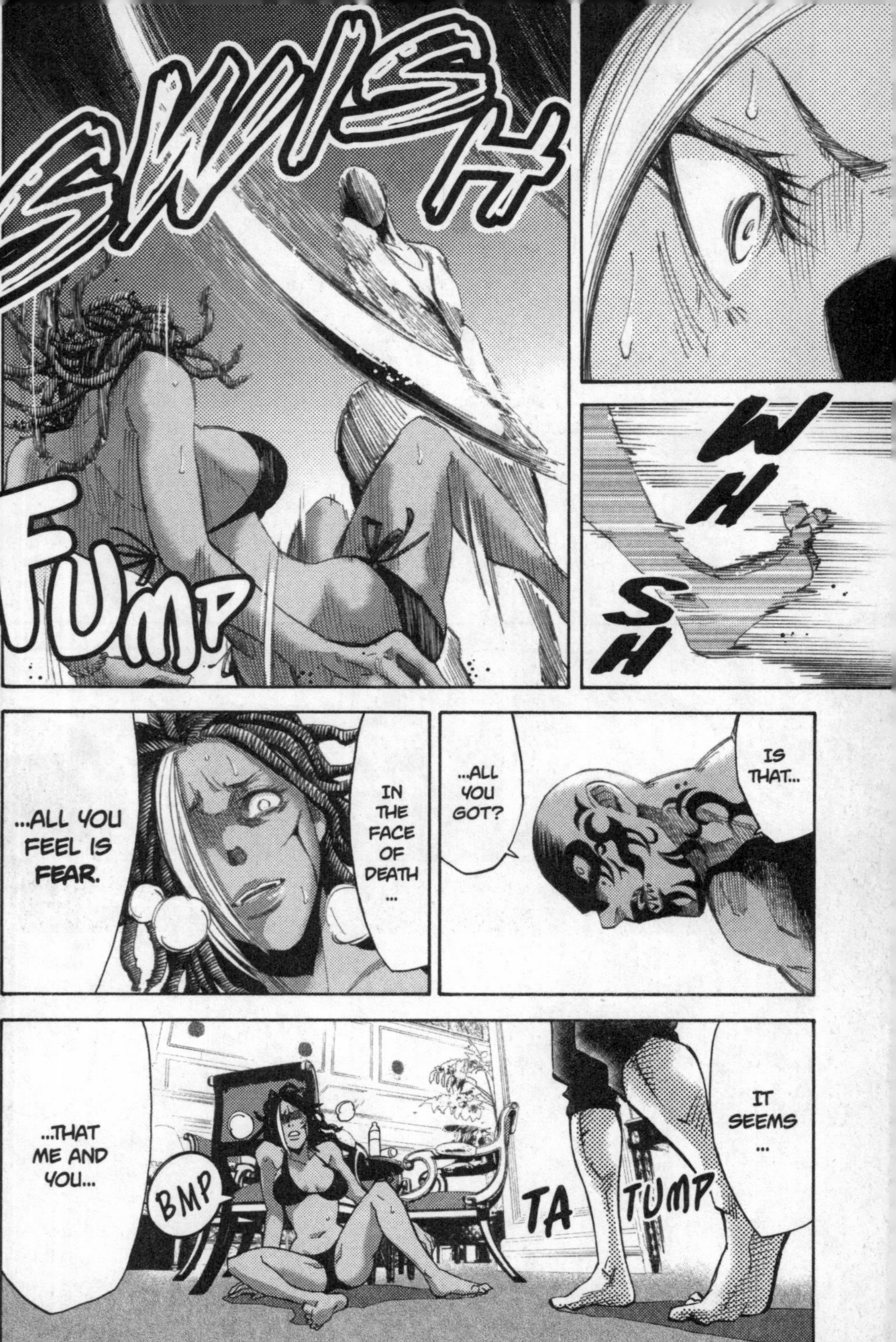
WHSH
SWISH
FUMP
IS THAT...
...ALL YOU GOT?
IN THE FACE OF DEATH ...
...ALL YOU FEEL IS FEAR.
IT SEEMS ...
TA TUMP
BMP
...THAT ME AND YOU...

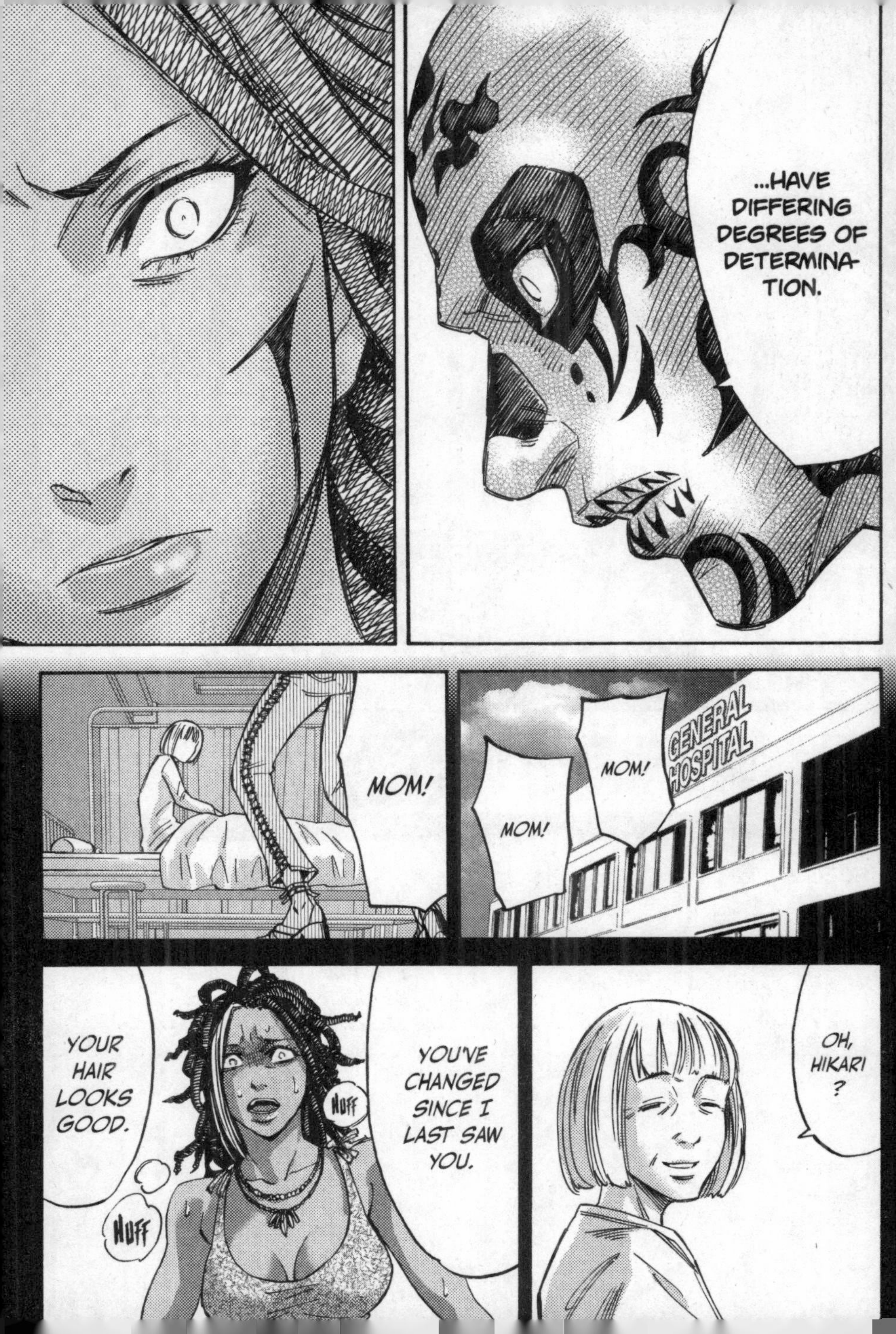
...HAVE DIFFERING DEGREES OF DETERMINATION.
GENERAL HOSPITAL
MOM!
MOM!
MOM!
OH, HIKARI?
YOU'VE CHANGED SINCE I LAST SAW YOU.
YOUR HAIR LOOKS GOOD.
HUFF
HUFF

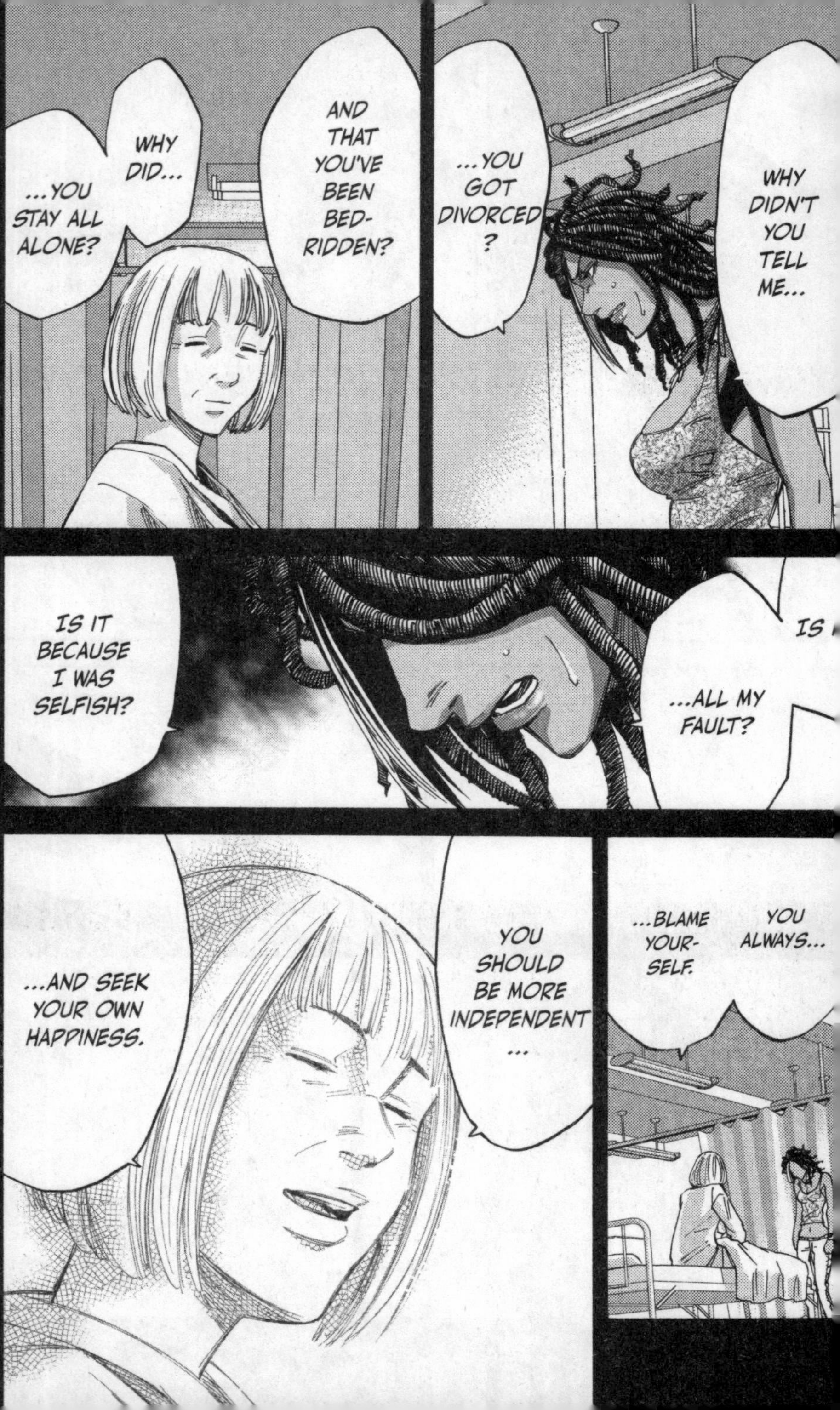
WHY DIDN'T YOU TELL ME...
...YOU GOT DIVORCED?
AND THAT YOU'VE BEEN BED-RIDDEN?
WHY DID...
...YOU STAY ALL ALONE?
IS
...ALL MY FAULT?
IS IT BECAUSE I WAS SELFISH?
YOU ALWAYS...
...BLAME YOUR-SELF.
YOU SHOULD BE MORE INDEPENDENT ...
...AND SEEK YOUR OWN HAPPINESS.

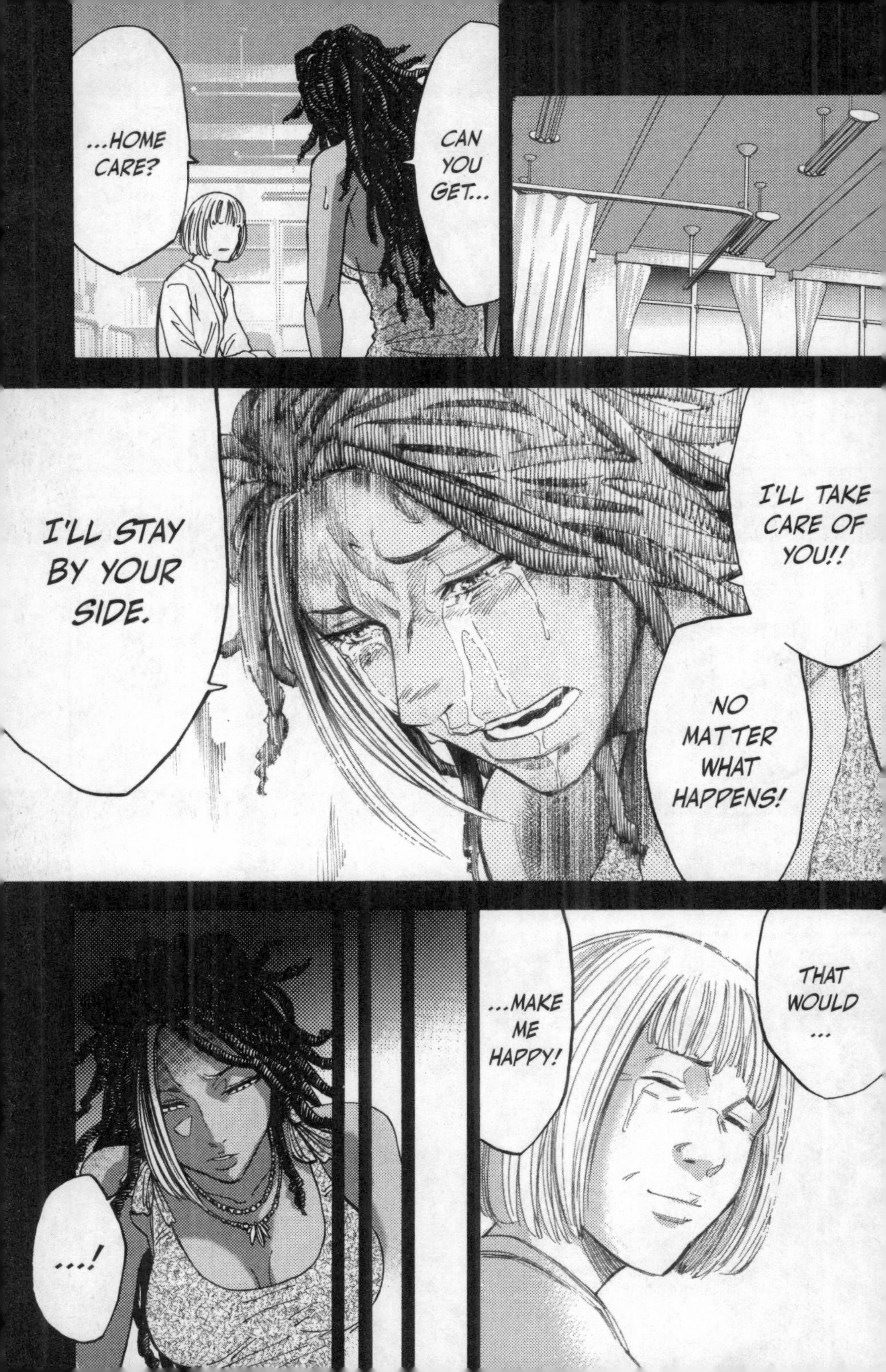
CAN YOU GET...
...HOME CARE?
I'LL TAKE CARE OF YOU!!
NO MATTER WHAT HAPPENS!
I'LL STAY BY YOUR SIDE.
THAT WOULD ...
...MAKE ME HAPPY!
...!

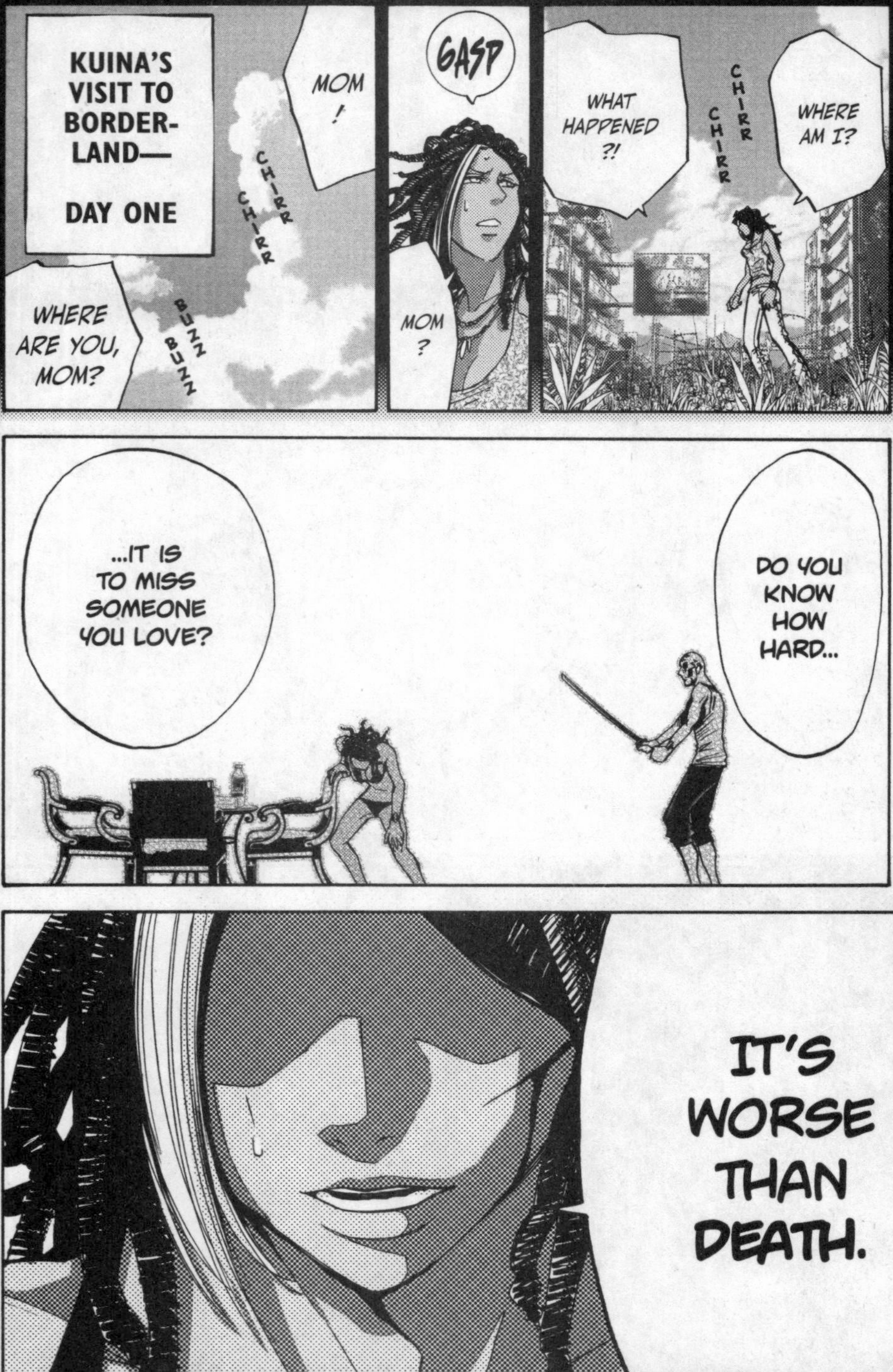
WHERE AM I?
CHIRR CHIRR
WHAT HAPPENED ?!
GASP
MOM ?
MOM !
KUINA'S VISIT TO BORDERLAND— DAY ONE
CHIRR CHIRR
WHERE ARE YOU, MOM?
BUZZ BUZZ
DO YOU KNOW HOW HARD...
...IT IS TO MISS SOMEONE YOU LOVE?
IT'S WORSE THAN DEATH.

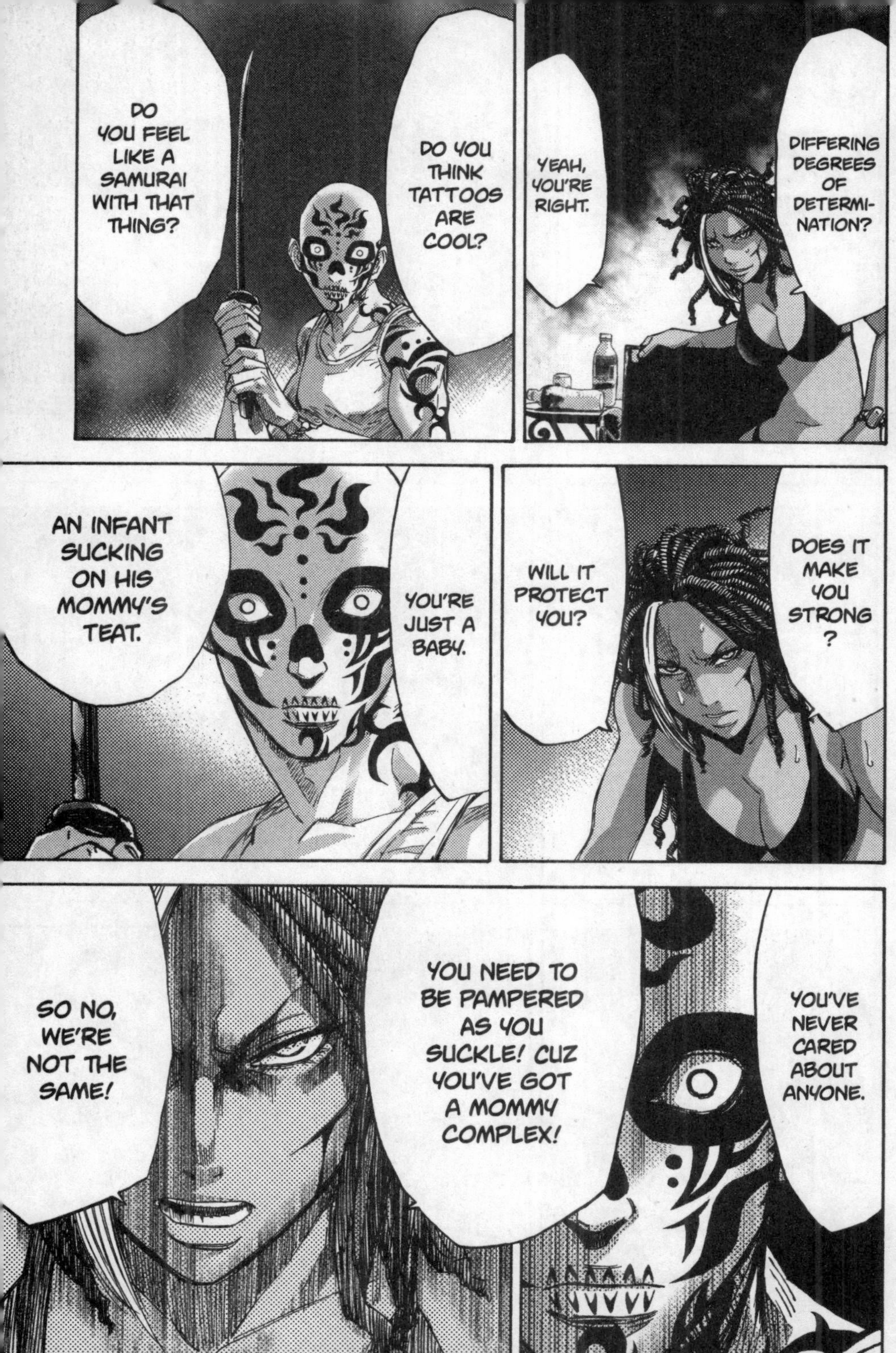
DIFFERING DEGREES OF DETERMINATION?
YEAH, YOU'RE RIGHT.
DO YOU THINK TATTOOS ARE COOL?
DO YOU FEEL LIKE A SAMURAI WITH THAT THING?
DOES IT MAKE YOU STRONG ?
WILL IT PROTECT YOU?
YOU'RE JUST A BABY.
AN INFANT SUCKING ON HIS MOMMY'S TEAT.
YOU'VE NEVER CARED ABOUT ANYONE.
YOU NEED TO BE PAMPERED AS YOU SUCKLE! CUZ YOU'VE GOT A MOMMY COMPLEX!
SO NO, WE'RE NOT THE SAME!

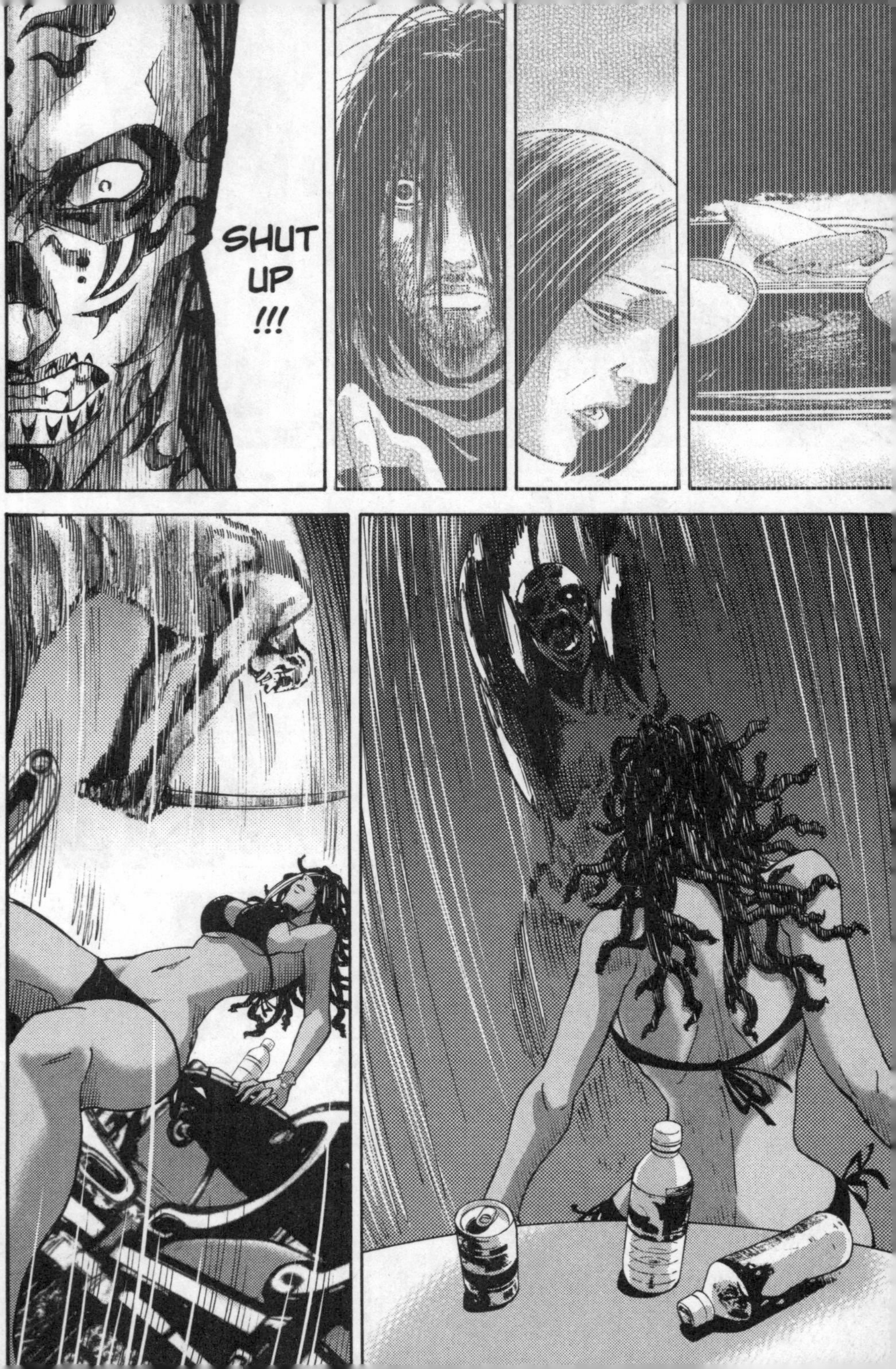
SHUT UP !!!

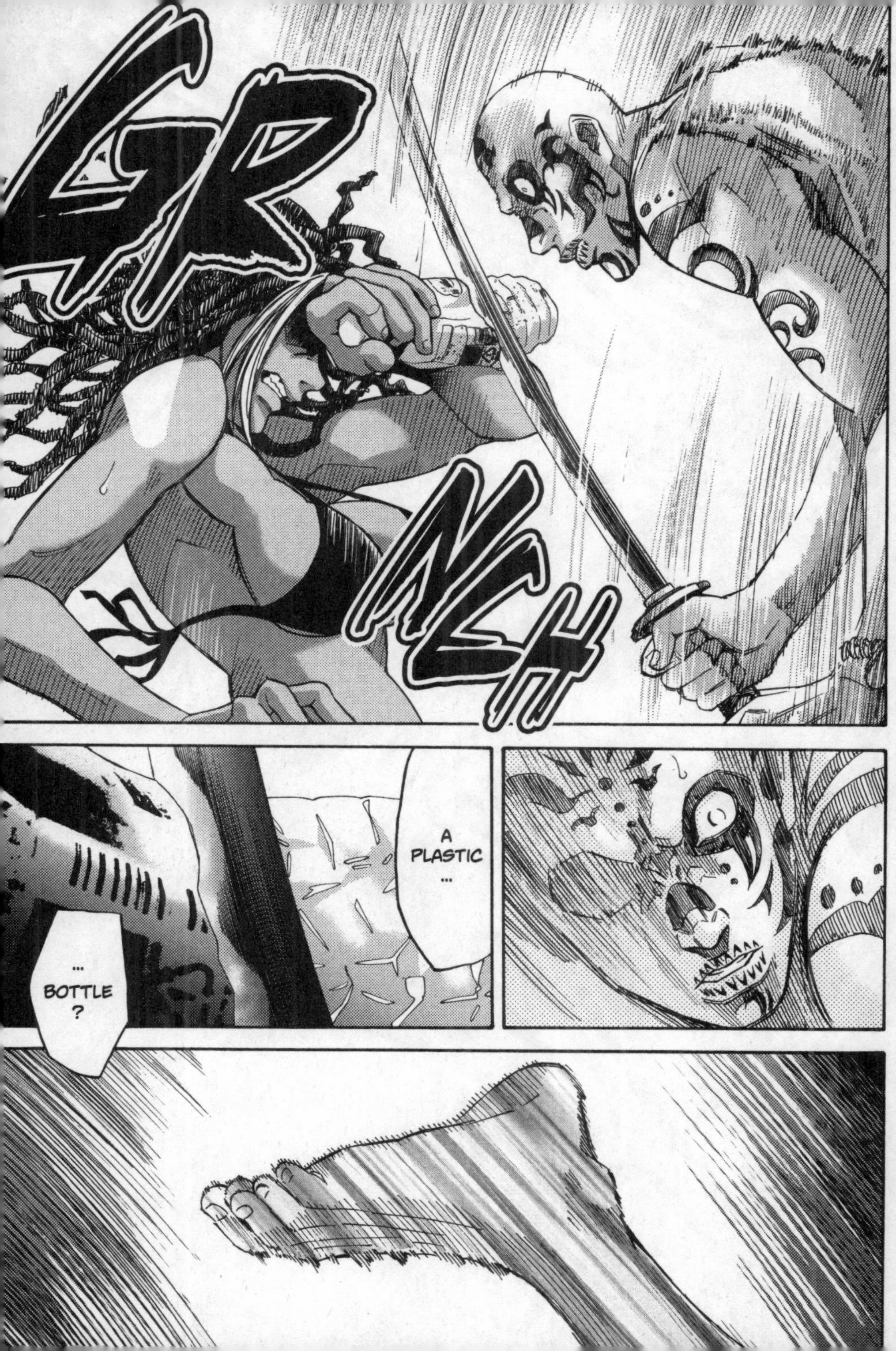
GR
NCH
A PLASTIC ...
... BOTTLE ?

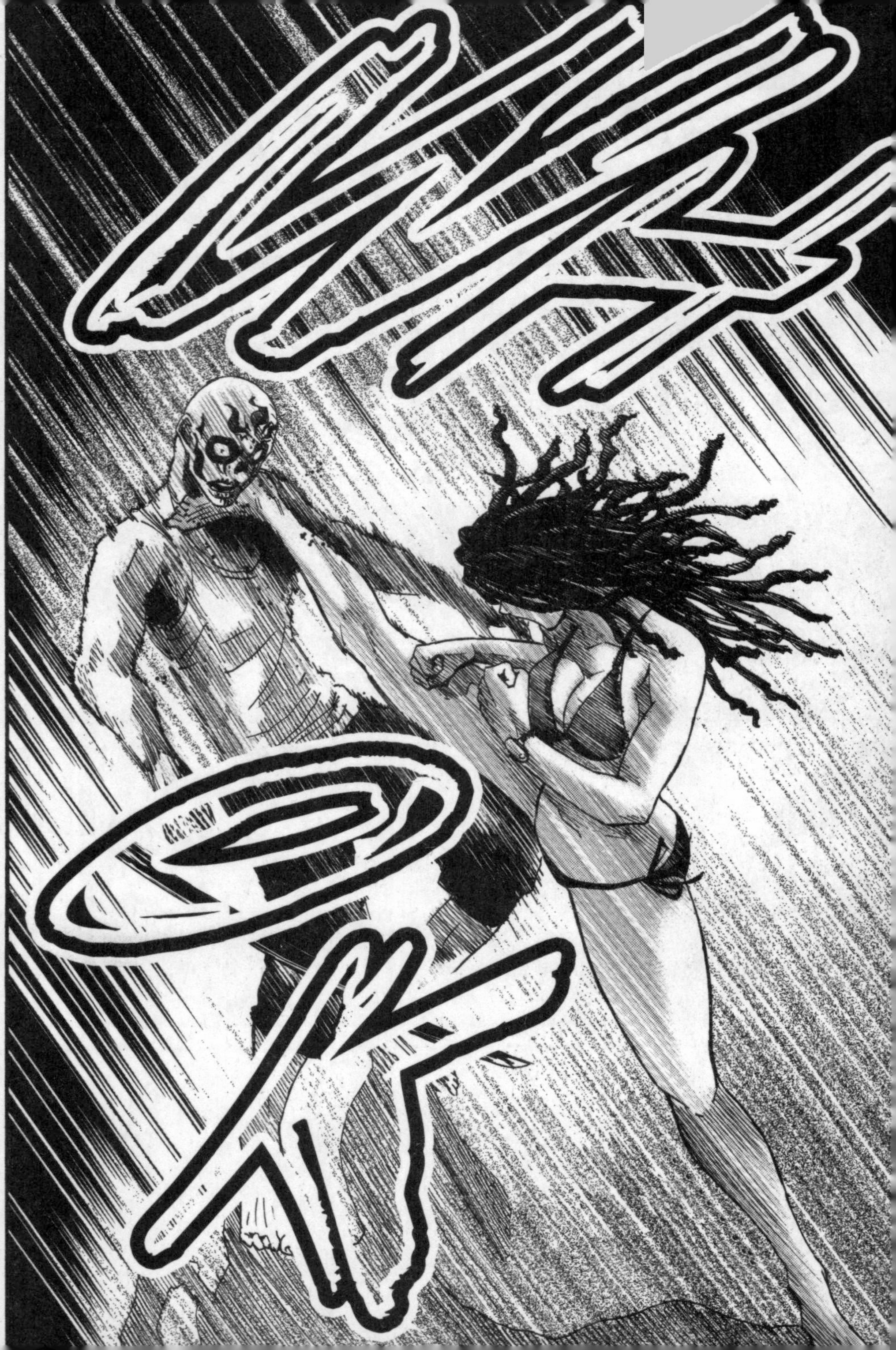

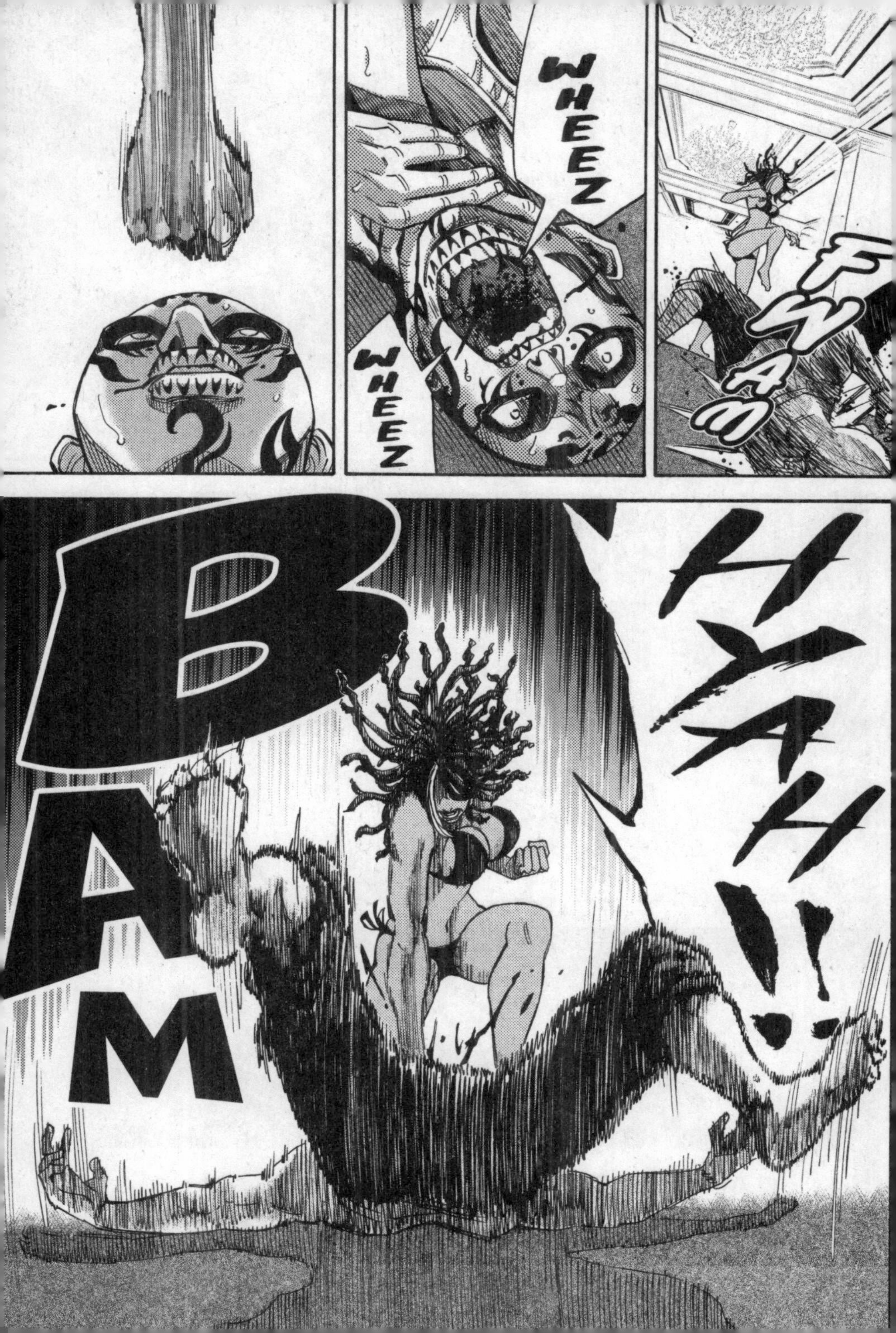
FWAM
WHEEZ
WHEEZ
HYAHH!!
BAM

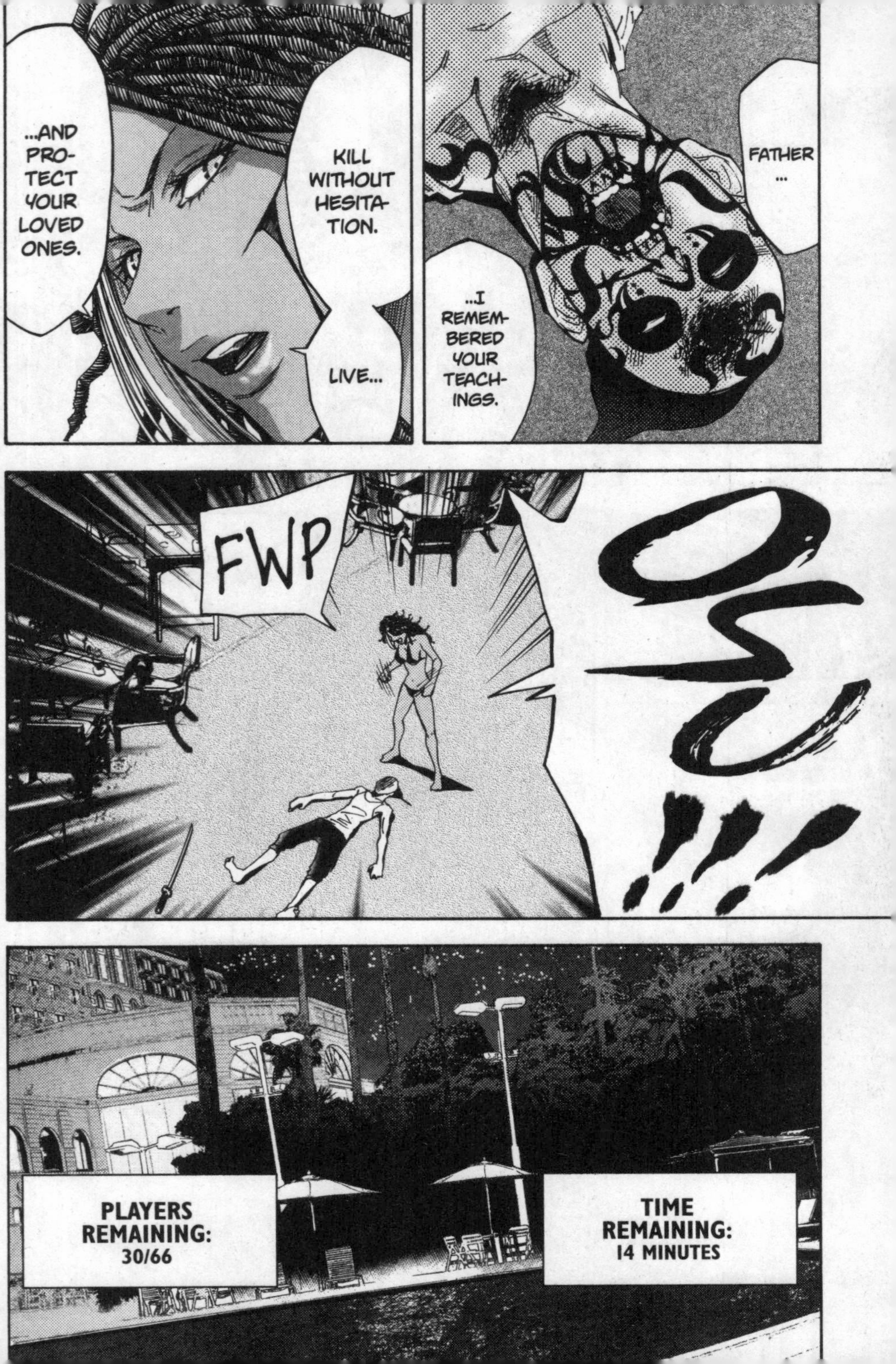
FATHER ...
...I REMEMBERED YOUR TEACHINGS.
KILL WITHOUT HESITATION.
LIVE...
...AND PROTECT YOUR LOVED ONES.
FWP
TIME REMAINING: 14 MINUTES
PLAYERS REMAINING: 30/66

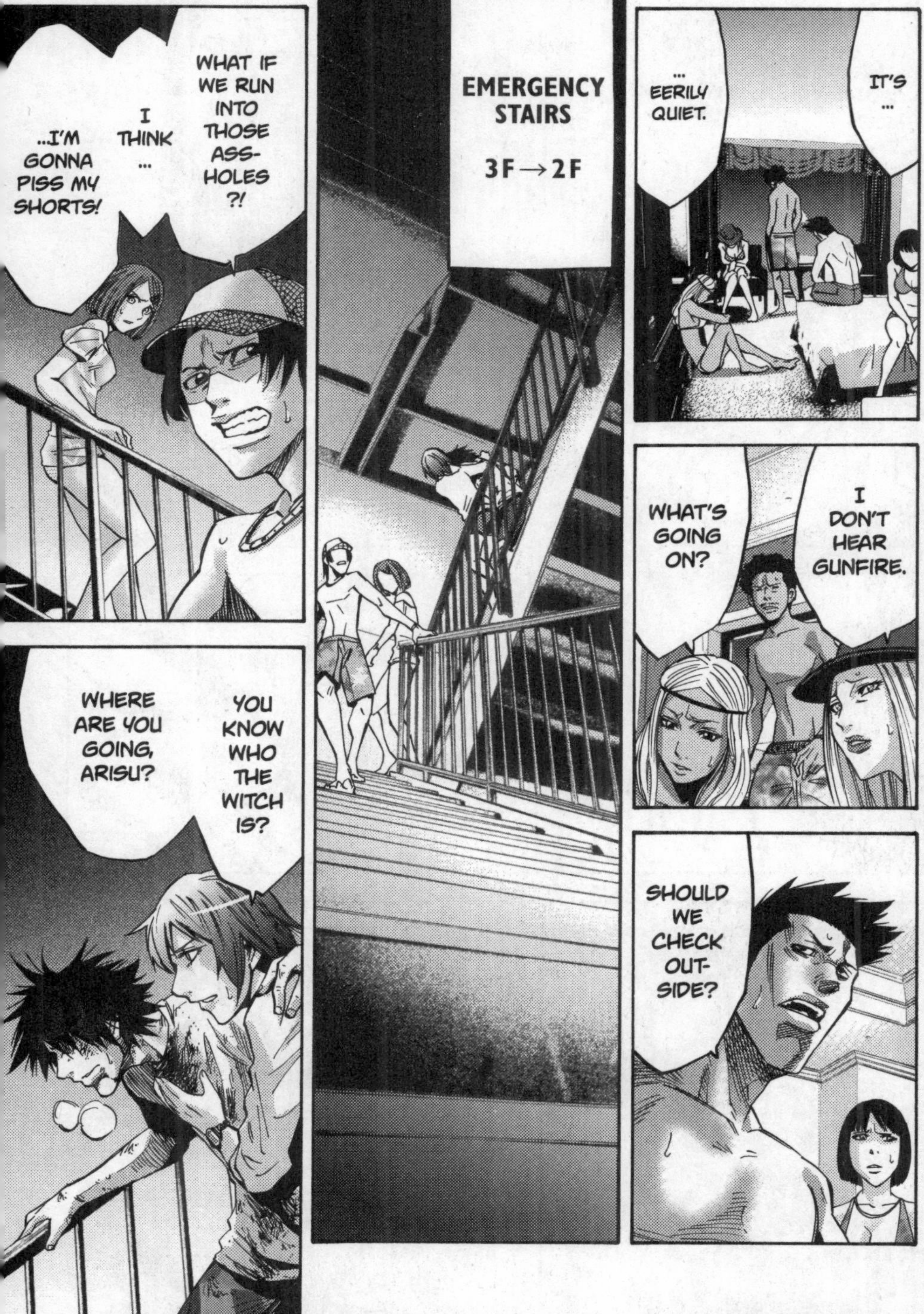
IT'S ...
... EERILY QUIET.
I DON'T HEAR GUNFIRE.
WHAT'S GOING ON?
SHOULD WE CHECK OUT-SIDE?
EMERGENCY STAIRS
3F → 2F
WHAT IF WE RUN INTO THOSE ASS-HOLES ?!
I THINK ...
...I'M GONNA PISS MY SHORTS!
YOU KNOW WHO THE WITCH IS?
WHERE ARE YOU GOING, ARISU?

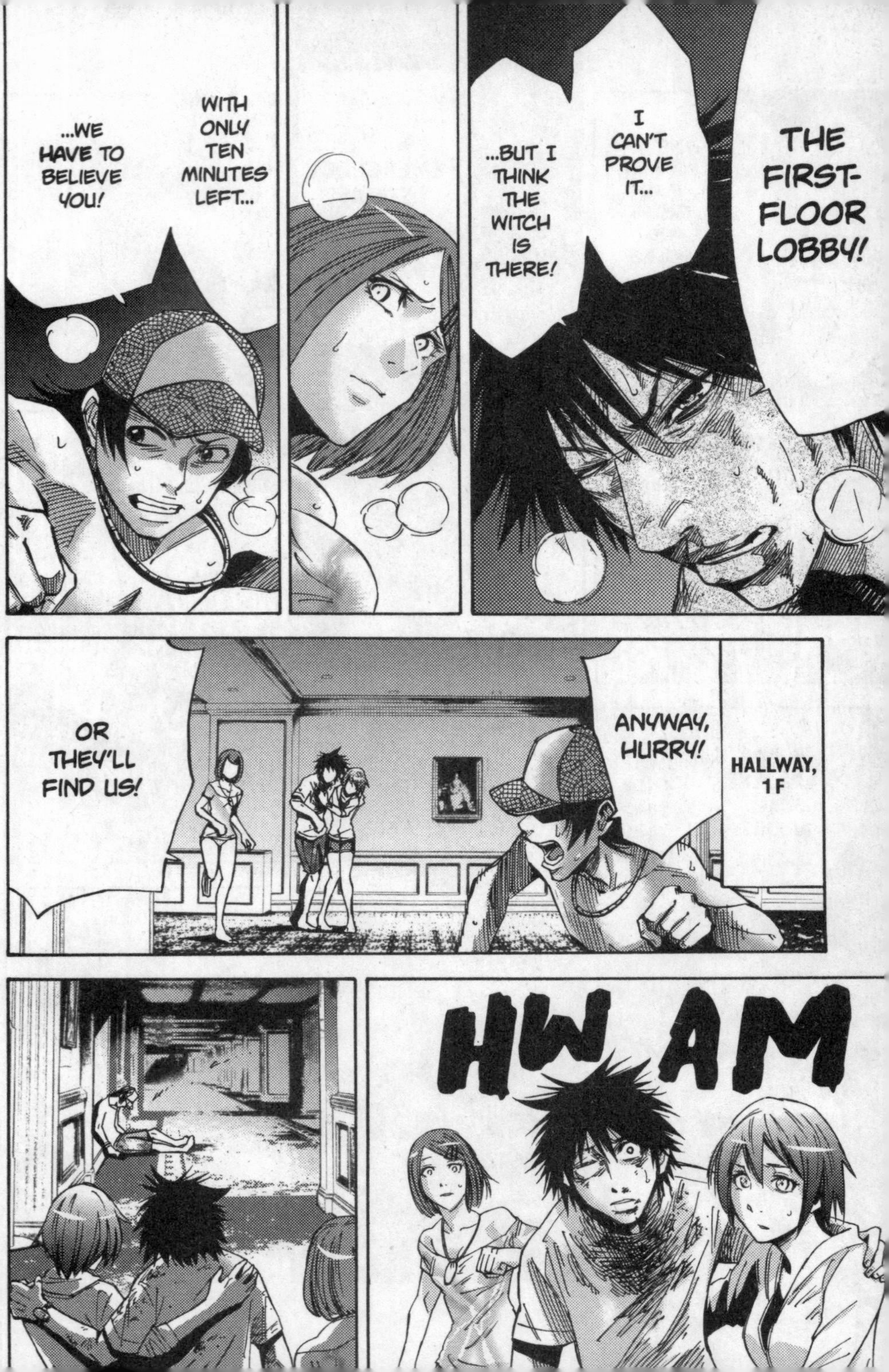
THE FIRST-FLOOR LOBBY!
I CAN'T PROVE IT...
...BUT I THINK THE WITCH IS THERE!
WITH ONLY TEN MINUTES LEFT...
...WE HAVE TO BELIEVE YOU!
HALLWAY, 1F
ANYWAY, HURRY!
OR THEY'LL FIND US!
HW AM

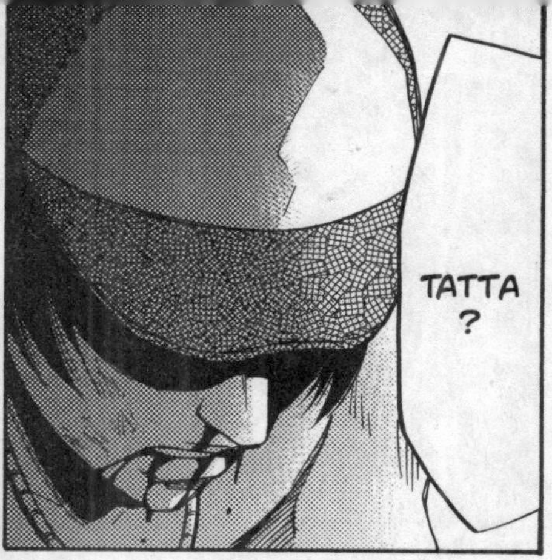
TATTA
?
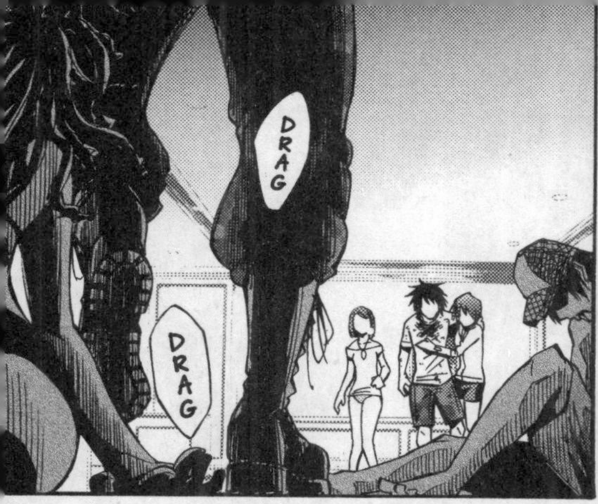
DRAG
DRAG
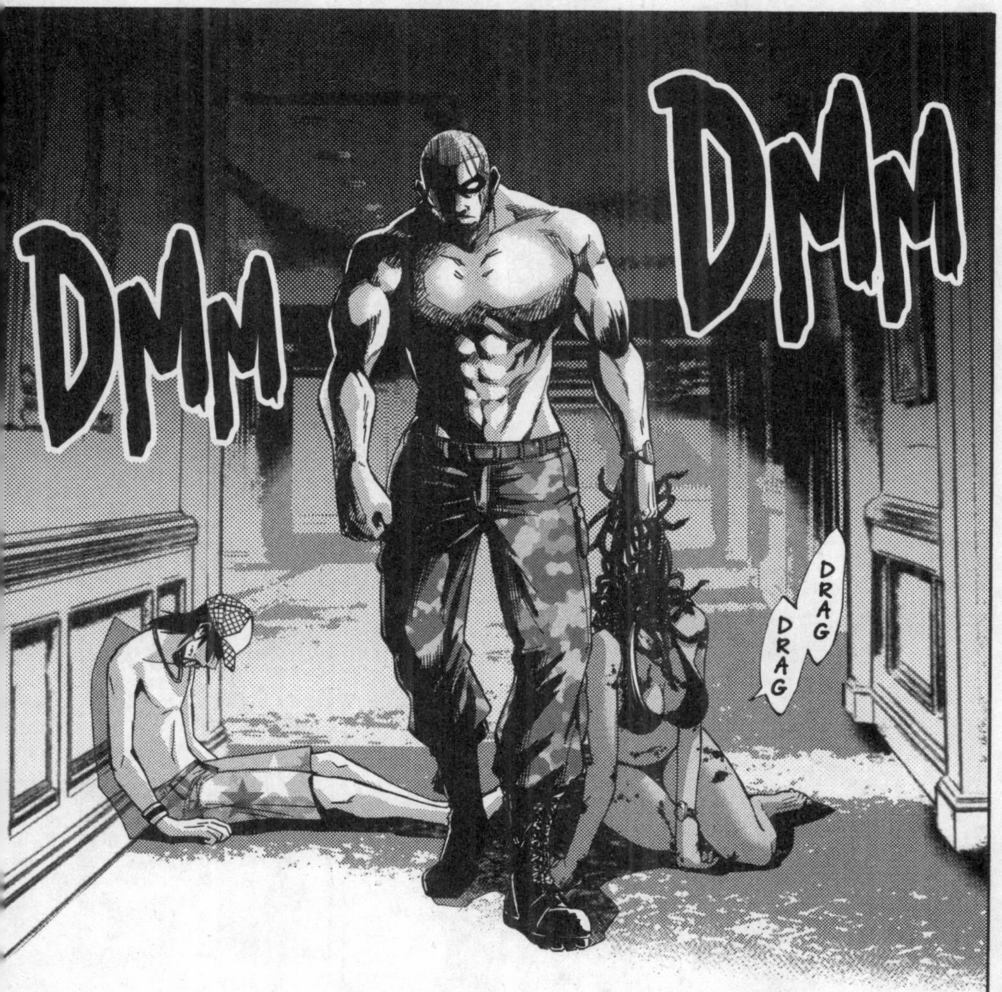
DMM
DMM
DRAG
DRAG

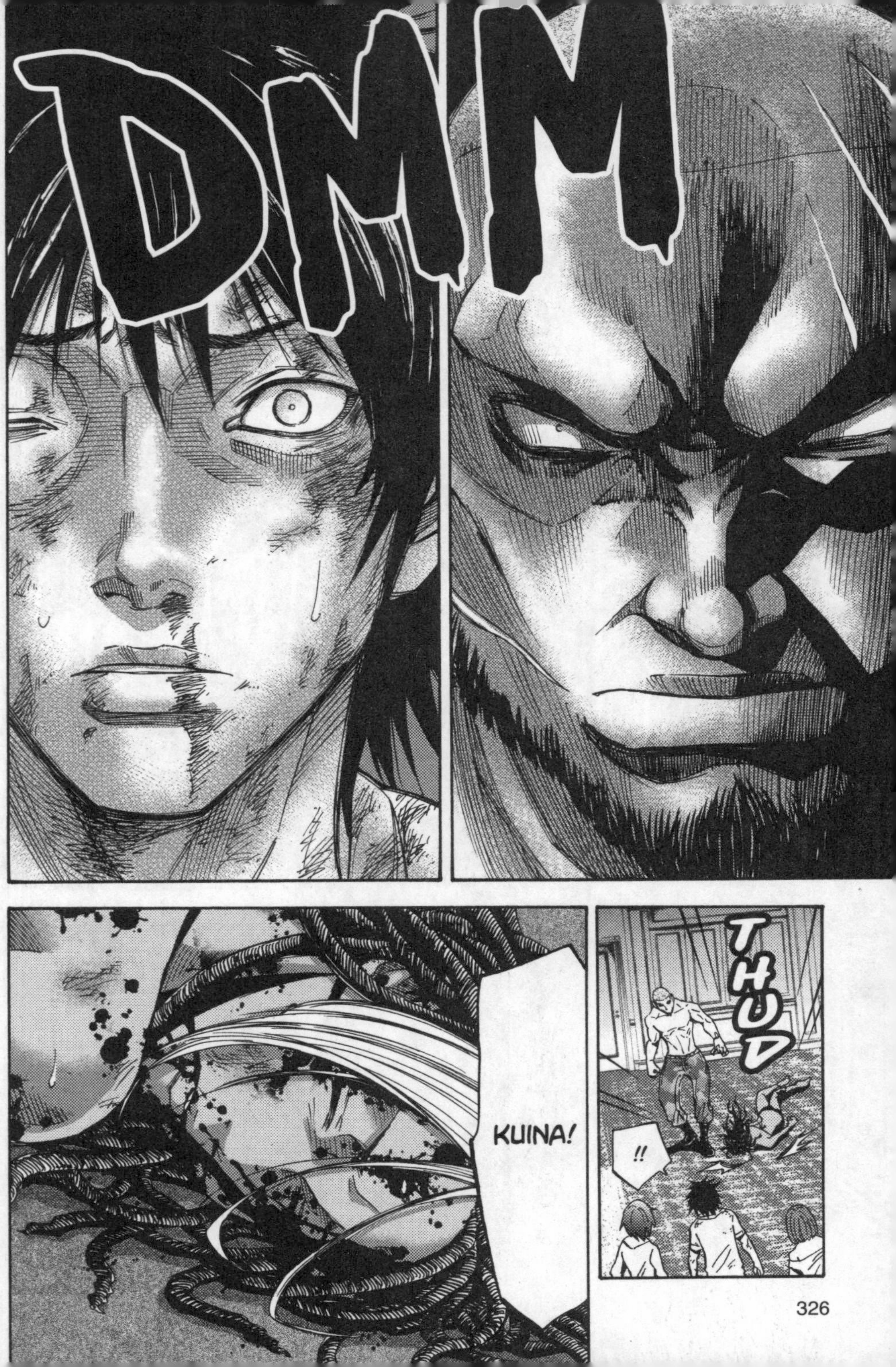
DMM
THUD
!!
KUINA!

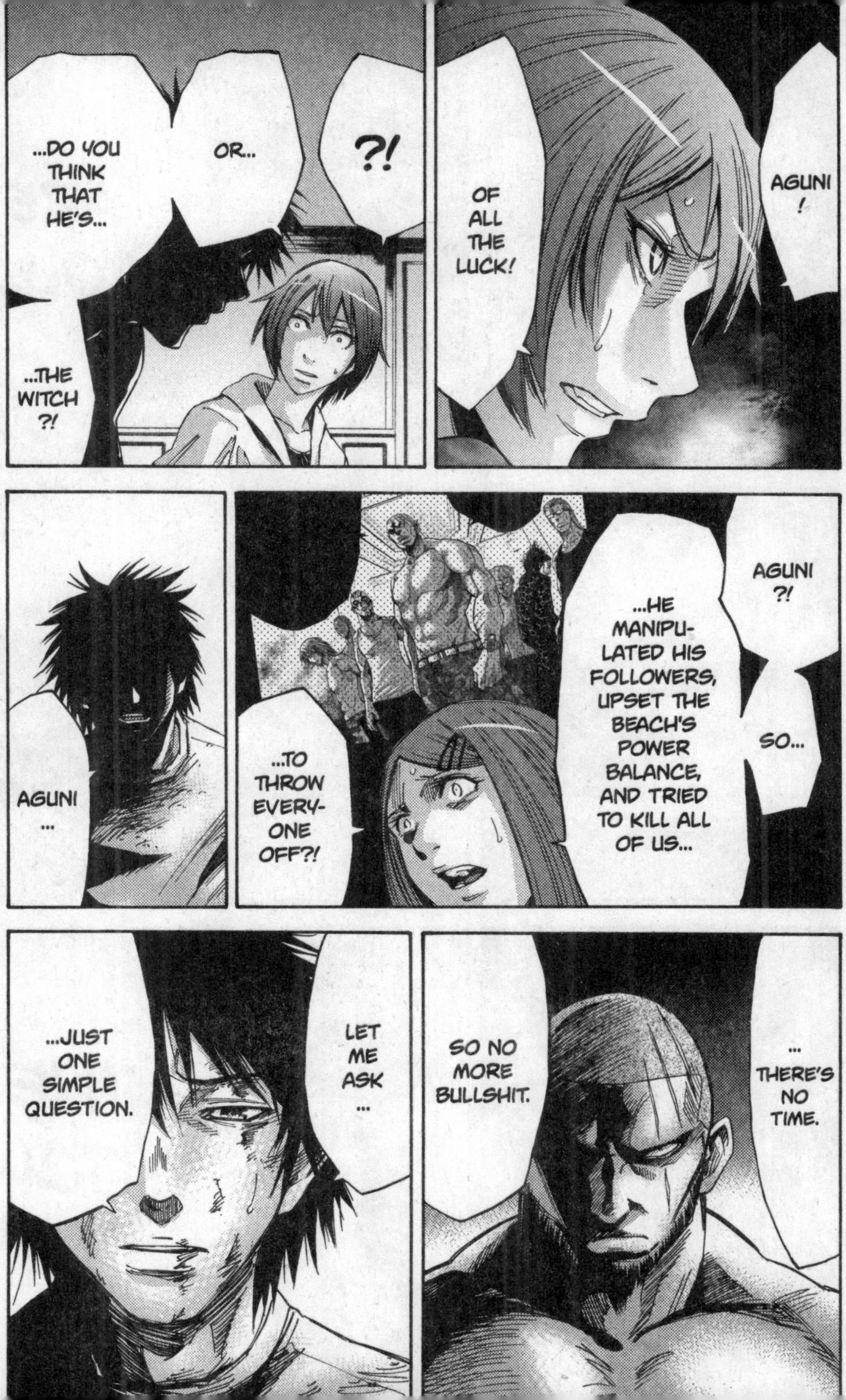
AGUNI!
OF ALL THE LUCK!
?!
OR...
...DO YOU THINK THAT HE'S...
...THE WITCH?!
AGUNI?!
SO...
...HE MANIPULATED HIS FOLLOWERS, UPSET THE BEACH'S POWER BALANCE, AND TRIED TO KILL ALL OF US...
...TO THROW EVERYONE OFF?!
AGUNI...
...THERE'S NO TIME.
SO NO MORE BULLSHIT.
LET ME ASK...
...JUST ONE SIMPLE QUESTION.

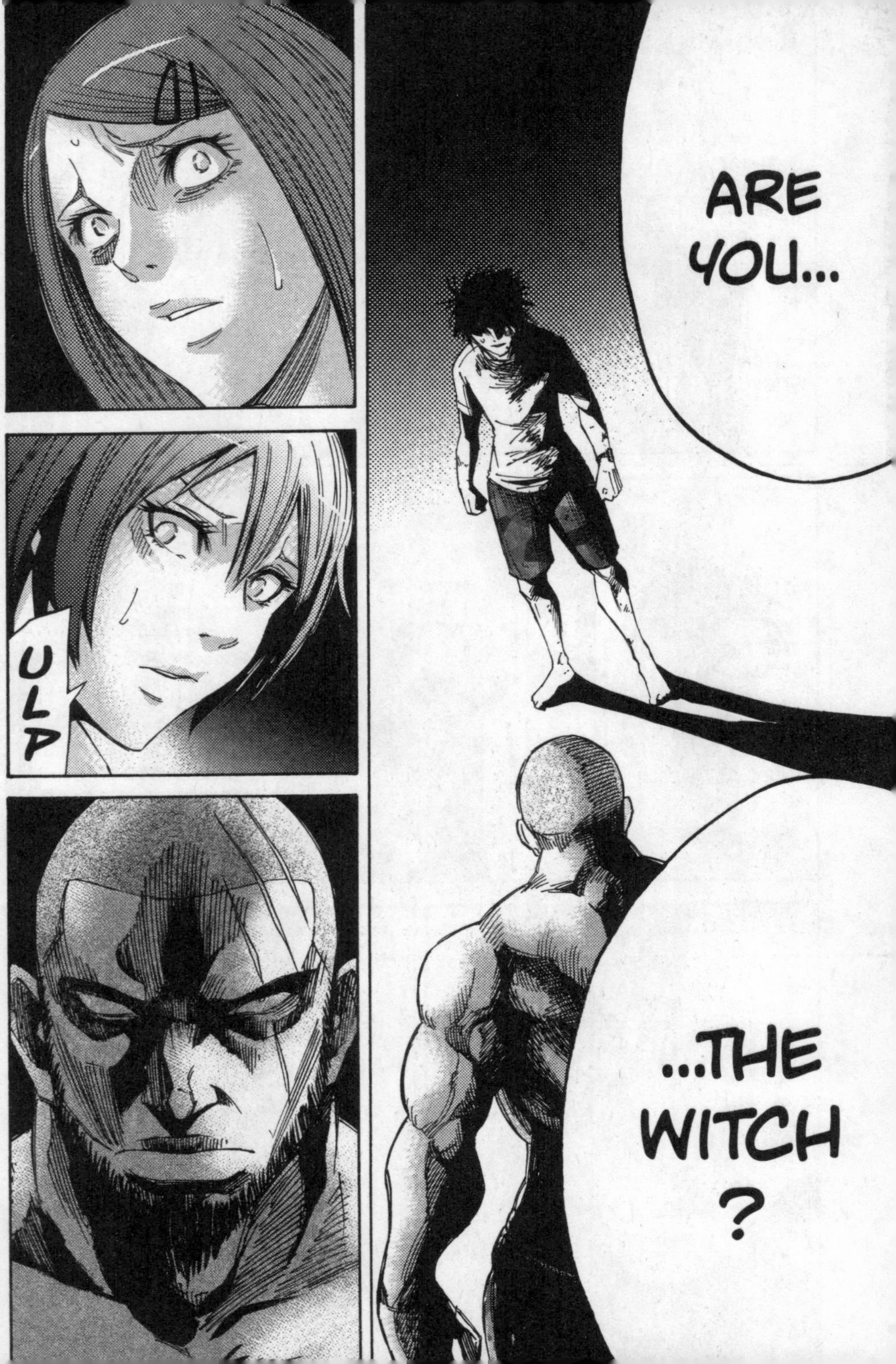
ARE YOU...
...THE WITCH ?
ULP

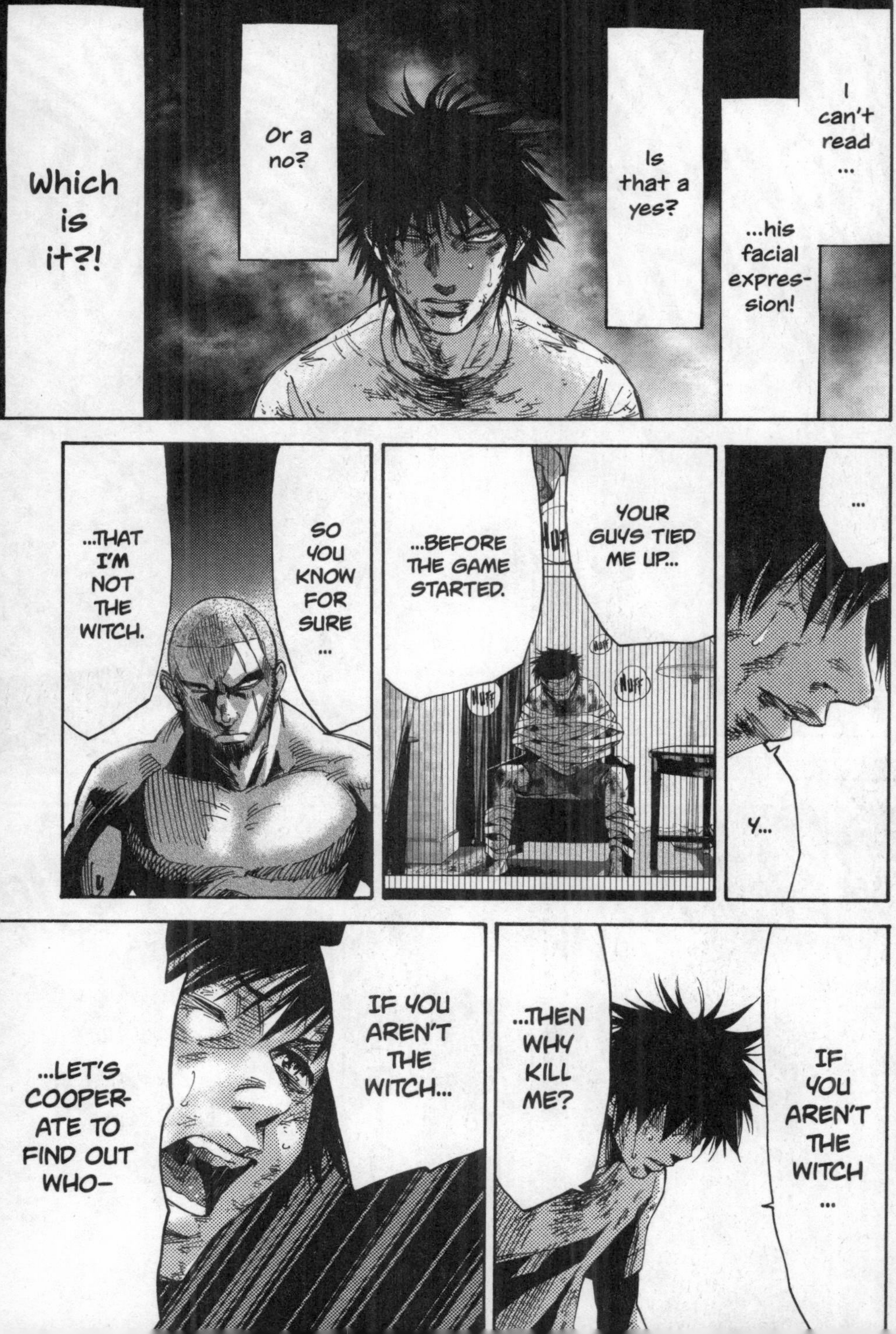
I can't read ...
...his facial expression!
Is that a yes?
Or a no?
Which is it?!
...
Y...
YOUR GUYS TIED ME UP...
...BEFORE THE GAME STARTED.
SO YOU KNOW FOR SURE ...
...THAT I'M NOT THE WITCH.
IF YOU AREN'T THE WITCH ...
...THEN WHY KILL ME?
IF YOU AREN'T THE WITCH...
...LET'S COOPERATE TO FIND OUT WHO-

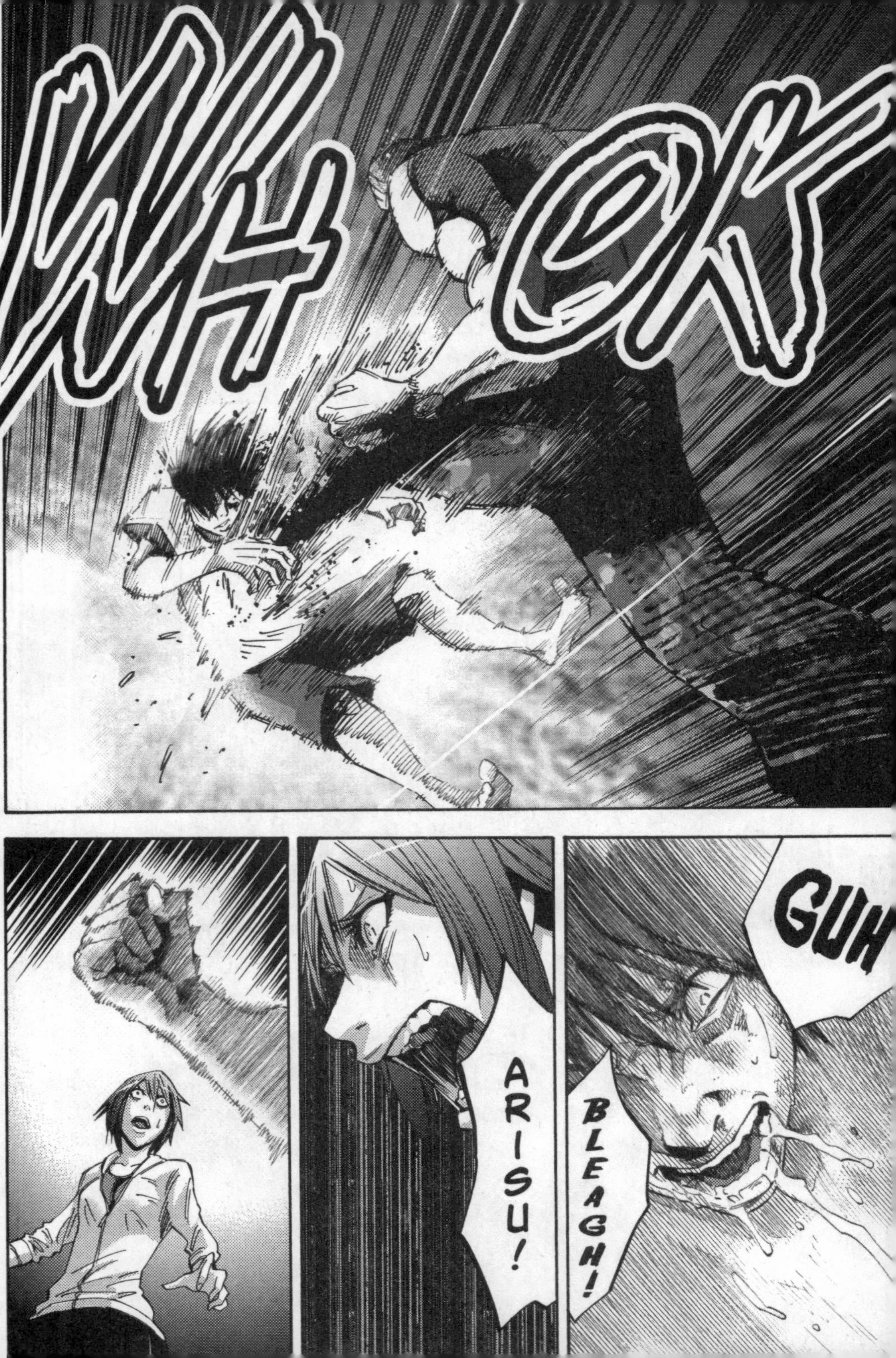
WHACK
GUH
BLEAGH!
ARISU!

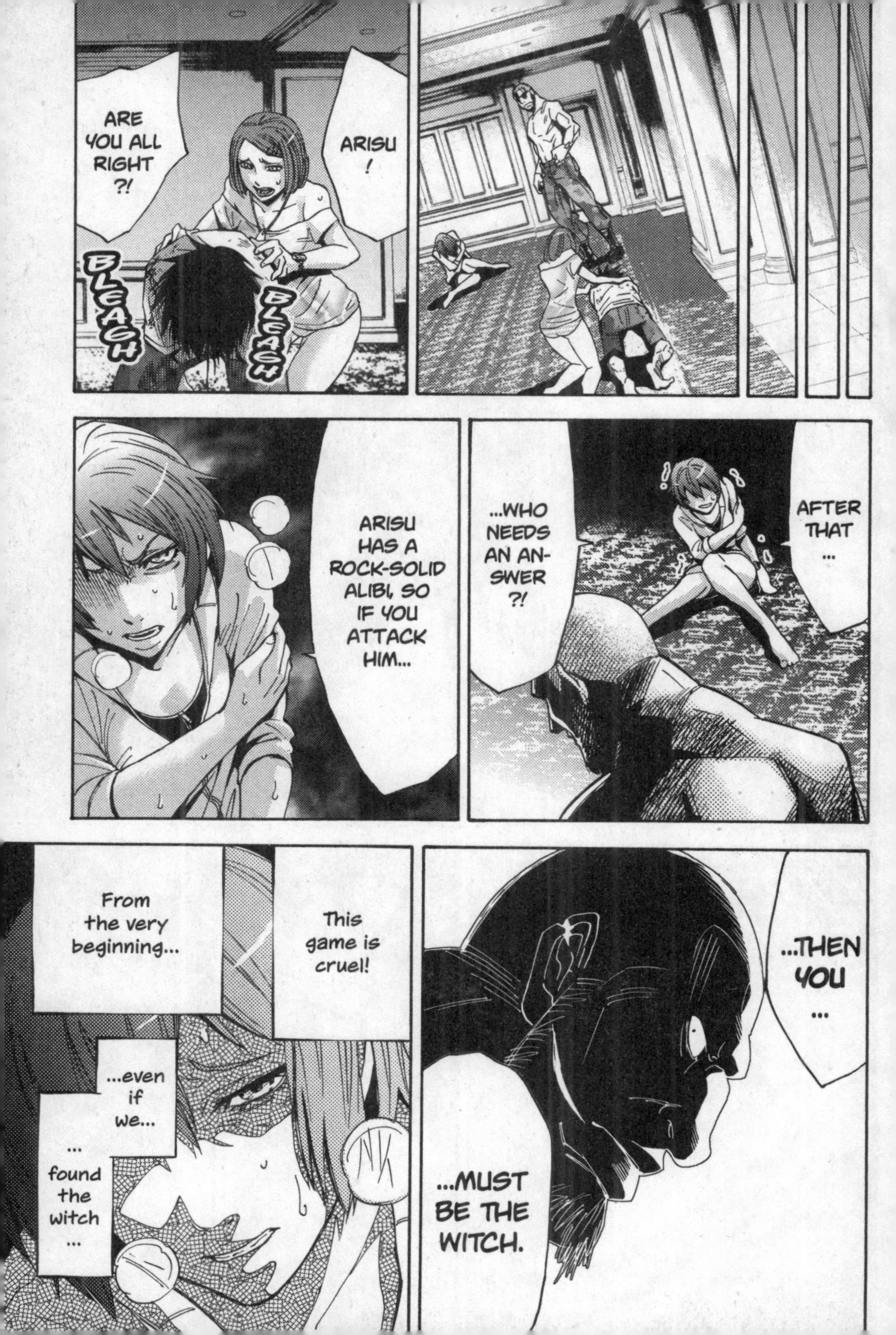
ARISU!
ARE YOU ALL RIGHT?!
BLEAGH
BLEAGH
AFTER THAT...
...WHO NEEDS AN ANSWER?!
ARISU HAS A ROCK-SOLID ALIBI, SO IF YOU ATTACK HIM...
...THEN YOU...
...MUST BE THE WITCH.
This game is cruel!
From the very beginning...
...even if we...
...found the witch...

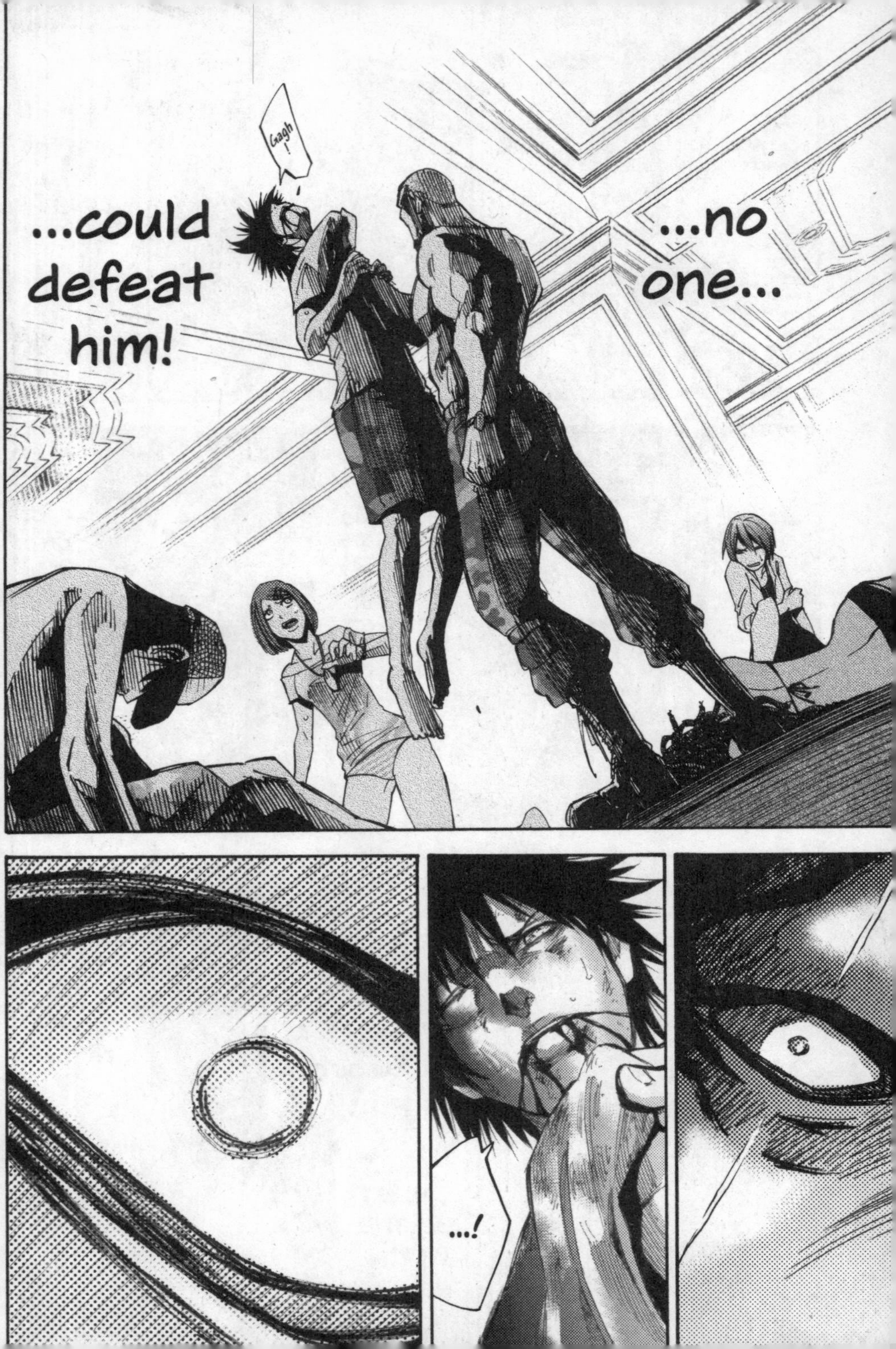
Gagh!
...no one...
...could defeat him!
...!

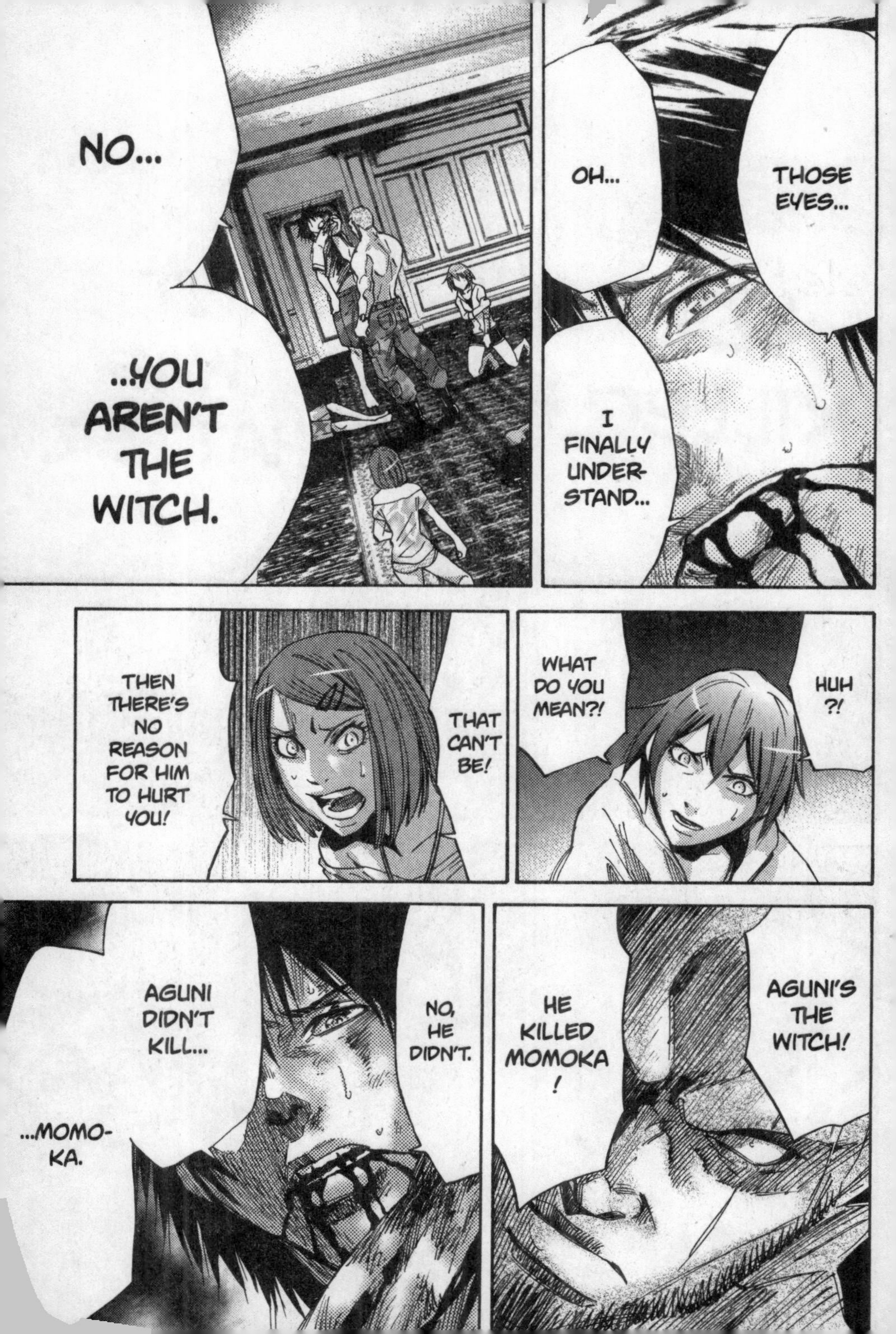
THOSE EYES...
OH...
I FINALLY UNDERSTAND...
NO...
...YOU AREN'T THE WITCH.
HUH ?!
WHAT DO YOU MEAN?!
THAT CAN'T BE!
THEN THERE'S NO REASON FOR HIM TO HURT YOU!
AGUNI'S THE WITCH!
HE KILLED MOMOKA!
NO, HE DIDN'T.
AGUNI DIDN'T KILL...
...MOMOKA.

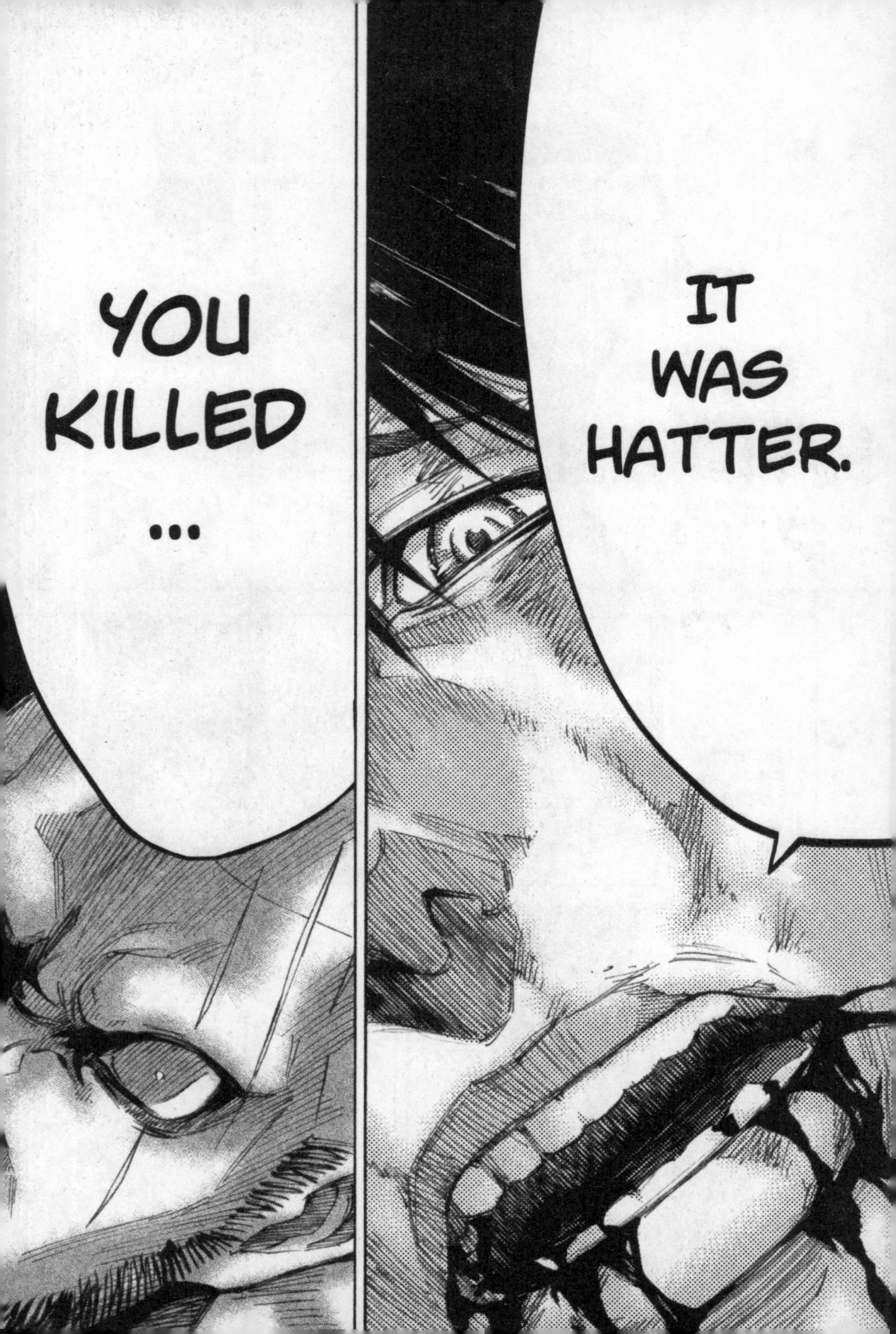
IT WAS HATTER.
YOU KILLED ...

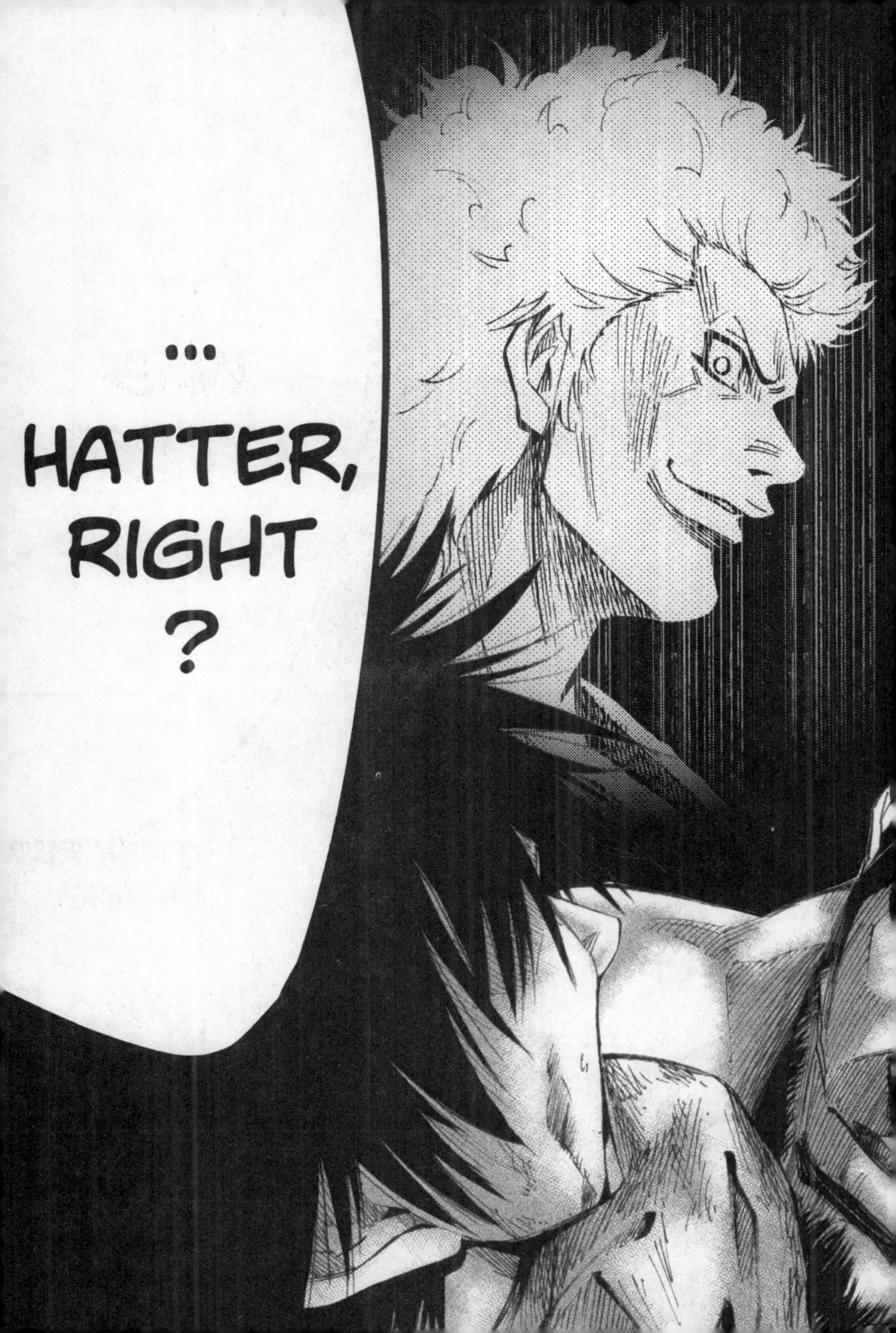
...
HATTER, RIGHT ?

...IN YOUR EYES.

I...

...CAN SEE IT...

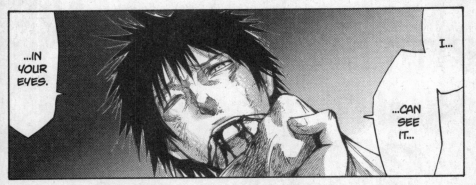

...YES.

THEY'RE SAYING...

It takes a lot of energy to trust someone. I never want to stint on that effort.

— HARO ASO

HARO ASO

In 2004, Haro Aso received *Shonen Sunday's* Manga
College Award for his short story "YUNGE!" After the
success of his 2007 short story "Onigami Amon,"
Aso got the chance to start a series of his own—
2008's *Hyde & Closer*. In 2010, his series *Alice in
Borderland* began serialization in *Shonen Sunday S*
and is now a Netflix live-action drama. *Zom 100:
Bucket List of the Dead* is his follow-up series.

ALICE IN BORDERLAND

VOLUME 3
VIZ SIGNATURE EDITION

STORY AND ART BY
HARO ASO

English Translation & Adaptation **JOHN WERRY**
Touch-Up Art & Lettering **JOANNA ESTEP**
Design **ALICE LEWIS**
Editor **PANCHA DIAZ**

IMAWA NO KUNI NO ALICE Vols. 5–6
by Haro ASO
© 2011 Haro ASO
All rights reserved.
Original Japanese edition published by SHOGAKUKAN.
English translation rights in the United States of America, Canada, the United Kingdom,
Ireland, Australia, and New Zealand arranged with SHOGAKUKAN.

Printed in Canada

Published by VIZ Media, LLC.
P.O. Box 77010
San Francisco, CA 94107

10 9 8 7 6 5 4 3 2 1
First printing, September 2022

viz.com   vizsignature.com

Three years ago the aliens invaded Tokyo.

Nothing was ever the same again.

But after a while, even impending doom starts to feel ordinary.

DEAD DEAD DEMON'S DEDE DEDE DESTRUCTION

INIO ASANO

By the author of **GOODNIGHT PUNPUN**

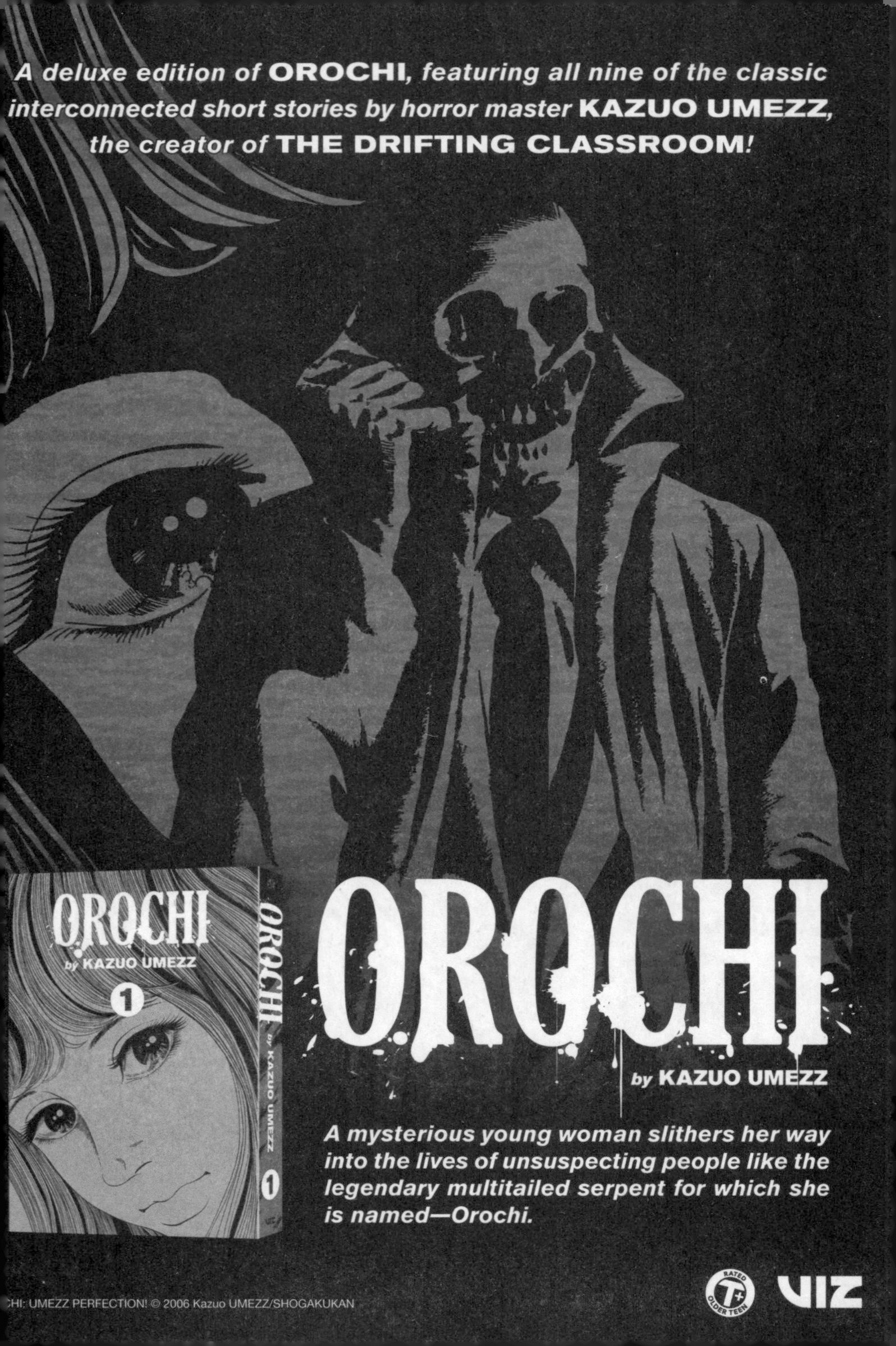
A deluxe edition of OROCHI, featuring all nine of the classic interconnected short stories by horror master KAZUO UMEZZ, the creator of THE DRIFTING CLASSROOM!
OROCHI
by KAZUO UMEZZ
1
OROCHI
by KAZUO UMEZZ
1
OROCHI
by KAZUO UMEZZ
A mysterious young woman slithers her way into the lives of unsuspecting people like the legendary multitailed serpent for which she is named—Orochi.
RATED T+ OLDER TEEN
VIZ
HI: UMEZZ PERFECTION! © 2006 Kazuo UMEZZ/SHOGAKUKAN